The Ancient English Morris Dance

The Ancient English Morris Dance

Michael Heaney

ARCHAEOPRESS

ARCHAEOPRESS PUBLISHING LTD
Summertown Pavilion
18-24 Middle Way
Summertown
Oxford OX2 7LG
www.archaeopress.com

ISBN 978-1-80327-386-0
ISBN 978-1-80327-387-7 (e-Pdf)

Front cover: Artwork by Francesca Heaney and Benedict Heaney

Back cover: Top: Chipping Campden Morris Dancers, 15 January 2007, photo © Keith Chandler
Bottom: Hag Fold Morris Dancers, 3 September 2022, photo © Duncan Broomhead

This book is available direct from Archaeopress or from our website www.archaeopress.com

For Francesca

Contents

PART V: REVIVAL (1899 – PRESENT)

List of Figures

Preface

This book had its genesis in the early 1980s, after I had done a few years' research into the history of the morris dance and realized how little was known. I was aware that gathering the evidence would be a long-term project, so I set a target date for myself of 1999, to celebrate the centenary of Cecil Sharp's meeting with the Headington Quarry Morris Dancers. Looking back, I realize what a meagre book that would have been, not just because I was ignorant of so much of the history but because in the interim the sources available to the would-be historian have multiplied many times over.

The first boost came when I found that John Forrest of the State University of New York was engaged on a similar exercise in researching early records of the dance, and we joined forces to assemble a corpus of primary source material for the period to 1750, several times larger than any previous research resource. The result of that was our chronological classified listing *Annals of Early Morris*, published by the Centre for English Cultural Tradition and Language in association with the Morris Ring in 1991; and an accompanying article, 'Charting Early Morris', in the 1991 issue of *Folk Music Journal*. These listed all the references to morris dancing that we could find up to the year 1750 and drew some preliminary conclusions. John Forrest published a book based on the research, *The History of Morris Dancing, 1458-1750*, in 1999. Since our joint work I have continued to accumulate references and that research corpus has increased from 851 listings in *Annals* to 1,444 for the same time period today.

A second boost came from the indefatigable researchers of the Records of Early English Drama team based in Toronto, aiming to gather all the primary source material up to 1642 relating not just to drama, but to performance and entertainment in general and including morris dancing. Forrest and I wrote in *Annals* (p. vii) of their extreme generosity both collectively and individually in sharing not just their published but many of their unpublished resources with us. That kindness has continued and contributed to the present work.

The third boost has been the explosion in the digitization of early texts. I have been able to make use of these primarily through the digital collections made available by and through my lifetime employer until retirement, the Bodleian Libraries. To have such a repository of physical resources literally surrounding me in my work has been an enormous privilege, but the digital dimension has transformed the ways in which we can access and research such material not just in one repository but worldwide. The response by publishers to the coronavirus pandemic had the unanticipated but welcome effect that significantly more resources were made available online to counter the difficulties in visiting libraries physically.

The Vaughan Williams Memorial Library of the English Folk Dance and Song Society is the nation's primary repository for folk music and dance, and I must pay especial tribute to successive generations of its staff. The library's initiative in digitizing not just a significant proportion of its own archival holdings but working with others across the globe to produce an unparalleled digital resource for folk-music scholarship has saved me a lifetime of travel.

My thanks go to all those mentioned above, but there are many other colleagues and friends who have been generous in their help over the years, and institutions visited whose custodians have invariably been helpful. The help has been provided over so many years that sadly some of them are no longer with us to receive my thanks personally. I thank the late Gordon Ashman, David Atkinson, Julia Bishop, Pruw Boswell, Elaine Bradtke, Duncan Broomhead, Theresa Buckland, the late Christopher Cawte, Bernie Cherry, the late Roy Dommett, Dave Evans, Vic Gammon, the late Bob Grant, John Jenner, Alison Jewitt, Alice Little, Chloe Middleton-Metcalfe, Chris Rose, Steve Roud, Steve Rowley, Ian Russell, Derek Schofield, Ron Shuttleworth, Paul Smith, Roy Smith, Garry Stringfellow, Barbara Tearle, Jennifer Thorp, Jameson Wooders and Lucy Wright; Chris Wildridge and Pete de Courcy for access to the Morris Ring's archives, and Roger Bryant and Velson Horie, in particular for access to the Manchester Morris Men's archives. (In so far as it resides with them, copyright in Manchester Morris Men's archives is retained by the Manchester Morris Men but free and unlimited access is allowed under a Creative Commons 4.0 BY-SA licence.) Taro Kobayashi kindly transcribed lute, guitar and viol tablatures into stave notation for me.

There are two people in particular to whom I owe a special debt, and in acknowledging this I do not in any way intend to diminish my appreciation of the help and friendship of others. The first is Keith Chandler, who has been a constant friend and inspiration for over 40 years. His ground-breaking research into the morris of the south midlands showed me what could be done to investigate and shed light on what I had previously thought to be intractable and unknowable. His unfailing geniality and generosity have been unbounded. The other is the late Roy Judge. Roy was the very model of the meticulous researcher, and I was fortunate enough to work closely with him on many an occasion. He had the additional gift of a strong sense of narrative, being able to weave a convincing and coherent account from refractory sources. More than once I had the benefit of his wise advice and he taught me much about research and writing. This was coupled with an irenic disposition which brought out the best in everybody who encountered him in his researches. I am hugely indebted to both of these gentlemen.

My son Ben has provided very practical help in bringing this book to market.

Last, but not least, my wife Francesca has not only put up with this invasion of our lives, particularly over the last five years, but has responded constructively to my ramblings and musings as I mulled over how to get all this down on paper. She has had the patience to read through the entire work four times and give me insight into what was good and what was bad, what was interesting and what dull; what else an intelligent lay reader might reasonably want to read about but I had failed to provide; where I had not expressed myself clearly; what could profitably be cut from a book which I knew to be far too long. Thanks don't begin to express it.

Needless to say, all errors are my responsibility alone.

Michael Heaney
October 2022

Textual note

I have on the whole transcribed texts exactly as I found them, with three exceptions. I have substituted Arabic numerals for Roman numerals except in regnal numbers. I have followed spelling except in the use of i/j and u/v/vv, where I have followed modern usage for ease of legibility. I have wherever possible avoided the reproduction in original sources of words which are nowadays seen to be grossly offensive.

Introduction

On 10 May 1589 a group of morris dancers from Herne in Kent was brought before the mayor at Canterbury. In the course of their interrogation the musician, one Henry Parkes, averred that 'he hath heard others say that it was never a merry England since men were to go with license being charged that he could not go [about] without license'. This is the first recorded time that anyone makes the equation of morris dancing and 'merry England', but it is an equation that echoes through the centuries and remains prevalent today. What is more, the concept comes not from a writer or thinker, but from a practitioner.

A few years before the Herne dancers' escapade, Robert Langham had described the visit of Queen Elizabeth to Kenilworth and the entertainments provided for her. These included 'a lyvely morisdauns, according too the auncient manner, six daunserz, Mawdmarion, and the fool'. Leaving aside for the moment the interpretation of the word 'auncient', this too is a first: the first time that a sense of history is attached to the dance.

I shall discuss both these accounts more fully later on, but it is worth a moment's reflection that the idea that morris dancing captures the essence of ancient Englishness, inherently carefree and merry, has been present for over four hundred years, and arose just one hundred and fifty years after the first evidence for the dance in England. This does not mean that the dance itself is either ancient (certainly not in the 16th century) or English, but it has served as a beacon of such ever since these first indications.

In *Revel, Riot and Rebellion* David Underdown showed how in the 17th century attitudes to the dance became one of the touchstones by which people displayed their allegiance to Royalist or Roundhead. The Royalist side (forgive this simplistic shorthand) used it as a symbol of traditional values – in other words, of ancient Englishness. The Roundheads, on the other hand, proclaimed it to be antithetical to Englishness: as heathen or Popish (take your pick). It was also associated with disorder, another thread that would return in later years.

The 18th century was the era of the dictionary definitions, which looked abroad to exotic origins among the Moors; but also of theatrical displays which continued to hark back to an English pastoralism. The theatre led indirectly to the interest taken in the morris dance by the early antiquaries, many of whom were interested in Shakespearean scholarship and in understanding the references to and performance of morris dances on the Tudor and early Stuart stage. The culmination of this was the first significant scholarly study of the dance by Francis Douce in 1807 in his essay 'On the Ancient English Morris Dance' published as an appendix to his *Illustrations of Shakspeare*, and from which this present work derives its own title. The pursuit of 'Merry Englishness' continued to form the focus of nineteenth-century interest, and at the same time the fear of unruly disorder continued as a subcurrent in what Alun Howkins called 'the taming of Whitsun',[1] whereby if the continuing practice of morris dancing among the lower social classes could not be brought within a middle-class framework of control, it was discouraged.

---

[1] Howkins.

The Victorian currents reached a watershed at the end of the 19th century with attempts to find and understand 'real' morris dances, culminating in the encounter between Cecil Sharp and the Headington Quarry Morris Dancers on Boxing Day 1899 and the start of the morris 'revival'. The moment remains iconic, even if its significance is sometimes overplayed. One of the drivers leading to the revival was a quest for 'authenticity', another the social Darwinian concept of seeking evolutionary origins and primitive forms. A consequence of the latter was an emphasis on the 'ancientness', and the re-assertion of the old Puritan idea that the dance represented something heathen and pre-Christian – except that now the concept was viewed with approbation rather than disfavour.

As ever, morris dancing continued to take on the flavour of the times. Social Darwinism led to an emphasis on the dances as exclusively for male dancers and a rejection of female dancers, and into some associations with race and ethnicity which in retrospect take on a more sombre aspect. The revived dances were now predominantly performed by the middle classes. The taming of morris was essentially complete. In the second half of the 20th century the exclusive maleness disappeared both on historical grounds and as part of the wider movement promoting the equality of the sexes. As we move further into the 21st century there are developments in its theatricality and in its links with other dance forms.

'Revival' is sometimes used pejoratively to deprecate the lack of either ancientness or authenticity, but it is undoubtedly the case that morris dancing is now practised more widely than ever before, in a wider variety of forms, and so is both revived and revivified. And so it continues. Among the practitioners and spectators of morris dancing it can evoke a sense of ancientness, of Englishness, and more broadly of connecting with the past and with the community. People also do it to keep fit, to socialize with friends, to find a partner, and to entertain and impress by artistry and skill in performance.

'Tradition' is a word invoking the sense of both the past and the community, and most morris dancing is certainly seen as a 'traditional' activity. But tradition is much more than the static re-enactment of something as it happened in the past. The tradition can be ancient but the form it takes inevitably renews itself in each generation. In an art form as fluid as the dance, where the sole method of transmission until the last century has been by direct demonstration and copying, each performance is necessarily a re-interpretation and re-invention. In a literate and technological society that can record its history in a variety of media, it is easier to know who creates and/or develops a work, be it a tale, or a song, or a morris dance. All 'traditional' works were of necessity created by someone, we just don't know by whom. Finding out how something 'traditional' was created or developed does not make it somehow suddenly non-traditional.

When people speak or write of 'morris dancing' they – and we as audience – have an idea, shared to a greater or lesser extent, of what it means. This book explores how that understanding has changed over the centuries. However, given the inherent fluidity, it can be difficult to know whether, when someone in the past writes of 'morris dancing', they are referring to something we would recognise as morris dancing today. At the same time, if people describe something that we now recognise as morris dancing, but do not name it as such, how can we know that they would share our understanding? This is a particular problem for artistic representations. As a general principle I start from the position that if it is called morris dancing, then it is morris dancing. If descriptions of activities do not identify themselves as morris dancing, then the evidence must be weighed in each case, and caution exercised in drawing conclusions. In some cases the designation is explicit but refers to something that appears to be known better today under other names (for example, sword dancing). Such instances are considered but not used to trigger a detailed examination of these other forms.

Throughout its history morris dancing has acted as a mirror to society, reflecting the concerns and mores of the times. My aim in this book is to use that mirror in reverse to illuminate the role and the significance of the dance itself. It is primarily a narrative history without an overarching framework of socio-cultural theory. I have also chosen to concentrate on the dance itself and have resisted the temptation to explore many of the wider societal factors such as rural economy, urbanization, or the ebb and flow of the Civil War, beyond what is necessary for the narrative. The book is already long enough, and the complexities of the development of morris dancing are, I hope, sufficiently engaging to hold one's attention on their own terms.

The story begins on 19 May 1448.

Part I: Emergence (1448-1569)

Chapter 1

First signs

The trade guilds known as livery companies represented the higher echelons of London society, including in their ranks the wealthiest and most powerful men in the capital. Their festivities, both public and private, lavishly displayed that standing. In the Wardens' Accounts and Court Minutes of the Worshipful Company of Goldsmiths is a set of payments made to entertainers, and for food and drink, at their annual feast on St Dunstan's Day, 19 May:[1]

Item. In primis paid un to the Ministrelles	*5. marc*
Item for 12. hattes for the Ministrelles	*10. s.*
Item for their drynk	*20 d.*
Item to Careawey harper	*12. d.*
Item to Johan Pyper	*2. d.*
Item to the Moryssh. daunsers	*7. s.*

The wardens were appointed at the feast on 19 May each year, and the retiring wardens rendered their account at the same feast. It is likely that payments were made after the event, after the goods and services had been delivered, and that this entry records the payment for the feast on the day of the wardens' accession, given as being 'from the ffest of Seint Dunston the 26 yeer of Kyng H. the VIth', i.e., 19 May 1448. This is the earliest evidence we have for morris dancers performing in England. The amount is comparable with the payment made to one of the musicians (the harper), once the 7s is divided among several dancers, but nowhere near the amount paid to the minstrels (£3 6s 8d; if there were twelve of them as implied by the purchase of their hats, then just over 5s 6d each). The wardens also paid for the hats and drink of the minstrels. Implicit in the reference is that both writers and their audience already knew what 'morris dancers' were without further explanation.

The immediate question this raises is where the dance came from. To attempt an answer we need to look at the earliest English evidence, the contexts in which we find it, and possible European analogues. In fifteenth-century English records there are only nine instances of the word 'morris', or one like it, being used to refer to a dance or similar performance. They arise in three contexts. These are trade guilds, courts of the nobility, and works of art. We shall look at these in turn (with occasional brief excursions into the 16th century) before considering how they may fit into the wider European context.

The only other record of a guild performance for a guild's own enjoyment is from the Carpenters' guild almost 60 years later, when morris dancers were paid 8d on their feast day, 11 November 1507.[2] Again, on that occasion a group of minstrels was paid much more, 3s 4d, but both amounts are much less than the money expended by the Goldsmiths 60 years earlier.

---

[1] Goldsmiths' Company, p 18; Lancashire, Anne and Parkinson, p. 165; Heaney, Michael, 'Earliest Reference'.

[2] Marsh and Ainsworth, 2:170; Lancashire, Anne and Parkinson, p. 283.

Between these two events, at the Midsummer Watch procession in 1477, the Worshipful Company of Drapers paid 28s 9d:[3]

> *for the morisse daunce and for the costs of the 9 worthi[es] as it aperith by a bill of parcells of the same.*

The midsummer marching watch of the mayor and sheriffs of the City of London was ostensibly a display of the citizens' readiness to defend the city but was really more of a splendid torchlit entertainment which had taken place, says John Stow in his *Survey of London*, from 'time out of mind'.[4] It was staged twice each year within a few days, beginning at 11 o'clock at night and continuing into the small hours of the following morning. The first began on St John's Eve, 23 June, and the second on St Peter's Eve, 28 June. The pageant element of the processions, however, is recorded only occasionally up to 1504 (as with the Drapers in 1477). Before that the strictly military elements predominated. We shall look at the guild processions in their heyday in Chapter 2.

The Drapers' payment of 28s 9d was made on St Peter's Eve, but it is not clear if this represents a payment just for that night, or if the dancers and Nine Worthies (major figures from history presented as chivalric role models) appeared on both nights of the procession and were also paid on the second. The general practice appears to be that the second night each year was a repeat of the first. If so, the payment equates to 14s 4½d per night. This was twice the payment for the Goldsmiths' dancers' private entertainment of 29 years earlier, albeit this time including the payments to those playing the parts of the Nine Worthies. These payments in turn contrast with the 8d paid by the Carpenters. We simply do not have enough context to understand the reasons for these wide variations in levels of remuneration. We know nothing of the costume or of the nature of the performance.

The two isolated fifteenth-century references from the London livery companies are indicative of how little we know of the history of the dance. No more references have been traced within the records of the Goldsmiths' Company. We may infer, however, that there was regular, if not annual, activity of a similar nature in England in the intervening period between the Goldsmiths' and Drapers' references, and between the latter date and the more frequent references extant from the beginning of the next century. They leave many unanswered questions.

The engagement of morris dancers by the wealthy Goldsmiths indicates that this was part of a lavish entertainment. The other source of our knowledge of morris dancing in the 15th century comes from an even more exalted source, the entertainments at the royal and aristocratic courts.

According to Sydney Anglo in his study of Tudor pageantry, court entertainments in England were in decline during the years of the Wars of the Roses.[5] Henry VII's seizure of the crown in 1485 signalled the end of this decline and the beginning of one of the most creative periods of English history and culture. During his reign the medieval disguising became more elaborate

---

[3] Lancashire, Anne and Parkinson, p.217; Johnson, A.H., 2:273.

[4] Stow, 1:101-04.

[5] Anglo, *Spectacle*, p. 98.

and within it we begin to find the first regular evidence of morris dancing. A disguising usually consisted of a dramatic prologue followed by a courtly dance, often reflecting a particular theme. During Henry VII's time new features were introduced, adopting Flemish themes and techniques imported from the French and Burgundian courts, including pageant cars.[6] A pageant in this sense was a mixture of carnival float and stage: it was an elaborate theatrical set, sometimes mobile, which supported a mime, playlet or dance, usually expounding a particular theme.

Disguisings were just one of the forms of English court entertainments in the reign of Henry VII. Others were typically provided by travelling players, fools, minstrels, waits, jugglers and bullbaitings. Anglo has brought together all the payments relating to court entertainments in Henry VII's time in the account books of the Treasurer of the Chamber. The first occasion on which a morris dance was performed for the king was 2 January 1494. On that day Henry paid 'for pleying of the mourice daunce ... 40s' (£2). On its own this entry, which refers to just one of the many entertainments of that Christmastide, tells us little; it is only by putting it into its context that we can begin to assess its significance. It is useful to look at similar entries from the accounts in the months on either side of which the payment for the morris dance occurs. The accounts show that payments were being made in coin presumably handed to the performers. The main unit of currency was the angel (6s 8d, one third of £1), also known as the angel-noble as it replicated the value of the earlier noble. The value of the noble itself had been raised to 8s 4d in 1464, and this was what a group of visiting Northampton waits was paid on 13 May 1493. Individual musicians such as the bagpiper who played three days later were paid 1 angel. The Lord of Bedford's tumbler was paid 2 angels on 15 January 1494. Visiting companies of actors from Essex, Wimborne Minster and France were each paid 3 angels in January 1494, but the king's own players were paid 7 angels. Diplomacy probably had a role in the reward of 12 angels to the French king's fool. The payment on 25 August 1493 of 60 angels to 'the young damoysell that daunceth' is extraordinary and suggests that she did rather more than dance.[7]

These were all apparently immediate payments in reward and are rather different from the payments to a Walter Alwyn for the overall celebrations described as 'revels' at Easter 1493, for which he was paid 25 angels, and from the 'disguising' at Christmastide that year, for which he was paid 44 angels the following February. The Easter ('Estermes') payment was made in November and some have suggested that it was in fact advance part-payment towards the Christmastide disguising.[8]

The 'mourice daunce' seems by its reward of 6 angels to have been quite elaborate and/or well-received. It is noteworthy that the performers are described as 'playing' rather than 'dancing', indicating perhaps something rather more than mere dancing, while not necessarily being wholly dramatic.[9] The context suggests that the morris dancers were a hired entertainment, much as the mayor of London had hired dancers in 1477. There is no individual payment for arranging the morris dance, so it seems that it was not specifically arranged or funded by the court. Morris dancing appears to have existed on a professional or semi-professional footing similar to that of the travelling players who also entertained the court. The Christmas

---

[6] Kipling, p. 96.
[7] Anglo, 'Court Festivals', p. 28.
[8] Streitberger, p. 27.
[9] Coldewey.

disguising paid for on 15 February does not appear to have any connection with the dance of 2 January 1494. The disguising was – as usual – the most elaborate element of entertainment that Christmas.

The only other fifteenth-century reference specifically to an event of this kind is in fact the earliest, and not from the royal court but from Cornwall at Christmastide in 1466/67. The entertainment is recorded in the household accounts of the home of John Arundell (the largest landowner in Cornwall) at Lanherne, in Mawgan-in-Pydar.[10] The event was a disguising, arranged by the household rather than presented for them by strangers. Several materials were bought from one 'Betty': red paint, tinsel, eight quires of paper, seven ells of Holland (linen) cloth (probably about nine yards) and three yards of buckram (stiff cotton or linen). Two white hats were bought for minstrels. An element of the disguising was a 'moruske':

> *Itm. 4 dosyn bellis for the Moruske of Betty*　　　　3s
> *It. 2 quayers paper for the moruske of Betty*　　　　　　7d
> ...
> *It. ½ li. glewe of Betty for the Morusk*　　　　　　　　2d

The paper and glue indicate perhaps some temporary costume or scenery, and there is a strong indication that bells were part of the costume. The disguising was clearly on a much smaller scale than those of the royal court, and the total sum which can be linked to it is 13s 9d (though this excludes the buckram, whose cost is not given). The moruske accounts for 3s 9d of this. The disguising was possibly also presented away from Lanherne, as the players were asked to go to 'Lord Stafford' (presumably Henry Stafford, the eleven-year-old Duke of Buckingham, who was already betrothed to the queen's sister, Catherine Woodville, and living in the queen's household).

'Morusk' is a variant on a word sometimes used to describe such events, 'morisk'. This and yet other versions of the word are found in contemporary descriptions of artwork. The exotic and sumptuous nature of the morris made it a suitable candidate for depiction in expensive works of art and craft to adorn the wealthiest homes. One such work was described in 1448, the same year as our earliest record of the dance itself. This was a tapestry which hung in Caister Castle, in Norfolk.[11] Caister Castle was built between 1432 and 1446 by Sir John Fastolf (1380-1459), who is said to be one of the models for Shakespeare's Falstaff, and who had made his fortune in the wars with France. After his death an inventory was made of the furnishings in the castle on 6 June 1462, including:

> *Item, 8 costers of aras, wherof somme grete and some smalle, wherof on is of the sege of Phalist, an other of the shepperdes and [t]her wifes, an other of the Morys daunse*

(A 'coster of aras' is a hanging tapestry made at Arras, in Flanders, the European centre of the industry.)

This was, in fact, the third such inventory: an earlier one is dated 'the laste day of October the 27 yere of King Henry the Sixte', i.e., 31 October 1448, and it lists:

---

[10] Hays, McGee, Joyce and Newlyn, p. 529; Douch, pp. 28-29.　　[11] Heaney, Michael and Forrest, 'Antedating'.

Item 1 clothe of aras of the morysk Daunce

An undated version of the inventory, dated, frustratingly, 'the last day of Octobre, the <blank> yere of the reyne of King Henri the Sixt', may well be an early draft of the dated 1448 list, and has:

Item, 1 clothe of arras of the morysch daunce

Tapestry was the ultimate symbol of wealth in late medieval households, and if 'Arras' is being used accurately here, and not as a term for any tapestry, then it is of Flemish/French origin, and clearly made before 1448. Nonetheless, the description is English, and the author(s) expected their audience to recognise what is being described. The tapestry was a large, expensive artwork on public display, so the depiction of the dance is unlikely to reflect a passing fad – it was an established component of aristocratic culture.

There are two apparent references to silverware engraved with a depiction of a morris dance. The first is in the will of Alice Wetenhale in 1458 (long thought to be the earliest English reference to the dance):[12]

lego Caterine filie mee ... 3 ciphos argenti sculptos cum moreys daunce cum unico cooperculo ad eosdem

[I leave to Catherine my daughter ... 3 silver bowls carved with a morris dance with one cover to the same]

The Wetenhales were a prominent London family of grocers, but Alice had previously been married to the wealthy Suffolk merchant John Edward of Bury St Edmunds. He was a wool merchant who had made his fortune in the expanding Anglo-Flemish wool trade of the early 15th century and had become a major local landowner.[13]

The second is also from a will of 1458, by Sir Thomas Chaworth:[14]

Sir Thomas praith his seid executors that ... thai delyvere to William Chaworth his aldest soon ... 3 peces of silver ... the which oon of thaym coveryth, another with a flatt knoppe and with a Moresk {th}eron

Chaworth was the sheriff of Nottinghamshire and Derbyshire and a member of Parliament.[15] The term 'Moresk' here may be merely indicative of a Moorish design (in which sense there are examples of the word from the 14th century) but the similarity of description (multiple pieces of silverware with a single engraved cover) suggests similar objects. Just after the end of the 15th century, Richard Jackson's will of *c.* 1510 referred to an apparently similar object, 'My cuppe w<ith> the morres daunce'.[16]

None of these artefacts survives, of course, so we remain ignorant of exactly what was depicted. It is not even certain that the artwork is of English origin. These are expensive pieces and may well be imported from the continent of Europe. They tell us only that the words were being used and were expected to be understood in England in the middle of the 15th century, so there must be some English cultural milieu which informed that understanding.

---

[12] Wetenhale.
[13] Copinger, 1:387, 396; Gottfried, p. 140.
[14] Chaworth, p. 226.

[15] History of Parliament: Chaworth.
[16] Jackson, Richard.

This completes the small corpus of known fifteenth-century instances of the word in England, and consideration of the forms those words take may throw some light on origins. Four relate to events, five to objects (three of those to the same item):

1448: moryssh daunseres (Goldsmiths' dance)
1448: morysk Daunce (Caister tapestry)
c.1448: morysch daunce (Caister tapestry)
1458: moreys daunce (Wetenhale will)
1458: Moresk (Chaworth will)
1462: morys daunse (Caister tapestry)
1466: moruske (Lanherne disguising)
1477: morisse daunce (Drapers' dance)
1494: mourice dance (Westminster Palace dance)

Even within these nine references three threads are discernable. Three instances apparently end in the sounds /sk/, three in the sound /s/, and three (moryssh, morysch and possibly morisse) in /sS/, where the capital /S/ represents some additional fricative or sibilant. The form of the first triad, ending in /sk/, is clearly French in origin, from 'morisque' and 'moresque'. The other two forms are more complex. The last triad in /sS/ suggests a form not found after the 15th century (though a Drapers' Company 1512 reference to a dance described as both 'morys' and 'morishe' should be noted).[17] It may indicate an attempt to transcribe the Flemish form /morisx/ (i.e., 's' followed by the sound of 'ch' as in 'loch'). The Flemish territories of the Duchy of Burgundy were the locus of an efflorescence of European culture in the 15th century, and it would not be surprising to find Flemish cultural influences reaching England at that time, especially given the close ties between the countries in the wool trade and Henry VII's desire to emulate the courts of Europe. The Flemish ending /sx/ easily simplifies to /s/ and does so even in Flemish. It would not be surprising if English speakers simplified the unfamiliar sound-group similarly or took it from Flemish directly in the simpler form. The forms in /s/ and /sS/, therefore, point strongly to Flemish influence, and it is the simpler of the two which became the dominant English word, 'morris'.

The Caister tapestry is crucial in showing that 'morris' and 'morisk' can be used interchangeably, although we shall see that the early sixteenth-century references may suggest nuances of difference while confirming the words' overall identity of meaning. The words themselves do occur earlier in English in contexts suggesting the meaning 'Moorish', i.e., relating to Moorish culture. A will made in 1394 (misprinted 1494 in the published text) refers to a vessel 'sculptum cum litteris de moreske' ('sculpted with Moorish letters')[18] and a 1434 text refers to a 'hullyng [covering] of black, red and green, with morys letters'.[19] Neither of these suggests the depiction of a performance of any kind, nor does an even more enigmatic form, 'Moricz', from a court case in 1341, again apparently indicating a Moorish design on a cover for a vessel.[20] Our first indications of a dance or performance remain firmly in the middle of the 15th century.

The often proposed links with other European customs rest on uncertain grounds, and this book does not pretend to be a search for unknowable origins. However, as I am suggesting

---

[17] Lancashire, Anne and Parkinson, pp. 310-11.
[18] Vavasour, no. 362. I am very grateful to Christopher Cawte for drawing my attention to the misdating of this will.
[19] 'Moorish' (OED).
[20] Thomas, 1:203.

that the etymology indicates that the dance most probably came into England via the Low Countries with perhaps some French influence, it is worth briefly reviewing some of the European evidence most closely related to the possible antecedents of the English dance.

There is not much evidence available. What is generally cited as the earliest reference, on the occasion of the marriage of the Aragonese queen Petronilla to Ramon Berenguer IV, count of Barcelona, in Lérida (Catalan Lleida) in August 1150, does not use the word at all, referring merely to a dance which featured 'moros y cristianos que figuraban un reñido combate' ('Moors and Christians who figured in a close combat').[21] The author of the 1855 work bringing this to public notice was citing a manuscript seen only by a colleague. Other proposed early European textual references or iconographic evidence before the 15th century also fade on inspection into supposition and inference from non-explicit accounts.

Figure 1.1: Israhel von Meckenhem, The Morris Dancers (The Art Institute of Chicago, CC 0 public domain).

[21] Soriano Fuertes, 1:125-26.

The first occasion on which we know a named dance was performed is at the Burgundian court in 1427-28, when the valet of the chamber was asked to make seven luxurious, colourful and exotic costumes 'propices à danser la morisque' ('suitable for dancing the morisque').[22] A performance in Nuremberg *c.* 1491, described in a contemporary poem, has a pipe-and-taborer, fool, six Moors and a lady holding an apple. The piper 'dhönt ein morisckendantz' ['plays a morris/Moorish dance'] and the Moors adopt various contorted postures in the dance.[23]

Israhel van Meckenem was a goldsmith and copper-engraver from Bocholt in Westphalia. It is thought that at least some of his engravings arose in the course of his goldsmith's work. Prints of over 500 engravings and works by him are known, most of them religious in character. One of his engravings from the same period as the Nuremberg poem, nowadays identified as a 'Moriskentanz', shows four such dancers, one of whom wears a fool's costume, dancing around a lady, holding this time a ring, to the music of a pipe-and-taborer.[24] (Figure 1.1).

Although matching contemporary images to named dance forms can be subjective, in one case we do have contemporary confirmation that a set of images represents a 'Moriskentanz'. These are the wooden figures carved by Erasmus Grasser for Munich's Old Town Hall in 1480, for which we have the record of the payment of £150 4s (German currency) for '16 pilden maruschka tanntz' ('16 figures of a morris/Moorish dance').[25] Though some of the figures (including the lady) have been lost, several survive, two of which are shown in Figure 1.2. One figure in the set has a black African's face, but the others, including the two shown here, do not. The figures are

Figure 1.2: Erasmus Grasser, Morris dancer with headgear like a hunting cap; Morris dancer with a white headband, from the ballroom of the Old Town Hall, Munich, 1480 (Münchner Stadtmuseum, Sammlung Angewandte Kunst, Inventory nos K-Ic/228, K-Ic/223, CC BY-SA 4.0).

[22] Laborde, 3:252.
[23] Welker, p. 70.
[24] Geisberg, no. 363.
[25] Müller-Meiningen, p. 7.

in a variety of contorted poses. These and similar references suggest a dance featuring contorted or exaggerated postures performed in the presence of a lady and seeking her favour.

When more detailed information about morris dances is recorded in the early sixteenth-century English sources, many are of a type similar to those attested in continental Europe from the mid to late 15th century. That raises the question of how morris dancers (described explicitly as such) appeared in the Goldsmiths' Hall as early as 1448. Peter Stabel states that the craft guilds in Flanders and the Brabant, like their English counterparts, shaped public culture and enriched cultural life by the promotion of 'public pageants, cavalcades, processions, games, and even theatre and music, ... but also more private ceremonies such as funerals, dinners, and investment in works of art'.[26] However, they are lacking in direct evidence of morris dances being performed in those environments. The Burgundian court, on the other hand, does provide evidence, beginning with the event of 1427-28 for Philip, Duke of Burgundy. More pertinent is probably the occasion of the marriage of Philip's son Charles the Bold to Margaret, sister of the English king Edward IV, just outside Bruges on 3 July 1468, at which seven monkeys emerged from a tower and danced a 'morisque' to pipe-and-tabor accompaniment played by one of them, and later in the proceedings twelve 'knights of the sea' emerged from a whale's mouth, leaping 'in the manner of a morisque'.[27]

The relevant sixteenth-century English evidence begins with an event within a group of festivities at the English court, probably occasioned by the celebrations held prior to the marriage in November of Prince Arthur to Catherine of Aragon. On 15 October 1501 the King paid 'to theym that daunced to mores daunce 26s 8d' (7 angels).[28] This was probably the same sort of event as occurred during the further festivities of 18-21 November 1501, for which Jacques Hault and William Pawne were instructed to 'devise and prepare disguisings and some morisks after the best manner they can'.[29] Hault and Pawne did not in fact complete their preparations; the disguisings were arranged by William Cornish and John English. The latter was Master of the King's Players, who performed an interlude immediately before the second of the four disguisings. The interlude consisted of a pageant of a lantern and arbour, from which the morisk may have emerged.[30]

We can be reasonably confident in this presumption because more about the nature of this entertainment emerges just two months later. Having successfully (or so he thought) secured the future of the Crown Prince, Henry VII turned his attention to relations with Scotland, to which purpose his daughter Margaret was betrothed to James IV. On 24 January 1502 at Richmond there were celebrations to mark the betrothal, during which a pageant car with an enormous glass lantern was brought in, 'out of which sorted divers sorts of Morisks. Also very goodly Disguising of Six Gentlemen and Six Gentlewomen, which danced divers Dances.'[31] This was the same pageant as had appeared two months earlier, and this time we know that John English was responsible.[32] It had evidently been a great success, hence its repetition. As in this case the morisk which emerged from the pageant was contrasted with the dances that followed, it may be that the morisk was more dramatic than terpsichorean.

---

[26] Stabel, p. 191.
[27] La Marche, pp. 153-54, 197-98.
[28] Anglo, 'Court Festivals', p. 37.
[29] Kipling, p. 100.

[30] Kipling, p. 106.
[31] Leland, 4:263.
[32] Kipling, p. 176.

This series of festivities cannot be separated from the image of the English court which Henry VII was fostering. The old palace at Sheen burned down during the Christmastide celebrations of 1497, and the replacement palace of Richmond was an architectural and artistic statement of Henry's claims for England as an important and sophisticated European nation. Much of the inspiration for the palace – and many of the craftsmen who worked on it – came from the Burgundian Netherlands, whose court and culture were models for much of Europe in the 15th century. The festivities on the occasion of Prince Arthur's marriage were the first major celebrations to be held at the new palace.

Two weeks later, on 4 February 1502, Henry VII paid 'to one Lewes for a mores daunce 53s 4d' (8 angels, perhaps suggesting eight participants) at Richmond. This was probably the Lewes Adam who prepared a disguising the following Christmas,[33] showing in this case that the morris dance was arranged by a regular supplier of court entertainment, and that the morris dancers did not simply appear at court of their own initiative. The payment may have related to the entertainments for Princess Margaret's betrothal.

Morris dancing and morisks continued to be favoured diversions at the court of Henry VII at considerable expense, as evidenced by further records of court expenditure for 20 and 31 December 1507:[34]

Item to Master Wentworth for to make a dysguysing for a moryce daunce	13 li	6s	8d
...			
Item to Master Wentworth towarde the makyng of a disguysing for a moryce daunce		100s	

Here the morris appears to be a constituent part of a disguising, but at the same time it has become the main purpose of the disguising. A year later Wentworth was entrusted with the organization of the lavish spectacles arranged for the visit of the Flemish ambassadors on the occasion of the betrothal of the Archduke Charles to Princess Mary in December 1508. The records give a vivid description of the complex logistics needed to present a display of this kind, as men and materials shuffled between Richmond and London in preparation. They record transport costs, the expense of feeding the workmen, labouring costs for nearly three months, even the contingency expenditure of a dash to London at the last minute for an item of costume. The work included preparations for a 'moreske', which must have been the same kind of event as had been described as a 'mourice dance' the previous year:[35]

Item, for a bott fro Richemount bank to London and for a cart to cary <.>[?] standardes that came in the same bott with stuffe of the moreske	22d	
Also, Henry Wentworth asketh alowauns for his costes, being abought the besyness of the disguising and moreske by the kings commaundement, from the 27th day of September to the 27th day of December, at 8d be the day for 80 days	53s	4d

---

[33] Anglo, 'Court Festivals', pp. 38, 22.
[34] Anglo, 'Court Festivals', p. 43.

[35] Myers, pp. 127-28.

The 'stuffe of the moreske' was probably the existing costume elements, being brought from Richmond to London. The same event was marked by the contemporary publication of a tract in English and Latin versions, *The Spousells of the Princess Mary*.[36] The English text tells us that:

> There lacked no disguysynges, moriskes nor entreludes made and appareilled in the beste and richest maner

while the Latin text is a little more informative:

> *His igitur cenis, tam lautis tamque opiparis ut nihil omnino egregium quod vel terra vel freto aut flumine crescat illis abfuerit, non defuerunt ludi Maurei quas morescas dicunt, et saltantium juvenum generosa virensque propago, simul et comediarum tragediarumque hystrionica et ludicra queque spectacula previsa sane prius ac sumptuose preparata.*

> *[So with these feasts, so splendid and sumptuous that nothing extraordinary that exists either on land or on water was lacking, the Moorish plays they call morescas, and the vigorous noble offspring of dancing youths was not wanting, and at the same time dramatic and theatrical spectacles of comedies and tragedies as were ever seen before, lavishly prepared.]*

This confirms our impression of the dances as part of a quasi-dramatic entertainment and suggests that it required the participation of vigorous young men.

Although this book's subject is the English morris dance it is worth looking at the very similar entertainment in the Scottish court at this time, not least because, in contrast to its subsequent English history, the dance did not take root in Scotland. The first event there was a payment of £42 (about £10.5 English) by royal command at Stirling on 8 February 1502 'to the men that brocht in the morice dance, and to thair menstrales'; the next a more detailed account of payments for a performance on 6 January 1504, 'to Colin Campbell and his marowis that brocht in the Moris dauns, £14' (about £3.5 English; Campbell was given a further £5). The costumes were also specially made for that occasion: red and blue coats and hats for six dancers, blue taffeta for a woman's gown, lined in white, at a total cost of £39 3s 8d (about £9.9 English). The elaborate hats used more material than the coats and were delivered to 'French Master John'.[37] Similar purchases of costumes for six dancers with bells, and for a woman, were made at the court in Stirling for events in 1506, 1507 and 1508, but these were not identified as 'morris'.[38]

Apart from a couple of references in the middle of the century and the beginning of the next, no more is heard of the morris dance in Scotland after December 1512. This last evidence is again found in the accounts of the Lord High Treasurer:[39]

> *Item, the 5 day of December ... payt to Monsure Lamote servitoures, that daunsit ane moris to the King, 10 crounis of wecht;*　　summa 9 li

> *...*

> *Item, the 16 day of December, to Monsur Lamotis servitouris, that dansit ane uthir moris to the King and Quene,*　　5 li　8s

---

[36] Gairdner, p. 30.

[37] Dickson, Paul, McInnes and Murray, 2:135, 414.

[38] Mill, pp. 324-28.

[39] Dickson, Paul, McInnes and Murray, 4:399-400.

Monsieur Lamot was the French ambassador to the court. Scottish morris ends as it began, as a suitable entertainment in providing hospitality at the highest levels of society and associated with continental origins. It was a comparatively short-lived fashion which found no reflection in the lower orders of Scottish society, and which was evidently perceived as a foreign activity.

The earliest literary reference to the dance was written by the Scottish court poet William Dunbar in the early years of the 16th century, continuing to suggest that the morris dance was cultured entertainment for sophisticated tastes. In his 'Aganis the Solistaris [petitioners] in Court' he wrote how those seeking the king's favour tried to win it:[40]

> *Sum singis, sum dances, sum tellis storyis,*
> *Sum lait at evein bringis in the moryis*

In 1513 Gawin Douglas composed the first modern translation of the Aeneid. In Book XIII (a medieval addition to the original twelve) he alludes, in a passage only loosely associated with the original text, to the 'morysis, and sik ryot' ('morrises and such[like] riot') of Aeneas's men.[41]

In a poem which has variously been attributed to Kings James I and V of Scotland, the poet describes a musician:[42]

> *Thome Lular wes thair menstrall meit;*
> *O Lord! as he cowd lanss;*
> *He playit so schill, and sang so sweit*
> *Quhill Towsy tuke a transs.*
> *Auld Lychtfute thair he did forleit,*
> *And counterfutit Franss;*
> *He use him-self as man discreit*
> *And up tuke moreiss danss*

The poem describes in hyperbole the events at a village festival; and although the maid was dancing a 'transs' (a Celtic dance) the minstrel forsook this and brought in an alien dance tune from France. If this poem were by James I it must have been written before 1437 and would rank as the earliest English-language reference to morris dancing by over a decade. It fits much better in the 16th century (James V, 1512-1542). Even here, if James V is the author then it is remarkably late for Scotland.

The cultural links between the English and Scottish courts are brought out in one of just two references outside the royal palaces. In the household accounts of Lady Margaret Beaufort at Collyweston in Northamptonshire, 6s 8d was paid in 1503 'unto 6 Spaynerdes that daunsed the morice'.[43] The event marks the English court on the move, accompanying Princess Margaret on her marriage journey to Scotland and stopping at the home of the mother of Henry VII. This indicates clearly that the morris dance was an exotic entertainment, part and parcel of the king's desire to show England to be a sophisticated European nation. It was part of the language of court diplomacy of the day.

---

[40] Dunbar.
[41] Douglas, Gawin, 2:859.
[42] Douglas, George, p. 177.

[43] Beaufort, p. 121. I am grateful to Alan Nelson for drawing this to my attention (in a personal communication, August 1986).

At the start of the reign of Henry VIII the morris of the court continued to be popular. We have a near-contemporary account of the celebrations at Epiphany in 1511 from Edward Hall in 1550, which describes all the classic elements of a courtly morisk:[44]

> *Agaynste the 12. daye or the daye of the Epiphanie at nighte, before the banket in the Hall at Richemond, was a pageaunt devised like a mountayne, glisteringe by night, as though it had bene all of golde and set with stones, on the tope of the which mountayne was a tree of golde, the braunches and bowes frysed with gold, spredynge on every side over the mountayne, with Roses and Pomegarnettes, the which mountayne was with vices brought up towardes the kyng, & out of the same came a ladye, appareiled in cloth of golde, and the children of honor called the Henchemen, whiche were freshly disguised, and daunced a Morice before the kyng. And that done, reentred the mountaine and then it was drawen backe, and then was the wassail or banket brought in, and so brake up Christmas.*

There is a quasi-dramatic scenic construction, and young noblemen dancing around a richly apparelled lady. The primary source gives more details, including the fact that the role of a fool was involved.[45] There were 14 leather garters and 28 latten (brass) buckles all with 'belles of sundry bignes for the morryske'; there was a total of 1020 bells for five dancers and a fool. This suggests that the entire costume was covered in bells, not just the garters and buckles. The dancers are identified as the fool and four knights of different colours. The fool's coat and ladle had 144 bells, and each dancer (including the fool) had 108 bells on arms and legs. This accounts for 684 bells, but over 1000 were bought. The dancers were nobles, not professional dancers, and bells were hired for them to wear while they practised. The fool's ladle is both a device for collecting money and a symbol of female sexuality, which seems out of place in the elaborate elegance of the pageant. The lady's gown was equally ornate, using 16 yards of pleasance (a gauze-like fabric). The costumes of the lady and knights were adorned with 29,000 spangles.

Records of the court revels of this period are well preserved, and they give an indication of the diversity of the themes presented in these pageants. On 13 February 1511 was a pageant of 'The Golden Arbor in the Orchard of Pleasure', which included singing by the children of the Chapel, and the provision of 12 elaborate satin garments for the king and his retinue. The pageant-wagon took a month to construct and was so heavy that it broke the floor of the hall in which it was displayed.[46] At Twelfth Night in 1513 Sir Harry Guildford devised a pageant called 'The Rich Mount' which was over three weeks in the construction. The mountain had Plantagenet broom, and red and white roses. Again, complete satin costumes with spangles were provided for the King, six nobles and six ladies; gowns were provided for six minstrels who rode in on the mountain; there were two armed knights, four wodewoses (wild men) and four dancers.[47] In 1516 the Twelfth-night pageant was an embattled castle, which not only provided pageantry in its own right, but also acted as the setting before which two comedies were played. Morris dances or morisks were becoming less central features in such increasing variety and innovation.

In the Twelfth-night revel of 1514 at Richmond, Guildford devised a 'moreske' as part of an interlude. The moreske (also called a 'morysks') was performed by six men, two ladies and

---

[44] Hall, Edward and Grafton, pp. 516-17.
[45] Gibson, 21-28, reproduced in summary in Brewer, J.S., Gairdner and Brodie, 2.2:1493-94.
[46] Brewer, J.S., Gairdner and Brodie, 2.2:1495-97.
[47] Brewer, J.S., Gairdner and Brodie, 2.2:1501-02.

a fool. The bells supplied in this case – 288 – amount to no more than 48 for each dancer. They were sewn onto the dancers' jackets, which were made from white satin and had wide, pendant sleeves. The dancers also wore bells on their legs; these, 60 in number, were supplied from stock by Guildford. The dancers, but apparently not the fool, had 'slop hosen' to cover the bells on their legs. Black gowns were supplied to cover their costumes until the moment of the dance. The fool wore a jacket of yellow sarsenet edged with crimson. All the costumes were adorned with spangles.[48] There are no indications of elaborate settings, although there is, nevertheless, an indication of a theme in the presence of the two ladies, who are styled 'Beauty' and 'Venus'. The morisk was part of an interlude whose nature we do not know. As before, the fool appears to be an adjunct necessary to the dance. The roles of Beauty and Venus are unclear, but the very fact that there are two ladies here, and only one in the morris of 1511, suggests that none of them is necessary for the morris itself.

The new court served as a model for the great nobles of the day. Henry Percy, fifth Earl of Northumberland and a member of the court's most intimate circles, was renowned for the magnificence of his lifestyle. He was closely involved in patronage of the arts, retaining minstrels and players who performed at court. His Christmastide entertainments were particularly impressive. The manner in which Northumberland's Twelfth-night revels were conducted is described in an administrative manual known as the Second Northumberland Household Book, wherein the usher prescribes 'Thordoryng of the Hall upon the 12 daie when a great estate or an Erle shall sit their present opinly in the saide Halle'.[49] The entertainments described are similar in form to those we have seen at the royal court. Although the rules would have been drafted for a specific event (Ian Lancashire suggests the entertainments at the Earl's seat at Wressle, formerly in the south-western corner of the East Riding of Yorkshire, now in Humberside, *c.* 1515), they are couched in general terms suitable for any occasion, so the first part of the Twelfth-night entertainments, an interlude, may be 'aithir ... A comody, or trigidy'. Next, the disguisers enter the hall; as they enter, four minstrels strike up, and the disguisers 'daunce suche daunces as they be appointed'.[50] The disguisers may be all male, or equal numbers of both sexes. These then stand to the sides, to make way for:[51]

> the morris to come in incontinent [i.e., at once] as is apointyd yf any be ordeignid And when the saide moris cummes in the Midist of the Hall Than the said Minstrallis to play the daunces that is appointid for thiem And when they Here the saide minsrallis play than to com out oon aftir an outhir as they be appointid And when they Have doon to go furth inlike caas as they cam into the saide towr or thing devisid for theim Alwaies reservid to the maister of the disguisinges to order it as he shall think best and convenient and when the said moris is doone than the gentillmen to com unto the women and make {th}er obeisance and every of {th}ame to taik oon by thande and daunce togeder by the maister of the Revelles and that doon to bring the women to {th}er plaices againe and mak {th}er obeisance and then departe to {th}er own places wheir the stoid befoir.

The morris dancers emerge from a device – a tower is suggested – and perform several dances. They are distinct from the disguisers who precede them, and from the mixed dancing which follows. Here 'the morris' is those who perform the special dances. The setting as a whole,

[48] Brewer, J.S. and Brodie, 1122-23, note 2562.
[49] Lancashire, Ian, p. 23.
[50] Lancashire, Ian, pp. 34-35.
[51] Lancashire, Ian, pp. 35-36.

including the other parts of the performance, constituted the disguising and may have been what was termed a morisk.

The Earl of Northumberland's brother-in-law Edward Stafford, third Duke of Buckingham, built a magnificent new seat on his estate at Thornbury Castle, near Bristol, in emulation of the palace at Richmond.[52] Like Northumberland, the scale of his entertaining was renowned, with feasts for as many as 500 people. In the Thornberry wardrobe accounts of 1516 for one such occasion are the following items:

> ... 10. dd. moresbelles. 6 virge. 3 quarteria nigri bokeram & ½ virge rubri bokeram pro 2 tunicis pro le moresdaunce. & 3 virge Canvas pro linura unius dictarum Tunicarum ...

> [10 dozen morris bells, 6¾ yards of black buckram and ½ yard of red buckram for 2 coats for the morris dance and 3 yards of canvas to line one of the said coats...]

Although the material for only two costumes is recorded, the relevant accounts for the preceding years are not all extant, and it would be unsafe to presume that there were only two dancers in the dance. The need to line one coat but not the other suggests repairs to and renewal of existing costumes. However, the use of buckram rather than the satin and sarsenet of the royal court does suggest an entertainment rather less lavish than at Richmond, and Ian Lancashire has described Buckingham's entertainments as 'unimpressive' in comparison with Northumberland's.[53]

As court revels increased in complexity and sophistication, royal and aristocratic tastes appear to have moved away from the morris dance and the morisk. The last specific reference from Tudor royal account books does indicate that a morris dance was not considered subtle enough to meet the court's mature tastes. In 1522 the morris dance was a children's seasonal entertainment to amuse the six-year-old Princess Mary at Christmas. The event took place at Ditton Park although the court was at Eltham at the time.[54] Among the items recorded in the accounts is the following entry:[55]

> Item paid for hyering of 10 dds [dozen] bells, and 9 Morres cots, & for the losse of 12 bells percell of the same 10 dd [dozen]: 2s 4d

The materials were hired from and returned to some outside agent, while the dances themselves were presumably supplied by members of the household. Why as many as nine coats were required is a mystery; and if all were used, each dancer had on average only seventeen bells.

Apart from the few instances where morris dancers appear in association with the celebrations of the great livery companies, these early references suggest a dance with quasi-dramatic associations, fit for the entertainment of the highest personages in the land in lavish spectacles. Costumes are extravagant and require bells. There are hints of the physical demands of the dance, requiring fit young men either from the ranks of the aristocratic audience or supplied by dedicated performers.

---

[52] Harris, Barbara J., pp. 85-89.
[53] Lancashire, Ian, p. 15.
[54] Marshall, Rosalind K., p. 8.
[55] Hall, Edward and Grafton, p. 651.

Chapter 2

Guilds

The first half of the 16th century was the heyday of the Midsummer Watch processions, when the mayor and sheriffs marched through London overnight (from 11 p.m. to 2 a.m.) on 23-24 and 28-29 June in a display of both military preparedness and spectacular entertainment. For a general impression of the nature of the processions we can do no better than to turn to John Stow, who in his *Survey of London* (c. 1598) described those which he must have seen himself in his youth. In an oft quoted passage, he wrote:[1]

> *The marching watch contained in number about 2000 men, parte of them being old Souldiers, of skill to be Captains, Lieutenants, Sergeants, Corporals, &c. Wiflers, Drommers, and fifes, Standard and Ensigne bearers, Sword players, Trumpeters on horsebacke, Demilaunces on great horses, Gunners with hand Guns, or halfe hakes, Archers in coates of white fustian signed on the breast and backe with the armes of the Cittie, their bowes bent in their handes, with sheafes of arrowes by their sides, Pike men in bright Corlets, Burganets, &c. Holbards, the like Bill men in Almaine Rivets, and Apernes of Mayle in great number, there were also divers Pageants, Morris dancers, Constables, the one halfe which was 120. on S. Johns Eve, the other halfe on S. Peters Eve in bright harnesse, some overgilte, and every one a Jornet of Scarlet thereupon and a chain of golde his Hench men following him, his Minstrels before him and his Cresset light passing by him, the Waytes of the City, the Mayors Officers, for his guard before him ... The Sheriffes watches came one after the other in like order, but not so large in number as the Mayors, for where the Mayor had beside his Giant, three Pageants, each of the Sherriffes had beside their Giantes but two Pageants, ech their Morris Dance and one Hench man their Officers in Jacquets of Wolsted, or say party coloured, differing from the Mayors, and each from other, but having harnised a great many, &c.*

Stow suggests that the watch was held annually until 1539, then next held in 1548, though more recent scholarship shows that it continued throughout the first half of the 1540s.[2] Although he says that the procession had taken place from 'time out of mind', the pageant element in these processions (a tableau or short performance presented on a moving wagon) is recorded only occasionally before 1504. Before that the strictly military elements predominated, though there are earlier records of minstrels, and of course the morris dance of 1477. Stow's account suggests that the 'Wiflers, Drommers, and fifes, Standard and Ensign bearers, Sword players, Trumpeters' and the like all belong together as quasi-military elements, while the 'Pageant, morris dancers [and] Waytes' belong in an 'entertainment' group, as do the giants, a feature of processions attested across Europe but particularly in Burgundy from the 14th century.[3]

In an attempt to revive the processions in 1585, a writer whom Stow describes as a 'grave citizen' elaborated in great detail who should be responsible for which items of expenditure in the watch, and prescribed that the entertainments were to be provided by each of the mayor and the sheriffs 'uppone his owne cost'. Each was to supply 'One companie of morris daun"cers'. The writer directed that the morris dancers should lead the companies of each of

---

[1] Stow, 1:101-04.
[2] Lancashire, Anne, pp. 157-67.

[3] UNESCO.

the mayor and the sheriffs, after the first 'battaylle' of soldiers and military music had passed, while a second 'battaylle' should close the procession.[4]

Morris dancing and pageants certainly occur together in the records of the livery companies. All the companies provided elements of the watch, but the pageants and other entertainments were usually supplied by the companies from which the mayor and sheriffs for the year were elected, so were in effect restricted to the 12 Great Livery Companies. Only four or five of these have appropriate records for the period, but the preponderance of records from the powerful Drapers' Company is striking. We have already encountered the earliest record from them in 1477. The next record of a morris dance in the watch comes again from the Drapers' Company, 35 years later in 1512, although the morris dance provided at the Carpenters' feast in 1507 suggests that activity continued in the interim. The 1512 morris dance, like the 1477 dance, took place when a draper, Roger Achilly, was mayor:[5]

> *of the pageant money*
>
> *It' for the Charges of 3 pagentes that is to say Saynt Blythe. Achilles. and th'assumpcion and also a Morish daunce, beside the Castell of were that the Bachillers paid for them self Sma of our Charges as aperys in 220 parcelles 12 li 17s 9d*

The castle is not related to the 'tower' of the kind from which the Earl of Northumberland's morris dancers descended. The dancers and castle were separate, as later accounts reveal.

When a Draper was next mayor, in 1515, a 'morysdaunce' was provided once more.[6] A Draper was again mayor in 1521. In that year Lodovico Spinelli, the secretary to the Venetian ambassador, saw the setting of the watch and described the order of the procession. This consisted of a succession of sets of armed men, musicians, mechanical devices and pageants. After a pageant of Saint George and the Dragon:[7]

> *Then followed a company dancing the morris dance, preceding a fine band of the city constables in armour with doublets of silk and cloth of gold and [gold] chains.*

This is a nineteenth-century translation from the Italian, which reads, 'Poi a piedi sequivano alcuni che faceano la morescha' ('some followed on foot, doing the morescha').[8] Spinelli was probably using 'morescha' as the cognate equivalent in Italian of 'morris dance' without implying any choreographic or other relationship. The Drapers' own accounts noted that 'the Maisters [of the Company] had a morysdaunce before the Waytes', and further details were supplied:[9]

> *It' to Robert Greves for a morysdaunce & 2 mynstrelles riding at there own coste except 2 sylk cotes & 2 hors trapps that we lent them and we gave the said mynstrelles 2 white hattes & paid for the mores daunce for both nyghtes 14s*

The arrangements for the minstrels were like those for other minstrels: silken coats and horse trappings were lent, and hats given. A taborer and a fiddler paid elsewhere in the accounts received six shillings; on the other hand, a piper and a drummer received only 1s 4d. Other (single) musicians received amounts between 1s 4d and 3s 4d. This suggests that the morris dancers themselves were paid 8s or more.

[4] 'Booke Conteyning the Manner', pp. 396-98, 404-06.
[5] Lancashire, Anne and Parkinson, p. 311.
[6] Lancashire, Anne and Parkinson, p. 322.
[7] Brown, Rawdon, Brown and Hinds, 3:136-37.
[8] Sanuto, 31:95.
[9] Lancashire, Anne and Parkinson, pp. 381-85.

Over the following two decades, until the demise of the Midsummer Watch processions, morris dancers appeared regularly. Most of the recorded instances were on behalf of the Drapers' Company. In 1522 the usual procession was cancelled to make way for a reception for the Holy Roman Emperor Charles V on 6 June, for a part of which the Drapers arranged 'a morys daunce as was used the last yere', and instead of the planned pageant 'to fynd 30 harnest men ... and also to have the gyant a morisdaunce & 50 moryspykes with suche mynstrelles as shall nede and 8 bowmen & no more'.[10] This time, however, the actual payment is more informative, giving the number of men involved, and the payment:

> Item to William Burnet for a morysdaunce of 7 & 2 minstrelles riding in our apparelles. 2 hattes &<c> 18s

The next year in which a Draper was mayor was 1525, and at the same time one of the two sheriffs was also a Draper. The mayor had a set of dancers and the sheriffs one between them.[11] The mayor's dancers were organized by Walter Fount. The dancers supplied their own costume, but like most of the participants were given breakfast. The mayor, Sir William Bayley, was obviously impressed, additionally rewarding the dancers with money and ale:

> Item to Walter ffount & his company that is to say 8 persones with
> there mynstrell for a morisdaunce bothe nyghtes for the Mair' all   sma 15s
> goyng on fote bifore the constables
> Item for a Reward to the moresdawncers 4d And for Ale to the
> mynstrelles & moresdancers 2d   sma 6d

If 4d was a fitting spontaneous reward for a group of eight dancers, the 15s received by Walter Fount must have represented a considerable sum if distributed among them. The musician would have commanded several shillings, of course, but that still leaves a sum of around 8s-10s for the dance itself.

In the following year the mayor was a Mercer, but again one of the sheriffs was a Draper. In the Drapers' accounts, together with payments for six drums, a double pipe, and tabor is a payment of 8s for a morris dance 'for the 2 Shireffes serving them equally'. This appears to have been a payment of 8s for each night, as elsewhere in the accounts is the record that 'John Laurens told me that bothe the Shireffes at ther own charge hyred hym & his company for a morysdance completed bothe the nyghtes in every thing after 16s. for all things besides there brekefast money'.[12]

John Laurence appears again in the 1529 accounts (when the Draper Sir John Rudstone was mayor) as a taborer, paid 2s 8d to play on both nights, supplying his own costume. On this occasion Walter Fount, now identified as a grocer, was contracted to supply the morris dancers 'with 6 persons and there mynstrell all in there own apparel, summa 7 persons, and they to have 13s 4d and there brekefast money', for which 4d was advanced. One Thomas Stringer was employed to walk in front of them with a two-handed sword.[13] This is the first instance of an arrangement which recurs from time to time over the following centuries, a sword bearer to walk ahead of the dancers, clearing the way.

---

[10] Lancashire, Anne and Parkinson, pp. 402-03.
[11] Lancashire, Anne and Parkinson, pp. 436-41.
[12] Lancashire, Anne and Parkinson, pp. 447-49.
[13] Lancashire, Anne and Parkinson, pp. 475-76.

In 1530 a Mercer was mayor, a Draper one of the sheriffs. The Drapers again agreed to supply a morris dance for their sheriff. The contractual nature of this arrangement is clear. The Drapers were hiring rather than providing morris dancers:[14]

> Agreed with Wm Darrell letherseller for A moresdaunce of 8 besides the Mynstrell onelye for our shreve [sheriff] all in their own apparell their mynstrell Rydyng and they to have 16s beside their brekfast monye.

For the first time in this survey of the Midsummer Watches a morris dance not associated with the Drapers was recorded in 1532, when the mayor was a Grocer. In the Grocers' wardens' accounts 26s 8d was paid 'for the hyre of the morys dauncers'.[15] The state of incompleteness of the records, and a reminder that not every event may leave a record, is indicated by the fact that the Drapers lent a pageant to the Mercer sheriff, but no records of this occurs in the Mercers' accounts.[16]

In 1534 the Drapers made very similar arrangements with Walter Fount to those of five years previously:[17]

> Agreed With Walter fountes for hym & his companye that is to saye
> 8 persons with their Mynstrell for A morysdaunce bothe nyghttes   summa 18s
> for the Maiour in their own apprell
> Agreed With Thomas waren for bothe nyghttes With A twoo hand
> swerde before the Moresdaunce besides brekefast Moneye   summa 12d

The Skinners were in charge in 1535 and they too hired Walter Fount 'morris dancer, for himself and for six persons morris dancers and for their breakfast money, 25s'. In 1536, when a Draper was again one of the sheriffs, Fount was contracted to supply seven persons for a morris dance, for 15s 8d; he was advanced 5s as an earnest.[18]

1539 was the year which Stow identifies as the first in which there was no Midsummer Watch, it being cancelled by Henry VIII for reasons which remain unclear.[19] However, the cancellation took place when preparations were well under way, and the Grocers, one of whom was to be a sheriff, had already constructed two pageants at Leadenhall. They transferred them to their own hall and set them up there, and 'paid to porters for bringing them from leden hall to the Grocers Hall with a Morrys Daunce 8s'.[20]

Despite Stow's assertion that the next Midsummer Watch procession was in 1548, the Drapers' records show preparations for processions for their mayor, including morris dancers, in 1541; but they expressed fears about the mounting costs of the exercise, caused by the 'wanton and superfluous' profligacy of the Mercers:[21]

> The seyd Mr Wardeyns as concernyng the charges of this hows for my lord mayre in his Wetche, dyd recyte befor the sayd Assystens & thoder, that they for evyry grote in tyme past, ar now ffayne to gyve 5. and that in dyuers thinges as shall appere in the hyryng of Drumes mynstrelles flag dragers two hand swerd pleyrs, morysdaunsers & berers of the Gyaunte Which hath rysyne by a wanton and superfluows precydence begone by mayres

14 Lancashire, Anne and Parkinson, p. 486.
15 Lancashire, Anne and Parkinson, p. 502.
16 Robertson, Jean and Gordon, p. 21.
17 Lancashire, Anne and Parkinson, p. 523.
18 Lancashire, Anne and Parkinson, p. 551.
19 Lancashire, Anne, p. 161.
20 Robertson, Jean and Gordon, p. 31.
21 Lancashire, Anne and Parkinson, p. 628.

and Shereffes of the mercery, And after the same so recyted The seyd Assistens sayd what remedy but go through wyth all.

The Drapers acknowledged that if they wanted to meet and match the show put on by the Mercers, they would have to go through with it; and the grounds for the Drapers' fears are confirmed in the increased payments made. John Lymmyr, a bowstring maker dwelling in St John's Street, was paid 23s 4d for himself and his company of seven morris dancers and their minstrel for both nights, 'so that they may be well trimmed after the gorgeous fashion'.[22]

This is the last occasion on which the livery companies record a payment for morris dances. The vast majority of the references come from the Drapers' records and show that the dance was done by eight men, who were hired for their services from outside the company. We have some names for the morris dancers' agents: in 1521 one Robert Greves, in 1522 William Burnet, and in 1526 the taborer John Laurence. In 1530 the company was that of William Darrell, a leatherseller, and in 1541 John Lymmyr, a bowstring-maker. But the chief agent was William Fount, a grocer, whose company was hired in 1525, 1529, and in 1534-1536, performing on behalf of both the Drapers and the Skinners. Other tradesmen were involved. In 1515 John Lupton, a tailor and Christopher Lee, a leatherseller, together with a William Deane, sued for the return of morris bells to the value of 6s 8d from Robert Shipton.[23] From the levels of recompense – above the average daily wage but not reflecting high social status – the performers, or at least their agents, were middling tradesmen in their crafts, but not necessarily linked to the trade of the company which hired them.

The earliest payment records are embedded in much larger payments (£10-20) for multiple elements of the watch. Payments for dancers and their minstrels generally range between 13s 4d and 18s when the Drapers hired them, but 25s and 26s 8d for other companies. The exception is the final year of records, and the Drapers' complaint about expense when they had to pay 23s 4d.

The *Order of the City Watch* (by Stow's 'grave citizen' writing in 1585) calculated a company of dancers as two ranks. Eight dancers in two ranks implies either they danced four abreast, or the author envisaged companies of only four dancers. In dealing with the eight-man teams of the account books, the companies made payment to one man, the dancers' agent, who in some cases (where seven dancers are mentioned) may have been a dancer himself; or a foreman leading six dancers.

An element of the payment was sometimes explicitly for costume, in order that it should be fitting for the magnificence of the spectacle, and it is not unreasonable to assume that when the dancers appear 'at their own cost' or 'in their own apparel' a substantial element of the fee was expended on costumes (although the dancers hired by the Drapers in 1522 were clothed by the company). The possession of such costumes would then enable the dancers to hire themselves out on other occasions for a considerably lower fee which accorded better with their personal monetary status, as with the Carpenters' feast day in 1507, when they were paid 8d. The mayor who gave them an extra 4d in reward in 1525 was likewise not being parsimonious but rewarding them according to their rank.

Although pageants, giants and musicians went in procession with the dancers, nothing in the contemporary accounts suggests that the dancers were closely linked with any of them, apart

---

[22] Lancashire, Anne and Parkinson, p. 631.   [23] Lancashire, Anne and Parkinson, p. 324.

from their own musicians and, perhaps, a swordsman at their head. Each was an item in a series of independent spectacles in a long procession.

The heyday of the metropolitan guild processions was the first half of the 16th century. When the watch processions were cancelled in the mid 1540s the focus of mayoral celebration switched to the Lord Mayor's Show, for which dancers were apparently not hired. Significant activity continued, however, in much the same vein within metropolitan parish activities, to which we shall return in Chapter 3.

Although the morris of the court had European analogues in the morisks of the period, we have no European analogues for the processional morris through the streets. The Drapers' event of 1477 is one of the earliest references to a processional dance not just in England, but Europe-wide. It may be that the indoor events seen at the Drapers' feast in 1448 and the Carpenters' feast in 1502 form a bridge between the two forms, but the origin of the processional morris of the trade guilds remains unknown.

———————————

Outside of London it is sometimes difficult to discern if events were primarily led by trade guilds or by the civic authorities or involved parish activity. These three foci of community life overlapped in many ways. The earliest record is from Lydd in Kent, where in 1518 the borough chamberlain paid 14d 'in rewarde to the morisdaunceres of Winchelsey'.[24] We do not know if the Winchelsea dancers travelled the nine miles to Lydd as part of the festival known as a parish ale (see Chapter 3) or to participate in a civic event. At a similar occasion at nearby Rye in June 1534, morris dancers who travelled from Mayfield were paid 2s 8d by the Rye chamberlain.[25] If this is modern Mayfield that was a journey of over 20 miles.

Most of the records of guild or civic activity outside London are later than those of the London guilds, and primarily relate to the mid 16th century. At Southampton in 1562 3s 4d was given to 'the singers players and Morris Daunsers on Maye Daye',[26] while in 1564 morris dancers were paid 2s at Plymouth as part of the civic May-day celebrations, followed by payments of 3s 4d in 1567 (with another 5s for breakfast), 4s in 1568, and 5s in 1569 and 1570.[27] The Plymouth payments continued into the next century, and were clearly an accepted part of civic life.

At Chester the first explicit payment for morris dancers at the Midsummer Watch procession was in 1569 when 'the morres dauncers' were paid 6s 8d and their minstrels 16d.[28] Similar payments were made in the following decades and we shall pick these up later, but it is worth considering the 1577 payment now:[29]

> *Et solutum Thome Gillam pro saltacione sua vocata daunseinge ludi vocato morris dawns ad vigilitatem sancti Iohannis Baptiste ultimam preteritam 6s 8d*
>
> *[And paid to Thomas Gillam for his dancing called a dancing game called morris dance on the eve of St John Baptist last past 6s 8d]*

Compare this with payments made a decade earlier in 1564 and 1565:[30]

---

[24] Dawson, p. 100.
[25] Mayhew, p. 58.
[26] 'Southampton Book'.
[27] Wasson, pp. 236-240.
[28] Clopper, p. 87.
[29] Clopper, p. 120.
[30] Clopper, pp. 70, 74.

Item paid to houghe gillome for daunsinge at midsomer 7s

Item paid houghe gillome for daunsinge at midsomer by mr mayres apoyntment 6s 8d

Much as Walter Fount in London, the Gillam family in Chester was clearly the chief supplier of dancers to civic processions. There are two ways of interpreting the references to 'dancing' in the 1560s and 'morris dancing' later. Either the 1560s entries refer to morris dancing, but don't make it explicit; or some more generic dancing then was transformed into 'morris dancing' by the 1570s. The circumlocutory expression from 1577 suggests that the concept was unfamiliar to the scribe (despite the straightforward mention in 1569). If indicative of such a change, it is tempting, albeit speculative, to infer that the Gillams maintained a continuity in choreography. They danced as they had done before, but the costume, &c. of the dance may have changed to make it a 'morris dance'. An undated record made when a lot of the Chester pageant gear was being renewed indicates that there were in fact six dancers; by the time of the record they and their pipe-and-taborer were paid 20s.[31]

At Salisbury the earliest reference reflects an already established morris. According to the record of the assembly of the Guild of Tailors on 22 September 1564:[32]

> *At thys assembly was receyved for the putting owt of the Morrys Cots 3s 4d; and yt ys agreyd that Gregory Clerke shall have the kepynge of the ffyve morrys-cots, with 20 dosyn of Myllan-bells, for the space of 12 yeres, yf he so longe lyve, payeng yerely to the ocupacon 3s 4d and also the said Gregory do stand bound to the occupacon in the some of ffive pounds of lawfull money of England, to delyver the same ffyve morys cots and 20 doysen of Myllan-bells, at the end of the said 12 yeres, or at the oure of death of the said Gregory if he diye before, in as good case as he receyved it, and further the said Gregory byndyth hymself by these presents to delyver the said Cotts and bells at all tymes to the said occupation yf they wyll have them to the use of the occupacion, and yt ys agreyd that the said Gregory shalbe bound to the Wardens of the occupacion, by wrytyng, obligatory in the some of ffyve poundes.*

There is a wealth of information here. There were five coats and 240 Milan (steel) bells, implying 48 bells per person. The coats had earned 3s 4d for the guild by being hired out, and now Gregory Clerke was to pay that sum to the guild annually, presumably intending to hire them out enough times to make a profit on the deal. At the same time the guild could use them whenever they wanted. The value of coats and bells is £5, which Clerke had to pay to the guild if he failed to return them at the end of the contract. We shall see that the hire of morris costumes between communities was a common practice, to get a return on the not inconsiderable expense of acquiring the costumes. In 1568 and 1569 the guild agreed to pay for the morris dancers' 'meat, drink and wages' at its annual feast.[33] The evidence indicates that the guild judged the considerable outlay to be a sound investment.

The establishment of the Salisbury tailors' morris may have been recent in 1564. The detailed record of the contractual arrangement for the care of the coats, together with records thereafter for the engagement of morris dancers, occurs in a minute book which was commenced in 1517. If morris dancers had been engaged before 1564 we might expect to find that reflected in the earlier records.

---

[31] Clopper, p. 481.

[32] Haskins, pp. 171-72.

[33] 'Tailors' Guild' (1517), ff. 61v, 66v. I am grateful to Audrey Douglas for drawing the minute books to my attention (personal communication, 10 October 1990).

The fullest account of civic May-day festivities appears in the Ledger Book of Newport (Isle of Wight) which started in 1567, and which begins by asserting that it describes 'the auncient usages and olde customs of the borough of Newport within {th}e Isle of Wight dewlie continu[e] d from {th}e tyme {th}at memorie of man is not to the contrarie'. A Lord and his Vice (deputy) were appointed and on the Saturday after 1 May rode with a minstrel and a company of youths about the town, summoning the townsfolk to fetch may home from Parkhurst woods before dawn the next morning, on pain of a penalty. The foresters at Parkhurst met them and presented them with green boughs in recognition of their rights of pasture. Next the townspeople entered the wood to cut green boughs to decorate the town streets, then marched back to the town 'the comeners before, the keapers following them; next, ye minstrel, Vice, and moriss dancers; after ye Sergeants with their maces; then the Bailives and the Coburg's couples in their degree' (Coburg is a nearby settlement) to breakfast and a church service. After dinner the women walked for recreation the five miles to Bigbury, 'orderlie in their degree' behind the Lord, minstrel and morris dancers, returning for evening prayer and supper.[34]

Much of this description fits with the kind of event described for Helston's Furry Day in the 19th century and still practised there today (albeit with some antiquarian invention).[35] Two points which stand out are the close intertwining of civic and church life, with most civic ceremonies finding realization at some point in a church service, and the emphasis on good order and social rank. The bringing in of the may was observed in similar fashion in the chamberlain's accounts for 1553 at Gloucester:[36]

Also in reward gevyn to maister Arnoldes servaunts on May Day at the bryngyng in of may by the commaundement of the maire	*20s*
...	
And more to those persons that daunsed the moorys daunse the same tyme by like Commaundement	*5s*

Despite the widespread popularity of these occasions, the fear that such festivity might result in civil disorder was strong in Tudor England, and all kinds of popular entertainment were liable to be subject to bans and prohibitions. In London in 1527 the Court of Aldermen required aldermen and their deputies to keep watch on May Day Eve (till 4 a.m.) to prevent householders from going out of the city to collect greenery to erect at churches 'as afore this tyme [corrected from 'of olde tyme'] have been used'; and not to 'suffer eny maner May Games as Mores daunses & suche other lyke openly to be kepte within ther wardes'. A very similar injunction was made in 1530, not to 'suffre eny Trees to be sett up in the Stretes afore eny Churches or other places, Nor no Maye Games to be used, as the morres daunce & other lyke openly to be kepte in the Strettes within youre seyd warde'.[37]

On the other hand, disorder or the threat of it could be turned to the authorities' advantage. At Sandwich in Kent in November 1525 the mayor Henry Booll indulged what had been his practice throughout his mayoralty of asserting his authority by parading through the town accompanied by a gang of ruffians. On St Clement's Day (23 November) when the bailiff Sir Edward Ringeley (a rival locus of power to the mayor) attempted to gather the King's tolls at the annual fair, Booll had 20 men walk up and down the fair all day long, 'craking and swearing

---

[34] Stone, 'Ledger Book' [Part 1], p. 183.
[35] Toy, pp. 367-79.
[36] Douglas, Audrey and Greenfield, p. 297.
[37] Lancashire, Anne and Parkinson, pp. 455-56, 481.

to kill ... whosoever durst presume to gather any penny that day for the King'. The same night the rioters morris-danced about the town, armed with swords and bucklers. There were further revels, culminating in a free banquet enlivened with a 'tabber' and pipe-playing.[38] All in all, however, it is clear that morris dancing enjoyed widespread civic and mercantile support through the 16th century.

[38] Gardiner, Dorothy, pp. 153-54.

Chapter 3

Parish entertainments

In the closing years of the reign of Henry VII morris dancers appear in a new context, that of the parish entertainment. The location of their first appearance – Kingston-upon-Thames – is significant because it hints at methods of transmission as the dance spread. The socio-cultural scenarios in which we encounter morris dancing in its first 60 years are high-class: the court, expensive artwork, the guilds. Kingston-upon-Thames was just two miles from Richmond Palace, and their geographical proximity may be the key to the transition of morris dancing into a popular community entertainment.

The threads that linked court and people were manifold, lying not simply in the public display of royal pomp, but, as we have seen, in the use of artisans and craftsmen to make the props and costumes needed for royal events. Moreover, the people could come to court, as on 31 May 1505, when 3s 4d was given 'to the players at Kingeston towarde the bilding of the churche stiple in almns'.[1] This entry is confirmation that, besides undoubtedly supplying local labour for the palace, the community presented its entertainments to the court. I would suggest that it is not a coincidence, therefore, that the churchwardens' accounts of Kingston provide us with the earliest (and some of the most detailed) information about morris dancing outside the court and the great houses of England.

When morris dancers were being equipped at Kingston, they were being grafted on to existing parish entertainments. May games in their various guises often included a mock court and it is easy to imagine the people of Kingston, aware of the nature of court entertainments at Richmond, mirroring them. This may have been serendipitous chance: no such transition took place in Scotland, where the dance essentially died out after it ceased to be a court fashion. Likewise, the dance did not make the transition from court to people in most of Europe.

There is always the possibility that morris dancing in parishes took place before we find it at Kingston-upon-Thames in 1507 but was simply not recorded. It is certainly the case that records do not stretch back into antiquity. However, churchwardens' account books providing evidence for the nature of parish entertainments are commonly available from the 15th century, with no evidence of morris dancing as part of such events. Once morris dancing does appear, however, the association with the parish ale and its successors survived well into the 19th century, so it is worth spending some time considering the nature of these festivals at the start of the association.

The typical parish at the beginning of the modern age had various means of obtaining money for the upkeep of property and clergy. It could receive income from property; it might be left money for either general or specific purposes; and it received fees for the performance of particular services, such as burial. These are typified in the accounts from Thame, Oxfordshire, in 1458, which record receipts of 3s in land rental, 2s 6d for a rood light (candle) and 3s 6d for the burial of a parishioner.[2] Straightforward collections might be made, as the receipt of 4s 2d for 'diverse gatherings' recorded at Bishop's Stortford, Hertfordshire, in 1491.[3]

---

[1] Anglo, 'Court Festivals', p. 39.
[2] Lee, Frederick George, *History,* col. 45.
[3] Glasscock, p. 27.

In many places there is evidence that the parish as a whole expected groups within the parish to generate income for it in one way or another. Reflecting the close intertwining of civic, economic and religious life, these might be guilds of workers in the same occupation, as at Croscombe in Somerset in 1490:[4]

> *Comys the Tokers* [tuckers] *and presentith in 2s 9d*
>
> ...
>
> *Comys the Wefars and presentith in nowgte*

Here the weavers had failed to collect anything or had spent as much in collecting the money as they received. Such arrangements made in general for an uncertain income. Particular groups sometimes had real or nominal responsibility for separate aspects of the upkeep of the church, for example, the supply of candles. In some parishes there were social groups as well as or instead of occupational groups (which by their nature were found only in the larger communities). Two groups in particular recur in many accounts: the young men and the maidens of the parish. At St Lawrence's church in Reading, the churchwardens recorded in 1505:[5]

> *It. rec. of the maydens gaderyng at Whitsontyde at {th}e tre at {th}e church dore, clerly 2s 9d*

and much later, in 1557:[6]

> *Itm ye gatheringe of ye yonge folkes & maydens on Maydaye & at Whitsontyde – nichil* [nothing]

The method of raising money seems to have been variable. A hobby horse might parade, soliciting gifts, or a play might be staged, or an ale held. An example of the last is to be found in the Bishop's Stortford accounts of 1496:[7]

> *Received of the Bachelors of the said Town of the profit of a certain drinking called the May Ale 35s 4d*

An ale was the normal equivalent of what would now be a village fête. It received its name from the fact that ale was brewed in large quantities and sold. Usually, food was supplied as well. A collection would be taken from those assembled for the ale, and towards this end entertainments were provided. A piper or fiddler to play for community dancing was probably the commonest of the entertainers. Many of the preserved records of ales occur in churchwardens' accounts, but the ale was not a peculiarly ecclesiastical event. Any occasion might be marked by an ale.

Ales were not necessarily tied to the calendar, although many took advantage of the main holidays or local church feast-days. If financial pressures required it, more than one ale might be held in a year, for example at Marston, Oxfordshire in 1553, when the parish received £1 from a 'churche ale' and a further 5s 4d from a 'youngmans ale'.[8] The ale was often put in the hands of the youth of the parish. In his 1602 *Survey of Cornwall* Richard Carew described the process:[9]

> *...two young men of the parish are yerely chosen by their last foregoers, to be Wardens, who dividing the task, make collection among the parishioners, of whatever provision it pleaseth them voluntarily to bestow. This they imploy in brewing, baking, and other acates* [groceries],

---

4   Hobhouse, p. 18.
5   Kerry, *History ... St. Lawrence*, p. 228.
6   Kerry, *History ... St. Lawrence*, p. 228.
7   Glasscock, p. 22.
8   Weaver, F.W. and Clark, p. 18.
9   Carew, f. 68v.

against Whitsontide; upon which Holydayes, the neighbours meet ... contributing some petty portion to the stock ... for there is entertained a kinde of emulation between these Wardens, who by his graciousness in gathering, and good husbandry in expending, can best advance the Churches profit. Besides, the neighbour parishes, at those times lovingly visit one another, and this way frankely spend their money together. The afternoons are consumed in such exercises, as olde and yong folke (having leisure) doe accustomably weare out the time withall.

Where autonomous groups were responsible for the ale, the detailed accounts of the ale are separate from the accounts of the parish and do not appear in them. The churchwardens relied on the person responsible for organizing the event to produce the money, and only the net profit was recorded. At Marston in 1557 this was made explicit:[10]

Item John Ewen brought in for the youngmens ale which he made this yere 4s 4d

The formal process of handing over the money at the end of the financial year is made clear by the terminology at Croscombe, for example in 1484:[11]

Comys yong men and presents nowgte
Comes the maydyngs and presents in 16s 3½d

The ales often had a theme. A favourite was Robin Hood, witness the accounts of Tintinhull, Somerset, in 1512/13:[12]

It. of Robine Hoods All [ale] *only this once 11s*

and at Thame in 1474 and 1501:[13]

Ite. we recevyd of Robyn hodg Ale at Wytsontyde	*26s*	*9d*
...		
Itm. rec' of the may ale and of the gaderyng of Robyn Hodde in new Thame att whitsontyed clere	*20s*	

Robin Hood assumed the role here which in other events was taken by the 'Summer Lord' or 'May Lord' or 'King'. David Wiles has argued – and convincingly demonstrated in the case of Henley-on-Thames – that the same master of ceremonies might be called both 'Robin Hood' and 'the King'.[14] The event was sometimes termed a 'King game'. The 'Whitsun ale', named for its staging at that time of year, also had its lord or king.

The general form which these ales adopted can be ascertained, although the details remain comparatively vague. The typical setting was a bowery – a temporary structure decorated with may boughs, or an adapted barn – in which a Summer Lord (or King, or May Lord, or Robin Hood), chosen from the community, held a mock court. A maypole was erected close by. The 'fertility' aspects of maypoles have been discussed many times, but undoubtedly they also served the more prosaic function of an ale-stake, the traditional sign that ale was being brewed. They have been a symbol of festivity from their first appearance in the records in the 14th century.[15] Maypole and ale-stake were both garlanded poles, and one later writer explicitly equated the two.[16] A tall maypole was a signal highly visible to all the surrounding countryside.

---

[10] Weaver, F.W. and Clark, p. 19.
[11] Hobhouse, p. 12.
[12] Hobhouse, p. 200.
[13] Ellis, p. 22; Lee, Frederick George, *History*, col. 26.

[14] Wiles, p. 8.
[15] Hutton, *Stations*, pp. 233-37.
[16] Robertson, William, s.v. ale-stake, p. 64.

The impending ale was announced in the preceding days by its Lord and his retinue, who toured the district after his election. In the case of a Whitsun ale, this took place on Ascension Thursday, ten days before Whit Sunday, and was itself an occasion for celebration, as at Melton Mowbray, Leicestershire, in 1563:[17]

Imprimis Rd of Hawe [Holy] Thursday at the chosinge of the Lorde and Ladye 28s 10d

Visits by other parishes were returned, and as many of these festivals occurred at Whitsuntide, the mock court, or representatives of it, might lead the visiting parties to the neighbourhood community and provide a measure of reciprocal entertainment. In these circumstances some costs would fall on the visiting parish and may be recorded in the accounts. At Bishop's Stortford in 1489 the accounts show expenditure of 3s at 'Sabbisford [Sawbridgeworth] May et lytill Hadham May' and a further 6d at 'Thorleigh May'.[18] These were all local communities: Sawbridgeworth is five miles from Bishop's Stortford, Little Hadham three miles and Thorley just two miles.

The parishes visited in the initial perambulation might also incur costs. An example of this also occurs in the Bishop's Stortford accounts, when they record a visit in 1515 from Sawbridgeworth:[19]

Item pd for brede and ale the same day that Sabbysford may was whan thay of Sabysford did come rydyng to the towne to sett ther may 9d

The Lord had a retinue uniformed in his colours, or livery, and visitors to the ale were expected to buy 'small liveries' – strips of ribbon in the Lord's colours – which were pinned to their clothing to indicate that they had paid and could participate in the festivities. The chief entitlements were to watch any entertainments being provided, such as a Robin Hood play, and to partake of a meal in the Lord's mock court. So at Bramley, Hampshire, in 1531 the following receipts were recorded, including some from the neighbouring parishes of Pamber and Stratfield Saye:[20]

Rec. of the Kyng Ale at Whitesonday at Sopper	£1	0s	7d
On Munday at dynner		2s	0d
The seid Munday at Supper		10s	7d
On the Tuysday at dynner		6s	9d
Rec. the seid Tuysday of the parishe of Pamber		4s	0d
Rec. the said Tuysday of the parish of Stratfeldsay		9s	0d
The seid Tuysday at Supper		10s	6d
The Wennesday at dynner		1s	6d
For Calfs and Shepe Skynns		1s	9d
At Supper on Trinite Sonday		12s	6d
For tappyng money		7s	6d
Ex dono parochianorum		1s	6d
Summa rec. de Churche ale, de clero	£4	8s	2d

[17] Kelly, p. 65.
[18] Glasscock, p. 20.
[19] Glasscock, p. 34.
[20] Williams, J.F., p. 19.

These receipts also illustrate other typical aspects of ales: that left-overs from the preparations and feasts (here the animal skins) were sold to defray the expenses; that a common pattern was to hold a few initial days of feasting, starting with the grand occasion on the Sunday, and to have a final fling the following Sunday (and the falling off of income during the week shows just why this was done), and that neighbouring parishes visited ales in a body.

Naturally, the receipts of the ale had to be balanced against the expenses, and in some of the examples given above obviously did not meet them. The three main categories of expenditure were provisions (the ale and food), equipment (including the liveries, trestle tables, &c.), and fees for the minstrels, musicians and sometimes the chief personages of the festival. When ales were organized by autonomous groups within the parish, only net receipts are recorded by the churchwardens in their accounts; but if the churchwardens themselves were responsible for the organization of the ales, the detailed expenses and receipts may be listed. It is this circumstance which makes the Kingston-upon-Thames accounts so important. The reasons for the centralization of the organization of activities are not clear. Possibly it reflects the growth of the activities to a point beyond the resources and organizational capacities of individual guilds or other social groups.

The ales held at Kingston-upon-Thames in the early 16th century are important both chronologically and geographically. The first book of the parish's churchwardens' accounts covers the period 1504-38.[21] The accounts were normally made up to St Luke's Day (18 October) each year.

For 1504-06 we have summary accounts rendered in June specifically for the 'King game', which reveal only that a King and Queen were appointed.[22] In 1507 a marked change takes place, and the accounts become much fuller. As well as a King, Robin Hood appeared as a separate personage. Both collected money from Whit Sunday to Thursday. In addition, the King still had his King game on one of the days (probably the Sunday), for which a separate note of receipts appears in the accounts.[23] In other words, multiple attractions were being presented; perhaps this expansion necessitated the transfer of all financial responsibility to the direct control of the parish. It is in this year that the morris dancers appear:[24]

Item for garterynge of 4 dosen bellys		*3d*
...		
Item for payntyng of ye mores garmentes and for sarten gret leveres [liveries]	*2s*	*4d*
...		
Item for 4 plytes and a quarter of laun for ye mores garmentes	*2 s*	*9d*
Item for orseden for ye same		*10d*
Item for 4 hats		*6d*
Item for a goun for ye lady		*8d*
Item for ye makynge of ye mores garmentes & for yer met & for fetting of ye ger at London	*9s*	*4d*
Item for bells for ye daunsars		*12d*
...		
Item to Robard Felere for chone for ye dauncers	*4s*	*4d*

---

[21] 'Kingston Parish Records'.
[22] 'Kingston Parish Records', p. 40.
[23] 'Kingston Parish Records', p. 51.
[24] 'Kingston Parish Records', pp. 53-54.

This suggests quite strongly that the morris was being introduced for the first time. The materials had to be acquired in London and brought from there, the shoes ('chone') had to be made, the bells bought and fixed upon garters, the costumes made up, tinselled (the 'orseden') and painted. Painting of plain cloth was a commonly used inexpensive way of creating colourful costumes. If the hats were theirs, there were four dancers, each wearing a dozen bells. The accounts state that their shoes cost 4s 4d. If a pair was made for each dancer, then they cost 13d a pair; no other small number of dancers gives a figure in an exact number of pence. This is expensive: shoes bought the next year cost only 7d a pair; three years later they cost only 8d a pair, and even special 'double-soled' shoes bought in 1536 cost only 9d a pair.[25] The lady's gown shows there was a female role, but we do not know if she was the consort of Robin Hood, or of the King, or a more anonymous character attached to the morris. Later records provide evidence for a Maid Marion role often played by a boy, but the explicit reference to a 'lady' may be an echo of the role of the lady in the courtly morisk in Richmond Palace nearby.

Coats were hired from one John Edmund for Robin Hood, Little John and 'Gyllys Kempe', for 17s 4d. The last may have been playing the part of the Friar, who is mentioned explicitly the following year, 1508, when 3s is paid for his coat, 8s for Little John's, but 16d only 'for makyng of Robyn Hodes cote', i.e., making it from material supplied.[26] In 1507 a taborer was hired for 6s 8d. Later accounts indicate the daily rate was 8d, so this payment suggests he was hired for a total of ten days. In 1508 he is paid only 5s 4d, i.e., only eight days' hire.[27] In 1508 the King game and Robin Hood were again both presented, and again they were essentially separate events. Wine was bought for the King game company on their day for 1d (they are clearly a small company); while food and drink were supplied to Robin Hood and his men for 16d.[28]

The morris dancers in 1508 are mentioned only twice: 14d was spent on food and drink for them on fair day, and a further 14d on two pairs of shoes.[29] No expenditure on new costumes is recorded, so it is more probable that shoes were being replaced rather than that the number of dancers had increased. The parish visited King games in that year at the neighbouring parishes of Long Ditton, West Molesey and Hampton (all within about 3 miles), paying out of the church box 3s, 2s and 3s 4d respectively.[30]

By 1508 Kingston-upon-Thames had a comprehensive assemblage of morris costumes and an established feast. In 1510 the parish made 'official' visits to the King games at neighbouring Walton-on-Thames (5 miles away) and Sunbury-on-Thames (6 miles), and made payments out of parish funds at each, 3s 6d and 1s 10d respectively.[31] For Kingston's own ale, the main costs were for food and drink, and for 'great and small' liveries. The numbers expected can be gauged from the purchase of over 3000 pins – some to make costumes but undoubtedly the majority to pin liveries to clothing. Costumes were refurbished or refreshed: 7d was paid for silver paper for the morris, six new pairs of shoes bought for 4s and a fool's coat for 1s 2d. For the Robin Hood game a Friar's coat was acquired for 3s and Little John's for 8s 4d. For 'half of Robin Hood's coat' 7s 6d was paid out, and a further 1s 3d for Kendal green cloth for it. Two shillings were paid for the morris dancers' food and drink, and an additional 4d for the

[25] 'Kingston Parish Records', pp. 39, 19, 178.
[26] 'Kingston Parish Records', p. 53.
[27] 'Kingston Parish Records', pp. 64, 52.
[28] 'Kingston Parish Records', pp. 59-64.
[29] 'Kingston Parish Records', p. 62.
[30] 'Kingston Parish Records', p. 60.
[31] 'Kingston Parish Records', p. 16.

same when they performed on Corpus Christi.[32] There were now definitely six dancers. This expenditure relates to at least two distinct events: £4 was received from the King game and 4 marks (£2 13s 4d) for Robin Hood's gathering.

In 1514, Kingston received 9s 4d for 'Robyn Hoodes gaderyng at Croydon', nine miles away, surely a semi-professional dramatic or quasi-dramatic performance in a place outside Kingston's usual ambit.[33] In 1515 we learn the names of dancers. A group of entries in the accounts is headed 'Chones [shoes] for mores daunsars'; and to this heading someone has added in a different hand, '& Roben hod and his compenye'. Six (and possibly a seventh) recipients of shoes are identified by name, but two only as somebody's 'man'. These will have been apprentices or servants. Each is provided with a pair of shoes for 8d:[34]

ferst to Jhon at benes A peyer of chone	8d
tomas Kendauall A peyer chone	8d
...	
leycroftes man A peyer	8d
...	

A further four pairs of shoes were associated with Robin Hood's company. Further entries indicate the progress of the event:

Item to Harry Payntare for 900 of leveres	3s	9d
Item for 16 gret leveres		7d
Item for makeng of a croun for ye mores daunsers		2d
Item for met & drenk for ye mores daunsars vpon feyer daye		9d
Item to Roben Hod for hes labor		12d
Item to leytell Jhon for hes labor		10d
Item to ffreer tuk		8d
Item in money Amongest Roben Hodes men at nythe		8d
Item for A taberare apon may daye		8d
Item in mony to young men that tok Apon them to pleye the mores dauns		6d
Item for a taberar Apon feyer eve & feyer daye and for belles for ye daunsars		16d

The 16 'great liveries' would be for the performers at the ale, while the 900 ordinary liveries represent the anticipated audience for it. A crown was also made for the dancers (for an unknown purpose), money was spent on bells, and they were fed. The sixpence to 'young men that took upon them to play the morris dance' suggests that they were given a token payment. Young men constitute one of the common groupings within parishes who were expected to contribute towards the upkeep of the church, doing so here by providing the morris-dance element of the festival.

Apart from the original purchase of a lady's gown in 1507, the initial indication of a Maid Marion comes in 1509, when 'she' (as the accounts have it) was paid 2s for two years' work, and a skirt and gloves were made for her. She appears to be in Robin Hood's retinue along with Little John and the Friar.[35] This is in fact the first securely dated reference to Maid Marion in English. After

---

[32] 'Kingston Parish Records', pp. 16-20.
[33] 'Kingston Parish Records', pp. 21, 77.
[34] 'Kingston Parish Records', p. 84.
[35] 'Kingston Parish Records', p. 66.

minimal records of receipts from Robin Hood's gathering in 1517 and 1518, she re-appears in Kingston's records when costumes were again refreshed in 1519. The payments are 'for the May game and Robert Hood': canvas and Bruges satin to make coats, russet (coarse red woollen cloth) for the Friar's coat, and 14 coats in Kendal green ('the gift of the Masters of the town'). There are '8 payer of schewes for ye mores dansserers ye freer & made maryen at 8d ye payer: 5s 4d' and 16 hats and feathers acquired at London, also for 5s 4d. Money was paid for the loss of a hat and of 4 feathers, so it seems these were hired rather than bought. Two thousand liveries were prepared, with pins for each.[36] The bundling of Maid Marion's shoes with those of the dancers and the Friar suggests that by this time she had a dancing role as demanding as that of the dancers. The text suggests also that Robin Hood has been absorbed into the May game (or *vice versa*).

Net receipts for Robin Hood alone were recorded in 1520 and 1521 (8s and 8s 6d respectively). In 1522 the King game reappeared: it brought in £6 13 4d, while Robin Hood brought in £2 6s 8d. If these are net figures they may reflect not just growth in the scale of the entertainment, but also the inflationary pressures that Tudor England was experiencing. The itemized expenditure has no entries for food or drink, but the morris dancers' costumes were refurbished yet again:[37]

Item paid for 8 yerdes of ffustyan for ye Mores daunsers cotes	4s
Item paid for 12 dosyn of belles	3s
Item paid for a dosyn of gold skynnes for ye mores	10d
...	
Item paid for 4 yardes of bokeram for ye morenys Cote	16d
Item paid for 4 Estrygge [ostrich] ffethers for Robyn Hode	20d
Item paid for 2 peyre of shone for Robyn Hode & lytell John	21d
Item paid for makyng of ye Mores cote	5d

The character of a Moor (the 'morenys', 'Mores cote' above) has been introduced, separate from the morris dancers, and an elaborate coat which uses four yards of material is made for him. The parish continued to invest heavily in its morris dancers. Eight yards of fustian are not sufficient to reclothe the entire set of dancers, and they and the gold skins must have gone towards making the existing costumes more elaborate, in which case the fustian was probably cotton velvet rather than the coarse cotton of ordinary fustian. There is an absolute increase in the number of bells on the costumes, regardless of whether the gross acquired here replaces or supplements the bells already acquired. Robin Hood's hat was embellished with ostrich feathers.

In 1524 all of Robin Hood's company of 20 wore hired hats (and had to pay for one lost), and 1500 liveries were made specifically for his event. This is significant because once again the receipts record both a King game and Robin Hood. The former brought in £9 10s 6d, the latter £2 5s 4d. No expenditure on food was recorded. The King game by this time seems to be entirely autonomous, as the churchwardens were responsible only for Robin Hood. The following year, the very word 'Kinggame' disappeared, being crossed out in the accounts and replaced by the more prosaic 'church-ale', i.e., a basic communal feast without any accompanying ceremonial

---

[36] 'Kingston Parish Records', p. 97.   [37] 'Kingston Parish Records', p. 112.

or entertainment. Net receipts ('all thyng deducte') for church ale and Robin Hood together are given as £3 10s 5d. The accounts record no expenditure on food. Robin Hood and one or two others had new satin coats made for them, and new liveries were made, but otherwise no relevant expenditure was recorded.[38]

In 1525 the church ale brought in £7 15s, Robin Hood £1. A tantalising hint of some of the other activity going on during the year is provided by the following isolated entry:[39]

Item paid for drynke for ye daunsers on May day 6d

In the period 1526-30 no church ale was recorded, only the annual income from Robin Hood, and minimal costs of maintenance for his coat were recorded, in 1529 and 1530.[40]

No relevant income was recorded in 1531; there is a gap in the accounts from 1532 to 1534, and no relevant income was recorded in 1535. In 1536, however, the May game and Robin Hood reappeared, possibly because extensive roof repairs costing £21 were being made to the church. The May game brought in £2 0s 4d, Robin Hood £5 6s 8d. The morris dancers and Robin Hood all had to be re-equipped, reflecting the fact that there has been next to no investment in the equipment for a decade. Five hats and four purses were purchased for the morris dancers, and new sets of bells together with garters on which to fix them. Material was bought to make new morris dancers', fool's and friar's coats and Maid Marion's skirt, and payments made for the making of them. Two sets of shoes (one single-soled, one double-soled) were purchased for six dancers. The total expenditure on this re-equipping was £2 3s 7½d, representing about one third of the eventual receipts. The dancers were evidently worked hard, as 3s 8d was paid for their refreshments when this would be no more than a few pence a day. The purchase of two sets of shoes, some heavy-duty, is another indication of a demanding performance schedule. In addition, a minstrel for them was paid 10s 8d, and visits were made to Croydon, Twickenham and Walton-on-Thames. Whereas in 1515 900 liveries were prepared for paying customers, on this occasion 1300 were made. [41]

Having re-established its entertainments, Kingston did not hold any the following year. In fact it may have cancelled those planned, for a deleted entry in the accounts refers to payments for 600 liveries for Robin Hood. Instead, the church lent out its morris coats to another (unidentified) parish for the sum of 2s, offset by the 4d cost of cleaning them.[42] There was an event in 1538, generating an income of £1 3s 8d, with fairly minimal expenditure. [43]

This marks the end of the account book. Towards the end is an inventory of goods in the wardens' keeping:[44]

Lefte in the kyping of the wardens nowe being a fryeres Cote of Russett & a Kyrtell of wostedde weltyd wt Redd cloth a mowrens Cote of Buckrame & 3 morres Dawnseres Cotes of whitte fustyan spangelyd & 2 gryne saten Cotes and a Dysarddes [fool's] Cote of Cotten and 6 payre of garderes w<ith> Belles

Given that the event had recently been re-equipped, this is a valuable indication of how it was organized. Robin Hood's coat was not in the keeping of the churchwardens, so was evidently

---

[38] 'Kingston Parish Records', pp. 120-26.
[39] 'Kingston Parish Records', p. 129.
[40] 'Kingston Parish Records', pp. 127-29,133,136-38,143-61.

[41] 'Kingston Parish Records', pp. 173-78.
[42] 'Kingston Parish Records', p. 179.
[43] 'Kingston Parish Records', p. 188.
[44] 'Kingston Parish Records', p. 185.

kept by the protagonist despite being supplied by the church. Similarly, and as one might expect, the morris dancers kept their own shoes. This in turn suggests that the dancers in 1538 were not those of 1536; or that the dancing was so strenuous as to wear all the shoes out. The morris dancers were still six in number including a fool, and they had elaborate coats in the keeping of the churchwardens. For the first time we know the colours of the coats, and perhaps this is the general colour of the Kingston livery. If so, then it surely no coincidence that the colours are those of the livery of the royal household two miles away at Richmond, the Tudor green and white. Although the dancers were apparently associated more with Robin Hood than with the King game, there were signs of links between the two, most notably in the purchase of a crown for the dancers in 1515. Perhaps the mock court of Kingston's King game was a mirror of the court at Richmond, and the morris dancers were introduced at the mock court to reflect the morisk of the Tudor court entertainments.

The comprehensive nature of the Kingston accounts also tells us more of the significance of the events. The May game and Robin Hood were not 'ritual' in the sense of a ceremony repeated every year with symbolic significance. They were staged in response to economic pressures and need not be staged at all. Many of the players performed without payment, fulfilling a social obligation. The events developed and changed during the 30 years, in the way in which Robin Hood and his company took over aspects of the King game, and Maid Marion may have developed as a character in the early stages of this process.

––––––––––––

The Kingston-upon-Thames accounts book ends in 1538. Thirty miles up the Thames from Kingston, the parish of St Lawrence in Reading paid for ale for morris dancers in 1513 on the church's dedication day, 10 August. Sixteen years later the parish invested in its own equipment for morris dancers, but apparently only for three: three hats were bought for 6d and bells were bought for 3s 6d (just over half the cost of the Kingston bells seven years later). Material for a coat for Maid Marion was bought for 1s 5½d. For the morris dancers three yards of buckram were acquired – obviously not for coats, perhaps for baldricks (the crossed sashes). The following year another 144 bells were bought for 3s and ten years later the morris coats were repainted.[45]

In one of Reading's two other parishes, St Mary's, morris dancers were equipped in 1556 and paid to perform on May Day, the following Sunday (3 May) and at Whitsuntide (around 24 May). Five pairs of shoes were bought for 4s, and the dancers' coats were painted for 2s 8d and sewn for 7d. Four dozen bells were bought for them for 2s. Theirs and the minstrels' food and drink were bought at Whitsuntide, when a 'Lord' presided over the festivities, and at one point the minstrels were boarded overnight. On May Day a hobby horse made an appearance – one of the earliest instances of its association with morris dancers.[46] A further 20 miles up the Thames from Reading, the parish of St Helen's in Abingdon bought 24 morris bells for 2s in 1560.[47] South of the Thames, 15 miles from Kingston, the 'morris gear' owned by Holy Trinity church, Guildford, was hired out for 10d in 1530.[48]

Although the spread of morris dancing along the Thames valley is well documented, there are outliers which indicate that the practice in fact was more widespread at an earlier date (see the map at Figure 3.1). There is a single entry from Sherborne in Dorset, datable only to the

[45] Kerry, *History … St. Lawrence*, pp. 226-28.
[46] Garry and Garry, pp. 28-29.
[47] Ward, J., p. 15.
[48] Palmer, Philip, p. 8.

period *c.* 1505-1508, 'Receyvyd of Hewe Honybrewe for a pott of ale of the Morys daunce'.[49] At St John's Bow, Exeter in 1525 there is a note that nothing was received in payment for bells for the morris dance. Although there is only this one reference to dancers, we know that the parish staged a Robin Hood play over several years from at least 1488 to 1544.[50] At Maldon, Essex in 1540 morris dancers were paid 8d and a further 4d was paid 'for the waste of the dancers' bells', implying that they were damaged or lost.[51] In 'The Book of the Fraternity or Gild of the Holy Trinity of Luton' there is a payment of 4d to morris dancers *c.* 1542.[52]

These isolated examples may well be the tip of an iceberg of unrecorded activity. However, there does seem to be a hiatus in known events during the 1540s. External factors may be in play. First, there was the economic situation, which led the Drapers to complain of the expense of the occasion in their preparations for the 1541 watch. The drain on their finances must have been caused in part by the massive inflation which resulted partly from developments common to all Europe caused by the influx of silver from the New World and by rapid population growth, and partly from Henry's policies pursued in trying to satisfy his voracious monetary requirements. Similar constraints may well have prevented churchwardens and other custodians of community funds from committing themselves to expenditure of this kind. Second, and more significant in its implications, was the ascendancy of Protestantism during the reign of Edward VI in the six years 1547-53. Henry VIII's split with the Church of Rome had not in itself engendered any major disruption in church practice or parish life, but the accession of Edward VI in 1547 led to the establishment of a distinctly Protestant Church of England, including the abolition of the Catholic mass, the use of English in services, the abolition of celibacy for the clergy and a degree of iconoclasm. There is little evidence that the people of England became committed Protestants in the period – in fact, given the risings of the reign, quite the reverse – but altars were being removed, images destroyed, the fabric of the Church subject to unheard-of upheaval. Churchwardens had more important things on their minds than morris dancing and May games.

The accession of Mary in 1553 signalled a return to the less solemn, more festal approach to church life after Edward VI's Protestantism. One of Mary's acts was to order the restoration of altars, images and other trappings to the churches. These, however, had been taken away, broken up or sold, and could not be replaced without expense. Articles were sent out to churches enquiring about the alienation of church goods, and the reply from St Lawrence's, Reading, is illuminating:[53]

> *Debts:*
>
> *It. upon John Saunders, th'apparells of the mores dauncers. He saith he delyvered them to Mr Bukland.*

This last entry – 15 years after the last recorded activity – may suggest that the use of them was in abeyance.

An atypical morris solo dance has been reported from Grimsthorpe Castle in Lincolnshire in a payment recorded in Richard and Katherine Bertie's household accounts to 'a morris dancer', but the Records of Early English Drama project at the University of Toronto has published the authoritative text which reveals that this was a payment of 2s to 'a moresse dawnce of Little Bytam' (3½ miles away), i.e., to a set of dancers, on 18 May 1562.[54]

---

[49] Hays, McGee, Joyce and Newlyn, p. 250.
[50] Wasson, pp. 108, 118, 121-23, 145.
[51] Mepham, pp. 135, 137.
[52] 'Book of the Fraternity'. I am grateful to Barbara Tearle for bringing this to my attention.
[53] Kerry, *History ... St. Lawrence*, pp. 226-28.
[54] Willoughby, Gilbert, p. 467; Stokes, *Records ... Lincolnshire*, p. 356.

At Crondall in Hampshire in 1555 the parish laid on an entertainment for the visiting Marchioness of Exeter, who was probably staying at nearby Itchel Manor:[55]

To the mynstrell for playing with the morysplayers before my lady Marques of Exeter 4d

There is no record that the dancers were hired, nor that any money was expended on them, so they had probably existed as a parish resource before that date. At Thame in Oxfordshire, however, which had staged Robin Hood gatherings and May ales for the better part of the last century, '9 dorsn daunchyng Bells' were bought for 3s 6d as part of the preparations for a May ale in 1557, in the first indication of morris dancing there. For the same occasion 13 yards of green cloth were acquired for coats, and minstrels were hired at a cost of £1 for their wages, 8s expenses and 6s board. The Lord of the May Ale was paid 5s. In the same year the rood screen was replaced, and an image of Our Lady erected there, quite possibly from the proceeds of the ale.[56]

By the time of the early years of the reign of Elizabeth there are records from across the southern half of England (Figure 3.1). At Leicester, 3s was paid 'for a morris dance of children' on Palm Sunday 1558; and morris dancers from Spalding (12 miles away) and Whaplode (6 miles) entertained at Long Sutton in Lincolnshire in 1562, receiving 2s and 6s 8d from the churchwardens respectively.[57]

At West Tarring in Sussex the churchwardens received 5s for the use of their morris bells held 'in store' in 1561. To illustrate the vagaries of recording, and the dangers inherent in drawing conclusions from such fragmentary data, it is worth pointing out that the same wardens made an inventory on the same day of 'All the churche stuffe', in which list the morris bells are absent.[58]

At Winterslow, Wiltshire, 16d was paid to hire morris gear in 1564 and 12d in 1567, quite possibly hired from the tailors at Salisbury six miles distant, where in the first of these years 3s 4d had been received for the hire of costumes, suggesting three or four hires a year were being agreed.[59] Wandsworth similarly invested in their kit: their morris coats were mended for 4d in 1565 and hired out in 1568 for 2s.[60] Morris coats made at Battersea the following year cost 2s.[61] At Thatcham, Berkshire, in 1566 dancers' coats were painted and 60 bells were bought,[62] while at Northill in Bedfordshire a servant was sent seven miles to Bedford to get two dozen bells, paper and red lead, morris coats were made, and 5s 8d was spent on morris dancers' shoes. Three shillings was spent on the morris bells and a vice's (fool's) coat was mended. Two years later the shoes were replaced (seven pairs, 5s 10d) and morris bells and leather bought.[63] All of these records suggest a thriving profitable trade in the hiring of morris dancers' costumes.

In London, parish and civic festivities in the middle of the 16th century were recorded by Henry Machyn. Machyn was a merchant taylor whose main business was the provision of funeral trappings. Little is known of him except that he kept a vivid diary of events in the

[55] Williams, J.F., p. 119; Stooks, p. 24.
[56] Lee, Frederick George, *History*, col. 73.
[57] North, p. 80; Stokes, *Records ... Lincolnshire*, p. 227.
[58] Pressey, p. 81.
[59] 'Winterslow', pp. 45, 54.
[60] Davis, pp. 152, 158.
[61] Taylor, John George, p. 350.
[62] Barfield, 2:93.
[63] Farmiloe and Nixseaman, pp. 6-7, 10.

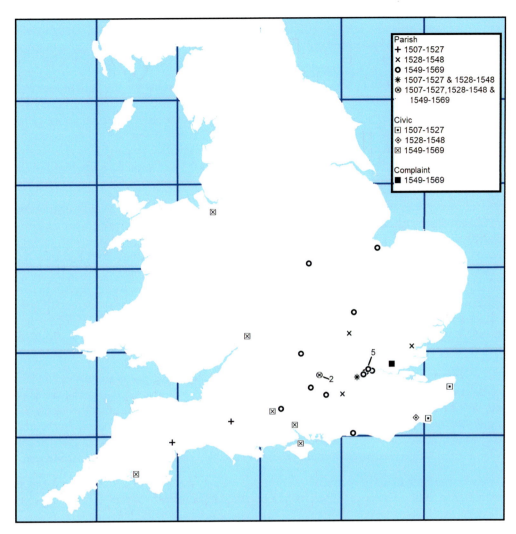

Figure 3.1: Morris activity, 1507-1569.

capital from 1550 to 1563. He was not concerned with matters of state, nor with his personal life. What he recorded was the life he saw around him: petty crime, accidents, the funerals of prominent citizens (in which he had a professional interest), and above all the pageants and festivities of the court, the civic authorities, the guilds and the parishes.

Notwithstanding the effect of Edward VI's Protestantism on parish activities, his court itself was not at all sombre or solemn, despite the influence of the Reformation and the ill health of the boy king. Court and public revels were still held; indeed, this was the era of the greatest of the Lords of Misrule, George Ferrars, who staged a series of lavish entertainments for the king. Lords of Misrule presided over licensed disorder, inverting the norms of a society normally acutely aware of rank and its privileges. Machyn recorded one such in his diary for January 1552, when Ferrars, as the King's Lord of Misrule, came from Greenwich to Tower Wharf by river, and proceeded from there to Cheapside accompanied by knights on horseback, guns and fireworks, musicians, a large retinue of followers, 'then the mores danse, dansyng with a tabret, and afor 20 of ys consell on horsbake', then the Lord. All wore 'a balderyke of yelow and grene abowt ther nekes'.[64]

Machyn's is not the only record of this event. The Revels accounts for the Lord of Misrule's Christmas festivities contain payments for, among other things, costumes for Ferrars and his immediate retinue, a fool, juggler, three dancers who danced a vigorous dance called a trenchmore, 105 uniforms for yeomanry and 20 mail shirts. There are no payments for costumes for some of the elements in the procession to London; in particular, the massed musicians and the morris dancers are not accounted for.[65] They were, perhaps, hired in the same way as the guilds' dancers were hired.

The following year, 1553, Machyn saw a similar event. The King's Lord of Misrule again came to Tower Wharf with a retinue including 'ye mores dansse'. On this occasion he was met by the Sheriff's Lord of Misrule with his own retinue, also including a 'mores dansse, with tabrett'. Both retinues had baldricks of blue and white; and this year the King's Lord had (possibly mock) gaolers and prisoners in the procession. All progressed to Cheapside, where the King's Lord 'knighted' the Sheriff's; then they dined with the Lord Mayor. Thereafter the King's Lord returned to Tower Wharf, 'the sreyff's lord gohyng with hym with torche-lyght, and ther the kinges lord toke ys pynnes [pinnace] with a grett shott of gonnes, and so the shreyffes lord toke ys leyff of ym and cam home merele wyth ys mores dansse danssyng and so forth'. As before, the Revels accounts are silent on many aspects of this performance.[66]

The visit by one mock lord to the 'territory' of another (in this case, that of the City of London), complete with retinue, the observance of inverted or mock ceremonial, and the communal feast, are each elements which have their parallels in the reciprocal entertainments of the parish May games. But none of these wholly follows a hallowed 'ritual', for novelty could be introduced from year to year. The King's Lord was not met by the Sheriff's in 1552, the livery changed with the year, and the King's Lord brought some prisoners for added entertainment in the second year.

Two months later Machyn recorded another procession, this time of the sheriff of London, with giants, hobby horse, mounted men, a morris dance, minstrels, armed men, 'my lo[rd justice?] late behyng lord of myssrulle', a devil and a sultan, a priest shriving Jack-a-Lent (a straw effigy used as a scapegoat), and a pageant car with minstrels.[67] This motley array goes to show that many of its elements existed independently of one another, just as a carnival procession today will have generally predictable elements, such as floats and marching bands, but their particular form and any extra displays will vary according to the ingenuity, enterprise and resources of the participants.

Machyn recorded May games with morris dancers and other entertainments at Westminster and St Martin's in the Fields in 1555 and in Fenchurch Street in 1557. The May game he reported on 24 June 1559 at St John Zachary's had a giant, guns, drums, pageants, the nine worthies, St George and the dragon, morris dancers, Robin Hood, Little John, Friar Tuck and Maid Marion. The next day the same May game went to entertain Queen Elizabeth at Greenwich (a journey of over five miles, or six by river).[68] This gallimaufry combined elements of the former guild processions with parish May games.

[64] Machyn, p. 13.
[65] Feuillerat, pp. 77-81.
[66] Machyn, pp. 28-29; Feuillerat, pp. 117-25.
[67] Machyn, p. 33.
[68] Machyn, pp. 89, 137, 191.

Although the king and sheriffs sanctioned Lords of Misrule, the fear of civil disorder among the populace at large remained high at all times during this period. In the spring of 1554 the Lord Mayor and aldermen, on Queen Mary's behalf, charged that no-one should prepare any 'mayegame or moryce dawnce or eny enterludes or Stage playes, or sett upp any maner of maye pole … or sounde eny drume for the gathering of eny people'; and ordered that any maypoles already set up should be taken down.[69] One of Machyn's earliest entries reflects the same attitude. On 26 May 1552 (Ascension Day, often the beginning of Whitsuntide festivities) Machyn recorded that a maypole had been erected in Fenchurch parish, with accompanying morris dancers and a giant, but that the Lord Mayor ordered its immediate taking down and destruction.[70] The specific reasons for these prohibitions are not made clear.

The overarching impression of this period is of uncontentious enjoyment of feasts and parades, supported by significant financial investment by parish, guild or town. Where opposition was voiced it was on the grounds of fear of disorder rather than any view of the moral rightness of such activities.

[69] Lancashire, Anne and Parkinson, p. 777.   [70] Machyn, p. 20.

Chapter 4

The first 120 years

Before moving on to the developments over the next century, there is the matter of the surviving early iconography to consider. This is inherently speculative in that our interpretations are based on *post facto* assertions that the images in question do depict morris dancers. Contemporary records do not tell us.

The fifteenth-century ornamental vessels and tapestry described in Chapter 1 do not survive and we know little of their appearance.

Two sixteenth-century sets of images which do survive appear to be related to each other and perhaps can give some insight into the ways in which images of 'morris' were transmitted in the 15th and 16th centuries. Both of them are well known to morris researchers, but the exact nature and the closeness of their relationship is not always recognised. Moreover, comparisons tend to be made at the level of the entire image, not at the level of the individual images within them.

These two images are the Betley window, now in the Victoria and Albert Museum (Figure 4.1) but originally from Betley Hall in Staffordshire, and a carved panel from Lancaster Castle (Figure 4.2). Both probably date from the mid 16th century. There are other images which have been asserted to depict 'morris' but none is convincing, being too early and unsupported by contemporary textual evidence, and/or choreographically distant from what we know of the dance at this stage – for example solo dancers, or dancers lacking bells, or holding swords.

The Betley window consists of 12 diamond-shaped quarries set into plain glass in a window 28 inches by 14 inches. From left to right, top to bottom, the images in four rows of three are a fool, three images of dancers, a maypole, a musician, a dancer, a hobby horse, two images of dancers, a lady holding a flower, and a friar.

The window has been well known for 250 years, being mentioned in one of the earliest essays touching on the dance, in Samuel Johnson's and George Steevens's critical edition of Shakespeare's works (1778).[1] This was written by George Tollet of Betley Hall in Staffordshire, the original home of the window. (See Chapter 10 for a discussion of the essay.) The dating is problematic. The Victoria and Albert Museum suggests that the window was made *c.* 1621 when the Hall was built, and notes that the dark blue colour used in the window was not produced before 1550.[2] If the window is of the 17th century, then it becomes a politically charged statement in the context of the dissensions of the time. If it dates from the Marian period or the early part of Elizabeth's reign then it is a much more innocent affirmation of the sentiment expressed in the window's quarry of a maypole, 'A Mery May'.

The Lancaster Castle panel is a small carved wooden panel (14 inches long). The panel is difficult to date and when the Victoria and Albert Museum was asked for an opinion in 1933 it could suggest only 'sixteenth century'. It may be relevant that the castle was refurbished

---

[1] Tollet, 5:425-34 + plate following p. 434.   [2] Victoria and Albert Museum.

Figure 4.1: The Betley window (Image © Victoria and Albert Museum, London, C.248-1976).

Figure 4.2: Lancaster Castle panel (Image courtesy of Vaughan Williams Memorial Library, Picture Folders/Folder 6/20).

by Queen Elizabeth about 1580.[3] The figures are, left to right, a lady, a musician, four dancers and a fool.

The images are related in a complex way. Analysis of the postures reveals that several, but not all, of the figures in the window and the panel are apparently based on a copperplate engraving by Israhel van Meckenem from about 1490, of which several prints survive. It has been surmised that the van Meckenem engraving (Figure 4.3) was intended as the basis for a design for a piece of gold ware.[4] The work appears to have direct influence on the two English images. The image is different from van Meckenem's roundel later called 'Moriskentanz', reproduced as Figure 1.1 (p. 9). In the fullest catalogue of his work it is described as 'Querfüllung mit dem Tanz der Verliebten' ('Panel with the Dance of the Lovers').[5] Several examples of prints from the engraving are known, scattered throughout Europe. There are examples in Cambridge, London and Oxford, and it is clear that it had some currency in artistic circles. On stylistic grounds the engraving is confidently dated to the 1490s. It was much copied, and in some copies the figures are reversed left-right.

The image consists of three dancers on the left, a fool, a central lady holding an apple, a pipe-and-taborer, and three dancers on the right. The dancers are all in contorted postures, a common depiction in European iconography. Two of them wear bells at ankles and wrists.

Figure 4.3: Israhel van Meckenem, Panel with the Dance of the Lovers (in Francis Douce, Illustrations of Shakspeare, plate VIII, London: Longman Hurst, Rees & Orme, 1807).

[3]   Gilchrist, 'Carved Morris Panel'.
[4]   *Israhel van Meckenem.*
[5]   Geisberg, no. 465.

44

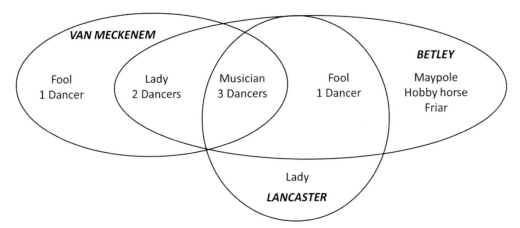

Figure 4.4: Correspondences of van Meckenem, Betley and Lancaster Castle images.

The figures in the Betley window are left-right reversed in relation to the others, and in the following comparisons those figures have been flipped to match them. The relationships and correspondences between the images are shown in Figure 4.4, and the images based on van Meckenem's third dancer are shown in Figure 4.5. Seven of van Meckenem's images can be seen in the window, but one of the dancers is unmatched in each. Betley introduces a new image for the fool, and of course has new images for the maypole, hobby horse and friar absent in van Meckenem.

The presence and position of circlets of bells varies between the images. Only two of van Meckenem's dancers wear bells, while all of the Betley dancers have them. However, the position of the bells does not match. Where van Meckenem has bells at ankle and wrist they have been replaced by bells at the knee in Betley, but other Betley images have bells at the ankle not copied directly from van Meckenem. The delineation of the Lancaster panel figures

Figure 4.5: Van Meckenem's third dancer image and its correlates in Betley window and Lancaster Castle panel.

is much less clear, and bells are generally not visible except perhaps at the knee of one dancer. The maypole, hobby horse and friar tie the Betley window very closely to what we know of English May games, and in turn the link to May games strengthens the identification of the dancers as morris dancers. The Lancaster panel has a distinct 'lady' but otherwise copies the window, including two figures introduced by the window artist.

The copying of the images means that little can be said with any certainty about the appearance of the figures. The costumes, for example, give no clue as to the dating. Although the lady is undoubtedly copied (given the cut of the dresses and the holding of an apple or a flower), in the window she has a crown instead of the conical hennin. She may represent the Lady of the May game rather than the Maid Marion, but the presence of the friar suggests a Robin Hood play may be involved. The hobby horse's bonnet hat is distinctly Tudor, and the cheeks of the face of the human 'rider' of the hobby horse are pierced by two daggers. This is entirely enigmatic. Christopher Cawte has pointed out that the only other information we have relevant to this depiction is from Ben Jonson's 1599 play *Every Man out of his Humour* where a hobby-horse dancer describes his proficiency, including 'I have the method ... for the daggers in the nose'.[6]

The lady on the left in the Lancaster panel is carrying a ladle and may be a Maid Marion figure, collecting money. However, the Lancaster panel also depicts what appears to be a boy personating a woman as the first dancer, with short hair and apparently fake breasts. The figure may be intended to be unclad but the carving around the loins is close to the codpieces represented in the original van Meckenem print. 'Adam and Eve' was a common theme in medieval and early modern pageants, with the actors wearing netting to simulate nudity.

The fact that the Betley window's images are reversed but the Lancaster panel's images are not suggests that there was an intermediate image following on from van Meckenem's, which introduced the Betley fool and a new dancer figure, and which was then copied at both Betley (reversing the images) and Lancaster. This implies that this was a group of images circulating quite widely in England in the 16th century, of which the surviving examples are just a fraction.

This is an appropriate moment to pause to review what the first 120 years of records tell us. This work does not attempt to explain the 'origin' of morris dances. There are those, for example Violet Alford and more recently Juan Antonio Urbeltz, who have sought or identified close parallels in other current or recent European traditions.[7] Given the inherent fluidity of dance forms, the centuries of development in their local milieux, and the lack of documentary sources, it is difficult to give any credence to theories which rely on such parallels. Moreover, it is important to distinguish four aspects in talking about the history and origins of morris (and any other kind of) dancing. Each of them may be subject to different influences in their development. The first is the name – this is essentially a question of etymology. Second is the choreography – the dance *qua* dance. The third is what may be termed the appurtenances of the dance – the non-choreographic performance elements, such as costume and characters, which distinguish it from other forms. Finally, there is the sociocultural context of performance.

We discussed the etymology in Chapter 1. The most common phonetic form suggests an immediate source in Flanders (a part of Burgundy), but at the same time we must acknowledge

---

[6] Cawte, *Ritual Animal Disguise*, pp. 43, 58; Jonson, 'Every Man', p. 295 (II.i).

[7] Alford, *Sword Dance*; Urbeltz.

that this is not supported by explicit documentary evidence in Flemish from the region's towns, nor from the Burgundian court, where the French-language forms occur. The form in /sk/ suggests a parallel borrowing from French morisque. It is not at all surprising that the two main forms of the word in early records point to our nearest geographical neighbours, Flanders and France.

The bilingual *Spousells of the Princess Mary* (see p. 13) is valuable corroboration that a moresk can be the same as a morisk, which can translate 'moresca' (a term which we encounter in European accounts); and that the performance can be described as a 'Moorish game/play'. The Latin text also distinguishes between this and the dances. Contemporary usages of the words strongly indicate that the reference was to things Moorish, and that the particular form of the word was not particularly significant, in that different forms could be applied to the same item or event. If there is any distinction to be made, it is that morisks are most often court entertainments and seem to be specifically devised for an occasion. Morris dances may be devised, but equally a set of dancers may be hired, or simply rewarded upon their appearance. Moreover, 'morris' is most often qualified explicitly as a dance, 'morisk' not.

As for choreographic elements, at this stage we have only tentative indications. The numbers apparently involved in dances varies. The payment by the Goldsmiths in 1448 implies perhaps seven participants, with a similar number involved in the court display in 1502. At Kingston there is stronger evidence for four dancers, but with supernumeraries; and perhaps two more dancers were added in the second year of attested performance, when more shoes were bought. At Reading five pairs of shoes were bought, perhaps for four dancers and a supernumerary.

Some of the early translating dictionaries can shed some light on choreography. The earliest, Horman's *Vulgaria* of 1519, is idiosyncratic:[8]

> *Let us daunce the haye/shypmens/sarson/and maurys daunce: Saltemus geranion*

– i.e., 'Let us do the crane dance', possibly alluding to the leaping dance of that name known from Ancient Greece, in which the dancers trace the path of a labyrinth.[9] In 1530 Palsgrave equated English 'morris' with French 'morisque' – he was but the first of many lexicographers to make that equation in translation – while also indicating perhaps an association with loss of inhibition (*debrise* = 'break up'):[10]

> *Let us daunce a morrasse this Christmasse: Dancons une morisque ce temps de nouel;*
>
> *I foote a daunce or morisque: Je me debrise*

Thomas Cooper's 1548 dictionary is even more informative. Cooper sees the use of hand gestures as being a distinguishing and defining characteristic of the dance:[11]

> *Chironomia, ..., a facion of gesture with the hands, used in dauncynge, as in a morys daunce, or in kervyng of meate ...*
>
> *Chironomia saltatio, the morys daunce.*
>
> *Chironomus, ..., he that teacheth one to make gesture, or he that daunceth with gesture of the handes in a morys.*

---

[8] Horman, f. 279r.

[9] Armstrong.

[10] Palsgrave, ff. ccv, ccxxxix.

[11] Elyot and Cooper, sig. Nvii, verso.

As for figures, the court dances appear to have a lady as a central figure but there is no hint of the same in the guild morris. In Kingston there is a female character, who may be a translation of the courtly lady onto the Maid Marion figure of May games or Robin Hood games.

Apart from Cooper's 1552 definition of the dance as requiring hand gestures, we have no other information about the elements of the dance at this time except for a broadside ballad of 1569, 'Good Fellows Must Go Learn to Dance':[12]

> *A bande of belles in Bauderycke wyse*
> *would decke us in our kynde a:*
> *A shurte after the Moryce guyse,*
> *to flounce it in the wynde a.*
> *A wyffler for to make the waye,*
> *and maye brought in with all a:*
> *Is braver then the Sunne I saye,*
> *and passeth round or brall a.*
> *For we wyll tripe so tricke and gaye,*
> *that we wyll passe them all a.*

'Tripping' the dance is not very informative, but the dance is claimed to be better than a round or brawl (bransle). An earlier verse speaks of 'a Braule come out of France', so this verse is implicitly celebrating the Englishness of the morris – the first such text to do so. This is also the first mention of a whiffler to clear a space for the dancers (although Stow, writing later, mentions them in his description of the earlier Midsummer Watch processions).

Our third thread takes in the typical costume elements of the dance. The bells on baldricks mentioned in the 'Good Fellows' ballad are not otherwise attested, but it also has an indication of a loose shirt. In the 16th century the chief costume elements mentioned in connection with dancers are special coats, often painted (22 references), and bells (27 references). Hats and shoes are each mentioned on nine occasions, and baldricks on three.

The coats at Stirling in 1505 were made of red and blue taffeta; at Kingston in 1507 the garments were 'painted' and adorned with tinsel. The Scottish hats cost more than the coats and took 39¾ ells of material. If these are Scottish ells that is about 120 feet, 20 feet for each dancer: if French ells (being delivered to a Frenchman), half as much again. In contrast, the hats at Kingston cost just 6d, 1½d each, and must have been modest affairs. At this stage there is no explicit reference to scarves, napkins or handkerchiefs, all of which appear later. Instead the allusions are to special shirts or coats and the images show streamers attached to the arms and shoulders. Shoes are mentioned only at Kingston (4s 4d for four in 1507, 14d for two further pairs in 1508). In the Lanherne morisk of 1466 48 bells were bought for 3s; at Kingston in 1507 12d (1s) was spent on bells for the four dancers.

From the parish entries it would seem that morris bells were in great demand. For the single year 1567/68 we have records of the amounts of various goods landed at the port of London. In that period, over 10,000 morris bells were imported into the country: surely indicative of a growth industry.[13] Most if not all of these bells were shipped from Antwerp. Simply because 'morris bells' were being imported we cannot presume that their use was for morris dancing

---

[12] *Good Fellows.*

[13] Dietz, pp. 45-82.

(one importer brings in 'coarse morris bells' on one ship and 'coarse bells' on another), but the mere fact that they are normally identified as such must imply that morris dancing was one of their chief uses. This may not always have been the case, and the terminology may also reflect the contemporary upsurge of interest in the morris. In a Tudor book of customs rates of 1507 'Bellys the small grosse' are rated at 12d;[14] in a similar book of 1582, 'Belles called horse belles or moris bels course the groce' are rated at 5s.[15] At the local level a Wallingford trader had horse bells at 6d a dozen and morris bells at 6d for five dozen in 1583.[16]

The Kingston-upon-Thames references are to 'mores garments' which may be read as 'Moor's garments' for a drama, but the number required and the immediate context of the purchase of bells and shoes for dancers make it almost certain that these are references to morris dancing.

The transition of the dance into new socio-economic contexts further down the social order, from court to town and parish, inevitably involved evolution to allow the dance to be incorporated into the existing structures of their customary festivities. In the case of the procession through the streets of the midsummer watch it is difficult to discern how that may have happened, but Henry Machyn's diaries show that the processional morris of the guild could easily meld with the perambulations of morris dancers in May games as they visited their neighbouring parishes.

Although morris dancing apparently fell out of use as an entertainment in royal and aristocratic circles, over the first 70 years of the 16th century it became embedded in the festive life of the country. Parishes embraced it as part of the entertainment at May games and invested resources in equipping themselves to present dancing, by purchase or hire. May games might be held around May Day or Whitsuntide, but parish patronal feasts were also popular. Church ales continued to be popular as a means of fund-raising for parishes even after the 1552 Poor Act gave them the ability to levy local rates.[17] Within urban communities merchant guilds were often involved and dancers paraded in midsummer watch processions and similar events, and civic authorities paid for dancers. The close ties between civic, mercantile and church life sometimes make it difficult to pinpoint the locus of the initiative. However, the carefree sentiments expressed in the ballad 'Good Fellows Must Go Learn to Dance' were about to come under challenge and attack.

---

[14] Gras, p. 695.
[15] Willan, p. 8.

[16] Prior, p. 80.
[17] Slack, pp. 59-60.

Part II: Contention (1570-1659)

Chapter 5
Rumblings 1570-1599

The later events in parishes described in Chapter 3 were taking place in the religious turmoil that overtook England during the middle of the 16th century, with swings to Protestantism, back to Catholicism and a return to Protestantism again. But apart from some indications of a drop in activity in the 1540s, there is no suggestion that the morris dance, or associated festivities, were symbolic or representative of any political or religious belief or attitude. The dance was simply an entertainment. Before 1570, only one record of activity seems to have negative overtones. The return made in response to the ecclesiastical visitation (an inspection and interrogation) of the parish of Shenfield in the archdeaconry of Essex in 1565 complained of a parishioner who 'danceth the morris in service time'.[1] There are just two other early minor indications of the beginning of a negative approach to morris dancing on religious grounds. The first was from the Bible translator Miles Coverdale, who while in exile in 1541 wrote *The Old Faith*, in which he complained about the lack of religious piety among the populace:[2]

> *Even so, if any play a wise man's part, and do as he is warned by Gods word, he shall have a sort of apish people, a number of dizzards and scorneful mockers, which, because the man will not dance in the devil's morrice with them, nor keep their company in the bondage of sin and vice, ... laugh him to scorn ...*

In 1552 Hugh Latimer (chaplain to Edward VI, later burned at the stake in Oxford for his Protestant views) spoke against 'our clergymen which go so gallantly now-a-days. I hear say that some of them wear velvet shoes and velvet slippers. Such fellows are more meet to dance the morrice-dance than to be admitted to preach.'[3] Both Coverdale and Latimer disdained morris dancing as an example of worldly activity, but only in the sense that all things temporal are to be rejected in favour of godliness.

The Marian years had done much to stimulate May games and other festivities and their trappings, partly as a means of raising funds for the restoration of churches, partly as a symbolic expression of the re-establishment of the 'old faith', the order of things before the Protestant reforms of the 1540s and the early 1550s. The actions of the followers of Edward VI and Mary Tudor had between them politicized the relation of the laity to the Church. When Elizabeth ascended the throne, there was an air of hesitant expectancy about the course she would adopt: whether she would accept the reconciliation with Rome accomplished under Mary or support the Protestants who wanted to sweep away everything associated with Roman Catholicism. In the event she did neither, steering instead a Henrician middle course. The Acts of Supremacy and of Uniformity of 1559 restored the position obtaining during her father's reign, and ensured that the bishops derived their power through, and were the servants of, the state. Within a few years all the Marian bishops had been replaced, but Elizabeth stoutly resisted the more radical revisions desired by the most zealous disciples of the European Reformation.

---

[1] Emmison, *Elizabethan life*, p. 186.
[2] Coverdale, p. 4.

[3] Latimer, 'Sermon', p. 83.

Religious reforms had been simmering for decades. In a sermon of 1549 Latimer had spoken about the undesirable consequences of parish festivals:[4]

> *I came once myself to a place, riding on a journey homeward from London, and I sent word over night into the town that I would preach there in the morning, because it was a holiday; and me thought it an holiday's work ... I thought I should have found a great company in the church, and when I came there, the church door was fast locked. I tarried there half an hour and more; at last the key was found, and one of the parish comes to me and says, 'Sir, this is a busy day with us, we cannot hear you; it is Robin Hood's day. The parish are gone abroad to gather for Robin Hood; I pray you let them not.' ... It is no laughing matter, my friends, it is a weeping matter, a heavy matter; a heavy matter, under the pretence of gathering for Robin Hood, a traitor and a thief, to put out a preacher, to have his office less esteemed; to prefer Robin Hood to God's word; and all this hath come of unpreaching prelates.*

Latimer identified the class of activities of which Robin Hood's gathering is a part as incompatible with acceptable Christian behaviour on holy days. This attempt to proscribe the behaviour of the lay populace lay at the heart of the struggle to come.

In the early years of Elizabeth's reign the turmoil caused by the succession to Henry VIII lessened, and the religious question had apparently faded somewhat into the background. The status of the Anglican communion *vis à vis* Rome remained uncertain, but a decade had passed since Elizabeth had re-asserted her supremacy in the English Church, and still she had not been cast out explicitly by the Pope. It was a situation with which most English people, in a broad spectrum from Catholic to Protestant, could live. The relatively unexpected action by Pope Pius V on 25 February 1570 changed that situation overnight.

––––––––––––

What the Pope did on 25 February 1570 was to publish a bull excommunicating Queen Elizabeth and declaring her reign to be illicit. Not the least of its effects was to make the English clergy alert to the slightest sign of rebellion, including signs of adherence to old ways. The ecclesiastical establishment was now beginning to view such activities as incompatible with the life of the Church. On being appointed Archbishop of York, Edmund Grindal issued injunctions to clergy in 1571, in which he required:[5]

> *that the minister and churchewardens shall not suffer anye lordes of misrule or sommerr Lordes or ladyes or anye disguised persons or others in christmasse or at may gammes or anye minstrels morice dauncers or others at Ryshebearinges or at any other tymes to come unreverentlye into anye churche or chappell or churcheyeard and there daunce or playe anye unseemelye partes with scoffes ieastes wanton gestures or rybaulde talke namely in the tyme of divine service or of anye sermon.*

In the visitation articles associated with the injunctions he proceeded to enquire whether any of these activities had been allowed in the parishes of the province.[6] Visitation had been (and still is) a long-established church practice, whereby questions were posed to the clergy and parish officers about their conduct and the life of the parish. Grindal's were not the first to appear in printed form, but they were the first to enquire about morris dancing. There is evidence that he carefully considered the content of his injunctions and articles on his

[4] Latimer, 'Sixth Sermon', p. 208.
[5] Johnston and Rogerson, p. 358.
[6] *V.A. York* (1571), sig. Cij; also in Frere, p. 271.

appointment to the northern province, as rushbearing – the practice of bringing rushes to the parish church annually to strew on the floor for comfort and warmth – was primarily a northern custom.

No articles from Grindal's time survive from the other dioceses in Grindal's province, but the extant metropolitan and diocesan articles from the Province of Canterbury did not copy his example. When Grindal himself moved to Canterbury in 1576, the first articles he issued followed the existing Canterbury model,[7] but the following year he replaced them with articles based on those he had issued from York six years before. The significance which might be read into their adoption is, perhaps, lessened by the fact that careless changes were made which rendered the text ungrammatical:[8]

> Whether the Minister & Churchwardens have suffered any Lords of Misrule, or summer Lords, or Ladies, or any disguised persons, or other in Christmas, or at May games, or any Morrice dauncers, or at any other times, to come unreverently into the church or churchyard & there to daunce, or play any unseemely parts, with scoffes, jeastes, wanton gestures, or ribald talke, namely in the time of common prayer. And what they be that committ such disorder, or accompanie or maintayne them.

In this second text Grindal (or one of his staff) elided the reference to rushbearing, which may have been thought irrelevant to the southern province, but failed to appreciate that 'at Ryshebearinge' refers to a specific time of year. What is more remarkable is that the error was repeated in the articles for the dioceses of London the same year, Exeter in 1579, Lincoln in 1580, and Salisbury in 1581, and reproduced again in the articles for the Province in 1580 and 1582.[9] The persistence of the error shows that texts were copied rather mechanically, so the presence of the question in the articles for a particular diocese does not necessarily imply dancing activity in the diocese, or even that the bishop of the diocese had a particular interest in the topic.

Only in 1583 did the articles for London acknowledge the error and change the text, but in doing so changed the sense – apparently inadvertently – to imply that morris dancers were associated with Christmastide:[10]

> Whether the minister & churchwardens have suffered any Lords of misrule: or sommer Lords or Ladies, or any disguised persons, or others, or maygames, or any Morice dauncers at Christmas, or at any other tymes to come unreverently into the church or churchyard, & there to daunce, or play any unseemely parts ...

This new text, with its new sense, was used again for London in 1586 and was copied for Coventry and Lichfield in 1584. The uncorrected and ungrammatical text was still in use, however, at Winchester in 1584 and Lincoln in 1585.[11]

London corrected the text again in 1589, to ask about 'any Lords of misrule, or Summer Lords, or Ladies, or anie disguised persons, or May games, or anie morrice dancers at anie times', so for the first time in 12 years the text now matched Grindal's apparent intention of 1577. The

---

7   *V.A. Canterbury* (1576).
8   *V.A. Canterbury* (1577), sig. Cii.
9   *V.A. Canterbury* (1580), sig. Ciii; *V.A. Canterbury* (1582), sig. Ciii; *V.A. London* (1577), sig. C1; *V.A. Exeter* (1579), sig. B3v; *V.A. Lincoln* (1580); *V.A. Salisbury*, sig. B4.
10   *V.A. London* (1583).
11   *V.A. London* (1586), sig. B3v-B4; *V.A. Coventry* (1584); *V.A. Winchester* (1584), sig. Bij-v; *V.A. Lincoln* (1585), sig. Bij-v.

new text was in use for the next surviving London diocesan articles of 1598 and 1601, and was also used by Winchester in 1597; but Gloucester was still using the unreformed 'Christmas' text in 1594.[12]

Meanwhile Archbishop Sandys, who had replaced Grindal at York, introduced in 1577 a simplified variant of Grindal's words in his articles for the province:[13]

> *Whether any moricedauncers, rishe bearers, or any others have come unreverently into the church or churchyard, and there daunced, or played any unseemely [part ...].*

This re-introduced the reference to rushbearing. Bishop Chaderton at Chester also included rushbearing in his own original 1581 text for the second-most important diocese of the northern province:[14]

> *Whether ... your said church, chapel or churchyard be abused or profaned by any unlawful or unseemly act, game, or exercise, as by Lords of Misrule, Summer lords or ladies, pipers, rushbearers, Morris dancers, pedlars, bearwards, and such like; then through whose default, and what be the names of the offenders in that behalf?*

He then took the text with him and used it again in the articles for Lincoln 18 years later, and again in 1601.[15] While Grindal and his successor texts asked whether the churchwardens had allowed these prophane practices, Sandys and Chaderton asked merely if they had happened. This casts the net wider from complicity on the part of parish officials to embracing the whole population of the parish.

Other dioceses also departed from the standard family of texts. In 1584, local articles for Shrewsbury asked 'Whether there have bene any lords of mysrule, or somer lords or ladies, or any disguised persons, as morice dauncers, maskers or mumers, or such lyke, within the parishe, ether in the nativititide or in somer, or at any other tyme, and what be their names?'[16]

Not every bishop specifically included enquiries about morris dancing in their articles. Bishop Wickham of Lincoln did not do so in the articles of 1588, 1591 and 1594 (in contrast to both his predecessor and successor); nor did the Bishops of Chichester in 1586 and 1600, nor of Exeter in 1599.[17] Those that omitted specific mention, however, may have simply included them in a more general rubric, as in Bishop Westfaling's articles for Hereford in 1586:[18]

> *Whether the minister and churchwardens have suffered any lordes of misrule, dancers, plaiers, or any other disguised persons to daunce, or play any unseemely partes in the church or church-yarde, chappell or chappel-yarde, if they have what be the names of such lordes of misrule, dauncers, plaiers &c. And whether there are any plaies or any drinkings kept in any of the said places, who maintain and accompany suche?*

One public rationale for the inclusion of such articles in visitation enquiries was explained by Bishop Cooper of Winchester in 1585. Morris dances and similar activities were, according to him, inappropriate as a means of supporting the church:[19]

---

[12] *V.A. London* (1589), sig. B3v; *V.A. London* (1598), sig. B4-B4v; *V.A. London* (1601), sig. B4; *V.A. Winchester* (1597), sig. B3; *V.A. Gloucester*, sig. C3.
[13] *V.A. York* (1577).
[14] *V.A. Chester* (1581).
[15] *V.A. Lincoln* (1598), p. 1; *V.A. Lincoln* (1601), p. 1.

[16] Owen, Hugh and Blakeway, 1:333.
[17] *V.A. Lincoln* (1588); *V.A. Lincoln* (1591); *V.A. Lincoln* (1594); *V.A. Chichester* (1586); *V.A. Chichester* (1600); *V.A. Exeter* (1599).
[18] Klausner, *Records ... Herefordshire*, p. 58.
[19] Cited in Atkinson, *Tom*, p. 245.

whereas a heathenish and ungodly custom hath bene used before time in many partes of this lande about this season of the yeare [Whitsun] to have Church Ales, May games, morish dances, and other vaine pastimes upon the Sabath Dayes, and other dayes appointed for common prayer, which they have pretended to be for the relief of theire Churches, but indede hath bene only a meanes to feed the mindes of the people and specially of the youth with vaine sight which is a strange perswasion among Christians, that they cannot by any other means of contribution repaire theire churches but must first do sacrifice to the Devil with Drunkenes and Dancing and other ungodly wantonnes. These are therefore to charge all Ministers and Churchwardens and other like Officers that they suffer not any such Church Ales, Morish dances or Riflings [possibly in the sense of gambling] *within theire parishes.*

In 1592 the secular state in the form of the Privy Council wrote to the Earl of Derby, Lord Lieutenant of Lancashire not to suffer 'certaine May gaimes, morryce daunces, plaies, bearebaytinges, ales, and other like pastimes used ordinarilye in those counties under your Lordship's Lieutenancie on the Sondaies and Hollydaies at the tyme of Divine service and other Godlie exercyses, to the disturbance of the service'.[20]

The responses to visitations were presentments, in which parish officials or parishioners were reported to and sometimes brought before ecclesiastical courts and, if found guilty, punished or made to do penance. Presentments made by individual parishes in response to visitation articles are, of course, manuscript records and so survival is much more fragmentary than for the printed articles, but they do provide real evidence of activities in parishes.

In the earliest presentments concerning morris dancing, those presented were the church officials rather than the parishioners. At Huntley, Gloucestershire, in 1576 the parson was presented 'for suffringe the may lorde and the morice dauncers (to) come into the churche', while at Canon's Ashby in Northamptonshire it was reported in 1578 that 'the curate is not in orders and is reported to be a morris dancer'.[21] In 1576 Richard Hackney, the rector of Cranoe in Leicestershire, admitted that he had allowed puppet plays in the church. He was discharged but enjoined that he 'in no wise hereafter shall suffer any such order eyther by morrys daunce or otherwise to be in his Churche but shall beforehand complaine unto the Justices thereof'.[22] The churchwardens of Weaverham in Cheshire reported in 1578 that there were 'morris dances and risshbearings used in church',[23] but did not present anybody or appear to regard this as an offence. The churchwardens at Finningley in Nottinghamshire were less fortunate, being fined ten shillings for allowing morris dancers into church, while the wardens of Wivenhoe, Essex, were presented in 1598 for not reporting the morris dancing which took place there on Sunday 9 July.[24] At Didcot in Berkshire in 1580, the churchwarden was presented because he 'withholdeth towelles from the churche'. He answered that 'theire towells be lost but not throughe his negligence & saith ffurther they weare fett owte of his howse by the morrice Dancers in his absence'. The dancers were not prosecuted, but the churchwarden was ordered to make good the loss.[25] We shall encounter further examples of dancers appropriating church property in later years.

Dancers came close to prosecution in Headcorn, Kent in 1583 when Thomas Young was presented because he 'verie disorderlie & loudelie upon the sabothe day did play upon his

20 Dasent, p. 549.
21 Price, p. 11; S., H.R., p. 57.
22 Foster, pp. 137-38.
23 Purvis, p. 65.
24 Hodgkinson, 'Extracts', p. 58; Emmison, 'Tithes', p. 202.
25 'Archdeaconry of Berkshire Act Book', f. 89.

fedle aboute the Churcheyard & certeine morris daunsers beinge disgised followinge of him to the great offence of manie'. Young replied that 'after evensonge he went to the alehouse who yoyneth upon the churchyarde and thither came certeyne morrys dauncers from Bocton Munchelse & requested [him] to playe with his Instrument and thereupon [he] went to a certeyn sportynge place the way leadyng thoroughe the churche yarde and sayth that Henry Jenkynson of Bocton Munchelsey was one of the said morrys dauncers'.[26] A margin note suggests that Jenkinson should be called to testify, but there is no evidence that he was. Young was instructed to admit his fault before the parish and pay sixpence towards the upkeep of the poor. The circumstances which apparently brought the dancers the six miles from Boughton Monchelsea without a musician are not clear. They may have been acting speculatively on their own initiative, or, less likely, been part of a parish festival.

Young was cited because he entered the churchyard, but from Cambridgeshire there are three cases where morris dancers or their musicians are presented for dancing elsewhere and being absent from church. These are the only such cases until the end of Elizabeth's reign, and reflect perhaps the incipient strength of Puritanism in East Anglia. At Witchford in 1590 three men were cited because they 'were daunseinge the morris in eveninge prayer tyme < ...> Holye Thursdaye Laste', and one of them 'did ride aboute three Sabbothe Dayes togither & was not at his parishe churche'. At Sawston the following year, John Loughtes, a minstrel, was presented for 'pipeinge or playinge before the morice dauncers at Sawston upon Trinity Sondaye and twoe Sondayes before midsomer daye, beinge then absent from his parishe churche'; while at Stretham in 1600, seven men were presented merely 'for morres dancing on ye sabbath daye'.[27] Dancing was being prosecuted not just for disrupting church services but also for luring those involved away from religious observance.

———————

Despite the emergence of presentments, for many parishes life appears to have gone on as usual. In the parish of Battersea, Thomas Twyford was paid two shillings to make morris coats in 1570, and bells were bought for the parish of St Mary at Hill in London as late as 1591.[28] In the Thames valley, in 1571 the churchwardens of Wantage bought a dozen morris bells.[29] In the same year the morris dancers at Axbridge in Somerset organized an ale to support the church, which brought in the enormous sum of £1 7s 6d.[30]

A long series of accounts from the parish of St Columb Major in Cornwall from 1585 to 1597 details the costume in the possession of the churchwardens from year to year. At first there were five morris coats, a friar's coat, and 24 bells. In 1585 the number of bells recorded drops to 20, and the friar's coat disappears (this is the first year explicitly identifying the coats as 'morrish' coats); but in 1591 a sixth coat was recorded. In 1595 the churchwardens recorded that 'Thomas Braben hath brought in hys dancyng Coate ... There Remaynethe in ye wardens kepyng ... syxe old moryse cotes & a new moryshe Coate wt ye wardens'. The seven coats remained in the churchwardens' keeping until the end of the record in 1597.[31]

The churchwardens of Great Marlow hired out their morris coat in 1595, and paid fourpence to have the coat carried to Maidenhead, where presumably it was used.[32] In 1596 the

[26] 'Archdeacon's Court Book', ff. 144-45, 148.
[27] 'Ely' (1601), f. 153; Owen, Dorothy M., p. 187; 'Ely' (1593), f. 213.
[28] Taylor, John George, p. 350.
[29] Wantage, f. 2r.
[30] Knight, Francis A., p. 404.
[31] Hays, McGee, Joyce and Newlyn, pp. 507-09.
[32] 'Great Marlow', f. 5v.

churchwardens of Camborne in Cornwall paid 12d to each of two sets of visiting morris dancers from quite distant parishes, St Levan (all of 20 miles away) and Gunwalloe in Lizard (10 miles).[33]

Away from the mixed messages found in the context of the parish church during this period, morris dancing still flourished and on the whole received civic and guild support in towns (Figure 5.1). At Plymouth, the civic payment to the morris dancers rose from 2s at their first mention in 1564 to 3s 4d (plus 5s for their breakfasts) in 1565, 4s in 1568, 5s in 1569, 1574 and 1575, and 10s in 1585. Thereafter the amounts fluctuated: 6s 8d in 1587, 14s 6d in 1594, and in 1595 Peter Anthony was paid 6s 8d 'for charge of morris danssers'.[34] In 1575 particular efforts appear to have been made to put on a splendid show: 23s 8d was spent on procuring and decorating a new maypole, and a hobby horse was made for 2s and paraded about the streets, the dancer being paid 6d.[35]

In Chester the arrangements for the morris dancers remained stable until 1594, two dancers being paid 6s 8d.[36] The northernmost record of dancing occurred in a lavish display in Liverpool in 1577, when to honour the Earl of Derby, 'There was manye thinges done & pastymes made as A morres daunce over & besides the premisses which were all so orderlye & trymlie handled as was to the great lykinge & pleasure of the said right honourable erle, the lyke wherof was never sene or knowen to be done in this said towne of Liverpole'.[37]

The arrangements for the morris dancers in Salisbury were regularized in 1568 and reaffirmed at intervals thereafter. The minutes of the Tailors' Guild Book recorded in 1568 that 'the stewardes for the tyme beinge as well now as herafter shall always fynde meate and drinke unto suche morrys playes and others as shall please the hole Companye to appoynte And that at such tymes as they for theyr direcyon shall think good to call them and shall also be charged with the wages for the same'.[38] In 1579, however, it was agreed 'that the gyaunt shalbe lett downe and goe nomore by cause of the charge whiche he causeth yearely to this companie'.[39] This is the first mention of the giant (who in later years was identified as representing St Christopher) which continued to be a feature of Salisbury's civic processions across the centuries.

In 1584 an arrangement was made very similar to that made 20 years before whereby a member of the guild took charge of the coats:[40]

> *At this assembly it is agreed that mr Thomas Barker shall have the morris and the mayde marrian's cotes and therten score millen bells with ther lethers and the velvet cappe and hobby horse and all his furniture and all other the appurtenances to them belonging, for ten yeres next ensuing, yelding and paying therfor yearly to this companie during the term aforsaayed, two shillings and six pence at their audit and in the ende of the years aforesayd to deliver the coates and all other the premisses up to the companie agayne the sayed companie to have them all at their commaundement every mydsommer feast usuall in thes company yff they thinke goode, gratis, and hereunto the sayed mr barker being present gave his consent and covenanted with the companie to observe and performe the condicions and covenantes above specified in witness wherof he hathe here unto set his hand.*

---

[33] Hays, McGee, Joyce and Newlyn, p. 476.
[34] Wasson, pp. 239-40, 242-43, 245, 250, 255-56.
[35] Wasson, p. 243.
[36] Clopper, pp. 94, 120, 137, 151, 155, 162, 166, 173.
[37] Twemlow, 2:245-46.
[38] 'Tailors' Guild' (1517), f. 61v
[39] 'Tailors' Guild' (1575), f. 21r.
[40] 'Tailors' Guild' (1575), f. 47r.

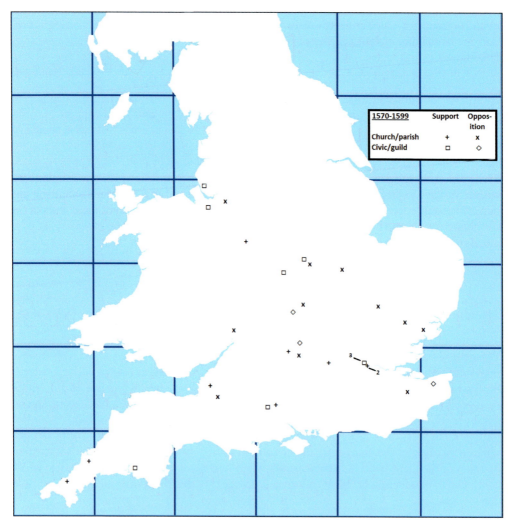

Figure 5.1: Civic and church support and opposition, 1570-1599.

The changes in material from 1564 include 20 extra bells of Milan steel, and the addition of apparel for Maid Marion and a hobby horse. The entry suggests that Maid Marion was now a character associated with the morris dance outside of the Robin Hood game. The value of the contract was smaller, 2s 6d a year instead of 3s 4d; and unlike Clarke, Barker did not have to agree to pay £5 in case of default. Seven years later, in 1591, the Guild agreed that 'the morrys coates shalbe new made agaynst our feast'.[41] Where this stands in relation to Barker's agreement, which should have run for ten years, is not clear. If it was still in force, then it seems clear that Barker was not responsible for maintenance; he was merely putting up the money to earn the right to sub-let the coats, while the Guild remained responsible for their upkeep. Again, this contrasts with the terms imposed on Clarke, who had to deliver the gear when needed, and eventually surrender it, 'in as good case as he receyved it'.

---

[41] 'Tailors' Guild' (1575), f. 83r.

In 1576 the inventory of effects of John Maulden, a weaver from Bildeston in Suffolk, listed 'sarten parelle for morres dancers and other empellements with the bels', valued at 20 shillings, so it seems that entrepreneurs of the kind found in the first half of the century were still to be found in the second.[42] There are further occasional references in municipal accounts for payments to visiting morris dancers, as at Dunmow in 1575 when they were paid two shillings, and at Coventry in 1596 when dancers from Stoneleigh were paid 3s 4d.[43] Such payments suggest that as parish support was withdrawn morris dancers were performing on their own initiative and soliciting payment, instead of being hired on a contractual basis.

We find increasing evidence that where they were not directly sponsored by powerful elements within the town, morris dancers now found that they ran the risk of official disapproval and punitive action. An early example of this is also one of the most circumstantial accounts of the social forces at work in both the establishment of and the burgeoning resistance to groups of morris dancers. At Canterbury on 10 May 1589 a group of morris dancers from Herne, six miles away, was examined before the mayor and two aldermen after dancing 'against Mr Mayor's door'.[44] The testimony they gave sheds much light on the mechanics of a morris side of the time. The side consisted of four male dancers, a boy dressed as Maid Marion, a vice (both fool and leader of the side) and a fiddler, who also had a 'man' to assist him. The fiddler was 26 years old; the boy, 12; the vice and two of the dancers 20; the third dancer, named Seers, was 24, but he claimed only to have joined the side that day as a substitute for another who was sick. The last dancer was 19 years old. The vice and one dancer were identified as servants.

J. Turfrey, the vice, stated that he had hired Henry Parkes the fiddler about two weeks previously (i.e., c. 26 April) until St Peter's Day, probably 1 August rather than 29 June, as the former marked the termination of many contracts. Parkes himself said that they had hired him to play with them in serving their turn in the morris dance from May Day and for Ascension Day (8 May) and 'doth think they will hire him for tomorrow being Sunday but does not clearly know'. He was not engaged for the whole of the period to St Peter's Day but had agreed to perform on such days as they required him until then. He was paid 4s a day, an impressive sum when worker's average wages were between 3d and 5d a day.[45]

The dancers' itinerary can be pieced together from their testimonies. They danced in Herne itself on May Day (a Thursday), and again on Sunday 4 May, mainly, said one, in the afternoon. The following Thursday, 8 May, was Ascension Day and they danced at Reculver, four miles from Herne, in the morning (though one dancer says they danced at Chislett in the morning, after attending the service there) and at Hothe, doubling back five miles, in the afternoon. On the Friday they moved on eight miles to Patrixbourne and Bridge, just outside Canterbury. On the Saturday they came into Canterbury itself, went to the George inn and there put on their morris gear ('the bells & furniture for the morris dance with maid marrion being a boy in woman's apparel'). The presence of a Maid Marion but no other characters from Robin Hood confirms that 'she' is now independently attached to the morris dance. They danced at St George's Gate, and were moving towards St Stephen's where they intended to solicit contributions from one Peter Manwood, without his foreknowledge. On the way they passed along the High Street and when they were outside the mayor's door one suggested that they dance there. They did so, and as a result first the musician, then the rest were hauled inside

[42] Dymond, pp. 3, 4.
[43] Smith, J.R., p. 9; Ingram, Reginald W., p. 346.
[44] 'Interrogation'.
[45] Aughterson, pp. 201-02.

to be examined. Parkes said that the dancers had told him that the 'Baron's son wanted them to play at Nackington that day'. In perhaps the most telling comment of all the statements, Parkes said that 'he hath heard others say that it was never a merry England since men were to go with license being charged that he could not go about without license'. 'Merry' here bears its original meaning of pleasant or agreeable, but it is this context of usage which enabled the change of meaning to its present connotation of joviality. The general idea had been current for centuries, but it was only a generation before that it had been expressed in these terms, when John Caius wrote in 1552 of 'the old world, when this country was called merry England'.[46] More important is Parkes's identification of morris dancing and fiddling with a rose-tinted image of an already bygone England, implying that it represented more than mere contemporary entertainment. The dancers were presumably acting on their own initiative but with the opportunity to make arrangements in advance to perform, as at Nackington.

Another example in which festivities were conducted without official sanction comes from Oxford in 1598, when the university authorities complained that 'The inhabitants assembled on the two Sundays before Ascension Day, and on that day, with drum and shot and other weapons, and men attired in women's apparel, brought into the town a woman bedecked with garlands and flowers named by them the Queen of the May. They also had Morrishe dancers and other disordered and unseemly sports, and intended the next Sunday to continue the same abuses.'[47] The university wanted the town to bear down on such disorders.

In Leicester in 1599, Richard Woodward, a shoemaker, took part as a morris dancer in a procession with five other young men, most of them servants, to accompany a maypole into the town. The mayor had sanctioned the pole, then changed his mind and had it taken down and chopped to pieces. The remnants of the pole were re-erected and Woodward was then brought before the judge after he was overheard to say that 'within theise six yeares it maye bee theire will bee more morrys Dawnsinge in the Towne'. The statement was seen as a threat of insurrection. Woodward's defence was that he was merely referring to the fact that one Mr Hunter, who was due to be mayor in future, had promised to allow such activity out of service time.[48] This is redolent of the famous Banbury maypole controversy, happening at the same time, when a group of Puritans tried to suppress the erection of a maypole. Precepts were issued by Richard Wheatley, Constable of the Hundred of Banbury, to local constables 'to take down all May-poles ... and to repress and put down all Whitsunales, Maygames, and Morrisdances, and utterly to forbid any wakes or fairs to be kept'. This brought a protest from the sheriff of Oxford against 'the bad proceedings of Anthony Cope and others of the town of Banbury, who under the plea of religion were practising to abolish most pastimes used in the country, as Maypoles, Morrisdances, Whitsunales, and others to the great discontentment of Her Majesty's loving subjects'. Cope replied that he 'has never restrained Whitsunales and Morrisdances'.[49]

Individual members of the gentry still appeared to be supportive. Performances before them could attract reward, as at Hengrave in Suffolk when the steward of the household of Sir Thomas Kitson paid 2s 'In reward to the morres-dauncers at my mr. his return into the country', probably in 1583; he also paid 2s 4d for a song for the occasion.[50] Sir Humphrey Gilbert presumably thought dancers to be an asset, since on his voyage to Newfoundland in

---

[46] Cited in Hutton, *Rise*, p. 89.
[47] *Calendar ...Hatfield House*, 8:201.
[48] Kelly, pp. 100-01, 230-32.

[49] Lemon, 2:601-02.
[50] Gage, p. 206.

1583 he took 'the least toyes, as Moris dancers, Hobby horse, and Maylike conceits to delight the Savage people'.[51] On an earlier voyage in 1578 he carried two firkins of manilios (bracelets) and morris bells to trade.[52]

———————

At the same time as the first ecclesiastical enquiries about morris dancing, the polemical tracts which were beginning to circulate were revealing other attitudes to and information about the dance. The son of the Puritan Samuel Clarke reported his father's struggles against Whitsun ales and morris dancing at Oundle in Northamptonshire in the 1580s, while the Marprelate tracts (a set of Puritan pamphlets published under variations of the pseudonym Martin Marprelate in the late 1580s attacking the Anglican episcopacy) contain references which, although they may be invented, have the ring of genuine topical allusion. Clarke's account is one of the earliest examples of a moral crusade by a Puritan minister against his parishioners:[53]

> ...the generality of them, were very ignorant and ungodly, and much addicted to the Prophanation of the Lords Day, by Whitsonales, Morris dancing, &c., which sinnes Master Clark in his Ministry much set himself against ... but they, having alwaies been trained up in such practices, and having their hearts hardened against admonition, still persevered in their former courses ... but the judgment of God found them out for this their wickednesse. For shortly after, on a Lord's day, the Leader of the Dance, being a lusty young man, in the midst of their prophane pastimes suddainly fell down and died. Yet these obdurate persons (though a little affected for the present) soon shaked off their fears, and returned to their vomit again.

The theme of divine judgement would recur in the following decades; but Clarke was early in his antipathy to worldly activity not just in the precincts of the church, but anywhere at all on the Lord's Day. Marprelate, on the other hand, saw the morris as mere empty buffoonery, typical of the attitudes of simple country clergy:[54]

> There is a neighbour of ours, an honest priest, who was sometime (simple as he now stands) a Vice in a play, for want of a better. His name is Glibbery of Halstead [....] Essex. He goes much to the pulpit. On a time, I think it was the last May, he went up with a full resolution to do his business with great commendations. But see the fortune of it. A boy in the church, hearing either the Summer Lord with his Maygame, or Robin Hood with his Morris Dance, going by the church out goes the boy. Good Glibbery, though he were in the pulpit, yet had a mind to his old companions abroad (a company of merry grigs, you must think them to be, as merry as a Vice on a stage), seeing the boy going out, finished his matter presently, with John of London's Amen; saying, 'Ha, ye faith, boy! Are they there? Then, ha' with thee.' And so, came down, and among them he goes. Were it not then pity that the dignity of such a priest should decay?

Marprelate's references to the Summer Lord and Robin Hood recall the situation at Kingston-upon-Thames 80 years before. His linking of Robin Hood and the morris was re-inforced in another of the tracts, which contended that:[55]

> Anderson, parson of Stepney, should make room before him [John Bridges, Dean of Sarum, whom Martin is proposing as Archbishop of Canterbury] with his twohand staff, as he did once before the morrice dance, at a market town in the edge of Buckingham or Bedford shires, where he bare the potter's part.

[51] Hayes, p. 396.
[52] 'Chancery Case', p.206.
[53] Clarke, Samuel, p. 160.

[54] Martin the Metropolitan, pp. 226-27.
[55] Martin Senior, pp. 369-70.

A note expanded on Anderson as follows:

> *This Chaplain robbed the poor men's box at Northampton, played the Potter's part in the morrice Dance, and begot his maid with child in Leicestershire; and these things he did since he was first priest.*

The suggestion that the morris dance had a 'potter' is unique; but the potter does have a part in the cycle of Robin Hood plays and ballads,[56] and Marprelate's main text suggests that the potter simply preceded the morris dance in some form of procession. The transference of the meaning of 'morris dance' from the dance itself to the whole event with which it is associated is a recurring feature which causes confusion throughout the centuries.

One of the first writers to reveal the attitudes prevalent in this phase of the Reformation was Lawrence Ramsey in *The Practice of the Divell* in 1577. This outwardly Puritan poet found it much easier to put life into his descriptions of worldly pursuits than he did to extol the virtues of a devout life:[57]

> *Suffer all sclaunder, against God and his trueth,*
> *And prayse the olde fashion, in King Arthur's dayes:*
> *Of Abbaies, of Monasteries, howe it is great rueth,*
> *To haue them pluckt downe, and so the eldest sayes:*
> *And howe it was merries, when Robin hoods playes,*
> *Was in everie Towne, the Morrice and the foole,*
> *The May poll, & the Drum, to bring the Calfe from schoole.*

The literary association between Robin Hood and the morris was maintained by George Gilpin in *The Beehive of the Romish Church*, a 1579 translation of a Dutch original, but much adapted for the English reader:[58]

> *In summe, a man doeth often spende a penny or two, to see a play of Robin Hood, or a Morisse daunce, which were a great deale better bestowed uppon these apish toyes of these good Priests, which counterfeite all these matters so handsomely, that it will doe a man as much good to see them, as in frostie weather to go naked.*

However, of all these only Marprelate actually provided a thematic link between Robin Hood and the morris. Ramsey and Gilpin each merely juxtaposed them (in the latter case contrastively) as the two main threads of popular amusement. Gilpin went further, and used 'morris' in a novel way, in satirising the elements of ritual of a Catholic mass in order to denigrate both:[59]

> *Why the Preist doeth trim him selfe in such mumming garments ... why he doeth first put a biggin [hat] upon his head, and then a long garment like a woman's smock aloft upon his gowne ... why he doeth turne sometime his tayle to the people, and sometime his face; why he trippes sometime to the one ende of the Altar, and sometime to the other side of the Altar, as though he were daunsing the Maides Morice.*

'Maids Morris' was, a century later, a country dance. Whether Gilpin was referring to an actual dance by women, or to Maid Marion's part in the morris, or is simply using 'morris' in the sense of nimble dancing, is now impossible to say.

---

[56] Knight, Stephen and Ohlgren, pp. 57-79.
[57] Ramsay, sig. Cij.
[58] Gilpin, f. 207r.
[59] Gilpin, f. 217v.

The tone of the visitation articles was being repeated in sermons at St Paul's Cross, the centre of Puritan demagogy. John Stockwood declared there that Sunday:[60]

> Is homblye prophaned by divellishe inventions, as with Lords of Misserule, Morice dauncers, insomuch that in some places, they shame not in ye time of divine service, to come and daunce aboute the Church, and without to have men naked dauncing in nettes, which is moste filthie ...

Some writers were content with broad-brush attacks, as Henry Barrow, who wrote in 1590 of the 'heathenish maner of keeping those feastes with idlenes, riot & gluttony, with their maygames, morrice dance, & sommer Lords &c.'.[61] Christopher Fetherston, writing, like Stockwood, in 1582, went into more detail in his *Dialogue agaynst Light, Lewde, and Lascivious Dauncing*, and described three ways in which May games and morris dances were offensive:[62]

> The first wherof is this, that you doe use to attyre men in womans apparell, whom you doe most commenly call maymarrions, whereby you infringe that straight commaundement which is given in Deut. 22.5. That men must not put on womens apparrell for feare of enormities. Nay, I myself have seene in a maygaime a troupe, the greater part wherof hath been men, and yet have they been attyred so like unto women, that theyr faces being hidde (as they were indeede) a man coulde not discerne them from women. What an horrible abuse was this? what abhominable sinnes might have hereupon ensued?
>
> The seconde abuse, which of all other is the greatest, is this, that it hath been toulde that your morice dauncers have daunced naked in nettes: what greater entisement unto naughtines, could have been devised? The thirde abuse, is, that you (because you will loose no tyme) doe use commonly to runne into woodes in the night time, amongst maidens, to fet[ch] bowes, in so muche, as I have hearde of tenne maidens which went to fet[ch] May, and nine of them came home with childe.

Fetherston brought morris dancing into the general ambit of play-acting, using a similar method of argument to that used by many Puritan writers, and which has already been demonstrated by the writers cited above. He identified particular activities as undesirable, then attributed the same characteristics to other activities which he also wished to condemn. Thus, the specific offence of boys acting 'maymarrions' is extended to men whose costume is not explicitly transvestite at all, of whom Fetherston complained that it is hard to tell the sex – which may amount to nothing more than gaudy attire seen through the polemicist's eyes. The claim that morris dancers have 'danced naked in nets' (made also by Stockwood) is also unsubstantiated in the literature. Fetherston was simultaneously condemning this form of costumed dancing by extending the pejorative 'morris' to it, and reinforcing the sinful nature of morris by attaching to it other manifestations of enormity. The 'naked dancing' in question is probably a reference to the sort of display presented by the guild pageants in Chester, where six 'naked' boys (probably representing savages) capered round the dragon in the midsummer watch, beating at it with sticks.[63] The stage depiction of nudity was usually achieved by the use of net costumes.

Fetherston continued his diatribe with an attack on the portrayal of fools and devils, conflating the fool of the morris dance with the 'devil', a character not associated with the morris, but sometimes found in midsummer watch processions and pageants. In so doing Fetherston confirmed the fool's position as a central character in the organization of the dance:

[60] Stockwood, p. 334.
[61] Barrow, *Brief Discoverie*, p. 80.
[62] Fetherston, sig. D7-D8v.
[63] Clopper, p. 481.

What mere madnes is this, that a man whome God hath endued with witt & reason, shoulde put on a noddies coate, and feigne him selfe to bee a foole, and to be destitute of both these most precious giftes? doeth hee not thinke that if the Lorde shoulde deale with him in Justice, that hee doeth deserve to be made a foole against his will, which playeth the foole so willingly? What a shame, nay what a sinne is it for him, who wilbe angrie with that man which shall not call him a Christian: to play the part of a divel, who is an utter enemie to Christ and al Christians? But truely these two persons, I meane your foole and your divell, doe make manifest what you are when you use suche wicked exercises. By your foole (who is most commenly amongst the thickest) men doe playnely see, that al the company are but fooles: and by your divell you doe manifestly declare, that you doe followe the divell and not God, so long as you are so idlely occupied. And this is to be noted that your divell doeth always leade the daunce.

The most famous rant against parish festivals came from Philip Stubbes's *Anatomy of Abuses* of 1583. The passage has been quoted many times before but is worth reproducing in full not least because of the circumstantial detail Stubbes provides. He does not identify 'morris' dancing explicitly but the depiction in the chapter 'Lords of Mis-rule in Ailgna' [England] is unambiguous:[64]

First, all the wilde-heds of the Parish, conventing togither, chuse them a Graund-Captain (of all mischeefe) whome they innoble with the title of 'my Lord of Mis-rule', and him they crowne with great solemnitie, and adopt for their king. This king anointed chuseth forth twentie, fortie, threescore or a hundred lustie Guttes, like to him self, to waighte uppon his lordly Maiestie, and to guarde his noble person. Then, everie one of these his men, he investeth with his liveries of green, yellow, or some other light wanton colour; And as though that were not (baudie) gaudie [sic] enough, I should say, they bedecke them selves with scarfs, ribons & laces hanged all over with golde rings, precious stones, & other jewels: this doon, they tye about either leg 20. or 40. bels, with rich handkercheifs in their hands, and sometimes laid a crosse over their shoulders and necks, borrowed for the moste parte of their pretie Mopsies & looving Besses, for bussing them in the dark. Thus al things set in order, then have they their Hobbyhorses, dragons & other Antiques, togither with their baudie Pipers and thundering Drummers to strike up the devils daunce withall. Then, marche these heathen company towards the Church and Church-yard, their pipers pipeing, their drummers thundring, their stumps dauncing, their bels jyngling, their handkerchefs swinging about their heds like madmen, their hobbie horses and other monsters skirmishing amongst the route: and in this sorte they go to the Church (I say) & into the Church, (though the Minister be at praier or preaching), dancing & swinging [t]heir handkercheifs, over their heds in the Church, like devils incarnate, with such a confuse noise, that no man can hear his own voice. Then, the foolish people they looke, they stare, they laugh, they fleer, & mount upon fourmes and pewes to see these goodly pageants solem[ni]zed in this sort. Then, after this, about the Church they goe againe and again, & so foorth into the church-yard, where they have commonly their Sommer-haules, their bowers, arbors, & banqueting houses set up, wherin they feast, banquet and daunce al that day & (peradventure) all the night too. And thus these terrestriall furies spend the Sabaoth day.

Stubbes's description of the dancers' costume is one of the fullest we have, and the depiction of the choice of a Lord and the march through the parish to the Lord's summer bower evocative. It also contains the first reference to the use of handkerchiefs. Given that he adds the hobby horse, it seems an odd omission on Stubbes's part not to fulminate even more strongly against

---

[64] Stubbes, 1:147.

a Maid Marion figure. Like many of his period, his chief complaint is against the encroachment into the church, especially in service time, but he also conveys a sense of the general fear of disorder among the populace.

––––––––––––––––––

Stage plays and their associated festivities were prime targets of Puritan writers from the first. Stephen Gosson in 1582 attacked the temptations provided by:[65]

> *Gearish apparell maskes vauting, tumbling, daunsing of gigges, galliardes, morisces, hobbihorses, showing of iudgeling castes, nothing forgot, that might serve to set out the matter, withe pompe, or ravish the beholders with varietie of pleasure.*

In contrast to the views of the polemicists, literary texts and dramas presented on the whole a far more favourable view of the morris dance. Robert Langham's description of the entertainments provided for Queen Elizabeth at Kenilworth in Warwickshire in 1575 is on one level a factual description, but is also an evocative literary piece. One of the entertainments was a mock representation of a country wedding, in which bride and bridegroom went in procession.[66] Of the man playing the bridegroom Langham wrote:

> *It was no small sport too mark this minion in hiz full appointment, that throgh good schoolation becam az formall in his action az had he been a bridegroom indeed: with this speciall grace by the wey, that ever az he woold have framed him the better coountenauns, with the woors face he lookt.*

The bride also cut a comic figure:

> *ill smellyng waz she: a 35. yeer old, of couler brounbay, not very beautifull indeed but ugly fooul ill favord: yet marveloous fayn of the offis, bycauz she hard say she shoold dauns before the Queen, in which feat she thought she woold foot it as finely az the best.*

The bridegroom was accompanied by riders on horseback, and Langham continued:

> *Well syr, after theez horsmen, a lyvely morisdauns, acording too the auncient manner, six daunserz, Maudmarion, and the fool.*

The import of this reaches far beyond the mere performance of the dance. Langham distances himself from the performance; his perceptions are removed from those of the participants. The country entertainment is just that, and Langham sees the difference between it and the more cultured entertainments with which he is familiar. The display was thought by its participants to be fit for the Queen, but it was certainly not what the court itself would have presented for her except, as here, in affectionate mockery.

Langham perceived not just a cultural disjunction, but a temporal one. His use of the word 'ancient' has been the subject of comment before now. It can (and could then) bear two meanings, of course, and some commentators have seen it as meaning 'very old' and have suggested that a dance termed ancient in 1575 must be ancient indeed. But Langham was not writing a historical piece, and no reliance can be placed on his use of the word in this sense other than to say it may date from before his time, which fact we know already. In its other sense it may have more significance. Langham may be saying that in his day the characteristics of morris dancing were different from what they were in his youth. We have already found indications of this from elsewhere, and it is significant that Langham's

---

[65] Gosson, sig. E1. [66] Langham, *Letter*, pp. 50–51.

characterization (six dancers and two supernumeraries) is close to what we found 55 years previously at Kingston-upon-Thames, when dancing shoes were bought for six dancers, Maid Marion and the friar. In either case there is the implication that morris dancing is validated by its status as a traditional pursuit, in the sense of having a continuity over time. It is the sentiment echoed by Henry Parkes when he referred to 'a merry England' before the mayor of Canterbury 14 years later.

Langham evoked a happy pastoral scene with no hint of the incipient contention and dissension that would convulse the next 80 years. The vast majority of the literary allusions of the period to morris dancing also inhabited this alternative carefree universe. They presented morris dancing solely as a light-hearted, positive feature of English life. William Warner wrote in 1586:[67]

> At Paske begun our Morrise: and ere Pentecost our May:
> Tho Robenhood, liell john, Frier Tucke, and Marian deftlie play,

while a madrigal of 1597 by composer and cathedral organist Thomas Weelkes (1576-1623) had:[68]

> Our country swains in the morris dance
> Thus woo and win their brides:
> Will for our town! Kate the next prance!
> The hobby horse at pleasure frolic rides.

An earlier madrigal by Thomas Morley (1594) described the dancers as follows:[69]

> Ho! Who comes here all along with bagpiping and drumming?
> O 'tis the Morris-dance I see a-coming,
> Come ladies, out, come quickly!
> And see how trim they dance and trickly.
> Hey! there again! how the bells they shake it!
> Hey ho! Now for our town! And take it!

'Trim' is an adjective often used to describe the dancers. The ballad *The Merry Life of the Countryman* (1589) has:[70]

> And then in may, by breake of day,
> with morrice daunces trime
> his men and he doth quickly agree
> to fetch their maypowle in.
> ...
> The lorde and lady, so merry as may be all day,
> like kinge and queene, will there be sene,
> all in their best array.

The verses capture the community pride and the festive context of the maypole and Lord and Lady of the May game. 'Trimness' is a nebulous concept embracing in the 16th century competence and excellence, and also the idea of being well equipped with all the appropriate and necessary appurtenances and characteristics. Underlying that is the sense that there exists

---

[67] Warner, William, p. 108.
[68] Weelkes, 'Madrigals to 3, 4, 5 and 6 Voyces', p. 282.
[69] Morley, p. 143.
[70] 'Mery Life', f. 19v.

a 'proper' way to present a morris dance and that people will recognise it. The same idea was present in a prose work of about 1590, *The Famouus Hystory of George a Greene Pinder of Wakefield* in which, when King Richard passed through 'Bradstead' (Bradford is probably intended):[71]

> *The shoo makers came and presented the Kinnge with a coontry morryce dance in wh<i>ch nothinge was omitted that coold bee prepared on the suddeine to give content which was so well ordered that it much pleased him.*

Robert Greene's 1591 text *Farewell to Folly* embodied all the typical features of the period. He described how Maesia, a nobleman's daughter, leaves the court for the country, where she meets 'with a wealthy farmers sonne, who handsomely deckt up in his holy day hose, was going very mannerly to be a foreman in a Morice dance'. The sense of community pride is signified by the fact that 'he had on his fathers best tawnye worsted jacket: for that this daies exploit stood upon his credit'; and the rest of the costume consists of 'a strawne hat steeple wise, bound about with a band of blue buckram ... a pair of hose of red kersies close trust with a point afore, ... a newe muffler for a napkin, ... tied to his girdle for loosing: he had a paire of harvest gloves on his hands as shewing good husbandry, & a pen and inckhorn at his backe: for the young man was a little bookish, his pompes were a little too heavie, being trimmed startups made of a paire of bootelegges, tied before with two white leather thongs'.[72] ('Start-ups' are a kind of high shoe, which the *Oxford English Dictionary* says were 'worn predominantly by unsophisticated rural people, and consequently also worn for comic effect by clowns and actors portraying such people'.)

When writers wanted to evoke the characteristics of the dancers in metaphor, the predominant images were of uninhibitedness or witless folly. In 1589 Lyly spoke of 'a wild Morrice daunce' and Robert Greene said that his love-sick character Ned 'is become Loves morris dance'. John Eliot wrote that a thunderstorm was as if 'five hundred thousand hundred millions of Divels dance the morrice'.[73] Greene sometimes used allusion to exemplify the morris as an empty-headed pastime. In *Groatsworth of Wit* he described how 'my yong master ... was very forward in dauncing, to shew his cunning: and ... laid on the pavement lustely with his leaden heeles, corvetting, like a steede of Signor Roccoes teaching, & wanted nothing but bels, to be a hobby horse in a morrice'; and in *A Quip for an Upstart Courtier* he derided the courtier's use of make-up as 'mak[ing] the foole as faire forsooth, as if he were to play Maidmarian in a May game or Moris-daunce'.[74]

Thomas Nashe also invoked witless folly in 1591 in his Preface to Sidney's *Astrophel and Stella*:[75]

> *Indeede, to say the truth, my stile is somewhat heavie gated, and cannot daunce Trip and goe so lively, with oh my love, ah my love, all my loves gone, as other Sheepheards that have beene fooles in the Morris time out of minde.*

Not only did Nashe invoke the love-sick fool, his morris was hallowed by time – it was ancient. Nashe used similar imagery in *The Return of Pasquil*.[76] He is one of the few literary authors whose works were explicitly anti-Puritan, and this text of 1589 was a riposte to the Marprelate tracts. In it Nashe made fun of 'The May-game of Martinisme' with Martin Marprelate himself as 'Mayd-marian, trimlie drest', and went on to give some idea of the stage business between her/him and the fool, in which the fool's exaggerated expressions of love for the maid

[71] 'Famouus Hystory', p. 177.
[72] Greene, 'Greene's Farewell', pp. 265-67.
[73] Lyly, p. 419; Greene, 'Frier Bacon', p. 21; Eliot, p. 111.
[74] Greene, 'Groats-worth', p. 98; Greene, 'Quip', pp. 248-49.
[75] Nashe, 'Preface', p. 332.
[76] Nashe, 'Returne', p. 83.

have become a byword for senseless infatuation. Martin as the maid (accompanied by Giles Wigginton, a prominent Puritan and purported author of some of the Marprelate texts) has:

> ...his face handsomlie muffled with a Diapernapkin to cover his beard, and a great Nosegay in his hande, of the principalest flowers I could gather out of all hys works. Wiggenton daunces round about him in a Cottencoate, to court him with a Leatherne pudding, and a woodden Ladle.

The characterization as uninhibited wildness was found in dramatic texts too, as in Shakespeare's 'I have seen / Him caper upright like a Wild Morisco / Shaking the bloody darts as he his bells',[77] capturing both the movement and the double meaning of 'Morisco' to conjure up images both of morris dancers and Moors. In *Henry V* he evoked the image of the innocent empty-headed pastime: '... let us do it with no show of fear; / No, with no more than if we heard that England / Were busied with a Whitsun morris-dance.'[78] In a play of unknown authorship, *The Pilgrimage to Parnassus*, the appropriately named Stupido claims ' ... studie not these vaine artes of Rhetorique, Poetrie, and Philosophie: ... why, the[y] are more vaine than a paire of organs, or a morrice dance'.[79] Munday's *The Downfall of Robert, Earl of Huntingdon*, while not having a morris within the play, has Little John speak of 'merry Morices of Frier Tuck, ... pleasant skippings up and downe the woodde'.[80]

In this period the earliest instances of the depiction of morris dancing itself on stage occur. One fifteenth-century dramatic work, John Lydgate's *A Mumming at Hertford* (1430), is sometimes supposed to allude to morris dances indirectly. It has the stage direction 'demonstrando 6. Rusticos' ('pointing to 6 countrymen') at the line 'Lyke as theos hynes, here stonding oon by oon, / He may with hem upon the daunce goon'.[81] In the context of the overall picture of the development of the morris dance, however, it seems more likely that this is an indication that there was a tradition of dance on to which the characteristics of morris were later grafted.

Given Puritan antipathy to the stage, it is not really surprising that those writing for it did not share their animosity to morris dancing. The first explicit indication is the title of a 1579 piece unfortunately now lost, entitled *Morris Mask*. Another lost title is Thomas Dekker's *Madman's Morris*, revived in 1598.[82] Around 1589 Anthony Munday's *John a Kent and John a Cumber* has a group of rustics planning for a morris with Maid Marion, played by a boy, and a Fool (into which role they intend to trick John a Kent). After John a Kent is given a new fool's coat they exit dancing, with their leader Turnop saying 'now Thomas [the taborer] lustily, and let us jerk it over the greene, seeing we have got such a goodly foole as Mr. John a Kent'.[83]

In John Marston's 1599 play *Histrio-mastix*, which is thought to have been an Inns of Court Christmas production at the Middle Temple aiming to pack in as many participants as possible,[84] morris dancers 'crave admittance' and the Clerk of the Market rewards them with ale.[85] And Jonson's *Every Man out of his Humour* the same year had the hobby horse mentioned earlier in connection with the Betley window (Chapter 4). The passage opens with the words 'you shall see him turn morrice-dancer, he has got him bells, a good suit, and a hobby-horse' – linking the hobby horse closely with the morris.[86]

---

[77] Shakespeare, *King Henry VI Part II*, p. 78 (III.iii).
[78] Shakespeare, *King Henry V*, p. 50 (II.iv).
[79] Pilgrimage, p. 113 (Act III).
[80] Munday, *Downfall*, sig. I2.
[81] Lydgate, p. 676.

[82] Harbage, *Annals*, pp. 48-49, 68-69.
[83] Munday, *John a Kent*, p. 44 (IV.i).
[84] Geckle, p. 34.
[85] Marston, 'Histrio-mastix', p. 262 (II.i).
[86] Jonson, 'Every Man', p. 295, II.i.

As the Elizabethan period drew to a close the expressions of disapproval of morris dancing in association with church activities were becoming well entrenched. Secular festivities 'abused and prophaned' church premises and were 'unseemly'. Parish officers were prosecuted for allowing them, although some stubbornly held on to the investment they had made in equipping themselves to stage them. Outside of the church, morris dancing could still be presented in civic contexts as in Liverpool and Salisbury, but even here signs of dissent were emerging, as in the controversies at Leicester and Banbury. The period also saw the emergence of writings in which morris dancing was not just an entertainment, but embodied polarizing attitudes to society and morality, whether positive in the evocation of innocent merriment or negative in the fulminations of mainly Puritan polemicists. The 17th century would see irreconcilable attitudes harden to the point where they became emblematic of allegiance in the approaching Civil War.

Chapter 6
Attack 1600-1629

As the 17th century began and the Elizabethan era drew to a close morris dancing began to be seen as one of the defining markers of a particular world view that was coming under increasing attack.

Variants on the visitation articles first used by Grindal in 1571 (see p. 54) continued to be used in the 17th century. There were three main lines of inquiry. The first was the role of the parish officers, as when Winchester and Bristol in 1603 simply asked 'whether your Minister and Church-wardens have suffered any lord of misrule ... or morice dancers... to come unreverently into the church or churchyard', though Bristol also wanted to know if the offenders had used 'scofes, jestes, wanton gestures, or ribauld talke'.[1] The second continued the approach first taken by Bishop Chaderton at Chester in 1581 and used by him at Lincoln, when in 1601 he asked whether the 'Church, chappell, or churchyard be abused or prophaned' by such activities, regardless of the connivance or otherwise of the parish officers.[2] He also inquired 'what be the names of the offenders in that behalf'. Pursuing the parishioners as well as the parish officials in this manner constituted the third line of inquiry, with many articles asking 'what they be that commit such disorder, or that accompanied or maintayned them'.[3] The Church Canons of 1604 provided a new model for ecclesiastical law, but laid responsibilities only upon the parish officers:[4]

> *Churches not to be profaned.*
>
> *The Church-Wardens or quest-Men and their Assistants shall suffer no Plays, Feasts, Banquets, Suppers, Church-Ales, Drinkings, Temporal Courts, or Leets, Lay-Juries, Musters, or any other profane Usage to be kept in the Church, Chapel or Church-yard...*

Bishop Chaderton may have been responding to the canons when he amended his articles for Lincoln in 1607 by omitting the enquiry about the offenders. It was also dropped by his two successors but used there in 1618 by George Montaigne and again in 1622, then at Winchester in 1628 and the Archdeaconry of Bedford in 1629.[5]

The Archbishop of York, Tobias Matthew, introduced a new form of enquiry for the Archdiocese of York in 1607, singling out pastimes taking place during church services or sermons:[6]

> *Item, Whether are there within your saide parish or Chappellry any Rush bearings, Bullbaytings, Bearebaitings, Maygames, Morricedances, Ailes, or any such like prophane pastimes or Assemblies on the Sabboth to the hinderance of Prayers, Sermons, or other godly exercises.*

Matthew's text was widely adopted. It was used in the Diocese of York (1610, 1619, 1623) and again in the Province (1629); and at the northern dioceses of Chester (1617) and Carlisle (1629).[7]

---

[1] *V.A. Winchester* (1603), sig. B3; *V.A. Bristol*, pp. 10-11.
[2] *V.A. Lincoln* (1601), p. 1.
[3] *V.A. London* (1604), sig. B4; *V.A. Coventry* (1610), sig. B3-B3v; *V.A. Leicester*, sig. B2; *V.A. Oxford* (1619), sig. B2v-B3; *V.A. Oxford* (1622), sig. B2v-B3; *V.A. Oxford* (1629), sig. B3v.
[4] *Constitutions*, sig. O4.

[5] *V.A. Lincoln* (1607), sig. A3; *V.A. Lincoln* (1618), sig. A2; *V.A. Lincoln* (1622), sig. A2; *V.A. Winchester* (1628), sig. A2; *V.A. Bedford* (1629), sig. A2.
[6] *V.A. York* (1607), pp. 8-9.
[7] *V.A. York* (1610), pp. 8-9; *V.A. York* (1618), item 39; *V.A. York* (1623), pp. 8-9; *V.A. York* (1629), p. 9; *V.A. Chester* (1617), sig. B2v; *V.A. Carlisle* (1629), p. 7.

The differing texts of the visitation articles offer a range of interests, from the identities of the individual parishioners to mere enquiry about whether the activities had hindered church activities, but the presentments bear little relation to the letter of the articles. Moreover, most of the records come from areas whose articles do not explicitly refer to morris dancing – dancers were being prosecuted under more general prohibitions against dancing.

Comparatively few presentments were made against parish officers. However, the churchwardens at Glastonbury in 1617 failed to keep a proper register book and 'they kept the church ale uppon the saboth daie with the Morysh daunce coming into the church'.[8] The churchwarden Thomas Statherne offended in a more personal capacity at Benington in Lincolnshire in 1609. He missed Sunday prayers because he was at a morris dance; when he did enter the church during the sermon he 'was warned to fetche the rest of the companie unto sermon but he sette still in the churche & did not'.[9] At Yazor (Herefordshire) in 1619 the churchwardens Hugh Stringham and Hugh Winney were presented 'for havinge a greate morris daunce upon the sabaoth daie at eveninge praier tyme'.[10]

The Archbishop of York's concerns about dancing in service time had been anticipated in a case early in King James's reign. In South Weald in 1603 Henry Graye was presented for 'making preparation, with others, for to dance the morris in the sermon time'. This is already a wider interpretation in which not just dancing, but preparing for dancing, was prosecuted. There is clearly another thread running through this prosecution, however. This was part of a wedding feast (weddings could be large-scale community events, often termed 'bride-ales'). The presentment goes on to say that 'they met with the bridegroom, and came dancing the morris home with them'.[11] John Burt of Wimborne in Dorset was presented 'for being at Robert Fulford's house with the morrise dauncers at sermon time' on 13 May 1608, while his colleague James Fabin was cited 'for help drawing a summer poole [maypole] in a carte at morning prayer time'.[12] At Ribbesford (Worcestershire) in 1616, Thomas Weaver was presented 'for dauncinge the morris upon the Lordes day and providinge himself for it at the tyme of devine service and sermon and for many misdeameanours then committed'.[13]

Great importance was attached to Sunday observance in one's own parish. While Puritans were often accused of 'gadding' out of their parishes to sermons, the equivalent offence on the other side of the argument appears to have been dancers dancing out of their parishes. In 1604 Henry Briggs and six others of Thetford 'did prophane & abuse the sabboth day by dauncing of the morrice from towne to towne And so to Wilberton feaste, as well in service tyme as otherwise to the high displeasinge of Almighty God And the offence of manye'.[14]

In 1617 John Stent of West Lavington in Sussex, his wife and five children combined preparing during the service and dancing out of the parish. The churchwarden also came under scrutiny:

> upon Trinitie sonday last past [they] did empty a kiln of pottes and did lade them into a Carte in the morninge before service began and moreover in tyme of divine service at our Church his sayde Children with divers other youthes of our parishe made them selves ready in a morrice daunce and a hobby horse and a mayde marryan and went for myles to Cockeinge to daunce the morrice and ... [John Joy] Churchwarden and his eldest daughter went after the sayde youthes the same Daye to Cockinge wheare they spent all that whole sabboth.

8   Stokes, *Records ... Somerset*, p. 129.
9   Stokes, *Records ... Somerset*, p. 26.
10 Klausner, *Records ... Herefordshire*, p. 183.
11 Emmison, 'Tithes', p. 201.
12 Hays, McGee, Joyce and Newlyn, p. 287.
13 Klausner, *Records ... Herefordshire*, pp. 387-88.
14 'Ely' (1600), f. 151.

Joy declared he had had to leave early for the following day's fair and had attended the service at Cocking. The rest were said to have missed both morning and evening services. All were fined.[15]

Dancing out of parish was the main grievance at Yazor in Herefordshire in 1619 when ten dancers were cited for dancing between morning and evening prayer, most of them out of their parishes. The clerk to the court dutifully noted down their home villages (all in a five-mile circle around Yazor): Bishopstone, Bridge Sollers, Byford, Mansell Gamage, Mansell Lacy, Staunton on Wye, and Weobley.[16] Still in Herefordshire, the innkeeper Edward Hall 'thee actor and morrice daunier' of Ledbury, was cited with two others because they 'have gone out of the parrishe to other placces with gune and drume bothe in the night to the disturbance of the kinges subjectes and the profanation of the Sabaoth daie in the morning'.[17]

The combination of leaving one's parish and dancing during service time was doubly offensive. In 1602, a group of people was presented at the church court simply for being present, some out of their parishes, at a morris dance at Tedstone Delamere in Herefordshire during divine service. Nineteen people (13 men and six women) were presented: they came from Tedstone Delamere itself and the surrounding parishes of Cradley and Avenbury. One, Milo Conney, was presented 'ffor prophaininge the Saboathe day and daunsinge and revelinge with morrice daunces' during service time, others 'for beinge at a Morrice Daunce', and others beside 'for the same'; it is not clear who was dancing and who watching. As at Headcorn in 1589 (see pp. 57-58), the musician was singled out for attack: the records note 'Let each one from this wanton crowd be asked especially about the taborer'.[18]

John Wikes of Tedstone Delamere in Herefordshire made the double mistake of arranging an event in 1605 at evening prayer time out of his own parish, and was charged with 'recieving Morrice Dauncers of the parishe of Bromyard And other parishes thereaboutes upon the Saboath daie at the time of devine service videlicet at Evening prayer time'. Perhaps because he had only arranged it and not participated, he was let off with a warning.[19]

At Ross-on-Wye in Herefordshire in 1629 seven men and three women were presented 'for daunceing the morris at time of evening prayer' (one man is specifically accused of morris dancing, the rest, including the women, are presented 'for the same'). One turned up to the hearing and was dismissed with a warning; another claimed innocence of the offence. Some of them repeatedly refused to appear before the court and they were excommunicated until they submitted, when those who did were dismissed with warnings.[20] Excommunication – barring the offender from participation in church life, including from the church as the path to eternal salvation – was among the most serious sanctions that ecclesiastical authorities could impose.

For its more zealous opponents merely dancing on the Sabbath was enough to warrant prosecution. At Stretham in Cambridgeshire in 1600 Thomas Rewell and six others were presented for doing so.[21] Richard Roberts of Chatteris, Cambridgeshire, was presented in 1614 'for mainteyninge of his three sonnes to profane the Saboth day by setting them to daunce the morrise about the Towne he himselfe followinge of them & incouraginge them so to doe'.[22]

---

[15] 'Diocese and Archdeaconry of Chichester', ff. 107v-108.
[16] Klausner, *Records ... Herefordshire*, pp. 182-86.
[17] Klausner, *Records ... Herefordshire*, pp. 142-43, 283.
[18] Klausner, *Records ... Herefordshire*, pp. 169-72, 250-54.
[19] Klausner, *Records ... Herefordshire*, p. 172.
[20] Klausner, *Records ... Herefordshire*, pp. 161-62.
[21] 'Ely' (1593), f. 213.
[22] 'Ely' (1614), f. 28.

There is one unusual example from 1610 of a woman being presented explicitly for morris dancing:[23]

> *Maria Goodenoughe. Notatur for abuseing of her selfe upon the saboth day, by dancing the morris very uncomly from Witcham to Coveney.*

In 1616 Thomas Cooper of West Ham was fined 7s upon being convicted of morris dancing on the Sabbath 'drawinge many Idle & Dissolute people to ale howses at unseasonable tymes upon that Saboth', even after being warned.[24] At Bradmore, Nottinghamshire in 1618 a company of ten dancers and two pipers was presented 'for prophayninge the Saboth by morrice dauncinge'. Those that appeared before the court were dismissed, but those who failed to appear were excommunicated.[25] At Stanton Lacy, Shropshire in 1611 William Wilkes 'counterfaited the divell in the morrice dance upon the Saboath daie' (an atypical charge, perhaps echoing Fetherston's 1582 equating the fool in a morris dance with the devil) and was excommunicated.[26]

These examples indicate a hardening attitude toward morris dancing, but in 1618 King James intervened. In 1617 *en route* from Scotland to London he had been petitioned in Lancashire by parishioners wanting to pursue Sunday recreations in contravention of edicts issued by local justices of the peace. He gave them leave to do so and the following year issued his decision nationally, as *The King's Majesties Declaration to his Subjects Concerning Lawfull Sports to be Used*. In the national re-issue he added Whitsun ales, maypoles and morris dances to the list of permitted activities:[27]

> *Our pleasure likewise is, That after the end of Divine Service, Our good people be not disturbed, letted, or discouraged from any lawfull Recreation; Such as dauncing, either men or women, Archerie for men, leaping, vaulting, or any other such harmelesse Recreation, nor from having May-Games, Whitson Ales, and Morris-dances, and the setting up of May-poles and other sports therwith used, so as the same be had in due and convenient time, without impediment or neglect of divine Service: And that women shall have leave to carry rushes to the Church for the decoring of it, according to their old custom.*

The key here is that the recreations are permitted after the Sunday service. But if there were both morning and evening services, there was scope for either a liberal or a strict interpretation of what the phrase meant, and some took advantage of it.

Although the effectiveness and influence of the *Declaration* has been much debated, by far the greatest concentration of presentments connected with morris dancing occurs immediately after its publication, with a peak in 1619. Many of the presentments in James's reign after the publication of the *Declaration* do refer only to dancing during services, suggesting that it was having a direct influence on the practice while simultaneously encouraging action against breaches. William Edwards of Marden (Herefordshire) was presented in 1620 'for dauncing the morris at Wellington on a saboath day before evening prayer', following the strict letter of the *Declaration*.[28]

It may be that the *Declaration* encouraged people to oppose church strictures. At Windsor in 1619 there was a complaint when the morris dancers directly challenged the minister:[29]

---

[23] 'Ely' (1609), f. 71v.
[24] Smith, J.R., p. 11.
[25] Hodgkinson, 'Morris Dancing', pp. 320-21.
[26] Somerset, pp. 323-24.

[27] James VI and I, p. 107.
[28] Klausner, *Records ... Herefordshire*, pp. 183, 173.
[29] Peyton, p. xix.

upon the feast day of the Ascension last past, when one of the morrice dauncers had leaped and daunced in the face of the minister standing before his owne doore [and] did before a great number of people, revile and abuse the minister, with these reproachful speeches, sc. that the morrice dauncers should daunce before his doore and before him in spite of him and in spite of his teeth and that they should ridd the towne of him; asking him disdainfully what he was.

At Clee St Margaret in Shropshire, also in 1619, the morris dancers decided they needed the communion cloth from the church at Abdon for a flag to lead their dance. Extremely detailed records of the subsequent case survive.[30] Nicholas Millichap persuaded the churchwarden at Abdon to lend him the cloth, implying that it was for a widely approved communal purpose but not specifying that purpose precisely. He and the dancers then used the cloth as a flag over two days of revelry around Clee St Margaret on Whit Monday and Tuesday. Most of the dancers swore that they had not known the flag was a communion cloth until they turned up for the dance. There were eight dancers, a fool ('the lord's vice or son') the flag bearer, a sword bearer, hobby horse, friar and a drummer as musician. Whether Millichap and his fellows were seeking to obtain implicit church sanction, or to defy or ridicule the church, has been the subject of detailed speculation.[31] The events in Clee St Margaret contrast, however, with those at Didcot forty years previously, where the churchwarden, not the dancers, was presented when the dancers took 'towels' from the church. Churchwardens did remain liable for church goods: at Ellenhall in Staffordshire Simon Tayler was excommunicated in 1619 'for lending the surplasse to daunce the Morrice upon May day'.[32]

William Hartley of Wollaton in Nottinghamshire was charged in 1618 that 'uppon a Sabaoth daye since the feaste of Pentecost laste paste he went to Trowell in companie of Morris dauncers in tyme of divine service'. Although he admitted the offence, he refused to do penance and was excommunicated.[33] Even when dancers outwardly expressed repentance, it might count for little. John Allen and three others were presented at Stratford-upon-Avon in 1622 for dancing in service time and he was ordered to confess his fault in church. He said he would 'never commit the lyke' again, but was resummoned the following month for doing precisely that. He was excommunicated and ordered to carry out his penance. The others were treated similarly, but all were absolved in the end. Francis Palmer, servant to John Hobbins of Shottery was presented 'for being the Maid Marrian' but was pardoned, perhaps because he was probably a mere boy.[34]

Although he was not strictly dancing, Richard Fire of Kinver in Staffordshire could hardly have expected less than the excommunication he got in 1620 'for fartinge & pissinge in the Church in sermon time & gingelinge of Morrice Dauncers bells'.[35] Fire evidently held the Church in some contempt if it interfered with his recreations.

At this remove we can know little of the motives behind prosecution of dancers and dancing. They may well have been grounded in religious ideology, but in many cases there may have been more immediate local or personal drivers. At Dundry in Somerset in the 1620s there was a long-running battle about communal dancing and maypoles in the churchyard, but this seems to have been driven in part by economic motives on the part of the curate and a personal vendetta between the two churchwardens.[36]

---

[30] Somerset, pp. 40-50.
[31] Winerock, 'Reformation', pp. 334-47.
[32] 'Archdeaconry of Stafford Visitation Act Book' [a].
[33] Hodgkinson, 'Morris Dancing', p. 319.
[34] Brinkworth, pp. 150-53.
[35] 'Archdeaconry of Stafford Visitation Act Book' [b].
[36] Winerock, 'Churchyard Capers', pp. 251-53.

While there are numerous records of presentments, especially in the west midlands and East Anglia, there is an area around the Thames valley in which church support apparently continued (Figure 6.1). Four morris coats and five garters of bells (the 240 bells for which were bought that year for 20s) were in the keeping of the churchwardens at Bray in 1602, and 21 years later they still had 'foure coats for morrice daunsers and for the mayd maryan & a payre of breeches and dooblet for the foole & a cupp'.[37] At Stanford-in-the-Vale in Berkshire (present-day Oxfordshire) the churchwardens recorded among the parish goods on 26 April 1607, '4 garters of morris belles, and one brasse bell' together with a drum.[38] At Great Marlow in Buckinghamshire the parish's morris coats were hired by the nearby parish of Beysham for 1s 6d in 1612, and in most years from 1606 to 1628, 'fower paire of morris bells, fower morris Coates and a fooles Coate, ffower ffeathers' were recorded as being in the keeping of the churchwardens; from 1621 they were the responsibility of the churchwardens but were 'in the hands of Edward Wooden'.[39] Also in Buckinghamshire, 2s was paid by the churchwardens of Aston Abbotts in 1620 'for leathering for the morris belles', indicating that they were still in use.[40] In the north of the region, at Brackley, a paten inscribed with the names of the morris dancers is said to have been presented to the church from the proceeds of a Whitsun Ale in 1623.[41]

In 1600 the diplomat Dudley Carleton wrote from Rycote, to the east of Oxford, to his friend the noted correspondent John Chamberlain, that if Chamberlain could send him news 'I will repay you and write you large discourses of Whitsun ales and morris dances'.[42] Unfortunately, the promised letter, if written, seems not to have survived, but Carleton's letter suggests a high level of activity in the area.

At Milborne Port in Somerset in 1603 the parish decided to hold a May game to raise funds to repair the church bell, and went with 'flagges gunnes and weapons in merriment and in the fashion of a May game' to the neighbouring parish of Poyntington. This was said to be at the instigation of Sir Edward Parham, who with his brother John 'have procured and Caused ... many great Bulbaytinges, Morishdaunces, the said Sir Edward beinge one of the Morishdauncers the better to gette the love and affection of the common people'; but a bill of complaint was laid against them that they were Popish recusants and encouraged riotous assembly. So although the parish was supportive and had aristocratic backing and even participation, the accusation not just of disorder but of religious dissent from the established church was raised in opposition.[43]

Whereas, outside the Thames valley, the ecclesiastical evidence was by now almost uniformly hostile, municipal records reveal mixed attitudes to the morris during the first 30 years of the 17th century (Figure 6.1). The grounds for hostility, where it is present, appear to lie in the threat of disorder in the events of which the morris is a part. Many local orders were passed banning revels, wakes, ales and the like, but at the same time such events might be instigated by the dignitaries of the town as markers of civic life. At the very beginning of James's English reign, at Leicester in 1603, a maypole was erected close to the house of Simon Yng, who 'raged' at it. On being told 'the King did allow of them', he declared that the

[37] 'Bray', ff. 1v, 4, 17; in part also in Kerry, History ... Bray, pp. 29-30.
[38] Howse, p. 304.
[39] 'Great Marlow', ff. 17v, 25, 32, 34, 36v, 43v, 45v, 47, 49, 51, 53, 55, 57, 59v.
[40] 'Aston Abbotts', f. 35.
[41] Baker, George, 1:576.
[42] Green, Mary Anne Everett, 5:436-37.
[43] Stokes, Records ... Somerset, pp. 167-70.

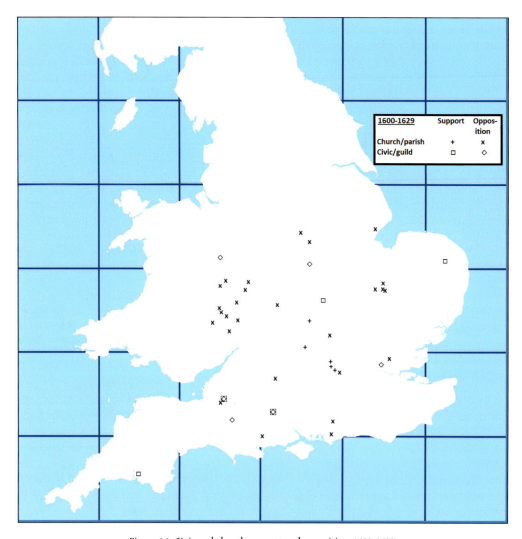

Figure 6.1: Civic and church support and opposition, 1600-1629.

King had no laws, and he would obey only Queen Elizabeth's laws, under which, one of the parties later asserted, 'they have been heretofore for many yeares forbidden & restrained amongst us'. The mayor took fright and hastened to assure the judge that although 'theire is a reporte suggested that myselfe should since that tyme give countenance unto the Morrice dauncers, whoe soe disorderlye did assemble themselves togeyther, I doe assure your Honor, that itt is, and hath beene, farr from me and my affection ...'. Disorder seems to have been the chief worry: there were 'Morrices and a great number of Idle, rude companie, many of them armed with shot, followinge them, morninge & eveninge, the wholle towne throwe out'. Nine men were named as dancers. One was a tailor's servant, the others in various trades (baker, saddler, shoemaker, smith, glover, butcher). The mayor's change of heart led him to order the taking down of the maypole, but this itself created further tension, with one man overheard to say 'he would see Mr Maiore hanged as heighe as the topp of the hall before he would be at his comaund, either for the cuttinge doune of May Poles or any thinge els'.[44]

Similar discord and mixed receptions for the morris can be seen in Wells, Somerset. The famous Wells May game, so called by C.J. Sisson in his commentary on Tudor and Stuart drama,[45] was a complex series of events. Sisson laid his own, sometimes inaccurate, interpretation on it, but the basic sequence of events has since been made clear by James Stokes. Stokes sees the events between 30 April and 25 June 1607 as 'a concerted attempt to re-establish traditional festive entertainments ... suppressed during the late sixteenth and early seventeenth centuries'.[46] The mayor and dean of the cathedral, in favour of an ale ostensibly to repair church bells, were ranged against John Hole, a clothier then holding the office of constable, and his Puritan colleagues. The events began as a May game but continued thereafter in a series of events resembling guild pageants. The May game had all the usual elements of a Lord and Lady, morris dancers, and even a Robin Hood. St George and the dragon and a giant also appeared. Unusually, at least one morris dance (on 10 May, Rogation Sunday) appears to have involved dancing with drawn daggers ('there wer Morrys Dauncers dauncinge there with naked daggers and rapyers in their hands'), who mocked a woman who had complained about the maypole, and at the dancing on Whit Sunday (24 May) there were songs mocking Hole himself. Direct satire was more prominent in the later events, especially that of 18 June, and in the show of 19 June Hole was accused of adultery. Although many of the same people were involved in May game and shows, and the morris dancers appeared independently of the May game, the morris is not mentioned during the show events.[47]

The result of all this activity – which lays bare the interweaving of complex motivations arising from religious, civic and personal rivalries and attitudes – was a series of court cases which reached the Star Chamber two years later. What is perhaps more surprising is that a mere six years later in 1613 the various guilds presented a series of pageants for Queen Anne, about which there was no dissension, but which featured many of the same elements as in 1607 (minus the libellous and slanderous additions). This time there were morris dancers in the shows: the Hammermen and the Cordwainers each presented a morris dance, while the Mercers presented a 'Morrice daunce of Younge children'.[48] It would appear that context is critical: what was unacceptable on one occasion was acceptable on another, and perhaps the use of children here was intended to mollify opinion.

A similar conjunction of approval and litigious conflict can be found in Salisbury. Here the Guild of Tailors continued its well established practice of entrusting the morris apparel to the chamberlain, who then had use of it. In 1603 the apparel was transferred from the outgoing chamberlain Nicholas Longman to the incoming Cuthbert Watson. In 1610 the guild agreed 'that the usuall ffeastes & accustomes called the midsomer ffeaste shalbe holden & kepte at the usuall place upon the sondaye sevennighte after St Peters day [i.e., 8 July] ... And yt is agreed that the morrice Dauncers shalbe ymployed as heretofore yt hath byn'.[49] The next year, however, the mayor issued an order at the last minute – after dinner on Sunday 23 June 1611, the day of the procession – saying that 'heretofore the Lordes Sabbaoth Day hath bene prophaned by some ydell and evill dysposed persones with the Morrys Dauncers and dromers from the churches and in tyme of prayers', and that this was to cease immediately.

---

[44] Kelly, pp. 237-43.
[45] Sisson, pp. 162-88.
[46] Stokes, 'Wells Shows', p. 132.

[47] Stokes, *Records ... Somerset*, pp. 261-367.
[48] Stokes, 'Wells Cordwainers' Show'.
[49] 'Tailors' Guild' (1597), ff. 39v, 65v.

The Tailors' wardens replied that they could not prevent it at such short notice, but 'willed their messingers to tell him that the Morris dauncers shold not showe them selves that Day before that eveninge prayer shold be donne & ended in all churches. And so accordingleye it was performed, for after the eveninge prayer donne at our Lady churche the whole company came fro there with the drome & Morris dauncers before them as their Ancyent custome was to their Hall to supper and daunced not any more nor any other where els that day.' Despite this, the wardens maintained, the mayor's sergeant had tried to obstruct them at every turn.

The mayor summoned the wardens the next Wednesday, accused them of profaning the Sabbath and demanded sureties against an appearance at the next sessions. The wardens replied that if they had profaned the Sabbath, it was not an offence over which he had jurisdiction. Moreover, they asserted that 'that which they did was not mislyked but lyked of by the best in the cittye and what they had donne, was donne for tyme out of mynde of man and always approved by the best of the cittye'. Despite the appeal to the dance's antiquity the mayor then gaoled them without even allowing them home to order their affairs, and they remained in gaol until bail was found for them two days later. The further particulars of the case are not known. The next record of the morris in Salisbury is the entry for the handing over of the apparel to the incoming Chamberlain in 1618.[50]

At Shrewsbury in 1619 there occurred an incident embodying, as at Salisbury, the complex relations between ecclesiastical and civil offence. A group of morris dancers in the Stonegate district of the town – a Lord of Misrule, flag bearer, eight dancers and a whiffler – became involved in an affray while they were performing at the residence of a Lady Buckley. The whiffler, Richard Morrey, appears to have been over-eager or overbearing in fulfilling his role of clearing the way for the dancers, knocking over one Philip Speake. The ensuing brawl seems to have involved Lady Buckley's servants and others rather than the dancers, of whom only David Plum, the flag bearer, is reported to have struck anyone; but all the side (except, apparently, Morrey) ended up in prison. Here most of the dancers expressed a willingness to see their Lord of Misrule, Ralph Whoode, put in the stocks; they all petitioned the bailiffs for clemency, admitting that they had danced outside their parish, had missed evening prayer, and had committed other misdemeanours.[51] They were released, but the episode shows how dancers could be arrested by the civil authorities and detained for an ecclesiastical offence, once the authorities had been given the opportunity by the commission of a civil disturbance.

Early in James's reign the corporation of Plymouth paid 6s 8d, as they had been wont to do during Elizabeth's reign, for 'Morrice dauncers & Musitians on Maye day', but thereafter municipal payments for dancers cease.[52] There is an undated record from Chester which may relate to this period. It reviews the costs of staging the midsummer show and notes that 'the morris dancers had 10s from city but now have no fee but the Curtesye after the show at eich house what the[y] please'; in other words, city support had been withdrawn but the dancers were allowed to solicit money on their own initiative.[53] The May-day activities at Newport, Isle of Wight, were circumscribed in 1621, on the ostensible ground that they encouraged the 'idle poor' (people who refused to work, in contravention of the 1601 Poor Relief Act) and thereby the threat of disorder:[54]

---

[50] Green, Mary Anne Everett, p. 50; Haskins, pp. 179-80.
[51] Somerset, pp. 309-12.
[52] Wasson, p. 261.
[53] Clopper, p. 478.
[54] Stone, 'Ledger Book' [Part 2], p. 216.

...for that the fetching of wood out of the forest under pretence of custome is founde rather to encreace the nombre of idle poore in the toune then to relieve the poore ... It is now ordered and decreed ... that the custome and priviledge of the Maior going to the Wood Ovis and the fetching of boughs of wood out of the forrest shall be utterly left off yealded uppe and abolished.

There are reports of a set of geriatric morris dancers performing before King James in Herefordshire in 1613,[55] but this seems to have been a fictional account probably based on the extravagant 1609 pamphlet *Old Meg of Hereford-shire, for a Mayd-Marian: and Hereford Towne for a Morris-daunce, or, Twelve Morris-dancers in Hereford-shire, of Twelve Hundred Yeares Old*.[56] This is a wildly encomiastic story, full of circumstantial detail, of a dance supposedly performed at Hereford races by twelve dancers and six supernumeraries whose average age was 103 years, the oldest being Old Meg Goodwin herself (an old woman rather than a young boy acting the Maid Marion), at 120, the youngest 89 (and the next youngest 96). The description of William Mayo is typical:

...William Mayo of Egelton, an old Souldier, and now a lustie laborer and a tall man, fortie yeares since being grievously wounded, he carried his liver and his lights home halfe a mile and you may still put your finger into them, but for a thin skin over them; and for all these stormes he arrives at fourescore and seventeene, and dances merrily.

In addition to the dancers and Maid Marion, there were two musicians, four whifflers with staves (to clear the way) and a hobby horse. The coats were 'of the old fashion... sleeves gathered at the elbows, and hanging sleeves behind'. There was an awareness here of changing styles, implicitly indicating that streamers attached to shoulders and arms were being supplanted by napkins, as Philip Stubbes described.

The fantastical literary style of the *Old Meg* pamphlet resembles that of much of the prose fiction of the day. However, drama historian David Klausner gives the account the benefit of the doubt, concluding that however exaggerated the style, a real event probably lay behind it. Some of the dancers' surnames and places of residence match those of the presentments being made around that time. The opening paragraphs confirm the county's reputation as a hotbed for morris dancing:

Hereford-shire for a Morris-daunce, puts downe, not onely all Kent, but verie neare (if one had line enough to measure it) three quarters of Christendome.

The pamphlet's celebration of the longevity of Herefordshire folk reverberated in repeated tellings and inventions of supposed similar feats throughout the next 300 years, with some confusions as to numbers of dancers (eight, ten or twelve) and even place ('Herefordshire' was miscorrected to 'Hertfordshire' as early as 1704). Later authors alluding to it relied for the most part on the references to it in Francis Bacon's *History ... of Life and Death* of 1638 (where he gives the number of dancers as eight) or in Sir William Temple's *Of Health and Long Life* from *c.* 1699.[57]

Oxford still saw morris dancers as a suitable way to greet the king. When King James visited the University in 1605 it bought six sets of morris costumes with bell pads 'for the Playes at ye Kinges comminge'. F.S. Boas surmises, on uncertain grounds, that the dance was one of the

---

[55] Fuller, Thomas, p. 33 [2nd sequence].
[56] 'Old Meg'.
[57] Bacon, Francis, p. 135; Temple, p. 277.

elements which James found so tedious that he almost walked out in mid-performance.[58] However, James witnessed another academical drama in Cambridge in 1623, *Fucus Histriomastix*. This is mostly in Latin, and at one point a stage direction calls for '4 comites saltantes' ('dancing earls'). They are dancing to the tune 'Come Helpe Me over ye Water ye Bony Bony Booteman', after which the stage direction 'Saltant' ('leaping' or 'dancing') occurs twice. After more dialogue comes another stage direction, this time in English, 'The morris dance'. Later, in Act V, is the stage direction 'Chorus sc. Morisdaunceres et caetera turba comitum' ('and the rest of the crowd of earls').[59] Henry Moll recorded some circumstances of the performance in a poem about the event:[60]

> *A Foole and a Morris provided was for his*
> *Good Majesties greater delight*
> *When a suddaine mischance might have spoyled ye dance*
> *Theire bells were forgotten quite*
> *But at a dead lift there were freinds for a shift*
> *To whom they became great debters,*
> *For the Hawkes of the Court to farther {th}eir sport*
> *Did give up their bells to their betters.*

If true, the morris on this occasion seems to have been a much-valued element of the performance, but at the same time the failure of the organizers to acquire bells contrasts with the careful preparations at Oxford; and indicates, perhaps, that for some sections of the population morris dancing was beyond their ken or care.

Back in Oxford a Christmas revel called *The Christmas Prince* was staged in St John's College in 1607:[61]

> *some of the Princes honest neighbours of St. Giles's presented him with a maske or morris,*
> *which though it were but rudely performed, yet itt being so freely & lovingly profered, it*
> *could not but bee as lovingly received.*

Although elected at a different time of year, a Christmas prince was a figure chosen to preside, like a May lord, over a period of festivity or misrule. The college is situated in the parish of St Giles, and its parishioners played a part in the revel. The organizer of the revel and author of the description and text may have been John Sansbury, who became vicar of St Giles about the same time.[62] The revel straddled the boundary between parish feast and the more refined entertainment of the masque, of which more below. It also placed Oxford firmly within the continuing support for morris dancing in the area of the Thames valley.

Outside of the formal civic and parish sphere, dancing on the initiative of the participants still took place. At Scopwick, Lincolnshire on 1 May 1602 Elizabeth Hickson let morris dancers into her father-in-law's house which was standing empty and so offered space for dancing, to an audience of 'most of the wives & other the inhabitants' of the village.[63] The use of an indoor space is not typical and may indicate a different kind of performance. Dancers who came to Felbrigg Hall in Norfolk the following year were given 3s 4d,[64] while Lord Berkeley gave the morris dancers of Kenilworth 2s 6d when they visited him at Coventry on 30 May 1605.[65] The

---

[58] Boas, pp.252-53.
[59] Ward, Robert, pp. 33 (II.v), 77 (V.ii).
[60] Moll.
[61] *Christmas Prince*, p. 55.
[62] Harbage, 'Authorship'.

[63] 'Jackson v. Swann'. I am grateful to Dr E.C. Cawte for providing me with this reference (pers. comm. September 1986).
[64] Galloway and Wasson, p. [6].
[65] Greenfield, p. 23.

same amount was given to dancers visiting Lord Cavendish in London on 1 May 1606.[66] Some years later, a reward to a single dancer was recorded in the account book at Hengrave Hall, when 12d was given to 'ye morish dancher at ye gate' in 1627.[67]

Several of the polemic writers of the day echoed the sentiments being put forward in the ecclesiastical visitation articles, and many used phrases directly lifted from them. In 1607 the preacher William Crashaw railed against 'the horrible abuse of the Sabbath day, in this citie, and over this kingdome: in some places by Faires and Markets, by May-games and Moricedencers, by Wakes and Feasts', while in 1611 the obdurate Puritan Henry Barrow wrote that 'if it be a common custome to have the Lords holy Sabbaths profaned with Beare and Bull baiting, with dicing and carding, with May games and morrice dance, with laciviousnes and luxurie, with rifling or revelling, &c. then all is good, and all may be done'.[68] In one of his many diatribes Henry Burton attacked the Royalist archdeacon (later bishop) John Cosin who had defended 'the joyfull festivitie' of Sunday allowed by the Church, by which, Burton claimed, 'he meaneth all kinde of Festivity, and jollity, and joviality, such as he termes necessary recreations: for example, Rush-bearings, Whitson Ales, Morice-dances, setting up of May-poles, hearing of a play, or seeing of a Maske, or Dicing and Carding, or bouling or bowsing, or whatsoever other Glosse the carnall vulgar may make of this unlimited joyful Festivity or necessary Recreation'.[69] 'What Church?' Burton asked, 'surely none other ... but his holy mother Church of Rome', thereby equating Sunday recreations with Roman Catholicism.

This equation was afforced by polemicists who juxtaposed the ceremonial of a high-church mass and the supposed licentiousness of Sunday recreations. In 1606 the anti-Catholic Dean of Exeter Matthew Sutcliffe derided the priest who 'is apparrelled like a moriske-dancer, and skippeth and danceth about the altar like an ape in a chaine. His head is shaven and well greased, his hands washed, but his hart uncleane.'[70] Four years earlier the Puritan minister William Burton had excoriated 'masking & mumming Masse Priests, in all glorious shew to the eye, with piping & singing, with belly cheare, with their Robinhoods, & morrice dances, & all their relegion like a stage play, ful of carnal delights, & bewitching vanities'.[71] The logical conclusion was to extend the condemnation to the papacy itself, as did Alexander Cooke in 1621, who claimed that Rome had 'had one boy Pope of twelve yeares old, viz. Benedict the ninth: and a May-pole-morrice-dancer Pope of 18. yeares old, viz. John 12. alias 13. who made the Lateran a plaine Stewes'.[72]

Samuel Harsnett's *A Declaration against Egregious Popish Impostures* placed morris firmly in Hell, danced by the devils themselves. He described the devils possessing a woman named Sara Williams:[73]

> *Frateretto, Fliberdigibbet, Hoberdidance, Tocobatto were foure devils of the round, or Morrice, whom Sara in her fits, tuned together, in measure and sweet cadence. And least you should conceive, that the devils had no musicke in hell, especially that they would goe a maying without theyr musicke, the Fidler comes in with his Taber, & Pipe, and a whole Morice after him, with motley visards for theyr better grace.*

Harsnett's allusion to 'motley visards' (painted face-masks) seems to indicate a rather different morris from that we know, perhaps existing only in his literary imagination.

---

[66] Riden, 3:386, entry 702.
[67] Galloway and Wasson, p. 168.
[68] Crashaw, p. 172; Barrow, *Platform*, sig. K8.
[69] Burton, Henry, *Tryall*, sig. F3v.
[70] Sutcliffe, Matthew, p. 194.
[71] Burton, William, p. 168.
[72] Cooke, pp. 21-22.
[73] Harsnett, p. 49.

The Marlborough minister who told midsummer merrymakers in 1618 'that they served the devil by it and not God, and that it was an idol which they served, meaning thereby that one played the part of a morris dancer'[74] was attacking such practices as undesirable in themselves, not just when they disturbed Sunday observances. The preacher Richard Rogers wrote to similar effect in 1603:[75]

> it were to be wished hartily, that the notable ill practises, customes and fashions in townes and companies of men, which uphold and mainteine the olde world and cursed fellowships in it, were overthrowen, and with the tables of the money changers cast downe: as houses of play and baudry, where they are knowen to be; stage-plaies, May-games, Lord of misrule, Morice-dancings, flockings and meetings together at victualling houses...

Barnabe Rich, a writer with a background in the military, was especially troubled by what he saw as effeminacy in society. In 1613 he complained of 'legges ... so over pestered with Garters and Roses, that they are fit for nothing unles for a Moris dance'. The following year he asked 'from whence commeth this wearing and this imbroidering of long lockes, this curiositie that is used amongst men in freziling and curling of their hayre? this gentlewoman-like starcht bands, so be edged, and be laced, fitter for Mayd-Marion in a Moris dance, then for him that hath either that spirit or courage that should be in a gentleman?', and in 1618 he wrote:[76]

> Mee thinks it were good therefore, and as well for men as for women, to determine with themselves how they would be accounted, and so to sute themselves in their apparell accordingly. Let men shew themselves to be like men, that doe now shew themselves like women, to looke like Maid-marrian in a Morris dance, fitter for a Sempsters shop, then to fight for a Countrey.

Even those who apparently had no great antipathy felt morris dancers in the body of the church to be an impropriety. The minister John Spicer wrote in 1608 that 'I think there bee not any heere but can away with honest recreations in time & place, but what if any of your dancers should come in their morish attire, I meane disguised into the Church, and the foole with his bable [mock staff of office] set them all on laughing?'[77] One or two were more indulgent of these recreations. When the Archdeacon of Gloucester Samuel Burton preached in Warwick in 1619 he wished 'that those painefull and zealous Preachers, whiche seeme so dearely to tender the instruction of the people, would for a time forbeare these May-poles and morrice-dances, and other such trifles, upon which they spend too much of their strength; and would press this point of Obedience more closely to the Consciences of the people'.[78]

———————————

Outside the wars of words, the presentation of morris dancing in the literature of the period continued for the most part to be benevolent. The *Old Meg of Herefordshire* pamphlet described earlier (p. 81) fits into this pattern. Another pamphlet, published in 1600, describes a unique event that was part drama, part literature and part dance. This was William Kemp's 'nine days' wonder', his morris dance from London to Norwich undertaken between 14 February and 11 March 1600.

William Kemp was the most celebrated actor, stage clown, dancer and acrobat of his day. The zenith of his stage career was as the comic actor in Shakespeare's company, the Lord

---

[74] Cited in Ingram, Martin, p. 103.
[75] Rogers, Richard, p. 578.
[76] Rich, *Opinion*, pp. 53-54; Rich, *Honestie*, p. 50; Rich, *Irish Hubbub*, pp. 21-22.
[77] Spicer, John, p. 408.
[78] Burton, Samuel, p. 13.

Chamberlain's Men, from 1594 to 1599. Apart from his roles in the plays, he was also prominent in devising and performing in jigs, the comic song-and-dance postludes to the main play in many theatrical entertainments.

In 1599 Kemp left the theatre company and his dance from London to Norwich the following year was a self-promotional stunt. He laid wagers at three-to-one that he could complete the dance; he collected money *en route*; and he sold souvenirs (gloves, 'garters' and 'points', i.e., bell pads and clothing ties) to spectators. He then published the pamphlet in which he gave a self-aggrandizing hyperbolic account of his feat.[79] This pamphlet also provides the first explicit contemporary depiction of an English morris dancer in the woodcut on the cover showing Kemp performing the dance, accompanied by his taborer Thomas Slye (Figure 6.2). The woodcut depicts the napkins

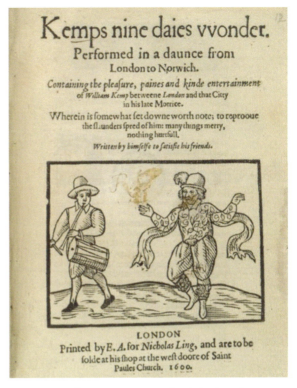

Figure 6.2: William Kemp, Kemps Nine Daies Wonder, *cover. London: Printed by E.A. from Nicholas Ling, 1600.*

attached to Kemp's upper arms, rather than held in his hands. When a young maid asked to dance with him at Chelmsford, he describes her as wanting to 'have the olde fashion, with napkins on her armes', a preference which was to be echoed in the *Old Meg* pamphlet nine years later. The presence of feather in Kemp's hat recalls the expenditure on feathers in the hats of morris dancers in May games. His waistcoat is decorated with a pattern of leaves. On his feet are 'buskins', from the illustration meaning in this case calf-high rather than knee-high boots.

Kemp rarely danced along his route on consecutive days and spent nearly a week at Bury St Edmunds (being delayed there by snowfall), so the entire exploit lasted 25 days. He reached Norwich after 22, but his overseer George Sprat, engaged to guarantee that he had accomplished the feat, made him dance the last section again three days later because he had lost Kemp in the crowds on his arrival and so had not been able to verify his dancing.

On several days Kemp had company. The maid at Chelmsford has been mentioned. At one point two 'country fellows' joined him but could not cope with the poor road conditions on the way to Braintree, while coming out of Braintree 'a lusty, tall fellow, a butcher' accompanied him for half a mile but gave up as he could not keep pace with Kemp. The butcher was immediately followed by a 'country lass' who put on a spare set of bells and danced with him for a mile. Kemp calls her 'my merry Maydemarian' and gave her money and drink afterwards. When he

---

[79] Kemp.

left Long Melford his host's fool danced with him and on his leaving Hingham five young men ran (not danced or walked) with him the seven miles to Barford. Whifflers cleared the way at Norwich, but they were not inherently associated with Kemp's morris.

Kemp brought in Maid Marion as a relevant related figure, and mentioned the 'forgotten' hobby horse in the common saying of the time, probably only to make the rhyme in a piece of doggerel:

> I had the heaviest way that ever mad Morrice-dancer trod; yet,
> With hey and ho, through thicke and thin,
> The hobby horse quite forgotten,
> I follow'd, as I did begin,
> Although the way were rotten.

As to choreography, Kemp mentions a 'hey-de-gaies' and the country girl who danced with him 'thumpt it on her way / With a sportly hey de gay'. The hey-de-gay is a movement whose precise meaning is now lost. He refers to 'jumps' and 'leaps' on more than one occasion, and to 'tripping lightly'. Apart from these hints, and the depiction of his dancing on the cover, we have no information about the nature of his dance; but notable are the facts that this is a solo dance (naturally, given Kemp's love of individual showmanship) and that women danced with him on at least two occasions.

In reward, Kemp says, 'The Maior [of Norwich] gave me five pound in Elizabeth angels; ... [and] 40.s. yeerely during my life, making me a free man of the marchant venterers'. In fact he was given just 40s on 8 March and there is no record of any further payments.[80]

Kemp's dance lived on in poetic and literary allusion for several years after the event. A throwaway line in Dekker and Webster's *Westward Ho* (c. 1604) has one character exclaim 'Sfoote weele dance to Norwich' in an allusion clearly expected to be understood by all.[81] In two poems celebrating Thomas Coryate's travels on foot across Europe and Asia, John Taylor wrote 'This Gentleman thy travels doth advance / Above Kemps Norwich anticke Morris-dance' and 'Kemp yet doth live, and only lives for this / Much famous, that he did dance the Morris / From London unto Norwich. But thou much more / Doest merit praise'.[82] In an elegy on Kemp's death Richard Brathwait wrote:[83]

> Welcome from Norwich, Kempe! all joy to see
> Thy safe return moriscoed lustily.
> But out, alas, how soone's thy morice done!
> When Pipe and Taber, all thy friends be gone
> And leave thee now to dance the second part
> With feeble nature, not with nimble art;
> Then all thy triumphs fraught with strains of mirth,
> Shall be cag'd up within a chest of earth:
> Shall be? they are: th'ast danc'd thee out of breath
> And now must make thy parting dance with death.

Soon after Kemp's dance to Norwich he journeyed across Europe and in the Cambridge University students' play *The Return from Parnassus (Part II)* (1602), in which he appears as a

---

80 Galloway, pp. 114-15.
81 Dekker and Webster, p. 377 (V.i).
82 Taylor, John, 'Incipit ... This Gentleman'; Taylor, John, 'Incipit ...Thou Cravest'.
83 Brathwait, 'Upon Kempe'.

character, a student greets him with the words 'welcome M. Kempe, from dancing the morrice over the Alpes'.[84] There is no evidence that he actually performed such a feat.

Almost immediately after Kemp's dance the boys' acting company the Children of Paul's performed John Marston's *Jack Drum's Entertainment* (entered in the Stationers' Register in September 1600 and published in 1601). The character Sir Edward Fortune says:[85]

> *...what newes at Court sweete sir?*
> *I had rather that Kemps Morice were their chat,*
> *For of foolish actions, may be theyle talke wisely, but of*
> *Wise intendments, most part talke like fooles.*

Morris dancing as vacuous foolishness is one common theme in the literature of the period, and another is that of the carefree rustic celebration. The play goes on to evoke that sense, too. A pipe and tabor strike up and Sir Edward exclaims 'Oh a Morice is come, observe our country sport; / Tis Whitson-tyde, and we must frolick it'. The dancers enter and dance to the lyrics 'Skip it, and trip it, nimbly, nimbly, tickle it'. Led by a fool, they are dancing to Highgate Green from Holloway and want to uphold the honour of their village, dancing so as to wear out their shoes and 'spare for no leather'. There are jokes about the inversion of roles as a signifier of freedom from care, the fool saying 'beggers are become Lordes sonnes'.[86]

Morris dancers on the stage, dancing for honour, recur in Thomas Dekker's *The Shoemakers' Holiday*, where they perform 'all for the honour of shoe-makers'. The carefree celebration is reflected in the lord mayor's injunction to them 'And to make merrie as you homeward go', to which end they are given beer money.[87] In Thomas's Nashe's *Summer's Last Will and Testament* the morris dancers and hobby horse dance 'for the credit of Wostershire'.[88] In Beaumont and Fletcher's *The Knight of the Burning Pestle* (1613) Ralph is the May Lord with his 'scarfes about him, and his fethers and his rings and his knacks' and will 'dance the morrice too for the credit of the Strand'.[89]

Although we should not lose sight of the fact that plays are literary constructs whose authors want to convey a message, portrayals of morris dancers in the drama of the period such as this, and *Jack Drum's Entertainment,* are invaluable when they occur in plays depicting contemporary Tudor and Stuart life, as they can provide insight into attitudes and social relations that dry factual records cannot. In *The Knight of the Burning Pestle* Ralph gives a speech in his capacity as May Lord, exhorting the spectators to enjoy and participate in the festivities, and adding a veneer of patriotism to the more usual invocation of innocent country merriment. He concludes:

> *With bels on legs, and napkins cleane unto your shoulders tide,*
> *With Scarfes and Garters as you please, and Hey for our Town cri'd:*
> *March out and shew your willing minds by twenty and by twenty,*
> *To Hogsdon or to Newington, where Ale and Cakes are plenty:*
> *And let it nere be said, for shame, that we the youths of London,*
> *Lay thrumming of our Caps at home, and left our custome undone.*
> *Up then, I say, both yong and old, both man and maide a Maying,*
> *With Drums and Guns that bounce alowd, and mery Taber playing.*
> *Which to prolong, God save our King, and send his Country peace,*
> *And roote out Treason from the Land, and so, my friends I cease.*

---

[84] 'Second Part', p. 338 (IV.iv).
[85] Marston, 'Jacke Drums Entertainment', p. 181.
[86] Marston, 'Jacke Drums Entertainment', pp. 181-85.
[87] Dekker, 'Shoemakers' Holiday', pp. 57-58 (III.iii).
[88] Nashe, 'Summers Last Will', pp. 239-40.
[89] Beaumont and Fletcher, pp. 75-77 (IV, interlude).

Another play reflecting attitudes in contemporary social life is Dekker's and William Rowley's *The Witch of Edmonton* (1621), a play based on actual events in Edmonton that year. The rustic Cuddy Banks is arranging a morris dance. He wants refurbishment of the pipe and tabor, asking for a 'new head for the Tabor, and silver tipping for the Pipe', and treble bells. Punning on the names for the lower-register bells, he says 'we'll have neither Mean nor Base in our company'. Dekker's and Rowley's contributions were not always seamlessly integrated, and at the dance itself later in the play they have a fiddler not a taborer, and apparently differently pitched bells. The hobby horse (which Banks wants to forget) is to have new or refurbished bridle, caparisons, snaffle and tail. When they prepare to dance they have the hobby horse and Maid Marian but Banks wants to add a witch (in development of the play's plot).[90]

John Fletcher's *Women Pleas'd* (*c.* 1620) is set in Italy but contains a rural morris dance which is wholly English. The servant Soto challenges the dancers to show 'your Bells ... Your Rings, your Ribanes, and your clean Napkins'. There is the community spirit: Soto cries 'Now for the honour of our town, boys!' The Puritan Bomby is a reluctant hobby horse: 'His pace is sure prophane, and his lewd wihies The Songs of Hymyn, and Gymyn, in the wildernesse'.[91] Lewd (and literal) horse-play was one of the defining characteristics of the hobby horse, and its intermittent association with morris dancers was further grounds for Puritans to condemn the dancers.

Bomby, participating unwillingly in the morris in *Women Pleas'd*, was the inverse of Zeal-of-the-Land Busy in Jonson's *Bartholomew Fair* (1614), who condemns 'your Stage-players, Rimers, and morrise-dancers, who have walked hand in hand, in contempt of the brethren' but is nonetheless drawn to the fair. The character John Littlewit recalls how before his conversion Busy was a baker and 'those Cakes hee made, were serv'd to Bridales, May-poles, Morrisses, and such prophane feasts and meetings' – echoing the language of ecclesiastical visitation articles.[92] These two plays are unusual in reflecting the controversies of the day. It is not surprising that plays paint a favourable view of morris, given Puritan antipathy against the theatre in general and morris in particular, and most did so without a hint that this may be a contentious activity.

Although allegorical in nature, Barton Holyday's *Technogamia* (produced by the students of Christ Church, Oxford in 1617), included a morris dance. The characters represented abstract qualities, and in the play Musica finds some morris bells, waistcoats and napkins and is regretting the absence of a taborer when one enters, accompanying a hobby horse. The stage direction reads 'The hobby-horse rushes on them, and throwes them all downe'; they all 'dance three times, the hobby-horse over throwes them all againe, kisses Musica and runnes away with the Tabourer'.[93] Ralph Trapdoor in Dekker's and Thomas Middleton's *The Roaring Girl* says 'The gingling of Golden bels, and a good foole with a hobby-horse, wil draw all the whores i'th' towne to dance in a morris'.[94]

One of the primary vehicles for allegorical presentation in this period was the masque, which in some respects was the lineal successor of the disguisings that had graced the early Tudor court. It was certainly seen as fit for royal and upper-class entertainment. Jonson's *A Particular Entertainment of the Queene and Prince their Highnesse to Althrope* (commonly known as *The Entertainment at Althorp*) was a masque performed on 25-27 June 1603 welcoming the new

---

[90] Dekker and Rowley, pp. 507-09 (II.i), 520-24 (III.i), 533-35 (III.iv).
[91] Fletcher, pp. 495-501 (IV.i).
[92] Jonson, 'Bartholomew Fair', pp. 293 (I.iii), 410 (V.v).
[93] Holyday, sig. K4-L4 (IV.v).
[94] Dekker and Middleton, p. 24 (I.ii).

king James's consort Anne and son Prince Henry on their progress from Scotland to London. There is a satyr (the presenter), and elves and fairies. The masque's commentary tells us that 'there was a speech sodainly thought on, to induce a morris of the clownes thereabout, who most officiously presented themselves, but by reason of the throng of the countrey that came in, their speaker could not be heard'; they are introduced by 'Nobody', describing himself as a 'huisher' (an usher or whiffler, clearing a space for the dancers):[95]

> *We are the Huisher to a Morise*
> *(A kind of Masque) whereof good store is*
> *In the countrey hereabout*
> *...[They] as the Pipe*
> *shall inspire them, meane to skip ...*
> *Come on clownes, forsake your dumps,*
> *And bestirre your hob-nailed stumps*
> *...*
> *But see, the Hobby-horse is forgot.*
> *Foole, it must be your lot,*
> *To supply his want with faces*
> *And some other Buffon graces.*

This continues the theme of innocent rustic merriment, but more exotic themes were introduced by Beaumont in his *Masque of the Inner Temple and Gray's Inn* performed on 20 February 1613. He introduced an antimasque, with 'a May-daunce or rurall daunce, consisting ... not of any suted persons, but of a confusion, or commixture of all such persons as are naturall and proper for Countrey sports', ushered in by a one characterized as a 'Pedant' and consisting of:[96]

May Lord,	*May Lady.*
Servingman,	*Chambermaide.*
A Country Clowne, or Shepheard,	*Countrey Wench.*
An Host,	*Hostesse.*
A Hee Baboone,	*Shee Baboone.*
A Hee Foole,	*Shee Foole.*

This is clearly a mixed-couple dance, and is not specifically identified as a morris, but it was so popular that Beaumont's frequent co-author John Fletcher took it, expanded it and inserted it into the play he co-wrote with Shakespeare, *Two Noble Kinsmen*, in which the pedant (recharacterized as a schoolmaster) announces 'We are a merry rout, or else a rable, / Or company, or, by a figure, chois, / That 'fore thy dignity will dance a morris'.[97]

Anne Daye has noted that turning the pedant into a schoolmaster puns on meanings of 'usher'. She points out that although this was certainly a dance of mixed couples and the performers in the masque were paired, in the dramatic performances the women's parts would have been performed by men, as women were not allowed on stage at this period.[98] At the presentation of her paper at the conference underlying her article, a reconstruction of the dance was performed by the group lightningtree (Figure 6.3).

[95] Jonson, 'Particular Entertainment', pp. 410-12.
[96] Beaumont, pp. 127, 133-35.
[97] Fletcher and Shakespeare, pp. 63-73 (III.v).
[98] Daye, 'Morris', pp. 27-28.

Figure 6.3: Gray's Inn antimasque: May Lord and Lady, Fools and Baboons, performed by lightningtree (Photo © Michael Heaney).

Terming this performance a 'morris dance' is unusual; perhaps the only other reference of this era which hints at a similar, mixed-couple country dance is the 1593 work *A Passionate Morrice* which featured eight pairs of matched couples. These were incongruous pairings such as a 'passionate ass' and a 'peevish wench'; and a 'miserly churl' and a 'rich widow', but there are no intimations of morris or other dances beyond the title, which may be being used simply to indicate disorder.[99]

The depiction of the morris in the literature and music of the period as a whole closely reflects what we find on the stage. Thomas Weelkes often used such rural scenes in his madrigals. He wrote appreciatively of the morris in 1600:[100]

> *Hark! hark! I hear some dancing*
> *And a nimble morris prancing.*
> *The bagpipe and the morris bells*
> *That they are not far hence us tells*
> *Come let us all go thither,*
> *And dance like friends together.*

William Fennor's *Pasquil's Palinodia* (1619) spoke of the pleasure of seeing 'the Country-gallants dance the Morris'.[101] Less typically, his *Cornu-copiæ, Pasquils Night-cap* (1612) described an urban procession in which 'The Waites did play & all the bels did ring, / Bag-pips plai'd horn-pips, som did dance the Morris, / Some wind their horns, & som with cornets flourish'.[102] The anonymous *The Runaway's Answer* (1625) promised a picture 'in which the Londoners and countrey-men dance a morris together', but sadly did not provide it.[103]

The rustic nature could be portrayed as oafish or clownish (in both the modern and the older senses), reminiscent of Robert Langham's characterization of the Kenilworth morris before Queen Elizabeth in 1575. The poet Samuel Daniels warned against abandoning sophistication

---

[99] A., 'Passionate Morrice'.
[100] Weelkes, 'Madrigals of 5. and 6. Parts', pp. 291-92.
[101] Fennor, *Pasquil's Palinodia*, sig. B3v.
[102] Fennor, *Cornu-copiæ*, p. 49.
[103] *Run-awyaes Answer*, [title page].

in *The Queen's Arcadia* (a loose adaptation of Giovanni Guarini's *Pastor Fido*), attributing the morris to the simple folk:[104]

> *Ah, you would loath to have your youth confin'd,*
> *For ever more between th'unskilful Arms*
> *Of one of these rude unconceiving Swains,*
> *Who would but seem a Trunk without a Mind;*
> *As one that never saw but these poor Plains,*
> *Knows but to keep his Sheep, and set his Fold,*
> *Pipe on an Oaten Reed some Roundelays*
> *And dance a Morris on the Holy Days.*

Nicholas Breton, a prolific author popular in his day, advised his readers in *The Mother's Blessing* (1602) to 'leave the Lout, to tread the morris-daunce', while in 1614 Robert Rablet likewise held his nose (semi-literally) against the aroma of the countryside and disdained the lewd associations of the hobby horse and also of Maid Marian:[105]

> *It was my hap of late by chance, oh pretty chance;*
> *To meet a Countrey Moris-dance, oh pretty dance;*
> *When cheefest of them all the foole:*
> *Plaied with a Ladle and a toole, oh pretty toole:*
> *When every Younker shak't his Bels, oh pretty Bels;*
> *Till sweating feete, gave fohing smels.*
> *And fine Maide-Marian with her smoile, oh pretty smoile:*
> *Shew'd how a Rascall plaid the Roile, oh pretty Roile.*
> *But when the Hobby-horse did wihy, oh pretty wihy;*
> *Then all the Wenches gave a tihy, oh pretty tihy.*

Breton made frequent allusion to the morris in his works, most often using it to illustrate the fool's central role. In *Pasquils Passe, and Passeth Not* he wrote 'When morrice dancers leave their bells, / The foole his bable by will lay ...';[106] and in *A Poste with a Packet of Mad Letters*, in which the fool and Maid Marion constitute a mock couple, he wrote:[107]

> *In the parish of Saint Asse, at the sign of the Hobbi-horse, Maid Marrian and the Foole fell together by the eares with the Piper: so that had not the good-man of the Pewter-Candlesticke set in for the Morisdance, the May-game had been quite spoyled: but when the game had gone round, and their braines were well warmed, their legges grew so nimble, that their heeles went higher then their heads ... your steeple-tire, it is like the gaud of a Maid-Marion, so that had you a foole by the hand, you might walke where you would in a Moris-dance.*

Very few poets and other writers voiced antipathy against morris dancing and popular entertainments. The few who did so looked down on it rather than condemning it, such as Henry Farley's attitude of resigned regret when he wrote in 1621:[108]

> *To see a strange out-landish Fowle,*
> *A quaint Baboon, an Ape, an Owle,*

---

[104] Daniel, p. 172.
[105] Breton, 'Mother's Blessing', p. 7; Rablet, sig. D3-D3v.
[106] Breton, 'Pasquils Passe', p. 12.
[107] Breton, 'Poste', p. 33.
[108] Farley, sig. E4-E4v.

A dancing Beare, a Gyants bone,
A foolish Ingin move alone,
A morris-dance, a Puppit play,
Mad Tom to sing a Roundelay,
A Woman dancing on a Rope;
Bull-baiting also at the Hope;
A Rimers Jests, a Juglers cheats,
A Tumbler shewing cunning feats,
Or Players acting on the Stage,
There goes the Bounty of our Age:
But unto any pious motion,
There's little coine, and lesse devotion.

Sir Henry Spelman, an early antiquary, was on the whole moderate in his religious and political opinions,[109] but was contemptuous in his satirical *Vox Graculi, or, Jacke Dawes Prognostication* for 1623.[110] He scorned the lowly populace but was more ambivalent about their practices. For him, the maypoles were idols but he had little sympathy for those who condemned them. He likened the passing months to a line of six morris dancers with a hobby horse:

Behold them [the first six months] therefore at hand, how they come frisking in single file one after another, like so many Morrice-Dancers, (my selfe being the Hobby-horse) and every Month wearing in his Cap, instead of a Feather, Foure unhansome wholesome Rimes; conformable to the fashion of our Neotericke Prognosticators. And thus heere the Foreman of the Morice delivers his speach.
January:
...

To Islington and Hogsdon, runnes the streame
Of giddie people, to eate Cakes and Creame

The 'giddy people' were described in more detail in the prognostication for May:

On the first day betimes in the morning, shall young Fellowes and Mayds be so inveloped with a mist of wandring out of their wayes, that they shall fall into ditches one upon another ... in the after-noone, if the skie cleare up, shall be a stinking stirre at Picke-hatch,with the solemne revels of Morice-dancing, and the Hobbie-horse so neatly presented, as if one of the Masters of the Parish had playd it himselfe ...

This day shall be erected long wooden Idols called May-poles; whereat many greasie Churles shall murmure, that will not bestow so much as a Faggot-sticke towards the warming of the Poore: an humour, that while it seemes to smell of Consciences, savours indeed of nothing but Covetousnesse.

Although literary and dramatic references abound, the woodcut depicting William Kemp dancing (Figure 6.2) remains the only image from this period unambiguously known to depict a morris dancer. There is another woodcut (Figure 6.4) attached to both the broadside ballads *Roaring Dick of Dover* and *Money is my Master*. The former has been dated to 1632, the latter to anywhere between 1624 and 1680, but woodcuts deteriorate with repeated use, and the

---

[109] History of Parliament: Spelman.   [110] Spelman, pp. 49, 62.

condition of this woodcut suggests that the latter should be dated slightly later than 1632. Neither of the ballads concerns or even mentions morris dancers, but the illustration depicts a man standing with bell pads on his legs, doffing a hat with a feather in it to a second man, not distinctively attired, who is holding a drinking cup.

There is a painting usually dated to around 1620 and once believed to be painted by the Flemish artist David Vinckenboom but now described more generally as 'Flemish school'. It is one of a pair depicting Nonesuch and Richmond Palaces respectively. The one now entitled 'The Thames at Richmond, with the Old Royal Palace'

Figure 6.4: Woodcut from Money is my Master. *London: for Francis Coules, n.d.*

has a group of dancers in the foreground which matches what we know of morris dancers of the period and in all probability is a depiction of them (Figure 6.5). There are only three main dancers together with a female figure, probably a male Maid Marion, dancing in two pairs in a single file. Also in line but facing sideways is a hobby horse. The three main dancers have white shirts and breeches of different colours; they and the hobby horse have feathers in

Figure 6.5: 'The Thames at Richmond, with the Old Royal Palace', c. 1620 (detail)
(Image © The Fitzwilliam Museum, Cambridge, accession number: 61).

their hats. The main dancers have ribbons at their elbows but no other sashes or baldricks, nor napkins. They also have bells on their legs. If the hobby horse and Maid Marion have bells, they are obscured by their costumes. To the left a fool in motley, with jags at the shoulder and waist, collects money in a ladle from the bystanders, and he too wears bells. To the right is a pipe-and-taborer. The dancers are performing different steps. One dancer has joined hands with the female figure facing him, while the other two, also facing each other have their hands by their side and are performing the same step. Both the well dressed and more commonly dressed people are watching them, and one of the former is putting money into the fool's ladle. The dancers appear to be performing on their own initiative, as there is no indication of the accompanying retinue of an ale.

One more work of art, or rather craftsmanship, now lost, is described in detail in the record of the transfer of a salt cellar from the king to the Duke of Buckingham and the Earl of Holland in 1625.[111] Sir Henry Mildmay, the Master of the Crown Jewels, was instructed to hand it over 'to be disposed of by them for Our especiall Service according as Wee have given unto them private Directions'. This was no ordinary salt cellar but a spectacular piece of decorative gold tableware, described as 'one salte of Goulde, called the Morris Daunce'. It weighed 9½ lbs and was decorated with 9 sapphires, 51 diamonds, 99 rubies, 14 large pearls and 186 garnishing pearls. Five morris dancers and a taborer stood about the base, the salt itself being held by a lady apparently standing at the centre. This is very much the image of the court morris at the beginning of the 16th century, and the item itself may well date to that period. Additionally, a smaller 'cup with a morris dance' was listed in an inventory of James I and VI's gold plate in 1606.[112]

In this chapter we have seen how the opening decades of the 17th century saw a wholesale onslaught against the association of morris dancing with the Church. Only the Thames valley showed signs of continuing support. In other contexts there was undoubtedly opposition, especially where particularly zealous reformers held positions of authority, but the dance was still widespread. The dance and its associations became one of the focal points in the wars of the polemicists, but for the most part the writers and dramatists presented a more old-fashioned view of the dance as innocent and frivolous country sport. Some appeals were made to antiquity, as when the Salisbury tailors protested that their custom had been 'done for time out of mind'. In a rather more belligerent argument Simon Yng of Leicester disavowed King James and looked to Queen Elizabeth for his authority.

As events in the political sphere moved to a climax in the middle of the century, morris dancing found itself even more in the eye of the coming storm.

---

[111] Sanderson, p. 238. [112] Herrick, William, f. 239.

Chapter 7

Suppression 1630-1659

In 1629 Charles I dissolved Parliament and began a period of personal rule. This was one of the signal moments defining the interplay of religion, royal prerogative and parliamentary power that played out over the coming decades. The beginning of this thirty-year period saw the last known occasion on which morris dancers were used in support of church fund-raising. On Ascension Day (10 May) 1632 the churchwardens of St Mary Magdalen, Oxford paid a guinea 'for a dinner for the morris dauncers and for flowers and for other necessaries'. The 'Whittsontide sport' the following week raised £7 6s 7d but a separate account was made of 'money that was gotten by the Morris dauncers', 9s 2d.[1] No other similar records have been found. It is significant that this last evidence of church support, in the Thames valley, comes from the future royalist stronghold and is at the heart of the south midlands, which were a focal point for future developments.

The visitation articles of the period continued to prosecute morris dancing and other recreations vigorously. The Diocese of Rochester used a well-rehearsed text in 1638, asking 'Whether the Minister and Churchwardens have suffered any Fea[st] banquet church-ale or drinking [.....] [s]ummer Lord or Ladie or any disguised persons, & players of May-games [or a]ny Morrisdancers, at any time to come irreverently into the Church or [Chu]rch-yeard'.[2] However, most diocesan visitation articles of the period did not single out morris dancers, typically asking more generally about 'Playes, Feastes, Suppers, Church-ales', as at Chichester in 1638.[3] The majority of enquiries about morris dancing were now found in the articles issued by archdeaconries within dioceses. The archdeaconry of Berkshire included 'Maygames, Morricedancings' after the plays, feasts, etc., of the general diocesan texts, in three sets of articles issued in 1631, 1635 and 1638.[4] Other archdeaconries used close variants of the text adopted by the province of York in 1633,[5] echoing the one introduced at Chester in 1581; for example the archdeaconry of Norfolk asking in 1634 whether the church or churchyard had been 'abused or prophaned' by any of:[6]

> *fighting, chiding, brawling, or quarelling any playes, lords of mis-rule, Summer lords, Morris-dauncers, Pedlers, Bowlers, Bearewards, Butchers, Feasts, Schooles, Temporall Courts or Leets, Lay-Juries, Muster, or other prophane usage...??*

Versions of this text were also used in the archdeaconries of York in 1635 and 1638,[7] Bedford in 1636[8] and Nottingham in 1639.[9]

At the same time presentments in ecclesiastical courts were also falling away, because the Church had already successfully repressed the offending activities (Figure 7.1). We have records of only four from this period. At Yarlington in Somerset the rector complained in 1634 that:[10]

---

[1] Briscoe, pp. 269-70.
[2] *V.A. Rochester*, sig. B3-B3v.
[3] *V.A. Chichester* (1638), sig. B2v [*recte* A2v].
[4] *V.A. Berkshire* (1631), pp. 2-3; *V.A. Berkshire* (1635), p. 3; *V.A. Berkshire* (1638), p. 3.
[5] *V.A. York* (1633), sig. A2.
[6] *V.A. Norfolk*, sig. B2.
[7] *V.A. York* (1635), sig. A3; *V.A. York* (1638), sig. A3.
[8] *V.A. Bedford* (1636), sig. A2.
[9] *V.A. Nottingham*, sig. A3.
[10] Stokes, *Records ... Somerset*, p. 400.

there is a common fame that upon Midsomer day last in time of Morning prayer and sermon a company from Gallington in the parishe of North Cadbury, and other places [came] with a Morrice daunce, and with ffidlers, and with a drume, and held on their sportes soe neere unto the Church, and Churchyard of Yarlington that the minister was disturbed in discharge of his funcion, and was faine to send out the Churchewarden Richard Slade, and others to require them to [make] leafe makeinge such a noyce at least twise within the saide time of Morninge prayer, & sermon, but they would not give over makeinge the said noyse.

Four dancers were named (but there were more); there were fiddlers and a drummer. The drummer was claimed to be a lodger in the churchwarden Richard Slade's house, so Slade may have been less than diligent in carrying out the minister's instructions. The offenders were excommunicated.

In the same vein, at Wombourne, Staffordshire in 1636 William Mulliner was presented 'for resorting together with other companie near to the church in sermon time with feathers in their hats, with bells, drums, taber and pipe makeing so great a noise that the congregation should scarce hear what was delivered by the minister'.[11] Though not explicit, these have many of the characteristics of morris dancers.

In the northernmost record of morris dancing in England the church official at Hornby, Lancashire complained in 1633:

contra inhabitantes de Horneby for bearinge Rushes on the Saboath day & prophaneing the[ir] saboath with Morrice dances & greate fooleries their lord of Misrule, their Clownes Piclers like Giantes ougly shapes Crosses & Crucifixes upon their Rushes Marching like warriors, longe staves Pikes, shooteing with gunns & Muskettes.

This was clearly a major event and they may have taken the crosses and crucifixes from the church without authorization (as with the other appropriations of church furniture reported in earlier periods); on the other hand, rushbearing (carrying rushes to renew the floor of the church) was a church-focused celebration so their use may have been seen as fitting. Eight offenders were named and dismissed with a warning.[12] The citation of rushbearing echoes the visitation articles for Carlisle issued in 1632, repeating the wording of 1629 and continuing the tradition of many of the northern articles:[13]

are there within your sayd Parish or Chappelrie any rush-bearing, Bull baitings, Beare-baitings, May-games, Morice-dances, Marriage-offerings, ales, or any such like prophane pastimes or assemblies on the Sabbath?

The last known ecclesiastical presentment took place at Lutton in Northamptonshire in 1639, when Phillip Kester was arraigned 'for daunceing of morris on A Sunday aboute ye country all evening prayer time and comeing into Lutton Church in ye morning attyred with scarfes teyes and other indecent apparel'.[14] After 1640 no more visitation articles were published until 1662.

———————

During the 1630s activities were still taking place in non-church contexts. In a rather obscure secular legal case in Mark, Somerset in 1635 morris dancers were mentioned incidentally in the context of another case. It is not clear what the offence was, but it shows that dancing was still taking place apparently without contention:[15]

[11] Johnson, D.A. and Vaisey, p. 11.
[12] Baldwin, George and Mills, pp. 19-20.
[13] *V.A. Carlisle* (1632), sig. B2.
[14] 'Peterborough Diocesan Records', f. 39v.
[15] Stokes, *Records ... Somerset*, p. 162.

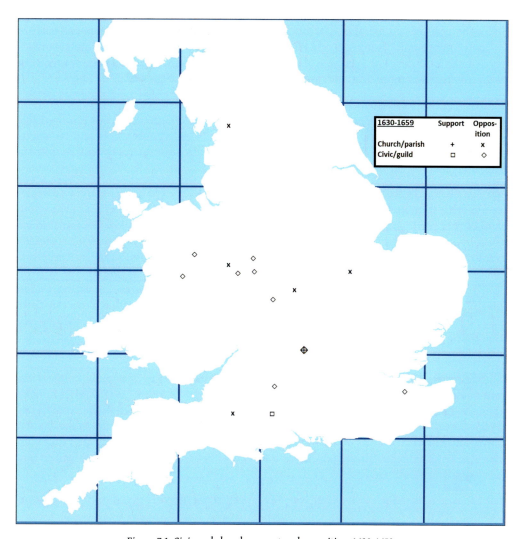

Figure 7.1: Civic and church support and opposition, 1630-1659.

upon Marke Revell Day last was Twelmonth being the 27th Day of May 1635 he [one William Reines] sawe one Mary Butcher sitting in Marke Streat upon a horse, and one Wiliam Andrewes standing by her, and talking with her, expecting the coming of some morrice Dauncers whoe shortly after came, and when they had ended their Daunce this examinate and divers others together with William Andrewes went into ane Alehouse in Marke, ... and William Andrewes sayd unto them, my masters, what saye, if I goe and bring in a pretty wench to drinke with us ... and there upon he went out unto the aforesaid Mary Butcher, and brought her in unto us, who stayd drinking in our company about one hower or there a boutes.

The general acceptability of morris dancing was, however, increasingly being called into question in the civic sphere. The tailors of Salisbury agreed in 1632 that 'It is thought fitt by the Maior parte of this Corporacion beinge here present that the Gyant and morris daunce shall go at the ffeast as in tymes past',[16] but even here there were voices of dissent. The

---

[16] 'Tailors' Guild' (1631), f. 6.

following year a guild member, Christopher Smith, was fined 5s 'for deridinge and scoffine Augustin Creed and Thomas Jarvis Wardens of this Company by uttering theis words ... praie make an Order that everyone of this Company may weare Belles on their legges'.[17] He obviously thought morris dancers were beneath the dignity of the guild.

In 1633 Charles I re-issued his father's *Declaration to his Subjects concerning Lawfull Sports to be Used*, and in this form it became known as the *Book of Sports*. Charles required that ministers read it from the pulpit, but this engendered fierce controversy and resistance from ministers who objected to doing so. The battle was already essentially lost, despite the king's support.

In December 1634 the Privy Council sent for the late mayor of Maidstone and two others on a certificate of Justices of Peace, who had an order to examine a petition of the young men of that town about morris dancing.[18] We do not know the details of the petition but the minister at nearby Otham, Thomas Wilson, was a fierce opponent of such activities. He refused to read the *Book of Sports*, whereupon he was deprived of his curacy and moved to Maidstone. His biographer (and son of his patron), George Swinnock, said that 'Maidstone was formerly a very prophane Town, insomuch that I have seen Morrice dancing, Cudgel playing, Stool-ball, Crickets, and many other sports openly and publickly on the Lords Day'; but Wilson was zealous in promoting strict Lord's Day observance.[19] It may be that the young men of Maidstone were petitioning to the civil authorities against such a crackdown.

The disorder which the authorities often feared in connection with popular celebrations was evident at Long Newton, Wiltshire on Trinity Sunday, 20 June 1641. Morris dancers themselves are not mentioned, but this was an affray in which one John Browne, 'sometymes a chymney sweeper', with a hobby horse and bells on his legs, came from Malmesbury to Long Newton with dozens of others to wrest from its residents a garland which they were carrying in procession, 'thereupon there was a great fight, and many of the Newnton men were sorely beaten'.[20]

For the whole duration of the Civil War, 1642-1651, there are records of only two relevant events, both from the Oxford area. For much of the war King Charles I was based in Oxford, and the contrast in attitudes exhibited by the reports of the two instances reflected changing fortunes as the war progressed.

The first was a pamphlet, *The King Found at Southwell, and the Oxford Gigg Playd, and Sung at Witney Wakes*, published in 1646.[21] The copy in the British Library Thomason Tracts has the date '7 May', possibly the date of publication. On that date Oxford was under siege and would shortly capitulate to Parliamentary forces. Witney wakes were held in September, so it is probable that the date of the events described is 1645, when the previous siege of Oxford had been lifted. However, the pamphlet also implies that they took place shortly before Charles went from Oxford to Southwell on 5 May 1646. It may be that the event (if not fictitious) described May festivities rather than the wakes of the title.

The whole depiction is of a celebration commanding general community support. The nature of the festivity is well summarized in the opening paragraph of the pamphlet:

[17] 'Tailors' Guild' (1631), f. 9v.
[18] Bruce, p. 378.
[19] Swinnock, pp. 12, 40-41.
[20] *Report* (1901), 1:107-08.
[21] Loyd.

> *Witney is a towne neere Oxford whither divers Courtiers and Officers of Oxford Garison went*
> *to the Wakes to bee merry, where they sung and drank themselves out of all their sences, on*
> *the Wake day early in the morning they went out of Oxford ...*

Various songs were sung and verses composed, and these are incorporated in the text. They are said to have been the work of a Captain M. Loyd. Some of the same verses appeared in an anonymous pamphlet *Recreation for Ingenious Head-peeces* published in 1650,[22] and in an expanded form in 1654[23] as a poem called 'The Wake' attributed to Sir John Mennes, one of Charles's major commanders who was appointed Governor of North Wales in 1644 and Commander-in-Chief at the Downs (a naval post, though Charles had lost the navy in 1643) in 1645.[24] Mennes was a noted wit and poet and may be the true author of the pamphlet, though by the time of the later publications he was in exile with the king.

The Oxford cavaliers 'had appointed certaine morris-Dancers to meete them at the Wakes, as also severall Musitians, with various sorts of Musicke, viz., the Country Fidler, a Taberer; a payre of bagge-Pipes, and a Harper'. The pamphlet continues:

> *the morris-Dancers, and the Musick being ready to attend them, first of all began the morris-*
> *Dancers to caper before them, with one who gave the Lords favour to divers Gentlemen*
> *that gave him some a shilling, some 6; some more, some lesse for the common stocke of the*
> *company. There were some 6. or 7. Country fellowes with Napkins, and Scarfes, and Ribons*
> *tyed about them, and bells at their knees, according to the manner of that sport, and with*
> *them a Mayd-Marian, and two fooles, who fell a dansing and capering before the Oxford*
> *blades, and made them sport a good while.*

This is a typical set of dancers and supernumeraries, apart from the presence of two Fools, and they are selling liveries (the 'favours') for the performance. The entry of the dancers is heralded by a song. The implication is that this was recited or sung at the time, but it is more likely that this is interpolated by the author. The image conjured up is of a lusty country fellow, strongly shod and dancing energetically:

> *The Song at the entry of the Morris-Dancers before them.*
> *With a noyse and a din,*
> *Comes the Morris-dancer in*
> *With a fine linnen shirt;*
> *But a buckeram skinne.*
> *O! he treads out such a peale,*
> *From his paire of legs of Veale*
> *His quarters*
> *and Idolls to him,*
> *Nor doe those knaves inviron*
> *Their toes with so much Iron*
> *Twill ruin a Smith to shooe him,*
> *I and then he flings about,*
> *His sweate, and his Clout,*
> *The wesest thinke it too ells:*

---

[22] *Recreation*, sig. X1v.
[23] Mennes.
[24] Knighton.

Whils the Yeomen think it meet.
That he jangle at his feete,
The forhorse right eare jewells.

When the verse was reprinted in 1650 it was accompanied by a woodcut showing a dancer wearing bells and baldricks, with a feather in his hat, and holding napkins in his hands (Figure 7.2). This is the first image to show napkins held in this way.

Later in 1646 Oxford fell to the Parliamentary forces. The second recorded event from there is an account written two years thereafter by Anthony à Wood. He described the very different atmosphere on 1 May 1648, which involved not just opposition but direct intervention to destroy any offending objects and prevent music being played:[25]

Figure 7.2: Woodcut from Recreation for Ingenious Head-peeces, *sig. X1v. London: Printed by M. Simmons, 1650.*

> *This day the Visitors, Mayor and the chief of the well-affected of the university and City, spent in zealous persecuting the young people that followed May-Games, by breaking of Garlands, taking away Fiddles from Musicians, dispersing Morice Dancers, and by not suffering a green bough to be worn in a hat or stuck up at any door, esteeming it superstitious, or rather a heathenish custom.*

Once the Civil War was over and the Commonwealth established, persecutions of morris dancing by civic authorities continued apace. In 1652 inhabitants of Astley Abbotts in Shropshire complained to the bailiff and justices in Much Wenlock that 'upon Munday in Whitsunday week being the 7th of June last past there came a Morrice daunce forth of the Parish of Broseley, with six sword bearers and a rude companye of followers throwe ye whole bodie of this our saide Parish being uninvited or desired by any one within the said Parish that wee doe know of'. Astley Abbotts is 5 miles from Broseley; *en route* the company stopped at Nordley and, the petitioners claimed, failed to pay for their drinks and abused the landlady of the alehouse as well as 'approved frendes and servants to ye Parliament of England'. The dancers' leader was termed a Lord of Misrule and he had a Vice: both are named. Also named are Thomas Lee, the sword bearer, 'who formerly and also in ye last service att Worcester bore armes againstt ye Parliament', and John Evans, who had been a soldier for the Parliamentary side in the Civil War but 'sayes hee will now continue a cavelleire as long as he lives'.[26] There could not be a clearer indication of the association of morris dancing and Whitsun ales with Royalist sympathies and as explicitly antithetical to the Parliamentary cause.

The ways in which these companies were assembled is revealed in another court case in the Quarter Sessions records for Wiltshire in 1652.[27] On Sunday 16 May Edward Smyth and Edward

---

[25] Wood, Anthony à, *History*, 2.2:577.
[26] S., F., p. 54.
[27] Cunnington, p. 221-22.

Hawking went from Woodborough to All Cannings (2½ miles to the east) and arranged for about a dozen men to meet them with muskets the next day. At the same time Robert Golfe went from Woodborough to Marlborough (8 miles to the north-east) to find a drummer, returning with one at one o'clock in the morning. A fourth man went to Easton Royal (6 miles west) to hire a fiddler. On the Monday:

> three hundred persons or there aboutes were assembled and gathered together in a Riotous Routous Warlicke and very disorderly manner with Musketts pistolls bills swords drawne and other unlawful weapons, who upon Munday the said 17th of May did march together to the parishe of Pewsey and there very disorderly daunced the Morrice daunce and committing severall other misdemeanors there as drinkeing and Tipling in the Inn and Alehouse till many of them were drunke.

In yet another case from 1652, a company of tailors danced in Wolverhampton on 1 July 'in contempt of several ministers that were arbitrating a difference between two gentlemen in the house of Mr. Richard Francis'. There were ten dancers, a pipe-and-taborer, a sword bearer with three persons accompanying him, a fool and a flag bearer. The case seems to have arisen because one of the dancers was arrested 'lying drunk in the minister's porch that he could not stand nor go and the rest were but little better'. It is possible that these tailors were members of a merchant guild, as at Salisbury, but there is no evidence that this was a guild event. They were bound over to be of good behaviour.[28]

Drunkenness was the pretext for several prosecutions. There are a few records from Wales (which by the 17th century was governed as part of England) which show very similar circumstances, indicating that they took place in the same cultural space as events in England itself. On 23 June 1653 William Lucas of Llansantffraid-ym-Mechain in Montgomeryshire was asked to play pipe-and-tabor for a company of six morris dancers at Bwlchycibau, 3 miles away. While they were dancing outside an alehouse some soldiers and countrymen came by and there was an affray in which three men (none of them dancers) were wounded. Lucas did not know how it began or ended, 'for he sayeth that he ranne away and hid himselfe in a bush a little from the said house, untill a child brought him his pipe and tabor'. The alehouse keeper's wife said that she had come out and one of the newcomers hit her so she struck back with a cudgel, then the newcomers ran off up the hill pursued by some of the morris dancers and others. From the statements of other witnesses it appears that one of the newcomers asked a spectator (who may have been the son of one of the dancers) to surrender a sword he was carrying, and the fight broke out when he refused. At least some of the dancers in the fight also had swords, but there is no intimation that the swords were used in dancing.[29] In a separate case Jane David of Caersws in the same county was accused that she had been maintaining an 'unnecessary' alehouse and that on Friday 24 June 1653 she had entertained morris dancers there.[30]

In 1654 the Commonwealth Parliament passed an *Ordinance for Ejecting Scandalous, Ignorant and Insufficient Schoolmasters*. The test of such behaviour was that they 'shall be proved guilty of ... or do incourage and countenance by word or practice any Whitson-Ales, Wakes, Morris-dances, May-poles, Stage-plays, or suchlike Licentious practices, by which men are encouraged in a loose and prophane Conversation'.[31] Not just the practice, but the encouragement of dancing

---

[28] Marriott.
[29] Klausner, *Records ... Wales*, pp. 230-35.
[30] Klausner, *Records ... Wales*, p. 235.
[31] Firth and Rait, p. 977.

and like entertainments was to be prosecuted. In this vein the authorities at Henley-in-Arden in 1655 took steps to stamp out any such activity before it began. Noting that 'usually heretofore there have been at Henley in Arden in this county several unlawful meetings of idle and vain persons about this time of year for erecting of maypoles and may-bushes and for using of morris dances and other heathenish and unlawful customs, the observation whereof tendeth to draw together a great concourse of loose people and consequently to the hazard of public peace besides other evil consequences', they instructed the bailiff and constables to suppress any such meeting and to issue notices to that effect. The inhabitants were forbidden not just to indulge in the activity, but also had to 'forbear to meet about the setting up of any maypoles or may-bush or about the aforesaid morris-dances or other unlawful sports'.[32]

The minister of the parish of Lapley in Staffordshire petitioned the county justices complaining that the 'great part of the wake-weekes is spent in promiscuous danceing, maurice-danceing, tipleing, gameing, quarrelling, wantonnesse'. This was in connection with the wakes kept on 6 May 1655, organized by Walter Brindley and others. There were said to be two companies of morris dancers. In the first, from Lapley, nine men and four women are named. 'All of which men and women danced promiscuously'. They included three of Brindley's sons, his female servant Ellen Perry and Ann Perry, possibly her sister, both unmarried. Several were identified as Papists who had failed to attend church on several Sundays. The apprentice to (and possibly relative of) another of the organizers 'danced in Women's apparel', presumably as a Maid Marion. The dancers also included a fool, and they had a musician hired from Church Eaton, four miles away. The second company of morris dancers came from Stretton in the neighbouring parish of Penkridge and numbered about 16, three of whom were named. One of the organizers was accused of selling ale without a licence, and one of the drinkers also for 'being married contrary to law formerly'. The grievance seems to be about those accused being recusant Papists as much as anything, and the minister drags up any and every aspect of potential misbehaviour. 'Morris dancing' is used to smear the entire company, and the large numbers implicated may suggest that as well as the morris dancing (which undoubtedly took place) there was general 'promiscuous' dancing, so that we can no longer tell who did what.

In this period one area of life where morris dancers could perform without causing contention was at private houses, often those of the gentry. In the household accounts of Framlingham Gawdy, the rather inactive MP for Thetford, are payments of 2s to one set of morris dancers and 1s 6d to another who each visited the family seat at East Harling on 28 December 1633.[33] Also in Norfolk, on 29 November 1635, Lady Townshend of Stiffkey Hall ordered 1s to be given to visiting morris dancers, though her husband was more favourable to Puritan attitudes.[34] On Christmas day in 1636 'Wassellers and the Morris dauncers' at Hatfield Broad Oak were given 5s at the Barrington family's home though Sir Thomas Barrington was an anti-Royalist MP. Twenty years later, during the Interregnum, Barrington's son, who had succeeded him, gave 'the men that danced in their disguise and to the fidler, at the making an end of Christmas' 4s 6d on 6 January 1657.[35] The last recorded payment during the Interregnum was, perhaps unsurprisingly, at the home of the Sir Francis Throckmorton, the recusant Roman Catholic owner of Coughton Court in Warwickshire. In the spring of 1658 (probably at Whitsuntide) he gave visiting morris dancers a generous 6s.[36]

---

[32] Ratcliff and Johnson, pp. 275-76.
[33] Galloway and Wasson, p. [5].
[34] Galloway and Wasson, p. 197.

[35] Smith, J.R., p. 11.
[36] Barnard, pp. 36-37.

The mid-century polemical tracts continued the themes of the first part of the century. The majority of those excoriating morris dancing were published before the outbreak of the Civil War. The Puritan William Prynne, whose extreme views led him eventually to rail against the Commonwealth government much as he had against the established church, was a particularly vocal critic. His most famous passage occurs in his *Histrio-mastix* (1633), a tirade against plays and associated activities:[37]

> *The way to Heaven is too steepe, too narrow for men to dance in, and keepe revell rout: No way is large or smooth enough for capering Roisters, for jumping, skipping, dancing Dames, but that broad beaten pleasant road that leads to Hell. The gate of Heaven is to strait, the way to blisse to narrow, for whole roundes, whole troopes of Dancers to march in together: Men never went as yet by multitudes, much less by Morrice-dancing troopes to Heaven.*

Elsewhere in the book he returns repeatedly to the theme of the abomination of clergymen taking part in such activities: they 'shall not intermixe themselves in publike morrices, galliards and dances'; 'Let clergy men never put on vizards, let them abstaine from acting and beholding comoedies, Stage-playes, morrices and dances'.[38] The book was seen (erroneously) as a direct attack on the behaviour of the royal family, as a consequence of which it was publicly burned and Prynne had his ears cut off in punishment.

Even the strictures of visitation articles were not enough for Prynne. He attacked the established church for 'justifying both in their visitation Articles and printed Bookes; That dancing, piping, Morrisses, Wakes, Ales, Sports and Bacchanals, are meet exercises for this holy day, and so no place fitter for them then the Church'[39] – an interpretation at odds with the texts themselves. The prelates, he says:[40]

> *spurre men on to Popery and superstition, but especially to profane the Saboath, to use dancing, Morrisses, May-games, erect Ales, May-poles, Bacchanalls, drinke, swill, and play the Epicures, the Pagans, even on Gods owne sacred day (and that whiles we lye all under Gods scourge & plagues for this very sinne) to tumble them headlong into hell, and draw downe all Gods wrath and plagues upon us from heaven at once, to our speedy certayne ruine.*

In his *A Quench-coale* Prynne described those upholding the 'Church of Rome', (i.e., anyone disagreeing with his view) as 'Traytours, who would blow up our Religion and our Church at once' for allowing 'Morrises, Dancing, Sports and Pastimes' on the Sabbath.[41] He attacked Bishop Goodman of Gloucester as 'a Papist or popishly affected, he hath beene a great encourager of Revells, Maygames, morrices and Dauncing meetings on the Lord's Day'.[42] As Goodman eventually converted to Roman Catholicism, Prynne was at least accurate in his target in this case.

When he edited the second edition of his friend Henry Burton's *A Brief Answer to a Late Treatise of the Sabbath Day* in 1636 Prynne introduced a direct attack on the king, challenging him 'to restrain the abuse and scandalous profanation of the Lords day' and to say 'what hee thinks of promiscuous meetings of wanton youth in their May-games, setting up of May-poles dauncing about them, dauncing the morrice, leading the ring-daunce, and the like'.[43] Burton

---

[37] Prynne, *Histrio-mastix*, p. 246.

[38] Prynne, *Histrio-mastix*, pp. 611, 633-34.

[39] Prynne, *Unbishoping*, p. 142.

[40] Prynne, *Looking-glasse*, p. 23.

[41] Prynne, *Quench-coale*, pp. 62-63, 66.

[42] Prynne, *Antipathie*, unpaginated leaf between pp. 304 and 305, sig.¶¶3.

[43] Prynne and Burton, p. 31.

himself continued to inveigh against sports and pastimes, although he was on the whole less vitriolic than Prynne. In a 1640 work he asked 'what Good Manners doth our May-pole-dances, and Moris dances teach us?', citing the popular paraphrase from Cicero, 'Nemo saltat sobrius', 'No man Danceth that is sober'.[44] In an anecdote picked up by several later polemicists he described how the villagers of Wolston in Warwickshire held a Whitsun ale with maypole and morris dances but were visited by divine retribution when shortly afterwards a spark from the blacksmith's forge set fire to the room where ale had been brewed and from there 'set the house on fire, and presently flew to the barn in which their disorder was, and burnt the same with thirteen dwelling houses more, most of whose Inhabitants were actors or abetters in the same'.[45]

Thomas Beard, a Puritan schoolmaster who had taught Oliver Cromwell at school, also claimed that divine retribution could be visited on transgressors. Writing in England in 1643 with the implication that this was a contemporary event, he described how in the village of Ossemer in Germany:[46]

> As the Popish Priest played the minstrell to his parishioners that danced the morris before him, and rejoyced in their merry May-games, a tempest arose, and a thunderbolt struck off his right hand, together with the harpe which he played on, and consumed about twenty foure men and women of the company a just punishment of so prophane a Priest.

The original German text simply described the priest playing for a 'dance' at Whitsuntide, and the event supposedly happened in 1203, long before 'morris' or anything like it was known in Europe.[47] Beard was grafting contemporary English concerns onto events in thirteenth-century Germany.

Those defending such practices could not find strong counter-thrusts but only modest, almost neutral arguments. Gilbert Ironside, refuting the charge that 'May-games and Morice-daunces [are] carnall and brutish delights' could only reply that 'no man will say that they are in themselves and in their own natures sinfull, but only by use or abuse'; and that if people might be thinking about forthcoming pastimes during a divine service, 'this is an inward and spirituall wickednesse of their secret thoughts, which none is able to discover, and therefore none should presume to judge'.[48]

Another respondent to Burton's *A Brief Answer to a Late Treatise of the Sabbath Day* (1635), Francis White, the Laudian bishop of Ely, claimed that the ferocity of the invective against Sunday recreations was a substitute for the weakness of the arguments:[49]

> Brother B. is destitute of firme Arguments, to prove that all bodily exercise, and civill recreation is simply unlawfull, upon any part of the Sunday: and therefore he imitates that Sectarian, and declaimeth against lascivious and prophane sports and pastimes.

When 'the envious man demandeth, what wee thinke of promiscuous meetings of wanton youth, setting up May-Poles, &c.', White wrote, 'Our answer is, that when hee hath proved by sound arguments, such meetings and pastimes as the lawes of our kingdom, and the Canons of our Church, have permitted (after that the Religious offices of the day are performed) to be ... dishonest or vicious, we must proclaime them to be unlawfull at all times, but especially upon

44 Burton, Henry, *Replie*, p. 294.
45 Burton, Henry, *Divine Tragedie*, pp. 7-8.
46 Beard and Taylor, p. 289.
47 *Chroniken*, 7:125.
48 Ironside, pp. 271-72.
49 White, p. 122.

the holy day' – in other words, exhorting the Puritan polemicists to go beyond mere assertion to reasoned argument.

Some turned to the *Book of Sports*, Charles I's re-issue of his father's *Declaration*, but this was somewhat vitiated by the Sunday Observance Act of 1625 which forbade 'Bearbaiting, Bullbaiting, Interludes, common Plays, and other unlawful exercises and pastimes upon the Lord's day'.[50] The 'other pastimes' could be interpreted broadly or narrowly according to the commentator's wish, although the wording closely followed James I's original *Declaration* in what it forbade, so by implication continued to allow those activities legitimized in the *Declaration*. Henry Burton was one adopting a broad interpretation of the prohibition in his *Brief Answer*, citing the Act and then averring:[51]

> *Hence it is plaine, that all manner of sports and pastimes are unlawfull on the Lords Day; for Beare-baiting and Bull-baiting are prohibited as unlawfull on this day, which els are made lawfull on other dayes. And therefore dancing, Maygames, Morrices and the like, however men may account them lawfull on other dayes, yet for the very reasons afore-sayd ... on this day at least, they are unlawfull.*

The clergyman William Twisse also adduced the Act in 1641, but fixed specifically on the broader prohibition of all sports and pastimes outside of one's own parish (which, as we have seen, often led to prosecutions):[52]

> *that Act made in the first yeare of King Charles to preserve the Lords Day from profanation, wherein are forbidden expressely and by name, bearebaiting, bulbaiting, enterludes, common playes, and in generall all other unlawfull exercises and pastimes; and over and above all meetings and assemblies or concourse of people out of their owne parishes for any sports or pastimes whatsoever; and consequently no man ought on the Lords Day, goe forth of his owne parish to any may-game, or to see a Morrice-dance, or dancing about May-poles.*

As, unlike his father, Charles I required that the *Book of Sports* be read from pulpits, ministers were punished for not doing so. We have already noted Thomas Wilson's refusal to read it. He declared 'I say Archery, May-poles, May-games, Dancings, Morrice-dancings, and the like, be not exercises of Gods true Religion and Service'.[53]

Richard Culmer, vicar of Goodnestone, wrote to Sir Edward Dering on 8 January 1641, 'I have had very ungracious dealeing from the Lambeth Patriarch, by whom I have bene deprived of my ministry, and all the profitts of my Liveing three yeares and seaven moneths, having myselfe, my wife and seven children to provide for; such is the Prelate's tyranny for not consenting to morris daunceing upon the Lords day'.[54] Dering himself complained that year about the excising by a chaplain to the Bishop of London of a passage about Sabbath observance which had maintained that 'we are to occupy ourselves in a serious contemplation of the Sabbath day'. The like-minded Dering lamented that 'All this wholesome doctrine was expunged lest it should mar a ball, a wake or a morris dance upon the Lord's day'.[55] The centrality of morris and maypoles to the concepts of Sunday recreations in the *Book of Sports* was highlighted by Sir Benjamin Rudiard's speech in Parliament in 1640 when he spoke of the 'abuses of poore Ministers for not reading the Morris book'.[56]

---

[50] Sunday Observance Act.
[51] Burton, Henry, *Brief Answer*, p. 29.
[52] Twisse, p. 176.
[53] 'Articles Objected', p. 75.

[54] Frampton, T. Shipdem, p. 108.
[55] Hill, Christopher, pp. 198-99.
[56] D'Ewes, p. 6.

The poet and satirist George Wither was more scornful of Royalists than incensed by them. After the Parliamentarian victory his *The Modern States-man* (1653) mocked the delusions of those who thought everything would go back to the old ways after the conclusion of the Civil War. He imagines their lamentations:[57]

> *Where are those golden dayes we once had? Where are our Court-revellings and Masques? Where our Lord-Maiors Feasts and Shews, and all those joviall sports gone, in which England was wont to pride herself and triumph? not a Wake, not a morrice-Dance now to be seen, are these the effects of a Parliament? and is this that we have got by fighting? Alas poor souls! you dream't (I'le warrant) a Parliament would have made the Thames flow Custard, and turn'd the pebbles on the shore into Garoway-Comfits; have caused Bag-pudding to grow on every Bush, and each pond abound with beef and brewis; have commanded the conduits to run Sack and Clarret, and the Rivers and Brooks Ale and strong Beer; and welladay, your houses are not wall'd with Hasty Pudding, neither do Pigs ready roasted come and cry Come eat me; Lubberland is as far off now as ever, and you deceived of all your goodly expectations.*

During the Commonwealth some continued to try to make a case for moderation, relying on the *Book of Sports*. The clergyman Thomas Gataker argued in 1654 that the book did not give blanket approval to, nor disapprobation of, all sports, but discriminated between unlawful ones like cards and dice, and lawful ones:[58]

> *expressly therein named [are] Dancings, men or women, May-games, Whitsun-Ales, Morrice-dances, Rush-bearings, setting up of May-poles, and other sports therewith used...*

Likewise, when the Puritans of Shropshire petitioned in 1653 for a broader prohibition against 'keeping Wakes, setting up Morice Dances, and other prophane Sports, against which there is no particular Law', a published response by the Roman Catholic dramatist Richard Flecknoe argued that 'they fall foul [of] your Wakes and Moris-dances, meaning quite to overthrow the Hobby-horse, horse and man, holding him little better than the beast, and maid Marian the Whore of Babylon. Mean time, what harm the poor Moris-dancers do unto them, I do not see, but only that the melancholy Devil which possesses them is enemy of all mirth and harmlesse Recreation ... such as these would make rare Governors of the Commonwealth, who, whilst they should be making Acts, for the overcoming of our Enemies abroad, and rendring us formidable to all the world, would be making Acts against Moris-dancers, and Hobby-horses, to render us ridiculous unto every one.'[59]

Several polemicists also used morris dancing in negative analogies. Daniel Featly wrote in *Threnoikos, The House of Mourning* (1640), 'what a preposterous thing were it, for a man that hath one foote alreadie in the grave, and is drawing the other after, to desire to cut a crosse caper, and dance the morrice?'[60] In what was possibly a purposefully drawn analogy, John Goodwin in defending the execution of the king in 1649 wrote:[61]

> *To say that the Law we speak of was never extended unto or understood of Kings, and therefore neither ought now to be extended unto, or understood of them... Very possibly it was never (in such a sence) extended unto musitians, or moris-dancers, yet this, if it could be proved, would be no proof that therefore it was never understood or meant of them.*

---

[57] Wither, *Modern States-man*, pp. 35-37.
[58] Gataker, p. 20.
[59] Flecknoe, pp. 26-29.
[60] Featly, Day, Sibbs and Taylor, p. 823.
[61] Goodwin, p. 4.

The import is that the law applies to the monarch even though that is not specifically spelled out, just as morris dancers are covered by the law even though it may not specifically mention them.

––––––––––––

Although references to morris dancing are found in non-polemical writing of the period it was sometimes used simply as a familiar analogue to explain foreign customs. William Lithgow's account of travel through Roman Catholic Mediterranean countries was reminiscent of the polemics against 'popery'. He railed against the display of richly decorated statues of past religious personages:[62]

> *And what a number of livelesse pourtrayed Prioresses, motherlesse Nuns, yet infinite mothers, be erected (like the Maskerata of Morice-dancers) in silver, gold, gilded brasse, ... over-wrought with silk, silver and goldlaces, rich bracelets, silk grograims ...*

Other accounts of travels simply used the dance as a straightforward comparator. A 1634 account by a settler in America, William Wood, related the tale of a 'neere neighbouaring Indian' taken captive by a rival group and subjected to near-cannibalism before he made his escape:[63]

> *[He] was brought forth every day, to be new painted, piped unto, and hem'd in with a ring of bare skinned morris dancers, who presented their antiques before him. In a word, when they had sported enough about this walking Maypole, a rough hewne satyre cutteth a gobbit of flesh from his brawnie arme, eating it in his view, searing it with a firebrand, least the blood should be wasted before the morning.*

In the same year Thomas Herbert, a historian and courtier to Charles I, published his account of how at a Persian wedding feast 'Some of the bride-maids came out unto us, and after a Sallam or Congee began a morisko, their faces, hands and feet painted with flowres' and in another account that in the Persian Empire 'The vulgar sort delight in Morice dancing'.[64]

John Parkinson's botanical treatise *Theatrum botanicum* was an academic work rather than a travelogue, in which he aimed to describe all the plants of the known world. He described the American 'Ahovai Theveti' tree, comparing the indigenous people's use of its fruit with English morris dancers' use of bells:[65]

> *the wood stincketh most abhominably, bearing a white three square fruite, some what like unto the Greeke letter Δ. whose kernell within is most poysonous and deadly, and therefore the Indians ... abstaine also from using of the wood to burne, but having taken the kernell they putting small stones within the shells, and tying them with strings they serve them for bracers for their legges to dance with, as Moris dancers doe with bells with us.*

Robert Codrington's translation of the collections of tales written by Margaret de Valois, Queen of Navarre, used the term 'the Morice of Gascogny' to translate 'les bransles de Gascogne'[66] – a reminder that in some circumstances the description may be used as an implicit analogy, not tied to a particular setting or choreography.

Domestic imaginative literature and drama continued in this period to reflect the attitudes and customs prevalent at the time, with frequent allusions to morris dancing. For the most part they ignored the political overtones, but a few works did engage with the issues. In the

[62] Lithgow, pp. 270-71.
[63] Wood, William, pp. 57-58.
[64] Herbert, *Relation*, p. 113; Herbert, *Some Yeares Travels*, p. 233.
[65] Parkinson, p. 1633 (ch. XCV).
[66] Codrington, p. 257.

1630s Edward Catlin wrote a poem addressed to the Royalist clergyman and poet Thomas Pestell which directly addressed them:[67]

> *And yet I hate thinges Antichristian*
> *As Morris-dauncers doe a Puritan*
> *Or as the Puritans them selves some saye*
> *doe hate the beautious pole surnamed Maye.*

A hint of the underlying contentions can be found in Robert Chamberlain's 1640 comedy *The Swaggering Damsel*. When Trash, a rustic, says 'if the whole world were a Morris dance for foure and fortie houres outright, what shud, nay, what does thou thinke wud the good people of New England doe all that while?' (New England being a Puritan stronghold), the reply is 'I doe thinke they wud pray for a timely cessation of the noise of the superstitious bells hanging about their knees'.[68] They also emerge in Thomas Randolph's *The Muses' Looking-glass*, a comedy about vices and virtues, in large measure as applied to the theatre. In the play the virtues are compared to a dance. Bird, a Puritan (who is eventually persuaded of the legitimacy of the theatre) says 'What dance? / No wanton jig I hope: no dance is lawfull / But prinkum-prankum' (a rather odd view, given that prinkum-prankum is a kissing dance at weddings). His companion adds 'I hate a virtue in a morrice-dance! / O vile, absurd, maypole, maid-marian virtue'.[69]

Satirical works sit halfway between polemic and literature and some carried overt political biases. The Royalist poet John Cleveland mocked the Earl of Stamford's 1643 defeat in the West Country, comparing him to a whiffler 'before the show, ... one that trod the stage with the first, travers'd his ground, made a legge and Exit. The Countrey People took him for one, that by Order of the Houses was to dance a Morice through the West of England'.[70] A rejoinder to Cleveland turned the morris analogy around in celebrating Prince Maurice's failure to take the Puritan base Lyme Regis, describing the Prince as one 'who more properly may be sayd to have danc'd the Morris in the West, though he danc'd Lachrymae before Lyme'.[71] On hearing of the Earl of Essex's approach to break the siege, Prince Maurice abandoned it, causing another Parliamentarian satirist to pun that 'the Morris was done, and danced away' before Essex arrived.[72]

At the very tipping point from monarchy to Commonwealth in 1649, the satire *A New Bull-bayting, or, A Match Play'd at the Town-bull of Ely by Twelve Mungrills* appeared, with the bull representing Cromwell and the baiting dogs representing various polemicists. The dogs are set upon the bull by a named group of four leading figures among the Levellers, a group advocating for wider democratic participation in politics. By this time one of them, John Lilburne, was saying it would be better to have the monarchy restored than to have Cromwell's Commonwealth. The author puts the following words in bull-baiter Lilburne's mouth, suggesting that morris dancing is just a harmless pursuit:[73]

> *Lets set on another, this is a lovely Dogge with a thin pair of Chaps; another of Sir Iohn*
> *Presbyters breed, better to hang then to keep; how he drivels out Nonscence and Tautoligies;*
> *sure he has wasted his Lungs in confuting a May-pole, and entered into a dispute with the*
> *Maid-marrian in a Morrice-dance, about the unlawfulness of that innocent pastime; till the*
> *Hobby-horse confuted him with his tayle, and retorted his rebuke with his heels.*

---

[67] Catlin, p. 123.
[68] Chamberlain, p. [48] (Act IV).
[69] Randolph, 'Muses' Looking-glass', p. 260 (V.i).
[70] Cleveland, p. 4.

[71] *Full Answer*, p. 6.
[72] Vicars, sig. Ll[1].
[73] *New Bull-bayting*, p. 9.

Very few texts of the period openly espouse morris dancing. The *New Ballad of Bold Robin Hood* published at an uncertain date sometime in the century celebrates the Tutbury bull-running and describes a celebratory morris dance into the town.[74]

Some writers preferred to look backwards, describing the morris in much the same terms as those of the Elizabethan and early Stuart authors. One mainstream drama of the period that described a morris dance in some detail is William Sampson's *Vow Breaker* (1636). The character Miles the miller wants to be the hobby horse in the dance: he has 'practic'd my Reines, my Caree'res, my Pranckers, my Ambles, my false Trotts, my smooth Ambles, and Canterbury Paces... borrowed the fore Horse-bells, his Plumes, and braveries, nay, had his mane new shorne, and frizl'd'. Later he goes to 'borrow a few ribbands, bracelets, eare-rings wyertyers, and silke girdles, and hand-kerchers for a morice'. This harks back to the stage morrises of the previous generation and adduces all their main characteristics. There is also to be a Maid Marion, and also possibly a St George and dragon, reminiscent more of the urban processions of the previous century.[75] The hobby horse and Maid Marion are also used as shorthand to evoke the character of a morris in Philip Massinger's *A very Woman* (1634) when a Moorish city's atmosphere is described in the words 'How like an everlasting Morris-dance it looks, / Nothing but Hobby-horse, and Maid-marrian'.[76]

One of the few indications of a knowledgeable interest in the choreography and costume can be found in a spoof will of the moderate Parliamentarian the Earl of Pembroke, published in 1649 (when he was already unwell, prior to his death the following year). In it he bequeaths his new 'trusse of points' (bundle of lacework) 'to Mr Selden to keep's codpiece close; hee'l wear 'um for antick fashion sake' and adds as an aside 'the rogues took me for a morris-dancer in a morning before I was truss'd, when they came to crosse capers, and dance attendance before my honourable Worship'.[77]

James Shirley's *The Lady of Pleasure* (1635) also evoked the association with the Whitsun ale, the scarves and napkins (baldricks and streamers or handkerchiefs), bells, hobby horse and Maid Marion as the archetypal elements of the morris. At the same time it reflected the more fashionable view of the morris of this period as an unsophisticated country pastime. Aretina, the protagonist, refused to countenance spending time in the country as lady to the squire:[78]

> *I would not*
> *Endure again the country conversation*
> *To be the lady of six shires! The men*
> *So near the primitive making, they retain*
> *A sense of nothing but the earth*
> *...*
> *How they become the morris, with whose bells*
> *They ring all into Whitsun ales, and sweat*
> *Through twenty scarfs and napkins, till the hobbyhorse*
> *Tire and the Maid Marian, dissolved to a jelly,*
> *Be kept for spoon meat!*

While Shirley's urbane Aretina had no time for the country, three years later Thomas Nabbes's Dobson, unsophisticated servant to a country gentleman in *Covent Garden*, 'had rather see a Morris-dance and a May-pole, th[a]n ten Playes: what care I for with which I understand not?'[79]

---

[74] 'New Ballad', p. 447.
[75] Sampson, pp. 68-72 (V.ii).
[76] Massinger, p. 250 (III.i).

[77] Mercurius Elenticus, sig. A3v.
[78] Shirley, *Lady of Pleasure*, pp. 55-56 (I.i).
[79] Nabbes, 'Covent Garden', p. 9 (I.i.)

The morris as a rustic pastime was a popular theme. Robert Herrick's *The Country Life* speaks of 'Thy Wakes, thy Quintels, here thou hast, / Thy May-poles too with Garlands grac't: / Thy Morris-dance; thy Whitsun-ale; / Thy Sheering-feast, which never faile', and in his *Hesperides* the poet enjoins his lover to 'Go to Feast, as others do ... / Morris-dancers shalt thou see / Marian too in Pagentrie'.[80] In his verse history of the reign of Henry II, Thomas May anachronistically invoked the image of the 'country Ladds and Swains' entertaining Fair Rosamund at Woodstock with their 'jolly Maygames'; but if any rustic innocent looked too long on her beauty he would be smitten:[81]

> *What now (alas) can Wake, or Faire availe*
> *His love-sick minde? no Whitsunale can please,*
> *No Jingling Morris dances give him ease;*
> *The Pipe and Tabor have no sound at all;*
> *Nor to the May-pole can his measures call,*
> *Although invited by the merryest Lasses.*
> *How little for those former joyes he passes?*

Other writers continued to use morris dancing as a metaphor for rustic simple-mindedness. A comic work of 1647, *Newes out of the West, or, The Character of a Mountebank*, written in a strong west-country rural dialect describes how one character found Hodge (the archetypal name for a rustic):[82]

> *c'he thought, that c'had, had a Morice-dancer in's noddle, his joynts did so twitch, and his chaps did so taber, c'he was ene wishing for a nosegay, bels, and a blue handkercher.*

'C'he' is the dialect word for 'I'; some of the other words remain obscure, but the characterization is clear.

Thomas Randolph presented a more positive view. He had died sixteen years before when his comedy *Hey for Honesty* was published in 1651 (after being augmented by one F.J. around 1650). The work was anti-Puritan and published surreptitiously.[83] In it Stiffe, a country swain, exclaims that he 'could give a penny for a May-pole to dance the morris vor arrant joy' on hearing good news.[84]

Morris dancing could also, as in earlier periods, represent disorder. In the cross-dressing comedy *The Ghost, or, The Woman Wears the Breeches*, which was published in 1653 with an exculpatory note to declare that it had been written before the ban on theatres, three characters enter with Aurelia, the heroine, to be greeted with the words 'Hoida, a morris dance, and she the jester'.[85] Thomas Heywood's *Fair Maid of the West Part II* (1631) speaks of dancing 'wild Moriskoes' in a bridal procession and Clem, the rustic, says that the locals 'have so tir'd me with their Moriscoes, and I have so tickled them with Countrey dances, Sellengers round, and Tom Tiler'. These are, however, 'real' Moors of Morocco, and Heywood is playing on the analogy of Moroccan morisco (as imagined by him) and English morris.[86]

The water poet John Taylor painted a more ambivalent picture of morris as low life in his description of a river trip to Oxford in 1644. Taylor reflected the 'real-life' experience of

---

[80] Herrick, Robert, 'Country Life', pp. 229-31; Herrick, Robert, 'Hesperides', p. 255.
[81] May, Thomas, sig. I5.
[82] *Newes*, p. 17.

[83] Day.
[84] Randolph, *Pleasant Comedie*, p. 11 (II.i).
[85] *Ghost*, p. 8.
[86] Heywood, pp.352 (I.i), 355 (II.i).

people on different sides of the conflict. Falling in with 'rebels' (supporters of the Parliament), he describes them:[87]

> *My leash of Rascalls, were mad Blades, (right Bilboes)*
> *True tatter'd Rogues, in breech, shirts, skirts and elboes,*
> *They sung, and danc'd the Morris, like maide Marrian*
> *And sweat and stunk, as sweet as sugar Carrion.*

The masque *Raguaillo d'Oceano*, by the Earl of Westmorland Mildmay Fane (who was both Royalist and Puritan), written to entertain his family in 1640, echoed the uninhibitedness associated with the morris, when 'as if Enchanted by ye Lowd Musiks high Strain They All fall into a morrice & Mad Jomping Phantastike Daunce'.[88] Henry Glapthorne's *Argalus and Parthenia* of 1639 viewed the wildness negatively: shepherds dance but the protagonist does not want to view 'idle Morris-Dances' because only a man 'possest / With eminent frensie' would want to do so.[89]

Many of the allusions to the dance during the 1640s characterized it more innocently as light frivolity. Sir Henry Wotton described how the threat of invasion by the Armada had evaporated and 'proved but a Morrice dance upon our waves', repeating a phrase used by James Howell in his highly allegorical history *Dendrologia*, published the previous year.[90] The dance was seen as the antithesis of battle: Donald Lupton wrote in 1642 that 'Soldiers are not for sport and joust, but for earnest. Neither is war to be accounted a May-game, or a Morris dance, but as a plague and scourge.'[91] Howell again in 1643 described how the royalist troops at the battle of Edge Hill 'upon sight of the Enemies Colours ran as merrily down the hill, as if they had gone to a morris dance'.[92] John Done (son of the poet John Donne) wrote in 1650 that 'A bold foole hath great advantage in quiet over a sober wiseman; for the foole accounts an earthquake but the earth's Morice-dance, Thunder ... the warrs a may-game'.[93]

Much later, in 1658 George Wither returned to the idea of morris dance as empty foolery, enjoining that poets should write plainly and should not:[94]

> *... when our Sin, for Sober-Mourning calls,*
> *Play us a Jigg, or sing us Madrigals.*
>
> *...*
>
> *Look like solemnizing an Ordinance*
> *In Pious Duties, with a Morrice-Dance;*
> *Or, like their actings, who, against the Forces*
> *Of well-arm'd Foes, bring Troops of Hobby-horses.*

In the drama as in poetry, empty frivolity, foolishness and dissoluteness were continuing themes. When Rolliardo in James Shirley's *The Bird in a Cage* (1632) says that 'we are preparing a morris to make your grace merry; they have chosen me for the hobby horse' he is speaking metaphorically to say he has been made a fall-guy or fool;[95] while John Ford in *Love's Sacrifice* (1633) alluded to 'planets drunk at a morris-dance', and in describing a comically unlikely romance says that a 'morris dance were but a tragedy / Compar'd to that'.[96] Lewis Sharpe's

---

[87] Taylor, John, *Mad Verse*, p. 6.
[88] Fane, p. 91.
[89] Glapthorne, p. 12 (I.ii).
[90] Wotton, p. 11; Howell, *Dendrologia*, p. 67.
[91] Lupton, p. 87.
[92] Howell, *True Informer*, p. 31.
[93] Done, pp. 86-87.
[94] Wither, *Salt*, pp. 7-8.
[95] Shirley, 'Bird', p. 443 (I.i).
[96] Ford, John, pp. 20-21, 26 (I.ii).

Noble Stranger (1640) scorned audiences coming to see 'see Comedies, more ridiculous th[a]n a Morrice dance'.[97]

Masques continued to be a more acceptable form of drama, often performed in private for the aristocracy. Morris references ranged from the simple allusion, as in Milton's 'The Sounds and Seas with all their finny drove / Now to the moon in wavering Morrice move' in his masque *Comus*,[98] to performances. Morris dances in performance were often part of the comic anti-masque. Aurelian Townshend's *Albion's Triumph*, staged in 1631 with the king's participation, had an anti-masque which included six fools and seven 'Mimicks, or Morescoes' (who may have been morris dancers or Moors).[99] The antimasquers of the Inns of Court masque *Triumph of Peace* around 1633 included 'Jollity in a flame-coloured Suite, but trick'd like a Morise-dancer, with Scarfes and Napkins, his Hat fashioned like a Cone, with a little fall.'[100] Randolph's *Amyntas* (1638) imagined birds 'that could dance / The morrice in the aire'. Later in the masque the 'fantastic shepherd and fairy knight' Jocastus enters 'with a Morrice, himselfe maid Marrian, Bromius the Clowne', and says 'I did not thinke there had been such delight / In any mortall Morrice, they doe caper / Like quarter Fairies, at the least' – this seems to be a more realistic, less fanciful morris than other masque morrises.[101] An event which may have been held at Chirke Castle in Denbighshire in 1634, but whose first performance has also more recently been placed at Woodstock in Oxfordshire in 1612, personifies the seasons with 'a morrice dance brought in by Spring'.[102] In another royal masque in 1638, personified Time brings in May, who presents 'A Morisk Dance' (also described as a 'morris-dance').[103]

With the enforced closure of theatres in 1642 most dramatic activity came to an end. Performances continued at private houses or in fly-by-night productions in taverns. Some plays were still published, usually dating in performance from before the closure. A few expressed negative views of the morris. One such was Aston Cokain's *Trappolin Creduto Principe*, published in 1658 but perhaps written *c.* 1633. When petitioners come to plead with Trappolin he is contemptuous, calling them 'morris-dancers' and 'lobs'.[104]

Although the theatres had closed, we have noted several plays published thereafter which allude to their being performed before the prohibition was introduced. The most intriguing of these later published plays is *The Country Girle* by 'T.B.' (possibly Thomas Brewer), published in 1647 but as the title page declares, 'as it hath beene often Acted with much applause'. The theatre historian Alfred Harbage records that it was performed in 1632 and was entered in the Stationers' Register of works in 1640.[105] The play has more the feel of a Restoration comedy: the lecherous squire Sir Robert Malory tries to seduce the young Margaret, one of his tenants. In the midst of his seduction Sir Robert hears music approaching and says to Margaret, 'rot on their fiddle, and their fiddle strings, / Thou art my Musick. – hoyday, here's a Morice'. The stage direction then reads:

> *Enter six Country Wenches, all red Pettycoates, white stitch'd Bodies, in their Smock-sleeves, the fiddler before them, and Gillian, with her Tippet up, in the midst of them dancing.*

They force Sir Robert to abandon his attempt, and he later complains 'A vengeance of all morrice dauncers. / I am sure, they h'a mar'd, my dancing: that delicate dance / That I should

[97] Sharpe, Lewis, sig. G2v (Act IV).
[98] Milton, 'Mask', p. 89.
[99] Townshend, pp. 67-68.
[100] Triumph, p. 592.
[101] Randolph, 'Amyntas', pp. 246 (I.iii), 343 (V.vi).
[102] Brown, Cedric C., p. 84; Daye, 'Revellers', p. 123.
[103] Nabbes, 'Presentation', p. 266; Nabbes, *Springs Glorie*, sig. G1v.
[104] Cokain, pp. 462-63 (IV.i).
[105] Harbage, *Annals*, p. 130; *Transcript*, 1:2.

have had with my tenant' (i.e., his seduction of her).[106] He is not against the morris dance as such, only that it has interrupted his seduction.

This is remarkable because it appears to be the first instance of a fully female group of morris dancers. The early courtly ring morrises featured a central lady; wenches occasionally accompanied Will Kemp in his nine days' wonder, and there are a few indications of morris dancing by women in the presentments to church courts, but little else. Maid Marion is attested as being played by a male youth in several cases. Given the surmised date of original performance in the 1630s, the presence of women on stage – if they were not played by boys – is also innovative. Even if these are boys, they are still acting out a women's morris. The stage direction emphasises their femininity: 'red Pettycoates, white stitch'd Bodies, in their Smock-sleeves'. Women were officially prohibited from the stage until 1660, and the first women on the English stage – French actresses performing in 1629 – elicited outrage. Perhaps this indicates that *The Country Girle* was performed elsewhere than the mainstream playhouses, at venues where the restrictions were less rigidly observed.[107] Women were certainly involved in community-based or private entertainments more generally, if not on the stage itself.[108]

––––––––––––––

The years of the Commonwealth were the culmination of a process that had begun 90 years earlier and before moving on we should consider what that had entailed. The transformation in attitudes to morris dancing between 1570 and 1660 is remarkable. At the start of the period, although falling from favour as an entertainment among the upper classes and royalty, morris dances were very popular in parish and civic entertainments. Expenditure on costumes for the dance was considerable, and they could be seen as an exploitable investment. At the same the view was beginning to emerge that this was an activity which should not be associated with the church. Opposition to dancing in association with the church began in the 1570s and from the beginning of the 17th century evidence of church opposition outweighed evidence of support. First of all actions were taken against church officials. This spread to presentments against parishioners whose activities were thought to disrupt church activities. The final stage was the blanket association of morris dancing with ungodliness or attachment to 'popery', which was seen as a threat not just to the church but also to the state. By about 1630 the battle within the church was won: church-sponsored events were at an end. By the end of the 1630s church presentments had also dried up. Morris dancing no longer took place in ecclesiastical parish contexts. This was in the context of a debate relating not just to the activity as such, but to wider theological and doctrinal issues about Christian observances and authority. In many cases those prosecuted showed indifference to the proceedings or even contempt for them and the church.

Outside of the church, morris dancing continued to be promoted in civic and guild contexts into the 17th century. In some cases thereafter active engagement might cease without turning into outright opposition. Towns such as Plymouth simply stopped hiring morris dancers (or at least, stopped recording the fact). In other cases, such as at Banbury and Leicester, there was contention as different factions in the community sought to prevail. The personal views of prominent individuals often drove events, as when at Wells in 1607 the mayor was in contention with the Puritan constable John Hole and the inhabitants of the town took sides in support. In such situations morris dancers were invariably on the side

---

[106] Brewer, Thomas, sig. D3-D3v, E1v.
[107] McManus.
[108] Stokes, 'Women'.

of the 'old order', a Laudian approach to church practices and support for the king rather than the parliament in civic society. David Underdown has described this in the context of the emergence of a growing gulf between classes in society, and of 'parish élites who saw it as their duty to discipline the poor into godliness and industriousness, and who found in Puritan teaching (broadly defined) their guide and inspiration'.[109] From the 1620s to the 1640s evidence is sparse, no doubt due in part to the exigencies of Civil War in the latter part of that period; in the 1650s the evidence is wholly negative.

The prosecution of, or support for, morris dancing was just a part of what we might now call a culture war and polemic about the nature of recreation, culture, religion and society in general. Although this book traces the specific thread of morris dancing, it was just one element in a broad tapestry. There are scores of visitation articles, church presentments and, later, civil prosecutions which deal with ales, feasts, games, misrule, processions and suchlike activities without mentioning morris dancing. The battles over whether and how to celebrate Christmas were if anything even more contentious, leading to the 'plum pudding riots' and mob rule in Canterbury.[110]

Figure 7.3 illustrates the changes in the reception of morris dancing in public events from the 1550s to the 1650s. It is necessarily rather subjective in how the evidence is assessed, a process which, as John Forrest has pointed out in his history of the subject, is fraught with potential pitfalls.[111] It reflects only real-world events, not the worlds of literature, drama and polemic, and records instance of support and opposition in the church and civic or guild spheres. Where there are several recorded events relating to a single situation (as with the several occasions of dancing recorded in connection with the Wells May game) these are counted as just one piece of evidence. The repeated recording of the possession of morris costumes in the same parish over successive years is also counted as a single event within each decade. And, of course, the chart remains subject to the vagaries of recording and the survival of records. Nevertheless, it shows a more or less steady drift, first in the church context, then more widely, from overall support to total opposition, and the elimination of morris dancing in both church and civic contexts. The occasions on which dancers were prosecuted for removing church cloths for use in their performances illustrate how what was once seen as a legitimate and sanctioned consequence of the support of the church for parish celebrations was withdrawn on the one side but continued to be asserted by the other.

Dancers visiting the private estates of the upper classes would know the character of those they were calling on, and would only go to those where they might expect a welcome, so it is not surprising that the evidence from household account books shows support, as Sir Francis Throckmorton did at Coughton Court in 1658.

With the exception of Hornby in northern Lancashire in 1633, evidence of morris dancing before 1660 is confined to the south of a line drawn from the northern edge of the Mersey estuary to the northern edge of the Wash. Although records are relatively few in number, between 1570 and 1599 records in the south-west of the country indicate support, while those in the eastern counties are generally hostile to dancing. Elsewhere in the country the evidence is mixed. Between 1600 and 1629 there is a clear island of continuing parish support in a rather small area centred on the Thames valley, in an otherwise hostile sea. The apparent presence of concentrated opposition in East Anglia and the west midlands may be an artefact of the survival of records, but may reflect

---

[109] Underdown, p. 275.
[110] Durston.
[111] Forrest, pp. 28-36, 363-75.

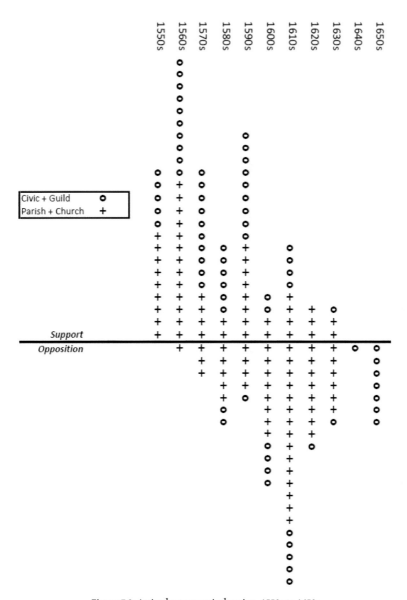

Figure 7.3: Attitudes to morris dancing, 1550s to 1650s.

on the one hand East Anglia's position in the forefront of the socio-cultural changes sweeping the country, and on the other, Herefordshire's reputation (as expressed in the *Old Meg* pamphlet describing the geriatric morris there) as a centre for morris dancing.

Most datable performances by dancers took place in May or June, often around Whitsun. Civic processions featuring dancers were held on May Day in Plymouth and at Midsummer in Chester and London. The Salisbury Guild of Tailors' dancers also performed at Midsummer, but additionally in July and August in some years. Dancers performed at other special occasions, such as the festivities in honour of Queen Elizabeth at Kenilworth in July 1575, and the reception of the Early of Derby at Liverpool in April 1577.

The east of England presents a different picture. Although some instances took place at more familiar times of year (for example, Witchford, Cambridgeshire and Wivenhoe, Essex in May/June; Scopwick, Lincolnshire, on May Day), others took place near the end of the year, usually at private houses: Stiffkey (Norfolk) in November, and Felbrigg, East Harling and Hatfield Broad Oak in December or January. At Hengrave it was a single dancer 'at ye gate'; but the Scopwick dance was indoors.

It is difficult to get a firm view on the numbers of dancers in a performance. Where dancers are presented in church courts, we do not always know whether all the dancers have been summoned, or just some; we do not know whether some bystanders have been caught up, or whether supernumeraries such as a fool or whiffler have been included among the dancers. Some of the clearest indications are from parishes holding costumes. At St Columb Major in Cornwall the churchwardens held five coats in 1586-89, six in the following two years, and seven in 1595-97; the number of dancers required may not be firmly fixed, but depend on resources. The churchwardens at Bray had four dancers' coats (plus Maid Marion's and Fool's costumes) in 1602 and 1623, and those at nearby Marlow also had four over the period 1615-29. The picture of dancers at Richmond-upon-Thames shows even fewer: three 'ordinary' dancers dancing with a Maid Marion figure (Figure 6.5 on p. 93).

There were six dancers in the troupe who entertained Queen Elizabeth at Kenilworth in 1575 and the one from Herne which perambulated around Kent in 1589. At Leicester, six were arraigned in 1599 but nine in 1603. Six coats were supplied for the dancers who entertained King James at Oxford in 1605. Six dancers were indicted in the presentment at Chatteris in 1614 and six named at Glastonbury in 1617.

There is a large arc reaching through Herefordshire, Worcestershire and Shropshire, and across to Staffordshire, where greater numbers of dancers were indicted or reported. When Thomas Weaver was presented at Ribbesford, Worcestershire in 1616 eight other dancers were presented with him. At Clee St Margaret in Shropshire there were eight dancers and at least five associated characters in 1619, and in the same year ten were presented at Yazor in Herefordshire and ten in connection with the affray at Shrewsbury. *Old Meg of Herefordshire* tells of twelve dancers. In Staffordshire, ten tailors took part in the dance at Wolverhampton in 1652 and as many as sixteen (though with some uncertainty, given the broadness of the accusations) at Lapley in 1655. The ten dancers fined at Bradmore, Nottinghamshire may represent an Eastern outlier of this arc.

A variety of characters is associated with the dance, but none of them is indispensable. The fool and Maid Marion are the most widespread, and at Kenilworth in 1575 their presence accompanying the dance was 'according too the auncient manner'. The dancers from Herne had both, and the painting of dancers at Richmond shows both, even with a depleted number of dancers (Figure 6.5 on p. 93). The cavaliers who travelled to the Witney wakes in 1646 met not only Maid Marion but also two fools. Each may appear on their own. As late as 1655 the minister who complained of dancing at Lapley mentioned a fool and an implicit Maid Marion in the male who 'danced in Women's apparel'. That Maid Marion's role is taken by a male – often a boy, as at Herne, reflecting practice on the stage – is apparently taken for granted, and is sometimes explicit. Kemp describes the lass who danced part way with him as his 'merry Maydemarian' but his whole exploit was an exceptional event. On another day a fool danced with him. It may be thought that Kemp was ensuring that he worked the expected characters into his narrative. The supposedly 120-year-old Maid Marion Meg Goodwin, she who was *Old Meg*, was also exceptional, and was a Maid Marion without a fool. On the other hand, the dancers from Clee St Margaret in 1619 had a large cast of supernumeraries, including a fool, but no Maid Marion. In the Thames valley, the churchwardens at Bray and Marlow had a fool's coat but no costume for Maid Marion. In 1652, both the morris dancers who came unwantedly from Broseley to Nordley and Astley Abbotts, and the tailors of Wolverhampton, had fools but apparently no Maid Marions.

Other characters were more tenuously associated with the dance. Apart from the proposed London city watch of 1585, which had sword bearers to clear the way (so acting as whifflers), sword bearers and whifflers are found only in that western arc, and then only occasionally: whifflers for *Old Meg* in 1609 and at Shrewsbury ten years later, and sword bearers at Clee St Margaret in 1619, and from Broseley and Wolverhampton in 1652. Sword bearers do, however, re-emerge in later periods (see Chapter 15). Flag bearers appeared at Wells in 1607, and again at Clee St Margaret and Wolverhampton.

The hobby horse is rather more complex. It appeared with morris dancers in civic contexts at Plymouth and intermittently at Salisbury. At Cocking in 1616 it was in the company of a Maid Marion, and along with several other characters there was one at Clee St Margaret in 1619. Its depiction by the Thames at Richmond (again, with Maid Marion) gives a good impression of its appearance. It was what is known as a tourney horse, in which a man wears a harness so that his upper body represents the rider, and the lower half the horse. It is noticeable that the hobby horse is found with the morris dancers in several plays of contemporary life around the London area, for example Hoxton and Stoke Newington (*The Knight of the Burning Pestle*, 1613) and Edmonton (*The Witch of Edmonton*, 1621). A hobby horse with morris dancers at Hoxton was mentioned again in Spelman's *Vox Graculi* in 1623. The enigmatic refrain about the hobby horse 'being forgot', common in the literature of the first quarter of the 17th century, has been examined by Christopher Cawte but remains a mystery.[112] The hobby horse disappeared after that time from the morris, except in literary allusion, but it also could have an independent existence, as in the affray at Long Newnton in Gloucestershire in 1641.[113]

There are several allusions to napkins, and some indication that the fashion of tying them, or streamers, to the arms and shoulders was considered to be old-fashioned by the beginning of the 17th century. Kemp's Chelmsford maid wanted to be dressed in 'the olde fashion, with napkins on her armes', and this is the style shown in the woodcut on the cover. In the *Old Meg* pamphlet the dancers' coats were 'of the old fashion ... sleeves gathered at the elbows, and hanging sleeves behind'. Stubbes's 1583 rant against dancing (p. 66) had been the first to allude to handkerchiefs, and the mid-century woodcut from *Recreation for Ingenious Head-peeces* (Figure 7.2 on p. 100) shows what is presumably the newer style of holding napkins, or handkerchiefs, in the hands. By the middle of the century what were to become the chief symbols of morris dancing in later periods – the bells and handkerchiefs – were in place.

The dancers in *Vox Graculi* were described as being in single file, and those depicted in the Richmond riverside painting are similarly shown. There were also dances – primarily in stage performances – indicating that dancers might be pairs of mixed couples.

---

[112] Cawte, *Ritual Animal Disguise*, pp. 48-49.

[113] *Report* (1901), 1:107-08.

Although the allusions are sometimes ambiguous, there are also a few references to women dancing. This is certainly the case where women accompanied Kemp on two occasions. Old Meg Goodwin herself is female. In some of the ecclesiastical court presentments, for example at Ross-on-Wye in 1629, women were arraigned along with male morris dancers, and may have been participants. In *The Roaring Girl* Ralph Trapdoor talks of drawing 'all the whores i'th' towne to dance in a morris'. This last certainly suggests the unseemliness of women's dancing, and it remained comparatively rare. The culmination came in the apparent all-female morris of *The Country Girle*.

We know very little about the music that accompanied the morris. In the popular and literary mind the appropriate instrument was the pipe and tabor. In 42 texts (plays, poems, polemics, etc.) of the period 1570-1659 the musician is identified as a pipe-and-taborer in over three-quarters of cases, but this masks a shift to more references to the musician being a fiddler as time progresses, so that by 1630-1659 one third of the instances are of this kind. Where there are records of actual events the picture is more complex. Just under half the 35 records which mention a musician refer to the combination of pipe and tabor, and over a quarter to the fiddle, rising to ⅝ of the references mentioning fiddle or fiddler in the period 1630-59. A word of caution should be sounded, however. There is evidence that a 'fiddler' may refer to any musician.[114] Henry Burton described how at Battersea in 1634:[115]

> God's judgement befell a fiddler, the youth of the town of both sexes, being assembled solemnly to set up a garland upon their May-pole, and having got a tabor and pipe for the purpose, he with the pipe in his mouth, fell down dead and never spake word.

At Kelvedon Easterford, Essex, John Ayly, an alehouse-keeper, was presented in the archdeacon's court in 1613 'for suffering of a fiddler to play with taber and pipe in his house upon the 9 of May, being the sabbath day, in time of divine service'.[116]

The most frequent accompaniment of the chief instrument was the drum, mentioned in over half the instances of events during the period, but in only one sixth of the literary references. The majority of occasions in which it is mentioned in the period are prosecutions or attacks of one kind or another, and the use of drums in such public situations may be seen as adding to the belligerency or disorder of such an event. In the literary sphere, however, while the polemics may have adduced the drum in evidence against the morris, the poems, masques and other works of the imagination favoured a more pastoral image where the drum would be out of keeping.

There is little information in this period about the actual tunes used. While some pieces of published or transcribed music do call themselves 'morrises' or similar, there is no evidence that they were actually used in performance. In the last decade of the period some dance manuals appear which include mixed-couple 'morrises'. (These will both be discussed in Chapter 8.) In *Fucus Histriomastix*, although the actors dance to 'Come Help me over ye Water ye Bony Bony Booteman' this is not directly linked with their morris dance. In *The Fair Maid of the West* Clem the rustic responds to Moorish dances with 'Sellengers round, and Tom Tiler' but these are country dances, not specifically morris dances. While the morris dancers are talking in *Summers Last Will and Testament*, three clowns (rustics) and three maids enter and dance to 'Trip and Go'; and in *The Witch of Edmonton* the fiddler for the morris has just played

---

[114] Heaney, Michael, 'Must Every Fiddler'.
[115] Burton, Henry, *Divine Tragedie*, p. 20. [116] Sharpe, J.A., p. 102.

'The Flowers in May', but, once again, it is not evident that this was for a morris dance. The closest we come to the identification of a morris dance tune comes in *Jack Drum's entertainment*, when the dancers enter and sing 'Skip it, and trip it, nimbly, nimbly, tickle it, tickle it lustily' – a song otherwise unknown and alluding directly to the events in the play, so perhaps composed specifically for it. Even here, there is no stage direction to indicate that the morris men were dancing as well as singing.

We also know little of the elements of the dance. Kemp tells us of the 'hey-de-gaies' figure, of skips, leaps and jumps, and of 'footing it'. The dancers in Jonson's masque at Althorp also 'skip'. At the Wells May game the mayor's sergeant denied that anyone 'dyd daunce in Roundes from the maye pole to his howse', but this may refer to general dancing. The geriatric dancers at Hereford could better anyone in keeping time by 'the knocke of the heele' and they too are described as 'footing' the dance. The cavaliers who went to Witney in 1646 described the dancers 'treading' the dance and 'capering'. All we can say from this is that the dance figures may have involved heys and rounds, and that the steps involved various leaps and capers. The painting of dancers at Richmond shows them in single file, facing in pairs.

There are rather richer descriptions in the literary sphere. The words most commonly used to describe the dance are hopping, skipping, 'tripping', frisking, and leaping or jumping. Sutcliffe in 1606 mocked the priest who 'skippeth and danceth about the altar' like a morris dancer, while John Taylor said that Kemp 'with antick skips did hop it'.[117] Christopher Wase in 1651 wrote that 'the leaping about with bells ty'd on the legs ... is not originally an European frolique ... but the name imports to dance Alla Moresca'.[118]

There are some more specific descriptions. In a 1646 sermon John Owen spoke of morris dancers 'that did rise and caper'.[119] Three writers in the 1640s speak of morris dancers' 'cross-capers', and one of them, Mercurius, adds 'levaltos'.[120] A cross-caper is probably akin to what today we would call an entrechat.[121] A levalto (or lavolta) is a dance with high leaps, reminiscent of Breton's description of the dancers whose 'legges grew so nimble, that their heeles went higher th[a]n their heads'. These descriptions suggest an origin in the dances of the sixteenth-century court.

Shakespeare's reference to Cade in *Henry VI, Part 2*, 'caper[ing] upright' named a specific dance movement,[122] and *The Most Famous and Renowned Historie, of that Woorthie and Illustrous Knight Mervine* (1612, by 'I.M. Gent', who may be Gervase Markham), did likewise in referring to a 'Morisco galliard'.[123] Both capers and galliards (altered in the course of time to 'galley') survived as names of dance steps in south-midlands morris dances into the 19th century.

Few references mentioned the arms and hands. Rider's 1595 dictionary defined a morris dance as a 'gesticula' (and a dancer as a 'gesticulator'),[124] while Higins's dictionary in 1585 adduced Cooper's referral to 'chironomia',[125] as did Thomas Blount's 1656 *Glossographia*.[126]

---

[117] Taylor, John, 'Incipit ... Thou Cravest'.
[118] Wase, p. 76.
[119] Owen, John, p. 1.
[120] Featly, Day, Sibbs and Taylor, p. 823; Mercurio-Mastix Hibernicus, p. 17; Mercurius Elenticus, sig. A3v.
[121] See Weaver, John, pl. 40. I am grateful to Jennifer Thorp for bringing this to my attention.

[122] Shakespeare, *King Henry VI Part II*, p. 78 (III.iii).
[123] Gent, I.M., p. 123.
[124] Rider, col. 963.
[125] Higins, *Nomenclator*, pp. 299, 521.
[126] Blount, *Glossographia*, sig. CC3v [signature mislabelled CC4].

The overall picture is of a dance performed mainly but not exclusively by men, with some characteristic steps, often to pipe and tabor but also to fiddle, and occasionally to other instruments. The numbers in the dance varied from as few as four to ten or more, and there are some indications of different characteristics in different parts of the country. A fool and Maid Marion were the most frequent accompanying characters, and sometimes a hobby horse, though the last also had an independent existence. None of them was essential to the dance. It was typically performed at a community's summer festival – a May game or ale – but on various civic occasions as well.

However, over the course of the ninety years from 1570 to 1660 the dance had gone from being a prime component of festive occasions to being unwelcome and prosecuted first in church, then in civic contexts. It was a victim of both doctrinal battles and the fear of civic disorder. The closure of theatres meant that it disappeared from the stage. By the end of nine years of Civil War and another nine of the Commonwealth, it was reduced to sporadic performances at the private estates of favourably inclined gentry, and to celebration in literature only in an idealized pastoral world and the refined stage of the masque.

It was close to disappearing altogether.

Part III: Fragmentation (1660-1800)

Chapter 8

Restoration and the later Stuarts

When Charles II returned to England in triumph at the Restoration in 1660 there were widespread celebrations. In his progress from Rochester to London on 29 May, he was met at Blackheath by 'a kind of rural triumph, expressed by the country swains, in a morrice dance with the old music of taber and pipe; which was performed with all agility and cheerfulness imaginable'.[1] A report from Richmond in Yorkshire speaks of a May game the same day, including Robin Hood, bowmen, the Bishop of Hereford (apparently in person), 60 nymphs following Diana, and 'Two Companies of Morris-Dancers, who acted their parts to the satisfaction of the Spectators'.[2] Though the account is very circumstantial, the author, Christopher Clarkson, gives no source, and North Yorkshire is an outlier in the known geographical spread. Elsewhere in the book Clarkson describes the 'sword or morisco dance' so it may be that a sword dance was being performed.

The Duke of Newcastle, William Cavendish, explicitly advised Charles to encourage a return to the 'old ways'. In a treatise on government he supported May games and morris dances to keep the populace happy and forestall disorder:[3]

> For the countreye recreations: Maye Games, Moris Danses, the Lords off the Maye & Ladye off the Maye, the foole, – & the Hobye Horse muste nott bee forgotten. – Also the Whitson Lorde, & Ladye, – ... The Countereye People with their fresher Lasses to tripp on the Toune Greene aboute the Maye pole, to the Louder Bagg-pipe ther to bee refreshte with their Ale & Cakes ... The devirtisments will amuse the peoples thoughts, & keepe them In harmles action which will free your Majestie from faction & Rebellion.

Cavendish is certainly evoking 'the good old days': the hobby horse had indeed been forgotten by his time. The people, however, were more than ready to comply. Daniel Defoe reported (with unlikely exactitude and probable journalistic exaggeration, but no doubt capturing the spirit of the times) that in the five years after the Restoration 6325 maypoles were set up across the country.[4] The revival was not simply directed by the ruling classes. Twenty-six villagers of Stowe in Buckinghamshire presented this petition to Sir Richard Temple:[5]

> That whereas the youth of ye parish of Stowe, having now ingaged themselves in reveiving ye antient Custome, of keeping a whisson Ale this year for ye divertissment of themselves, and this side of the Countrey, and are in good hope to performe it to their credit as well as some other their neighbour Townes have done it, with ye usuall countenance and assistance of the Gentlemen here about: some whereof have already granted them May Poles, with other favours, and therefore we make it our humble request,

> That you will be pleased to Looke upon your own Towns with the same Kindnesse & furtherance upon this occasion, in confidence whereof wee humbly subscribe ourselves, yer humble servants and poore Tennants.

[1] 'England's Joy', p. 428.
[2] Clarkson, pp. 305-07.
[3] Cavendish, William, p. 227.
[4] Defoe, *Great Law*, p. 62.
[5] 'Stowe MSS, Petition'.

And if they shall be so happy (pardon our presumption to see you here), they will bee the better inabled once in their lives to bid you welcome to their ignorent pastime and Countrey mirthe.

For Charles's coronation on 14 April 1661 there was 'Musick, (particularly a stage of Morrice-dancers at the Maypole in the Strand) in the several places all along his Majesties passage'.[6] The newly erected maypole was over 120 feet high, and morris dancers had performed at its erection. A contemporary tract describes 'a Morice Dance finely deckt, with purple Scarfs, in their half-shirts, with a Taber and Pipe the antient Musick, and Danced round about the Maypole, after that Danced the rounds of their Liberty'.[7] The use of purple was a direct evocation of the royal connection. However, the Covent Garden barber Thomas Rugg was less appreciative. He witnessed the setting up of the maypole, and 'under it a knot of morris dancers, the worst that ever were'.[8] He may have been right: perhaps people had indeed forgotten the finer points of how to dance. The Royalist preacher Henry Newcome, travelling from Lancashire to London in 1660, confirmed that there had been a generation's suppression of dancing; he 'found May-poles in abundance as we came, and at Oakham I saw a morris-dance, which I had not seen of twenty years before'.[9] Samuel Pepys, too, commented in the same vein on 1 May 1663, when 'about 7 or 8 a-clock, homeward ... In my way in Leadenhall Street there was morris-dancing which I have not seen a great while'.[10]

The initial enthusiasm in communities across the country seems to have petered out. Anthony à Wood reported that in Oxford on 31 May 1660 and thereafter:[11]

This Holy Thursday the people of Oxon were soe violent for Maypoles in opposition to the Puritans that there was numbred 12 Maypoles besides 3 or 4 morrises, etc. But no opposition appearing afterwards, the rabble flagged in their zeal; and seldom after above 1 or 2 in a year.

Henry Newcome viewed the morris dancers more in sorrow than in enjoyment or anger. He added to his diary entry, 'It is a sad sign the hearts of the people are poorly employed when they can make a business of playing the fool as they do'.

There is indeed a dearth of records of actual events until the closing years of the century. Those that exist are of two kinds. There are some civic events, including Charles II's restoration, in which dancers were engaged. For the others we are mainly reliant on information from payments made to dancers encountered by the gentry, together with other indications that 'self-organized' morris dancers were in action. Figure 8.1 maps these as 'civic' or 'encounters' respectively during the reign of Charles II, and shows a continuing concentration of records from the south midlands.

The Salisbury Tailors' Guild received 5s when their set of morris dancers' coats was rented out to dancers from Downton in 1663, and their chamberlain was paid 6d in 1665 and 2s in 1667 for the use of the morris coats by the guild.[12] In 1685 a civic celebration in Wells, on the restoration of its civic charter, involved food and drink, trumpeters, ringers and morris dancers, who were paid 5s in a total expenditure of £15 5s.[13]

[6] Heath, p. 206.
[7] *Cities Loyalty*, p. 4.
[8] Rugg, p. 175.
[9] Newcome, 1:121.
[10] Pepys, 4:120.
[11] Wood, Anthony à, *Life*, 1:317.
[12] 'Tailors' Guild' (1631), ff. 102, 109; Haskins, p. 190.
[13] *Bath Chronicle*, 8 November 1866.

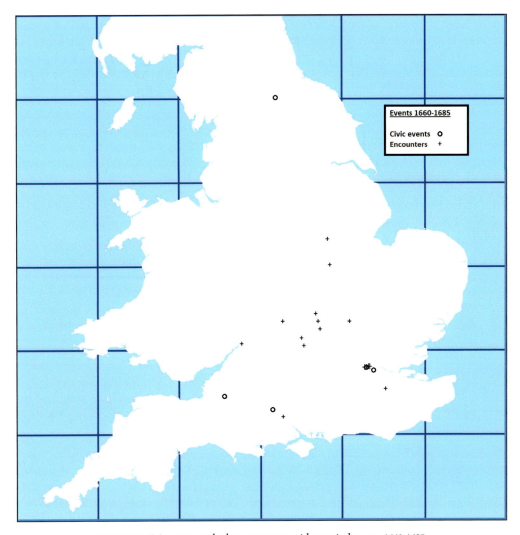

Figure 8.1: Civic events and other encounters with morris dancers, 1660-1685.

There are occasional records of payments to dancers by large households: 2s 6d to dancers at Belvoir Castle, Leicestershire on 30 May 1664; 6d to dancers in London on 9 June 1660; 1s to dancers at Frampton-on-Severn in 1674.[14] Hastings Ingram from Little Wolford gave morris dancers from Shipston-on-Stour 2s 6d when they visited on 7 June 1680 (Trinity Monday – very probably in connection with an ale).[15] Sir Richard Temple of Stowe (from whom the tenants had requested support for their Whitsun ale) was much more generous, giving morris dancers £1 at Buckingham fair day in 1680 and in 1681, and the following year 11s to the 'whitsunday Lordes'.[16]

The king's wife Catherine of Braganza also made generous payments of £1 to morris dancers on several occasions. In 1663 she gave money to some in Hyde Park on 25 June (the Thursday

---

[14] Manners, 4:542; Smith, J.R., p. 11; Clifford, John.
[15] Ingram, Hastings.

[16] 'Stowe MSS, Richard Temple, 3rd Bart., Ledger Book', ff. 55, 81; 'Stowe MSS, Richard Temple, 3rd Bart., Day book' [unfoliated].

in the week of Trinity Sunday). She next rewarded dancers on 23 and 24 July and 17 August, apparently at her residence, St James's Palace. It may be that the dancers were reacting to her generosity and specifically seeking her repeated patronage. In August 1663 she gave morris dancers in Tonbridge £2. The final record is from 10 July 1666 when she gave £1 to morris dancers at Sevenoaks in Kent.[17]

In justifying his Christmas spending at Claydon House in Buckinghamshire to his father, the young Edmund Verney claimed in 1665 that 'aussi nous avons eu Danceurs qu'on appelle Morice' ('we also had morris dancers'), though he does not say how much they were paid.[18] There were also morris dancers at Christmas at Wrest Park in Bedfordshire, home to the Earls of Kent. They were paid 5s on 20 December in 1672 and 1673.[19]

In 1679 Thomas Blount recorded the lamb ale (a variant on the Whitsun ale) at Kidlington in Oxfordshire, as a contemporary event:[20]

> *At Kidlington, in Oxfordshire, the custom is, that on Monday after Whitsun-week there is a fat live lamb provided, and the maids of the town, having their thumbs tied behind them, run after it and she that with her mouth takes and holds the lamb is declared the Lady of the Lamb, which being dressed, with the skin hanging on, is carried on a long pole before the lady and her companions to the green, attended with music, and a morisco dance of men, and another of women, where the rest of the day is spent in dancing, mirth and merry glee.*

Blount noted elsewhere that while he uses the term 'a morisco dance', 'The common people call it a Morris Dance'.[21] 'Kidlington' has often been taken to be an error for Kirtlington, four miles away, which maintained a lamb ale with morris dancers until the middle of the 19th century.[22] Blount's assertion that there were men's and women's morrises indicates a broadening of the understanding of what constituted a morris dance.

Fire had also gone from most of the polemics. New bishops were appointed and new visitation articles issued. One version of the new articles issued in 1662 asked 'Do you permit no Minstrels, no Moris-dancers, no Doggs, Hawks, or Hounds to be brought or come into your Church, to the disturbance of the Congregation?' This is from the Diocese of Chichester, but identical texts for that year survive from eight other dioceses. Only Durham added extra text to the sentence, 'but set your Sexton to keep them out, that the Congregation and the minister performing divine Service, or Preaching his Sermon, may not be disturbed by them?'[23] The articles were re-issued by some dioceses from time to time, the last to enquire about morris dancers being from Lincoln and Norwich in 1686.[24] They enquire only about dancers' presence within the church, and there is a sense that they are just going through the motions, based on past content, rather than reflecting real local concerns. Some articles were from dioceses with no records of morris dancing, for example Llandaff and St David's.[25] There are no records of presentments of morris dancers under any of these clauses.

A few polemicists did continue to fulminate. Thomas Hall in *Funebria Floræ, the Downfall of May-games* (1661) lamented that 'wee have those in our times that are mad on May-poles,

[17] Catherine of Braganza. I am grateful to Jameson Wooders for drawing these documents to my attention.
[18] Verney, Frances and Verney, 4:82.
[19] 'Lucas Archive, Account Book'; Grey, Anthony.
[20] Blount, *Tenures*, p. 1181.

[21] Blount, *Glossographia*, sig. CC3v.
[22] Dunlop.
[23] *V.A. Chichester* (1662), p. 13; *V.A. Durham*, p. 12.
[24] *V.A. Lincoln* (1686), p. 12; *Articles of Visitation*, p. 15.
[25] *V.A. Llandaff*, p. 10; *V.A. St David's*, p. 10.

Morrice-dancing, Drinking Healths on their Knees, yea in their hats (as in the Universitie by Scholars, &c.) doating on old, superstitious, prophane customes' and that the return of May games had brought in 'Ignorants, Atheists, Papists, Drunkards, Swearers, Swash-bucklers, Maid-marrions, Morrice-dancers, Maskers, Mummers, May-pole stealers, Health-drinkers, together with a rascally rout of Fidlers, Fools, Fighters, Gamesters, Whore-masters, Lewd-men, Light-women, Contemners of Magistracy, affronters of Ministery, rebellious to Masters, disobedient to Parents, mis-spenders of time, abusers of the creature, &c.'[26] Some looked backwards: Samuel Clarke recalled the divine retribution visited upon his father's flock at Oundle and Wolston for their morris dancing some 40 years previously.[27] (Nearly 40 years later William Turner's review of divine judgements rehashed the same anecdotes.)[28] The theologian Richard Baxter recalled his youth at Eaton Constantine in Shropshire, when 'sometimes shows or uncouth spectacles have been their sports at certain seasons of the year, and sometimes morrice-dancings and sometimes stage-plays and sometimes wakes and revels; and all men observed that these were the times of the most flagitious crimes... Sometimes the morrice dancers would come into the Church in all their linnen, and scarfs, and antick dresses, with morrice-bells jingling at their legs. And as soon as common prayer was read did haste out presently to their play again.'[29]

Another cleric, John Gaule, fretted over the immoderation of 'Feasting, and drinking of Healths, our Musick, and Pageantry, our May poles, and Garlands, and Morrice-dancers, and ringing of Bells, our Drummes, and Trumpets, vollyes of Shot, and shoutings'.[30] Thomas Taylor asked in 1697 'shall Drunkards, Sweaters, Morrice-Dancers, Stage-players, Gamesters of all sorts, and Hypocrites of all sorts, have liberty to meet together to dishonour [God's] Name, without danger and fear?'[31] Taylor was by this time a Quaker who retained the strongly Puritan views of his youth.

None of these tracts generated the same controversy that had accompanied those of the first half of the century. Most of the polemicists were shaking their heads at the immorality of the times rather than calling for action against such practices.

———

The sense of a return to the old ways was reflected in the verse of the day. Abiel Borfet wrote of Charles's triumphal return, 'His enterance, though contriv'd with costly Art, / Denying not the Morrice-Dance a part'.[32] Celebration extended to the victory over Puritanism. The anonymous author of the collection *Rome Rhym'd to Death* observed:[33]

> *The Sabbath-breakers Sins are less by far,*
> *Than the offences of Tub-preachers are.*
> ...
> *These Meetings are more dangerous by far,*
> *Than Bull-baits, Bear-baits or Cock-fightings are:*
> *Stage-plays and Morrice-dances, Masks and Shows,*
> *Wakes, May-games, Puppet-plays, and such as those*
> *More harmless are; for all their Mocks and Jears*
> *Are innocent, if but compar'd with theirs.*

[26] Hall, Thomas, *Funebria*, pp. 3, 19.
[27] Clarke, Samuel, pp. 160-61, 165.
[28] Turner, pp. 19-20.
[29] Baxter, p. 444.
[30] Gaule, *Admonition*, p. 7.
[31] Taylor, Thomas, pp. 139-40.
[32] Borfet, p. 2.
[33] 'Informers Lecture', pp. 102-03.

Figure 8.2: 'Cromwell Pypeth unto Fairfax' (in Edmund Goldsmid, Explanatory Notes of a Pack of Playing Cards, Temp Charles II, *9. Edinburgh: E. & G. Goldsmid, 1886).*

There were more subtle ways of rubbing in the rout of Puritanism. In a pack of cards issued shortly after the Restoration, the three of hearts depicts 'Cromwell pypeth to Fairfax'. Fairfax had been Cromwell's commander-in-chief during the Civil War but opposed the regicide and later supported the Restoration.[34] The image on the playing card (Figure 8.2) is a direct parody of the cover of *Kemp's Nine Daies Wonder* (Figure 6.2 on p. 85).

William Cavendish's wife, Lady Margaret, wrote several plays including *The Lady Contemplation*, in which the farmer's wife complains about her virtuous maid (helpfully called Virtue):[35]

> I never was merry since she was in my house, the May-pole is down since she came... And the Towns Green is a Meadow, and the poor Bag-pipers cheeks are fallen into a Consumption, hardly wind to speak withall; the Morris-dancers bells are silenc'd, and their crosse garters held superstitious, idolatrous, and profane; the May Lord and his Lady depos'd, and the Hobby-horse is forgotten; nay the Whitson-Lord and Lady are banish'd, Merry Wakes abolish'd, and the poor Ale-wives beggar'd.

Like her husband's recommendation to Charles II, this contains every element of the morris dance as part of a Whitsun ale from 50 or more years before. Much of *The Lady Contemplation* is about appropriate behaviour for stratified social classes, and in *Youth's Glory, and Death's Banquet* Lady Margaret returned to this theme: Lady Sanspareille argues for the benefits that theatres provide, and declares 'shall Kings, Princes or noble Persons, that dances, sings, or plays on Musick, or presents themselves in Masks, be thought, or called Dancers, or Fidlers, Morris-dancers, Stage-players, or the like, as in their masking attire: No'.[36] A noble did not become a mercenary actor simply by playing a role. On the other hand, outward appearance was important in signifying rank. Thomas D'Urfey's *Madam Fickle* (1677) picked up the theme: Sir Arthur is upbraided because 'methinks your Cloaths are not made according to Mode', and the speaker's companion adds 'I took him for a Morrice-Dancer'.[37] In Aphra Behn's *The Rover*, Blunt, a country squire in Naples, is revealed sitting in shirt and drawers, having been tricked: he declares 'a Pox on this Tayler tho, for not bringing home the Clothes I bespoke', and putting on old rusty sword, and buff belt, declares 'how like a Morrice-Dancer I am Equipt'. This is

---

[34] Goldsmid.
[35] Cavendish, Margaret, 'Second Part', p. 237 (IV.xxv).
[36] Cavendish, Margaret, 'Youths Glory', p. 127 (I.iii).
[37] D'Urfey, p. 27 (III.i).

a rare example of a sword being associated, but again it uses the morris-dancer analogy to demonstrate the incongruity of dressing out of one's class.[38]

Most poets returned to the existing tropes, such as morris as the epitome of empty frippery. Charles Cotton metaphorically chided Bacchus for being 'More like a Morris-dancer far, / Than any Son of Jupiter',[39] while Samuel Butler suggested in 1680 that empty oratorical rhetoric was 'like a Morrice-dancer drest with Bells, / Only to serve for Noise, and nothing else'.[40] Those continuing to press for moral sobriety used similar analogies. One writer warned that the last judgement 'Is not a May-game, nor like Morris-dance'.[41] The writer Edward Waterhouse echoed the phrase used by Sir Henry Wotton a quarter of a century previously, when he wrote that 'dangers formidable, like Spanish Armadoes and Invasions, he [God] changes into Morris Dances upon the Waves of dislustre'.[42]

Morris as innocent country amusement continued to be another favourite theme in literature. The well known ballad *Arthur of Bradly,* of uncertain date but most probably post-Restoration Stuart, has, in the earliest known of several variants of the lyrics:[43]

> *The chiefest youths in the Parish*
> *Come dancing in a Morris,*
> *With Country Gambols flouncing,*
> *Country Wenches trouncing,*
> *Dancing with mickle pride,*
> *Every man his wench by his side,*

Dancers were used by Maurice Atkins in his mock-heroic version of the Aeneid to typify country sport, providing a detailed picture of costume, music and the dance:[44]

> *A sort of Revellers were seen*
> *In holland Drawers, lac't Crevats,*
> *Hair tied with ribbands, but no Hats,*
> *Who wearing on their feet light pumps*
> *Trac't 'long the path with ambling jumps:*
> *One bore a kind of little Drum*
> *And fumpt it with finger and thumb,*
> *Which made the bells that round it were*
> *Sound like those at forehorses ear;*
> *Ask what they were, the vulgar answers,*
> *They were (as they call 'em) Morrice-dancers.*

The masque tradition continued to present morris as pastoral. In John Aubrey's *The Country Revel* 'enter country fellowes & countrey wenches & the Melancholy shepherd & shepherdess, then the Gypsies and Ld & Lady of the Maypole ... A Morisco-dance'.[45] In William Davenant's *The Rivals* (1668), an adaptation of *Two Noble Kinsmen* which itself incorporated the morris from Beaumont's *Masque of the Inner Temple and Gray's Inn*, countrymen dance a morris with Maid Marion, hobby horse and taborer, and referencing the fool's ladle.[46]

---

[38] Behn, p. 63 (IV.iii).
[39] Cotton, p. 126.
[40] Butler, p. 224.
[41] *Alarm*, p. 59.
[42] Waterhouse, *Gentlemans Monitor*, p. 164.

[43] 'Arthur of Bradly', p. 127.
[44] Atkins, pp. 68-69.
[45] Aubrey, f. 18 (III.iv).
[46] Davenant, pp. 266-68 (Act III).

Thomas Duffett liked to parody the works of other dramatists. His *Psyche Debauch'd* of 1678 parodied Thomas Shadwell's *Psyche*, and has a masque in which 'Enter a Countrey Crouder [fidler], followed by a Milk-maid with her Payl dressed up as on May-day:—After them a company of Morris-dancers, a Sylvan, and a Dryad.'[47] The milkmaids' May Day was an annual solicitation custom whose development from the 17th century on has been described by Roy Judge.[48] Dancing was associated with the custom but it was not at this time associated with morris dancing. Duffett's incorporation of their celebration into the scene is an indication of the blurring of morris dancing's associations at the edges, attaching it to other popular customs.

John Leanerd's *The Country Innocence* of 1677 was not a masque but a comic play. Nonetheless, its title suggests the same imagery. In fact Leanerd plagiarizes *The Country Girle* from 1647. The play calls for six morris dancers, and fidlers. This time the morris dancers are not explicitly female, but there is to be a dancing match between 'all the Maids of our Town Edmonton, and all the mad Wenches of Waltam'; the heroine, Gillian, gives her instruction, 'Fidlers lead the way, and Wenches follow your Leader', followed by the stage direction 'Ex[eunt] Fidlers playing, Gillian and the Morris-dancers following dancing', strongly implying a female set of dancers.[49]

In his poem *The Florists Vade-mecum* Samuel Gilbert emphasised the 'country bumpkin' aspect, writing that those who 'have not seen the Alamodes of France, / Swear none so gay, as at a Morrice dance'.[50] An early musicologist, John Wallis, suggested that because 'rusticks' did not hear much music, 'a little Musick will do great Feats. As we find at this Day, a fiddle or a Bag-pipe, among a company of Country fellows and Wenches (who never knew better) or at a County Morrice-Dance, will make them skip and shake their Heels notably ... they flock about a Ballad-Singer in a Fair, or the Morrice-Dancers at a Whitsund Ale.'[51]

It is a small step from the 'rustic' to seeing morris dancing as part of low life in general. In *Clod-Pate's Ghost* Justice Clod-Pate berates his clerk for suggesting he might 'quit the Gentile and Laudable Employ of a Justices Clerk to run rambling up and down the Country, and be the Buffoon to all the Wakes, May-games, Morrice-Dances, and Whitson-Ales'.[52] A character in the journal *Heraclitus Ridens* is excoriated because he 'might have taught the young one to have more wit, [rather than to have] brought his Morrice-Dancers to Town again, with their Bells and Bables'.[53] In its rival journal *Democritus Ridens* some 'Protestant morris dancers' sing a ballad about 'The pope's morris-dancers', which combines the associations of scurrilousness and popery:[54]

> *The first who began his bells for to gingle,*
> *Was a frisking old Piper who us'd to dance single;*
> *He long shook his heels to make our ears tingle.*
> > *Frick awhile Roger.*
> *But he pip'd and he danc'd, and he made a foul clutter,*
> *Till up flew his heels, and he fell in the Gutter;*
> *There lies the Popes Tumbler, the People did mutter.*
> > *Rise again Towzer.*
> *A dancing Baboon, yclep'd Heraclitus,*

[47] Duffett, Psyche, p. 6 (sc. i).
[48] Judge, *Jack-in-the-Green*, pp. 3-9.
[49] Leanerd, pp. 10-18 (Act I).
[50] Gilbert, p. 92.
[51] Wallis, pp. 298-99.
[52] Smith, Francis, p. 2.
[53] *Heraclitus*.
[54] *Democritus*.

With Tabor and Pipe began to delight us,
Till with his foul Earnest he thought to affright us.
> *Pull off your Vizzard.*
With Ribbons, and Gewgaws, and Bawbles well drest;
With sing-songs and Ballads, though none of the best,
He brings in his Monkey to dance, called Jest.
> *Higgledy Piggledy.*

...

Of the Popes Cause they are the Advancers,
They shew you their Fiddles, but hide their Snaphancers [pistols],
Though jingling Church-bells, they're Rome's Morris-dancers.

Thomas Tryon, painting a utopian vision of a vegetarian society, wrote that there would be 'no Festival Days, that serve chiefly to call the violent Rabble together; nor no Whitson-Ale, or Morris-dancing'.[55] In 1694 William Burnaby translated the classical writer Titus Petronius's 'Pantomimi chorum, non patris familiae triclinium crederes' (*Satyricon*, 31:7; literally, 'the chorus for an actor in a pantomime') as 'You'd have taken it for a morris dancers hall, not the table of a person of quality.[56] In *The History of Reynard the Fox*, a loose English translation made at the end of the century from a German text, Reynard makes free with hospitality, 'entertaining lewd Fellows, as Fidlers, Morrice-dancers, and the like'.[57]

The ballad *The Jovial May-pole Dancers, or, The Merry Morris* (c. 1690) contains no direct reference to the dance apart from the title, but is illustrated by a woodcut illustrating a circle dance of mixed couples dancing around not a maypole but a piper (Figure 8.3).[58] The woodcut is already quite worn, suggesting it had been in use for some time. The picture captures the fluidity of morris, maypoles and social dancing in the public mind.

Many of the travellers of the period, reporting on the customs of foreign lands, said they saw dances 'like morris dances'. These loose analogies do not really tell us much about perceptions of the English morris, except that the allusions presume a familiarity with it on the part of the reader. De Rochefort's *The History of the Caribby-islands* described 'some who anoint their bodies with a glewy oil, and blow on that the downe or smallest Feathers of divers Birds... and it were a pleasant sight to see a company of these Morris-dancers'.[59] The diplomat Sir Paul Rycaut

Figure 8.3: Woodcut from The Jovial May-pole Dancers, or, The Merry Morris. *[London]: Printed for J. Deacon, [c. 1690].*

[55] Tryon, p. 457.
[56] Burnaby, p. 55.
[57] *History of Reynard*, p. 157.
[58] *Jovial May-pole Dancers.*
[59] Rochefort, p. 256.

described the dervishes of the Ni'matullāhī order in the Ottoman Empire 'who taking hands Dance in a Morris'.[60] Occasionally they refer back to English practice, as, for example, the translation of Nicolas Sanson's description of the customs of Persian women 'richly attired, having about them costly Jewels, Pendants, Rings, having about their legs Bells, like Morris-dancers'.[61] John Ogilby's account of Persia described how, in the Festival of Roses in Isfahan, the servants 'Dance from Street to Street with great delight, and use several postures like our Morris-Dancers'.[62] Closer to home, Antoine de Brunel may have had the etymology in mind when he wrote of the Corpus Christi processions in Spain (he claims that the Moors introduced 'publick sports' there), describing 'a procession, whose first ranks are intermixed with several Hoboies, Tabors, and Castanettas, a great many habited in party coloured clothes, skip and dance as extrava[g]antly as at a Morrice'.[63]

The conceptual link being made between Moors and morris dancing is evidenced in Elkanah Settle's *The Empress of Morocco*, which sets the scene with 'a Moorish Dance ... presented by Moors in Several Habits, who bring in an artificial Palm-tree, about which they dance to several antick Instruments of Musick'. The published play contained illustrations engraved by Walter Dolle, one of which depicts this scene (Figure 8.4). The dancers carry tambourines and wear short tunics and conical hats. They are also in two ranks of three dancers, an arrangement which Dolle perhaps adopted from encounters with English morris dancers.[64] The palm tree stands in for a maypole. The following year, when Thomas Duffett came out with another of his parodies, also called *The Empress of Morocco*, he explicitly introduced morris men to represent the Moorish dancers. The dance in the play is not explicitly Moorish or morris, but the *dramatis personae* include 'Morris-dancers, Tapsters, Gypsies, Tinkers, and other Attendants', and there is 'a Heathen Dance ... presented by Tinkers and Jack-puddings, who bring in an artificial broad-spreading broom about which they dance to Drum-stick and Kettle, Tongs and Key, Morish, Timbrel and Salt-box, &c.'[65]

One more piece of verse should be noticed as the earliest use of the word 'morris' in the blackly humorous sense of 'to hang', making an analogy between a hanged body jerking on the end of a rope and the movements of morris dancers. The ballad *A New Touch of the Times* (1688) declared:[66]

> *As for the Lord Chancellor that climb'd up so high,*
> *He must climb higher before that he dye,*
> *That is to Tyburn, for to take a swing,*
> *And there dance the Morris in a Hempen string.*

———————————

At the same time as direct experience of morris dancing as practised before the Commonwealth was diminishing among the lettered classes after the Restoration, the concept was becoming more fluid. Starting with the publications of John Playford at the height of the Commonwealth, 'morris' dances began to appear in music and dance manuals. The occurrence of 'morris dances' in such publications reaches prominence in the later Stuart period, but spills over at each end. Apart from a couple of earlier examples, the heyday begins in 1651 and continues into the first third of the 18th century. It is useful to consider this extended period as a whole.

---

[60] Rycaut, p. 143.
[61] Sanson, [2nd sequence], p. 260.
[62] Ogilby, p. 72.
[63] Brunel, pp. 83-84.
[64] Settle, p. 13 and facing plate.
[65] Duffett, *Empress*, sig. B2v.
[66] 'New Touch', p. 113.

Figure 8.4: Moorish dance (in Elkanah Settle, The Empress of Morocco, *plate facing p. 13. London: Printed for William Cadema, 1673).*

Some tunes for 'morrises' or 'moriscos' had been written down in earlier years. There is a 'Morisco Gallyard' in the Osborn Commonplace Book dating from the mid to late 16th century.[67] Christopher Page has characterized this as 'seemingly designed to resist any but a vigorous and raking performance' to 'capture a wild and supposedly "Moorish" abandon, for this "morisco" galliard appears to be no simple Morris dance'.[68] There is a 'King's Morisco' in the *Fitzwilliam Virginal Book*,[69] which was published as 'The Kings Morisck' in the collection *Parthenia In-violata* around 1614.[70] Apart from these there are no less than eleven 'Moriscos' in Playford's 1662 publication *Courtly Masquing Ayres*, by six different composers,[71] and five (including a 'New' and two 'Scotch' moriscos) in his *Apollo's Banquet* of 1670.[72] There is little now to tell us what makes a morisco a morisco: sarabands and galliards are in triple time, and allemandes in duple, and there are known characteristics of the associated dance; but the moriscos offer no common thread. The 'Morisco Gallyard' is a typical galliard in triple time and the use of the word 'morisco' may not be significant. 'King's Morisco' is a complex piece with passages of varying lengths, in $\frac{2}{2}$ time. Playford's pieces are simpler, and *Apollo's Banquet* also expressly contains 'old country dances'. The measures for these are often 16 or 32 bars (but this is not distinctive), the time signatures mainly $\frac{4}{4}$ with a few in $\frac{3}{2}$ time; but his 'New Morisco' has a more complex four-part 38-bar structure. The moriscos are found in books and manuscripts in the European tradition of courtly music. *Apollo's Banquet* straddles this and Playford's country-dance works. The moriscos, however, appear to have little to do with the domestic culture of morris dancing.

When it comes to tunes entitled 'morrises' as opposed to 'moriscos' we know of 21 tune notations up to 1735, after which dance manuals stopped including 'morris' dances as the fashions in dancing moved on. Six of the tunes have associated dance notations, and there is also one dance notation lacking a tune.

Until Playford, most sources for these tunes are in undated manuscripts, so we have only an approximate idea of when they were written down, and it may be that some of them did not have much public circulation. The earliest are tablatures for lute, 'Stanes Morris' and 'The Moris', both from around the end of the 16th century.[73] 'Stanes Morris' was later printed by Playford in the first edition of his dancing manual, but these two inhabit the same milieu as the courtly moriscos. Another source of early 'morris' tunes are the masques. 'The French Morris' is found in Sir Nicholas Le Strange's collection of masque music,[74] and in her study of masque music Jean Knowlton assigns it to Ben Jonson's 1622 masque *Time Vindicated*.[75] The same collection includes 'The Maypole', which is the same tune as 'The King's Morisco' in the *Fitzwilliam Virginal Book*. Knowlton assigns it to the *Masque of the Inner Temple and Gray's Inn*.[76] This fluidity in the title reflects the general linking in the popular mind of morris, maypoles and rustic mirth.

The composer Giles Farnaby's 'Kempes Moris' was first known as 'Muscadin'. Richard Marlow has suggested that 'presumably the ... tune frequently accompanied his [Kemp's] dancing during this journey'; it is much more likely that the tune was re-named from 'Muscadin' honorifically after Kemp's dance.[77]

[67] 'Morisco Gallyard'.
[68] Page, p. 122.
[69] Maitland, Squire and Winogron, 'King's Morisco'.
[70] Hole, p. [4].
[71] *Courtly Masquing Ayres*, nos 114, 152, 188, 193, 206, 222, 226, 230, 267, 296, 298.
[72] *Apollo's Banquet*, nos 22, 79, 80, 108, 109.

[73] Spencer, Robert, 'Stanes Morris', f. 9v; Spencer, Robert, 'Moris', f. 8.
[74] Sabol, p. 237.
[75] Knowlton, 1:289.
[76] Knowlton, 1:288.
[77] Farnaby, pp. 96-97, 143.

Where they do not have a distinctive title, the musical notations for moriscos simply entitle them 'A Morisco', suggesting that 'morisco' is a generic term for a type of tune. The non-distinctive morris tunes, on the other hand, are usually '*The* Morris (dance)' – as if there is only one dance, although the tunes so entitled are quite diverse. In addition to 'The Moris' mentioned above, there are two tunes (one attributed to William Byrd) called 'The Morris' in a manuscript of English tunes compiled *c.* 1635 and held at the Bibliothèque Nationale in Paris,[78] and 'The Morice Dance' in the *Cromwell/Matthewes Gittar Book* from *c.* 1685.[79]

The earliest datable notation of a dance is in the first edition of Playford's *The English Dancing Master* in 1651. (Subsequent editions dropped the 'English' from the title.) Playford was a Royalist, as witness the presence in his *A Musicall Banquet* not only of 'Prince Rupert's Morrice' but also 'Prince Rupert's March' and 'When the K[ing] Enjoyes [his own again]'.[80] The last of these was written in 1643 in support of Charles I. All these titles evince strong support for King Charles despite being published during the Commonwealth. The dance in *The English Dancing Master* is named for the established tune 'Stanes Morris'.[81] It gives simple dance instructions for couples, 'longways for as many as will', that is, as many male-female pairs as want to take part (Figure 8.5). The figures of the dance are described rather than the steps or hand movements, apart from the instructions to the man to 'Take her by the hand' and 'Turn her halfe about, holding both hands, and salute her'. Despite the appellation of this dance as a 'morris', the figures do not have any characteristics distinct from the instructions for the other country dances in the book.

The tune 'Stanes Morris' and its dance were also included in the next edition of the book (1652), and the tune appeared in the third edition (1657/65), which, however, lacked dance notations. Dances termed 'morrises' then disappear until the third supplement to the eighth edition (1689), when 'Maids Morris' appears (and in all subsequent editions to *c.* 1728) (Figure 8.6).[82] Again, it is 'longways for as many as will' and is a straightforward social dance, a 'country dance'. This term had been in use for several decades by the 1650s,[83] but became especially

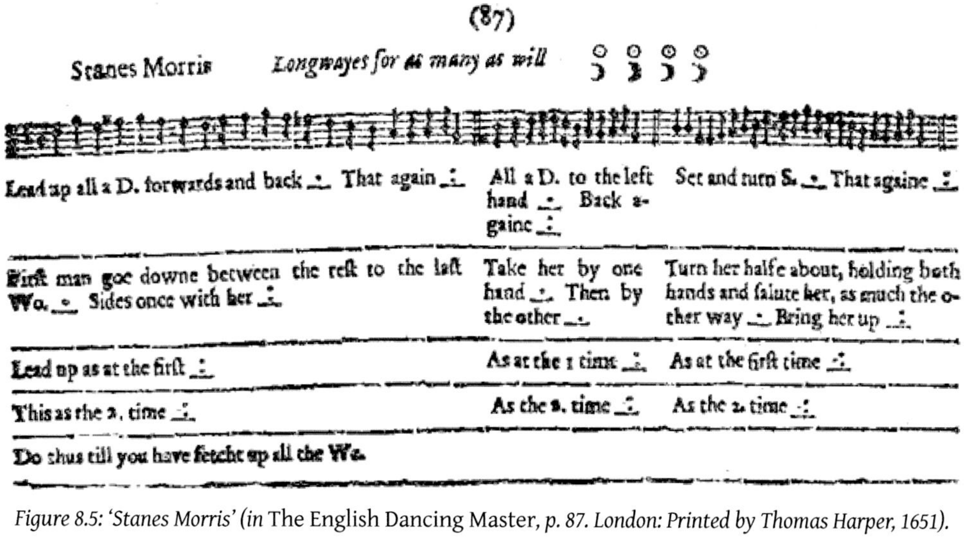

Figure 8.5: 'Stanes Morris' (in The English Dancing Master, p. 87. London: Printed by Thomas Harper, 1651).

---

[78] Maas, p. 54; Byrd.
[79] 'Elizabeth Cromwell', f. 5.
[80] *Musicall Banquet*, pp. 4-6.

[81] 'Stanes Morris'.
[82] 'Maids Morris'.
[83] 'Country Dance' (OED).

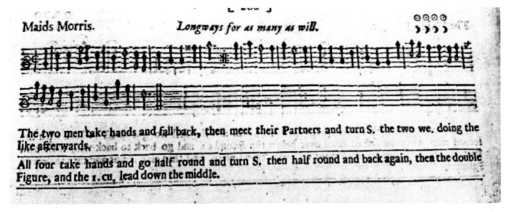

Figure 8.6: 'Maids Morris' (in The Dancing Master, *7th ed., 3rd supplement, p. 1. London: Printed by E. Jones, 1689).*

widespread thereafter. It describes dances by sets of several pairs of mixed couples, in which they move with the other pairs in the set sequentially. The emphasis is on the figures traced over the ground, rather than on particular kinds of step. These dances were popular with the developing middling and upper classes.

In defending the traditions of the Inns of Court in 1663, Edward Waterhouse specifically distinguished country dances from morris dancing, writing, 'With us we have onely *French* dancing and Country dancing used by the best rank of people. *Morris-dancing* is an exercise that the loose and vile sort only use, and that onely in faires and meetings of lewdness'.[84] This again raises the question of the extent to which the dances in the manuals are morris dances, or simply dances which use the word 'morris' loosely, with no further connotation of a particular kind of dance. 'Morris' dances of mixed couples had been known on the stage since Beaumont's 1613 *Masque of the Inner Temple and Gray's Inn* but these usually had allegorical overtones, and Anne Daye has proposed that the tune for Beaumont's dance is the 'Graies Inne Maske' in *The English Dancing Master*, where it is not designated a 'morris'.[85]

The 17th edition of *The Dancing Master* introduced 'The Fidler's Morris' in 1721.[86] Towards the end of its publishing life, extra volumes of *The Dancing Master* were issued, and volume III, published in 1727, contained both 'Scotch' and 'French' morrises.[87] All of these are standard country dances, longways for as many as will. So too was the last known such dance, the 'Welsh Morris Dance' published by J. Walsh in 1735.[88] There seems no rationale for the attribution of national origin to these dances, except perhaps for the 'French Morris'. This uses the tune to a different dance, a couple dance from 1716 devised by Francis Isaac, an English dance teacher who had trained in France and taught the highest echelons of English society. His expertise in the French style was recognised by his frequently being styled 'Monsieur' Isaac. He published a dance called 'The Morris' in 1716 in Beauchamps-Feuillet notation, a complex French method primarily used to notate dance duets (Figure 8.7).[89] Jennifer Thorp has considered the dance in depth and concludes that it is not a morris dance in any real sense, but also suggests that Isaac may have been displaying his credentials as a good Protestant (he was sometimes suspected of popery) and that the title alludes

84 Waterhouse, *Fortescutus*, p. 534.
85 Daye, 'Morris', p. 28.
86 'Fidler's Morris'.

87 *Dancing Master*, pp. 19, 195.
88 'Welsh Morris Dance'.
89 Isaac.

Figure 8.7: The first page of notation of Mr Isaac's 'The Morris'
(Image courtesy of Vaughan Williams Memorial Library, QL.5.4).

punningly to Colonel Maurice van Nassau, who brought hotfoot to London the news of the Jacobite defeat at Preston in November 1715.[90] It was in the French noble style of courtly dances, and its complexity can be gauged from the transcription in John Forrest's work, which analyses its 80 different dance moves.[91] The publication was still being advertised for sale eight years later.[92]

One country dance called 'The Maurice Dance' survives in an undated seventeenth-century manuscript in the British Library, on a sheet together with three other dances, 'Lavena', 'Newcastle – a round daunce for eight only', and 'Put up thy Dagger'.[93] The first two of these occur in the first edition of *The English Dancing Master*; the tune of 'Put up thy Dagger' can be found in the *Fitzwilliam Virginal Book*.[94] This suggests a date for the manuscript early in the second half of the century. There are only dance instructions, no tune. The instructions are:

> *Lead all ye Mates round ye Roome.*
>
> *1 ffig: The 1 & 2d Man meete the 1 & 2d woaman & passe through them to ye contrary sides & soe faces about then ye 1 & 2d Cu: take hands & meete each other then let goe hands & turne round all 4 single; then ye 1 man takes ye 2d man by ye right hand, & soe also ye 1 woaman & ye 2d woa: & turne {th}eir places & so caper, then doe ye same each with his mate & caper againe. Doe this all along.*
>
> *2d ffig: Th 1 Cu: cast off & goe downe into ye 2d place, whilest ye 2d Cu: lead up between them into ye 1 place & there change places one with another still holding hands; then ye 2d Cu: being in ye 1 place cast of & goe downe as ye first Cu: did before whilst ye 1 Cu: doe as ye 2d Cu: did before then ye 1 & 2d man take right hands & change places as in ye first fig: ye 1 & 2d woemen ye same at ye same time; then each change with his mate as in ye first fig: Doe this all along.*
>
> *3 ffig: The 1 & 2d men take hands, ye 1 & 2d woemen ye same; & fall back from each other, then meete & change places each with his mate; then ye 1 Cu: cast of & goe downe into ye 2d place whilst ye 2d Cu: goe up into ye first place betweene them, then ye 1 & 2d men ioyne both hands, & soe ye 1 & 2d woemen & meete each other slipping one foote before ye other;*
>
> *then slip apart againe ye men from ye woemen still holding hands, & soe Caper, then take hands each man with his mate, & change places with them then caper. Doe this all along.*

This is undoubtedly a mixed-couple country dance. However, the introductory circuit of the room suggests a ceremonial entry, and there are two specific instructions about the kinds of steps to do: there are 'capers' in the first and third figures, and in the third, pairs of women meet 'slipping one foote before ye other'. Morris dancers were often described as 'capering' in earlier texts, and in later times capers were certainly a specific step used in morris dances. The manuscript might be seen as a missing link between the morris and country dances.

Beyond the dance manuals, there were other indications of the nature of morris dances in the ballroom. A song from 1675 describes a dance by eight women, ostensibly at Brewers' Hall in London, at 'Mr. Young's ball', 13 April 1674. The setting is opulent (the Brewers being a livery company, and the hall new built after the Great Fire of 1666) but these are 'country girls':[95]

---

90 Thorp.
91 Forrest, pp. 386-91.
92 *Evening Post*, 12 March 1724.
93 'Maurice Daunce'.

94 *English Dancing Master*, pp. 59, 77; Maitland, Squire and Winogron, 'Put up Thy Dagger'.
95 Author of Westminster Drollery, 'Song'.

Some pretty Country Girls there were
Within an Arbour sitting:
Who when they did the Piper hear
They then left off their knitting
One bid him play
the Irish Hay
And th'other little Norris
At last they all
Both great and small
Did bid'em play the morris.
Their dress was tight, with wascoats white,
And well dyed Petticoats too;
And had you seen 'em on that Night
You think 'em pretty Coats too:
Their Coiffes were new,
And croft-cloaths too:
I'le tell you more then that too,
To keep 'em from
The burning Sun,
Each had a new Straw Hat too.
First lively Sm::: began the Dance
And humour'd it compleatly:
Then pretty Mu::: D: did advance,
Who danc'd all things neatly:
Brisk So:::i: then,
Did follow in,
And kept her measures duly;
And pretty C:::
That airy spark,
Did likewise dance it truly.
Then th'other lively Cl::: went on,
And danc'd with strength and vigour:
And pretty little Tr:::h:: then,
Did keep both time and figure:
Sweet Dal::: then
Did credit win,
To see her was a pleasure:
Young Sp::: too
She well did do,
Who danc'd good time and measure.
Thus have you heard the Morris, and
The Lass that did begin it
And how they march'd up hand in hand
And fixt within a minnit
Then everyone
When time was done
Did make their Curchyes gravely
Although so young
Yet all the throng
Did say, they did it bravely.

Figure 8.8: Three Morris Dancers trade token, c.1650 (Image © Museum of London, NN18007).

Figure 8.9: G. Barrett, The Three Morrice Dancers *[etching, c 1795] (Image © British Library, Maps K.Top.27.33.1).*

The imagery is strongly reminiscent of the all-female dance in *The Country Girle*, whose description emphasised the dancers' femininity. The 'arbour' suggests the bower of a Whitsun ale. There may be a satirical agenda here, now lost to us. The use of obscured names (e.g., 'Tr:::h::') was a common device to forestall accusations of libel. On the other hand, the song does not appear to be scurrilous or defamatory in tone. The following song in the collection is 'The Little Children's Figure Dance, at the Same Ball' and uses the same device.[96] It may be just what it implies, an affectionately humorous representation of events involving real people at an actual ball, and an all-female morris. This was five years before Thomas Blount's assertion of women morris dancers at Kidlington, noted earlier.

The 'Three Morris Dancers' inn in the Old Change in London was a popular venue as a meeting place and a venue in which to transact business, or recover lost or stolen goods, from the middle of the 17th century until it was pulled down at the beginning of the 19th. (Sometimes these meetings verged on the eccentric, as the society that met there every Monday 'to suppress the unlawful and slavish Practice of Shaving and Combing Perukes on the Lord's Day'.)[97] The owner in the mid 17th century, John Lisle, issued trade tokens for use at the inn depicting three male morris dancers in diverse poses, wearing pointed hats and with some indication of bells (Figure 8.8).

[96] Author of Westminster Drollery, 'Little Children's Figure Dance'.
[97] *Daily Post*, 19 November 1725.

The inn sign, on the other hand, depicted two male dancers and one female dancer, who is leaping or being helped into the air (Figure 8.9). If anything, the costumes are even earlier than Jacobean, and the image may be copied from a much older source, repurposed post-Restoration to match the contemporary image of morris dancing in the context of the country dances. Even the conical hats may add to this. The etching was made by G. Barrett in 1795. A version is reproduced by Jacob Larwood in *The History of Signboards*. He dates it to *c.* 1668, though Bryant Lillywhite has suggested that stylistically it is Jacobean.[98]

Figure 8.10: Morris dancers (in Randle Holme, The Academy of Armory, iii:[40]. Chester: For the Author, 1688).

One other image deserves notice. *The Academy of Armory* (1688) by Randle Holme of Chester began life ostensibly as a book of heraldry reproducing armorial devices, but became more of a wide-ranging idiosyncratic encyclopaedia. Many of the supposed armorial devices are fanciful, including one showing two morris dancers (Figure 8.10). Holme describes them thus:[99]

> He beareth Argent, two Morice Dancers in their Leaping, Dancing, or Fantastiek postures, variously cloathed, with Handkerchers in their hands, and Bells at their Caps, Shoulders, Knees Elbows, Or. Now some hold that to name Morrice-Dancers, is as much as to name all that I have before said, because they are ever drawn and set forth in such antick Dresses and Postures.

Holme says that dance movements, bells, handkerchiefs (which are held in the hands) and the hats are enough to identify them as morris dancers. One hat is conical, as in the inn sign. An earlier reference to such hats occurs in the pre-Commonwealth *The Masque of the Gentlemen of the Foure Honourable Societies, or Innes of Court, c.* 1633, in which Jollity enters 'trick'd like a Morise-dancer, with Scarfes and Napkins, his Hat fashioned like a Cone, with a little fall'.[100] Holme is silent about the fool with ass's ears at the foot of the illustration.

The diversification in styles of dancing in different geographical areas and in the perception of what was 'morris dancing' developed during this period. It becomes clear that when people describe or comment on morris dancing there is no longer a common understanding of what image that may conjure up.

The relative paucity of records of morris dancing after the Restoration continued through the time of the later Stuarts. Most of the evidence comes from the south midlands in the

---

[98] Larwood and Hotten, pl. 18 (after p. 480); Lillywhite, pp. 577-78.

[99] Holme, 3:[40], 169.
[100] Nelson and Elliott, p. 579.

form of household and personal account books and diaries. This may reflect the situation on the ground – that morris dancing continued to be practised in that area more widely than it did elsewhere – or it may be a consequence of the fact that this area has been more comprehensively researched than the others. The resurgence of records from other areas that we shall find from the latter part of the 18th century may indicate that dancing continued to be widely practised in these areas in the intervening period, or may be evidence of growing popularity there. It was probably a bit of both: there was a decline, but more evidence is waiting to be found, particularly outside the south midlands.

The account books of Thomas Cartwright of Aynho in south Northamptonshire, a long-serving Tory Member of Parliament and at various times High Sherriff of both Northamptonshire and Oxfordshire, are particularly informative. At Aynho in July 1696 he gave morris dancers 2s 6d, and in June 1706 gave '3 setts of Maurice dancers' 15s, i.e., 5s apiece. In May 1713 he gave 'to maurice dancers etc' £1 8s; the 'etc' may well have been a full procession associated with a Whitsun ale, as it far exceeds what the morris dancers alone might expect.[101]

Sir Robert Throckmorton was the son of Sir Francis who had paid morris dancers at the height of the Commonwealth in 1658 (see p. 102). On 16 June 1716 (Trinity Monday) he paid morris dancers at his second seat, Weston Underwood in Buckinghamshire, 2s 6d, and did the same on 27 December that year. On 1 January 1705 he gave 1s to a solo morris dancer from 'Stratford' – probably Stony Stratford, 8 miles away.[102] Records of solo dancers remain sparse, however. Nicholas Blundell, visiting Hatherop, near Fairford in Gloucestershire, from his Lancashire home in 1703, noted a visit by morris dancers on 17 May (Whit Monday).[103] At nearby Sherborne Sir John Dutton paid visiting morris dancers 1s on 18 and 21 May 1711 (the Friday before Whit Sunday, and Whit Monday).[104]

The local populace were entertained at the laying of the foundation stone for Blenheim Palace, Woodstock on 18 June 1705, where the festivities included 'three morris dances; one of young fellows, one of maidens, and one of old beldames', reminiscent of the men's and women's morrises at nearby Kidlington's (or Kirtlington's) lamb ale. There was 'plenty of sack, claret, cakes &c ... for the gentry and better sort; and under the Cross eight barrels of ale, with abundance of cakes, ... for the common people'.[105] Although these records are short on detail, they indicate that the morris survived in this area little changed from before the Commonwealth, as a community celebration centred around an ale. The presence of women dancing, however, represents some broadening of the concept.

At the south-western fringe of the south midlands, the local doctor at Wells, Claver Morris, paid 1s to morris dancers on 20 October 1714 (an unusual time of year but we do not know the stimulus for this appearance).[106] At Bath there had been a grand civic celebration upon the coronation of Queen Anne on 23 April 1704, witnessed by Celia Fiennes, who saw:[107]

> *four couple of Maurice dancers with their pranceing horses, in holland shirts with laced hats riboned, and cross swashes and garters with bells, with their two antiques drest in their formalityes, with hankershiefs in their hands danceing all the way.*

---

[101] 'Cartwright Papers' (1691).
[102] Throckmorton Family.
[103] Blundell, 1:35.
[104] Dutton, f. 44.

[105] Green, David, p. 50.
[106] Morris, Claver, p. 19.
[107] Fiennes, pp. 21-22.

This has many of the elements of what we should now term the south-midlands morris: good shirts, decorated hats, baldricks, bells on legs, waving handkerchiefs. There are eight dancers, not six, and two fools; the horses are out of place, unless they are hobby horses.

Although the north-west of England was to be a major centre for morris dancing during the 19th century, there is little evidence in this later Stuart period. There is, in fact, just one source, the diaries of Nicholas Blundell of Little Crosby, near Liverpool, whose family had been Royalist during the Civil War and continued to espouse Roman Catholicism. On 16 June 1714 (Trinity Wednesday) he wrote 'we saw the morris Dansers of Sefton as were going their Round in order to Rear a May-Pole in Sefton' (2.5 miles from Little Crosby); and the following year on 9 July (the Saturday after Trinity Sunday) 'The Little Boyes & Girles of this Town [Little Crosby] diverted themselves with Rearing a May-pole in the West-Lane, they had Morrys dansing & a great many came to it both old and young chiefly out of this end of the Town'.[108] This suggests that the pre-Commonwealth custom of morris dancing in association with a village feast and maypole continued here into the 18th century. That it was 'little boys and girls', however, again suggests a broadening of the concept. We have encountered children before, at Leicester in 1558 and Wells in 1613, but these events have been exceptional, in the context of adult festivities. Blundell appears to report this as a child-organized activity.

Although falling just outside the later Stuart period, it is worth noting Blundell's final reference to morris dancing, again associated with a maypole. On 24 June 1721 (the Saturday after Trinity Sunday), Blundell went to Moor Hall at Aughton, five miles from Little Crosby. He records that on the way back 'I overtook the Morris Dancers as were going to Flower [to garland] the May-Pole in Magull' (Maghull is halfway between the two).[109]

Around 1710 the Staffordshire antiquary Thomas Loxdale described the hobby-horse custom at Seighford as it had been practised until 1584. The custom provided money for church repairs: 'Ye Usual way of Repairing itt [the church] was by ye Hobbey horse money soe called, from ye publick manner of Collecting itt at Easter ... attended by a Piper & other persons in odd dresses, something like a Morris dance'.[110] This sounds like the dance which is still performed at Abbot's Bromley, and reflects the more fluid cultural space in which morris dancing was beginning to be perceived at the beginning of the 18th century.

There are isolated reports from elsewhere in the country. At the spa Epsom Old Wells during Queen Anne's reign a newspaper advertised, 'Whitson Tuesday will be Moris Dancing Set against Set, for Lac'd Hats, at 10 a Clock'.[111] This is the first example of morris dancing as a competitive display for public entertainment, and although Epsom remains a geographical isolate, competition is a strand which continues in the south midlands. The Epsom event is also the first example of dancing at a place where social entertainments were staged, in this case at a spa, outside the context of performance within a dramatic production.

Morris dancers were out in Lincolnshire on 28 December 1703 on the occasion of an earthquake. Daniel Defoe recorded that having 'danc'd and play'd their tricks' they were travelling from Grimsby to Laceby, five miles away, when the earthquake struck; and 'thinking that God was angry at 'em for playing the Fool, they returned immediately to Laceby in a great Fright, and the next Day home, not daring to pursue their intended Circuit

---

[108] Blundell, 2:138, 140.
[109] Blundell, 3:48.

[110] Cawte, *Ritual Animal Disguise*, pp. 17-18.
[111] Ashton, p. 244.

and Dancing'.[112] Dancing at Christmastide is something that would characterize east-midlands activity in future years. Here as elsewhere payment to morris dancers did not necessarily indicate positive appreciation. In the Massingberd Mundy household accounts from Gunby in Lincolnshire is the note from 6 January 1665, '1s gave the Morris Dancers when I would not have them come in and play'. The estate owner, Sir Henry Massingberd, had been High Sheriff of the county under Cromwell.[113]

———————

The trade guilds at Shrewsbury held an annual show at Kingsland across the River Severn from the town centre on the Monday after the feast of Corpus Christi. In 1688 and 1689 the Glovers' Company accounts include the following entries relating to it:[114]

> *[1688]*
> *pd to the Bedlam morris*   00 01 00
> *pd to the keepers*   00 04 00
>
> ...
>
> *[1688]*
> *pd to ye bedlom morris*   00 10 00
> *pd ye keepers*   00 04 00
>
> ...
>
> *[1689]*
> *pd the Bedloms*   00 05 00
> *pd the keepers*   00 02 00

This raises several questions. What was 'bedlam morris'? Was it a description of the dance, or the dancers? Or were they from the Shropshire village of Bedlam, 22 miles away? In 1688 'Bedlam' was already in common use as a term for madness and the mentally ill. There was no specific asylum in Shrewsbury at the time, but the original Bedlam, the Hospital of St Mary of Bethlehem in London, had been rebuilt and enlarged twelve years before, so the word was in the public mind. The *Oxford English Dictionary* has instances of the figurative use in the sense of 'confusion' or 'uproar' from 1661.[115]

The fact that the payments are immediately followed by payments to 'keepers' might suggest that the bedlam morris had to be chaperoned (since the term was used to indicate someone who had charge of the sick), but there were payments to 'keepers' in other years, without the bedlams, sometimes in association with music, as in 1693 when 3s was paid 'to trumpet and keepers'.[116]

The other aspect to note is that the word is considered necessary. This is not just a 'morris', but a particular kind of morris that needs to be distinctively labelled to distinguish it from 'ordinary' morris. It implies that this is a new kind of morris dancing.

This is primarily a chronological account of the history of morris dancing but at this point we have to step outside the timeline to consider the other evidence for bedlam morris. There are only four primary sources that use the word, spread over 200 years, and it is useful to consider them all together at this point where the word first appears.

---

[112] Defoe, *Storm*, p. 231.
[113] 'Massingberd Mundy', [unfoliated].
[114] Drinkwater, p. 78.

[115] 'Bedlam' (OED).
[116] Drinkwater, pp. 79-80.

The first is this set of payments from Shrewsbury. It is not very informative in itself, but looking ahead to the nineteenth-century evidence this is an area where stick dances were later predominant. The second is an account published in 1814 but, on the whole, referring to the period around 1774. It was written by the antiquary Joseph Haslewood, and is primarily an account of May games, or Whitsun ales, as practised in the Wychwood Forest area of Oxfordshire, and in particular at Combe. The description was provided to him by an unnamed informant who clearly had first-hand and detailed knowledge of them. Most of the account describes the morris we are already familiar with: bells, ribbons, handkerchiefs or napkins, pleated shirts. The informant then adds:[117]

> *There were also the dancers of the Bedlam-morris. They did not wear bells, and were distinguished by high peaked caps (such as are worn by clowns in pantomimes) adorned with ribbons. Each carried a stick about two feet long, which they used with various gesticulation during the dance, and, at intervals, struck them against each other. A clown and a piper attended them.*

This is less circumstantial than the informant's account of the Whitsun-ale morris, and it is not clear how, or if, the two kinds of dancers interrelated. We have encountered conical hats in stage references to and depictions of morris dancing, but not linked to other unifying features.

Third is the description in Anne Baker's *Glossary of Northamptonshire Words and Phrases*, published in 1854. Like Haslewood, she was primarily describing the south-midlands morris of handkerchiefs and bells, in particular when associated with Whitsun ales. However, she adds:[118]

> *They sometimes dance with sticks, flourishing and brandishing them about; then placing them on the ground, with the points all meeting in the centre, they dance round them in a circle. This is called Bedlam Morris, and is probably a rude perpetuation of the ancient Sword-dance.*

Baker was writing in the middle of the century, and in some cases is evidently describing events from personal experience, but she also clearly had access to unpublished material from the end of the 18th century, so it is difficult to ascribe a date to this description. By this stage, however it seems that the bedlam morris was not a separate practice but was an element incorporated into the morris of Whitsun ales.

The last source comes at the end of the century, in 1897. At that time the Oxfordshire antiquary Percy Manning was collecting information about morris dancing in the county and across its borders, using his agent Thomas Carter as a field collector. Morris dancing was in decline at the time, and most of Carter's information came from old men who had danced in their youth. Carter meticulously collected information on the members of the morris side, when they danced, their music, and their costume. On 18 October 1897 he spoke to an informant from Marsh Gibbon in Buckinghamshire who told him that the sticks they used in dancing were 'Bedlam sticks'.[119]

The association of sticks with morris dancing is non-existent before 1688, and the first authority to link them explicitly is not found until 1756 (and will be discussed in Chapter 10). In her 1957 survey of early references to morris dancing Barbara Lowe mentioned 'four clattering staves and nine morris dancers' at the Christmas revels of six-year-old Princess Mary in 1522.[120] This

---

[117] Brydges and Haslewood, 4:337.
[118] Baker, Anne Elizabeth, 2:31.
[119] 'Manning MSS, March Gobbin'.
[120] Lowe, p. 77.

misinterprets the accounts, where the four dozen (not four) staves are grouped with pikes and other weaponry, several entries removed from a reference to morris dancers' coats.[121] Sticks have sometimes been seen as substitutes for swords. In the disturbances in Sandwich in 1526 the rioters walked about 'armed with swords, daggers and clubs' and 'danced a morrice about the town, with swords and bucklers'.[122] Similarly, in the disturbances at Wells in 1607 the dancers danced 'with naked rapiers & daggers in their hands' and people assembled with 'warlike munition with morrice daunces'.[123] In both cases the weaponry was present as part of the general disorder, not specific to the morris. In Higins's dictionary of 1572 the morris is 'Pyrricha saltatio', invoking Pyrrhus as a warlike dancer; and a morris dancer is 'Danseur de morisque ou entre les espees' ('A dancer of morisque, or between the swords').[124] Philemon Holland made the same equation in 1601 in his translation of Pliny, linking Pyrrhus with the 'morisk' and describing the practice of 'meet[ing] together in fight like sword-fencers, and to make good sport in a kind of Moriske daunce' (Pliny's 'saltantium', 'leaping').[125]

Paolo Lomazzo's Italian treatise on art described 'vibrando l'armi ad usanza moresca in atti diversi, di ripari, e simili', which Richard Haydocke translated in 1598 as 'shaking their weapons after the manner of the Morris, with divers actions of meeting &c.'[126] The 1623 translation of Mateo Alemán's *The Rogue* has 'morris dance' and explains it as 'Dança de espadas. A dance much used in the Kingdome of Toledo; they dance it in their shirts, and Breeches of Linnen, and night Caps on their heads, & bright Swords'.[127] John Marston's 1603 play *The Malcontent* speaks of ' Knight of the lande of Catito' who can 'Doe the sword daunce, with any Morris-dauncer in Christendome'.[128]

The majority of morris dance references to weaponry of any kind have been in association with general disorder of which morris dancers are a component; or in the translation of classical or continental texts making a simple equation of war and sword dances with morris dances. The Shrewsbury bedlam morris may be the first implicit indication of the use of sticks in English morris dancing. Shortly before the Shrewsbury references, Randle Holme described a 'Bedlamite' as having 'a long Staff and a Cow or Ox-horn by his side; but his Cloathing is more Fantastick and Ridiculous [than that of a tinker], for being a Mad Man, he is madly decked and dressed all over with Rubins, Feathers, cuttings of Cloth, and what not; to make him seem a Mad-Man, or one Distracted, when he is no other than a Dissembling Knave'.[129]

From this fragmentary evidence – tantalisingly allusory and spread over 200 years in four different counties – it seems that 'bedlam morris' was morris dancing performed with sticks that were clashed together and might be laid on the ground and danced around. It was to be distinguished from the morris dancing associated with May games and Whitsun ales, which were the lineal successors of pre-Commonwealth dancing in communities. There may be an association with beribboned costume. It is not until the late 18th century, however that substantial evidence of dancing with sticks is found, by which time the use of the term 'bedlam' had been lost in its apparent birthplace, the west midlands.

---

[121] Collier, 3:90-91.
[122] Gardiner, Dorothy, pp.153-54.
[123] Stokes, *Records ... Somerset*, p. 335.
[124] Higins, *Huloets Dictionarie*, sig. Eiv-v.
[125] Holland, *Philemon*, 1:189, 192-93.
[126] Haydocke, 2:54; Lomazzo, 1:254.
[127] Alemán, p. 155.
[128] Marston, 'Malcontent', p. 148 (I.iii).
[129] Holme, 3:161.

Chapter 9

Eighteenth-century entertainment

The 18th century continued the post-Restoration morris 'dark ages', which only begin to lighten in the last quarter of the century. There are records of dancers, but many are minimally informative, and one suspects continuing widespread traditions of dancing in areas barely represented in the records. However, two strands of activity developed during the century which cast other light onto the morris dance. One of these is representation on the stage and in entertainment venues, which reveals new conceptualizations of what morris dances were and who might participate. The other is the beginning of scholarship about the morris as lexicographers and antiquaries sought to define or explain morris dancing in an authoritative or illuminating way.

In the early part of the century a few plays continued to allude to morris dancing to conjure up associations familiar to the audience, such as the Maid Marion character referred to in William Taverner's *'Tis Well if it Takes* (1719). In this play the heroine, Corinna, has donned men's clothing as a deception. Prate, the manservant of the hero, is spying on her (in ignorance of the deception). When she talks to her maid about her petticoats, Prate exclaims '... Pettycoats! What, shall we have a Morrice-Dance, and does he play the Maid Marrion?'[1]

In discussing the nineteenth-century theatrical morris dance, Roy Judge distinguished three categories: the morris dance as an integral part of a play on the legitimate stage, as an interlude between such plays (a night's theatrical entertainment usually consisting of the main play, an interlude, and a light short play to close), and as an entertainment in the pleasure gardens.[2] Those same strands first emerged during the 18th century, with different elements coming to the fore as the century progressed.

The earliest eighteenth-century record is of an interlude accompanying the play *The Unfortunate Couple* at Lincoln's Inn Fields Theatre on 17 August 1704, when the additional entertainment included 'Italian Scaramouch by Layfield [and] A new Morris Dance by two men and two women'.[3] Eight years later in August 1712 the Drury Lane Theatre was staging a series of plays in repertory, together with 'The last new Morrice Dance by Prince and others'.[4] (One advertisement announced it as being 'by Mr Norris and others'.)[5] There was also a 'Morris Dance by Prince and others' on 13 July 1714 to accompany *The Taming of a Shrew; or, Sauny the Scot*.[6] Joseph Prince was the theatre's dancing master, while Henry Norris was one of the principal actors in the company. It was said of Prince that 'in all the dances he invents, you see he keeps close to the characters he represents'.[7]

On 10 January 1716 the players at Lincoln's Inn Fields Theatre performed 'a Comedy call'd, The Devil of a Wife. To which will be added the last new comic Masque, call'd, The mountebank; or, The Country Lass. With several Entertainments of Dancing by Mons. De la Garde, Mr. Thurmead, Mr. Shaw, Mrs. Bullock, and Mrs. Cross. Particularly a New Dance, call'd, The Morris,

---

[1] Taverner, p. 73 (V.ii).
[2] Judge, 'Old English Morris Dance', pp. 311-12.
[3] Avery, 2:73.
[4] Avery, 2:280-81.
[5] *Spectator*, 7 August 1712.
[6] Avery, 2:325.
[7] Highfill, Burnim and Langhans, 'Prince'; Mares.

composed by Mr. Isaac; and at the Request of severall Masters perform'd by Mons. De la Garde and Mrs. Bullock.'[8] This was the couple dance just published by Mr Isaac in Beauchamps-Feuillet notation (see Chapter 8). Charles Delagarde was a dancing master who performed at several of the London theatres and who had previously noted down other dances by Isaac. Mrs Bullock was one of a numerous family of theatrical dancers.[9]

The 'Moorish dance' presented with the play *The Committee* in 1730 at the New Theatre in Goodman's Fields on 17 January 1730, may have been just that, the more so in that it was presented again on 21 March, when 'several Entertainments of Dancing, particularly The MOORISH DANCE' were staged in conjunction with the play *Oroonoko*, adapted from Aphra Behn's work about an enslaved African prince. The dancing was by three men and two women, led by the dancing master Thomas Burney.[10]

The legitimate theatre was keen to pander to public taste. In a supposed discussion between the managers of the Covent Garden and Drury Lane theatres, published in 1743, the Covent Garden manager claimed that 'I have a fresh Cargo of Tumblers and Morris-dancers coming over, and Mr. a--- a--- has been furbishing up a vast Heap of old Scenes, which I intend to exhibit as new Ones next Season, and the foolish Town will come and gape at them as usual'. The Drury Lane manager lamented that he had none, and was recommended to 'send circular Letters to the several strolling Companies, and cull from them what you can'.[11]

There was a spectrum of popular entertainment from the legitimate theatre to theatrical booths both permanent and erected for fairs, and actors and dancers could each move between them. At one end were the creations of the dancing masters of Drury Lane, at the other, events like Harlow Bush Fair, described in a poem of 1723 as having 'fidlers, Tumblers, Morrice-Dancers, / And Mountebanks, that's come from France, Sirs'.[12]

Concern about the use of theatres as a platform to criticise the government led to the enactment of the Licensing Act in 1737. Drury Lane and Covent Garden theatres operated under letters patent from the monarch, as did provincial theatres royal. From 1737 all other theatres could only present dramas for hire, gain or reward if they were licensed, and players at unlicensed premises were treated as vagabonds. This led to the rise of subterfuges such as the incorporation of other entertainments into the production, with the drama as a free addendum to the main programme, and what would today be termed 'pop-up' theatres at the fairs. At the annual Bartholomew Fair in 1739 the proprietor of Hallam's Great Theatrical Booth declared that 'the Town will be humorously diverted with a New Entertainment call'd Harlequin turn'd Philosopher; or, The Country Squire Outwitted [...] with several Entertainments of Singing and Comic Dancing, particularly The Milk-Maid, or, The Merry Morrice-Dancers'.[13]

Some wanted to distance uplifting legitimate drama from the *demi-monde* of the more popular end of the spectrum. A correspondent wrote to the *Universal Spectator* in 1732:[14]

> *Tis not to be doubted that the Stage, well regulated, is of considerable Service to the Publick... And, I would fain persuade some noble Genius to undertake the glorious Task of delivering us from the wretched Slavery of Harlequins, Morris-Dancers and Ballad-Singers, and restore us to the Use of common Sense...*

[8] *Daily Courant*, 10 January 1716.
[9] Highfill, Burnim and Langhans, 'Delagarde'; Highfill, Burnim and Langhans, 'Bullock'.
[10] *Daily Journal*, 17 January 1730, 21 March 1730.
[11] *Case between the Managers*.
[12] 'Description'.
[13] *London Daily Post*, 20 August 1739 [and following days].
[14] *Universal Spectator*, 9 December 1732.

The development of popular entertainment was the subject of debate, with some regretting the introduction of European models. 'What is there in any of these new Entertainments, to which the Slight of a Jugler, the Agility of a Morrice-Dancer, or the Movements of a Puppet-Shew, are not at least equal?', asked one correspondent in 1725.[15] The performers themselves echoed the sentiment. *The Humble Petition of the Humerous and Diverting Company of Jack-puddings, Tumblers, Morrice-dancers, Jumpers thro' Hoops, Dancers on the Slack-rope and with Swords, Spinners of Glass, Puppet-show, and Cups and Balls Men* declared in 1738 that 'they have made it their Business for many Years to cultivate the Activity of their Limbs at the Expence of Their Heads', so are but simple folk, who 'humbly pray, that tho' most of them are Britons, they may have a fitting Encouragement given them, and not be sent to the Plantations to make way for Strangers who (tho' their Ignorance may not be so intelligible), are not a Grain more deserving than themselves'.[16] In other words, they claimed that the public taste for foreign entertainments and entertainers was driving British entertainers out of business. The company which the petitioning morris dancers kept extended from acrobats to the street fraudsters using the cup and balls legerdemain, associated more with the likes of Bartholomew Fair than the legitimate theatre.

The association with low life is reflected in literary texts which often associate morris dancing with roguery and the picaresque. The supposed autobiography of Thomas Munn, hanged for robbery, is an example. Rather than continue hard work in the flax trade, he:[17]

> *learnt to play upon the Flute, and was famous for dancing of Jiggs and Hornpipes, so went into Sussex and commenced Dancing-master, and got a Set of young Fellows as undiscerning as myself, that I had taught to caper a little, to go with me to morris-dancing, as it is called in that County: I was Master of the Ceremony, and was Fool enough to have 'em to some Relations, for which my Uncle gave me a smart Reprimand, and told me the Folly of spending my Time in such an idle manner, and the Scandal it was to every Body that was related to me, to hear or see me capering about the Country like a Vagabond, and begging for Money to spend idly.*

The travelling entertainer in Thomas Berington's *News from the Dead* 'was very good at a morrice-Dance and Stage-play, and won many a Prize at Cudgels and Quarter-staff [and] perform'd several juggling Tricks by Slight of Hand'.[18] Another fictional travelling entertainer was 'Rosanno ... a young spouster from the Morris-Dancers, whom we shall pass over in silence, being convinced he had studied the taste of porter in preference to acting' ('spouster' in error for 'spouter', an amateur actor).[19]

The most macabre aspect of the association of morris dancers with the low life was the persistence of the meaning 'to be hanged'. Some dictionaries of thieves' cant indicated this figurative meaning of the word: the *New Canting Dictionary* (1725) gives an additional definition of 'to morris' as 'to hang dangling in the Air, to be executed'[20] (recalling the 1688 ballad usage), and the popular genre of ballads sold at hangings, purportedly being the subject's real-time gallows confession, included *Jack Sheppard's Epistle*, in which 'By the gullet we're ty'd very tight; / We beg all spectators, pray for us; / Our peepers are hid from the light, / The tumbril shoves off, and we morrice'.[21] At the end of the 18th century James Caulfield's *Blackguardiana*

[15] *London Journal*, 17 April 1725.
[16] 'Humble Petition'.
[17] Munn, p. 5.
[18] Berington, p. 58.
[19] *Memoirs*, 2:26.
[20] *New Canting Dictionary*, sv morisco, morris.
[21] *Daily Journal*, 16 November 1724.

defined the verb as 'morris, come morris off, dance off, or get you gone, allusion to morris'. Humphrey Potter also defined 'morris' as 'to run away' but had additional entries capturing morris dancers themselves as low elements in society:[22]

> *Abramers: naked, ragged, dirty beggars, the lowest order of vagrants*
>
> *...*
>
> *Anticks: morris dancers; a species of abram men, called merry-andrews.*

'Antic' had been a common epithet applied to the dance, conveying a sense of both ancientness and grotesquerie.

A satirist writing in the *London Chronicle* in 1763 described a dream in which he was at the rotunda in the fashionable Ranelagh pleasure gardens when 'a parcel of jack-puddings, who had been diverting the multitude without, rushed in, followed by a crew of buffoons, French ballad-masters, strolling players, merry-andrews, and morris dancers. – They made such confusion, that all the persons of elegant taste left the room immediately.'[23] What was suitable as street entertainment was deemed inappropriate when it burst uninvited into the refined and controlled space of the pleasure garden.

In the unregulated theatrical sphere an intriguing advertisement appeared on the occasion of Bartholomew Fair in 1743, this time at Yeates, Warner, and Rosoman's Great Theatrical Booth. It promoted a play plus interlude, and it is the interlude that is a little different: 'during the short Time of Bartholomew-Fair ... will be presented a pompous Tragedy, call'd The Cruel Uncle ... With the surprising Performances of the famous Bath Morris-Dancers...'.[24] It is unusual to have a group of dancers named as hailing from a particular place, and it suggests that they were not drawn from the theatrical dancing-master tradition, but perhaps had roots in their community of Bath and morris dancing as performed there. The first notice of the Bath Morris Dancers had appeared a month earlier, in a letter to the *Daily Advertiser* which was placed, as likely as not, as a covert advertisement for them:[25]

> *Sir, A few Days ago I was invited by the Calmness and Serenity of the Evening, to make a little Excursion into the Fields. As I was returning home, being in a gay Humour, I stopt a little at a Booth near Sir John Oldcastle's, to hear the Rhetorick of Mr. Andrew. He used such Eloquence to persuade his Auditors to walk in, that I (with many others) went to see the Entertainments he mention'd; and I assure you, Sir, I never was more agreeably amus'd than with the Performance of three Men, who call themselves The Bath Morrice-Dancers. They shew'd so many astonishing Feats of Strength and Activity, so many amazing Transformations (if I may be allow'd the Expression) that it is impossible for the most lively Imagination to form an adequate Idea thereof. As the Fairs are coming on, I presume these admirable Artists will be engaged by some Body to entertain the Town; and I assure your Readers, they can't spend an Hour more agreeably, that in seeing the Performances of those wonderful Men. I am, &c.*

'Feats of strength and activity' suggests more of a gymnastic display, and the presence of just three men also militates against our placing this within the known folk-dance tradition; and, of course, the exhortation that they be engaged for the fair was taken up by Yeates, Warner, and Rosoman.

---

[22] Potter, pp. 42, 10.

[23] *London Chronicle*, 13-15 September 1763.

[24] *Daily Advertiser*, 22 August 1743.

[25] *Daily Advertiser*, 27 July 1743.

Even greater fame was to await them. At the end of the fair on 26 August 1743 their performance is said to have been viewed by the Prince and Princess of Wales, Princess Amelia, and Princess Louisa, attended by 'several Persons of Quality'. This report was published in both the *Daily Advertiser* and the *Daily Post and General Advertiser* on 27 August,[26] but these newspapers went to press in advance of the intended royal visit. However, the royal seal of approval for the Bath Morris Dancers was trumpeted throughout the following months: for example, in an advertisement in the *Daily Advertiser* of 10 September 1743 for 'the surprising Performance of the Bath Morrice-Dancers, that gain'd so universal an Applause in Bartholomew Fair, before their Royal Highnesses the Prince and Princess of Wales'.[27] In these circumstances, it is unlikely that the performance before royalty did not take place.

The main purpose of the item in the *Daily Advertiser* of 27 August 1743 was, in fact, to announce that the Bath dancers had been engaged by Mr Hallam at the New Wells:

> *As the Bath Morrice-Dancers, who performed at Bartholomew Fair, have not only given the greatest Pleasure, but Surprize, to all who could have an Opportunity of seeing them; we hear that Mr. Hallam (who always studies to entertain the Town in the best Manner) has engaged them for a certain Time, to exhibit their extraordinary Performances at his Wells, the Bottom of Lemon-Street, Goodman's Fields; and that they will appear there this Night for the first Time.*

This was the first of an entire season of performances at the New Wells which lasted until the end of the year. Their performances were advertised no fewer than 64 times in the *London Daily Post and General Advertiser* between 30 August and 31 December 1743.[28]

Six weeks into their season the dancers introduced 'several new Performances', and a few days later appeared at a booth at Southwark Fair.[29] Back at the New Wells after the fair in Southwark, 'new scenes' and 'several new Exercises' (not 'performances') were announced again on 7 October.[30] The major change came ten days later, however, when three more dancers were apparently incorporated into the displays. The New Wells proudly advertised 'a new Morrice Dance, never perform'd upon any Stage, by six Morrice-Dancers, just arriv'd from Bath'.[31] While it is conceivable that other members of the theatre company had simply been assigned to provide the increased numbers, the announcement is quite explicit in stating that the dancers are from Bath and that they have just arrived. This begins to sound very much like a morris dance that we would recognise it today. On 3 November the *Daily Advertiser* announced 'The Morrice Dancers will perform a new Morrice of Three, and a new Morrice of Six'.[32] For the final month of their performances, we return to 'The Morris-Dancers will perform a new Morris of Three' in the first half of the month,[33] and to 'the diverting Performances of the famous Bath Morrice Dancers' until the end of the year.[34]

The phenomenon of dancers from the provinces coming to London to dance and then working their way back home, interspersing working and dancing, is known from the 19th century,[35] and it may be that the Bath dancers were originally engaged in a similar enterprise before being sucked into the London entertainment scene for nearly half a year. There were certainly

---

[26] *Daily Advertiser*, 27 August 1743; *Daily Post and General Advertiser*, 27 August 1743.

[27] *Daily Advertiser*, 10 September 1743.

[28] Data from the Gale Cengage British Newspapers 1650–1900 database.

[29] *Daily Advertiser*, 15 and 19 September 1743.

[30] *Daily Advertiser*, 7 October 1743.

[31] *Daily Advertiser*, 17 October 1743.

[32] *Daily Advertiser*, 3 November 1743.

[33] *London Daily Post*, 8 and 13–15 December 1743.

[34] *London Daily Post*, 19–22 and 26–31 December 1743.

[35] Chandler, *Ribbons*, pp. 93–95.

morris dancers in Bath in the first half of the 18th century. An account of an ox-roast to celebrate King George II's birthday in 1727 describes a procession through the town, 'with two Sword Bearers, a set of Morris Dancers, and Martial Musick before them'.[36]

The Bath Morris Dancers appeared again at Bartholomew Fair the following year, 1744, this time in association with a Punch and Judy show,[37] and once more in 1745. It may be relevant that Punch's Theatre, where they appeared in 1744, had been established 34 years previously by the showman Martin Powell, who gave the Punch and Judy show its modern form and who first appeared in Bath in 1709.[38] The advertisement repeated the characterization of their appearances as 'surprising Performances'. [39] On these occasions, however, their appearance did not lead to an engagement for the season. They were clearly a single-season wonder.

After 1745 we hear no more of the Bath Morris Dancers. It is not difficult to imagine that the Bath dancers' performances had some influence on the staging of morris dances by the professional dancers in the New Wells company, and *vice versa*. However, the use of morris dances in theatres and booths, whether provided by dancing masters or from the community, dies down thereafter, before reviving in the last quarter of the century.

The description of the Bath dancers' gymnastic abilities suggests that their dances required more athleticism than the social dance. As long ago as 1662, an anonymous author writing on exercise had recommended leaping while holding 'counterpoises of Lead ... (as our Morrice Dancers oftentimes wear leaden Pumps, that they may be the more nimble when the same are lay'd off). It is not clear whether he was describing practice among stage dancing masters, or in community-based dancing, but it reveals a mindset dedicated to achieving excellence in performance.[40]

The distinctiveness of dancers' costume was also commented upon. James Ralph's *The Touch-stone* (1728) parodied the published guides to London low life. If a dancer wanted to be recognised as a morris dancer, he wrote, he should be 'adorn'd with Garlands of flowers, fetter'd with silken Cords, and deck'd all round with Bells'.[41]

A writer with a unique perspective was Giovanni-Andrea Gallini, the director of dancing at the Royal Theatre in London's Haymarket. His fellows were certainly devising morris dances for the stage, and Gallini may well have done the same. His 1762 treatise on dancing brought out the disjunction between artistic representation and morris dancing in the 'low' culture of the community, while at the same time expressing a desire, perhaps, to validate the depiction on stage by incorporating a degree of 'authenticity'. His thoughts are worth quoting in full:[42]

> *I do not know whether I shall not stand in need of an apology for mentioning here a dance once popular in England, but to which the idea of low is now currently annexed. It was originally adopted from the Moors, and is still known by the name of Morris-dancing or Moresc-dance. It is danced with swords, by persons disguised, with a great deal of antic rustic merriment: it is true that this diversion is now almost exploded, being entirely confined to the lower classes of life, and only kept up in some counties. What the reason may be of its going out of use, I cannot say; but am very sure, there was not only a great deal of natural mirth in it, but that it is susceptible enough of improvement, to rescue it from the*

---

[36] *Country Journal*, 11 November 1727.
[37] *Daily Advertiser*, 25 August 1744.
[38] Speaight.
[39] *Daily Advertiser*, 23 August 1745.
[40] *Another Collection*, p. 253.
[41] Ralph, p. 107.
[42] Gallini, pp. 185-86.

contempt it may have incurred, through its being chiefly in use among the vulgar; though most probably it may have descended among them from the higher ranks. For certainly of them it was not quite unworthy, for the Pirrhic or military air it carries with it, and which probably was the cause of its introduction among so martial a people. Rude, as it was, it might require refinement, but it did not, perhaps, deserve to become quite obsolete.

As an immigrant to England (he was born in Florence in 1728) Gallini may not have seen such dancing for himself. The allusion to swords suggests that he may have seen a sword dance if anything. He is nonetheless aware that dancing continues in some parts of the country and wants to rescue and revive it. In this he was anticipating the activities of some antiquaries over a century later. Just ten years later, a woman encountering and appreciating a performance by south-midlands morris dancers at Fairford in Gloucestershire wished 'that the playhouses had adopted a scene of this kind in their representations of rural life' and 'wondered that they had never done it'.[43]

———————

Gallini may have encountered an event at one of the pleasure gardens which sprang up during the century. A sword dance proclaimed as a 'morrice dance' was presented on 31 January 1788 in the Pantheon, which had opened in Oxford Street in 1772 as an indoor entertainment centre paralleling the outdoor pleasure gardens. It was one of the largest and most popular of such venues. The dance appears to have been a single performance, which was widely reported. The *Morning Chronicle and London Advertiser* gave a circumstantial description of the event, apparently before over 1200 spectators:[44]

> *A set of Morrice Dancers from the North, gave an excellent display of the Cumberland Sword Dance. Five of them, dressed in their shirts, trimmed with ribbons, performed their athletick exercise; and the remainder of the nine consisted of Bessey, a Minstrel, Jack, and his Master, who in the characters of Ring Sweeper, Fidler, Songster and Interpreter, added much to the hilarity of the place.*

An even fuller account appeared in a cutting from a journal as yet unidentified, but probably the *Westminster Magazine*, preserved in the Mander & Mitchenson Theatre Collection at the University of Bristol:[45]

> *The most striking and eccentric groupe which appeared in the rooms, was a set of Morrice Dancers, consisting in all of nine characters, five of whom, dressed in their shirts, trimmed with variegated ribbons, performed what we took to be the Cumberland Sword Dance; a spectacle of all others the most novel and whimsical to a London company. The different manoeuvres were most unaccountably and dextrously managed; and, together with the athletic appearance of the Dancers (all of whom were of the Horse-guard standard) gave us a high opinion of our northern countrymen. – The remaining four characters consisted of a Bessy, a Minstrel, Jack and his Master; who in their several departments of Ring-Sweeper, Fidler, Songster and Interpreter, acquitted themselves with a very good effect. Their dresses were in a style entirely different from the Swordsmen. Old Bessy exhibited an old woman in true northern style. The Musician was a whimsical satire on Palmer's musicals – and represented Apollo turned Stroller, with the Royalty Pegasus at his back, in the semblance of an ass with his ears cropped. This character would have been an exceeding laughable*

---

[43] 'Sentimental Journey', p. 101.
[44] *Morning Chronicle*, 2 February 1788. [45] 'Mander & Mitchenson'.

one independent of the groupe. Jack and his Master, the profest masking drolls of their own country, exhibited two Herculean figures in canvas frocks [frock coats], embellished most curiously with rustic devices, and occasionally gave a song adapted to the dance, and the place it was performed in.

This description accords closely with what we know of the sword dance of the north-east from the late 18th century, except of course that it is attributed to Cumberland instead of Northumberland or County Durham.[46]

The *Public Advertiser* reproduced in full a handbill that was distributed by the dancers:[47]

ADDRESS

To the mirth-loving crew, who can laugh and be jolly,
Here met in full glee, at the Temple of Folly;
To the belles, and the beaus, that are buzzing about 'em;
The wise-heads with tongues – and to black-heads without 'em;
To Lords, out of breath, in the midst of their leisure;
To Harlequins, hopping in minuet measure;
To Temple-Bar Highlanders – Scotch Petit-Maitres;
To the whole corps of songsters, from all the Theatres;
To house-maids and hay-makers, fair, young, and civil;
To dominos, peevish, and black as the devil;
To petticoat Gentlemen – Ladies in breeches;
To shepherds and sailors – wits, wizards, and witches;
To non-descript figures – Automaton stalkers;
To the lollers, the loungers, the leapers, the walkers;
To the grinners, the growlers, the huffers, the pleasers;
To all the un-character'd character teazers;
To clowns, sweeps and soldiers, nuns, rakes, and old women;
Kings, cobblers, fools, conjurors – Ladies and Gem'men:

The merry morrice-dancers from the north country present their compliments: – being Folly's own children; begotten upon Mirth, they have ventured into the Pantheon, and beg leave to consider themselves at home; while their northern manners are one degree less barbarous then the present prize-worthy standard in the south; they not only expect the indulgence, but the protection of the company; and should their behaviour rise but one degree above that standard, they should justly hold themselves beneath its notice. Their aim is to please and be pleased – the first part of which may be difficult to accomplish, but of the latter they entertain no doubts, for in all places, and in all companies, Folly is ever pleased when dancing to the music of its own bells!

Vive le Bagatelle!

From the foot of Skiddau

Jan. 31, 1788.

This remarkable text confirms their Cumbrian origin (perhaps Keswick). It confirms their self-identification as 'morrice dancers' – this is not a designation imposed upon them by the unknowing London press. It may even suggest (in the last line of text) that they wore bells.

---

[46] Heaton, pp. 14–18. [47] *Public Advertiser*, 4 February 1788.

It is indicative of the broadening scope of 'morris dance' as an umbrella term for groups of dancers performing to entertain, in some specific setting or context. Around 90 years earlier Sir Daniel Fleming of Rydal Hall in Westmorland had paid 'morris dancers',[48] but morris or sword dancing is otherwise little known in the Lake District at this time.

The event, fascinating as it is, raises a string of questions. What brought them 300 miles to London? Who wrote the text? Was it composed by the dancers themselves? Did they engage a local or a London hack to write it for them? If it was their own work, who acted as scribe? The date on the handbill is the actual date of performance, which suggests that it was created in London after their arrival. Whoever composed it, it reveals the dancers as something more than mere rustics – there is a sophisticated knowingness about their presentation as performers. There is self-awareness here of this as a performance event, purely for entertainment's sake. The dancers are outside of the home community, it is out of the usual Christmas/New Year season, there is no cadging. Given the prominence afforded by the press to their appearance, and their positive reception, it is both surprising and disappointing not to find accounts of further performances at the Pantheon or elsewhere.

The Mander & Mitchenson cutting also includes the text of the handbill and follows it with an additional passage, which may or may not have been part of the handbill: 'N.B. For information of gentlemen unacquainted with North-country diversions, an interpreter, who can speak a little English, attends the dancers, to answer all questions. – An interpretess for the ladies.' The Cumberland dancers were depicted as exotic and remote – needing an 'interpreter', even if only in jest. The dances and dancers were characterized primarily by their agility and novelty. This was a masquerade for the upper echelons of society – tickets for such events typically cost half a guinea or more, and food was extra. As with the Bath Morris Dancers' performances 50 years before, the Prince of Wales attended the event, with the Duke of York. Like the Bath Morris Dancers, the Cumberland dancers blur the distinction between morris in the community and its depiction on the stage, and in this case blur the distinction between morris and sword dances.

––––––––––––––

Gymnastic ability of the kind exhibited by the Bath and Cumberland dancers continued to be a defining characteristic in public perceptions of morris dancing. Astley's Amphitheatre presented both dramatic and circus-related entertainments, and in 1787 this included the acrobat Joseph Lawrence (famous for his somersaults and prodigious leaps), who performed his composition 'The Tumblers Morris'.[49] The combination of morris dance and acrobatics was repeated at the theatre in Stamford, Lincolnshire in 1792, when after the main play, 'A Favorite Dance, call'd The Tambourine; Or, Morris Dancers', was performed by Mr Lassells who, together with his wife and son, 'will kick several Tambourines near Eight Feet high'.[50] Another performer was Jean-Baptiste Dubois, whose 'Morrice-dancing and Italian singing' in Charles Dibdin's harlequinade *Chaos* in 1800 were 'fine specimens of burlesque acting'. Dubois was a multi-talented clown, acrobat, rope dancer and egg dancer (dancing around eggs laid on the floor, without breaking them).[51]

Towards the end of the century theatrical performances began to present morris dances within stage representations of May-day festivals. *Pygmy Revels, or Harlequin Foundling* was

[48] *Carlisle Patriot*, 8 January 1897.
[49] 'On Monday Next'; Highfill, Burnim and Langhans, 'Lawrence'.
[50] *Lincoln, Rutland and Stamford Mercury*, 29 June 1792.
[51] *Morning Post*, 19 August 1800; Highfill, Burnim and Langhans, 'Dubois'.

presented at the Drury Lane Theatre in 1772. The reviewer noted the incorporation of 'the morris dance so much approved of in the opera of the *Rose* (deservedly damned three weeks since)'.[52] (*The Rose* was apparently taken off after one performance, the actors being booed off the stage. Sadly, its reviews fail to mention the morris dance.)[53] *Pygmy Revels* also presented a dance of chimney sweeps with their May-day garland, as part of the general collocation of springtime celebrations in the popular mind.

Allusions in plays maintained the earlier associations with rustic fellowship. Leonard MacNally evoked them in his 1784 play *Robin Hood*, when Little John is asked to arrange the 'nuptial sports and pastimes' and exclaims 'we shall have bull-baiting and morrice-dancing – Oh how I long to be capering!' (In a surprisingly modern touch, Robin chastises him for wanting to inflict cruelty upon animals.)[54] Charles's Dibdin's comic opera *Liberty-hall* had as alternative title, 'A Test of Good Fellowship', and included in song the rhetorical questions 'Do curates crowdies [fiddles] love to play? / Or peasants morice-dancing?'[55]

In the later part of the century as in the early part, the morris dance could be a stand-alone addition to the main entertainment. The Whitsun-week entertainment at the Drury Lane Theatre in 1787 added 'a Grand Dance, called *The Morris Dancers*' to the topical opera *Botany Bay*.[56] The Royal Circus in St George's Fields, Southwark, announced on 27 April 1789 that it would soon present 'A new Musical Piece, called, The What Is It? And a new Dance, called, The Morris Dancers, or Humours of May-Day'. After the entertainment commenced the billing was soon reversed, the advertisement reading 'Besides the favourite Ballet, The Morrice Dancers, or Humours of May Day, which is so justly admired by all ranks of spectators, a New Musical Piece was produced on Monday, called, The What Is It? ...'. The ballet was also advertised without mention of *The What Is It*.[57] It was composed by John Holland and he performed it with Auguste Ferrère, Madame Sala and Mademoiselle Fuozi ('Fowzi'). John Holland was both dancing and equestrian master (as indeed the Royal Circus presented both kinds of entertainment), and his fellow dancers were all from dancing families of French or Italian extraction.[58] We know nothing more of it, but the subtitle indicates that it took the form of a May-day festival.

In a play which reflects attitudes now entirely unacceptable, William Macready's *The Irishman in London, or, The Happy African* (1793) presents an African slave girl Cubba, who claims 'my fader great King', to which the Irishman Murtlock responds (in a caricature of an Irish accent) 'It's King of the Morice-dancers she manes; ay, ay, that fellow had a black face – I saw him yesterday'. Cubba points out that her father is in Africa, so it is clear that Murtlock is referring to morris dancers with blackened faces.[59] The same year, Archibald MacLaren's farce *London out of Town* poked fun in similar vein at a pair of rustics preparing for a wedding. The level of humour can be gauged from the rustic Cuddie's words 'We'll have a town dance, -- such as I see'd when I wur in London at the hopera ...they call it hopera, because they hop about so much'. When the coachman suggests 'we shall have Bob o'the Bolster, -- Jack o'the Green, -- or Morrice Dance', Cuddie is dismissive: 'Poh! poh! That be all vulgar stuff!'[60]

[52] *Morning Chronicle*, 28 December 1772.
[53] *London Chronicle*, 1-3 December 1772; *Morning Chronicle*, 3 December 1772.
[54] MacNally, pp. 38-39.
[55] Dibdin, p. 32 (I.v).
[56] *World and Fashionable Advertiser*, 1 June 1787.

[57] *World and Fashionable Advertiser*, 27 April 1789, 1 May 1789, 7 May 1789, 11 May 1789.
[58] Highfill, Burnim and Langhans, 'Ferrère'; Highfill, Burnim and Langhans, 'Fuozi'; Highfill, Burnim and Langhans, 'Holland'; Highfill, Burnim and Langhans, 'Sala'.
[59] Macready, p. 37 (II.i).
[60] MacLaren, pp. 10-11 (III.i).

Most of the traceable references to theatre activity come from the London entertainment scene. There must have been similar activity in the provinces, but little evidence for it in the 18th century survives. There was the acrobatic Mr Lassells in Stamford (and he performed widely on the provincial circuit).[61] Besides that, the Leeds theatre in Hunslet presented *Measure for Measure* in 1776, including, for one night only on 15 July:[62]

> *End of Act second, (for that Night only), A New Grand Pastoral Ballet Dance, call'd*
> *The Irish Milk-maids, or,*
> *May Pole.*
>
> *To be performed by Twenty-five Children of this Town, all to be dressed in New Dresses for that Purpose, as it was performed at the Theatre-Royal, Drury-Lane, Twenty three Nights successively, and repeatedly performed Last Winter at the Theatre-Royal, York, with universal Applause. – To conclude with a Grand Garland Ballet by Mr and Miss West, the Irish Milk Maids, and Twelve Morris Dancers.*

This brought together the metropolitan (it was performed at Drury Lane) and the local (25 local children), and a total of three sets of dancers – the Wests, the milkmaid child dancers, and 12 morris dancers (whose origin is not given) – in a grand garland ballet celebrating May Day. The Wests were the adult children of D. West, described as 'a minor performer at Drury Lane Theatre' who is known to have performed in York and other northern towns with his wife around that time.[63] Elements of this spectacle were also performed in Manchester the following year, in circumstances which make it useful to defer consideration until eighteenth-century morris dancing in the north-west is examined in Chapter 12.

The sword dancers from Cumberland who performed at the Pantheon in 1788 were participating in the culture of the masquerade, which developed in such pleasure gardens during the 18th century and involved both professional entertainers and audiences who might dress in character as part of the entertainment. It transformed the aristocratic masque into a more general participatory entertainment open to a wider – though still upper- to middle-class – public. Masquerades were also held in private houses. Carlisle House in Soho was the abode of Teresa Cornelys, an opera singer of whom Casanova, one of her many lovers, said coyly, 'her good fortune had not depended entirely on her talent; her charms had contributed to it more than anything else'.[64] Her home was the place to be seen for those seeking upper-class entertainment, and on 12 April 1771 it was patronized by a couple who arrived as 'two nimble, well-dressed Morris dancers, with bells &c.'[65] On 14 February 1774 Carlisle House hosted a 'reception of those masks who wished a rehearsal of their intended amusements at the Opera-house'; about seventy characters were named, including 'a Morrice Dancer'.[66] These will have been mere fancy-dress costumes, with no suggestion that the masqueraders were performing morris dances.

The Carlisle House entertainments were held up as the standard to meet. In 1791 a report of a masquerade at the Vauxhall gardens claimed that 'Since the days of Mrs. Cornely's, we have not witnessed such a scene of mirth, happiness, and festivity, as this delightful spot exhibited on Friday night', at which those attending in character included 'a Morris dancer; a Jack in the

---

[61] Highfill, Burnim and Langhans, 'Lassells'.
[62] *Leeds Intelligencer*, 9 July 1776.
[63] Highfill, Burnim and Langhans, 'West, D.'.
[64] Casanova, 3:342-43.
[65] *Craftsman*, 20 April 1771.
[66] *General Evening Post*, 15-17 February 1774.

Green, with a group of milkmaids, and a good fiddler',[67] embodying several different elements of May festivities.

At the royal residence of Frogmore Gardens, Windsor, George III arranged a fête for the 51st birthday of Queen Charlotte on 19 May 1795, and engaged James Byrn, dancing master at Covent Garden Theatre. Byrn brought 'a select company of morrice dancers' who 'did much credit to their profession'.[68] His production *Merry Sherwood; or, Harlequin Forester* at the theatre later that year also included a morris dance.[69]

In an item entitled 'Mrs. Walker's Masked Ball' in 1800 *The Oracle and Daily Advertiser* described how the ball 'attracted most of the Fashion in Town to her house in Stanhope-street... six hundred Visitors attended the fair Hostess about half past ten o'clock'. Among the masqueraders in fancy dress were 'Mr. Sheridan, jun., and his partner, as Morris Dancers', who 'figured away with much spirit and agility'.[70] Alethea Walker was the wife of a Liverpool shipping magnate and noted society hostess whose London masquerades attracted royal favour.[71] 'Mr. Sheridan, jun.' was Thomas Sheridan, the 24-year-old son of the playwright and manager of Drury Lane Theatre Richard Sheridan.

Not everybody liked masquerades. The male author of *An Enquiry into the Duties of the Female Sex* (1797) was much against masquerades because the masked participants could create a sense of allure by hiding their identities, with pernicious consequences. Remove the masks, he said, and 'the pageant would almost instantly become insipid; and the sultans, the chimney-sweepers, the harlequins, the shepherdesses, and the nuns, would speedily regard each other with the indifference with which they would view the motley tinsel of a group of morrice-dancers or the kings and queens of gilded gingerbread at a fair'.[72] Morris dancers were a curiosity to be looked on with detached amusement, but ideas about them could be appropriated into the theatre and the higher echelons of society.

Morris dancing as a staged entertainment could engender a variety of responses. The evocation of May revels devised by the professional dancing masters and their companies of dancers was admired and popular. Dancers coming to London from provincial communities could occasionally break through at least into the pleasure gardens and theatrical booths. At the same time there could be a distinct odour of low life intruding into the more refined sensibilities of the upper and middle classes.

---

[67] *Public Advertiser*, 6 June 1791.
[68] *Sun*, 21 May 1795.
[69] Judge, 'Old English Morris Dance', p. 317.

[70] *Oracle*, 29 May 1800.
[71] 'Richard Walker'.
[72] Gisborne, pp. 143-45.

Chapter 10
Lexicographers and scholars

We have already looked at how some of the early dictionaries mentioned in their definitions elements relating to gestures (see Chapter 4). Early lexicographers were all too ready to copy definitions, so the same themes recur in several publications.

Definitions of 'morris dance' occur most often in the translating dictionaries, sometimes little more than the bare equation of morris = French morisque = Italian moresca = Spanish morisco. John Minsheu's 1617 *The Guide into Tongues* added Dutch, German, Latin, Greek and Welsh, the last a semi-translation into 'chware-morris', 'morris-play'.[1] After the 17th century, however, the inclusion of 'morris' in translating dictionaries died away: only *The Complete Vocabulary in English and French* of 1785 had it, as 'Morisco or morris dance: Danse Moresque'.[2] Two more eighteenth-century translating dictionaries include it, but they were aimed at the internal market of the British Isles: Ó Beaglaioch's Irish dictionary of 1732 gave a literal translation of morris dance as 'Damhsa muirisig', while the entry in John Roderick's Welsh dictionary of 1737, 'chwaryddiaeth, llamsach' ('play' or 'sport'; 'to jump, hop or caper') was slightly more indicative of his view of the nature of the dance.[3]

Minsheu's 1617 polyglot dictionary also included the equation of morris dancing with the warlike 'Pyrrhic dance' described in classical texts:[4]

> *pyrrhicho saltator, i. a morice-dancer. Nota Pyrrhum hanc saltationem in armis militibus instituit.*
>
> [... Note: Pyrrhus instituted this dance among soldiers in arms]

This theme was picked up by Edward Phillips in 1658, who rather more tentatively defined a 'Morisco' as 'a kind of Dance which seemeth to be the same as that which the Greeks call Pyrrhica, we vulgarly call it the Morris Dance, as it were the Moorish Dance'.[5]

Another who used the analogy was Francis Gouldman, defining a 'morrice-dance' as 'Gesticula, f. chironomica saltatio, ludus Pyrrhichus' ('gesture, a gesturing dance, a Pyrrhic game or play'). He went on to define 'chironomia' as 'A kind of gesture with the hand, either in dancing or carving of meat, or pleading: also the Morice-dance';[6] directly copying Cooper's definition from a century earlier. Thomas Holyoke did the same in 1677, while the last to make the connection was Robert Ainsworth in 1736.[7]

Edward Phillips's 1658 definition was the first to equate 'morris dance' with 'Moorish dance' explicitly, in 1658, though Minsheu had included 'Saltatio Maurica, the Moorish-d[a]nce' in his multilingual list under 'morice dance'. The reviser of the 1663 edition of Bullokar's *An English Expositour* was more dogmatic, defining a 'morisco' as 'A certain dance used among the Moores; whence our Morris-dance'.[8] From then on it became an unquestioned equation,

---

[1] Minsheu, p. 315.
[2] *Complete Vocabulary*, p. 215.
[3] Ó Beaglaioch, Mac Cuirtin and Mac Cuirtin, sv morris dance; Roderick, sv morrice dance.
[4] Minsheu, p. 315.
[5] Phillips, *New World of English Words*, sig. Cc4.
[6] Gouldman, sig. n5v, N8.
[7] Holyoke, sig. U4v, Z1; Ainsworth, Robert, sv morisco, morrice.
[8] Bullokar, sig. L4.

for example in *Gazophylacium Anglicanum* in 1689 ('Morrice-dance, from the Ital. A la Moresca, or the Fr. G. Moresque; q.d. a Dance after the fashion of the Moors, q. Moorish-dance') and Sheridan's pronouncing dictionary of 1780 ('Morris-dancer, mor'-ris-dansu, one who dances the Moorish dance.').[9] Most non-English translating dictionaries made the simple equation of morris = Moorish, though Prokhor Zhdanov's English-Russian dictionary of 1784 described it as 'арапской танец с колокольчиками', a 'blackamoor's dance with little bells'.[10]

Franciscus Junius's *Etymologicum anglicanum* was not published until 1743, but Junius himself had died in 1677, compiling the work throughout his life. Junius was Dutch, Francis Du Jon, and a major philologist; his use of a Latinate form of name was common among the European scholarly community at that time, and the language of communication was Latin. After the usual European-language equivalents to 'morrice dance', he explains why it is so called in the various languages:[11]

> *... nam faciem plerumque inficiunt fuligine & peregrinum vestium cultum assumunt, qui ludicris talibus indulgent, ut Mauri esse videantur, aut e longius remota patria credantur advolasse insolens recreationis genus advexisse.*
>
> [*... because for the most part they dye themselves with soot and adopt a foreign style of clothing, they indulge in such acting so that they are seen to be Moors, or are believed to have flown hither from a further remote homeland, to bring a kind of exotic entertainment*]

Junius dwelt in England for 20 years from 1621, in the employ of the Earl of Arundel, but in 1642 moved back to the Netherlands. He made frequent visits back to England in 1650s, returning to London two years before his death.[12] His description of morris dancers 'blacking up' to represent Moors has sometimes been seen as evidence for the practice in the English morris dancing tradition, but it is clear from the context that Junius is writing for a pan-European scholarly audience and taking a holistic view, primarily based on continental forms of performance with quite different characteristics, perhaps including the reference in Arbeau's famous treatise *Orchésographie* (1589) to 'un garçonnet machuré et noircy' ('a blackened boy') performing the morisque.[13]

A few dictionaries gave other hints about the nature of performance. Florio's Italian-English lexicon of 1598 translated 'ballonchio' as 'a countrey hopping or morrice dance', and perhaps more unexpectedly, 'sonagliera', as 'a mans privie parts. Also a set of bels as morris dancers dance'.[14] In 1611 Cotgrave translated French 'moulinet' as 'a Morisdauncers Gamboll', and by 1660 James Howell chose to translate 'morris dance' as a 'peasant dance' in Italian and Spanish, while holding to its equivalence to 'morisque' in French.[15] We noted earlier Thomas Blount's allusion to 'chironomia', but his definition in his *Glossographia* of 1656 went further. He defined a 'Morisco dance', 'wherein there were usually five men, and a Boy dressed in a Girles habit, whom they call the Maid Marrian'.[16] This is descriptive of the dances of the south-east: and his use of the past tense is telling. Blount used his definition again in 1707 (without the use of the past tense), and it was picked up by John Kersey in his dictionaries of 1702, 1706 and 1708.[17]

---

[9] *Gazophylacium*, sig. R4v; Sheridan, sv morris-dancer.
[10] Zhdanov, sv morris.
[11] Junius, sig. Bbbb2.
[12] Romburgh.
[13] Arbeau, f. 94.
[14] Florio, pp. 37, 375.
[15] Cotgrave, sv moulinet; Howell, *Lexicon-tetraglotton*, sv morris.
[16] Blount, *Glossographia*, sig. CC3v.
[17] Blount, *Glossographia Anglicana*, sig. Ccc2v; Kersey, *New English Dictionary*, sig. S2; Phillips, *New World of Words*, sig. Sss1v; Kersey, *Dictionarium*, sig. Uu1v.

A developing sense of history began to seep into commentators' awareness of morris dancing during the 18th century. At its simplest level this was based on a few key texts, primary among them the continuing echoes, with varying degrees of accuracy, of the *Old Meg* pamphlet describing the geriatric morris of Hereford, which was adduced regularly throughout the century, mediated through Francis Bacon's and William Temple's texts. To cite just two examples: *Geography Epitomiz'd* (1718) averred that 'Not many Years ago eight old Men danced a Morrice-Dance, all living in one Manor in the West of England, whose Ages, put together, made 800 Years'; while the article 'Instances of the Longevity or Length of Life in some Persons' in 1794 ostensibly quoted from but in fact paraphrased Bacon in writing '"A while since in Herefordshire, at their May-games," saith my Lord Bacon, "there was a morrice-dance of eight men, whose years put together made up eight hundred, that which was wanting of an hundred in some, superabounding in others."'[18]

One text from 1789 which at first glance is yet another allusion to *Old Meg* refers to 'a May-game or Morrice-dance ... performed by the following eight men, in the county of Hereford, whose ages united amounted to eight hundred years'; but the eight men are named (with their ages) and the names are entirely different from those in *Old Meg*. The author's source, hence his veracity, remains unidentified.[19]

Another primary text for commentators was the royal declaration permitting some Sunday recreations, the *Book of Sports*, either in its King James incarnation or that of King Charles, and the associated controversies. Some of these were plain statements of the fact of the declaration, for example Richard Burn's *The Justice of the Peace, and Parish Officer* in his description of the law relating to Lord's Day observance.[20] In proposing new laws to allow some agricultural work to take place on Sundays, James Roper Head looked back to King James's *Declaration* for support but thought that 'the sports of may-games, Whitsun-ales and morris-dancing, are objects certainly of a very secondary nature' compared with the desirability of workers' earning their daily bread.[21] John Brown's church history disinterestedly described how 'Dr. Bound published a tract on the due sanctification of the Lord's day. All the Puritans relishing his sentiments, distinguished themselves by their Sabbath behaviour. Hereon the customary shooting, fencing, bowling, interludes, and May-games, and Morris-dances on it, began to be diluted and disliked.'[22] Others were more polemical, for example William Harris's account of the reign of Charles I: 'It certainly is a very odd way to express a pious care for the service of God, by encouraging Morice-dances, May-games, and May-poles, on the day set aside for his worship'.[23] A few were still fighting the battles of the previous century, as the author of the letter attacking Laurence Echard's *History of England* for its generally favourable attitude to the Stuarts: 'No, god be praised, the impious and unchristian book of sports on Lords Days, viz. Morris-Dances, May-Games, &c. Many Hundred conscientious Ministers, rather chose to be suspended or depriv'd of their Livings, than to read it in the House of God, and so far encourage Prophaneness'.[24]

A few historians were aware of Robert Langham's description of the morris dance at the entertainment for Queen Elizabeth on her visit to Kenilworth in 1575. One of these was John Collinson in his *The Beauties of British Antiquity* in 1779 and Francis Grose another in *The*

---

[18] J., G., p. 20; 'Instances', p. 72.
[19] *Chester Chronicle*, 10 July 1789. For a discussion of the confused sources see Klausner, *Records ... Herefordshire*, pp. 280-82.
[20] Burn, 2:138-39.

[21] Head, pp. 10-11.
[22] Brown, John, p. 154.
[23] Harris, William, p. 58 (footnote).
[24] Country Layman, 1728, p. 5.

Antiquities of England and Wales in 1783.[25] The work itself was republished in 1784.[26] Other events known to writers included the Midsummer Watch as described by Stow, and Queen Elizabeth's 1559 visit to St Mary Spittle.[27]

The painting of morris dancers at Richmond-upon-Thames (Figure 6.5 on p. 93) was described by Horace Walpole in these terms in 1765:[28]

> *At the lord viscount Fitzwilliam's, on Richmond Green, are two very large pictures which came out of the old neighbouring palace: they are views of that palace, and were painted by Vinckeboom, who, I never knew, was in England. The landscape in both is good, and touched in the style of Rubens; the figures are indifferent, the horses bad. In the view to the green is a stag-hunting: in the other morrice-dancers, and a fool collecting money from the spectators. By the dresses they appear to have been painted about the latter end of James I or beginning of Charles, for some of the ruffs are horizontal, some falling on the breasts, which latter fashion was introduced at that period.*

Nine years later a print of the painting was published, price 2s 6d, describing the scene as 'a representation of a Mumming or Masquerade, with Morris Dancers'.[29] The conjoining of three different kinds of entertainment in the description of the print shows just how fluid the various concepts had become over the course of the century.

The earliest attempt to define morris dancing in a historical context was written by Henry Curzon in his encyclopaedic *The Universal Library* in 1712. He lifted (without attribution) Thomas Blount's 1679 description of the lamb ale at Kidlington, but went on:[30]

> *The Custom of morisco, or Morrice Dancing, (the Name whereof is derived from the Moors) is much used in several Parts of England, especially on May-day, Whitsontide and the like times, the Practice being to be Clad in White Wastcoats, or Shirts and Caps, having their Legs adorned with Bells, which Gingle merrily as they Leap or Dance, and the Leaping about with Bells on their Legs after a Hobby and a horse (quasi hobbyhorse) is not Originally an European Frolick, tho brought first among the English by the Spaniards, but the Name imports to Dance – Alla Moresca.*

This is the first description which tries to explain the origin of the dance and to describe its characteristics – which are those of the by now 'traditional' morris (smart clothing, bells on the legs, leaping) – in a non-polemical way. Curzon went beyond the etymological association with the Moors and suggested a potential route for the dance to enter England, from Spain.

The description first used by Blount in 1656 and copied by John Kersey in his dictionaries to 1708 was also used by Nathan Bailey in his 1721 dictionary. Bailey was, like Junius, primarily a philologist, interested in explanation as much as in definition of the words he listed. In 1730 he produced a definition with new text, closely based on Curzon:[31]

> *Morisco, a Morris Dance, much the same with that which the Greeks call'd Pyrrhica. Span.*
>
> *Maid Morion/ Maid Marrion, a Boy dressed in a girl's Habit, having his Head gaily trimmed, who dances with the Morris-Dancers.*
>
> *…*

25 Collinson, p. 166; Grose, 6:7.
26 Langham, *Laneham's Letter*.
27 *London and its Environs*, p. 37; Bailey, *Antiquities*, p. 129.
28 Walpole, p. 38.
29 *Morning Chronicle*, 12 March 1774.
30 Curzon, 1:354.
31 Bailey, *Universal Etymological Dictionary*, sv. maid marrion, morris dance; Bailey, *Dictionarium*, sig. 5T.

> *Morris Dance (or a Dance a le Morisco, or after the Manner of the Moors; a Dance brought into England by the Spaniards) the Dancers are clad in white Wastcoats or Shirts and Caps, having their legs adorn'd with Bells, which make a merry jingling, as they leap or dance.*

Curzon's ascription of the dance's entry to England from Spain was expanded upon by the antiquary Francis Peck in his 1740 commentary upon Milton's masque *Comus*, in which there had been a brief allusion to the dance:[32]

> *The morris or moorish dance was first brought into England, as I take it, in Edward III. time, when John of Gaunt returnd from Spain, where he had been ... This dance was usually performed abroad by an equal number of young men, who danced in their shirts with ribands & little bells about their legs. But here in England they always have an odd person besides, being a boy dressed in a girl's habit, whom they called Maid Marian. The place where they danced was often in the field & called the five, seven, or nine, men's morris ... I cannot forbear observing on the boy dressed in girl's cloaths introduced into this dance, that tho' the young folks of England had, by this Spanish expedition, got a new diversion, yet they could not forbear dashing it with their old favorit one of Maid Marian.*

The attribution to John of Gaunt in Edward III's time (i.e., before 1377), is entirely speculative, antedating the earliest records of the dance in England (themselves unknown to Peck) by up to a century. Peck was simply looking for plausible links between England and Spain which might support such an origin. He likewise sought a rational explanation for the introduction of a Maid Marion figure. Unfortunately, his quest for probable causes led him astray in associating nine-men's morris with a dancing-ground. Nine-men's morris is a game usually played with counters on a board, but which could also be marked out on the ground. Nonetheless, Peck's remains the first attempt to go beyond assertions of origins and seek historical causes and effects. The idea of transmission via Spain was repeated by the anonymous author of the *Agreeable Companion* in 1748, who copied much from Peck, but added that 'It was much used in England before the late Civil Wars, and though the Custom be mostly laid aside, it is observed in some parts of the Nation to this Day'.[33]

Ferdinando Warner's *The History of Ireland*, published in 1763, provided an alternative theory of origins which was not picked up for nearly two hundred years. He suggested that the celebrations of morris dancers and milkmaids on May day derive from the pagan Celtic festival of Beltane. He added, cautiously, that 'this is merely my own conjecture, and of no sort of moment whether it is right or wrong'.[34]

Samuel Johnson's 1756 *A Dictionary of the English Language* was conceived as a direct successor to Nathan Bailey's work, and an interleaved copy of the 1736 edition of Bailey's work (which contained the same definitions as the 1730 edition) was used as the basis for it.[35] Johnson introduced a new lexicographical element, attribution of an authority for his entries, based on the citation of a source text. His entries for our relevant headwords are:[36]

> *Maidmarian, n.s. [puer ludius, Latin] A kind of dance, so called from a buffoon dressed like a man [sic], who plays tricks to the populace.*
>
> *A set of morrice-dancers danced a maidmarian with a tabor and pipe. Temple.*
>
> ...

---

[32] Peck, Francis, pp. 135-36.
[33] *Agreeable Companion*, p. 29.
[34] Warner, Ferdinando, p. 220.

[35] Rogers, Pat.
[36] Johnson, Samuel, *Dictionary*, 2:sv morisco, morris.

Mori'sco. s. [morisco, Spanish.] A dancer of the morris or Moorish dance. Shak.

...

Mo'rris / Mo'rris-dance. s. [that is, moorish dance.] 1. A dance in which bells are gingled, or swords or staves clashed, which was learned by the Moors. 2. Nine mens Morris. A kind of play with nine holes in the ground. Shakespeare.

Mo'rris-dancer. s. [morris and dance.] One who dances à la moresco, the Moorish dance. Temple.

While adopting some of the standard ideas about sources, and dispensing with some elements of Bailey's definition, Johnson's primary definition of the dance as one in which 'bells are gingled, or swords or staves clashed' introduced a new element. This was the first time in which staves were mentioned, and there are no literary antecedents upon which Johnson can have drawn his definition. It must come from personal experience. Johnson was born and raised in the centre of Lichfield, which had an annual Whitsuntide celebration – the Greenhill Bower – featuring morris dancers. This will be discussed in more detail later, but Lichfield lies in that arc north and west of Birmingham where we find stick dances – bedlam morris – in the 19th century (see Chapter 15), and there exists an early nineteenth-century illustration of the Lichfield dancers showing them dancing with sticks (Figure 15.2 on p. 244).

Two years after Johnson, his friend the Oxford librarian Francis Wise, after a discussion of Hungarian sword dances, added in a footnote that 'The common people in many parts of England still practise what they call a Morisco dance, in a wild manner, and as it were in armour; at proper intervals striking upon each others Staves, and winding their Horns; which seems to be a low imitation of the Corybantine rites'.[37] Although the assertion about armour is baseless, the blowing of horns made from birch-bark was certainly an aspect of Whitsun festivities in Wychwood, Oxfordshire, in the 19th century.[38]

The writer George Gregory also noted in 1788 that morris dancing was still practised in some parts of the country but not others, writing at the end of his discussion of Ancient Greek drama that 'something like this state of drama we see in the rude exhibitions of mummers and morrice-dancers in the inland parts of this kingdom'.[39] One 'Lucius', writing 1785, claimed that 'In the counties familiar to Milton, at harvest-homes, sheep-shearings, meadow-mowings, lamb-ales, as they are stiled, and other rustic celebrities, more especially at the Whitsun-sports, the tabor and pipe, and the morrice-dance, are still in high request'. This is perhaps a somewhat odd statement in view of the fact that Milton spent most of his life in London and its environs, but it may indicate the patchiness of the survival of morris dancing across the country.[40]

Another strand in the developing understanding of morris dancing as a historical phenomenon was in the interpretation of Shakespeare's plays and other pre-Commonwealth drama. The earliest does not inspire confidence. In 1748 John Upton followed Francis Peck when he dismissed another commentator's (reasonable) definition of the game of nine-men's morris (from *A Midsummer Night's Dream*, II.i) as 'a kind of rural chess', writing 'Nothing like it. I have writ the following in my Shakespeare: i.e. The place where the Morisco, or morrice dance was wont to be performed by nine men is filled up with mud, so that they must leave their sport.'[41]

---

[37] Wise, p. 51 (footnote).
[38] Little, Alice.
[39] Gregory, p. 41.
[40] Lucius.
[41] Upton, p. xl.

In 1765 Samuel Johnson reverted to Nathan Bailey's definition of a Maid Marion in glossing the term's occurrence in *Henry IV, Part I*: 'a man dressed like a woman, who attends the dancers of the morris'.[42] Edward Capell was able to make more connections in his *Notes and Various Readings to Shakespeare* (1774), telling us that Maid Marion is 'one of the personages that make up the morris dance, along with her companions of the famed Robin Hood, to who (it seems) she is mistress: these dances were historical; presenting actual characters of this or that hero and none oft'ner than the man abovemention'd'.[43]

Shakespeare studies reached a new level of maturity with the publication of Samuel Johnson and George Steevens's critical edition of his works, in particular the 1778 edition, which contains 'Mr. Tollet's Opinion Concerning the Morris Dancers upon his Window' as an appendix to *Henry IV Part I* (presumably on the basis of the 'Maid Marion' reference in it).[44] George Tollet's window was the Betley window (Figure 4.1 on p. 43) and this was the first notice of it in print. The essay was accompanied by a plate reproducing an image of the window, and the presence of this illustration was heavily promoted in most of the advertisements for the book in this and subsequent editions. For example, a 1785 advertisement announced that 'On Thursday the 15th inst. will be published the Plays of William Shakspeare... To which are added, Notes by Samuel Johnson and George Steevens ... and a Plate representing the Figures of ancient Morrice-Dancers, &c.'[45]

Tollet had read Peck's origin theory, and Johnson's reference to swords or staves, pointing out that the characters in his window lack them, and do not have dark faces. He described each figure in detail, and was aware of the possible resonance of the lady and the friar with Maid Marion and Friar Tuck from the Robin Hood cycle. He identified the dancer at bottom left as the 'bavian' or a fool, and alluded to that character in the mixed-couple morris performed in *Two Noble Kinsmen*. Steevens thought the dancer to the right of the hobby horse to be the lady's paramour, but Tollet saw the pouch at his waist and used it to identify him as the morris dancers' treasurer. He noted the references by Jonson to the hobby horse, and to the mysterious daggers through the cheeks, and identified its ladle as a collecting device. In an overly close analysis of the costume and physical appearance (he did not know of the antecedent of the images in van Meckenem's print), he deemed the dancer to the left of the hobby horse to be a peasant or yeoman, and the dancer to the left of the maypole a franklin. He noted the history of the maypole, and its prohibition then return at the Restoration, but added (p. 431) that 'they are now generally unregarded and unfrequented'. He reckoned the pipe-and-taborer to be 'a minstrel of the superior order' (p. 431). He noted that others had proposed that the dancer at top left was a Spaniard or Moor, and that at top right a Fleming. For his part he thought the latter might be a nobleman, and suggested that the window represents all the social classes. The Fool was for him a 'counterfeit fool' (p. 432) and he proposed reading the window as a procession beginning and ending with fools, and with the social classes in their due order between them. He suggested that the window dates from the early part of the reign of Henry VIII. For all its inadequacies, Tollet's essay was a significant step forward in the efforts by scholars to reach a detailed understanding of the morris dance, and it drew on a number of sources to do so.

The essay came hard on the heels of two other contributions, by Sir John Hawkins and John Brand. Sir John Hawkins published his *A General History of the Science and Practice of Music* in

---

[42] Shakespeare, *Plays*, 4:91.
[43] Capell, p. 43.

[44] Tollet.
[45] *General Evening Post*, 3–6 December 1785.

1776. He accepted unquestioningly the Moorish origin and suggested that morris dancing was introduced to England in Henry VIII's reign. Of the morris dance, he says that 'there are few country places in this kingdom where it is not known' and notes the shirts, bells, ribbons, and baldricks, also Maid Marion and the hobby horse. Like most commentators, he was aware of the Hereford geriatric morris, *via* Sir William Temple's work.[46] In 1777 John Brand published his *Observations on Popular Antiquities*, one of the first works to consider systematically popular lore and custom. In this first edition he did little more than note the remarks of earlier writers, in particular John Stow and Thomas Blount.[47] In its later editions, under Henry Ellis, Brand's work would become a significant source for scholars.

In the last decades of the 18th century Joseph Strutt was working on his history of sports and pastimes, which was finally published in 1801, entitled *Glig-gamena Angel-ðeod* (a rendering in Anglo-Saxon of its alternative and more commonly used title, *The Sports and Pastimes of the People of England*). Like Tollet, Strutt knew his sources, and was sceptical of the simple equation of morris = Morisco or Moorish dance on the grounds of the clear differences between English and Spanish dances. He suggested instead that it derives from the medieval fools' dance. He was aware that the dance was often associated with pageants, processions and May games with associated characters, and of its representation on the Tudor and Stuart stage. Bells were a defining characteristic, and the leader of a side might be more finely dressed than his fellows. He noted reports of differing numbers of dancers, and the presence of the hobby horse as 'almost inseparable' from the dance.[48]

Henry Curzon, Nathan Bailey, Samuel Johnson (in his dictionary and jointly with George Steevens and George Tollet in the critical edition of Shakespeare), John Hawkins, John Brand and Joseph Strutt were all grappling over the course of the century in the developing fields of antiquarianism, proto-folklore and social history, to come to an understanding of the history and nature of the morris dance itself. They paved the way for the developments of the 19th century, to which we shall return in Chapter 13.

---

[46] Hawkins, 2:134-35.
[47] Brand, *Observations* (1777), pp. 257-61, 404.

[48] Strutt, *Glig-gamena*, pp. 171-72.

Chapter 11

Hanoverian communities and Whitsun ales

It is time to turn to morris dancing in the communities of Hanoverian England in the 18th century. The evidence for activity can be hard to find. Despite the activities of the theatres and scholars, morris dancing in communities was for the most part beneath the notice of the lettered classes. The personal and household accounts of the major families of a district often recorded payments to visiting dancers, or to those encountered on their travels. Sometimes the activities of dancers were recorded in newspaper reports, often incidentally to the main subject of the story, or in diaries. The larger-scale festivities in which morris dancers were involved – most notably, Whitsun ales in the south midlands and rushcart festivals in the north-west of England – also attracted attention, particularly, as the century progressed, among those harbouring antiquarian interests. Some occasions on which morris dancers were incorporated into political or civic celebrations were recorded.

In early Hanoverian England, where morris dancing still flourished the dancers would visit the large houses on a tour of their district, soliciting contributions. Sometimes this would be in support of a general community festivity, such as a Whitsun ale. In many cases we do not know the nature or details of the event, because all we have is a record of a payment made to dancers. On some occasions more than one team of dancers would apparently turn up at the same time. Figure 11.1 shows the locations where we know payments were made to morris dancers from household or personal accounts between 1715 and 1750.

The clustering in the midlands may be an artefact of the known survival of records. The most common amount given to dancers was 5s, and after that, 2s 6d. The records from Aynho, in Northamptonshire, just over the border from Oxfordshire, are a major source and give a typical picture. In the account book of Thomas Cartwright for 1722 to 1735 are payments made not just to Aynho morris, but to morrises from eleven surrounding communities, the furthest being from Syresham twelve miles away (Figure 11.2).[1] In June 1726:

gave Heath Morrice dancers	– 5	–
& Mixbury	5	
& Whitfield	10	6

Brackley morris dancers also received 10s 6d on the two occasions they visited. After 1730 the standard amount given dropped from 5s to 2s 6d. Most of the entries are uninformative beyond the month, the amount and the origin of the dancers, but a late entry was made in 1731 which confirms the likelihood of a Whitsun ale:

pd Mr Blisse w[hi]ch he gave Dunstew Morrice in Whitsun weeke by my Mastrs order 2-6

The consecutive June 1726 payments suggest that the teams visited together. A similar occasion occurred in 1731:

gave a Croughton morris	– 2	6
gave another Croughton Morris	– 2	6

---

[1] 'Cartwright Papers' (1722).

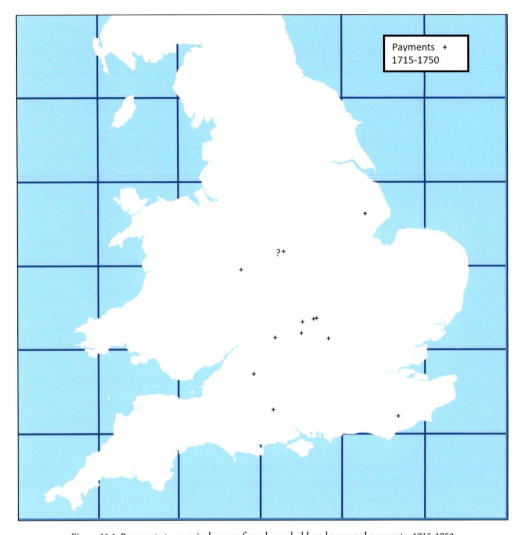

Figure 11.1: Payments to morris dancers from household and personal accounts, 1715-1750.

'Another' suggests that, unusually, two teams from the same village turned up to perform.

A further major source are the records of Stowe House in Buckinghamshire. In the period to 1750 these take the form of the personal account books for Richard Temple and his nephew Richard Grenville-Temple. It is not always clear where they were when they made the payments. Richard Grenville-Temple only acquired Stowe in 1749, and for most of the time under review lived at Wotton House, Brill.

Richard Temple may have been in Aylesbury when he paid 5s 'To Morerish Dancers' eight days before Whitsunday in 1722.[2] This was the same level of payment as we found at Aynho. Richard Grenville-Temple was more generous. In 1737 (probably on the occasion of his wedding) he paid no less than £6 15s to a 'Set of morrice dansers, fidlers &c' – of course,

[2] 'Stowe MSS, Richard Temple, 3rd Bart., Money Received', [unfoliated].

all kinds of extras could be hidden in the '&c.' Two years later he paid morris dancers 7s 6d and at Christmas 1739 paid '[blank] Morrice dancers' 10s 6d. Evidently his steward intended to add where they came from but failed to do so. In 1742 he paid the Brill morris 5s, and at Christmas paid morris dancers 10s 6d. In May 1743 he recorded £1 11s 6d given to dancers – this may represent three sets paid at 10s 6d each. Nearby payments relate to his property in Eyam in Derbyshire, where dancers are known in the early 19th century, but a location in Buckinghamshire seems more likely. (The Eyam location is indicated with a question mark in Figure 11.1.) Certainly there were three sets of dancers in May 1748 at Brill, when they were apparently

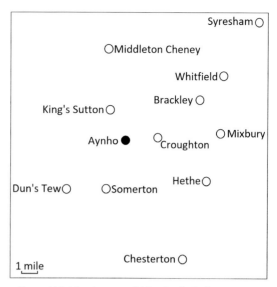

Figure 11.2: Morris teams visiting Aynho Park, 1722-1735.

paid £1 0s 6d (an anomalous amount which may be an accounting error for three payments of 10s 6d, totalling £1 11s 6d). On another occasion that year he paid dancers 8s. Finally, in 1750 at Stowe he paid Buckingham morris 10s 6d.[3]

Other south-midlands records include the 5s paid when the Northleach dancers travelled 5 miles to Sherborne House in 1731 and a similar gift for 'Kertling[ton] Morris at the Lamb Ale' by Sir James Dashwood a year later.[4] Elizabeth Purefoy and her son Henry at Shalstone Manor in Northamptonshire made payments varying from 1s to 3s 6d between 1735 and 1748 to dancers from Shalstone itself, Turweston and Buckingham (the latter two each four miles distant). On 7 June 1742 (Whit Monday) they apparently made separate payments to the Shalstone dancers, Elizabeth giving them 3s 6d and Henry 2s 6d. None the less, they were apparently not that close to their tenants' lives: on 13 May 1748 Henry noted in his diary: 'Persons I conversed with: one of ye Shalstone Morrice Dancers to whom I gave money (whose name I know not)'. Although that date was not close to Whitsun, most were, and on 10 May 1743 (12 days before Whitsunday) Elizabeth gave 'the Whitsun ale folks' 2s 6d.[5] A payment for a different kind of seasonal event is recorded when James Leigh at Adlestrop gave morris dancers 1s at the annual mead mowing.[6]

Outside the south midlands records are scattered. At Lacock in Wiltshire the Davenport family regularly gave 2s 6d to dancers between 1722 and 1724 (on 7 May 1722, 5s to 'morris dancers and harp'). In 1724 the payment was 'to 7 morris Dancers' – perhaps a supernumerary to the dance was included in the count.[7] At Brightling in Sussex John Fuller made two Christmastide payments of 2s to 'Morris dancers and Fidlers' on 20 December 1737 and 6 January 1738.[8] Between 1744 and 1761 the Arundell family in Salisbury gave morris dancers 1s as a Christmas

[3] 'Stowe MSS, Richard Temple, 2nd Earl', pp. 70, 92, 96, 118, 126, 159, 175, 189.

[4] Dutton, f. 98; Townsend, James, p. 15.

[5] Purefoy and Purefoy, p. xxv; Cawte, pers. comm.

[6] Leigh, James.

[7] Davenport, Barbara; Davenport, Mrs; Davenport, Henry. I am grateful to Jameson Wooders for bringing these and other records to my attention.

[8] Fuller, John.

box; these may have been the Tailors' Guild dancers, but there is nothing in Guild records to corroborate this. The payments stop before the end of the account book, so the dancers may not have appeared in later years.[9]

One more outlier in the first part of the 18th century is Revesby in Lincolnshire, where Christmastide payments were made on 7 January 1724 ('Gave Moris Dancers 6d') and 26 December 1724 ('Given to the Morice Dancers 1s').[10] Although these payments are not in themselves particularly informative, they are important because of the significant role of Revesby later in the century, for which see Chapter 12.

For those households and estates which record multiple payments, Aynho, Stowe and Shalstone in particular, there is an inherent uncertainty in extrapolating the evidence. On the one hand, they may be seen as evidence of widespread activity – the tip of an iceberg. On the other, there are many years in these runs of accounts when no payments are recorded. Given the overall richness of detail, does this absence of evidence constitute evidence of absence – does it indicate that there was no activity? Henry Purefoy's note of his meeting with a morris dancer in 1748 may give a hint. Although he says he gave the dancer money, there is no corresponding record in his accounts to corroborate this. There are other instances where an expected corroboration is not found. My inclination is to suggest that, rich as they are, these records remain but a partial record of the levels of activity, particularly in the south midlands.

Newspaper reports can be more informative than brief entries in account books. In 1727 a correspondent sent a riddle in verse to the *Gloucester Journal*:[11]

> *On a place big enough for Work or for Play,*
> *A Carpet was spread on a bundle of Hay,*
> *Of neat morrice-Dancers full fifty met on it,*
> *Now perhaps you'll expect both a Jigg and a Sonnet,*
> *But, alas! of all these there was never a one*
> *Cou'd whistle Moll Peatley, or sing Bobbin Joan:*
> *However they trip it and trip it about,*
> *Ev'ry one in their turn, not a Couple stood out.*

An answer in verse the following week identified the dancers as bobbins used in lace-making.[12] The riddle is one of the earliest pieces of evidence for the tunes used in what is presumably the Whitsun-ale morris. 'Moll Peatley' was a tune printed in the third edition of *The Dancing Master* in 1665.[13] It had disappeared from the repertoire of south-midlands morris tunes by the time of the collectors in the early 20th century, but 'Bobbin Joan' (a phonetic rendering of 'Bobbing Joe', which appeared in the first edition of *The English Dancing Master*)[14] survived in several morris communities under various phonetic renderings. Their use here suggests that the dancing manuals were a significant source of tunes for morris dances, even if those specifically named as 'morris' tunes within them were not incorporated into the repertoire.

At Litchborough in Northamptonshire morris dancers helped to celebrate the marriage of ninety-year-old John Butcher in 1731,[15] and ten miles away at Great Brington morris dancers

---

[9] 'List of Christmas Gifts' (1744).
[10] Revesby.
[11] *Gloucester Journal*, 23 May 1727.
[12] *Gloucester Journal*, 30 May 1727.
[13] 'Moll Peatly'.
[14] 'Bobbing Joe'.
[15] *Read's Weekly Journal*, 12 June 1731.

were advertised as an attraction at the statute (hiring) fair on 17 September 1747: 'on the Statute Day will be the famous Blakesley Morrice at the same Place' (the Black Swan inn).[16] Blakesley was 13 miles away from Great Brington so the organizer – one Brooks Wright, a wrestling promoter describing himself as a 'gamester'[17] – must have been sure of a good return on his investment. A few years later the October statute fair at Towcester was the venue for a competition, when in 1766 'six Pair of Gloves ... will be given to be danced for by Morris Dancers: No less than three Setts to dance'.[18] Another competition was advertised at Coln St Aldwyns, Gloucestershire in 1744, as part of general Whitsun festivities organized at the Swan inn there:[19]

> NOTICE is hereby given
>
> That on Whitsun-monday next, at the Sign of the Swan, In Cown-allins, near Fairford, Gloucestershire, will be given a HAT of a Guinea Price, to be play'd for at Backsword, by five or seven Men of a side, and that Side that can break the most Heads shall be entitled to the Hat, each side to appear on the Stage by One o'Clock.
>
> Likewise, on the Morrow, there will be six exceeding good KNOTS to be Morrice-danc'd for, Free Gift, and Six Pair of Gloves to be Bowl'd for at Nine-Pins.

The number of knots (rosettes) indicates that six-person sets were expected. These advertisements, presumably placed by the landlords of the inns to attract customers, demonstrate that morris dancing was seen as a potential source of revenue for dancers and entrepreneurs, and, in the case of Towcester, an explicit indication that several sets of dancers from the surrounding area were available to be potential competitors.

Morris dancing as an income generator was demonstrated in another way by a report in the *Gloucester Journal* from 1733 (widely picked up and re-reported by other newspapers nationwide). The first part re-echoes the casual approach to physical violence adduced by the head-breaking backsword fights at Coln St Aldwyns, before the report moves on to a domestic tragedy:[20]

> Last Tuesday Evening [15 May] *some Men of Barton-street, went to take away a May-Pole from Wooton near this City, and the People of the Place having Notice thereof, arm'd themselves with dangerous Weapons, so that a desperate Fray ensu'd, wherein one of the Barton-street Men had his Arm almost cut off, and several others very much wounded.*
>
> *About the same time, two children were burnt in a terrible Manner, at Hempstead near this City, one of which is since dead, and the other lies dangerously ill: It is observable, that the affectionate Father was then attending upon a Company of Morrice-Dancers with his Tabor and Pipe, and when the News of this melancholy Accident was brought to him, he refus'd to return Home, saying, He would not lose his Whitsontide. – It is greatly wish'd, that not only this, but the aforesaid kind of Whitson Sports, the Consequences of which often prove fatal, were suppressed.*

It is easy to understand the journalist's outrage, and this is an early indication of the tide of fear of the disreputable lower orders among the developing respectable middle class, and its desire to control them. Looked at another way, it is an indication of the economic importance

---

[16] *Northamptonshire Mercury*, 7 September 1747.
[17] 'Brooks Wright'.
[18] *Northampton Mercury*, 6 October 1766.
[19] *Gloucester Journal*, 1 May 1744.
[20] *Gloucester Journal*, 22 May 1733.

Figure 11.3: 'Country around Dixton Manor' (detail) (The Cheltenham Trust and Cheltenham Borough Council © The Wilson/Bridgeman Images).

of morris dancing to its participants while community support was maintained. In the one or two weeks of Whitsuntide the dancers, and even more so the musicians who played for them, could expect to earn more each day than they would normally earn in a week (see Chapter 14).[21] By continuing to play for the morris the unfortunate Hempsted musician could bring in much-needed money to support his surviving family.

A report from Hillmorton in Warwickshire also reflects the casual violence, with a hint too, perhaps, of the community rivalry that lay behind it, when 'a Fray happened between some Morrice-Dancers ... wherein two of them were so much bruised, that they died soon after'.[22] The October date of this report is outside the Whitsun season and may be related to a hiring fair or similar occasion.

One other remarkable witness to morris dancing in the early 18th century is similarly ambiguous in the message it conveys. This is a painting of an uncertain date – dates between 1715 and 1730 have been proposed – in The Wilson art gallery and museum in Cheltenham. It is a huge painting, 9 feet by 3 feet, titled 'Country around Dixton Manor' but more commonly known as 'The Dixton Harvesters', and it depicts the various scenes in a country harvest (some of which happen sequentially, but all are shown together) taking place at Dixton, north of Cheltenham. Mowers scythe, the hay is raked and gathered into stooks, to the accompaniment of a piper; waggons ply to and fro; another piper leads a group of men and women towards another task; some are watching, having a picnic (or preparing food for the workers). And in the bottom of the picture a line of morris dancers dances away (Figure 11.3).

<hr>

21 Heaney, Michael, 'With Scarfes'.

22 *Whitehall Evening Post*, 26 October 1754.

The depiction is tiny, occupying no more than about 7½ inches of the 9-foot canvas. The six dancers brandish large white handkerchiefs, wear tricorn hats, white shirts, baldricks (alternately blue and red down the line of dancers) and black breeches; indistinctly painted bells may be present. They are led by one man similarly dressed, who carries what may be a sword upon which a garland has been affixed, or a fool's long stick. They are preceded by two men in coats who may be flag bearers or whifflers to clear the way: these two carry poles with flags or garlands on top. No musician is visible. Four of the six dancers are kicking their left legs out, one his right leg out and one his right leg across his body.

It all appears to be a representation of an idyllic rural scene, but the painting is one of a pair: its companion, of equal size, 'Dixton Manor, Gloucestershire' shows the other side of the hill, depicting the manor house and the Higford family who owned it (and who, it is presumed, commissioned both paintings) standing outside.[23] The contrast between them could not be starker. Our painting shows over 100 people working an immense open field. The companion picture shows around two dozen enclosed fields in a similar area. Sheep and cattle graze, but apart from the family and household around the manor house the scene is almost devoid of people. Dixton itself had been enclosed early in the 16th century, and that is what is shown in the companion piece; our painting shows the scene to the east of the manor, in the parent parish of Alderton, which was not enclosed until early in the 19th century.[24] The true message of the paintings is ambiguous. They seem to have been created soon after 1715, when William Higford succeeded to the manor upon the death of his brother, and they recreate the landscape with almost photographic accuracy. Many of the fields can be identified: the open field with all the activity is Mickle Mead.[25] William Higford might simply be celebrating the acquisition of the estate, but the paintings may be a statement representing his view of the good and the bad in contemporary English agricultural practice. In the absence of supporting evidence we do not know whether Higford is affirming the benefits of proprietorship and productivity in the picture of the manor, or the vibrant community life of the open field system represented by Mickle Mead in the picture of the harvest.

Another kind of testimony comes from William Savory of Brightwalton on the Berkshire downs. He kept a commonplace book in which he recorded village memories. His uncle John Savory was a wheelwright who was active in village life, being a bell-ringer, involved in the church choir and keeping parish accounts. William included the following account of his uncle's activities in the middle of the 18th century:[26]

> *he was very fond of Card playing - Dancing &c - him with more of his Companions went to Morris Dancing and ornamented themselves with Snail shells instead of Bells. Their Squire was one Robt Brown who lived at a little Cottage House in the way to Farnbro & occupied his own land. ... their Musitioner [sic] was Betty the wife of Stephen Taylor now living at Brightwalton.*

This is unusual in several respects. The use of snail shells was innovative, the location is not in an area known for its dancing, and there was a female musician. Savory himself was more than just a labourer, and Jameson Wooders has established that Robert Brown, the squire (leader) for the team, was a yeoman farmer with his own freehold land. This suggests, perhaps, a middle-class representation that may have had a hint of self-parody about it.

---

[23] 'Dixton Manor Paintings'.
[24] Elrington.
[25] Sale.
[26] Wooders, p. 559.

One more allusion from this period, by Richard Wilkes, reveals the general broadening of the conceptions of what constitutes a morris dance. Around 1710 Thomas Loxdale had described the hobby-horse custom at Seighford in Staffordshire as 'something like a Morris dance'. Abbot's Bromley, 15 miles away, also had (and still has) a hobby-horse custom described as such by Dr Plot in 1686.[27] Wilkes, probably writing in the second quarter of the 18th century, was more decided in his assertion.[28] The dancers use:

> six Elks Heads ... with which, a Bow and Arrow; Sword, & Pot Lid, & a thing made in the shape of a Horse, with Hoops and Cloaths, they dance the Morrice, on particular occasions.

Throughout the 18th century the Whitsun ale continued to be a popular recreation, particularly in agricultural communities in the south midlands, that is, Oxfordshire and the contiguous areas of Gloucestershire, Warwickshire, Northamptonshire and Buckinghamshire. They were not entirely looked upon with favour. A minister near Stow-on-the-Wold in Gloucestershire was to some extent fighting the battles of the previous century when he wrote in 1736 *A Serious Dissuasive against Whitsun Ales*, but his writing this does suggest that Whitsun ales were prevalent around him. The text is now lost to us, but it is cited in John Brand's *Observations upon Popular Antiquities* (1813 edition). Ales were 'acts of foolery and buffoonery – but children's play, and what therefore grown-up persons should be ashamed of'. Worse, 'Morris Dances, so called, are nothing else but reliques of Paganism'.[29] Most complainants, however, were simply aggrieved by the clamour and disorder which assaulted their refined tastes. The lament of Lady Fermanagh at Claydon House in Buckinghamshire in 1716 is well known:[30]

> We have whisen ayls all about us, which brings such A Bundance of rabble & the worst sort of Company round us that I wish noe mischifes Happens. ... I can't help giving the Morrises monny when they come, for they tell me everybody doing it is the best way to send them going – there is one at Steeple Claydon, one at Hoggshaw, one at Buckingham and one att Stratton Audley.

This confirms our earlier supposition that ales and morris teams were common. Though Steeple Claydon is the 'home' team, and Hogshaw just 2½ miles distant, the other two locations are over five miles away. At the same time Lady Fermanagh reveals that making a gift to them does not necessarily imply approval. Ann Tracy, daughter of the house at Stanway House in Gloucestershire, was similarly annoyed, expressing increasing exasperation in her diary as the household staff prepared for an ale in 1724:[31]

> May 25th: Vast preparation among the servants that our Morrice might out-do all the rest at the Whitsun Ale.
>
> May 28th: Almost distracted with ye perpetual noise of morrice in ye morn.
>
> May 30th: Almost stunned with Morrice Dancing.

The nature of a Whitsun-ale feast is described in several contemporary accounts, of which the best is that published by John Haslewood, mentioned earlier in considering the bedlam morris (Chapter 8).[32] Other accounts vary in details, as the ales themselves must have done, but this is the best single account and elements of it can be tested against other sources. Writing in 1814,

27 Plot, p. 434.
28 Wilkes, p. 388, cited in Cawte, *Ritual Animal Disguise*, p. 67.
29 Brand, *Observations* (1813), 1:227.
30 Verney, Margaret, 2:41.
31 Winkless, p. 206.
32 Brydges and Haslewood, 4:335-38.

Haslewood related the description given to him by a first-hand informant of a typical Whitsun ale (although he calls it a May-game) as held at Combe in Oxfordshire around 1774, and it is worth quoting in full. He begins:

> The May-games were, at that period, planned by the sons of wealthy farmers, who undertook the burthen of the expense in case the want of success should leave any undefrayed. Some convenient spot, near the middle of the village, where the use of a barn could be obtained, was fixt upon, and with a green sufficiently contiguous, where the bower and May-pole could be erected. The intended festival was then announced by the Morris-dancers upon Maundy-Thursday, (if that day fell conveniently,) who made a rotary visit to the halls of the neighbouring gentry, where they usually obtained a seasonable contribution. It was also made known upon the market days at all the adjacent towns.

The informant is a little confused about dates, using the term 'May-game' and attributing the start of proceedings to Maundy Thursday. In fact, the preliminaries for a Whitsun ale usually began ten days before Whit Sunday, on Ascension Day. This was a practice carried over from before the Civil War, as evidenced by records such as those from Melton Mowbray in 1563 and Oxford in 1632 (see Chapter 7). Both Ascension Day and Maundy Thursday are also known as 'Holy Thursday', and this may have misled the informant's memory. The dramatic elements sometimes associated with pre-Commonwealth feasts – Robin Hood and the like – have disappeared in favour of simple horseplay.

We have seen plentiful evidence of morris dancers' visits to the houses of the gentry in the lead up to and during a Whitsun ale, and the payments received. There is also evidence that the ale was announced in nearby towns. On 26 May 1753 an announcement appeared in *Jackson's Oxford Journal* about a proposed ale at Cumnor (just over the border from Oxford in Berkshire), which the authorities wished to prohibit on the grounds of a smallpox outbreak. The ale had been 'cried' in Oxford and in Abingdon.[33]

Haslewood's extended description continues:

> The May-pole, and a thrave of boughs, to form the bower, were occasionally purchased, but more commonly obtained as a donation. The first, when erected, had the top adorned with a garland of flowers, and the latter being arched over, was made sufficiently capacious for the country-dances.
>
> In the barn, or, as named for the occasion, the Lord's mansion, there were placed several barrels of ale, brewed for the purpose, with cakes newly baked, (for a daily supply of which some neighbouring oven was engaged) and a large quantity of ribbons. The sale of these articles usually exonerated the promoters of the games from any loss.

Beer was certainly brewed in quantity. At an advertisement for a Whitsun ale in Moreton-in-Marsh, Gloucestershire, in 1785, it was announced that the entertainment 'will begin on Monday, and continue so long as their Stock of Liquors will last, which consists of eight Hogsheads of Beer, of an exceeding good Quality, with the best Cakes that can be provided'.[34] Eight hogsheads are equivalent to 7680 pints of beer.

Ribbons were used to make favours – in pre-Commonwealth terms, liveries – to show that a participant had paid to take part. At a Whitsun ale held in 1721 in Churchill, Oxfordshire,

---

[33] *Jackson's Oxford Journal*, 26 May 1753.   [34] *Jackson's Oxford Journal*, 23 April 1785.

1580 yards of ribbon of varying widths were purchased on a sale-or-return basis; 595 were returned, which means 985 yards were used, for favours and presumably for elements of the characters' costumes and regalia.[35]

Haslewood next turned to the protagonists and their retinue:

> *In chusing the Lord and Lady of the May, care was taken to select a smart active and handsome man, as well as a lively pretty woman, the daughter of some respectable farmer, and to whom it often proved the prelude of obtaining a husband. It is doubtful whether the Lord derived any pecuniary advantage from the revenue that supported his state, though the Lady was allowed daily new shoes and twenty yards of ribbon, and, at the end of the sports, complimented with a guinea.*
>
> *In procession the Lady carried a bouquet, which was called her mace, and herself and Lord held each the end of a ribbon, as did their attendants, called my Lord's footman and my Lady's maid, part of whose province was to sell ribbons. The maid also carried a mace, which might be named the mace of mischief, as, to tickle the noses of her admirers, the flowers were often mischievously enwoven with pins as well as briar.*

Others go into more detail about the retinue. Simeon Moreau, writing in 1783, said that they were 'attended by the Steward, Sword, Purse and Mace Bearer, with their several badges of office, ... they have likewise in their suit a page or train-bearer, and a jester, dressed in a party-coloured jacket. The Lord's music, consisting of a tabour and pipe, is employed to conduct the dance.'[36] Moreau was the first Master of Ceremonies at the Assembly Rooms in Cheltenham as it developed into a fashionable spa town. It was his job to provide entertainment and diversion for visitors, and he was describing the ale as a quaint local custom.[37]

Anne Baker provided details of the Lord's and Lady's retinue at two Northamptonshire Whitsun ales, Greatworth in 1785 and King's Sutton *c*. 1800.[38] Each had a Lord's son, a fool, and two or three providers of music. Each had two treasurers to collect and look after the money, and two 'butlers' responsible for dispensing drink. King's Sutton had two sword bearers, and 'servitors', who may have been equivalent to the footman and lady's maid at Combe; Greatworth had unspecified 'supporters'. Greatworth's procession was also led by a constable, absent from other accounts.

The next part of Haslewood's account dealt with the Squire, or fool:

> *Another attendant, whose province gave life to the show, was called the Squire. His dress was a fanciful compound of those genuine Mimes, the Harlequin, Clown, and Scaramouch. He was furnished with a weapon to prevent the crowd incommoding his Lord and Lady in their progresses. It consisted of a short stick, having at one end a narrow round sand-bag, sewed in tan leather; at the other end, the dried tail of a calf. From the last, the incorrigible, on whom the weight of the sand-bag had repeatedly fallen without effect, seldom ventured to provoke a second stripe. The Squire was noted for his loquacity, and was expected to have a wise or foolish speech ready upon every occasion; for by the laughter his nonsense occasioned, was commonly decided his ability to support the character.*

The fool is confirmed as a key character by several accounts. Though Haslewood's informant speaks of his carrying a small sandbag, in other accounts he has an inflated pig's bladder.

---

[35] 'William Smith MSS, Whitsun Ale'.

[36] Moreau, p. 63.

[37] *History of Cheltenham*, p. 47.

[38] Baker, Anne Elizabeth, 2:433-35.

Anne Baker referred to 'the usual badge ... an inflated bladder with beans, fastened to a staff about two feet long, or ... attached to one end of a short stick, and a calf's tail at the other'.[39] A description by a Mr Horne (as reported by Cecil Sharp) of an ale at Milton-under-Wychwood, Oxfordshire in 1780 tells us that he 'carried a stick with a bladder at one end and a calves tail at the other end and did not fright to use them about the boys backs'.[40]

Baker and Mr Horne each refer to the fool's dress. Horne refers to his having one black and one white shoe, ditto stockings, loose print trousers reaching below the knee, his jacket having 'T.F.' ('Tom Fool') on its back. Baker says that he is 'variously, but always grotesquely, attired, sometimes with a cow's tail at his back, sometimes covered with skins; and, in the neighbourhood of Brackley, he is called the squire or fool, and has a gridiron and fish drawn on his back'. The Brackley fool found himself in trouble in 1766 when, as *Jackson's Oxford Journal* reported from Oxford, 'Yesterday the Squire of a Whitsun-ale, attending his company of Morrice-Dancers in this City (which he had imported from Brackley in Northamptonshire) having been somewhat insolent as well as troublesome in playing the Fool, had the misfortune to get himself committed to Brideswell as a vagrant'.[41] We do not know whether this was an ale in Oxford (which is a rather more urban environment than that usually associated with ales, with a consequent difficulty in getting strong community support), or if this was an ale at Brackley and the fool and dancers were touring the area to generate income and engagement. If at Oxford, the Brackley dancers may merely have been visiting the ale, or they may been engaged as the morris dancers for the ale itself. Brackley is 25 miles from Oxford, which is a significant distance to travel in the 18th century. What this event does tell us is that the fool/squire is a key figure in a Whitsun ale, and that he is particularly associated with, if not in charge of, the morris dancers.

Moving on to describe the conduct of the ale, Haslewood wrote:

> *Early upon May morning the Lord and Lady, with their attendants, waited by the May-pole for visitors, whom they preceded in due form, their Squire and two servants leading the way, first to the bower and then to the mansion. Here the company were shown the curiosities, viz. a flail, hung over a beam, as my Lord's organ; the portrait of a lion for my Lady's lap-dog, and that of an owl for her parrot. The regulations and forfeits of the mansion were also communicated, and finally the party invited to partake of the refreshments. That being done, the duty of the Lord and Lady ceased, and they returned, with their attendants, to their former station, to wait other visitors. If while they were engaged, as it frequently happened, there arrived a set of Morris dancers, often with all the good folks of their village in company, the whole halted at a distance until the cavalcade could be preceded in due state to the mansion.*
>
> *No inconsiderable portion of good humour arose from the non-payment of the forfeits. To call either of the above named curiosities by any other appellation than that assigned to it, incurred a fine of sixpence; and he that refused to pay was forced to ride my Lord's horse. This was a wooden machine, about four feet high, borne upon poles, and having the head of a horse with a bridle. Upon this my Lady first mounted, sideways, holding the rein; then the delinquent was placed behind her, and both carried by two men round the May-pole. A fine was often wilfully incurred, as during the ride it became the duty of the swain to salute my Lady; and whether he was bashful or a gay gallant, the elevation and the deed always proved a subject of merriment for the spectators.*

[39] Baker, Anne Elizabeth, 2:31.
[40] 'Sharp MSS, Mr Horne'.
[41] *Jackson's Oxford Journal*, 31 May 1766.

Baker corroborated the account of transgressors being made to ride a wooden horse, and added 'if they were still more unruly, they were put into the stocks, which was termed 'being my lord's organist'. She also averred that (outside Whitsun ales) morris dancers may be accompanied by 'Molly', who carries a ladle to solicit contributions (much as the fools did), and surmised that this was a descendant of the Maid Marion role. Her description on this point, however, has little corroboration elsewhere in the south midlands, except in the Forest of Dean on the edge of the region (see Chapter 15).[42]

Haslewood continued:

> To these festivals the Morris-dancers came in sets far and near. Those from a distance, commonly on horseback, with the manes and heads of the horses decorated with flowers, &c. They usually wore a shirt closely pleated, buckskins, or white linen breeches, cotton stockings, and pumps. Six bells, fixed upon the outside of each leg, the whole dress tastefully adorned with ribbons and white handkerchiefs, or napkins, to use in dancing. In procession, first came the fool, next the piper, and then the dancers; of whom twelve seem to have been the customary number. It was not uncommon for persons to attend them, whose only task was the care of their clothes.
>
> ...
>
> The greatest number of Morris dancers, in that part of England, always assembled in the Whitsun-week at Dover Hill, near the vale of Evesham, in the neighbourhood of Campden, Weston, and Longmaston. There were many booths erected, with various rural sports and gymnastic exercises.

Haslewood's description of the morris dancers' costume matches what we already know: a closely pleated shirt, white breeches, and pumps; bells on the legs, ribbons over the costume and white handkerchiefs or napkins in the hands. Horne's depiction of the Milton-under-Wychwood dancers in 1780 had them wearing high box hats, pleated shirts, white breeches, ribbons and a sash and cross-belt, and bells riveted to leather pads.[43] Baker made more distinctions. She described the morris dancers 'without their coats and waistcoats, and with the cleanest and best shirts they can procure, gaily bedizened with pendant ribbons and rosettes of various colours'; but dancers at ales were 'more gaily attired, and had a larger number of bells'; they had 'scarfs or belts of broad ribbon, one over each shoulder, crossing in the centre, ornamented with bunches of blue and red ribbons, or blue and orange', with five rosettes on them on the chest and five more on the back; the hats beribboned in the same colours.[44] The reference to arriving on horseback suggests a rather more prosperous community than that of most Whitsun ales, and has little corroboration beyond, perhaps, Celia Fiennes's description of 'Maurice dancers with their pranceing horses' at Bath in 1704 (see p. 142).

Haslewood mentions 12 dancers at a time. Baker says that most morris dancers are in sets of six or eight, while at a Whitsun ale there may be six couple; having said that, in describing the ales at Greatworth and King's Sutton she specifies six dancers at each.[45] Horne's account of the Milton-under-Wychwood ale also mentions six dancers.[46]

Haslewood concludes:

---

[42] Baker, Anne Elizabeth, 2:435, 30-31.
[43] 'Sharp MSS, Mr Horne'.
[44] Baker, Anne Elizabeth, 2:30-32.

[45] Baker, Anne Elizabeth, 2:31, 434-35.
[46] 'Sharp MSS, Mr Horne'.

At the village of Finstock, near Charlbury, Oxfordshire, the Morris is held by prescription, with a right of common, of a considerable extent, by the forest of Whichwood. The young men and maidens claim the right of procuring from the forest as much materials for the bower, as, with the May-pole, they can draw away, always preserving the leather harness for that purpose, and when the sports are ended the bower and May-pole are sold, and the money expended in malt, from which is brewed ale for the ensuing year. At Woodstock and Longcombe those articles are usually donated by the donation of the Duke of Marlborough.

'In conclusion,' said my informant, 'I may assert that in forty years I have never seen so much mirth, pleasure, and happiness, enjoyed by numbers, as in those meetings. Early in the day the fiddle was heard in the bower, the young were ready, and happy in their mates, and the dance continued, almost without stopping, until the evening, for when some wished to rest there were others crowding near and waiting the opportunity to join the merry throng. The old folks, gaily dressed, were always cheerful, and seemed to have left their little ailments at home. ...'

The Churchill Whitsun ale mentioned above comes to us from William Smith, the surveyor and 'the father of English geology', whose observations led to his publishing the first detailed geological map of England. His great-grandfather (of the same name) was treasurer for a Whitsun ale held in Churchill in 1721, and the family preserved the accounts for the ale.[47] These give a sense of the scale of an ale. Expenditure was £52 13s 5¼d, and receipts £59 7s 0¼d, considerable sums of money for the time. Much of the material for the ale – ribbons, cakes, etc. – was provided on credit, and the bill settled after the income had been received. It suggests that the organizers were creditworthy. The fact that they declared and paid the excise on the beer brewed also indicates a degree of respectability. The excise duty was £4 7s 11d, indicating that an enormous amount of beer was brewed; and the bill for cakes was £6 2s 9d. The fool was paid £1 and the fiddler 10s 6d. Three men were paid for bells: one 6d, the second 1s and the third 'for dancing and belles', 1s 6d. If the unit price for a set of bells was 6d, then this is enough for six sets, implying six dancers. The set of morris dancers was paid 6s and five maids were paid 2s 6d each, as was the Lady of the ale. The participants visited the neighbouring villages and there are costs associated with each visit: £4 13s at Bledington, £5 3s at Kingham, and 6s at Sarsden. The first two amounts are substantial and may reflect formal visits to neighbouring ales.

Comparative figures are available for an ale held towards the end of the century, at King's End, Bicester in 1790.[48] A draft of the announcement declared that 'in the course of Whitsun Week there Will be a Whitsun Ale held on Monday, Tuesday, Friday & Saturday in the said week ... Thare have been no meeting of that kind in that parrish for upwards of thirty years'. The ale was organized by the tradesmen of the town, with three victuallers providing £20 worth of beer. All the ribbons, blue and pink, were supplied by Mrs Humphries. These were the colours of the Dashwood family at Kirtlington five miles away, and a donation of 5s was received from Sir Henry Dashwood. William Hadland supplied half the cakes, three other bakers the rest. Hadland was also one of the six morris dancers, as were William Boffing (one of the beer suppliers) and Richard Humphrey, probably related to Mrs Humphries. Two more Humphreys were among the two treasurers and two butlers. Most of the identified dancers were born in the 1760s so were in their mid twenties at the time. Later in life Hadland was an agricultural labourer and a butcher, but died a pauper; William Boffing was a shoemaker in 1851.[49] The

---

[47] 'William Smith MSS, Whitsun Ale'.
[48] Dunkin, manuscript notes in the copy at Bodleian Libraries G.A. Oxon 8o 257, interleaving between pp. 268-69.   [49] Chandler, *Ribbons*, pp. 141-42.

dancers and other officials were sternly admonished 'The[y] that flinch from their proposed plases if the[y] are able to sarve them shall forfeit the Sum of Five Shillings'. This – and the length of time since the last ale – suggests that the dancers may have been novices, and one wonders where and how they learned their craft. One of the dancers was also nominated as Lord of the ale. A donation of 19s 9d was made towards the purchase of their bells. The most profitable day was Whit Monday, when they took £22 15s 2d; on the other three active days they earned around £13 a day. Total receipts from all sources were £68 6s 8d; the bills came to £59 17s 2d. One of the aims of the ale was to raise funds for a funeral pall for the church, and this was bought for £2 6s. Eleven payments of half a guinea (10s 6d) were made – probably to the main participants in the ale; 7s 8d was left in hand.

William Smith had noted that in addition to the Churchill ale in 1721, there was one in 1775/76, implying no others; but in his diary is a note of his attending a 'Youth ale' there at Whitsun in 1789.[50] In the same year an advertisement for a Whitsun ale at Woodstock declared that it would be held 'by the youths of the town'.[51] This and the Bicester account suggest ales were occasional events in many communities, but there are also examples of annual and septennial ales, for example at Kirtlington and Woodstock respectively. From payments made, it seems there were often several ales taking place within a few miles of each other every year.

Haslewood and others identified the young people of a community as prime movers in organizing an ale. His comment that the 'The young men and maidens claim the right of procuring from the forest as much materials for the bower, as, with the May-pole, they can draw away' and the fact that the Duke of Marlborough supplied wood for maypoles, highlight the role of an ale in cementing community relations and obligations. An instruction from Lord Temple's estates manager at Stowe in 1782 to his forester Henry Beauchamp exemplifies this. He gave precise guidance:[52]

> Lord Temple gives the people of Whitchurch a Maypole, which they are to fetch on Wednesday, you will therefore get some Timber down in Grenville's Wood as fall [sic] as you can, in order to have some proper for the purpose. I fancy it must be of three pieces, viz. – a Stock, middle piece, and Spire. The Stock I suppose to be about 25 feet long, and 18 or 20 inches square at the bottom, which will diminish 5 or 6 inches, as it may happen, the next piece of course must diminish in proportion, and be 20 or 25 feet long as it happens, and then any long taper Small Tree for a spier. If such pieces as I have described are not proper let them have such as are so.

Beauchamp's reply confirmed that he had supplied three pieces: 27 feet of oak timber 19½ inches round, 28 feet 12 inches round and 40 feet 7 inches round, giving a total height of 95 feet, at a cost of £7 15s. The occupants of Stowe were consistent supporters of these customs over 200 years. The other major family in the county, the Verneys at Claydon House (from where Lady Fermanagh complained of the 'whisen ayls' in 1716) were less so. Between 1688 and 1698 the villagers of Steeple Claydon asked for a maypole almost every year and were rewarded, but only to the tune of 10s a year in lieu of the actual timber.[53]

At an earlier period we have evidence of the sense of entitlement mentioned by Haslewood. At Preston Bissett in Buckinghamshire in 1661 the villagers took a thirty-foot tree from Tingewick

[50] 'William Smith MSS, Biographical'; 'William Smith MSS, Diary'.
[51] *Jackson's Oxford Journal*, 23 May 1789.
[52] 'Stowe MSS, Letter from Joseph Parrott'.
[53] Claydon House.

Wood and then came to the estates steward at Great Horwood to haggle about paying for it. Five years later six youths paid over 6s as compensation for a 'stolen' tree: 2s 6d of it was given to the wood's keeper, 1s 6d to the landowner (New College, Oxford) for the trespass, and 2s back to the youths 'as being knaves'. In 1670 'about 7 or 8 of the young maidens of Tyngewyke … entreating pardon for being soe bold they desired a tree to make a May-pole', and 'to increase good neighbourhood and love among them … and to weane them from conventicles, a tree was granted to them'. (Conventicles were meetings of hard-line Protestants opposed to the church as re-established at the Restoration.) In 1672 when two trees were set aside for use as laths in transpired that 'one of them is already cut downe & brought home & sett upp in a May-pole by the young men of Stanton' (Stanton St John, Oxfordshire).[54]

Many of these instances embody a kind of indulgent tolerance, as when William Snooke at the Manor house in Bourton-on-the-Water recorded paying 'Whitsun fools from [Great] Rissington' and from Wyck Rissington 1s each in 1774; the following year he had visits in Whitsun week from morris dancers from Wyck Rissington, Icomb and Stow-on-the-Wold (all within four miles of his home).[55]

Back at Stowe, there was a similar concentration of visiting sides in 1797, when four sets of morris dancers visited on 5 June (Whit Monday) from Westbury, Shalstone, Newton Purcell and Twyford and were each given 10s 6d. The following day a team from Marsh Gibbon visited: they were identified as freeholders, and were given a guinea (£1 1s). Clearly, being of a higher social status merited a greater reward.

At the other end of the scale was an event which allowed newspapers full rein to call upon the authorities to 'suppress such nurseries of idleness and drunkenness as Morrice-dancings have generally proved'. William Kealey, a prominent morris dancer, had been training the Chipping Campden morris dancers two weeks before Whitsun in 1772 when he followed and murdered a gardener who had been unwise enough to flash his just-paid wages at the Fish inn on Broadway Hill. At one point he accused the team's musician, pipe-and-taborer James Warner, as an accomplice, but later recanted. (The Warners were a respected family of clockmakers and musicians in the town.) Kealey was hanged on 3 August 1772 and his body hung in chains on a gibbet on Campden Hill.[56]

While some members of the upper classes tolerated or actively supported morris dancing, it was easy for others to be almost unaware of it outside of fashionable entertainments. When John Byng saw some dancers in Wallingford (then in Berkshire) in 1781, he noted 'a set of Morris dancers pranced away in the street: these, with other old rural sports I Fear'd had been lost'. Three years later in Cheltenham, however, just as Simeon Moreau was adducing morris dancing and Whitsun ales as quaint customs, the dancers Byng saw in the town, with their fool, appeared 'tedious, and as little enjoyed by the performers, as the spectators'. He commented 'the genius of the nation does not take this turn'.[57] The dancers in Wallingford may have been from Abingdon, nine miles away; two years later they were seen 45 miles from home at Richmond-upon-Thames, with their fool, who said they were 'were Berkshire husbandmen taking an annual circuit to collect money from whoever would give them any'.[58] Later accounts confirm dancers would go to London and work their way home, combining their usual labour with dancing (see Chapters 14 and 15), and if the Abingdon dancers were

54 Rickard, pp. 12, 77.
55 Snooke, William.
56 Heaney, Michael, 'Morris Murder'.
57 Byng, 1:5, 124-25.
58 Jonson and Waldron, p. 255.

following the route of the Thames they may have been doing just that. Travelling so far from home, and doing it annually, indicates that they must have been sure of a profitable journey.

Whitsun morrises were also found in the Forest of Dean, though without the formal setting of a Whitsun ale. At Brockweir in the 1780s 'they issued, as formerly, at Whitsuntide and ... in every ancient device (except that of the hobby horse), the Maid Marian and the Clown being preserv'd'.[59] An account from 1799 tells us that at Doward on the northern edge of the forest, at a piece of open ground called the Bailie, 'Many years ago, when the return of May was welcomed with external marks of joy, the village train used here to assemble, and indulge in all the frolic joys peculiar to the day, -- Among which sports, the entertainment of the Morris Dancers held a distinguished rank'. This implies that the custom was no longer observed.[60] Eight miles west of the Forest of Dean, Francis Douce reported morris dancers around the end of the century at Usk in Monmouthshire. He says that they had a fool, Maid Marion and hobby horse, and that they claimed a three-hundred-year ceremonial tradition.[61] The hobby horse is unusual (it having been 'forgot' elsewhere for almost two centuries), and there is no other evidence for this kind of longevity in the area, but in later years other teams of dancers would make similar unsubstantiated claims, perhaps based on second- or third-hand accounts picked up from the general literature.

The overall impression is of a thriving morris-dancing culture in the south midlands which in many respects continued practices from before the Commonwealth, but while it was prevalent among the unlettered populace it remained for the most part invisible to the middle and upper classes.

---

[59] Byng, 1:272.
[60] *Excursion*, sv Doward.

[61] Douce, 'On the Ancient English Morris Dance', p. 481.

Chapter 12

Beyond the Whitsun ale

The evidence for morris dancing in the north-west of England before the middle of the 18th century remains sparse. The diary entries of Nicholas Blundell of Little Crosby early in the century (see Chapter 8) show a continuing association between morris dancing and maypoles in west Lancashire. On 5 August 1755 Thomas Gerard of Garswood near Wigan paid morris dancers £1 1s, but we have no context for the payment apart from the date.[1] A report from the mid 19th century suggests that morris dancers performed at nearby Abram in 1794. The Abram dance as collected early in the 20th century has a circular formation, and although no maypole survives there the adjacent land houses Maypole House Farm and, latterly, the Maypole Colliery. A later antiquary, writing in 1882, surmised that in the mid 18th century morris dancers performed annually at the piece of ground in question.[2]

The date of Thomas Gerard's payment may indicate that it was connected with the rushbearing festivals of late summer that had been popular, particularly in the north of England, for centuries. The custom itself was essentially practical. Rushes were strewn on the floors of churches as a clean renewable cover for earthen floors, and as a means of keeping warm. When churches were provided with flagstone floors the practice often continued, to provide warmth and comfort when kneeling. Rushbearing has an excellent historian and chronicler in Alfred Burton and his still unsurpassed 1891 book with that title.[3] The communal effort involved in gathering and strewing the rushes made it a natural focus around which to engage in a community celebration. This in turn led to enquiries about the practice being included in Tudor and Stuart ecclesiastical visitation articles and injunctions, from Archbishop Grindal's very first in 1571, asking about 'may gammes or anye minstrels morice dauncers or others at Ryshebearinges or at any other tymes'.[4] The churchwardens at Weaverham in Cheshire reported 'morris dances and risshbearings used in church' in 1578;[5] and in 1631 Richard Brathwait, describing the character of a pedlar, says that 'A Countrey Rush-bearing, or Morrice Pastorall, is his festival'.[6] All of these are mere collocations, and the majority of such references do no more than echo the litany of possible affronts to ecclesiastical dignity. The only clear direct association of rushbearing with morris dancing at this time is that from Hornby in 1633 when morris dancing was one of a variety of entertainments that apparently accompanied the rushbearing (see p. 96).[7]

Rushbearing itself is well attested with a variety of associated customs. Those at Grasmere and Ambleside continue to this day, involving rush maidens carrying the rushes to church, some made into garlands or other shapes.[8] King James I's *Declaration* identified it as a specifically female custom: 'women shall have leave to carry rushes to the Church for the decoring of it, according to their old custom'.[9] After the Restoration we still find references in church records, as at Wilmslow in 1679 when the churchwardens spent 2s 'on ye Rushbearing on those which come to prevent disorder in the Church'.[10]

[1] Gerard.
[2] Bearon, 'Abram Morris Dance', p. 56.
[3] Burton, Alfred.
[4] Johnston and Rogerson, p. 358.
[5] Purvis, p. 65.
[6] Brathwait, *Cater-character*, p. 19.
[7] Baldwin, George and Mills, pp. 19-20.
[8] Rawnsley.
[9] James VI and I, p. 107.
[10] Earwaker, 1:116.

John Lucas of Warton, near Preston, writing *c.* 1743, described how the parishioners collected the rushes 'and then Dress them in fine Linen, Ribons, Silk, Flowers &c ; afterwards the Young Women take the Burdens upon their Heads and begin the Procession ... which is attended with a great multitude of People with Musick, Drums, Ringing the Bells and all other Demonstrations of Joy they are able to express'. He went on to say that in the evening there is 'Dancing about a May Pole adorned with Greens, Flowers &c'; a good example of how the different elements of festive celebration could come together.[11] It is quite easy to imagine how, if they were available, morris dancers could become part of the celebration.

From the 18th century we begin to find references to the rushes being brought to church on a rushcart. The earliest of these is from Prestwich in 1726. Sir Holland Egerton, residing at Heaton Hall, Prestwich, wrote to the antiquary Browne Willis:[12]

> as to ours of Prestwich, we have nothing but a Custom of bringing Rushes to Church in a cart, with great Ceremony. Dancing before it, and Cart and Horses adorned with Plate, Ribbons, and Garlands. The time anciently and usually observed is about St Bartholomew's Day [25 August].

The earliest use of the word 'rushcart' is from Didsbury, Lancashire, in 1733, when 1s was 'Given to Withington Rushcart and setting a frame for the Garlands'. Similar payments were made annually for many years thereafter.[13] In 1744 at Ashton-under-Lyne the Methodist John Bennet met 'many men dressed with ribbons, drums, pipers, fiddlers, etc. The cart was drawn with men.'[14] Rushcarts were also recorded at Taxal in Derbyshire in 1762 and 1774.[15] The first explicit indication of morris dancing in association with these activities comes from Nether Alderley in Cheshire. From 1683 the churchwardens spent small sums on 'rushburying', until 1720 when 'Our allowance at ye Rushburying day' was 1s 4d. There is then a gap until 1748 when we have these entries:[16]

Charges at ye Rushburing & on ye Morice Dancers	*00*	*17*	*06*
P<ai>d ye Musick at ye Rushburing & As<...> to get ye Rushes	*00*	*05*	*09*

Unfortunately, there are no further records of payments, but there is the distinct implication that the event in 1748 was something new, and at a larger scale than in previous decades. The large payment may well have included a number of different activities; when morris dancers were engaged at the rushbearing in Chapel-en-le-Frith in north-west Derbyshire in 1758 they were paid 3s.[17]

In the second half of the 18th century records of morris dancers become more numerous (Figure 12.1). Nether Alderley associated the morris dancers with the general rush-bearing custom, but the earliest direct linking of morris dancers specifically with rushcarts comes from a later account relying on contemporary documents. Henry Fishwick wrote in 1875:[18]

> *Rushbearing: This form of annual Wakes, although peculiar to the north of England, is too well known to require description. Not only the town of Rochdale, but Milnrow and*

[11] Roper.
[12] Burton, Alfred, p. 63.
[13] Cawte, 'Early Records'.
[14] Bennet, p. 85.
[15] Earwaker, 2:548.

[16] 'Nether Alderley'. I am grateful to Garry Stringfellow for bringing these to my attention.
[17] Bunting, p. 104.
[18] Fishwick, p. 533.

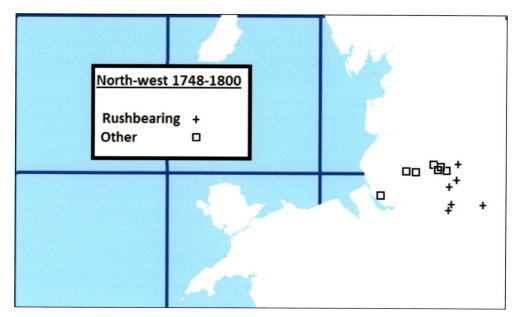

Figure 12.1: North-west morris contexts, 1748-1800.

Whitworth each had their festival, with the accompanying rushcarts, morris dances, and garlands. As the population increased the ancient custom appears to have been abused; in 1780 Dr. Hind the vicar found it necessary to forbid the rushes being brought into the Parish Church on the Saturday, and also to order the sexton not to give out the usual notice to bring them.

A concise but informative account similar in tone comes from Wilmslow, also in 1780:[19]

In order to ornament the church for this festival (that of the Wakes or dedication), there is a custom called a Rushbearing, for two townships in their turns to bring in a cart-load of rushes, nicely dressed and ornamented with flowers, on the Saturday but one preceding the festival. They often vie with each other in finery, in morrice dancing and in tinsel, painted paper and flower garlands. The Rushes are spread upon the floor in the farmers' pews, and between the benches, and serve to keep their feet warm in winter and to kneel upon at their prayers, and the garlands are fixed up in the church and make a tearing show. It is however unfortunate for the parish that the Wakes happen in the midst of their harvest, when the people ought to be all at work, instead of amusing themselves with Races, Riot, and Drunkenness.

Alfred Burton described equivalent festivities at Gorton, Lancashire in the same year, outlining the route taken by the rushcart, the replacement of the garlands in the chapel, and how 'On the Sunday, the morris-dancers, and other officials connected with the rush-bearing, all attended the chapel, when an appropriate sermon was preached'.[20]

The most extraordinary account of festivities of this nature comes in a pamphlet which may be a gross exaggeration of events, but has an underlying ring of authenticity. It is *The History*

---

[19] Earwaker, 1:81 (footnote). [20] Burton, Alfred, p. 57.

of Eccles and Barton's Contentious Guising War, published in 1777.[21] Eccles wakes were among the most renowned in the county and had a long history, which was noted by Sir Holland Egerton as early as 1726.[22] An undated handbill lists the entertainments provided one year, including bull-baiting, foot races, donkey races, a smock race, cock-fighting, and a fiddling match.[23]

Just four months before the events of the guising war, a performance was presented at the Theatre Royal, Manchester (four miles from Eccles),[24] being an adaptation of the performance staged at the Leeds Theatre seven months previously (see Chapter 9). That performance had been a 'pastoral ballet dance', *The Irish Milk-maids, or, May Pole*. It had been performed by 25 local children and was followed by a 'grand garland ballet' by Mr and Miss West, the Irish milk maids, and twelve morris dancers. William and Louisa Margaretta West were brother-and-sister dancers who had performed in London as well as touring provincially.[25] In Leeds it had been part of a full evening's entertainment including a performance of *Measure for Measure*, with dances between each act, and a pantomime to finish. In Manchester the play was *The Brothers* (a romantic comedy by Richard Cumberland) and the entertainment included some of the same *entr'actes* and some new ones, described in the advertisement:

> *A new Grand Pastoral Ballad Dance, altered from the Milk maids May-pole, call'd ECCLES WAKE; with the Humours of PENDLETON POSEY. And the original Morris Dancers – tune to be accompanied with the Tabor and Pipe.*
>
> *To be performed by forty Children of this Town, all to be dressed in new Dresses for that Purpose...*
>
> *To conclude with a Grand Garland Ballad, by Mr. and Miss West; the Milk Maids, twelve Morris Dancers, and fourteen Bower Dancers.*

This was the performance from Leeds (and other earlier presentations), adapted to take account of local interest in Eccles wakes. The announcement shows local knowledge – the fame of Eccles wakes, the reference to a 'posy', being the local name for a garland; and Pendleton is a neighbouring community to Eccles which would also feature in the imminent guising war. In a change from the Leeds advertisement, the morris dancers are described as 'original' with pipe-and-tabor accompaniment, which may have been a theatrical conceit for antiquity or perhaps a reflection of local practice. The 40 children – 15 more than at Leeds, but again recruited locally – may include the morris dancers, or refer to the milkmaids, distinct from them. The dancers were to re-appear in a 'grand garland' ballet, which also included fourteen 'bower dancers' as well as the milkmaids. The garland ballet may be a garland dance as performed with hoops of flowers by later teams in the north-west, but the nature of a bower dance is obscure.

This is the context in which the guising war pamphlet was published. It records a series of events from June to October 1777. The author, 'F. H**r**g**n' (probably Harrington) declares himself a recent arrival to Eccles, unfamiliar with local customs but familiar with the milkmaids' May-day garland in London and the survival of a few maypoles across the country.

The tale he relates is that one Mr Chorlton of Monk's Hall, Eccles (a real residence, so his readers would be able to judge Harrington's veracity) had men digging marl. This was a labour usually reckoned to be gruelling, and at the conclusion of a season a celebration was held[26] such

---

21 Harrington.
22 Burton, Alfred, p. 63.
23 Harland and Wilkinson, pp. 127-28.
24 *Manchester Mercury*, 25 February 1777.
25 Highfill, Burnim and Langhans, 'West, Louisa Margaretta'; Highfill, Burnim and Langhans, 'West, William'.
26 Rocke.

as the occasion in 1712 which Nicholas Blundell described as the 'flowering' of his marl pit, for which he trained sword dancers, gathered tinsel for garlands to decorate a barn, made special caps, had a bull-baiting at the bottom of the marl pit, a maypole, and a feast with dancing.[27] According to John Harland, 'guisings' were synonymous with marling celebrations.[28]

Youths at the Catch inn in the settlement of Barton-upon-Irwell, neighbouring Eccles, constructed a garland (a 'posey') to bring to Mr Chorlton's marl pit and provided a gift of 3s 6d to buy drink. When the marlers displayed the garland in Eccles, some locals took umbrage that another township had seen fit to do this, and a rivalry began, which the pamphlet describes in terms of a military conflict.

Eccles youths took a rival garland to the marl pit on 16 June and regained the marlers' allegiance by providing them with 4s 6d for drink. A fortnight later, Barton folk came to Eccles 'marching into the very heart of the town in triumph, with their usual dancing method of marching' (suggesting a processional dance). The invaders morris-danced through the streets of Eccles, encouraged by the pub landlords, and re-bribed the marlers to support them once more, laying down over £5. Harrington says that in such disputes 'those who are most in number, make the grandest appearance, bring the most money to some public use, and come last, are looked upon to be conquerors'. The Eccles people in return raised over £13 and considered using it to fund-raise for a communion plate or a church organ, but decided upon applying it to poor relief. On 14 July they returned to Barton, with a King and Queen, Robin Hood and Little John, Adam and Eve (dressed in leaves), drums, flags, music and about 32 morris dancers, with over 100 people in various uniforms. Again they swayed the marlers by presenting the £13.

Barton residents responded by offering to raise money for the communion plate considered and rejected by Eccles, and came again to Eccles on 4 August, in slightly fewer numbers than Eccles had raised, and did not buy over the marlers. Money was displayed (but not necessarily spent) in a show of wealth, to the sum of £37. Despite this poorer spectacle, Eccles nonetheless responded, but delayed doing so till Eccles feast on 1 September. On that day about 150 went in procession to Pendleton (two miles east of Eccles), and the respective Kings and Queens of the two communities agreed mutual support. Eccles people then 'retook' Barton, again with a display of wealth, over £347.

Barton's response was to ally with Stretford (3 miles away), to provide 220 people (Harrington notes that women were as well represented as men, as 'Queen's Maids of Honour') and on 24 September the township started by firing cannon, then marched upon Eccles. The full order of procession gives a detailed view of such events (allowing for hyperbole and exaggeration in the account):

1. *A bull with bells about his neck, and his guides;*
2. *Two light horse;*
3. *Two garlands and one colour;*
4. *Two hatters, each with a basket upon their heads, and an artificial rabbit in them;*
5. *Two drummers and two fifers;*
6. *Ten men with spikes;*
7. *A small garland, one drummer, one fifer, and two colours, with a guard of light horse;*

---

[27] Blundell, 2:25-27.   [28] Harland.

8. [omitted from the list]
9. *Two farriers to the light horse, with their hatchets in the usual form on a march;*
10. *Robin Hood and Little John with bows and arrows;*
11. *A colour, with six light horse to guard it;*
12. *Twenty-eight light horse to guard the king and queen ('Her royal highness the queen made a fine figure on horseback, which was even allowed by her enemies');*
13. *Thirty-four maids of honour, who made the best appearance in the field that day;*
14. *A colour, and thirty light horse to guard the maids of honour;*
15. *Five blues and ten light horse;*
16. *About twenty foot soldiers, who frequently fired ('These troops were thought very unsuitable for a Guising war');*
17. *A few young boys and girls dressed;*
18. *About twenty couple of morris-dancers ('These have always been imprudently placed behind, but are most proper to lead up an affair of this sort');*
19. *A good band of music in the centre of the morris-dancers;*
20. *The grand garland, near the centre of the army, drawn by four good horses, and proper attendance;*

The procession returned to Barton, visited their 'allies' (i.e., went to Stretford), and back to Barton, where presumably there was a village feast. The amount of wealth displayed was over £644.

The last sally in the war came from Eccles, with help from Pendleton, on 20 October. Two hundred horsemen, 100 on foot, 56 maids of honour in their finery 'had all watches by their sides' and the morris dancers 'dressed equally as gay, watches only excepted'. Harrington adds 'these light infantry go through the most difficult part of the duty'. The procession went from Pendleton to Salford, then to Barton, and finally to Eccles. Over £1,811 was in the exchequer. One commentary on the pamphlet notes that the sums involved in all these displays (nearly £3000 in all) 'do not seem to have been spent, but only exhibited ... They were probably lent for one hour, and returned to the pockets of their owners, except so much as may have been expended in horse-hire and other expenses, and in ale, &c., for the feast'.[29] The displays are best seen as visible expressions of community solidarity, support and prosperity.

Apart from the reference to Eccles feast on 1 September, this has no explicit connection with rushbearing or wakes, but has obvious close affinities with them. The listing above puts morris dancers in their context as recognised skilled exponents of their craft, bringing added spectacle to a procession, and shows that they could be mustered in considerable numbers. The whole episode expresses the same community pride as we find associated with Whitsun ales in the south midlands, and evoked in pre-Commonwealth drama such as *Jack Drum's Entertainment* and *Women Pleas'd*.

The presence of morris dancers in Pendleton is confirmed by the *Star* newspaper in 1792, which reported them paying an annual visit to Salford on 30 July, 'adorned with all the variety of colours that a profusion of ribbons could give them, and had a very showy garland'.[30] A

---

[29] Harland and Wilkinson, p. 91.

[30] *Star*, 9 August 1792, cited in Ritson, 1:cxxii.

slightly less favourable assessment was given by Dorning Rasbotham in July 1783 at Farnworth, Lancashire (which until earlier in the century had been a hamlet of Barton-upon-Irwell), who noted good prices for agricultural produce, and wrote 'I met a very large procession of young men and women, with fiddles, garlands, and every ostentation of rural finery, dancing morris dances in the highway, merely to celebrate an idle anniversary, or what they have been pleased to call for a year or two a fair, at a paltry thatched alehouse upon the neighbouring common.'[31] If Rasbotham's words are not merely based on the vagueness of his understanding, this is the earliest indication of women dancing the morris in the north-west.

Wakes were held as far west as Wavertree (now a suburb of Liverpool) in 1794, when morris dancers were hired for £1 19s 6d, on the instruction of the local magistrate, but then had trouble getting their payment.[32]

There are rushcart accounts from Didsbury (which had its rushcart from the 1730s) during the last decade of the century in the pages from the accounts of the parish clerk Thomas Wood listing rushcart and wakes payments. In 1791 he paid for garlands, bell ringers and fiddlers, competition prizes, food and drink, and in 1792 6s for 'Morris dancers Porter & Wine'. Similar payments were made in subsequent years to the end of the century. Payment was always for drink, not for the performance itself.[33]

A native of Mottram-in-Longdendale (in Cheshire, near the Derbyshire border on the western edge of the Pennines) recorded his memories from the 1830s, but with a footnote mentioning a writer in 1795 who averred that 'The festival of the Wakes is still kept up, with all the ceremony of dressing up rush-carts'. The memories summarise the community pride in decorating the rushcart with silverware and plate, the preparation of garlands, and the additional personal pride of the morris dancers:[34]

> The Morris-dancers were dressed in ribbons in such a style that none but women whose heart was in the work could have attained; and proudly did the village maids look upon the favoured young men who took part in the dances. The village band headed the procession, the clearers cracked their long whips, the dancers waved their arms and handkerchiefs high over their heads, the flags floated from one side of the group to another.

The opportunity afforded by participation in the rushcart festival for finding a partner, alluded to here, complements the observation of the Combe informant of John Haslewood, that being chosen as Lady of an ale was often a prelude to finding a husband.

―――――――――

The morris at Chapel-en-le-Frith in Derbyshire looked north and west to find its fellows. Across the Pennines and at the other end of the county, at Normanton in Derbyshire (now a suburb of Derby itself), John Byng noted a maypole in 1789 and was told that people 'danced in the morrice-way' around it each 29 May (the date celebrating the Restoration).[35] Much later, Thomas Ratcliffe reminisced in 1914 about his grandmother's memories from her Derbyshire youth around 1770, saying that she 'talked a good deal about morris dancers, mummers, and dancing about the maypole, and her talk was to the effect that two of these dancings were widely distinct. That, in fact, sword dancing was not morris dancing, but that dancing about the maypole was really morris dancing. In her young days ... these amusements were fairly

---

31 Barton, 1st series, p. 263.
32 'Wavertree'.
33 Wood, Thomas, pp. 44, 166, 349.
34 Earwaker, 2:137.
35 Byng, 2:29.

common in all country places.' Ratcliffe went on to talk about Plough Monday customs.[36] The nub of his grandmother's memories is that, for her, the usage of the term 'morris dance' shifted from a dance around a maypole to a sword dance in her lifetime.

Writing of 'Nottinghamshire Centenarians' in 1878 George Stevenson noted the death in 1825, aged 95, of Richard Pearce of Basford (now a suburb of Nottingham), and recorded that 'he took pleasure in teaching the young villagers the mysteries of the mazy or morris dance, in which art he was considered a proficient', and that he also taught them violin. Presuming he did this when himself young to middle-aged, this suggests activity around 1760-1780, but with little indication of what shape this took.[37]

John Byng again, many miles away in Silsoe, Bedfordshire, commented in 1795 on the wretched poverty of the inhabitants, but was told that, nevertheless, 'there are Mayers (alias Morrice Dancers) who go about with a Fool, A Man in Womans Cloaths (the Maid Marian), and Musick'.[38] The 'Woburn Abbey Morrice dancers' appeared in Bletchley at Whitsuntide in 1766. A correspondent of *The Gentleman's Magazine* suggested in 1821 that they were retained as part of the Duke of Bedford's household, but it is much more likely that this was the serving staff of the household behaving much as those at Stanway in 1724, entertaining themselves at a Whitsun ale.[39]

Although some of these records suggest the continuation of morris dancing in association with May customs, the later records from the east midlands suggest a different kind of event. Perhaps the event mentioned in *The Gentleman's Magazine* as happening in Risby in Suffolk in autumn 1774 was a one-off, arranged, it is suggested, by some freemasons at the marriage of one of their number.[40] At the marriage celebrations there was a semi-comic procession referencing several aspects of the butcher's trade, as 'The corpse of a sheep, borne on a tray by two Butchers' as well as more expected elements such as garlands, and maids strewing flowers. At the head of the procession were two men to clear the way, followed by four morris dancers.

The easternmost counties of East Anglia are almost devoid of morris references not just in this period, but also into the first half of the 19th century. However, Joseph Ritson asserted in 1795 that 'morris dancers are said to be yet annually seen in Norfolk', before mentioning their widespread occurrence in Lancashire.[41] A set of accounts from Burton Hall in Burton-by-Lincoln, home of the Barons Monson, recorded Christmastide payments to men (receiving 2s 6d) and boys (receiving 1s) identified as morris dancers in 1767 and 1768. In December 1771 two sets of dancers including one from Nettleham (three miles away) each received 2s 6d.[42] For most of the years 1781-1790 payments of 2s 6d were made to 'Lincoln Morris Dancers (as usual)' each December, often glossed as a 'Christmas box', suggesting perhaps that it was a consideration in respect of dancing at other times, but a reward for a performance at the time of donation seems more likely.[43]

Also in Lincolnshire, the antiquary John Cragg of Threekingham noted in his diary in 1795 that 'a number of young men join together, and strip to their shirts, which they pin all over with ribbons ...They are called Maurice or Morris dancers', but he offers no further information.[44]

---

[36] Ratcliffe.
[37] Stevenson.
[38] Byng, 4:100.
[39] Cole, p. 46; 'On the Burlesque Festivals', p. 323.
[40] Report (1813).
[41] Ritson, 1:cxxii.
[42] 'Household Accounts' (1767), ff. 13, 35v, 110, 110v.
[43] 'Household Accounts' (1781), ff. 5v, 32, 45v, 58, 69v, 79, 90, 111.
[44] Helm MSS, f. 11.

A few years earlier, Aulay Macaulay had noted in 1791 that 'On Plow Monday I have taken notice of an annual display of Morris-dancers at Claybrook, who come from the neighbouring villages of Sapcote and Sharnford' (within three miles of Claybrooke Magna).[45]

None of these records tells us much, apart from the presence of dancers termed morris dancers, associated with maypoles at first but also appearing in winter. The Christmas payments at Christmastide at Revesby in 1723 and 1724, however, augured a much more complete description from there in 1779. The Revesby sword play is well known. For many years the sole source was a fair copy of the script of a performance, headed 'October ye 20, 1779, The Morrice Dancers acted their merry dancing, &c., at Revesby'.[46] The characters in the play are the Fool, Pickle Herring, Blue Breeches, Pepper Breeches, Ginger Breeches, Mr Allspice, Cicely, and 'Fidler, or Mr Musick Man'. All parts were played by male actors. The play also features a Hobby Horse and a 'Wild Worm' (and a Dragon is mentioned in the text), but it is not clear who, if anyone, played these parts.

The action consists of a series of episodes. First, the Fool calls on the five actors mentioned next in the *dramatis personae* in turn, then the animal figures are introduced, the Fool fighting with the Hobby Horse. This scene ends with a dance. The second scene consists of a series of executions of the Fool by the same actors in a sword dance in which the swords are interlocked round the Fool's neck. The third scene is a series of sword dances using dance figures similar to the figures found in current longsword dances, without the climax of the interlocked swords. The fourth part consists of a wooing play, which opens with a morris dance augmented by each character as he enters. Pickle Herring then woos Cicely, being assisted in his task by Blue Breeches and Ginger Breeches, but Cicely prefers the Fool. The whole play ends with a sword dance and an obeisance to the master of the house.

The manuscript is signed and dated 1780 by Sara Sophia Banks, sister of the naturalist and President of the Royal Society Sir Joseph Banks. Its uniqueness and peculiarities have led to the suggestion that it was a literary creation, perhaps even by one of the Banks family. That theory was effectively demolished by the discovery of the rough copy on which the British Library copy was based, and of correspondence from Sir Joseph to Francis Douce in 1808 describing the performance and saying that 'our morrice dancers in Lincolnshire were in perfect preservation in my time tho now I believe extinct'.[47]

A lot of ink has been expended trying to make sense of the different kinds of 'folk play' and to classify them. This has been particularly important for those who see them and related customs as primitive survivals of an older system of belief and custom, the 'species' from which one can divine the nature of a common ancestor. Hybrids like the Revesby play do not fit. What they do confirm is that elements of cultural practice could flow, migrate and gather around different central loci much more freely than we sometimes realize, and that the working people in rural areas did not necessarily have a localized and blinkered worldview but were able to see, copy and innovate from a wide variety of cultural influences. Thomas Pettitt has called Revesby 'A medley of distinct and miscellaneous items roughly coordinated into a continuous performance'.[48] More recently Peter Harrop has drawn attention to its context within the variety of amateur theatricals performed at all levels of society in the 18th century.[49]

[45] Macaulay, p. 128.
[46] *Morrice Dancers.*
[47] Preston and Smith, pp. iv-vi.
[48] Pettitt, p. 16.
[49] Harrop, pp. 83-92.

The rough copy of the text in fact terms the performers 'modes dancers', corrected to 'morrice' in the fair version, which form is also used in the corroborative evidence; 'modes' was probably either a transcription error or a mishearing of what was said. The term applies to the performers as actors in the dramatic elements, and to their role in the sword dances and the separate dance explicitly designated a 'morris dance'.

The morris dance is introduced by the characters speaking in turn, starting with Pickle Herring, who says:[50]

> *In first and foremost do I cum for all to lead*
> *This race seecking this country fare and near*
> *So fair a lady to Im brace ...*
> *O so fair a ladey did I never see so cumbly in*
> *My sight ...*
> *Masters all behould*
> *tis know for sum prity dancen time*
> *<-> and wee will futit fine [the next is blu bretches*
> *He said] I am a youth of Jollatree whear is thear*
> *One licke unto mee ...*
> *I a golly youth proper and tal thearfoar*
> *Mester musick man what so ever may be mee chance*
> *It is for mee ladis louve and mine strik up*
> *The modes dance [then they footit once round*
> *The next man ginger bretches he said]*
> *I am a iolly young man of flesh blood and boan*
> *...*
> *Musick man what so ever may be my chance*
> *It is for mee ladys louve and mine strike up the*
> *Modes dance [then they footit round*
> *the next man cauld in pepper bretches*
> *He said] I am my fathers eldest son and air of*
> *All his land and in a short time I hope it will*
> *Fall into my hands ...*
> *...*
> *A fair lady I wish shee was my wife*
> *I louve her at my hart and from her I will never*
> *Start thearfore mr musick man play up*
> *My part [the fool said] and mine toou [then cums*
> *In mr all spice and they foots it round*
> *pickel herrin suter to sislay and tackes her*
> *by the hand and walcks about the room...]*

The dancers in turn, led by Pickle Herring, woo the lady, and as each comes in they 'foot it round' in the morris dance, suggesting that they dance around the lady. Although this is more reminiscent of the morisks of the early Tudor court than of the other kinds of morris we know about, the absence of any evidence for the survival of morisks anywhere in England

---

[50] Preston and Smith, f. 8r-9r.

in the intervening 250 years militates against such an interpretation. The Revesby dance remains an outlier which tells us more about what we don't know than what we do.

————————————

In other areas of England evidence is sparse, and none of the surviving records tells us much about the nature of the dances performed.

The Arundell family's Christmas gifts to morris dancers in Wiltshire continued sporadically: in 1767 1s was given to some 'Lettell Moris Dancers' (i.e., children) from Tollard Royal.[51] Thirty years later the list of Christmas boxes included 'Moriss Dancers 2s'.[52] At Loseley Park in Surrey morris dancers from nearby Compton were given 1s 6d on 29 December 1769 and '3 Morris Dancers' were given 2s on Boxing Day the following year. Another gift of 3s to dancers was made on 19 December 1771.[53] The time of year, and the number of dancers, again suggest something moving away from the earlier conceptions of morris dancing linked to summer festivals. An account from Puttenham, three miles from Loseley Park, tells us that it used to have morris dancers. The last to be remembered as wearing bells was a carter named Thomas Furlonger 'by far the best dancer in the whole neighbourhood, the bells on his legs and ankles keeping wonderful time with the musician'.[54] Thomas Furlonger was born in 1744 so this probably relates to the later 18th century, though he lived on till 1840.[55]

In the arc of the west and north midlands, which had larger numbers of dancers before the Commonwealth and the first hint of bedlam morris after it, there is very little evidence for community morris in the 18th century. The Davenport family in Worfield, Shropshire, recorded a payment of 2s there (undated, but c. 1730) to 'morris boys'.[56] The *London Evening Post* reported in March 1756 that 'a few Days since died at Willey, within three Miles of Bridgnorth, Margery Brider, aged 113, who retained her Senses, and was never known to be ill, till a Fortnight before her Death. Last Summer she followed a set of Morris Dancers to a neighbouring village, and supplied the Place of one who was disabled by some Accident.'[57] In fact she was buried on 21 January, and as one of her children was baptised in 1701 it is unlikely that she had reached so great an age.[58]

Joseph Moser recalled seeing in Shrewsbury at some time in the 1780s 'a company ... consisting of Morris dancers, a kind of Clown or Merry Andrew, and Maid Marion'.[59] The Maid Marion hints at a Whitsun-ale kind of morris, but more we cannot say.

On 26 September 1761 John Campbell, son of Lord Glenorchy, had married Willielma Maxwell, and on 8 October they, with his parents, returned to the family seat at Sugnall just outside Eccleshall in Staffordshire. Lord Glenorchy described how the people of Eccleshall had welcomed them. The streets were decorated with boughs and flowers, and 'Several girls dress'd in white stroud [strewed] flowers as we went, & morrice dancers preceeded us'.[60] There were hogroasts and bell ringing, and a hogshead of beer was provided. Part of the celebrations were funded by subscription from the major inhabitants and farmers, but Lord Glenorchy added that 'it cost me 20 £ but luckily 'tis a Case which happens seldom'.

51 'List of Christmas Gifts' (1756).
52 'List of Christmas Gifts' (1744).
53 'Loseley Manuscripts'.
54 Kerry, 'Antiquarian Papers', 6:121.
55 'Thomas Furlonger'.
56 Davenport family.

57 *London Evening Post*, 2 March 1756.
58 Ashman, Gordon, 'Customs', pp. 142-43.
59 Moser, p. 346.
60 'Lucas Archive, Correspondence'. I am grateful to Jameson Wooders for drawing this to my attention.

This celebration obviously relied on the availability of local dancers and was not tied to a seasonal feast, but it occupies the middle ground between self-organized community activity and externally inspired civic support, when the authorities and influential citizens encouraged popular support for public events. The Lichfield morris dancers also benefited, as we shall see shortly, from continuing civic support over many years, but this enabled them to visit local gentry to solicit donations at festive times. They visited Shugborough Hall 12 miles north of the city, home of the Anson family (later the Earls of Lichfield) regularly at Whitsuntide (when they also performed in the city) and at Christmastide, and there are records of their receiving a guinea (£1 1s) in most years between 1784 and 1789, for which period records survive.[61] The same account book also records four smaller payments of 5s to "Brownhill Colliers M: Dancers' at Christmas. The smaller amount probably reflects the fact that the Lichfield dancers also had some civic status in their community, while the Brownhills dancers did not. The Brownhills dancers, however, must have had some expectation of reward to travel the 15 miles from their home to Shugborough.

———

The Lichfield dancers straddle different contexts in which dancing took place. The civic procession and feast each Whitsuntide that is the Lichfield Greenhill Bower is attested as far back as 1698, and from December 1765 there are payments to morris dancers of one guinea at Christmas and at Whitsuntide for every year until 1822. The first of these was made to six dancers, identified as 'freemen'.[62] We have surmised that Samuel Johnson's 1756 definition of the dance involving the clashing of staves arises from his observation of the Lichfield dancers. In 1779 he said that he had not seen the procession for fifty years, i.e., since he had been a twenty-year-old around 1729.[63] In 1779 it was 'much degenerated', he said; but this may be the standard reaction of the staid middle classes to popular recreation. In 1795 Anna Seward wrote that in the 1750s it had been 'a day of festal and social enjoyment for all ranks', but that the gentry had come 'to despise such a promiscuous, and innocently democratic celebration, and to consign its noisy and gaudy pleasure to the vulgar'; she called it a 'morris-dancing revel', suggesting that although in earlier accounts the morris had not been seen as a particularly significant element, by then it had become a defining feature of the Bower procession.[64] Certainly by 1795 the dancers had a leading role. John Jackson recounted that 'Early in the Morning of that Day, the high-Constables of the City, attended by Armed Men, Morrice-dancers, &c. with Swords and staves, escort the Sheriff, Town-Clerk, and Bailiffs, to the Bower', from where the procession wound through the town led by the morris dancers, gathering ward constables and other dignitaries and officials.[65] (The 'swords and staves' may have been taken from Johnson's dictionary.) Three years later, Stebbing Shaw, largely copying Jackson, adds that there were eight dancers, accompanied by a fool, and drums and fifes.[66]

The only other city in which we know there were regular civic events during the 18th century is Salisbury. An inventory from 1709 reveals that the Guild of Tailors in Salisbury still retained their giant, hobby horse and clothes for five morris dancers.[67] If there were processions they do not merit mention in the newspapers, but during the 1740s John Wyndham of Norrington recorded payments in Salisbury to the morris dancers and giant

[61] Judge, 'Morris in Lichfield', p. 134.
[62] Judge, 'Morris in Lichfield', p. 134.
[63] Johnson, Samuel, *Letters*, 3:166.
[64] Seward, 4:84.

[65] Jackson, John, pp. 27-28.
[66] Shaw, 1:316.
[67] Haskins, p. 197.

in a procession, giving each element 1s.[68] In 1746 in celebration of the defeat of the Jacobite rising at Culloden, the guild:[69]

> ... agreed that the Giant, Hobnob and Morris Dancers be made use of, on the next general thanksgiving day, and that a new banner and two new scarves be bought, to be worn as occasion shall offer, and this Corporation may direct; and that the same be bought by direction of the Wardens and the Chamberlain.

The *Salisbury and Winchester Journal* described the event, reporting that 'To divert the populace, the "Giant" (a colossal figure, near 25 feet high) with Hobnob, his renowned 'squire, encircled with morris dancers, went up and down the town'.[70] In 1763 at the celebration of the peace after the Seven Years' War and in 1784 on the peace following the American War of Independence, morris dancers again appeared, accompanying the Salisbury giant and the hobby horse Hobnob.[71]

At Stratford-upon-Avon morris dancers making a Whitsun perambulation were given 5s from the town chamberlain's accounts on the mayor's order in 1717 and 1732, showing if not civic sponsorship, at least civic support.[72] Other examples are celebrations of individual events. To mark the new king's birthday in 1727 officers in the militia at Bath gathered 160 'gentlemen volunteers' to arms and led them into the town market-place headed by two sword bearers, morris dancers and a band playing martial music. One officer, the jeweller Captain Goulding, who saw himself as a rival to Beau Nash and sought to upstage him by promoting his local interests in the town,[73] made the mistake of stuffing the buttocks of the ox roast with some of his precious stones, making the populace so eager to find them that 'they flung themselves over the Heads of the Officers into the Dish, and stood over their Shoes in Gravy, and one was stuff'd into the Belly of the Ox, and almost stifled with Heat and Fat'. The officers had to leave the table to protect their uniforms, but continued to watch from a safe distance.[74] The following year Goulding arranged a similar celebration for the arrival of the Princess Amelia, which involved:[75]

> the Mayor, Recorder, and principal Citizens, a Company of Grenadiers, all Inhabitants here, dress'd in Red Breeches with Silver Lace, and their Shirts Sleeves ty'd with Red Ribbons, as also by a Company of Morris-Dancers; the Streets were strew'd with Flowers, and the Houses without the Gate had all green Trees nail'd up before them.

This passed off without the indignity of gravy-bespattered officers, but the provision of matching clothing for the populace, and the decoration of the streets, must have entailed similar levels of expenditure. It may be no coincidence that Bath was suspected to harbour Jacobite (i.e., Stuart) sympathies, and the morris dancers may be the lineal ancestors of the famous Bath Morris Dancers who graced the London stage 15 years later.

Putting on a warm welcome for visiting royalty clearly had its reward, as when the town of Marlborough gave the Prince and Princess of Wales a similar welcome when they stayed at the Angel inn in the town overnight on their way to Bath on 16 October 1738:[76]

[68] Wyndham, entries for 21 May 1741, 18 May 1747 and 24 April 1748.
[69] Haskins, p. 203.
[70] *Salisbury and Winchester Journal*, 13 October 1746.
[71] Haskins, pp. 205, 208.

[72] Stratford-upon-Avon, Accounts (1701); Stratford-upon-Avon, Accounts (1730).
[73] Eglin, pp. 80-84.
[74] *Country Journal*, 11 November 1727.
[75] *London Evening Post*, 23 April 1728.
[76] *London Daily Post*, 26 October 1738.

After the Charges of the House were Paid, his Royal Highness was pleased to present the Landlady with a Purse of Thirty Guineas; and left Ten Guineas for the Servants: His Royal Highness also gave Four Guineas to the Ringers, Two to each Church; and Two Guineas to a set of Morrice-Dancers and Musick, who met their Royal Highnesses at their Entrance into this Place: his Royal Highness was likewise pleased to give Ten Guineas to the Poor.

At the end of the century, in 1794, there were national celebrations at the naval victory known as the 'Glorious First of June' in the French Revolutionary wars. At Woodstock on 13 June there was a procession through the town and beneath the triumphal arch at the entrance to Blenheim Palace. *Jackson's Oxford Journal* reported that in addition to the members of the four friendly societies with their flags, 'what added greatly to the Chearfulness of the scene, was an excellent and well attired Company of Morris Dancers ... preceded by a numerous Band of Music'.[77]

In all of these instances the community was coming together in celebration and it is perfectly obvious that morris dancers were still very much in the public eye. From the freemen of Lichfield onwards, the impression is that the dancers were a rung above the rural poor, and could command some respect.

Civic celebrations easily became entwined with the political. Robert Hucks had been elected as member of Parliament for the borough of Abingdon in the spring of 1722. A resident of nearby Clifton Hampden, on returning there on 9 October he was met by Abingdon's town music and 300 mounted men, and proceeded to the borough, where 'all the Streets were strew'd with Rushes and Flowers, the Houses cover'd with Garlands and Greens, the Windows crowded with People, the Morrice-Dancers and several young Maids dress'd in White with Garlands of Flowers, met them at the Foot of the Bridge, and went before them thro' the Town'. There was bell-ringing, and barrels of beer for the populace.[78] It may be this was a delayed post-election celebration. In the 1727 election the poll at Woodstock was held on 21 August, and the Marquess of Blandford's election accounts record that one guinea was paid to morris dancers 'at the election' on 23 August – very likely in connection with the celebratory chairing of the successful candidate.[79]

The election of 1754 was one of the most corrupt in Parliamentary history, and Wootton Bassett in Wiltshire was particularly egregious in this regard. The candidates John Probyn and Thomas Cresswell spent nearly £6000 in bribes and lavish entertainment.[80] Nearly a year before the actual election:

There was a grand Entertainment given by them on Tuesday at Pinkney, near Great Sherston; at which were present above 150 Persons, who, the next Day, went in Procession through Malmsbury, to Wotton Basset, where they were received and attended through the Town by the Corporation, the Bells ringing, the Musick playing, and Morrice Dancers dancing before them all the Way.

The dancing may have been 'all the way' through Wootton Bassett itself, rather than the ten miles from Malmesbury or 15 from Pinkney, but we cannot be sure.

The most notorious of all the constituencies in that election was Oxfordshire, bitterly fought and with a contested result. The Duke of Marlborough, supporting the Whig candidates, held a

---

[77] *Jackson's Oxford Journal*, 21 June 1794.
[78] *Daily Post*, 13 October 1722.

[79] Blenheim Papers, f. 183.
[80] Pugh and Crittall.

rally at the George inn in Burford on 18 June 1753, and when he entered the town, 'Before his coach caper'd a long train consisting of Grenadiers, Sword-bearers and Morris-Dancers'.[81] It was probably no coincidence that this was Trinity Monday, a week after Whitsun, when morris dancers would be expected to be active in any case. Local knowledge of Whitsun ales had been used in May of that year in a spoof declaration using the pseudonym 'Thomas Motley' as the Fool of a Whitsun ale to comment at length on the forthcoming Oxfordshire election. He is there 'to preserve Order and Decorum', and jokes that people should not say he has turned his coat because sometimes they see the yellow of its motley and sometimes the blue, and continues:[82]

> *Every Body knows what a Whitsun-ale is, knows that the Fool, or more properly the 'Squire, claims the Privilege of cracking jokes upon the Women, and exercising the Calves Tail, the immemorial and tremendous Ensign of his Office, upon the Men. – We never pretended to a Right of flogging the Ladies. – Never fear me Lady – you need not put on your Breeches; the most I shall have to do with you will be a brush at your Petticoats: but as to the Men, especially those that crowd where they have no Business, and break in upon the antient and undoubted Rights and Privileges of the Morris Dancers, I shall have no mercy on. My brave Boys of Oxfordshire are going to begin a Dance, and I shall endeavour to keep a clear Stage for them.*

Motley had started by posing the rhetorical question, 'As everyone will be asking, Whose Fool is this? I will begin by giving an Answer to that Question; I am my own Fool. Whose Fool are you?'. Later he singles out one voter:

> *There's no reason I should be the only idle fool in the County. – Stand by there; who's that? Mr. R—d—r! ... dear Sir, did you not play a little in my Character, when you threw away your Ale in a Town where you could not possibly get a Vote, for the Sake of raising rough Musick to entertain one of my Morris Dancers?*

Motley suggests that Mr. R—d—r had used rough music (discordant beating of pots and pans as a sign of disapproval) against the opposition at an election rally. The only R—d—r with voting rights in the election was John Ryder of Great Milton, who voted for the Tory interest,[83] from which we may conclude that the author supported the Whigs, as did the Duke of Marlborough.

When George Grenville was chaired around Buckingham after the election for the borough in 1741 (his first election; he would go on to become Whig prime minister 1763-65) he did not pay any morris dancers, but he had used them extensively in the course of the campaign. He hired '8 Morrice given by Chandler, 3 by Doggett' to perform in ten villages in the county, paying them a total of £5 15s 6d, i.e., half a guinea (10s 6d) for each outing.[84] The villages range from Turweston, seven miles north-west of Buckingham, to Dinton, 14 miles south. Doggett was a common surname in Adstock, one of the communities entertained by the dancers, so it may be that he was from there. Chandler is a common Buckinghamshire surname, but not in the communities named; there was, however, a family of that name in Marsh Gibbon, which features in other morris-dance payments recorded in the Stowe manuscripts. Grenville's total election expenses were £926, so the morris dancers are clearly only a minimal expense. Much more was spent on bands of music, on ringers and on food and drink for the populace.

[81] *Jackson's Oxford Journal*, 23 June 1753.
[82] Motley.
[83] *Poll*, p. 101.
[84] 'Stowe MSS, Buckingham Election Accounts'.

At the election in Abingdon in 1768 Nathaniel Bayly arrived to try to win the seat. He was marginally defeated in the election, but this was overturned on appeal and he took his seat in 1770. As he began his campaign, there was a grand procession around the town, although it was in January:[85]

> *First came the Morrice-Dancers; after them, Drums, Fifes, Hand-bells and Violins; next, the Horsemen, two and two; these were succeeded by the Post-Chaises and other Carriages; then came a Landau and Six, with Gentlemen in it; after that, two Post-Chaises and Four with the new Candidate and Mr. Rook; a Band of French Horns brought up the Rear.*

We know nothing about the morris dancers at Great Marlow in the 1774 election except that they were engaged by the unsuccessful independent candidate William Dickenson, who paid them a total of £1 11s 6d.[86] When George Grenville (son of the former prime minister) was elected for Buckinghamshire in the same election, he 'was attended to the place of election by an almost incredible number of Gentlemen and Freeholders of the County, who breakfasted with him at Wootton, and from thence marched in procession to Aylesbury, preceded by a very large band of musick, several flags, and a Morris, dancing all the way'.[87] This is a much clearer indication of an extended processional dance than was Wootton Bassett. The distance between the towns (Wotton Underwood is meant) is nine miles.

Where there were civic connections it was probably inevitable that morris dancers should be recruited for election purposes. At Salisbury in 1768 they were hired at the Parliamentary election for Wiltshire, even though the two members were returned unopposed. The event was on 22 March, just one week after polling opened, and was probably for a celebratory chairing. The city's bell-ringers, music, drummers and trumpeters were hired, bailiffs employed and four hogsheads of strong beer bought for the people. The morris dancers were paid 5s out of a total expenditure of £32 5s for the day.[88] At Lichfield the dancers were hired at 13 general elections and four bye-elections (most of them uncontested) between 1774 and 1830. At the chairing in 1774 they were paid two guineas (£2 2s); and two days after the declaration of an election result on the 14 January 1795, James Thacker, one of the morris dancers, signed a receipt for the payment: 'Received of the Rt Honble Granville Leveson Gower by the hands of Chas Simpson Esq Two Guineas due to the Morris for dancing before the Chair on the Election Day'. In 1831, however, there is evidence of a reluctance to engage the dancers, and election accounts cease to feature them.[89]

We shall see later (Chapter 15) that the morris dancers of Lichfield were generally falling out of favour at that time, but the Reform Act of 1832 fundamentally changed the nature of the electorate and of political campaigning, and it makes sense to continue to follow through the involvement of the morris in elections to its natural conclusion. The last such link is in 1832 itself, and is in fact tangential to the election process. A Banbury correspondent to *Jackson's Oxford Journal* wrote in June 1832 to support the potential candidacy of J.H. Pye (probably Henry John Pye), of Chacombe in Northamptonshire, in the election which took place at the end of the year. In the event Pye did not run and the election was unopposed. The correspondent reported:[90]

> *It appears that it is the annual custom of the Club of that village to assemble on Whit-Monday, with their banner, music, morris dancers, &c., to enjoy the usual convivialities of*

[85] *St. James's Chronicle*, 9 January 1768.
[86] Sigma.
[87] *Jackson's Oxford Journal*, 22 October 1774.
[88] 'Expenses for the Election'.
[89] Judge, 'Morris in Lichfield', pp. 132-33, 139.
[90] *Jackson's Oxford Journal*, 16 June 1832.

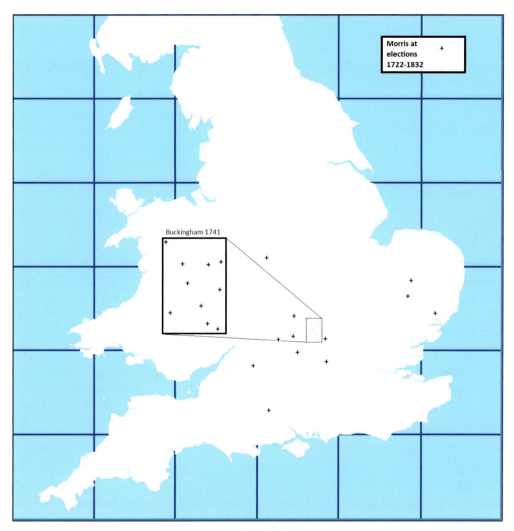

Figure 12.2: Morris at elections, 1722-1832.

villagers. On this occasion, to mark their respect for the worthy resident of the Priory, who at this time aspires to the honour of representing the freemen of Banbury in Parliament, the villagers had manufactured a flag in their rustic way, kept out by sticks, to exhibit more conspicuously the very honourable motto – a more gratifying one than King's could give – viz., 'Mr. Pye, the Poor Man's Friend'.

In a satisfying inversion (especially in the light of the fool's declaration at the Banbury election 80 years before), instead of the politician using morris dancers to gain support, here the populace and dancers are using their Whitsun ale to express support for the politician. It does, however, highlight the relation between politicians and their electorate. Politicians would not use unfamiliar, unpopular or controversial elements in seeking expressions of support or celebration, so where they do use morris dancers it must be because morris dancing is both prevalent and popular. The cluster of evidence from the south midlands here is telling, although caution must be maintained, as other areas of the country may still be under-researched.

Outside of the south midlands dancing at elections is reported only from urban centres with civic support (Figure 12.2).

There is a small cluster of East Anglian examples from the first part of the 19th century. At Bury St Edmunds in Suffolk, James Oakes was a prominent banker and businessman in the town, and owner of the Green Dragon inn, the scene of several election celebrations. His diary records payments to morris dancers at three elections. In his diary for 1802 he noted that six morris dancers were paid 9s each (i.e. £2 14s in all) in a total election expenditure of £477.[91] A couple of months before the election the town had held a procession celebrating the recent peace, at which 'A female was carried round the town, personating the Goddess of Peace, and several emblematical representations of the woollen manufactory, with a Jack of the Green [the figure from the sweeps' May day, dressed in greenery], and morris-dancers, accompanied the procession; but there was no regular celebration of Bishop Blaze, or St. Crispin, as was expected'.[92] (Bishop Blaize was the patron saint of clothworkers and Oakes was a yarn merchant.)

In 1807 at an uncontested election the elected members 'were chaired round the town, (preceded by a garland and morris-dancers) amidst the loudest plaudits of the populace; among whom 12 barrels of beer were given away'.[93] According to Oakes's diaries, in 1812 the dancers were paid £4 7s, and in 1820 £3 6s.[94] The following year came a report which may have signalled the end of the practice:[95]

> Died [on 21 December 1821]..., aged 63, William Lomax, who had been for 36 years grave-digger, in this town, and still longer, we believe, morris-dancer at the Borough elections. How many members he had preceded we know not, but he had been the 'strong builder' of nearly 6000 graves.

This suggests an unrecorded history of morris dancing at Bury St Edmunds elections going back to around 1780. At the same time there is a hint that the dancers only ever appeared at election time.

In Ipswich in 1820 the election celebrations included a long procession in which morris dancers are not listed as such, but appear to have been present nonetheless, as the local newspaper reported that 'Considerable life and interest were given to the scene, from the introduction into the procession of a groupe [sic] of morris-dancers, who were dressed with great propriety, and whose activity on the "light fantastic toe" excited a good deal of admiration'.[96]

Election celebrations did not entirely disappear after 1832. At Norwich in 1835 the newly elected members were chaired through the streets in a cavalcade of 'horsemen, music, banners and the partizans on foot'. At Thetford, Norfolk, on the other hand, 'The chairing, flower strewing, morris-dancing, and music were dispensed with, but a dinner was given to three hundred in the evening'.[97] Morris dancing may already have been on the way out there – an expenses list, possibly from the June 1790 election, includes a payment of 10s to 'one morris dancer'.[98]

---

91 Oakes, 1:124; 2:22-24.
92 *Bury and Norwich Post*, 12 May 1802.
93 *Bury and Norwich Post*, 13 May 1807.
94 Oakes, 2:161-62, 252.
95 *Bury and Norwich Post*, 26 December 1821.

96 *Suffolk Chronicle*, 6 July 1820.
97 *Norwich Mercury*, 10 January 1835 [a]; *Norwich Mercury*, 10 January 1835 [b].
98 H., A.L.

Coleshill in Warwickshire was the election town for North Warwickshire and a description of the nomination of candidates, written in 1854, mentions the playing of the tune 'Ole Dan Tucker', a minstrel song of the mid 1840s. The writer adds:[99]

> *A band of music, headed by a large party of men in straw hats, with short sticks, something resembling those of Morris dancers, kept time to the music.*

This is the only record to link dancing with sticks with an election event, and the author seems unsure whether these really were morris dancers.

By the end of the 18th century the concept of what constituted a morris dance had become broader and somewhat fragmented. Up to the beginning of the Restoration period there had been a common understanding of what was meant by a 'morris dance'. Although it had moved from the royal courts and aristocratic households, there is little evidence that the basic nature of the dance had changed significantly thereafter. We know that it involved bells and napkins or handkerchiefs, ribbons and baldricks, and other elements of expensive clothing. It involved specific dance steps, notably capers. It was certainly an element in civic processions and in local festivals, and local rivalries sometimes came to the fore. What had changed were the attitudes to the dance and to what it represented, in terms of both morality and the increasing differences between the strata of society – their lifestyles, interests, attitudes and experiences. There were only the merest hints of regional differences.

In the early years of the Restoration there was a distinct effort to roll back the clock and recapture the spirit of the pre-Commonwealth era, with explicit appeals towards life as it was lived before the contentions of the previous generation. Sometimes the nostalgia went the other way, for those polemicists who regretted the return to a less censorious society. In masques and literature the vision was more of the pastoral idyll, where the morris was an innocent amusement or at worst, empty frippery. Masques, interludes and plays formed a spectrum allowing scope for professional dancing masters to shape the presentation, and mixed sets and female morris dancers became part of the generalized and idealized pastoral May Day. The use of the word 'morris' to describe country dances (though the links between them and morris dances as practised are hard to find) also helped to broaden the general concept of what a morris was, who could dance a morris and in what circumstances.

Outside the manufactured world of the theatrical morris and May Day, the upper echelons of society sometimes looked with disfavour and even repulsion on the divergent lifestyles and entertainments of the lower classes. Morris dancers and their retinue could be disreputable rogues, depicted in the literature as at best picaresque. The local gentry might support their local festival but at the same time could express their dislike or contempt for them. This was very much an individual thing. Some gentry were more supportive of their tenantry and the local populace than others. Social conditions – such as the persistence or not of open field systems in different communities – could encourage or discourage community cohesion. But whether supportive or not, for most members of literate society morris dancers and the life of their communities were beneath notice.

In these circumstances it was easy for regional differences to arise. What we might term the Whitsun-ale morris of the south midlands retained most of the characteristics of the earlier

[99] *Coventry Herald*, 5 May 1854.

church ales, in which the morris dancers were embedded in a quasi-dramatic staging of a mock court and its retinue, with all the appurtenances of costume of the earlier festival. Dances were primarily static, being performed in specific places (such as the local manor, or in the mock court) by a set number of dancers (usually, six) as money was solicited. We have some indication that distinct tunes were associated with the dances. There is evidence that in the first half of the 18th century similar circumstances existed in the north-west of England, with morris dancers continuing to be associated with maypoles if not with ales. In the second half of the century the parallel custom of rushbearing developed with the introduction of rushcarts, and with it the participation of morris dancers into the procession bearing the rushes to the church. The emphasis was on the processional element, and there could be large numbers of dancers. The celebration often coincided with the local wakes holiday weeks. Dancers could be involved in other local celebrations, such as the completion of work in marl pits, and as with the Whitsun-ale morris, strong local rivalries could develop and there was a sense of the morris dancers embodying community pride.

In the east of England evidence is harder to come by, but there is a distinct shift towards morris dancing being a Christmas custom, and in the Revesby play (anticipating evidence from the 19th century) it is becoming part of the ambit of mumming plays and Plough Monday customs. There is a single instance of what we would now call a sword dance being termed a morris dance; again, this will be a characteristic of some nineteenth-century accounts.

We have also the first intimations of a different kind of dance, the bedlam morris involving sticks. What little primary evidence we have stretches from Shropshire to Buckinghamshire. Indirectly (and again, anticipating the nineteenth-century evidence) we also see it in Lichfield and continuing in Shropshire and surrounding English counties, as well as penetrating the area of the Whitsun-ale morris. In the mid century, for the first time, some books also indicated that staves might be involved in morris dancing. Isolated records can be found from other parts of the country. Those from Surrey, with the three morris dancers at Loseley Park and the last dancer at Puttenham, suggest a custom in decline.

This is not to say that morris dancing was entirely divorced from the broader elements of society. The Bath Morris Dancers, the sword-dancing morris men from Cumbria and the theatrical presentation of the Eccles wakes with local talent straddled the boundary between community activity and theatrical performance. The Tailors' Guild in Salisbury continued to field morris dancers, and the Lichfield men were engaged in a range of activities. The Lichfield dancers were also freemen, and we have the payment of double the standard gift when the Marsh Gibbon freeholders turned up at Stowe. The organizers of the Whitsun ale at Bicester were tradesmen, and the dancers using shells at Brightwalton were certainly of the middling sort. The civic authorities would happily use morris dancers in expressions of popular celebration, and politicians would reward them well to participate in electioneering.

The developing fields of lexicography and historical enquiry enabled scholars to move beyond the polemicists' assertions that morris dancing was sinful and/or a relic of popery, and to seek linguistic and historical sources to explain it. Despite starting with etymological equivalences, those taking the initial steps sought, as in most things, classical analogues and in particular the *saltatio Pyrrhica*. Once the link had been made between linguistics and history – that the name indicated that the dance had come from the Moors – the next step was to find a mechanism to enable such an origin, and it was found in John of Gaunt's Spanish adventures. Just a few key texts (in particular the *Old Meg* pamphlet and the *Book of Sports*) informed historians of the dance within this country, until Shakespearean scholarship produced the Johnson and Steevens critical edition of his works, which not only brought the Betley window to the attention of the world, but also adduced a number of other Tudor and Jacobean literary and dramatic allusions to the dance. This laid the foundations upon which antiquaries like John Brand and Joseph Strutt could build. In society at large the term 'morris dancing' could now embrace a wide variety of concepts beyond the core lineal developments allied to Whitsun ales and wakes, including mixed dances in the assembly rooms and by theatrical dancing troupes, and almost any performance by men soliciting largesse, from sword dances to mummers and plough boys.

The beginning of the 19th century saw the scholarly study of morris dancing take a great leap forward in the publication of key antiquarian texts which informed scholarly understanding of morris dancing for the rest of the century, and we shall now turn our attention to these.

Part IV: Re-emergence (1801-1899)

Chapter 13

Antiquaries and artistes

Francis Douce (1757-1834) was an antiquary who amassed an enormous collection of illuminated and other manuscripts, prints, drawings and early books. For a time he was Keeper of Manuscripts at the British Museum, but fell out with the Museum and left his collections to the Bodleian Library in Oxford. His interests revolved around the social history revealed by the works in his collection, particularly that of the ordinary people. The images in his medieval illuminated manuscripts showed people working in the fields and in trades, at worship and at play, writing, singing and dancing. In 1807 he published his *Illustrations of Shakspeare* [sic], *and of Ancient Manners*.[1] The body of the text consists of explanatory glosses to words and phrases in Shakespeare's plays, taken one after another. These are followed by three longer dissertations: on Shakespeare's clowns and fools; on the medieval tales known as the *Gesta Romanorum*; and a 'Dissertation upon the Ancient English Morris Dance'.[2] Over fifty pages long and meticulously researched, it became the definitive study of the morris dance for the rest of the century.

Douce began by stating his intention to 'fill up a chasm in the history of our popular antiquities'. He looked at the origins, noting that all commentators had uniformly linked the name of the dance to 'Moorish', while recognising that, as for the form of the dance, 'there is scarcely an instance in which a fashion or amusement that has been borrowed from a distant region has not in its progress through other countries undergone such alterations as have much obscured its origin'. Noting the John of Gaunt theory, he dismissed it and relied on the documentary evidence, saying that 'it is much more probable that we had it from our Gallic neighbours, or even from the Flemings. Few if any vestiges of it can be traced beyond the reign of Henry the Seventh.' Joseph Ritson had tied the dancers to Robin Hood in his 1795 study of the character,[3] but Douce noted their appearance in wider contexts of ales, watch processions and with the lord of misrule, and how elements of 'several recreations were blended together so as to become almost indistinguishable', so that there was little distinctiveness in the context of morris dancers' appearances.

For all his originality Douce based much of the remainder of his dissertation on a discussion of George Tollet's account of his Betley window (see p. 165). With his own extensive collections for reference, Douce noted that the costumes depicted in the window were from the mid 15th century, and that they derived in part from van Meckenem's engraving; the lettering of 'A Mery May' on the window, on the other hand, was at least a century later. He then discussed in turn each of the characters of the window and others frequently associated with morris dancers. He spent little time on the characters of Robin Hood, Little John and Friar Tuck, but considered Maid Marion in detail. He equated her with the queen or lady of the May and was not immune to the general proclivity of early antiquaries to seek classical antecedents, saying that 'There can be no doubt that the queen of the May is the legitimate representative of the Goddess Flora in the Roman festival'. Addressing the coarser character of the transvestite Maid Marion associated with the morris, he noted that 'although the May-lady was originally

[1] Douce, *Illustrations*.
[2] Douce, 'On the Ancient English Morris Dance'.
[3] Ritson, 1:cx-cxxiii.

a character of some delicacy and importance, she appears to have afterwards declined in both respects'. In discussing the fool he corrected Tollet's misidentification of two fools in the window and noted the fool's continuing association with the morris.

In his consideration of the hobby horse he noted its frequent 'forgottenness' and lamented the Puritans' attitudes:

> *During the reign of Elizabeth the Puritans made considerable havoc among the May-games, by their preachings and invectives. Poor Maid Marian was assimilated to the whore of Babylon; friar Tuck was deemed a remnant of Popery, and the Hobby-horse an impious and Pagan superstition.*

Having examined all the associated characters, Douce turned to the dancers themselves. As regards costume, he noted the streamers attached to the sleeves in several early pictures, and the richness of costume, including feathers, in the accounts from the time of Henry VIII. He noted the variant numbers of dancers and associated characters in different accounts and depictions: nine in van Meckenem's engraving, eleven in the Betley window, the twelve in the *Old Meg* pamphlet and the seven in the Vinckenboom-school painting, and Blount's definition of five men and a boy-Marion. He ended by mentioning the continuing practice of dancing at the end of the 18th century at Usk, Pendleton, in Norfolk and at Richmond-upon-Thames by men from Abingdon, saying that 'It has been thought worth while to record these modern instances, because it is extremely probable that from the present rage for refinement and innovation, there will remain, in the course of a short time, but few vestiges of our popular customs and antiquities'.

Douce brought order to the half-understood or misconceived analyses of morris dancing by others before him. He correctly identified the etymology, probable source and subsequent native development of the dance, and the main features of it at least in the Tudor and Stuart period. He drew on a wide range of sources (his footnotes identify over 60). His closing remarks, however, bring out the limitations in the armoury of an antiquary at the start of the 19th century. He was reliant primarily on literary sources and historical texts, and the first-hand evidence of the dance as practised in his time was consigned to a few closing sentences at the end of the dissertation, without analysis. Nevertheless, his work remained the first port of call for many of his successors through the century.

The year after Douce's dissertation, Joseph Strutt's novel *Queenhoo-hall* was published, which was intended to bring to life the customs of the English as set out in his *Sports and Pastimes* book.[4] Strutt himself had died in 1802, leaving the work unfinished, and it was edited for publication, and brought to a rather peremptory conclusion, by Walter Scott, who apologised for the rather jarring unpolished state of the dialogue between the late medieval characters (it is, frankly, execrable).

The opening chapter depicts a May game in the middle of the 15th century. It involves the Robin Hood characters, various groups of maidens and young men, a maypole drawn by eight oxen, and Gregory the jester as the hobby horse, whose dialogue is modelled closely on that of Sampson's *Vow Breaker* of 1636 ('no man can jerk the hobby, or rein him, or prance him, like me'). Although the hobby horse is attendant upon a morris ('if the hobby-horse be not performed, the morris will be stark naught'), no overt morris is described. The character of

---

[4] Strutt, *Queenhoo-hall*.

Much the miller's son, however, confusingly called Morris, capers with bells on his legs, and there is a general dance of the maidens and young men about the maypole to pipe and tabor accompaniment.

Douce's successor as Keeper of Manuscripts at the British Museum was Henry Ellis, who shared many of Douce's interests. Ellis had John Brand's own copy of his *Observations on Popular Antiquities*, heavily interleaved and annotated with additions, and also had access to Douce's similarly interleaved and annotated copy of the same work.[5] He used these as the basis for a revised edition of Brand, published in 1813.[6] He was also able to make frequent use of Douce's own conclusions, based on his dissertation. In the 1813 edition the additions were largely in the form of notes to the original text, often taking up the bulk of the page. In later editions (also overseen by Ellis) they were incorporated into the body of the text. The work was, therefore, much more Ellis's than Brand's. Ellis cited an even wider range of sources than Douce in his notes on the morris dance and Whitsun ales. He relied heavily on the evidence of churchwardens' accounts which were now beginning to be published, in particular the first publication of the Kingston-upon-Thames churchwardens' accounts published in Daniel Lysons's *Environs of London* in 1792[7] (a source briefly noted but otherwise neglected by Douce). However, even where he adduced new sources he frequently concluded by summarizing what Douce has had to say about the subject, and like Douce, framed much of what he wrote around Tollet's description of the Betley window.

The works of Douce, Brand and Strutt underpinned much of the received wisdom concerning morris dancing throughout the nineteenth century. Although *Queenhoo-hall* is a work of fiction, it was taken to represent the reality of the May game. Nathan Drake, in his *Shakspeare and his Times* (1817), was unequivocal: 'Mr. Strutt ... has introduced a very pleasing and accurate description of the May-games and Morris of Robin Hood'; a phrase picked up and repeated in an article on 'May Day' in *The Literary Chronicle and Weekly Review* in 1820.[8] In his compilation of interesting facts and customs *The Every Day Book* (1827) William Hone (who was later to edit Strutt's *Sports and Pastimes*) wrote that 'It is scarcely possible to give a better general idea of the regular May-game, than as it has been here represented'.[9] Even where commentators had Douce to hand, elements of Strutt's thesis which had been refuted by Douce were still adduced. A reviewer of a work on Herefordshire customs noted that 'The Morris Dance, kept up with great spirit, is deduced by Strutt, with probability, from the Fools' Dance at Christmas, part of the antient Feasts of Fools and Saturnalia; at least, no better origin is assigned; and Mr. Douce, who has very deeply investigated the subject, admits a connection with the Pyrrhic Dance'.[10] In a fictional account of a sword dance in the north of England, Edward Duros wrote 'The practice seems clearly a vestige of the old English Morrice games: but as we have neither Strutt nor Brand at elbow, we will not plunge into the question'.[11] Authors and magazines thought nothing of reproducing extended extracts from these works *literatim* or with minimal editing, as the *Brighton Herald* did in 1829 for Strutt's analysis of the May game.[12] Some authors were less accurate than others. John Timbs, writing in his magazine *The Mirror of Literature, Amusement, and Instruction* in 1837, wrote that Douce dated the dance's introduction to John of Gaunt's time, and after noting that Douce's etymological analysis settled the Moorish origin,

---

[5] Brand, *Observations* (1777), copies at Bodleian Libraries MSS. Eng. misc. e.242-43 and MS Douce d.46.
[6] Brand, *Observations* (1813).
[7] Lysons, 1: 212-56.
[8] Drake, 2:167; 'May Day'.
[9] Hone, 1:278.
[10] 'Popular Customs', p. 221.
[11] Duros, p. 150.
[12] Cited in Judge, 'Old English Morris Dance', p. 327.

Figure 13.1: Henry Stacy Marks, 'May Day', 1867 (Image © Victoria and Albert Museum, London, FA677).

introduced Strutt's attribution of the origin to the fools' dance. For some reason he thought the Betley window was in Uxbridge.[13]

Douce, Brand and Strutt were all reprinted and new editions issued during the century. In addition, as well as the general magazines which carried secondary articles from time to time, William Hone's *Every Day, Table* and *Year Books*, and journals such as *The Gentleman's Magazine* and *Notes and Queries*, provided a steady stream of antiquaries' observations, both theoretical and of real encounters, and provided the general reader with at least a hazy notion of morris dancing, albeit mostly as imagined and only occasionally as practised.

Strutt's description of the May game in *Queenhoo-hall* undoubtedly informed the artist Henry Stacy Marks's 1867 depiction of May Day on a triptych panel that was originally displayed in one of the Victoria and Albert Museum's dining rooms (Figure 13.1). All the elements that Strutt described are present, though in much reduced numbers (no doubt to enable Marks to depict the scene in sufficient detail), including the cart drawn by oxen, hobby horse, dragon, characters from the Robin Hood stories, and three morris dancers with single garters of bells around their legs who are waving wands.

In a more general nod to the public's penchant for the depiction of English customs, in 1859 the Alhambra theatre hosted a re-enactment of the Dunmow Flitch ceremony. This is the custom of awarding a flitch of bacon to a married couple who swear that they have not quarrelled during the year, and it had recently been revived following the publication of William Ainsworth's novel about it in 1854.[14] The play opened with festivities on the village green including 'wrestling, quarter-staff fighting, single-stick, and the mummers' sword-play, … practised in succession with a fidelity to the ancient usages of such rough games as would have delighted the heart of Strutt to have seen so accurately illustrated from his authority. Morris dances and the spirit-stirring "Sir Roger de Coverley" give additional animation to the scene.'[15] But this was just one instance of an entire culture of such representations which evolved over the course of the whole century.

We have seen how morris dances in the theatre developed as an entertainment during the 18th century, occasionally featuring in plays, or as an autonomous element in an evening's entertainment either in the theatre or in the pleasure gardens; and how those attending a ball or masquerade could personate dancers in a kind of fancy dress. The blossoming of antiquarian studies and interests at the beginning of the 19th century led to an increase in the depiction of dances on stage and in gardens. These developments have been comprehensively reviewed by Roy Judge, and the following paragraphs owe much to his work.[16]

---

[13] Timbs.
[14] Dunmow Flitch Trials.
[15] *Era*, 23 October 1859.
[16] Judge, 'Old English Morris Dance'.

While eighteenth- and early nineteenth-century newspapers and playbills advertised simply a 'morris dance' in theatrical performances, the title of Douce's essay began to influence the description, and from 1820 the appellations of 'ancient', 'old' and 'English' began to be attached to the phrase. The first of these was at Astley's Amphitheatre in October 1820, when the evening's entertainment concluded with a 'never performed, an entirely new Broad Farcical Melo-Dramatic Pantomimical Drama, called *When The Clock Strikes; or, The Bandit Farmer*. In the Course of the Piece, A Village Festival, in which will be introduced The Ancient Morris Dance.'[17] The phrase was also picked up by the newspapers. The reviewer of *Harlequin at Home; or the Magic Fountains* reported that 'The ancient morris dance was introduced, and most deservedly encored'.[18] This dance was devised by Frederick Hartland, whom Judge identifies as one of the prime choreographers and performers of morris dancing on the stage. It was danced by six men; another, performed by Hartland in 1837 in a production of *Fair Rosamund*, involved twelve.[19] 'Englishness' was highlighted at the Vauxhall fête on 23 July 1821 to celebrate the coronation of George IV, where 'Groups of Quadrille and other dancers will enliven the festive scene, and pourtray [*sic*] the Dances of various Nations, particularly the celebrated English Morrice Dancers'.[20]

A crime melodrama, *The Victim*, presented at the Adelphi in December 1833, included a 'morris-dance in an illuminated barn [which] was not by any means the least effective part of the performance'.[21] It must have been very successful, because six months later the theatre appended 'the celebrated Old English Morris Dance, from *The Victim*' as an independent addition to a production of *Victorine, or, 'I'll Sleep on it'*.[22] In the provinces the trio of Messrs Brown, King and Gibson, usually with three female partners, used the same phrase in advertising performances in Liverpool and Birmingham in the 1830s. By the time these performers appeared at the Adelphi in 1836 it was the even more encomiastic 'Fine Old English Heart-Reviving Morris Dance'.[23] This was in fact a return to the metropolis, for the same trio had been part of the Adelphi company from at least 1829, and from there had graced the Duchess of St Albans's fête, a booking which they promoted in their provincial advertisements.

The duchess's *fêtes champêtre* at Holly Lodge in Highgate were the manifestations of the change in fashion from costume masquerades to fêtes employing professional entertainments. At the beginning of the century masquerades could still be encountered, as for example at Mrs Thellusson's masquerade in 1804 when a Mr and Mrs Shaftoe appeared as morris dancers. At Mrs Dupre's the following year a Mr James dressed as one, and at Mrs Richards's masque ball in 1809 a Mr Hornby did the same.[24] At Almack's masked fancy dress ball in June 1819 – Almack's being the top London assembly rooms patronized by the highest levels of society – were 'Captain Clayton and Mrs. Lamb, as Morrice Dancers' (or, according to another report 'Messrs. Lamb and Capt. Clayton, Morris-dancers' – this may say something about the efficacy of the costume!). A month later 'among the most prominent characters were ... Mr. Munroe, at the head of a group of Morris-dancers'.[25] It may be that this was a group of professional dancers hired for the occasion, but at an Almack's ball in 1825 'Mr. Henry Villeboys, at the head of a party of morris dancers, gave novelty, and added life to the scene'; in 1826 he repeated

[17] *Morning Chronicle*, 9 October 1820.
[18] *Morning Post*, 13 June 1821.
[19] Judge, 'Old English Morris Dance', pp. 313-14.
[20] *Morning Chronicle*, 21 July 1821.
[21] 'Adelphi'.
[22] *Morning Chronicle*, 22 March 1834.

[23] Judge, 'Old English Morris Dance', pp. 321, 327, 330.
[24] *Morning Post*, 2 June 1804; *Morning Post*, 17 May 1805; *Morning Post*, 14 June 1809.
[25] *Morning Post*, 25 June 1819; *Morning Chronicle*, 25 June 1819; *Morning Post*, 7 July 1819.

the appearance, but this time the list of names is clearly one of high-society attenders: 'Mr. Villeboys, Mr. Herbert, Mr. Bruce' came as 'morrice dancers' while his sisters turned up in Turkish costume.[26] At a similar event a week before Henry Villeboys's first appearance 'among the Eccentricities were: Greek Slaves, Arabs, Russians, Morris Dancers (Mr. Mark Ker being at their head); Mary Queen of Scots'. This was a 'Caledonian' fête but Mary Queen of Scots had to share the arena with some distinctly non-Scottish fellows.[27]

By 1815 dance companies began to be involved. At Albinia, Countess of Buckinghamshire's 'masked fête' in 1815, based round a theme of Sir John Oldcastle (as precursor to Falstaff) there were 'fire-works, water-works, bear-baiting, morrice-dancing, tumbling, twisting and turning in all directions'.[28] The morris dancers at the Duchess of St Albans's fête in 1829 came from Covent Garden, together with an Italian concert, Tyrolese minstrels and other national entertainments,[29] while in 1830 the entertainment was 'Professedly intended to commemorate the ancient English pageants of May-day' and was 'enlivened by several of our national games – by the exhibition of the May-pole with its garlands, and the morris-dancers with their antics; – a show replete with reminiscences of Shakespeare and Queen Bess'.[30] The nostalgia and the distinct evocation of 'Merrie England' are unmistakable.

In some ways it is surprising that the Covent Garden dancers returned to the Holly Lodge fêtes because in 1828 they had been aggrieved by their treatment there. On arrival they had been obliged to leave their carriages some distance from the entrance and walk the rest of the way in full costume to the derision of the locals, then were sent off to a remote part of the grounds when the duchess indicated she did not want them near her. The correspondent of *The Age* who complained about this remarked tartly that 'if this truly arrogant Lady condescended to send for these people, she ought to have treated them at least with civility, not forgetting she was once a member of the same class' (she had been an actress in her early life). The occurrence is a salutary reminder that while the upper classes might revel in the idea of 'Merrie England', social rank remained important. The complainant described the Covent Garden *corps de ballet* as providing 'humble, not to say coarse entertainment'.[31]

In 1833 the morris dancers at Holly Lodge 'from one of the Theatres Royal ... exhibited their skill by sylph-like movements around the gravel-walks of this delicious Eden'. The event the following year was more concert-like, with a musical performance followed by 'a group of morris-dancers, [who] most effectively did ... support their parts, being the corps de ballet of the principal Theatres, led by Oscar Byrne' [sic].[32] Oscar Byrn was the son of James Byrn, who had organized the Frogmore fête nearly 40 years before.

Notwithstanding their appearance on stage in *The Victim*, morris dances were overwhelmingly associated with the light-hearted carefree pantomimes, more often than not signalled to the audience by the flagging of 'Harlequin' in the title, from *Harlequin and Mother Goose; or, The Golden Egg* in 1807 to *The Pretty Bluebells and the Ugly Beast; or, Harlequin King of Coin Castle* in 1860. There were at least fourteen such titles over that period.[33] By the 1830s the pleasure gardens were also regularly presenting morris dances, often calling upon the theatrical troupes to supply them. The Surrey Zoological Gardens appear to have been the first, in

[26] 'Morning Post, 8 June 1825; Morning Post, 8 May 1826.
[27] Morning Post, 1 June 1825.
[28] Morning Post, 26 June 1815.
[29] 'Varieties'.
[30] Judge, 'Old English Morris Dance', p. 329.
[31] Age, 11 May 1828.
[32] Lincoln, Rutland and Stamford Mercury, 24 May 1833; Morning Post, 2 June 1834.
[33] Judge, 'Old English Morris Dance', p. 340); Standard, 27 December 1860.

1834.[34] Others followed. In 1836 the Royal Beulah Spa in Norwood engaged Messrs Gibson, King and Brown with their female partners to 'dance in character. A Chinese Comic Dance, a Comic Bedouin Arab Dance, and an old English Maypole Morris Dance, as danced by them at the Duchess of St. Alban's Fete Champetre.' A few days later the newspaper reported that their morris dance 'elicited loud expressions of approbation'.[35] The provincial fêtes joined in: a gala fête at Leicester cricket ground during a race meeting in 1839 anachronistically advertised an 'Old English Morris Dance, as in the 14th century', and a fancy-dress ball in Liverpool the following year included 'Messrs. Brecknell, Watson and Williams, and their partners, [who] danced the old English morris dance in a handsome style, and were much applauded by the company'.[36]

At the Royal Surrey Zoological Gardens in 1845 (the 'Royal' was added by the proprietor to capitalize on visits by members of the royal family) a two-day fête in honour of Prince Albert's birthday made the most of its antiquarian credentials by opening the proceedings with 'the peculiarly English sport of the Maypole, with its Morris Dancers, Friar Tuck, Maid Marian, Pipe and Tabor, &c.'[37] Five years later the 'Morris Dance on the Platform by the ladies and gentlemen of Herr Deulin's powerful Ballet Company' concluded the entertainments at a similar festival in honour of Prince Albert at the Cremorne Gardens.[38] (Niccolo Deulin was a dancer at the Adelphi in 1845; he had a 'rustic character dance' in his repertoire.)[39]

1851 saw the emergence of Richard Flexmore (son of another dancer of the same name) as an organizer of morris dances. His first essay was something of an anticlimax: at the Scottish fête in Holland Park 'there was to have been a morris dance round a Maypole ... The performers were ready dressed all day, but, up to the hour at which we left the ground, the state of the weather made the notion of dancing round a Maypole the most dismal of tragedies.' The weather improved the following day, and 'Mr. Flexmore had his happy peasants duly rigged out in what is considered pastoral attire by the idealising costumiers of theatres – and a merry round they danced among the garlands of the maypole, finishing off with the quaint morris step', although we do not know what this step involved.[40] A few weeks later the Royal Surrey Zoological Gardens engaged 'the party conducted by Mr Flexmore, who lately exhibited at Holland House' for their display of morris dancing with all the trimmings of Robin Hood first shown six years before.[41] At the Surrey Gardens the two years later 'Mr. Flexmore, with his troupe of 50 artists, portrayed with considerable ability "The Bye-gone Sports of Merrie England", when Robin Hood and Maid Marian led the dance in "Merry Sherwood", and introduced the popular dance of "Pop Goes the Weasel" together with may-pole and morris dancing'.[42] In another historical re-creation in 1855, 'the renowned Flexmore' was at Kenilworth Castle recreating Queen Elizabeth's 1575 visit, as part of 'a morrice dance, by a number of ballet-dancers from the London Theatres, dressed in the rustic garb of Queen Elizabeth's time, [which] was performed with very pleasing effect, and was greatly applauded by the thousands who surrounded the circle in which it took place'.[43] Flexmore was still only 29; he died just five years later, reputedly 'of consumption brought on by the violent exertion he underwent in his professional duties'.[44]

---

[34] *Age*, 22 June 1834.
[35] *Morning Post*, 16 August 1836; *Morning Post*, 20 August 1836.
[36] *Leicester Chronicle*, 7 September 1839; *Liverpool Mercury*, 23 October 1840.
[37] *Lloyd's Weekly Newspaper*, 3 August 1845.
[38] *Reynolds's Weekly News*, 8 September 1850.
[39] Adelphi Theatre Project.

[40] *Morning Chronicle*, 11 July 1851; *Glasgow Herald*, 14 July 1851.
[41] *Examiner*, 26 July 1851.
[42] *Standard*, 17 May 1853.
[43] *Jackson's Oxford Journal*, 18 August 1855; *Era*, 12 August 1855.
[44] Boase.

'Maypole and morris dances' as a set piece were standard fare at Cremorne Gardens and elsewhere in the late 1850s and were becoming *passé* to the extent that the *Daily News* described them as 'The usual garden performances of maypole and morris dances'.[45] They had to compete for attention with 'Ethiopian serenaders' (black-face minstrels), acrobats and troupes of performing dogs. Attitudes were becoming ambivalent. *Lloyd's Weekly Newspaper* commented about their appearance at the Royal Surrey Gardens in 1857, 'An old English morris dance was performed, a highly exciting reminiscence of the "days that are no more", thank heaven!'[46] Describing performances at the Crystal Palace, *The Morning Post* lamented, 'There were old English Morris dances, but with scarce the vivacity which we remember in our younger days – unless, indeed, it be that our feelings have changed with advancing years'.[47] When the Royal Dramatic College staged an event in 1860, *The Morning Post* was again condescending:[48]

> A variety of innocent recreations, designated somewhat ambitiously in the programme as 'Old English sports and pastimes', were conducted with great spirit and success ... but lest posterity should be misled by a too highly coloured narrative, it is due to historical candour to state that of these drolleries by far the most frequent and the most popular was the noble game of 'Aunt Sally'. Maypoles there were to be sure, and African opera troups, and morris dances by boys and girls dressed in pastoral costume, to represent in these bleak latitudes the shepherds and shepherdesses of sunny Arcadia; but 'Aunt Sally's' attractions were supreme, and she bore away the palm from all rivals.

Judge has noted, moreover, that 'With the end of the [eighteen-]forties any popular fashion for morris in the orthodox theatre had gone'. This was reflected in theatre programmes. In 1849 *The Country Squire* was put on twice in London; at the Marylebone it still included 'A Morris Dance', but at the Strand this had become an 'Old English Country Dance'.[49]

Perhaps the nadir in decline was Hengler's Cirque in Liverpool in March 1868, presenting 'Morris Dancing on Horseback'.[50] The company was still presenting the spectacle in its staging of *The Dunmow Revels* in 1872, when the reporter for *The Era* was impressed:[51]

> so many animals are employed in this that the marvel is how the rapid evolutions, as they thread the mazes of the dance, are gone through without hitch or accident.

Another report from 1874 mentions the 'ladies and gentlemen on horseback' and 'the ease and rapidity with which they execute complicated and constantly changing movements'.[52] These suggest that the riders were executing a plaited maypole dance.

Despite indications of decline, morris dances continued to be presented in theatres and at fêtes up and down the country. Sometimes the worlds of theatrical and community morris overlapped. At a banquet for the Crimean battalions of the Guards in Surrey Gardens in 1856 there were official entertainments in the form of acrobats, bands and 'Ethiopian serenaders', but in addition some old soldiers from the ranks 'gave practical evidence of their rustic origin by a vigorous exhibition of morris dancing, barring the sticks and the ribbons, but with fife accompaniment, to the amusement of the lookers-on, and to their own profit, some silver coins being occasionally flung into the midst of the arena at the close of the performance'.[53]

[45] *Daily News*, 14 June 1859.
[46] *Lloyd's Weekly Newspaper*, 30 August 1857.
[47] *Morning Post*, 6 April 1868.
[48] *Morning Post*, 2 June 1860.
[49] Judge, 'Old English Morris Dance', p. 334.
[50] *Liverpool Mercury*, 11 March 1868.
[51] *Era*, 17 March 1872.
[52] *London Evening Standard*, 7 April 1874.
[53] *Lady's Newspaper*, 30 August 1856.

What kind of dance did the dancers on stage and in pleasure gardens perform? Undoubtedly the dancing masters devised the dances, and what little evidence we have suggests two kinds of dance. One is the 'morris dance, with sticks and handkerchiefs' performed at the Garrick Theatre in 1831, or the one in the 1848 production, *Lady Godiva and Peeping Tom of Coventry*, which had 'a Band of Morris Dancers with Sticks and Handkerchiefs'. Despite the obvious salaciousness of the play's title, the dance was claimed to be 'from undoubted authorities in the possession of the Society of Antiquaries'.[54] In 1860 the Royal National circus promised to tour the southern counties of England with an unrivalled spectacle:[55]

> it is proposed to present, with all requisite dress and paraphernalia, the Sports and Pastimes of bygone days in Merrie England, A Rural Fete and Archery Contest, shooting at Target for the Prize – 'A Silver Arrow'; bold Foresters habited in Lincoln green will crowd the arena to contest for the victory. The minor parts of this exciting production will introduce the once-famous Morris Dancers, with Gay Ribbons and Jingling Bells, and Short-stick Evolutions, May Pole Dance, Single Stick Players, and quarter Staff Combat, altogether forming a coup d'oeil never before presented on such a scale.

None of the most consulted authorities (Douce, Strutt and Brand) mentioned stick dances, as they relied primarily on literary sources from the time before they were used in the morris, so where did this come from? It may be that the dancing masters saw them in the provinces on their travels, but perhaps more likely is that they saw them in the streets of London. In the early 19th century it was common practice for dancers, especially from the south midlands but also from elsewhere, to travel to London in the spring, earn some money dancing in the capital (not least because of their novelty value as street entertainers), then work and dance their way back home, helping with the hay harvest in each place as they went.[56] The Abingdon dancers met by John Byng in 1783 may have been doing this (though we have no evidence for Abingdon dancers using sticks). The spectator of the Crimean soldiers certainly expected to see sticks in a morris dance. A writer to *The New Monthly Magazine and Literary Journal* in 1822 described the scene at Brook Green fair in Hammersmith the previous spring, where he had met 'six young and healthy-looking country lads. They were gaily decked in ribbands, with small bells attached to their knees and ancles – one hand waving a white handkerchief, the other flourishing a smooth stick. The step was regular and graceful, and when crossing in the dance, the sticks were smartly struck against each other, making, with the jingling of the bells, a new, but not displeasing accord with the music.'[57]

The unnamed contributor to *Gentleman's Magazine* in 1830 made an explicit link with the hay harvest, and also helpfully described three kinds of dances, including stick dances:[58]

> It is pleasant, just before the beginning of hay-harvest in the environs, to observe the monotony of some 'long dull street' of dingy houses, broken by the simple music of the pipe and tabor, and the ringing of bells on the legs of the morris-dancers. It tells of the country and its delights to dull ear of the Londoner, while, moreover, there seems a patch of old-time merriment in the active but not mincing motions of the ruddy and sun-burnt countrymen who thus endeavour to gain a few pence by the exhibition of their own peculiar pastimes to those ' pent up in populous city.' They generally perform three (perhaps more) different dances, one with sticks, the rattling of which, struck against one another, keeps time to the

---

[54] Judge, 'Old English Morris Dance', pp. 313, 333.
[55] *Era*, 8 April 1860.
[56] Chandler, *Taking*.

[57] 'Brook Green Fair', p. 559.
[58] 'Scraps', p. 24.

music;— another with handkerchiefs, which are gracefully waved in various directions; and a third, in which the hands are clapped in unison with the pipe and tabor. All are pleasing, when executed with precision.

Perhaps the most telling contribution came from the 'J.R.P.' who wrote to William Hone in 1826. In a detailed description (asking why Hone did not publish more about morris dancing) he wrote:[59]

In June, 1826, I observed a company of these 'bold peasantry, the country'[s] pride', in Rosoman-street, Clerkenwell. They consisted of eight young men, six of whom were dancers; the seventh played the pipe and tabor; and the eighth, the head of them, collected the pence in his hat, and put the precious metal into the slit of a tin painted box, under lock and key, suspended before him ... The dancers wore party-coloured ribands round their hats, arms and knees, to which a row of small latten bells [brass or similar] *were appended, somewhat like those which are given to amuse infants in teeth-cutting, that tinkled with the motion of the wearers.*

He went on to describe a handclapping dance (but omitted mention of a stick dance); identified the tune 'Moll in the Wad', said the dancers were from Hertfordshire and identified the musician as one Lubin Brown (sadly, no one of that name and period has emerged from genealogical sources). It is significant because J.R.P. was James Robinson Planché, and when he penned this letter he was the in-house writer and librettist at the Covent Garden theatre. In the course of his career between 1818 and 1852 he moved between the Adelphi, Lyceum, Olympic, Haymarket and Sadler's Wells theatres and the Theatres Royal at Covent Garden and Drury Lane.[60] He was an eminent historian of costume who consulted Douce in his quest for authenticity in the presentation of historical drama. It is entirely plausible that he brought his expertise and experience to bear on the staging of the dramas at his playhouses. Although Rowley's Jacobean comedy *A New Wonder, a Woman Never Vexed* does not have a morris dance, Planché's 1824 revival of it added one.[61] A later likely candidate is the 1840 production at Covent Garden of *The Fortunate Isles, or The Triumph of Britannia*, written in celebration of Queen Victoria's marriage, in which 'A pastoral scene in the Weald of Kent, with a Maypole and Morris dancers, represents the golden days of Queen Bess'.[62]

This brings us back to the other strand of the representation of morris dancing on stage, the maypole. Here again we owe much to the work of Roy Judge, not just in his research into theatrical morris but also that on the history of the plaited maypole.[63] Maypoles had long since been used as the sign of an ale and continued to be so used into the 19th century. They were undoubtedly associated with morris dancers in the public mind for most of that period, not least because of the Puritan focus on those two elements as being the most egregious of the depravities of the age, but there is remarkably little evidence of morris dancers actually dancing round a maypole. The earliest is perhaps the 1589 Marprelate tract *Plaine Percevall the Peace-maker of England*, which alludes to dancers 'footing the Morris about a May pole'.[64] There were the dancers performing around the maypole in the Strand at the restoration of Charles II. There is the report from John Byng at Normanton in Derbyshire in 1789 that people 'danced the morrice-way' around a maypole, and the similar Derbyshire reminiscence from around the same period but reported 140 years after the event. The dancers at Abram probably also danced around a maypole.

---

[59] Planché.
[60] Roy.
[61] *London Courier*, 10 November 1824.
[62] 'Covent Garden'.
[63] Judge, 'Tradition'.
[64] Harvey, p. 8.

The clearest indications of morris dancing around a maypole are those from the professional London dancers both in the theatres and in other entertainments. The first of these is the Duchess of St Albans's fête at Holly Lodge in 1833. This is the occasion when the dancers (from one of the Theatres Royal) exhibited 'sylph-like movements'; later in the day 'the morrice-dancers again exhibited their skill around a maypole, which was profusely decorated with streamers, i.e. ribbons, blue, green, and yellow'.[65] This is also an indication that the maypole was plaited by the dancers. The following year the dancers decorated trees at Holly Lodge with garlands and then danced around them; this was advertised as the last of the duchess's fêtes.[66]

The first morris dancers with maypole on the stage that we know of came in the 1836 production of *Richard Plantagenet* at the Victoria Theatre. In this play the morris dancers appear first, then in a subsequent scene there is a maypole with streamers around which the knights and ladies dance. The next instance is similarly circumspect, and Judge has suggested that the maypole around which morris dancers danced did not have streamers to plait. He quotes the disdainful report of the 'Sylvan Fete' at the Royal Surrey Gardens in August 1845 from *Punch*:[67]

> *A gingling of bells announced the commencement of the peculiarly English sport of the maypole, with its morris dancers. We rushed to the spot with truly British eagerness ... Our disappointment at seeing the villagers was more poignant and agonising than can be possibly conceived...*
>
> *The peculiarly English sport at length commenced by the lads and lasses, one of whom looked ancient enough to be the original old lass of Richmond Hill, who began to twirl themselves round and round the maypole to the sound of pipe and tabor ...*
>
> *The 'peculiarly English sport' went off rather heavily, in spite of the efforts of an individual in a white waistcoat and long hair, who superintended the dance, and who, it was whispered, was the celebrated C. somebody or other from the Royal Pavilion, but whether Brighton or Whitechapel we could not exactly discover.*

The composer George Macfarren's 1849 opera *King Charles II* included 'the Morris Dance round the Maypole, accompanied by music redolent of the seventh [*sc.* seventeenth] century, [which] was picturesque and animated in the highest degree'.[68] Macfarren being a respected composer, the piece was subsequently performed independently in orchestral concerts (see Chapter 21). At the Scottish fête at Holland Park in 1851 'a group of morris-dancers ... gaily footed it through the intricacies of a maypole dance, garlanded with flowers'.[69] The following year's fête had a morris dance arranged by Richard Flexmore and later there was 'a dance around a May-pole, forty feet hight, gaily ornamented with garlands and streamers. Mr. Flexmore had arranged this dance so as to represent the weaving of a tartan with the variegated streamers, and the effect of the performance altogether, shared in by 32 people in appropriate costume, and seen under such advantageous circumstances, was extremely pleasing.'[70] Presumably both dances were performed by the same dancers in the same costumes so it is a moot point whether they were still 'morris dancers' when they danced around the maypole.

In the Christmas pantomime at the Theatre Royal in Manchester in 1853, Little Red Riding Hood was chosen as the May Queen (anything is possible in a pantomime). Then the 'morris dance around the Maypole' was described:[71]

---

[65] *Lincoln, Rutland and Stamford Mercury*, 24 May 1833.
[66] *Morning Post*, 18 June 1834.
[67] Judge, 'Tradition', p. 4.
[68] 'Metropolitan Theatres', p.366.

[69] *Dumfries and Galloway Standard*, 16 July 1851.
[70] *Morning Post*, 6 August 1852.
[71] *Manchester Courier*, 24 December 1853.

Figure 13.2: 'A View of the Rotundo, House & Gardens at Ranelagh' (detail),
(British Library 840.m.82, public domain).

...sixteen village lasses in boddices, short skirts, and conical caps, eight villagers of the opposite sex to dance with them, and sixteen children dressed like them to dance round the Maypole. Their dance proceeds with a great deal of rollicking action, but it is so arranged that they plait coloured ribbons round the summit of the pole, or slowly weave them into trelliswork midway....

It seems clear that mixed sets of theatrical morris dancers could dance around a maypole, and at least sometimes this involved plaiting it. The origin of the plaited maypole dance remains obscure, despite Judge's work. The sole example antedating the instances described here is the 1759 print of an image by Canaletto of dancers plaiting a maypole at Ranelagh pleasure gardens (Figure 13.2).[72] Perhaps significantly, those engaged in the dance include the Italian figures of the *commedia dell'arte*, Harlequin and Punchinello, as well as a Chinaman and sailor, and four others.[73] Other costumed figures adorn the scene. It may well be that the plaiting of a maypole emerged in the gallimaufry of cultural influences that arose in the theatres and pleasure gardens of the late 18th century (and the prominence of French and Italian dancing masters), and once the antiquaries had provided the grounds for theatrical interpretations of morris and maypoles early in the nineteenth, it was easy to associate the two even more closely.

We do have one image of theatrical morris dancers of the period, in a picture from 1858 of a performance at the Crystal Palace (Figure 13.3). Morris dances were performed at the Palace at both Easter and Whitsuntide, provided by 'eighteen of the principal Clowns, Harlequins, and Columbines of the metropolitan theatres', 'dressed in grotesque and characteristic costumes'.[74] The picture shows four of the nine mixed couples distinctly. The dancers as

---

[72] 'View of the Rotundo'.
[73] Alford, 'Maypole'.
[74] *Standard*, 25 May 1858; *Standard*, 6 April 1858.

Figure 13.3 'Morris Dancers at the Crystal Palace', Illustrated News of the World, *24 April 1858, p. 181.*

depicted have neither bells, nor ribbons or handkerchiefs, and the costumes are certainly not Elizabethan, more the image of eighteenth-century pastoral. The bringing together of different groups of performers to provide the entertainment suggests that there was not sufficient interest among any one of the theatre companies by this time. This is the event that elicited the *Morning Post*'s comment that the performance lacked vivacity.

We have seen that the publications of Douce and his fellow antiquaries provided the impetus for widespread presentations of morris dancing with assertions of its ancient Englishness and association with May festivals and maypoles, and stimulated a thriving industry of professional choreographers to devise appropriate spectacles in both theatre and pleasure garden. One aspect of this was the observance, and possible imitation by the choreographers, of morris dancers using both handkerchiefs and sticks in the streets of London. To investigate how this came about we have to return to the morris of the south midlands.

Chapter 14

South-midlands morris

Before looking at the development of morris dancing in the south midlands from a social and historical perspective, we need to return to matters of choreography. In reviewing the evolution of dancing in the period to the Restoration (Chapter 7), we noted some descriptions of what characterized the dance, including frequent mentions of 'capers' and 'cross capers', knocking of heels, and levaltos or galliards. These last could refer to any of several complex steps.[1] To review the nineteenth-century situation we must look at the information collected at the start of the 20th century from old men who had danced in their youth.

In the morris of the south midlands as collected at the beginning of the 20th century, mainly from dancers' memories of 50 years before, there were capers, slow capers (where the music slows to allow the dancer to execute a complex leap, sometimes akin to the entrechat to which the cross caper was likened), and galleys, a leaping spin with complex leg movements. It seems very probable that this complexity of steps was a conservative continuation, in the context of Whitsun ales, of the dance styles from those earlier times. While the characteristic steps may derive from court dances of the Tudor period, many of the figures in the dances are those of the country dances being done in social contexts after the Restoration. Dancers and musicians certainly saw a close connection between tune and dance. When the pipe-and-tabor fell out of general use around the middle of the 19th century, some dancers gave up dancing. The Bampton musician and dancer William Wells wrote in 1914:[2]

> They used to play much slower on the whistle and dub, but it was very beautiful and you could grasp every movement ... the music [now] is most of it too quick and the old graceful movements are slurred to keep pace with it. You see very little of the old backstepping now which was as pretty a thing as you could wish.

Another feature of this style of dancing is that specific dances were tied to specific tunes. One dancer put it simply, 'If you're a dancer, when you hears the tune playing, you knows how to foot it'.[3] This is in part a reflection of the complexity of dances – there can be as many as four different musical sequences, of different length, repeated several times over. Of course, new and alternative tunes were also constantly introduced, especially for the simpler dances. Some can be traced back to editions of *The English Dancing Master*, others are eighteenth-century, still others nineteenth-century. A striking example is the tune and dance most commonly known as 'Trunkles', one of the most complex dances. The tune derives (though with much adaptation to fit the complexities of the dance) from 'Trincalo's Reel', music composed by Charles Dibdin for a production of *The Tempest* for the Shakespeare jubilee of 1769.[4] In the name's garbled form as 'Trunkles' it became widespread across the south midlands, suggesting a single point of introduction, then mutilation of the name, then diffusion. 'Trunkles' exhibits increasing complexity as the dance unfolds. Typically, the 'chorus' figure when danced the first time through is performed with 'ordinary' morris steps; the second time, with 'plain capers', and the third and fourth times with slow capers, successively fore capers and upright or full capers

---

[1] Winerock, 'Competitive Capers', pp. 70-73.
[2] *Reading Standard*, 15 July 1914.
[3] Heffer, p. 259.
[4] Heaney, Michael, 'Trunkles'.

Figure 14.1: 'Trunkles' (adapted from the Headington version in Michael Heaney, 'Trunkles',
The Morris Dancer, 2, no. 9 (1990): 136-39.

(Figure 14.1). Another tune composed for the same festival and published at the same time, 'Warwickshire Lads', was in the repertoire of the Ilmington morris dancers 120 years later.[5]

Although south-midlands morris dancing includes both handkerchief and stick dances, no stick dance includes the kind of complexity described above for 'Trunkles', involving slow capers. To elucidate the reasons for this we need to look again at the bedlam morris. We noted in Chapter 8 that bedlam morris has just four explicit primary sources: the mere mention from Shrewsbury in 1688/89; the assertion from around 1774 in Oxfordshire that the bedlam morris dancers were separate from those of the Whitsun ale; the description from late-eighteenth-century Northamptonshire suggesting that the dancers who performed at Whitsun ales also danced bedlam morris; and the mention from Buckinghamshire in 1897 naming 'bedlam sticks' among morris dancers' accoutrements.

This suggests that bedlam morris, that is, dances using sticks, began as a separate kind of morris dancing but that, sometime around 1800, elements of it were incorporated into the Whitsun-ale morris to produce the sets of south-midlands dances that were collected at the beginning of the 20th century. There is a heartland in the south-midlands morris, centred on the upper Thames and its tributaries, where dances with the characteristic slow capers of the Whitsun-ale morris survived long enough to be recorded in detail. Some of these also lacked recorded stick dances. The repertoires of Bampton, Longborough and Kirtlington are examples. On the periphery of the area teams performing both stick and handkerchief dances were more common, and some of these teams' repertoires as collected, such as at Ilmington and Adderbury, lacked dances with slow capers altogether. The merest hints of the development over time can be found. We have the report of the squire of a Whitsun ale from Brackley in Oxford in 1766, but by the time Cecil Sharp was collecting early in the 20th century (see Chapter 23) nearly half the Brackley dances he found were stick dances, and it had no slow capers. Similarly, though Lady Fermanagh complained of the Whitsun ales at Steeple Claydon in 1716, when Sharp visited in 1922 he recovered only one dance, a stick dance.[6] The south-midlands morris as known today is very probably the result of a fusion of the Whitsun-ale morris with the bedlam morris to greater or lesser degree in the different communities.

---

[5] Judge, 'D'Arcy Ferris', p. 472. [6] Bacon, Lionel, pp. 96-109, 299-301.

Music and dance repertoires were inherently fluid. Dances from Leafield were collected at different times from three old dancers: George Steptoe and Henry Franklin, who danced in the same set of dancers, and Henry's younger brother Alec. Each of them named a group of dances, but the list in each case was significantly different. Out of 28 dances, only three were named by all three men, and Steptoe's and Alec Franklin's repertoires were otherwise entirely different.[7]

Fluidity in the choreography is well illustrated at Ilmington in Warwickshire. In 1912 Cecil Sharp published the dances in *The Morris Book* in a version he had reconstructed to recreate what he thought was the form the dances took in 1867. He also spoke to a dancer from the 1890s and to the Ilmington fiddler Sam Bennett in 1906. Bennett later taught a team of children whom another researcher, Kenworthy Schofield, saw in 1945. All of these gave different accounts of the way the dances were to be performed, and the steps to be used.[8] The Bampton fiddler and fool William Wells said, 'When I first started in the Morris they hadn't got no more than half the dances as they had when I finished, because I found a lot of dances'.[9] These were probably a mixture of his own creations and dances observed from elsewhere. Peripatetic musicians were a major source. Wells said:[10]

> *My Granpy used to say that he liked to get men from Fieldtown [Leafield], Finstock and*
> *Filkins to come in because they always brought a new tune or two with them. That's how we*
> *got new tunes. They explained the tunes and put them through it. Then the local men would*
> *pick them up and play them. There were several tunes picked up in that way.*

'Putting them through it' strongly implies that Wells is talking about the dance as well as the tune, echoing other dancers' assertions about the equation of tune with dance.

Despite the fluidity, and the ready incorporation of popular new tunes such as 'Getting Upstairs' (a tune that became popular following the introduction of minstrel shows), the recurrence of complex tunes with associated dances, such as 'Trunkles', is indicative of an interconnected community of dancers and musicians with a strong shared cultural identity. A number of other tunes and dances – for example, 'Constant Billy', or 'Shepherds' Hey' – also recur numerous times in the different communities.

As well as the most conspicuous elements of the south-midlands morris, the capers of the Whitsun ale and the sticks of bedlam, other kinds of dances can be found. Most solo jigs use the steps of the Whitsun-ale morris, but a few, such as the 'Bacca Pipes' jig (dancing over crossed churchwardens' pipes) or the broom dance, are better seen as 'jigs done by morris dancers' than as 'morris jigs' – dancing to show off prowess was a general feature of community entertainment (for example, the sailor's hornpipe).

Turning to the social and historical context, the history of morris dancing in the south midlands has been comprehensively covered by Keith Chandler in his definitive work on the subject, incorporating years of research and fieldwork. Though it is thirty years since it was first published, his *Ribbons, Bells and Squeaking Fiddles* and its companion volume of primary data, *Morris Dancing in the English South Midlands 1660-1900*, remain the standard works on the subject: nothing which has emerged since has changed the picture he paints.[11] Much in the following paragraphs derives from his work.

---

[7] Heaney, Michael, 'Disentangling', p. 71.
[8] Bacon, Lionel, pp. 207-24.
[9] 'William Wells', p. 5.
[10] Kettlewell, p. 11.

[11] Chandler, *Ribbons*; Chandler, *Morris Dancing ... Gazetteer*. A combined 2nd edition is Chandler, *Morris Dancing ... Aspects*.

At the start of the 19th century the Whitsun ale remained a primary focus of morris-dancing activity in the south midlands. *Jackson's Oxford Journal* claimed in 1837 that 'In no other part of the united kingdom [*sic*], we believe, are these old English revels celebrated with such spirit, and so much original character, as in the midland county of Oxford, particularly at Woodstock, Marston, Beckley, Headington, Hampton, &c. septennially, and at the village of Kirtlington annually in the week following Whitsun-week, under the well-known name of the 'Lamb-ale".[12] All of these (except Kirtlington, at eight miles) are within five miles of Oxford, and it is likely that the correspondent was writing from very local knowledge. He failed to mention, for example, the septennial ale at Charlbury, 15 miles to the north-west.[13] Alun Howkins adds to the list a further seven ales from this period in his study of Whitsun celebrations.[14] We saw that in the 18th century the organization of an ale involved considerable expense, and although an ale organized by youths was typical, there was an implicit appeal to attract the middling classes as well as the local clientele. An advertisement for the ale at Milton-under-Wychwood in 1808, saying that this was a once-in-twenty-years event, began with an appeal aimed distinctly above the heads of the average village labourer:[15]

> *Come then, ye votaries of pleasure, and pay your adorations to the shrines of Venus, Bacchus, and Comus: lose not this charming opportunity of hiding from care, in the bowers of love, festivity and harmony. You may not live 20 years more: hilarity, jocularity and rural simplicity, will move hand in hand, conducted with the greatest discretion, modest demeanour, and appropriate etiquette, by his Lordship, attired suitably for the occasion, assisted by his Lady, specially selected for the pleasing talk from the youth and beauty of the neighbourhood...*

The evocations of decorum and good taste may well have been tongue-in-cheek to an audience who would know what to expect. The ale was held, but marred by poor weather, so the following year the organizers broke with the twenty-year rule and held another, again advertising in the local newspaper:[16]

> *Those who beheld the scenes of festivity and mirth exhibited at the above place last year, must remember with such emotions of pleasure the hilarity, jocularity, and appropriate demeanour that attended the past happy days, as to induce them once more (perhaps the last opportunity) to witness a repetition of such delightsome pleasures; and those last year prevented by the unfavourable state of the weather, business, or other casualties, to them fortune again unfolds the golden doors of opportunity.*

This may have been an attempt to recover the investment. A twenty-year cycle suggests considerable planning (with perhaps the participants of one ale becoming the middle-aged organizers of the next). The home-brewed beer for the 1808 ale was claimed to have been made nine months before. That the twenty-year cycle was not a mere advertiser's hyperbole is shown by the occurrence of another ale there in 1828, again announced in uplifting terms:[17]

> *The preparations for the renewal of that enchanting Festival, called a Whitsun ale ... are great indeed.*
>
> *Casks of home-brewed beer, as fine and exhilarating as the fountains of Bacchus, are provided! and Ceres, from her bounteous hoard, has selected the finest flour, to be made into rich cakes for the fair, and to be carried away by the sprightly Morris-Dancers....*

---

[12] *Jackson's Oxford Journal*, 13 May 1837.
[13] Clifford, Jesse, p. 17.
[14] Howkins, p. 189.

[15] *Jackson's Oxford Journal*, 21 May 1808.
[16] *Jackson's Oxford Journal*, 20 May 1809.
[17] *Jackson's Oxford Journal*, 17 May 1828.

Haste, then, ye friends of rural pleasure and innocent mirth, and again pay your homage in the pleasing temples of festivity and love! An excellent band of musicians will attend, to add delightful harmony, and complete the fête.

Disorder and riot will not be admitted into our shades; but gentle peace, appropriate demeanour, and wakeful diligence, will be the guardians and attendants of those festive boards.

A description of the Woodstock ale of 1823 revealed a festival considerably less decorous than these advertisements suggest. This was Thomas Little's *Confessions of an Oxonian* (1826), a titillating (for the Regency reader) account of life as an Oxford undergraduate. The publisher (and possible author) was John Stockdale, who in the same year also attached Little's name to the notorious *Memoirs of Harriet Wilson*, the courtesan. Little finds himself at the septennial Woodstock ale:[18]

On elbowing through the throng, the first fellow I met, who was engaged as a party in the revels, was an old man, dressed up in the motley garb of a Tom Fool or clown, and I must say for him, he looked his character to perfection.

How do master? cried he. May I ask your honour, what do you call that yonder? pointing to a painted, wooden horse, placed in the middle of a ring.

A wooden horse, to be sure, said I. What should you think it was?

A shilling, Sir, if you please, answered the clown, a forfeit, if you please, Sir.

A forfeit! a forfeit! what for? I enquired. I'll give you no shilling, I assure you.

Bring out his lordship's gelding. Here's a gentleman wishes for a ride! ... His lordship's groom, hey! Tell her ladyship to be mounted!

Here I was seized by four or five clumsy clod-poles, dressed up in coloured rags, and ribbons. They were, forthwith, proceeding to place me on the wooden hobby, just mentioned, behind an ugly, red-haired, freckled trull, who personated the lady of the revels, I bellowed out that I would pay the forfeit without more to do; and thus, was I sconced of a shilling, for not calling the cursed, wooden hobby his lordship's gelding.

On his next error (failing to identify a stuffed owl as 'her ladyship's canary bird'), he is threatened with a mock marriage to a maid of honour, 'a fat, ugly wench, with a nose and cheeks, reddened with brick-dust,' and to avoid this and being pricked on the buttocks with a toasting fork, he has to pay another shilling (Figure 14.2).

Despite the indignities visited upon unwary participants, during the first half of the century Whitsun ales could still be presented as respectable affairs. The notice of the impending 1837 Woodstock ale announced 'one of the finest May Poles ever seen' and that on Holy Thursday (Ascension Day, ten days before Whitsun), 'My Lord and My Lady, with their usual attendants – the tabor, pipe, and fiddle, with an excellent set of morris dancers, paid their respects to their neighbours, to invite them to My Lord's Hall and Bower during the Whitsun week'.[19] In 1844 the *Oxford Chronicle* looked forward to 'fun, frolic and revelry', while a later, fuller account of the ale spoke admiringly of the 'set of Morris Dancers dressed in clean white trousers, frilled shirt fronts and sleeves, and many small bells nicely adjusted to their legs'.[20]

---

[18] Little, Thomas, 1:169-74.

[19] *Jackson's Oxford Journal*, 6 June 1837.　　　　[20] *Oxford Chronicle*, 25 May 1844; Taplin.

Figure 14.2: 'Whitsun Ale in Blenheim Park', 1823 (in Thomas Little, Confessions of an Oxonian, plate after 1:170 London: J.J. Stockdale, 1826)

George Rowell wrote in 1886 that 'In the early part of the present century Whitsun-ales were somewhat common in the neighbourhood of Oxford, but I have no remembrance of any but one Lamb-ale, which was held annually at Kirtlington'. Elsewhere he wrote that 'my memory will go fairly back to the first decade of the century' – he was born in Oxford in 1804 and intimates that he attended the ale from the mid 1810s; but there was also a lamb ale at Eynsham until, probably, sometime in the 1790s.[21] The Kirtlington lamb ale attracted curiosity and attention because of the additional elements of the maidens of the village chasing a lamb to catch it with their teeth (their hands being tied behind their backs), the lamb being subsequently the centrepiece of a feast. Though this had been asserted by Blount in 1679, Rowell suggested that the first part of it was fanciful. He wrote that the lamb, decorated with ribbons, was carried about on a man's shoulders, and 'From about sixty or seventy years ago, the lamb used in the lamb-ale has been borrowed and returned; but previous to that time ... the lamb was slaughtered within the week, made into pies and distributed, but in what way is uncertain'.[22] As for the morris dancers, Rowell wrote:[23]

> *The Morisco dance was not only a principal feature in the lamb-ale, but one for which Kirtlington was noted. No expense was spared in the getting up ... and, with the linen of the whitest and ribands of the best, the display of the Dashwoods' colours was the pride of the parish, and in my early time it was generally understood that the farmers' sons did not decline joining the dancers, but rather prided themselves on being selected as one of them.*

The emphasis on pride in representing the community is a thread extending back to Tudor times, and the accounts from earlier times of other morris sides visiting, representing their own communities, is also attested at Kirtlington. The Headington dancer William Kimber

---

[21] Rowell, pp. 107, 103; 'George Augustus Rowell'; Stapleton, pp. 160-61.
[22] Rowell, pp. 108-09.
[23] Rowell, p. 108.

referred to the competitions between morris sides at the lamb ale: 'all the morris dancers used to dance for a cheese and the ribbon and the Headington Team always won. As many as 20 sides used to compete but ours was the only one with sticks and jigs and drawbacks and set backs dances.'[24] Every dancer who spoke to researchers about competitions invariably claimed their own team won. Kimber is proud of the variety of the Headington dances, and incidentally confirms the innovatory intrusion of stick dances into the Whitsun-ale morris. Twenty sides is not at all impossible. In the mid 19th century there were at least 25 teams within a ten-mile radius of Kirtlington.[25] Fred Gardner of the North Leigh morris spoke of his participation in the last Woodstock ale (he called it a 'lamb ale' though there is no evidence for that element) and how, again, there were 20 teams competing: 'First they all danced before the Duke, and then repaired to a barn where they competed, "Nor Ly" (i.e. North Leigh) of course winning.' It may well be that they won because of an innovation: Gardner reported that North Leigh had the idea of substituting half-coconuts for bare hands in a hand-clapping dance ('Mrs Casey').[26]

However, the atmosphere was changing. Despite later favourable reports, as early as 1825 a pessimist had written in *Jackson's Oxford Journal* that 'The Whitsun ales, and other customs … are fast sinking into disuse'.[27] After the 'fun, frolic and revelry' which the *Oxford Chronicle* had anticipated would be found at the 1844 Woodstock ale, the *Banbury Guardian* in 1851 was at first more neutral, simply announcing 'Preparations are in progress at Woodstock for commemorating the septennial Whitsuntide Ale, which commences next Monday. There is to be a pageant, with morris dancing, &c.'[28] By the time the ale was under way the newspaper's correspondent had decided he didn't like it, even resurrecting the old antipathy on religious grounds:[29]

> The septennial mixture of buffoonery, profaneness and obscenity, called the Whitsun Ale, is this week in full vigour, and doing its work in corrupting the youth of both sexes. We are no friends to putting down Popery by law, but we think the Mayor and Corporation of this eminently Protestant borough might abolish this remnant of a dark age, particularly as the religious part of the pageant has ceased for centuries.

He was prescient. By the time the next ale was due in 1858, there was a new Duke of Marlborough, evidently less well disposed towards supporting it, and the 1851 ale was the last.

The demise of the Whitsun ale was relatively rapid. The Kirtlington lamb ale was the last survivor. The last documented ale in Kirtlington was in 1860, though there are indications that it survived a couple of years thereafter.[30]

As ales died out around the middle of the 19th century, other festive opportunities for morris dancers to perform were also disappearing, though dancers could also dance out on their own initiative. At Dover's Games, one of the inspirations for the modern Olympics, just outside Chipping Campden, there were various country contests such as wrestling, hurdle races, jumping, singlestick (fighting with cudgels), as well as opportunities to eat, drink, dance and gamble. The games had been started in 1610, suspended during the Civil War, but revived soon after the Restoration.[31] Teams of morris dancers would turn up and compete for the privilege

[24] 'Sharp MSS, Extracts from William Kimber's Letters'.
[25] Dunlop, p. 253.
[26] 'Sharp MSS, North Leigh Morris'.
[27] *Jackson's Oxford Journal*, 21 May 1825.
[28] *Banbury Guardian*, 5 June 1851.
[29] *Banbury Guardian*, 12 June 1851.
[30] Chandler, *Ribbons*, p. 73.
[31] Whitfield, pp. 61, 76-77.

of dancing at the games themselves (with the opportunities for collecting money that it afforded), and at one of the last meetings the team from Guiting Power beat five other teams, including one from Sherborne (Gloucestershire), which had travelled 16 miles to compete.[32] At the last meeting of all in 1852 the team from Longborough is said to have been victorious.[33] A correspondent in 1826 gave an idea of the efforts that went into presentation:[34]

> *The morris dancers are not like what I saw in London streets a few days back – country fellows in their dirty working dresses scratching the pavement to pieces, but they are spruce lads sprigged up in their Sunday clothes, with ribbons round their hats and arms, and bells on their legs; they are attended by a jester called the Tom Fool. He carries a large stick with a bladder tied to one end, with which he buffets about and makes room for the dancers; one of the finest looking fellows among them is generally selected to carry a large plum cake with a long sword run through the middle of it, the cake resting on the hilt, on the point of the sword is a large bunch of ribbons with about a dozen streamers flying, of divers colours, a large knife is stuck in the cake, and when the young man who carries it sees a favourite lass or any one that is rather bountiful towards them he treats them with a slice.*

The fool was an integral part of the team, often the leader, while the sword bearer had come across from the retinue of a Whitsun ale as a means of soliciting contributions, selling crumbs from the cake in return for good luck. In their later years the games were organized by the innkeepers of Chipping Campden, who paid a rent of £5 to the parish for the privilege, but then rented out licences for booths at the fair: £4 for advance payment for drinking booths (£5 for later payment), and variable amounts for food booths, according to size.[35]

The Whit Hunt in Wychwood Forest was a customary right for communities around its boundaries to hunt deer. Given the time of year, and the fact that several of the communities had morris teams for much of the period, it was also a time for them to perform, typically in a different village each day. On one occasion the Ducklington morris team were upbraided for failing to dance around the newly erected maypole before setting off to the hunt (one of the few confirmations of dancers dancing around a maypole in the south midlands).[36]

The Wychwood Forest Fair was a more recent institution, having begun in 1795, initiated, ironically, by Wesleyans from Witney as a civilized picnic to escape from the debaucheries of Witney wakes, held in September each year. By the 1820s thousands attended the fair, and by 1831 it had become so disorderly that the authorities attempted to ban it.[37] By 1834 it was back. In the 1840s the authorities seemed to acknowledge the losing battle, and while announcing in 1844 that no fair was authorized, said at the same they would be taking action against anyone found selling alcoholic drinks in the forest. The next year they simply said that no fair involving the sale of alcohol was permitted. The year after that the local newspaper reported 'This most delightful of all holidays was the present year, if possible, more delightful than ever', with over 20,000 visitors.[38] There were military bands, Wombwell's menagerie, and games of cricket; boxing and theatrical booths, and a 'Vauxhall dancing saloon'.[39] There was also morris dancing. In 1847 one of the Leafield dancers, Emmanuel Dixon, married on the morning of the fair then went to dance there while his bride worked on a refreshments stall.[40]

[32] Wortley, 'Cotswold Olympicks'.
[33] 'Sharp MSS, Mr Horne', pp. 43-44.
[34] Real Lover of Old English Pastimes, p. 355.
[35] Whitfield, pp. 75, 77.
[36] Sharp and MacIlwaine, *Morris Book, Part I* (1912), pp. 23-24.
[37] *Jackson's Oxford Journal*, 3 September 1831.
[38] *Jackson's Oxford Journal*, 7 September 1844; *Jackson's Oxford Journal*, 30 August 1845; *Jackson's Oxford Journal*, 19 September 1846.
[39] Clifford, Jesse, p. 8.
[40] Willoughby, Maurice.

Both the Whit Hunt and the Forest Fair ceased when Wychwood Forest was enclosed in 1858.

Teams of dancers would also tour the district independently, soliciting contributions from the wealthier members of the community. It was hard work. Bucknell morris used to dance the whole of Whitsun week without returning home.[41] Emmanuel Dixon left his special dancing shoes on all Whitsun week because his feet had swollen so much after the first day's dancing that he couldn't get them off again.[42] There were frequent fights (which many dancers anticipated with enthusiasm). On one occasion the dancers from Little Barrington went over to Sherborne to dance in rivalry with the dancers there, but they took the precaution of hiring a prize fighter from Leafield (in fact George Steptoe, one of the Leafield morris dancers) to act as their fool. The resultant fight was one of the 'choicest memories' of the Barrington dancers.[43] There did not even have to be a rival team to fight. Ben Moss of Ascot-under-Wychwood named the dancers in his team and recounted:[44]

> these Danced at Pudlicot House on Whit Monday Morning and the Gentleman then Living there after Seeing there Dancing Set them Boxing for Money the First to Draw Blood to Receive 2/6 the Second 1/0 - they Reseved 14/- that Morning for the Entertainment and as Much Beer as they Liked to Drink.

On the other hand, meetings could also be amicable. Jesse Clifford of Charlbury recalled seeing 'twelve young men of Finstock and Leafield' dancing together on 29 May every year, 'dressed in knee-breeches and white stockings; and six rows of little goggle bells ... tacked on red braid, from knee to ankle, adorned each leg; a white wand and a large silk handkerchief formed the equipment of the dancer'.[45]

There were, of course, other opportunities for dancing. Morris dancers performed at the Bloxham statute (hiring) fair in October in the middle of the century.[46] Special occasions also encouraged performance. On the wedding of the Prince of Wales in March 1863 local celebrations included morris dancing at Buckingham, Longborough and Milton-under-Wychwood.[47]

In the right context morris dancing could survive. Abingdon's morris dancers were associated not with a Whitsun ale but with a mock-mayor ceremony which was held at the time of the town's June fair. The much repeated story of the origin of the custom invokes a fight at an ox roast in 1700 in which the inhabitants of Ock Street, in the east of the town but outwith the borough boundaries, who wanted the trappings of a mayor as in the borough proper, fought with the west-enders for possession of the horns of an ox. The current dancers still parade with a set of horns emblazoned with the date '1700'.[48] Regardless of the historicity of this aetiology, there is evidence of the custom and its dancers for the whole of the 19th century.[49] We also have the evidence of dancers in the 18th century, on a peripatetic circuit and in the context of parliamentary elections; and at the mock-mayor ceremony of 1849 the candidates adopted the names of the contestants in the 1847 parliamentary election.[50] As in parliamentary elections of yore, the successful candidate for the mock mayoralty is chaired along Ock Street in procession.

[41] Wortley, 'Bucknell Morris'.
[42] Willoughby, Maurice.
[43] Dommett, Morris Notes, 2.1:428; 'Wortley MSS, Notes on Cotswold Morris'.
[44] 'Manning MSS, Ascot-under-Wychwood'.
[45] Clifford, Jesse, p. 17.

[46] Heaney, Michael, 'Bloxham'.
[47] Bicester Herald, 27 March 1863; Jackson's Oxford Journal, 28 March 1863; Oxford Chronicle, 21 March 1863.
[48] Leach, Jonathan, Morris Dancing, pp.3-5.
[49] Chandler, Morris Dancing ... Gazetteer, p. 37.
[50] Berkshire Chronicle, 23 June 1849.

It is important also to bear in mind that dancing did not take place in a cultural silo. The dance itself could be used in other contexts. Many mummers' plays incorporated some kind of dance, and as early as 1780 the play text for the mummers at Islip in Oxfordshire concludes with the instruction, 'All dance the Morris'.[51] Similarly, in the play text noted at Thame in 1853, St George declaims 'Bring in the morres-men, bring in our band', which is followed by the instruction 'Morries-men come forward and dance to tune from fife and drum'.[52] An informant at Bloxham recalling the 1890s said that 'The mummers would do a dance similar to that of the Morris Dancers'.[53] Not just the form, but the people were involved in different activities. Jack Haynes, the fool for the Headington Quarry morris dancers in the mid 19th century, was also the informant who supplied the text for the Marston mummers' play and was presumably an actor in it.[54] Keith Chandler has described the multifarious and varied community activities of Richard Heritage, the Marsh Gibbon morris dancer.[55]

In the early part of the century there was the opportunity to earn significant money during the weeks around Whitsuntide. Elsewhere I have suggested that the money earned by a team dancing during one week could much more than double the expected earnings for each member in their regular jobs.[56] The detailed records from Stowe House in Buckinghamshire illustrate this. At Stowe the household accounts show that in 1819 the Marquess of Buckingham continued his predecessors' practice of generously supporting the Whitsuntide morris dancers who visited, paying £1 to each of the Gawcott, Westbury and Wotton morrises and 10s to an Oxfordshire morris, while the marchioness gave 10s to the Twyford dancers. Two years later the marquess gave £1 to each of the Westbury, Edgcott and Brackley dancers. In addition, the most local of the sides, Westbury, received 'their annual present' of one guinea (£1 1s) at Whitsuntide in 1818 and 1820.[57] The same volume of accounts records a payment of one guinea to dancers on 23 February, apparently as an entertainment for a tenants' social dance, and another guinea on 1 January 1819. Finally, it records election expenses in July 1818 which include payments of £1 each to Wotton and Waddesdon sets of dancers.

The Marquess of Buckingham was undoubtedly a keen supporter of the local morris dancers. Nowhere was this more evident than in family celebrations. In 1798 Matthew Lewsley the Buckingham saddler was paid three guineas (£3 3s) for supplying 'a new Sett of morris bells for 8 men' by the Marquess's order, and it is possible that these related to his son's coming of age the previous year, when hogsheads of beer were provided for the local populace. Lewsley billed the marquess for 410 bells, costing £2 11s 3d, suggesting 50 bells per dancer (with ten over).[58]

We have no written evidence of morris dancers at the next heir's coming of age, in 1818, but they are depicted dancing in the February snow in two pictures of the occasion. In a sepia-wash drawing they are on the north portico of Stowe House, performing a stick dance. Six dancers are depicted in beribboned top hats, white shirts, baldricks and dark breeches, and with crossed garters on their calves which may imply bells. There is a fool in a striped costume, pointed hat and carrying a long stick; and two musicians in the same costume as the dancers except for the garters, one playing a pipe and the other beating a side drum (Figure 14.3). The other picture is a watercolour. The main scene is of braziers being carried through the snow towards

---

[51] Preston, p. 171.
[52] Lee, Frederick George, 'Oxfordshire Christmas Miracle Play', p. 504.
[53] Huntriss, p. 219.
[54] Millington, 'Manning's Mummers' Plays', p. 202.
[55] Chandler, 'Popular Culture'.
[56] Heaney, Michael, 'With Scarfes', p. 501.
[57] 'Stowe MSS, Payments', [unfoliated].
[58] 'Stowe MSS, Stowe Household Accounts'.

Figure 14.3: 'View from the North Portico of Stowe House, February 1818' (Image courtesy of Bucks Archaeological Society, Discover Bucks Museum, AYBCM: Loan 321.18).

a temporary barn erected for the feast. The dancers in this picture are again on the north portico but are just a small detail at the edge of the larger scene. They appear to be holding hands in a circle; seven are visible in the dance, while an eighth sits astride a stone lion to the side of the steps (Figure 14.4).

For the coming of age of the next Marquess of Chandos in 1844 his father the duke made extensive preparations regarding the morris. One newspaper of the time reported:[59]

So anxious is His Grace to see restored the old fashioned custom of Morris dancing in the largest of his numerous parishes (as being within their moderate means of upholding and tending to divert the gross dispositions of young people from the beer-houses) that it is reported that His Grace has ordered no less than a dozen sets of their trappings to be made and presented to them forthwith.

Figure 14.4: 'An Outdoor Feast in Honour of the Coming of Age of the Duke's Heir' (detail) (Image courtesy of Bucks Archaeological Society, Discover Bucks Museum, AYBCM: Loan 321.17).

[59] *Buckinghamshire Herald*, 21 September 1844.

Figure 14.5: James Danby, 'Celebrations at the Coming of Age of the Marquis of Chandos, Stowe House, September 1844' (detail) (Image courtesy of Reeman Dansie).

The patrician duke was keen to entertain his tenants and estate workers, and the morris was an integral part. In planning for the coming celebrations, he wrote to his wife on 18 July 1844:[60]

> *I propose to give the Poor their dinner at Stowe, & then let them all come out on the <u>North Front</u> to drink the <u>Ale</u>, smoke, and dance with the morrice and other amusements, & the fireworks.*

The 'dozen sets of their trappings' were to supply a team at each of Stowe and the duke's second residence at Wotton, and the details give an insight into the costs of fitting out a team of dancers. The arrangements at Stowe were put in the hands of the house steward, William Jones. He contracted with Charles Camozzi (the Bicester ironmonger and silversmith) for the bells, James Goodwin for the breeches, George King (the Buckingham draper) for the shirts and ribbons, Elizabeth and Thomas Bason (shoemakers of Buckingham) for the shoes, and Benjamin Braggin (of Silverstone in Northamptonshire) for the Squire's (fool's) costume. Camozzi's bells were attached to six pairs of bell-pads, each pad bearing twenty-five bells and about thirty satin bows. Camozzi made four hundred bows, some of which may have been for the Squire's costume. Goodwin's breeches were supplied at two different prices, 6s and 6s 6d a pair, because, as Goodwin explained in a note, he 'had not a sufficient number corresponding in colour'. The Basons supplied the shoes for 9s a pair, and Braggin's charge for making the Squire's costume was £1 12s. The major beneficiary of the order was the draper, George King. He supplied the hats at 5s 6d each, the hose at 1s 3d a pair, and shirts and ribbons. Each dancer wore 20 yards of ribbon, and the total cost of King's bill for each dancer, including hat and hose, was 15s 5d. King also supplied large amounts of sarsnet and cambric silk, beyond the amount for the six dancers, totalling 94 yards. From the price and length of the material it would appear to have consisted largely of ribbon, and some of it may have constituted the

---

[60] 'Stowe MSS, Letter from Richard Grenville'.

material for the Squire's costume made up by Braggin, which according to the artist James Danby's contemporary picture of the occasion was certainly striped (Figure 14.5).[61] As in 1818, the 1844 picture shows six men, a pipe-and-taborer and a squire/fool. The dancers are performing a stick dance before the north front of the House, as the Duke had planned.

The costumes for the Wotton morris were largely supplied by Thomas Umfrey, a draper of Brill, except for the bells, which were again made by Camozzi. He charged the same as he did for the Stowe dancers, five guineas. As with Stowe, he supplied three hundred bells and ribbons; but here he reveals that the pads were made of morocco leather, and that they were made 'to pattern', that is, from a model supplied. Umfrey's hats cost 5s each (compared with 5s 6d at Stowe); the hose 1s 3d a pair (as at Stowe); the boots 8s 6d a pair (9s at Stowe); the breeches 6s 6d a pair (the same, or 6s, at Stowe). The only goods which we may confidently ascribe to the squire at Wotton are a 'fancy coat' and a 'fancy cap' for £2 10s, to be compared with the £2 14s 2¾d attributed to the Stowe squire's coat; but some of Umfrey's charges for ribbon should, perhaps, also be assigned to the Squire. The basic cost of each of Umfrey's shirts was 15s, whereas Stowe's were probably 16s.[62] The costs average out at the not inconsiderable sum of £17 10s per team.[63]

Without such patrician support the morris declined. The duke spent extravagantly on entertaining. Over 1,500 people dined at Stowe during that month.[64] Similar extravagance for the visit of Queen Victoria the following year resulted in the duke's bankruptcy. A generation further on, the *Buckingham Express* reported in June 1868 how Stowe villagers prepared for a village tea party:[65]

> *...on Monday several of the young men of the village set about raising funds for the purpose by decorating themselves in a variegated costume composed of all the colours of the rainbow and visiting Buckingham and its neighbourhood as morris dancers.*

This brought an immediate angry riposte from the vicar Edward Gardiner, one of the organizers of the treat:[66]

> *In the first place the day was Whit-Tuesday, not Whit-Monday as stated in your report; secondly, there are no morris dancers in any way connected with Stowe parish, the practice has been discontinued here for some years. Finally, it is not the custom to go to Buckingham or any other place begging alms for the expenses of the school treat; once a year, on May-day, the children of the school go round the parish with a garland, and the expenses of the tea are more than provided for out of the money collected on that day from parishioners only.*

The Stowe vicar's reaction exemplifies what Alun Howkins has called 'the taming of Whitsun',[67] the process whereby the Victorian middle class sought to control the disorderly pleasures of the lower orders by corralling them in a framework of Christianity, decorum and sobriety. The process affected a wide variety of popular customs. Steve Roud has put it succinctly:[68]

> *Increasingly during the nineteenth century, mass working-class customs were seen as harmful, distasteful, even dangerous, and those in authority began to condemn them and*

---

[61] 'Stowe MSS, Bills'.
[62] 'Stowe MSS, Abstract'.
[63] Heaney, Michael, 'With Scarfes', pp. 496-97.
[64] 'Stowe MSS, Abstract'.

[65] *Buckingham Express*, 13 June 1868.
[66] Gardiner, Edward I.
[67] Howkins.
[68] Roud, p. xii.

then actively interfere. In many cases, such as the celebrations surrounding May Day, their interference took the form of remodelling – cleaning up and constructing safe, child-based events.

The 'safe' (or at least, safer) event that replaced Whitsun ales was the club feast. Club feasts were the annual celebrations organized by friendly societies, whose main aim was to provide some insurance against illness, infirmity or hardship, in return for a modest subscription. Typically, at the club feast a procession through the community, accompanied by a brass band, was preceded or followed by a service and sermon at the parish church, and a sit-down meal. At Kirtlington the Provident Friendly Society, established in 1809, moved its club feast day from Easter Monday to Trinity Monday – the main celebration day for the lamb ale – around 1859. The diners at the feast were said then to have complained of the noise from the ale outside. The two were clearly in competition, and the club feast won. The society was 'under the fostering care of Major Dashwood', who in 1862 stopped providing an annual sum in support of the ale.[69]

A similar sense of the change in attitude can be seen in the reporting of Whit Monday at Bampton. The *Oxford Times* reported in 1865:[70]

Our friendly societies held their annual meeting on this day, attended Divine Service, dined together, passed pleasant hours in each other's company, discussed the wisdom of providing against sickness and old age, made converts to their notion of economy, &c., &c. A forcible sermon was given them by the Rev. T. Godson, and they will exhibit their wisdom if they follow his advice. Both societies are thriving, and adding to their numbers. The morris-dancers, a relic of bygone times, made their appearance, but did not attract the attention of many persons except the juveniles.

The reporter may have been particularly disapproving that year, as in 1870 the report is a more neutral but equally dismissive 'the morris dancers made their appearance in the streets'.[71] The point is clear: morris dancers, central to the Whitsun ale, are marginal to the club feast.

At the edge of the south-midlands area, at Yardley Hastings in Northamptonshire, by 1855 a vehicle accompanying the club processions contained members dressed in 'ludicrous and fanciful costume'. One was dressed as morris dancer.[72] The costume had become just an element in a fancy-dress parade.

Such changes in attitude were not entirely imposed from outside. Many poorer members of society converted to Methodism during the 19th century, and/or abstained from alcoholic drink. William Kimber senior of Headington Quarry and Daniel Lock of Minster Lovell both embraced religion towards the end of the century. Lock said he stopped morris dancing because of his wife's influence: 'She saw it lead to drinkin' and spendin' money and 'twere true enough'.[73]

Changes in attitude were clearly a significant factor in the decline. The economics of dancing compounded the problem. The records from Stowe show that it cost around £17 10s to equip a team, including about £2 10s for a fool's costume, making the cost per dancer for his kit also £2 10s. The majority of known dancers were labourers. Chandler's gazetteer of dance teams

---

[69] *Oxford Times*, 17 February 1902.
[70] *Oxford Times*, 10 June 1865.
[71] *Witney Express*, 9 June 1870.

[72] *Bucks Herald*, 2 June 1855.
[73] Chandler, *Ribbons*, p. 215; Hobbs, p. 229.

lists 56 known participants in Oxfordshire teams born in the decade 1821-1830.[74] These would have been in their twenties at the time of the 1851 census. Of the 51 who have been traced in the census, 34 (two thirds) were described as agricultural, farm, or general labourers. The £2 10s investment to equip a dancer was equivalent to around five weeks' wages (which were around 10s a week for labourers). Morris teams also needed a musician. These were in great demand, and could often be the making or breaking of a team. Joseph Woods, of Deddington, was said to have 'played for all the morrises for twenty miles around', and certainly played for at least four teams; John Potter of Stanton Harcourt is recorded as having played for eight.[75] In the 1860s, the morris team at Minster Lovell fetched a musician from Barrington, nine miles away, and the team folded when a subsequent musician left.[76] As a consequence of their scarcity musicians were relatively expensive. The two musicians who negotiated with the Ascot-under-Wychwood morris team in the 1850s wanted 5s and 7s a day.[77]

Analysis of sums paid to morris dancers evidenced in the household accounts of large estates such as Stowe shows that, so long as community support continued, teams of morris dancers touring the larger houses and surrounding villages and towns of a district might expect to collect over £60 in the usual week-long performing opportunity at Whitsun. The evidence outlined above for the cost of the costumes, lost wages and a musician account for about £23 of this, leaving a balance of £37 to be divided among the six dancers and a fool – a profit of over £6 per person.[78] There were often other supernumeraries to share the kitty, and takings would vary considerably from year to year, but it is clear that the earning opportunities considerably outweighed those of a week's work as a labourer.[79] The diaries of Richard Heritage of Marsh Gibbon confirm that sums of this magnitude were possible. On the village morris dancers' Whitsun tour in 1828 he received, on successive days, 9s at Bicester, £1 7s at Stratton Audley and around Marsh Gibbon, 6s at Poundon, Godington and Twyford, and 11s 4d at Wotton and Ashendon.[80] In a different context, Edwin Tanner of Finstock said people earned 10s or 11s a day when dancing their way back from London to Oxfordshire during the haymaking season in the first part of the 19th century.[81]

With the community support of a Whitsun ale such expenses could be met; without it, would-be teams needed a high level of confidence that they would get a return on their considerable outlay. Certainly, some of the later dancers claimed that they spent as much as, if not more than, they earned. Joseph Druce of Ducklington claimed to have been 'generally out of pocket over the dancing'.[82] When support fell away dancing became financially unsustainable. Daniel Lock of Minster Lovell said that the team had not been patronized enough, and Ben Moss of Ascot-under-Wychwood said that 'no one would give us anything, it got like begging which they [the dancers] didn't like'.[83] Moreover, new opportunities outside morris dancing did open up. Richard Heritage of Marsh Gibbon was also a member of the village band, which played at club feasts. Typically, his payments for that were smaller than the returns on dancing, but it was a secure sum for a contracted performance, and before parliamentary reform could be equally remunerative at elections.[84]

Keeping what rewards there were within the family was a significant incentive to dancing. There are many examples of family traditions. Although morris dancing is often described

[74] Chandler, *Morris Dancing ... Gazetteer*, pp. 121-213.
[75] 'Manning MSS, [Efforts]'; 'Manning MSS, Deddington'.
[76] 'Sharp MSS, Minster Lovell Morris'; Heaney, Michael, 'Disentangling', p. 64.
[77] 'Sharp MSS, Ascott under Wychwood Morris'.
[78] Heaney, Michael, 'With Scarfes' pp. 497-98.
[79] Heaney, Michael, 'With Scarfes', p. 501.

[80] Chandler, 'Popular Culture', p. 45.
[81] 'Sharp MSS, Finstock Morris'.
[82] 'Sharp MSS, Ducklington Morris'.
[83] 'Sharp MSS, Minster Lovell Morris'; 'Sharp MSS, Ascott under Wychwood Morris'.
[84] Chandler, 'Popular Culture', pp. 24-37.

in terms of place, thinking of the transmission of styles of dancing in terms of families may be more accurate. At Ducklington one team was composed entirely of members of the Fisher family.[85] Richard Eeles, the squire of the team based at Field Assarts in Oxfordshire, was the father of the George Eeles who was squire of the team based at Asthall Leigh a few years later; and of Richard Eeles, the squire of the Leafield morris. The younger Richard was the father of Stephen, also a dancer in the Leafield set. The three communities are within two miles of each other.[86] One of the most closely knit and densely populated family networks was at Bampton, its strength perhaps contributing to the persistence of dancing there until the end of the century. Keith Chandler has investigated the intertwining of the Portlock, Radband, Wells and Tanner families, illustrated in Figure 14.6. All of the men listed were morris dancers. Across four generations in the 19th century these four families provided 25 dancers.

Other societal changes were also at work. The nineteenth-century enclosures diminished the sense of community. Wychwood was disafforested in 1857 and enclosed the following year, leading to the immediate cessation of the Whit hunt and Forest Fair. The coming of the railways also had an impact. From the middle of the century excursion trains took people – most particularly the lower-middle and middle classes who might have given money to dance teams – out of their own communities to the seaside or other visitor attractions. The railway running through the Evenlode valley, heart of the morris dancing communities, opened in 1853.

From being the pride of their communities morris dancers became objects of mild amusement, indifference or disdain. Occasionally more sentimental memories were stirred. When the dancers from Brackley visited Banbury in Whit week in 1866, the local paper reported:[87]

> *A novel and amusing spectacle was afforded to young Banbury, on Whit Monday and Tuesday, by a set of morris dancers which perambulated the streets of the borough, dressed in many coloured ribbons, and other gaudy finery, and marshalled by the fool of the troupe, who was very active with his javelin, a cow's tail and bladder, and who displayed much witless buffoonery. The musical department consisted of the customary pipe and tabret, to whose doleful sounds the dancers performed their jigs with more strength than gracefulness. It is nearly 20 years since a similar exhibition of such a bye-gone pageant was witnessed in Banbury.*

A generation later, at an old folks' party in Shipton-under-Wychwood in 1889, 'Tea being over, the tables were speedily put aside, and so made room for other recreation and amusement ... the old morris dancing by the aged men causing much amusement'.[88]

As participation fell, dancers from different communities combined to provide a full complement of dancers, an example being when 'the Longborough and Lower Swell Morris dancers' entertained at the Swan Assembly Room in Moreton-in-Marsh in 1886; and when the following year three men from Bledington joined three from Longborough to dance.[89] Some of the morris teams that came together in the second half of the century were disparaged by the older dancers. This may simply be the perennial trope of the older generation despairing of the attitudes and capabilities of the young, or it may reflect the falling away of the traditions. Ben Moss said of a younger team at Ascot-under-Wychwood that it was 'nothing of a morris'

---

[85] 'Sharp MSS, Ducklington Morris'.
[86] Heaney, Michael, 'Disentangling', p. 50; Chandler, *Ribbons*, pp. 140-41.

[87] *Oxford Chronicle*, 26 May 1866.
[88] *Oxfordshire Weekly News*, 22 May 1889.
[89] Chandler, *Ribbons*, pp. 217-18.

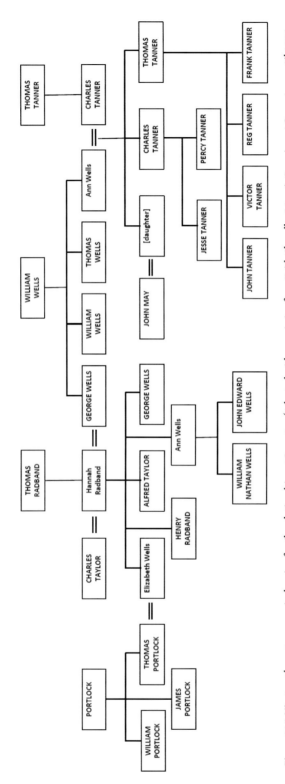

Figure 14.6: Nineteenth-century morris-dancing family relationships at Bampton (Adapted with permission from Keith Chandler, Morris Dancing at Bampton until 1914, p. 7. Eynsham: [The Author], 1983).

while Daniel Lock of Minster Lovell said that 'the young boys weren't willin' to work at the steps and such like, and so we given en up'.[90]

When the context for morris dancers to perform disappeared, performances in the south midlands essentially became just another form of street entertainment or busking. Towards the end of the century the grandson of the Finstock dancer and musician John Dore, Noah Buckingham of Hailey, would appear at Witney market acting as fool while one fellow villager, Jesse Jennings, played the concertina and another, Nokey Holloway, danced the morris jig 'Princess Royal'.[91] The team from Wheatley was reduced to three dancers and two musicians.[92] Although the Bampton team remained in performance, in the late 19th century their fiddler and fool William Wells also performed alone:[93]

> *I have done what no other known man ever attempted to do, I have been to village clubs, single-handed in full war paint, with Gosoon Dress, two sets of Bells on, Stick and Bladder, a stocking of a sort, Ribbons and Sashes, with my Fiddle in my hand. The jingle of the Bells would fetch the people out. They would shout, 'Here's the Bam Morris'. When they saw only one member, 'Where's the Morris?' 'Here's the Morris, says I. ... I have been out as far as Stow-on-the-Wold, Kingham, South Lea, Leafield, Kingston and dozens of other places and met with plenty of old Morris dancers that used to take part in sets that are broken up and gone.*

Dancers in the south midlands were predominantly adult (albeit young) and male. There are a few references to women dancing – Blount's account of the Kidlington lamb ale in 1679 tells us of a dance by men and another by women; at the laying of the foundation stone of Blenheim Palace at Woodstock in 1705 there were 'three morris dances; one of young fellowes, one of maidens, and one of old beldames', and at Spelsbury in the early 19th century there were sets

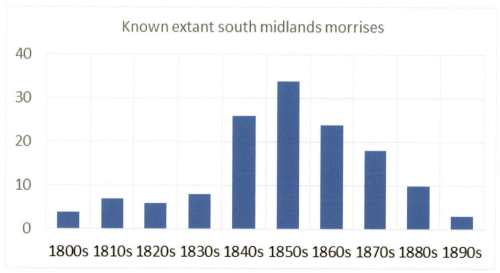

Figure 14.7: Known extant nineteenth-century south-midlands morrises (Adapted with permission from Keith Chandler, Morris Dancing in the English South Midlands, 1660-1900: A Chronological Gazetteer, *figure 5 (p. 17). Enfield Lock: Hisarlik Press, 1993).*

---

[90] 'Sharp MSS, Ascott under Wychwood Morris'; Hobbs, p. 229.
[91] Heaney, Michael, 'Disentangling', p. 69.
[92] 'Wortley MSS, Notes on Cotswold Morris', p. 17.
[93] 'William Wells', p. 12.

both of men and of young women. The latter were said to have danced on the church tower.[94] In each case, these were single-sex teams, in communities with male dancers.

Figure 14.7 uses data from Keith Chandler's gazetteer to track the number of known extant south-midlands sides for each decade during the 19th century. It may look as though these peaked in the 1850s but we have to bear in mind how the data were collected. The bulk of our knowledge comes from newspapers and researchers collecting at the turn of the 19th century. For the most part the researchers were interviewing men who were then old, having danced in their youth 40 or 50 years before, and familiar with the morrises in their and the surrounding communities. Records from the second half of the century are very probably comprehensive. For each decade before the 1850s we are increasingly reliant on the haphazard survival of documentary evidence. What it does show very clearly is an ineluctable decline through the second half of the century, once all the cultural supports had fallen away. The second inference one may draw is that, if the decline from a more or less steady state only began in the 1850s, and if the record from the 1850s on is more or less complete (which is likely to be the case) then the record we have from the early years of the century captures perhaps one sixth of the real levels of activity. The overall picture is clear. From being vibrant at the start of the 19th century, south-midlands morris had almost expired by its end.

[94] Blount, *Tenures*, p. 1181; Green, David, p. 50; 'Sharp MSS, Spelsbury Morris'.

Chapter 15

West-midlands morrises

The Forest of Dean on the west bank of the River Severn had a group of morris traditions of its own based in the forest and its surrounding communities in Gloucestershire, Monmouthshire and parts of Herefordshire. Post-Restoration records before the 19th century are few and were noted earlier (p. 182): Douce's report of dancers from Usk with fool, Maid Marion and hobby horse; John Byng's record of the dancers with Maid Marion and fool from Brockweir at Whitsuntide; and an account of 1799 of dancers on May day performing in Doward, adjacent to Symond's Yat on the Wye.

The Forest of Dean was relatively isolated, between the rivers Wye and Severn, subject to forest law, and with a substantial body of 'free miners' producing mainly iron ore and coal. Free miners are 'All male persons born or hereafter to be born and abiding within the said Hundred of St Briavels, of the age of twenty one years and upwards, who shall have worked a year and a day in a coal or iron mine [or 'in a stone quarry'] within the said Hundred', though the 'male' requirement was dropped in practice in 2010.[1] This led to a relatively independent population with a strong sense of community that was conducive to the continuation of customary practices such as morris dancing. The forest is well to the west of the communities of the south-midlands morris, and about ten miles south of those of the west-midlands morris dances with staves (Figure 15.1 on p. 243).

We know little about the details of the Forest of Dean dances or who the dancers were, although there are descriptions of their apparel. Cecil Sharp encountered some old dancers and musicians in 1909 but collected no dances, and some 40 years afterwards Russell Wortley visited the area and collected information about the dances done at Ruardean 75 years previously. Only one dance was remembered in any detail, a hand-clapping dance, 'Soldier's Joy'.[2] At Ruardean and May Hill former dancers were adamant that they had no stick dances, but did have handclapping dances. The same sources disagreed about handkerchiefs (Ruardean used them, May Hill did not), and it may be that this is indicative of the decline in tradition as the appurtenances of the dance style were lost.[3] Dancers' shirts were covered in ribbons of many colours, and they wore 'ruggles' on the legs (bell pads in which the bells are covered by numerous small strips of ribbon), but at May Hill the bells element in the ruggles had been lost. At Ruardean the dancers wore velveteen breeches, but at May Hill ordinary black trousers.

As in the south midlands, the dancers performed at Whitsuntide. For reasons unknown, a distinctive characteristic of the Forest of Dean morris was dancing on hill-tops: at May Hill itself (the hill's name, previously Yartleton Hill, reflects this),[4] at St Briavel's on Bailey Tump,[5] on Pope's Hill outside Littledean,[6] on the Bailie at Doward adjacent to Symond's Yat, from where the 1799 report comes. There are several accounts of dancing on Symond's Yat itself, including this from 1838:[7]

---

[1] Dean Forest.
[2] Wortley, 'Morris of the Dean Forest'.
[3] 'Sharp MSS, Mayhill'; 'Sharp MSS, Ruardean'.
[4] Rudder, p. 533.
[5] 'Karpeles MSS, Forest of Dean'.
[6] 'Sharp MSS, Longhope'.
[7] 'Wye and Monmouthshire'.

The morris dancers of Monmouth, the Forest of Dean and Lydbrook, generally assemble at Cymon's Yatt, at Whitsuntide, to celebrate their annual 'revels' on its summit.

Even a small eminence sufficed. The tump at St Weonard's (an old motte) was used for village festivities and 'especially morris dancing'.[8]

Another popular place for dancing was at crossroads, perhaps as neutral meeting places between communities. The Blakeney dancers danced at one in the middle of the forest. When Maud Karpeles investigated she was told that at Cinderford there were 'Traces of [a] processional [dance] to [a] dancing place, [an] open space in the forest (all the places evidently had a dance place in the part of the forest near, often at cross tracks)', while at Bream the morris was performed at the maypole that stood at the crossroads in the middle of the village.[9]

As in the south midlands, meetings between morris sides in the Forest of Dean were often the occasion for fights. At the Symond's Yat event in 1838, mentioned above, 'This year the parties contended for the possession of the post of honour, and a serious engagement took place which ended in several of the parties being carried from the field very seriously injured'. A Mrs Hands of Longhope remembered:[10]

The morris dancers ... came from Little Deane and danced on Pope's Hill. This latter was a great war place. Two parties of people met on the hill day by day and asked 'Is it peace or war'. One day it was war when blood ran down the hill in streams.

Maud Karpeles noted that there were fights between Brockweir and Tintern morris dancers.[11] The morris at Ruardean may have ceased when one of the dancers died after a fight at Plump Hill.[12]

The contest between the dancers from Lydney and Blakeney at a crossroads in the forest was said to be a 'mock fight' to determine who should dance first. It was fought with the swords which each side carried.[13] The role of sword bearer in the Forest of Dean was different from that in the south midlands and may derive more from the presence of sword bearers in processions. These had been a feature of the Midsummer Watch processions in sixteenth-century London and were found accompanying the morris dancers as late as 1727 in the celebrations for the king's birthday in Bath. In the west midlands no fewer than six sword bearers accompanied the procession of morris dancers from Broseley to Astley Abbotts in 1652; the dancers at Wolverhampton the same year had both sword bearer and flag bearer, as had those at Clee St Margaret in 1619. At Clee the flag was seen as so essential an adjunct to the dance that it was purloined from the church. Somewhat to the east of the forest but west of the Whitsun-ale area, in the eighteenth-century picture from Dixton near Cheltenham (Figure 11.3 on p. 172) the men leading the procession may be carrying flags or even swords with streamers. (Confusingly, there is another Dixton on the western edge of the Forest of Dean near Monmouth.)

At Clifford's Mesne the dancers danced in procession, with the flag bearer leading the left file and the sword bearer, carrying two swords, leading the right. Each waved their regalia around in time with the music. The sword bearer there did put the swords to use in a dance: they were laid crosswise on the ground and danced around as in the 'Bacca Pipes' jig of the south midlands,

---

[8] Robinson, Charles J., p. 295.
[9] 'Karpeles MSS, Forest of Dean'.
[10] 'Sharp MSS, Longhope'.
[11] 'Karpeles MSS, Forest of Dean'.
[12] Chandler, 'Morris Dancing in the Forest of Dean'.
[13] 'Karpeles MSS, Forest of Dean'.

to the same 'Greensleeves' tune.[14] At May Hill the 'Bacca Pipes' jig was also performed over churchwarden's pipes, while at Ruardean the swords were used in a dance in which the sword bearer manipulated them in a complex manner. Far from being supernumeraries, the flag and sword bearers were seen as the leaders of the team, the flag bearer being their 'foreman'. The flag itself was large, usually three feet or more square.[15]

Some teams also had a cross-dressing male character equivalent to the Maid Marion of earlier times but called 'Mad Moll'. John Byng had mentioned a 'Maid Marion' in 1787. Later records suggest a blurring in the roles of supernumerary characters, so that at Lydbrook 'Moll the ladle' went with the dancers, while at Blakeney the 'woman' had a horse's or cow's tail tied on his back (commonly attested for the fool of a morris) and there was a distinct 'ladleman'.[16] The ladle's use as a collecting device is attested from Tudor times and is depicted in the painting of the Thames at Richmond (Figure 6.5 on p. 93). The 'Moll' who accompanied the dancers from Woolaston and Alvington was identified as a 'fool' character. At May Hill only a fool was recorded.[17]

One Ethel Hartland wrote to Cecil Sharp in 1913 and told him that at Framilode, a ferry-crossing point on the east bank of the Severn opposite the forest, there was morris dancing using 'little crooks, like diminutive shepherds' crooks ... instead of plain sticks'. This fits with neither the Forest of Dean nor Whitsun ale morrises, and is not close to other communities with stick dances; it must remain an enigma.[18]

One of the earliest nineteenth-century accounts, from 1822, described all the elements at Blakeney: the beribboned shirts, flag bearer, swordsman with two swords and both a 'Tom Fool' and a 'Maid Marian'. The dancers 'cut the most ridiculous capers and contortions'.[19] The author was William Wickenden, and in 1851 he published (anonymously) a short story in Charles Dickens's magazine *Household Words*, which again captured many of the characteristics of the morris dances of the area:[20]

> *Now it was Whitsuntide ... In the Forest of Dean every hamlet has, at this season, its wake or festival; and morris-dancing is the business of life. Each morris-dancer throws aside his coat and waistcoat, to display a shirt covered with party-coloured ribbons twisted into rosettes for him by his sweetheart. Happy the maid who has decked out her lover with finery; she loves to see her ribbons glorified. Then the dancers pride themselves on feathers also, and hang bells about their knees. The foremost dancer wields a flag on which are inscribed the initials of the district to which his morris belongs. Our dancing-ground was Blakeney Hill. ... On the top of this hill is a level platform, where has always been held the Blakeney Hill wake. To this wake all the different forest districts used to send forth their sets of morris-dancers; each set had its own dancing-ground, and you might see twenty or thirty companies, of forty or more couples, all tripping it at one time merrily.*

The final sentence suggests a shift in Wickenden's narrative from morris to social dancing, but the specificity of the information (for example, the knowledge that the flag bearer was the leader of the dancers) confirms his first-hand credentials. Wickenden was the son of a Blakeney farmer, and in his autobiography he describes how he used to watch the morris dancers rehearsing for weeks before Whitsuntide on the village green in Blakeney, to the accompaniment of a fiddle.[21]

[14] 'Sharp MSS, Cliffords Mesne Morris'.
[15] 'Sharp MSS, Mayhill'.
[16] 'Karpeles MSS, Forest of Dean'.
[17] 'Sharp MSS, Cliffords Mesne Morris'.
[18] Hartland.
[19] Wickenden, Letter.
[20] Wickenden, 'Tale', p. 463; Lohrli.
[21] Wickenden, 'Sketch', p. xix.

At Ross-on-Wye in 1851 morris dancers were also present at the celebrations accompanying the passing of the parliamentary bill to bring a railway to the town, and in 1863 they appeared again at the festivities marking the wedding of the Prince of Wales.[22] In the latter year they were still putting in an appearance at the club feast in Westbury-on-Severn, although as in the south midlands they were described by the press in this context as 'old-fashioned'.[23] The report of the Newnham club feast in 1867 expressly stated that the feast had supplanted morris dancing, and a similar report from Lydney in 1871 averred that such clubs and their feasts 'have the benefit of the working man in view, and seek to inculcate provident habits. These celebrations are far preferable to the way in which Whit-Monday was formerly celebrated in Dean Forest, when the local morris-dancing troupes capered in the village.'[24]

Dancing did continue in some circumstances. In 1875 the boggy track over the top of May Hill was made up into a firm road, and according to the *Gloucester Journal* 'In the evening the workmen celebrated the event in a convivial manner, winding up with the old-fashioned morris dance'.[25] Almost the last reports of dancing in the area are from Ruardean in the early 1880s, ending with a tour by the Ruardean dancers to Mitcheldean and Ross-on-Wye.[26] Other information comes mainly from local newspapers. The context of the appearance of 'a set of morris dancers' at the annual demonstration and gala of the forest miners at the Speech House in the centre of the forest in July 1884 suggests a performance of the traditional type, but the 'quaint procession' with 'morrice dancers in attendance' at the 'Ancient shepherds' harvest home festival' in Ross-on-Wye two months later may have been a more contrived event of the kind seen by that time at fêtes up and down the country (see Chapter 18).[27] This was certainly the case for the historical fête at Chepstow Castle in 1890, where morris dancers performed in a scene from T.J. Dibdin's drama *Kenilworth*, a popular piece of theatre since its first production in 1821, recreating the visit there of Queen Elizabeth in 1575.[28] The same is true of the coming-of-age celebrations of J. Maclaren-Rolls at The Hendre, Monmouthshire in 1891, where the six male morris dancers 'attracted much attention by their contribution to the performance, … in excellent time to music dating from the 13th century played by the piper and taborer', with Robin Hood, Friar Tuck, etc., in attendance.[29]

At the end of the century there was a brief revival at Mitcheldean, led by the fiddler Stephen Baldwin. Baldwin was the son of the fiddler for the Clifford's Mesne dancers, but he had previously moved to Bromsberrow Heath in Gloucestershire. That village, although close to the northern edge of the Forest of Dean, had morris dances using sticks, in line with other dances from the west midlands. Baldwin had played for the morris dancers at Bromsberrow Heath, and it was those dances he introduced to Mitcheldean, rather than those typical of the forest.[30]

The communities a few miles north of the Forest of Dean marked the southern edge of that arc of dancing sweeping north through the counties of Hereford and Shropshire and north-east through Worcestershire to Staffordshire. We identified some traits emerging in this area as morris dancing declined through the 17th century, and the reference to the apparently novel bedlam morris of Shrewsbury late in the century, using staves. Unfortunately, there is an almost total dearth of information from this area during the 18th century. When sources

[22] *Gloucester Journal*, 21 June 1851; *Hereford Times*, 14 March 1863.
[23] *Gloucester Journal*, 30 May 1863.
[24] *Gloucester Journal*, 16 May 1868; *Stroud Journal*, 3 June 1871.
[25] *Gloucester Journal*, 12 June 1875.
[26] Wortley, 'Morris of the Dean Forest'.
[27] *Citizen*, 3 July 1884; *Citizen*, 1 September 1884.
[28] *Chepstow Weekly Advertiser*, 2 August 1890.
[29] *Monmouthshire Beacon*, 9 May 1891.
[30] Wortley, 'Bromsberrow Heath Morris Dances'.

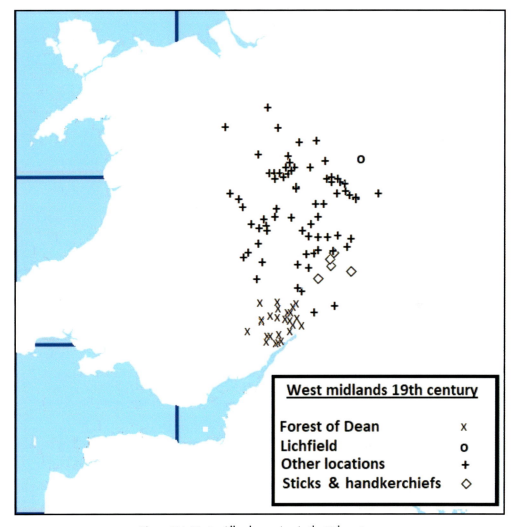

Figure 15.1: West-midlands morrises in the 19th century.

pick up again in the 19th, wherever there is information about the content of the dances, they almost invariably involve the use of staves; but the term 'bedlam morris' has been lost (Figure 15.1). Where it overlapped with the Whitsun-ales morris the term 'bedlam' survived (albeit minimally) as a contrast to dances using handkerchiefs, but where dances with staves were the only sort of morris dancing encountered there was no need to distinguish it from other kinds, and in those circumstances it is not surprising that the distinctive adjective might be dropped. It is speculative, but it may be that the Forest of Dean dances are the descendants of the earlier form of morris in the west-midlands area, before morris dancing using staves became the norm.

––––––––––––––

The Forest of Dean apart, the dances of the rest of this area have commonalities which we can bring together as 'west-midlands morris'. We shall see that many of its dancers were performing in contexts in which widespread community investment and support were lacking.

Figure 15.2: Charles Stringer,' The Lichfield Greenhill Bower Procession', c. 1800 (watercolour inserted at p. 353 in a copy of Thomas Harwood, The History and Antiquities of the Church and City of Lichfield. *Glocester: Cadell and Davies, 1806, Bodleian Libraries G.A. Staffs 4° 7, detail). (Image © Bodleian Libraries, University of Oxford).*

The morris dancers of Lichfield were an exception, but it is worth beginning with them partly because we can trace their development in detail from the start of the 19th century, but also because we have a unique visual record of them from early in the century (Figure 15.2).

Charles Stringer was an artist and house-painter who added numerous illustrations to his interleaved copy of Thomas Harwood's history of the city, published in 1806. His watercolour of the Greenhill Bower procession is undated. Most of the dated pictures in the book are from between 1812 and 1819, but Stringer depicts the procession as it once was, and includes the market house, demolished 1789, in the picture.[31] He may have been inspired by the resurrection of the procession in 1816 after a ten-year hiatus. His picture shows eight dancers clashing staves (six of which are clearly visible), confirming the description by Stebbing Shaw in 1795 of eight dancers in the procession.[32] Their shirts are covered in ribbons, and they have breeches in various colours. No bells are visible (although later reports mention bells), and they are hatless. In front of them, at the head of the procession, are a pipe-and-taborer, a man-woman figure carrying a bow, and a fool in motley carrying a ladle. Although the supernumeraries have full costumes, the beribboned shirts are all that distinguish the dancers apart from the staves.

The hiatus which began in 1806 was initiated by the city corporation, which described the Bower festival as 'as a custom no longer of any use, but the occasion of great expense to the Corporation and Constables and a great nuisance and inconvenience to them and the other

---

[31] Judge, 'Morris in Lichfield', pp. 137-38.   [32] Shaw, 1:316.

inhabitants of the City'; and Harwood himself described it in that same year as 'an idle and useless ceremony, adapted for the amusement of children'. When it was revived ten years later it was as an independent initiative supported by contributions from local gentry and others.[33] There was a rather more distinctly antiquarian feel to the proceedings, with the *Lichfield Mercury* in 1830 referring to 'the times of our merry forefathers' (and noting the dancers' accoutrements of sticks, bells and shirts with ribbons in many colours).[34] The last payment to dancers for chairing at a parliamentary election was made in 1831, and their last annual civic payment in 1833, after which the city chose to support other local activities instead, such as the cricket club and Mechanics' Institute.[35]

The morris dancers continued to appear at the Bower procession, and when the pipe-and-tabor accompaniment was discontinued in 1839 local protests led to its reinstatement the following year. However, other elements were taking over, Wombwell's menagerie among them, such that in 1837 the *Staffordshire Advertiser* repeated the 1779 description of the event as 'degenerated'.[36] Once the railway came, and a town-centre station opened in 1849, the Bower festival became a day out for visitors from the Potteries and the industrial midlands, and the morris dancers were well down the roster of attractions, listed after the bands, menageries, horse riders, theatrical shows and exhibitions.[37] The *Illustrated London News* described the event in 1850 and published a line drawing showing some of the dancers (Figure 15.3). Five dancers are depicted, carrying staves but apparently not dancing; also the pipe-and-taborer, fool and male Maid Marion. The men's costume does not seem to be particularly elaborate: they have beribboned shirts with crossed baldricks, but plain trousers (with no bells in sight) and what appear to be somewhat misshapen John Bull hats. The musician wears ordinary street clothes. Two of the emblems known as 'poseys' on poles carried by the 'dozeners' (city ward representatives) are shown.

Figure 15.3: 'Lichfield "Greenhill Bower" – the Morris Dancers', Illustrated London News, *25 May 1850, p. 364.*

The 1850 newspaper report marked a new direction for the Bower procession as, fixing upon the secondary name for the event of 'the Court of Array', it took on aspect of the re-creation of a medieval pageant, with knights in armour. A mounted knight is prominent in the *Illustrated London News* picture behind the dancers. The dancers still

[33] Judge, 'Morris in Lichfield', pp. 136-37.
[34] *Lichfield Mercury*, 4 June 1830.
[35] Judge, 'Morris in Lichfield', p. 139.
[36] *Staffordshire Advertiser*, 20 May 1837.
[37] *Staffordshire Advertiser*, 12 May 1849.

led the procession with pipe-and-taborer, fool and 'Maid Marian', until in 1860 they were demoted to follow Wombwell's band, which was on a cart drawn by an elephant and camels. Two years later they were even further down, as in addition to Wombwell's band and animals, the Rifle Volunteers and militia and juvenile bands and the dozeners (who previously followed the dancers) all took precedence.[38] At some time in the 1870s the dancers were dropped altogether.[39] The unique combination of stick dances and embedding in a community festival was apparently not enough to save the Lichfield dancers from disregard as fashions moved on and pseudo-historical pageantry and more modern entertainments supplanted them.

———————

The Lichfield dancers' chief appearance was at a Whitsuntide procession, though in the earlier period they also came out at Christmas and at elections. They had civic support, at least in the initial period and later tacitly. The only similar context in the west midlands is, firstly, a single report from 1847 relating to Droitwich in Worcestershire, where 'on the 27th of June, a large party of Morris Dancers still continue to parade the town and neighbourhood, it is said, in commemoration of a discovery of some extensive salt mines';[40] and secondly, the suggestion mentioned earlier (p. 201) of morris dancers at Coleshill, just to the east of Birmingham, at a parliamentary election probably in the 1840s.

The wider west midlands showed no such civic approbation. Writing of his youth, probably in the 1820s, John Randall of Coalport in Shropshire recalled morris dancers at Whitsuntide, 'with short thick sticks in their hands, which they brandished about to keep time to the dance, and their hats gaily decorated with parti-coloured ribbons, a few streamers being ... attached to their knees, trousers being little worn then by the lower classes' (implying that they wore breeches).[41] The majority of subsequent references come from the winter season, occasionally as an element in seasonal celebrations, more often as a response to privation.

One of the earliest and most detailed records of morris dancing in the west midlands comes not from the area itself, nor from winter, but from London in August 1817. In an episode reminiscent of the fate of the Canterbury morris dancers in 1589, a group of dancers performed outside the Alien Office in Queen Square and were hauled inside to face the magistrate. *The Times* reported the event on 8 August 1817, and there is a suggestion that, like some teams from the south midlands, the dancers were intending to work their way back home during the harvest season. There were eight dancers, carrying sticks, and a musician, who had a 'tambourine', apparently the only instrument. They dressed in 'all the colours of the rainbow, by means of ribands of various colours, white, red and yellow paper round the edges of their hats, to imitate silver and gold lace, and other absurd imitations of finery'. On a piece of paper on one of the hats was written 'Colliers from Shropshire'. Between them they had 2s in halfpennies, and they claimed that that was as much as they earned from dancing on any day. The rather benevolent magistrate ordered them to surrender their costumes, sticks and drum and to go back home by two different routes, in one group of five and the other of four, seeking work on the way, but not dancing. He paid each of them 2s 6d from public funds on their undertaking to do so.[42] Were it not for the absence of a mention of bells, these may even have been the 'eight Morris dancers with bells and time evolution staves, attended by the proper music, a tabor and pipe' seen two months earlier in St James's Street.[43]

[38] *Staffordshire Advertiser*, 2 June 1860; *Staffordshire Advertiser*, 14 June 1862.
[39] Judge, 'Morris in Lichfield', p. 143.
[40] Gutch, John, 1:346.
[41] *Salopian and West Midlands Monthly Illustrated Journal*, December 1879.
[42] *Times*, 8 August 1817.
[43] Carter.

Figure 15.4: George Scharf, 'Morris dancers, January 1841' (in Sketch book. Image ©The Trustees of the British Museum, 1900,0725.120.15+. All rights reserved).

The names of four of the dancers were given in the report, and Gordon Ashman was able to trace the name of one of them – John Cadman – to the Ketley area near Wellington (the other names remain untraced). There is more than one person of that name, so an exact identification is not possible, but all were colliers.[44] Twenty-five years later, in 1841, George Scharf sketched a party of Staffordshire boatmen he encountered in Francis Street, Westminster (Figure 15.4). He met them in January, in a year when hard frosts and frozen rivers kept boatmen out of work. The boatmen are carrying a placard, 'Turn out [*sc*. turned out of work?] Staffordshire canal boatmen'. The Staffordshire and Worcestershire canal ran from Great Haywood in the north (two miles east of Stafford, at the Trent and Mersey canal junction) through Wolverhampton and Kidderminster to the River Severn at Stourport-on-Severn. Scharf notes that there were 12 men, but sketches 11: eight dancers, a fiddler, a tambourine player, and a money collector holding the placard. He does not identify them as morris dancers, unlike the sketch of 'Moris dancers' [*sic*] immediately above it on the page, made in 1826, and showing what appear to be south-midlands dancers, again using sticks, in which each pair of the six dancers is performing a different element of the dance.[45] The Staffordshire boatmen are all clashing their staves, and are wearing much less ornate apparel, namely smocks and trousers, and a variety of hats.

The Shropshire colliers and Staffordshire boatmen had each travelled about 150 miles to dance in London and solicit money, and had probably walked all that way (unless the boatmen were able to use the waterways on unfrozen parts of the network). Indigence arising from loss of work was a common theme, and it may well have been the driver for the Staffordshire boatmen seen by Scharf. 'H.W.' saw some morris dancers performing stick dances beside the canal at Loveday Street in Birmingham in the 1830s 'kept out of work by the long and severe frost'.[46]

---

[44] Ashman, Gordon, pers. comm.
[45] Reproduced in Judge, 'Old English Morris Dance', p. 326.   [46] W., H.

The freezing of the River Severn at Worcester was the occasion of many reports through the century. In January 1838 the local newspaper reported that 'the almost exploded custom of morris-dancing has been revived in our streets: we noticed this morning a little group, with the usual accompaniments of a fiddle and two fools'.[47] Sometimes doubt was cast on the probity of the dancers. At Worcester in 1854:[48]

> *A number of watermen - generally most improvident men – having been thrown out of employ by the stoppage of the Severn and the canals, have paraded a boat round the town and solicited alms; while another party was to be seen in the streets yesterday habited as morris dancers, and assuming a gaiety if they did not possess it.*

Another newspaper describing the same events made similar imputations:[49]

> *Frozen-out watermen, real or pretended, commenced also to levy contributions on the tender-hearted, appealing to their sympathies through an attempt at enacting Morrice Dancers.*

Scepticism was also evident in Worcester in 1881 in town meetings to discuss relief for the poor in the severe weather. One alderman 'very much questioned whether by permitting morrice-dancers to beg in the streets much good was done', and said that they looked 'well clothed and well fed', while the mayor said that when 'he had told dozens of men that they could have work immediately [clearing snow] on application to the Borough surveyor, there had not been a single applicant; and when he suggested such a thing to some of the "Morris-dancers" they ran away from him'.[50]

As the century progressed morris dancers were dropping out of public consciousness. Six years later when 20 boatmen paraded Worcester 'decked out in coloured papers and fancy feathers, and carrying short sticks' collecting money, the *Worcestershire Chronicle* reported that 'Their strange appearance caused much curiosity, and there seemed to be an idea that their "get up" was intended to represent morris dancers'.[51]

Frozen-out boatmen also appeared on the streets of Cheltenham and Gloucester in 1855 among other years, overlapping in geography if not in time of appearance with the summer dancers of south-midlands morris.[52] Those in 1881 in Cheltenham were not specifically identified as boatmen by the *Cheltenham Journal*, reporting on the effects of the weather, but as 'labourers, gaily dressed in ribbons of various colours ... [who] treated the residents to some country dances to the tune of an accordian, beating time with their cudgels. It is some time since "morris dancers" have been seen in the town, and their appearance now is evidently an indication of the snowed-out state of the labouring classes.'[53]

Other outdoor trades also danced to relieve hardship. Bricklayers were recorded in Shrewsbury in the early 1870s. There was a fool, collecting, and five pairs of dancers. One of each pair held a stick, the other a trowel, which they beat together as in ordinary stick dances.[54] The trowels were probably an innovation to highlight their authenticity as out-of-work labourers, and may have been in response to a complaint from February 1865, when a Shrewsbury bricklayer wrote to complain to the local newspaper that 'A number of men have been going

---

[47] *Berrow's Worcester Journal*, 18 January 1838.
[48] *Gloucester Chronicle*, 7 January 1854.
[49] *Worcestershire Chronicle*, 11 January 1854.
[50] *Berrow's Worcester Journal*, 29 January 1881; *Worcestershire Chronicle*, 29 January 1881.

[51] *Worcestershire Chronicle*, 22 January 1887.
[52] *Gloucester Journal*, 17 February 1855; *Cheltenham Chronicle*, 20 February 1855.
[53] *Cheltenham Mercury*, 29 January 1881.
[54] M., M.

about the town with painted faces, and ribbons attached to different parts of their persons, morris dancing, representing themselves as bricklayers out of work. I beg to state, on behalf of the bricklayers of Shrewsbury, that there was not one bricklayer amongst them.'[55] Another bricklayers' dance with trowels was observed in Oldbury near Bridgnorth in 1884.[56] In 1878 it was the gardeners of Shrewsbury who attracted attention, and caused an onlooker to suggest in a letter to *Eddowes's Journal* that they be put to useful work:[57]

> It appears to me that the trees standing on public property in Shrewsbury require pruning. Would it not be advisable to employ some of the many frozen-out gardeners, who would prefer work to Morrice-dancing and guzzling the proceeds, to do the work at once?

Dancing in winter had its dangers. We do not know the occupation of Joseph Beardmore of Gnosall in Staffordshire, or if he was out of work and seeking to earn some money, but on Boxing Day 1836 as an 18-year-old he went morris dancing with his companions to Bradley, five miles away. On the way home, when nearly half-way there, he separated from his fellows to return to the pub at Bradley, but being drunk, fell shortly thereafter and died from exposure.[58]

The other circumstance which often led to hardship was going on strike, and there are several reports of striking colliers dancing to supplement their income. Colliers seem to have had a long association with the dance. The regular Christmas visitors to Shugborough Hall in the 1780s were colliers from Brownhills. The dancers in London in August 1817 were also probably colliers, but there is no hint that they were enduring hardship, and they had been approvingly described by the reporter for *The Times* as 'stout, well-made, and some of them rather handsome young men' once divested of their costumes. Out-of-work labourers could indeed travel far afield when morris dancing. In February 1858 some from Staffordshire were seen in Leominster, over thirty miles away, as reported by the *Hereford Times*.[59]

The dancers at Hockley Hill in Birmingham about 1835 were described as 'colliers on strike'.[60] A correspondent from Oldbury near Dudley recalled dancers around 1860, and suggested some of the cultural background:[61]

> If my memory serves me correctly, it was when there was a great strike amongst the miners of the district, and many of the elder men took to this mode of pleasing the public to gain a living, having been used to it in their youth, when they have told me it was frequently to be seen in most country villages, especially at Christmas time.

This may have been the strike of 1858 when according to one T. Hill writing to the *Birmingham Weekly Post* over 25 years later, the Oldbury dancers sang 'doggerel verses announcing their determination rather to starve than accept 4s per day'.[62] There is a hint in this report of evolution from a festive winter custom, recalled by the older miners, into solely a solicitation practice. In the 'great colliers' strike' of 1863-64 there were morris dancers in Wolverhampton, Bilston and elsewhere.[63]At Ironbridge the colliers paraded as morris dancers and ballad singers, sometimes accompanied by drum and fife bands, and despite the difficult conditions were praised for the way they were conducting the strike.[64]

[55] Bricklayer.
[56] Cawte, 'Morris Dance', p. 202.
[57] Arbor.
[58] *Wolverhampton Chronicle*, 4 January 1837.
[59] *Hereford Times*, 6 February 1858.
[60] Father Frank.
[61] G., W.H.
[62] *Staffordshire advertiser*, 7 August 1858.
[63] Hill, T., 'Local Notes ... [1479]'.
[64] *Wolverhampton Chronicle*, 19 October 1864.

Colliers went on strike again in 1884, and a correspondent of the *Walsall Advertiser* worried that it would produce 'a fearful amount of suffering', and added:[65]

> *Passing through Willenhall last week ... I observed about a dozen men, who were said to be miners out on strike. These men wore most grotesque head gearing, and were dancing a kind of Morris Dance, to the music of an accordion which was being played by one of their number, while another was going round with a box, collecting money. The dancers, who appeared pretty much exhausted, were beating time with sticks, as they danced to the music, somewhat after the fashion of stage fencers. I could not help thinking that if what these men were doing was called work, they would consider themselves badly paid if they got no more than they were getting when I saw them – for all they received was only a very few coppers.*

The strike continued, and five weeks later T. Hill, who in May 1884 had recalled the 'great colliers' strike' of the 1860s, reported that 'They have visited most of the towns in the Black Country during the last few weeks'.[66] When carpet-weavers went on strike in 1853, one Kidderminster reporter foresaw all sorts of problems (while remaining blind to the issue of child labour):[67]

> *Hundreds of children employed in factories have been dispersed over the country, begging, morris dancing, and the like, and will probably imbibe dissolute and vagrant habits.*

There was a strike at the Minerva iron works in Wolverhampton in January 1868 which also elicited a description in the *Birmingham Weekly Post* of the striking puddlers' morris dancing as 'begging'.[68] It may have been these same puddlers (iron workers) whom 'Archaeologos' described meeting in his regular column 'Jottings by the Way' a couple of months later. His notes provide an evocative description. He met them in Darlaston, four miles from the Minerva works:[69]

> *Near here we meet a party of puddlers in strange guise. They were engaged in what they term 'morris dancing'. Some six or eight of them, with sprig of green in their hats, and short sticks in their hands, were travelling the country round, and dancing to the music of an old fiddler, to pick up a few stray coppers. Their dance is one which, so far as Archaeologos could make out, was peculiar to South Staffordshire. Divided into two parties, they face each other in line, and advance and retire, striking their batons together each time they meet, after the fashion of the 'deadly ccombat' [sic] in a circus. We asked one of them if they made the thing pay. 'Well,' he said, 'we gets wir livin', and I suppose that's all we wants. I wish I was out on it, for one; but there, anything's better nor nothing'.*

Archaeologos shared the misconception of many other antiquaries of their local history, that morris dancing was extremely rare, and unique to their own district. The dancer he spoke to clearly saw it as a last resort rather than a festive customary celebration.

At least in the early part of the century the dance in the west midlands had been part of the general round of Christmas or winter festivities. Charlotte Burne described how in times past 'The players seem usually to be much more elaborately decked with ribbons and coloured paper than were the party at Shrewsbury [she was alluding to the dancers who

---

[65] *Walsall Advertiser*, 2 August 1884.
[66] Hill, T., 'Local Notes ... [1575]'.
[67] *Birmingham Journal*, 27 August 1853.
[68] *Birmingham Daily Post*, 30 January 1868.
[69] Archaeologos.

used trowels in their dance]: the music and dancing to be more lively, the antics of the fool more prominent', giving as her authority 'old John Thomas, in whose youth morris-dancing was a customary Christmas amusement of the young men around Bishop's Castle'.[70] In 1820 the American writer Washington Irving published his account of Christmas at Bracebridge Hall in *The Sketch Book of Geoffrey Crayon, Gent.* This was a work of fiction, but it became one of the most cited 'authentic' sources for descriptions of English festivities, along with Strutt and Douce. The model for Bracebridge Hall has been sought in various places, from Bracebridge itself, in Lincolnshire, to the various residences in which Irving is known to have stayed, but as the introduction to the critical edition of the work points out, 'the debate is purely an academic one. Bracebridge Hall is a noumenal English manor.'[71] One of the proposals has been Aston Hall in Birmingham, with an unsubstantiated claim that Irving spent a Christmas there. There is no doubt that he brought together his experiences and his knowledge accumulated from reading, and melded then together, but his account of the Christmas morris dance fits well with what may have occurred at Aston, and is without an obvious source in literature:[72]

> *We had not long been home when the sound of music was heard from a distance. A band of country lads without coats, their shirt sleeves fancifully tied with ribands, their hats decorated with greens, and clubs in their hands, were seen advancing up the avenue, followed by a large number of villagers and peasantry. They stopped before the hall door, where the music struck up a peculiar air, and the lads performed a curious and intricate dance, advancing, retreating and striking their clubs together, keeping exact time to the music; while one, whimsically crowned with a fox's skin, the tail of which flaunted down his back, kept capering round the skirts of the dance, and rattling a Christmas box with many antic gesticulations.*

The nature of the dance described by Irving in festive mode and seen by Archaeologos as a begging custom – advancing and retiring, and clashing sticks – is repeated in other descriptions. The dancers seen in Loveday Street, Birmingham did this. At Astwood Bank near Redditch in the 1830s, 'each of the party carried in his hand a short stick or staff, and when dancing face to face would, at intervals, strike their sticks together and wheel into a change of position'.[73] In his dictionary of Worcestershire words Jesse Salisbury wrote:[74]

> *The morris-dancers go through certain figures, country dances, 'the figure of eight', &c., and at certain parts of the dance stand face to face and mark the time with short sticks.*

As Salisbury indicated, most figures, as in the south-midlands morris, were country-dance figures. Ella Leather described the dance from Dilwyn in Herefordshire as 'distinguishable from a country dance by the "stick rapping" only'.[75] The bricklayers in Shrewsbury in the 1870s faced each other to clash their sticks and trowels, then cast off to left and right, and circled back to place. Heys or reels were also common. The Loveday Street dance had one distinctive figure in which the dancers danced in a circle with their sticks pointing radially to the centre, while at Malvern in the 1890s 'In the final figure the men threw their sticks into the middle and danced around them, free form'[76] – each reminiscent in its own way of the figure described by Anne Baker for the bedlam morris.

---

[70] Burne, *Shropshire Folk-lore*, p. 478.
[71] Irving, p. xv.
[72] Irving, p. 178.
[73] Thornton.

[74] Salisbury, p. 24.
[75] Leather, p. 130.
[76] W., H.; Williams, A.R.

A report of an encounter with morris dancers at Bagot Street in Birmingham in 1843 'with ribbons flying and staffs in their hands' claimed that 'Most of them were noted characters for step dancing' (individual display dancing centred primarily on foot movements).[77] Twenty-five miles away and 80 years later, Maud Karpeles was told that at White Ladies Aston in Worcestershire in the 1880s 'The dancers sang carols and did step-dancing in between the dances'.[78] Despite this, unlike the south-midlands morris, there is virtually no evidence in the west midlands for complex steps in the dancing. In the dances that have been collected, when steps are described at all they are usually simple single (one-hop-two-hop) or double (one-two-three-hop) steps.[79] Few early accounts mention them. In an atypical event, the celebration in 1857 at the coming of age of George Wicksted of Cleobury Mortimer in Worcestershire 'The bells rang, cannon fired, morris dancers capered, the fiddlers fiddled',[80] but this is probably a generic usage rather than a description of a specific capering step. The *Worcester Herald*'s account referred to 'troups of morris dancers', and also gave a clue as to why the morris dancers were present: Wicksted was the heir to Betley, home of the famous window.[81] It may well be that this was one of those artistic representations of the dance, devised by the theatrical dancing masters.

The most characteristic features reported were the staves and the beribboned shirts and other clothes. The description of dancers at Smithfield in Birmingham in 1821 is typical:[82]

> The dancers were about eight in number, they were all uniformly dressed, they had on knee breeches, and were in their shirt sleeves, but their shirts were very gaily decorated with ribbons that were tied round their arms and arranged in small bows, as well as on the knees of their breeches and round the waist, and likewise there were attached to their dresses a great number of small round bells, that jingled very much when they danced. Each man was provided with a stout stick or truncheon about 2 feet long, and repeatedly in the dance they confronted each other and clashed their sticks.

Other early reports such as John Randall's from 1820s Coalport also implied breeches, but later ones have trousers, sometimes of corduroy. Although the Smithfield account mentions bells (apparently all over the body?), few others, even those with details of costume, did so. The Shrewsbury bricklayers had ribbons on their hats, while the fool had 'the pieces of ribbon on his coat, and more profusely distributed over his hat, while his face was coloured, and fastened to a strap passing round his waist was a bell, hanging down at his back'.[83] Jesse Salisbury painted a very similar picture in his dictionary. Mentioning the fool's bell but not other bells is a strong indication that in many cases the dancers did not wear bells. The dancers at Dilwyn, however, wore bells, as did half of those at Malvern.[84] Some of the later references explicitly exclude them. Maud Karpeles underlined her note from William Griffen, her informant for the Upton-on-Severn dances, 'They did not wear bells', and at White Ladies Aston she noted 'No bells or handkerchiefs'.[85] Cecil Sharp noted from Mrs Anne Morris that at Peopleton in Worcestershire the dancers had 'ribbons not bells round their knees', though another informant said they had 'Bells sometimes, but not on legs, [he] thinks on arms'.[86]

The reference to handkerchiefs needs explanation. The great majority of dances in the west midlands were stick dances, where sticks were held instead of handkerchiefs; but in the area

---

[77] Bilstonian.
[78] 'Karpeles MSS, Worcestershire Morris'.
[79] Jones, Dave, *passim*.
[80] *Hereford Times*, 7 February 1857.
[81] *Worcester Herald*, 7 February 1857.
[82] Silhill.

[83] M., M.
[84] Leather, p. 130; Williams, A.R.
[85] 'Karpeles MSS, Upton-on-Severn Morris'; 'Karpeles MSS, Worcestershire Morris'.
[86] 'Sharp MSS, Peopleton'.

of southern Worcestershire nearest to the south-midlands dancing communities – Evesham, Pershore and Upton-on-Severn – there was 'a stick dance' and 'a handkerchief dance' (indicated in Figure 15.1 on p. 243).[87] There does not appear to have been a fixed repertoire of dances, merely a sequence of figures danced to a variety of tunes. William Griffen of Upton-on-Severn said, 'Any hornpipe does for the stick dance and any jig for the handkerchief dance'.[88]

There were usually eight or more dancers and a fool, who had a bell tied at his back and sometimes had a blackened or painted face. The issue of whether the dancers blacked their faces, and if so, why, was to become a sensitive issue in the late 20th and early 21st centuries, and merits a careful examination of the sources. The evidence nation-wide before the middle of the 19th century is minimal. Junius's seventeenth-century dictionary definition was not grounded in English practice. Apart from that there is the hint in Macready's *The Irishman in London* of 1793 that an Irishman equated a black woman's father with morris dancers he had seen. An intriguing Irish reference from 1824 may suggest a similar equation. Describing the festivities at Irish wakes, Thomas Crofton Croker wrote:[89]

> *Dancing, or rather running in a ring, round an individual, who performs various evolutions, is also a common amusement; and four or five young men will sometimes, for the diversion of the party, blacken their faces, and go through a regular series of gestures with sticks, not unlike those of the English morris-dancers.*

After a childhood in Ireland Croker was living in London when he wrote this. It does confirm his familiarity with stick dances, but whether the blacking of the face is implied for them, or solely for the young Irishmen, is ambiguous. The early pictures from Lichfield and by Scharf do not show blackened faces, and some of the nineteenth-century commentators think it an innovation in their time. When 'F.S.' wrote to *Shropshire Notes and Queries* in 1885 that 'Broseley has always been noted for its "Morris dancers" and the custom is kept up to the present time, the dancers, with flying colours and black faces, making occasional excursions to the neighbouring towns and villages', he (or she) later added 'The blacking of the face is perhaps modern and detracts to some extent from the dance'; while another respondent wrote of the dance he had seen in Shrewsbury 1879, when 'The faces of the men were not blacked'.[90] The folklorist Charlotte Burne wrote 'One would think this a modern innovation, in imitation of "n****r minstrels"', but then adduced Junius and Walter Scott as evidence of historical authenticity. Junius is dealt with above; for Scott, Burne referenced his poem 'Old Christmastide' and its reference to maskers, 'smutted cheeks the visors made' in *Marmion* – which is irrelevant to the case.[91]

The Shrewsbury dancers in 1865 had 'painted faces' but the earliest date we can put on explicit blacking up is from Evesham *c.* 1875, based on information collected in 1940 and reported to Ralph Vaughan Williams in 1941 as 'ten dancers in their ordinary clothes with black faces and coloured paper on their legs, a clown with a bladder, two collectors, and a concertina player'; the men were also mummers.[92] The earliest contemporary reference is in the trial of John Bond, Alfred Hicks and George Hicks of Leigh, Worcestershire, for theft in 1879. Richard Baylis had lain aside his overcoat in the pub, while playing a game with his companion, named Stinton:[93]

---

[87] Jones, pp. 38, 46, 60-61.
[88] 'Karpeles MSS, Upton-on-Severn Morris'.
[89] Croker, p. 171.
[90] S., F.; Greg.
[91] Burne, *Shropshire Folk-lore*, p. 478.
[92] Cawte, 'Morris Dance', p. 206.
[93] *Worcestershire Chronicle*, 13 December 1879.

About 10 p.m. the three prisoners appeared, and, being morris-dancers with their faces blacked, asked if they should amuse the company, when Stinton said, 'Yes, after we have done playing our game of bagatelle'. Prisoners waited for about 20 minutes, and all left together. George Hicks, who sat on Baylis's coat, when he went out took it with him.

At the quarter sessions they claimed to have taken the coat by mistake but were found guilty. George Hicks was sentenced to 12 months' hard labour, the others to six. Hicks was just 17; Bond 36, and both were described as labourers; Alfred Hicks (26) was a brickmaker.[94] The fact that there were only three of them may imply that they were what we should now call mummers rather than morris dancers.

The next account to mention blacked faces is the Broseley one described above. When Cecil Sharp visited the area in 1909 he spoke to two people in their eighties who recalled that the dancers at Peopleton 'always blacked their faces'; he noted a similar recollection from White Ladies Aston. The earliest date for these memories would probably be the 1840s; on Maud Karpeles's visit in 1928 she was told the dancing had stopped around 1890. The memories could date from anywhere in this period. On the other hand, Sharp's informant for Pershore did not remember blacked-up faces, and Karpeles's informant was adamant that only the fool had one.[95] At Brimfield in Herefordshire the morris men were '4 dancers with melodion & tambourine man. Black faces with white paint, white eyes, etc.' (Figure 15.5).[96] This is a clearly the caricature make-up of a black-face minstrel. Several accounts of the morris in the early

Figure 15.5: Brimfield morris dancers, 1909 (Image courtesy of Vaughan Williams Memorial Library, Roy Dommett collection, RLD/2/5/5).

[94] *Worcestershire Chronicle*, 10 January 1880.
[95] 'Sharp MSS, Peopleton'; 'Karpeles MSS, Worcestershire Morris'.
[96] 'Sharp MSS, Brimfield'.

20th century mention the use of bones as a musical accompaniment, another indication of a derivation from black-face minstrelsy; and when Christopher Cawte researched in the area in the 1950s he found it difficult to get his informants to distinguish between morris dancing and what they themselves called 'n****ring'.[97] In describing gipsy music-making in Worcester in 1890, one reporter speaks of their use of instruments deriving from this strand of minstrelsy, including how 'should no instrument be handy, they rap two sticks together, somewhat after the manner of the morris dancers'.[98] In a case at Upton-on-Severn in 1855, a wedding couple were accused of stealing a pair of brass candlesticks from the Old Crown inn in the town. Their defence was that a party of morris dancers outside the inn had taken them to be used 'in the band as substitute for 'bones'' (another account has 'cymbals'), then handed them to the accused to return them inside, at which point they took them 'for a lark' without intending to steal them. To the surprise of the court the jury acquitted them on those grounds.[99]

The introduction of black-face minstrelsy into England in the 1830s is well known, and we have already met theatrical morris dancers performing at the pleasure gardens alongside 'Ethiopian serenaders', as they were often styled. It did not take long for theatrical performances to be translated into street entertainments. George Rehin has suggested that such performances were often not intended to be directly imitative of, or caricaturing, Black America, but that black-face 'helped buskers to act, to be uninhibited and symbolically to flout convention and authority, and to distance themselves from the close physical proximity of the audience'.[100] There are other theatrical and cultural antecedents for the use of 'blacking up' in folk performance but it seems clear that the blacking of dancers' faces is a late introduction to the morris of the west midlands, following on the heels of the enormous popularity of the minstrel shows from the 1840s on. It need not take long for something to become 'traditional'. Christopher Cawte was told in the 1950s that 'you're not a morris dancer without a black face'.[101]

There are more references to black-face at the turn of the century, in conjunction with an aspect less commented on, namely that some of the dancers are reported to have worn women's clothes. In 1957 Christopher Cawte was told that at Broseley (possibly around 1900), 'There were six or eight dancers, who wore women's dresses, feather boas, and flowered hats, and blacked their faces'. He recorded that at Much Wenlock, where a team performed intermittently from about 1880 to the 1930s, 'The dancers wore tags of cloth on their ordinary clothes, later the tags were paper, then the clothes changed to fancy dress reminiscent of circus clowns, and finally the tags were abandoned because boys used to set them alight. The dancers blacked their faces and hands, wore top hats, and some dressed as women.'[102] Maud Karpeles noted in 1928 at Pershore, where dancers had performed until around 1924, 'The dancers wore any old clothes or finery that they could lay hands on and decorated themselves with ribbons. Some of the dancers wore women's clothes.'[103] Finally, at Weobley in 1909 Cecil Sharp saw the 'Weobley morris dance' with stick tapping as at Brimfield, but danced by '8 couples as in country dance' in which 'women chassez to the left and men to the right'.[104] He collected several country dances on this occasion, but this appears to have been a morris dance proper, not simply a country dance with a 'morris' name. It may be that the women

[97] Cawte, 'Morris Dance', *passim*.
[98] *Worcestershire Chronicle*, 31 May 1890.
[99] *Worcestershire Chronicle*, 28 February 1855; *Berrow's Worcester Journal*, 3 March 1855.
[100] Rehin, p. 33.

[101] Cawte, 'Morris Dance', p. 206.
[102] Cawte, 'Morris Dance', p. 202.
[103] 'Karpeles MSS, Worcestershire Morris'.
[104] 'Sharp MSS, Weobley Morris Dance'.

were an integral element of the dance (and that is the simplest explanation); or that they were pressed into service to demonstrate a men's dance to Sharp; or that 'women' is simply the term used to designate one side in the dance set, regardless of actual gender.

Another possible influence on the use of black-face is the disguising element in mummers' plays, also performed at Christmas. Some commentators seemed to use the terms 'morris dancers' and 'mummers' interchangeably. Charlotte Burne discerned a distinction in Shropshire between '(1) morris-dancing; (2) the rude masque performed by the so-called morris-dancers of North-east Salop'.[105]

It is clear that in some cases a play included a dance; or a dance might include a quasi-dramatic element. The example of Revesby in 1779 is a clear case of a play incorporating a 'morris dance'. T. Caswell described stick dances seen at Atcham and Shrewsbury, then recalled an encounter at a farmhouse in Bromdon, Shropshire, in 1858:[106]

> Upon preparing for departure I was informed that the 'Morris Dancers' were expected, and invited to remain over their performance. The troupe differed but slightly in appearance from those I had seen previously, save that they were of a somewhat 'higher grade', whilst the dresses and general get-up were far superior. One of the performers, I remember, wore a turban, another a crown. The one wearing a turban had his face blacked, and was known as 'Melchior' or 'Melchisedec', I cannot remember which; another (I think) represented 'Judas Iscariot', and another the 'King of the Romans' – I will not at this distance pledge the correctness of these designations, although I believe them to be perfectly correct. One represented his Satanic majesty, another (a boy) a mischievous imp. There was also, of course, a clown, and there was a fiddler. Altogether they formed a very picturesque, well-equipped party. Upon entering the old kitchen they formed up two lines facing inwards. The conductor, stepping forward, made a short speech, after which the whole party, including the fiddler, performed a very graceful dance to the accompaniment of the clatter of the truncheons. After this the real Morris or Mummer dance began, interspersed with dialogue and figurative dumb show. There was in this little, if any 'patter'. I fancy it was intended to represent some episode or other, the true meaning of which I could not fathom. In fact, I question if the performers themselves knew more than the mechanical parts.

This account throws up all kinds of questions. Were the clattering truncheons part of the dance or an accompaniment to it? Why was this not the 'real' morris dance (which Caswell had just described at Atcham and Shrewsbury)? What kind of play was this? Judas is rarely represented as a character in mummers' plays, and Melchior/Melchisedec are otherwise unknown, though a turbaned/face-blacked Turkish Knight is common. Likewise the King of the Romans is not found elsewhere, though King George/William (or St George) may appear.[107] What it does show is the performers availing themselves of a variety of elements of popular performance to construct their entertainment; and the observer loosely attaching the name associated with any of these elements to the performance as a whole.

Almost simultaneously with Caswell's account, the *Illustrated London News* published a description, with a print, of a painting by Charles Cattermole depicting 'Worcestershire mummers'.[108] The painting remains untraced, but we have the print (Figure 15.6). The reporter seemed to have some direct knowledge, claiming that 'its truthfulness and admirable character

---

[105] Burne, *Shropshire Folk-lore*, p. 477.
[106] Caswell.

[107] Millington, 'Folk Play Scripts Explorer'.
[108] *Illustrated London News*, 15 January 1859.

Figure 15.6: Charles Cattermole, 'Worcestershire mummers', Illustrated London News, 15 January 1859, p. 21.

will be easily recognised by all who have witnessed the original performance in any of our rural districts at this festive season'. He noted that in Worcestershire morris dancing was practised at Christmas time when cold weather stops labourers from working. He continued (describing 'morris dancing' despite the 'mummers' in the article's title):

> Though it still bears the name, it is somewhat of a different nature to the morris-dancing described by Strutt ... the hobby-horse, Robin Hood, and Maid Marian, have given way to a foreman, or fool, and his company. The party generally consists of the fool, a musician, and six dancers. They are dressed in their best clothes, showing their shirt sleeves, which are adorned with bows and long ends of different coloured ribbons, and any other finery which their wives or sweethearts can furnish to them. The fool has, in addition to his own proper cap, a rabbit-skin on his back and a dog-whip in his hand. To the end of the whip is attached a bladder, full of air, which he swings about, and occasionally administers, in the form of slaps, to his company. The dancers have a short stick in their right hands, and stand in a double row, facing one another. The music strikes up, and they commence by beating time with sticks against their neighbours' opposite. The fool swings his bladder, and off they go into a figure somewhat resembling 'right and left', often ending in an impromptu figure of their own.
>
> ... It is a healthy amusement for the poor fellows, and much better than staying at home doing nothing; but it is to be feared that some of them are not content with the drink given them and spend, in the attainment of more, the money which they should have taken home for their wives and families.

In fact the picture has little connecting it to a mummers' play, but several features linking it to a morris dance. On the left of the group is a musician apparently playing a shawm. The others appear to be six dancers, with the fool in the middle of the dancing set. They are wearing a variety of clothing. The dancers all wear different hats, one has a smock, others jerkins, some wear breeches, others trousers. Three of the dancers whose legs are visible have a single line of bells round their knees, two do not. Only one of the dancers can be seen to be carrying a stick. The fool has a clown's pointed hat and a cane or whip with perhaps two bladders attached.

Caswell describes mummers and calls them morris dancers, Cattermole depicts morris dancers and calls them mummers. Cattermole's dancers appear to have a rather desultory approach to turn-out and costume, perhaps reflecting the general poverty of the performers. The reporter's note about the dancers' spending their receipts on drink is a common one not confined to the west-midlands morris, but it has other echoes here too. At Pershore in 1874 an inebriated Edward Cosnett, aged 17, was charged with attacking a police officer when asked to move on, and said 'I should not have done it if I hadn't had the drink along with the morris dancers'.[109]

The blurring of the boundaries between the performance elements is captured by the *Shrewsbury chronicle* under the heading 'Christmas minstrelsy', describing Ludlow in 1886:[110]

> *Several bands of carols singers, itinerant n****rs, and Morris dancers also turned out to serenade the residents; but from the reception some of these would-be vocalists received, we fear that they found that the occupation of the Christmas mummers had become a thing of the past.*

The history of the morris dance of the west midlands is yet another story of decline. A Christmas festivity favoured by particular groups of workers became associated primarily with economic hardship. Costumes became less elaborate, and elements were lost. In some cases the numbers dancing in a team declined. Other influences came in, from minstrels to mummers, eroding the distinctive characteristics of the dance. Christopher Cawte's comment about the team in Orleton in the early 20th century captures the essence:[111]

> *...there was a team at Orleton in the 1920s at Christmas. Two dancers carried bones in each hand, and the third a tambourine. The fourth, who sometimes also danced, played an accordion. They wore fancy clothes and top hats with feathers, and blacked their faces. They had neither bells nor sticks. The 'dance' consisted merely of circling round, feet well apart, and occasionally one foot thrown forwards. If indeed this was a morris dance, it must be near the nadir of such performances.*

---

[109] *Kidderminster Times*, 3 January 1874.
[110] *Shrewsbury Chronicle*, 31 December 1886. [111] Cawte, 'Morris Dance', p. 204.

Chapter 16

East of England

There are records throughout the 19th century for morris dancing in the area stretching north-east from the industrial midlands to the Lincolnshire coast, and down to Cambridgeshire, but this is more a geographical artefact than representative of a homogeneous cultural community of dancing. It is almost the absence of specific characteristics that defines them, except perhaps that the records are primarily of a winter custom. They also exhibit that diffusion of the name and the practice into other cultural forms which characterized the decline of the morris in the west midlands. Although instances can be found over all of the Christmastide period, much of the uncertainty revolves around its relationship to plough-jagging, a solicitation custom found over most of eastern England which involved a threat to plough up the threshold of unforthcoming households. The traditional day for plough-jagging was Plough Monday, the Monday following the 6 January feast of the Epiphany. In the following pages I shall concentrate mainly on those records which use the term 'morris' without attempting a broader survey of associated customs.

The terminology used by contemporary reporters can be irretrievably entangled. The *Lincolnshire Chronicle* in 1870 wrote that 'As if to remind us how customs are passing away, a band of mummers or morris dancers visited the lower portion of the city on Saturday night. Their antics caused great amusement and no little surprise in the minds of the many who witnessed their dances at the several inns.'[1]

One writer did try to tease out the characteristics, writing in January 1897:[2]

> *I remember a Plough Monday company of processionists and street actors in Derbyshire, who were variously called 'morris dancers' and 'mummers', that trailed a plough in their midst. It was decorated with ribbons. They had a 'fool' and a 'molly' in the company, and were a different set of persons altogether from the Christmas masqueraders.*

Just four weeks earlier, in December 1896 in Retford, John Henry Slaney had been charged that he 'not serving either in her Majesty's army or navy, did wear the uniform of one of these forces in such a manner as to bring contempt upon it'. He had a drawn sword in his hand and was wearing a Middlesex Regiment tunic, Army Service Corps cap and Sherwood Rangers Yeomanry trousers. He explained that 'he and three others were "Morris dancing"', and that he took the part of the 'Valiant Soldier'.[3] This role clearly indicates that there was a mummers' or plough-play element in whatever he was doing.

Besides the uncertainty (or indifference) as to whether mummers were morris dancers and *vice versa*, there were also conflicting reports as to whether plough-jagging was the same as morris dancing or whether these were two distinct customs. One of the earliest writers flags up the potential for confusion. After describing the Haxey Hood mob football game, the Lincolnshire antiquary William Peck described the plough jags, or plough bullocks in 1815:[4]

---

[1] *Lincolnshire Chronicle*, 14 January 1870.
[2] *People*, 17 January 1897.
[3] *Stamford Mercury*, 11 December 1896.
[4] Peck, William, 1:278.

The next day [after Twelfth Day] the plough-bullocks, or boggins, go round the town to receive alms at each house, where they cry 'Largus.' They are habited similar to the morris-dancers, are yoked to, and drag, a small plough; they have their farmer and a fool, called Billy Buck, dressed like a harlequin, with whom the boys make sport. The day is concluded by the bullocks running with the plough round the cross in the market-place, and the man that can throw the others down, and convey their plough into the cellar of a public house, receives one shilling for his agility

Of morris dancing itself, Peck said it 'has but recently been discontinued', but merely refers his readers to Brand, Strutt and Douce for further information. The association of the two customs is confirmed by a report from Kirton-in-Lindsey six years later, to the effect that "magistrates have determined to visit with exemplary severity the misconduct of persons who appear as morris dancers or plough bullocks or under any other name of similar character. The excesses of these persons have arrived at such a pitch that it would be impossible to bear them any longer, and it would be well if the country and the farmers in particular, would second the endeavours of the magistrates.'[5]

When Arthur Benoni Evans, headmaster of the grammar school in Market Bosworth, published his Leicestershire glossary in 1848 he defined 'plough-bullockers' as 'A name given … to persons who, like the Morris-Dancers … come round on "Plough Monday", dressed up in ribbons and women's gear, and dance with untiring agility before the houses of the more opulent, to obtain "plough-money", for the evening dance or festivity'. When his son Sebastian published the second edition in 1881 the instruction at 'morris-dance' was '*vide* Plough-bullockers', and at 'Plough-bullockers' was a much more detailed description, written in the past tense:[6]

On Plough-Monday it was the custom for some of the villagers to dress in grotesque masquerade and perform morris-dances before all the houses where they were likely to get money or drink. Sometimes they were accompanied by a gang of lads with raddled faces, half-hidden under paper masks, who dragged a plough, but this was unusual. Some of the performers, generally four, had on white women's dresses and tall hats. One of these was called Maid Marian. Of the other performers, one was the Fool, who always carried the money-box, and generally a bladder with peas in it on a string at the end of a stick, with which he laid lustily about him. Another was Beelzebub, in a dress made up of narrow bits of flannel, cloth, &c., with the ends hanging loose, yellow, red, black and white being the predominant colours. The rest were simply grotesques. The dance they performed was merely a travesty of a quadrille, with ad lib. stamping and shuffling of feet.

Sebastian Evans went on to recount how on one occasion (probably around 1840) the outwardly frightening Fool reassured him about who he was beneath his disguise. In the generation between his father's and his own account, the plough jags had moved from being 'like morris dancers' to being morris dancers, and not even requiring a plough. The mixture of male and cross-dressed male performers remained, and a dance was done. The dance was a straightforward social dance, inexpertly performed. The use of the name 'Maid Marian' may be a link to the older forms of performance, as is the money-collecting fool, while Beelzebub is a character from a mummers' or plough play. The 'raddled faces' confirm the practice of disguise, but in this case suggesting a red appearance rather than black.

---

[5] *Lincoln, Rutland and Stamford Mercury*, 22 January 1821. [6] Evans (1848), p. 68; Evans (1881), pp. 195, 215.

A description from Crowland in 1853 corroborates the occurrence of cross-dressing:[7]

> *Strange looking parties called 'Morrice Dancers' still perambulate the fens at this season; we believe that Crowland has the honour of sending forth a party of this kind. Imagine a lot of burly fellows, some decked in female attire, others with blackened faces, and flaunting rags and ribbands, with rusty sword and fiddle, and other theatrical accompaniments. These gentry assume the right of entering any house where the doors are not fastened against them, commencing 'Here comes I who'se niver bin yet'.*

At Melton Mowbray in 1851 there were 'fantastically dressed plough boys and morris dancers' and in 1858 'the juveniles were greatly enlivened by the odd antics and grotesque attire of several parties of ploughmen and "morris dancers"'.[8] At Little Bytham in 1882 and Castle Bytham in 1883 'The ploughmen and morris dancers paraded this and the surrounding villages and went through their performances in a creditable manner',[9] while in 1864 the *Stamford Mercury* was equivocal about their separate or joint identity in its report from Barton-on-Humber:[10]

> *During the last few days a party of morris dancers or plough-jarks, or both combined, have made Barton their head-quarters, whence to radiate into neighbouring villages, and a great 'racket' they have made.*

At the other end of Lincolnshire, Michael Barley's informant in Moulton Seas End was 'quite precise in remembering Morris dancers there at Christmas and the Plough Boys playing on Plough Monday'.[11] It was morris dancers who unexpectedly entertained workmen restoring the church at Caistor shortly before Christmas in 1862 by dancing within the church, but in December 15 years later the *Stamford Mercury* reported that 'Morris dancing is becoming a rarity ... but last week Caistor and the villages adjacent were visited by a full company of those rustic merrymen, the "Plough Jacks"'.[12] Colliers, not ploughmen, were reported as morris dancers in Hinckley in May 1859, 'practising country dances in the streets'. They may have shared the Christmastide dance custom or may have taken their lead from striking colliers in the west midlands, or a little bit of both.[13]

In 1870 Edward Peacock published his novel *Ralf Skirlaugh, the Lincolnshire Squire*.[14] Any work of imaginative literature must be treated with caution, but Peacock was an antiquary who spent his life at Brigg and Kirton-in-Lindsey. His daughter Mabel was the co-author with Eliza Gutch of a major account of Lincolnshire folklore.[15] His account of a Lincolnshire Plough Monday may well, therefore, reflect his own observations. In the novel, Ralf Skirlaugh's attendant Bob is about to be married but is asked to take part in the 'plew-jaggin'. Peacock explains that 'what the mummer is to some other parts of England, the plough-jag is to Lincolnshire', a 'comic drama'. He adds that 'it was a custom, probably as old as the performances themselves, to introduce local characters into the piece, for the purpose of satirizing anyone who was obnoxious'; this is a description more usually associated with rough music. The basic play is, however, based on 'St. George and the Dragon, and the sodgers and the Turk'.

---

[7] *Lincolnshire Chronicle*, 30 December 1853.
[8] *Lincolnshire Chronicle*, 17 January 1851 [a]; *Leicester Journal*, 15 January 1858.
[9] *Grantham Journal*, 28 January 1882; *Grantham Journal*, 20 January 1883.
[10] *Lincoln, Rutland and Stamford Mercury*, 15 January 1864.

[11] Barley, p. 79.
[12] *Stamford Mercury*, 26 December 1862; *Stamford Mercury*, 4 January 1878.
[13] *Leicestershire Mercury*, 21 May 1859.
[14] Peacock, quotations from 3:226-45.
[15] Gutch, Eliza and Peacock.

Peacock describes how on Plough Monday there were two sets of performers. 'Mummers' went round the village in the morning. 'Their costumes were gay with ribbons, they sang their old songs, and went through the rude histrionic evolutions which they had derived from the middle age mystery players.' In the afternoon half of them, described as 'the plough-jaggers of the morning' and 'arrayed very differently to what they had been in the morning's performance' went out again, with Bob and his fellows, for the plough-jagging. The performers arrived in parallel columns, led by a piper. The performance included a satire on a local lawyer and the local Justice of the Peace. Peacock does not call his performers 'morris dancers' but he gives a sense of the easy combination of elements of performance.

The party of 'Morris Dancers' from Brigg who travelled the nine miles to Scunthorpe on 7 January 1876 had:[16]

> the traditional 'lady' – a tall man, with hob-nailed boots, in woman's chignon, crinoline and petticoats; Aunt Jane, with her crying child; the 'fool', 'doctor'; and what seemed to us an innovation, a 'bullock', in the shape of a hobble-de-hoy with the headgear of a horse's clothing, the ears stuffed with straw for horns – a hoop round the waist with a broom handle, to which a tuft of hair was tied as tail, for the yoke – and a rug over the shoulders to represent the skin. By means of bones, a kettle drum, &c., the grotesque crew contrived to make a hideous din, but not to extort much money from the inhabitants.

This is a detailed description of the characters in a plough play; the 'bullock' hobby horse was in fact quite common in the area.[17] Possibly the most masculine performer was allocated the female role.

Some groups looked further afield for inspiration. For several years Matthew Kirk of Raunds in Northamptonshire played the 'lord' on Plough Monday dressed as an American Indian accompanied by a squaw.[18] In 1884 'the chief of these morris dancers having gained admission to the cottages and made a set speech, was followed by the others, who sang and danced, accompanying their songs and antics with grotesque performances on some musical instruments'.[19]

In 1825 William Hone published a picture of plough jags in the section of his *Every Day Book* on 'Plough Monday' (Figure 16.1). The drawing depicts the plough, musicians, the fool, and Bessy. A man dancing is holding handkerchiefs and wearing breeches. Hone confirmed an association between the customs. He writes:[20]

> In some parts of the country and especially in the north, they draw the plough in procession to the doors of the villagers and townspeople. Long ropes are attached to it, and thirty or forty men, stripped to their clean white shirts, but protected from the weather by waistcoats beneath, drag it along. Their arms and shoulders are decorated with gay-coloured ribbons, tied in large knots and bows, and their hats are smartened in the same way. They are usually accompanied by an old woman, or a boy dressed up to represent one; she is gaily bedizened, and called the Bessy. Sometimes the sport is assisted by a humorous countryman to represent a fool. He is covered with ribbons, and attired in skins, with a depending tail, and carries a box to collect money from the spectators. They are attended by music, and Morris-dancers when they can be got; but there is always a sportive dance with a few lasses in all their finery, and a superabundance of ribbons.

---

[16] *Lincolnshire Chronicle*, 14 January 1876.
[17] Barley.
[18] Frampton, George, 'Penny', p. 123.

[19] *Northampton Mercury*, 6 December 1884.
[20] Hone, 1: 36.

PLOUGH MONDAY.

Figure 16.1: 'Plough Monday' (in William Hone, The Every Day Book, *1: 36. London: William Tegg, [1868]).*

In this mingling of cultural forms are house-visiting morris dancers with cross-dressing, blackened faces, and swords, reciting lines from a mummers' play. Another indication that a sword dance may be performed is from Pishey Thompson's 1856 history of Boston, where he defined 'plough-boys' as 'Country-men, who go about dressed in ribbon etc., as Morris (Moorish) dancers on Plough Monday, perform the sword dance etc. One is dressed as "Maid Marion" and is called the witch, another in rags, and is called the fool, &c., &c.'[21] Evidence for sword dances south of the Humber is otherwise scanty. Llewellynn Jewitt wrote in 1853 of the plough bullocks' custom around Mansfield, 'with its plough, drawn by farmers' men, gaily dressed in ribbands, its drivers, with their long wands and bladders, its sword-dancers, its fool, and its celebrated Bessy, and hobby horse', referring readers to his description of Derbyshire customs (which mention simply 'a dance', and no hobby horse).[22] R.M. Heanley reported a sword dance by 'guisers' at Wainfleet near the Wash, who also had some dialogue to recite.[23]

Morris dancing – in whatever form in took – was by now primarily a solicitation custom in these districts. A writer in the *Huntingdon, Bedford & Peterborough Gazette* in 1837 alluded to the plaints of 'the morrice-dancers on Plough Monday – "just one ha'penny, sir; only one ha'penny, please sir"'.[24] The *Lincolnshire Chronicle* reported that at Melton Mowbray in 1851 'A goodly number of fantastically dressed plough boys and morris dancers with musical accompaniments visited

[21] Thompson, p. 718.
[22] Jewitt, 'On Ancient Customs ... Nottingham', p. 238; Jewitt, 'On Ancient Customs ... Derby', p. 202.
[23] Heanley, p. 40.
[24] *Huntingdon, Bedford & Peterborough Gazette*, 16 September 1837.

... as usual last Monday, to "levy coined remembrances" of the inhabitants'.[25] The same year '"Morris-dancers", as they call themselves' visited Lincoln from Washingborough and other local villages, 'bedecked with ribbons, swords, &c.', and the newspaper complained that their begging 'is the signal for a general locking of doors'.[26] It is not clear if the swords were for a sword dance, or as mummers' play props. Morris dancers, again from Washingborough and elsewhere, 'levied contributions in Lincoln being bedecked with ribbons, veils, and portions of female attire' on Plough Monday in 1852. The *Lincolnshire Chronicle* thought them 'silly' and noted that the money begged would be spent on a supper or a drinking bout.[27]

At Brinklow, east of Coventry, about 16 men, eight of whom were morris dancers wearing beribboned shirts, set out to dance on 10 January 1865, as they were out of work. They were accompanied by an 'old Moll' (also called 'mawther'), wearing women's clothes and with face blacked, and the rest of the company also wore ribbons. The party included a fiddler and treasurer. They were described as labourers, with one report calling them 'plough boys'. They made a circuit visiting Coombe and Brandon before reaching Wolston and returning to Brinklow. One of them was charged with robbing a fourteen-year-old boy of his pocket knife just outside Wolston. One dancer, called as a witness, said the accused had been his dancing partner the whole time. The Moll said that his job was to keep to the rear of the company all day. Another witness claimed that they were not drunk but 'right market merry', and there was an altercation when a policeman tried to arrest the accused.[28] There is no mention of sticks, or ribbons, or a plough; there is a hint that the dances involved couples (presumably in a double file), but not that either of the files was dressed as women. Only the Moll had a blacked face. The theft of a pocket knife at Wolston was relatively petty, as were the theft by a seventeen-year-old 'morris dancer' of a shaving brush from the pantry of the blacksmith's house in Corringham in 1880 (implying an indoor performance) and the theft of two tins of fish by five men from Messingham (four agricultural labourers and a pot hawker) from a grocer's shop in New Brumby in 1881. They were 'out dressed as Morris dancers or plough jags'.[29]

Drinking was, almost inevitably, a concomitant of dancing. On New Year's Eve in 1852 George Wilson, a gardener from Old Leake, was charged with being drunk and disorderly, and causing an obstruction in the street. He said that he had come to town (Louth, 27 miles from home) as one of a party of morris-dancers and had so exhausted himself with dancing and drinking that he laid himself across the footway 'in order to take a little repose'. A lenient magistrate fined him sixpence.[30] In 1863 four labourers from Timberland, 'part of a body of morris dancers', made what was claimed to be an annual visit to Metheringham on 22 December, when 'the inhabitants are compelled to fasten their doors to keep them out'. They knocked on the vicar's door and 'on its being opened by the servant girl followed her down the passage. Their strange attire frightened her very much.' They came round the next morning to apologise but the vicar pressed charges and they were each fined 5s with 7s 6d costs for being drunk and disorderly.[31]

There were, of course, attempts to suppress those real or apparent morris dancers who were intruding, thieving and causing disorder. A writer to the *Leicester Journal* in 1864 noted that

[25] *Lincolnshire Chronicle,* 17 January 1851 [b].
[26] *Lincolnshire Chronicle,* 17 January 1851 [c].
[27] *Lincolnshire Chronicle,* 16 January 1852.
[28] *Coventry Herald,* 20 January 1865; *Northampton Mercury,* 21 January 1865; *Rugby Advertiser,* 21 January 1865; *Coventry Standard,* 27 January 1865; *Rugby Advertiser,* 28 January 1865; *Northampton Mercury,* 28 January 1865.
[29] *Stamford Mercury,* 23 January 1880; *Stamford Mercury,* 14 January 1881.
[30] *Lincoln, Rutland, and Stamford Mercury,* 7 January 1853.
[31] *Lincolnshire Chronicle,* 2 January 1864 [b]; *Stamford Mercury,* 8 January 1864.

'morrice dancers and plough-bullocks are not suffered in towns because of the danger and annoyance to the public. I think there is perhaps as much in the county, and, if anything, more annoyance and harm from the practice. The hideous fellows meeting women in lonely roads are calculated to cause greater fright.'[32]

Drinking could lead to arrests for fighting, as at Spilsby on New Year's Day in 1882, when 'A party of morris-dancers, fantastically dressed, visited the various inns during the day. Towards evening it was apparent, some of the visitors had imbibed a little too freely, and fights ensued. As a result summonses to some will issue.'[33] At Scothern in 1857 some 'bumpkins... bedecked in tawdry habiliments and denominating themselves "morris dancers"' overturned a coal wagon left for the benefit of the poor, the newspaper calling for retribution.[34]

There are several instances of morris dancers being accused of theft, as at Brinklow. At the same time as the Metheringham incident, four labourers of Ingham, morris dancing at Willingham by Stow, were charged with stealing four chickens and two ducks; but the magistrate decided they had been entrapped into confessing, and dismissed the charges.[35] In November 1820 at Whaplode Fen-Ends in the south of the county thieves gained entrance to a house under false pretences, and being masked, they were mistaken for morris dancers. This may have been something in the nature of a mummers' play, performed indoors, that was expected by the occupants.[36] A similar instance occurred at Deeping St James on 15 December 1831 when a 'set of strolling vagabonds from Crowland calling themselves morris dancers, opened the door and entered a respectable person's dwelling ... and began to perform sans ceremonie, which frightened a little girl, who ran to give an alarm: in the interim they purloined a new cap'.[37] There is no doubt that some performances involved indoor dancing. Mary Kirby described how on Plough Monday in the 1830s at Thurcaston in Leicestershire 'a goodly troop of plough-boys, in the costume of ladies and gentlemen, opened the back-door, and filed into the kitchen ... and at once formed a circle, joining hands and beginning to dance a reel'.[38] There is no mention of their having a plough, nor were they termed 'morris dancers'. This is of additional interest as one of the earliest references to cross-dressing by men other than the Bessy.

As in the west midlands, these activities involved the solicitation of money, but in the east midlands there was a greater tendency to see it as mere begging, and this was sometimes characterized as going beyond solicitation into intimidation. There are also more reports from this area of outright theft. Other grounds were also invoked to discourage the practice. In 1866 the magistrates at Winterton were asked by farmers 'to stop the morris dancers from going round the different villages', to prevent the spread of rinderpest. The magistrates did not issue a formal ban, but asked the police superintendent to 'tell the morris dancers in their several beats that the magistrates wished them not to go about this year as they had been accustomed to do'.[39] At Market Harborough it was reported that 'In some places applications were made ... to prevent the assembling of "plough witches" and morris-dancers on Plough Monday, whose clothes might increase the cattle plague, but as no such application was made to the Market Harboro' Bench, these face-bedaubed and ludicrously attired fellows appeared in the town as usual'.[40] A rather unusual approach was taken by a youth who asked for permission for himself

[32] Countryman.
[33] *Stamford Mercury*, 5 January 1883.
[34] *Lincolnshire Chronicle*, 2 January 1857.
[35] *Lincolnshire Chronicle*, 2 January 1864 [a]; *Nottinghamshire Guardian*, 8 January 1864.
[36] *Stamford Mercury*, 10 November 1820.
[37] *Stamford Mercury*, 30 December 1831.
[38] Kirby, p. 44.
[39] *Stamford Mercury*, 5 January 1866.
[40] *Northampton Mercury*, 13 January 1866.

and five companions to go about Grimsby morris dancing at Christmas, 1870. 'The bench had no objection, but the morris-dancers are to give in their names to Supt. Campbell, and were cautioned not to annoy people.'[41]

A writer calling himself 'An Old Fogy', living in a quiet village in southern Derbyshire described his Christmas visitors in 1874, encapsulating in a single account the variety of overlapping activities that could take place in a community. Over a few days he saw carol singers, children singing hymns, a small brass ensemble, glee singers and also the following groups:[42]

> *Christmas Eve. 6 p.m. Six Morris Dancers, youths bedecked with old finery and scraps of paper, who danced and stamped about in the snow without much rhyme or reason to the music of an accordian, concluding with a Christy Minstrel melody.*
>
> *Christmas Eve. 6.30 p.m. A troop of Mummers, or Guizers as I think they are more usually called in Derbyshire, five in number, who entered the kitchen and acted a short play, the characters being St George, Slasher, the Doctor, and Old Bet. ...*
>
> *...*
>
> *December 26th, 3 p.m. A troop of seven morris dancers, but dressed more after the fashion of n****r minstrels than the traditional mummers, an effect which was increased by five of them having blackened their faces. The tallest and most ungainly of the party was caparisoned as a woman. To the sound of a concertina they danced burlesque waltzes and quadrilles, but happily they did not possess that French agility which leads to cancan steps. This incongruous medley of a performance was concluded by a 'walk round' of the whole company singing, with more vigour than accuracy, the very unseasonable and inappropriate glee, 'in a little boat we row'.*

The 'Old Fogy' encountered two kinds of morris dancers also termed 'mummers', mummers acting a play, and the pervasive influence of black-face minstrelsy. Other winter customs in the east of England included plough jagging, plough plays, sword dances and whip-cracking. Almost any of these could combine and recombine with one or more of the other elements. Where a dance is recorded in association with other elements, without further evidence we cannot know if this was something we might now characterize as a morris dance, or as a sword dance, or whether the observer or the participants would attach either of those names to it, or none.

South of the east midlands, in East Anglia a similar picture emerges in Cambridgeshire and its surrounds. On Plough Monday in 1854 'a party of men gaily decorated with ribbons of many colours' appeared; 'they had a violin and a banjo, and paraded the villages of Cottenham, Landbeach, and Waterbeach, as Morris-dancers'. They had been thrown out of work by the bad weather. The vigour of their dancing, far from the 'light fantastic toe' was commented upon.[43] One 'Flo. Rivers' wrote to *Notes and Queries* to enquire about 'morris dancing as observed on Plough Monday in Cambridge' in 1884, in order to compare it with what she had presumably seen in 1850.[44] Her enquiry did not elicit any response but the question suggests first, that she had seen 'morris dancers' then and second, that she suspected that the nature of the custom had changed. In fact her query had been answered two years previously, when 'W.R.' wrote in response to a similar question. He described the custom as it was around 1848:[45]

[41] *Lincolnshire Chronicle*, 9 December 1870.
[42] Old Fogy.
[43] *Cambridge Chronicle*, 14 January 1854.
[44] Rivers.
[45] R., W.

On Plough Monday troops or 'sets' from neighbour-villages annually visited the town. In the costume, which formed no small part of the rivalry of the sets, the most noticeable points were brown or black velveteen coats, covered with bows or streamers of bright ribbons; tall hats banded from brim to crown with ribbon and adorned with a plume of feathers. Each troop was accompanied by a 'Moll', a swain dressed as a woman, generally in white muslin or extravagantly in the latest fashion. Dances were formed at intervals through the main streets, and largess solicited. An important feature with some troops was a wooden plough drawn by four or six of the company; this formed the centre of a 'round dance'. The Madingley set was famous (about 1848) for their get-up and that of their 'Moll'. There was always a marked courtesy shown to the 'Moll', which may have had an origin in some earlier form of morris dancing ... I believe the custom is still observed, though possibly with 'maimed rites'.

Like Flo. Rivers, W.R. suspected that the nature of the event had changed over the previous thirty years. The association with the plough is loose at best. The costume is beribboned, but there is no mention of bells. Many of these details were confirmed in 1930 by a former dancer, who described how teams from Girton, Histon, Comberton, Coton, Madingley and Grantchester would converge on Cambridge market-place to dance, with six dancers (including the Moll) and half a dozen pulling a plough. He also commented that the dancers held handkerchiefs but did not wear bells.[46] The 'respect' accorded to the Moll may relate to the role of 'lady' used in some groups, accompanying a 'lord'; the pair led the dancers through the day, as evidenced at Hardwick, and later at Comberton and Boxworth. The lord wore a more elaborate costume than the others.[47]

There is plentiful evidence for some of the dancers cross-dressing. At Cambridge in 1859 'a party of Morris dancers, some of the fellows dressed in female attire, were ringing bells, cracking whips, and dancing', causing a horse and cart to bolt and run over a boy.[48] At West Wickham, apparently on Boxing Day, the dancers, 'some in women's clothes ... just jumped about, couldn't really dance'.[49] Similar evidence comes from Great Wilbraham in the 1890s, where there were about 16 in the group (some may have been employed to drag a plough), some dressed as women, with no special dance figures; they 'jumped about in couples'.[50] Just over the county border at Great Sampford in Essex, dancers went round with a plough on Plough Monday, some dressed as women.[51] Hannah Gawthrop of Cambridge recalled seeing 'Men in muslin dresses, with bows and ribbons, and others with bells on their ankles' from Histon and Girton towards the end of the century.[52]

The Moll often had a blacked face, but in some cases, particularly in later years, the dancers too blacked their faces. At St Neots on Plough Monday around 1880, brightly dressed men with blacked faces danced in a ring.[53] An early example came from Godmanchester in 1861, where the local newspaper complained about previous occurrence of importuning by 'solicitous "plough witches" or "morris dancers" who assumed to themselves a most horrible disfigurement of both face and form, and ... would not hesitate to plough up the road in front of one's house'; but expressed pleasure that 'this year ... the event would have passed unheeded at Godmanchester, but for a few farmers' boys, who appeared in the evening, with their faces

---

[46] Needham and Peck, pp. 80-81.
[47] 'Wortley MSS, Typed Details'; 'Wortley MSS, Field Notes on Comberton Molly Dancers';' Wortley MSS, Field Note on Boxworth'.
[48] *Cambridge Independent Press*, 15 January 1859.

[49] 'Wortley MSS, Field Note on ... West Wickham'.
[50] 'Wortley MSS, Field Note on Great Wilbraham'.
[51] 'Wortley MSS, Mrs Bolton'.
[52] Porter, p. 103.
[53] Tebbutt, p. 52.

besmeared with soot shaking their tin boxes, and offering the usual plea of "please to bestow a half-penny upon the poor plough boy"'.[54] Another writer added that they stuffed bundles of straw between their shoulders to give themselves a hunch-back appearance, but could not remember anyone's house being blocked by a ploughed furrow there.[55] In fact, verified instances of the actual use of a plough in this way are hard to come by.

As in Lincolnshire and the east midlands, in the Cambridge area the relationship between plough customs, dancing and morris dancers can be uncertain. At Fulbourn Russell Wortley's informant told him that men with whips went round with the dancers during the day and with the plough in the evening.[56] The Ely correspondent of the *Cambridge Independent Press*, on the other hand, equated the two, commenting in 1888 that formerly 'the streets were tolerably filled by village ploughmen, fantastically dressed, dancing to the strains of a violin, ploughs being dragged on the roads; but this year, these implements of agriculture were conspicuous by their absence, and fiddles were supplanted by concertinas. Some of the morris-dancers, it would appear, had no connection with agricultural pursuits.'[57] At Stretham in 1894 several ploughs were dragged round the village on Plough Monday, the men 'dressed up in all manner of costumes with their faces and hands coloured with all the imaginable hues' and on the Tuesday there were two or three groups of morris dancers.[58] As at Market Bosworth in the mid century, face colouring, not specifically blackening, was evidently intended primarily as disguise.

A Huntingdonshire calendar from *c.* 1845 noted that on Plough Monday a plough 'is made to traverse the streets, by strings of boys, accompanied by the rustic characters, called Plough-Witches ... In some parts of the county an imitation of the ancient morris-dance is given by ploughmen, dressed in white garb, exuberantly decorated with rosettes; but, the true morris-dancers themselves – the "old chaps" have "bolted"'.[59] This implies a falling away of the links between current practice and older custom within the writer's experience, and that the dancing that accompanied the plough in his day was not a continuation of 'morris dancing' as he knew it. It anticipates the questions of Flo. Rivers and W.R. in Cambridge a generation later when they suggested that the custom had changed, producing 'maimed rites' as W.R. characterized them.

Inevitably, for the more respectable elements in society there were negative associations, as for the correspondent who alluded unfavourably in 1837 to the solicitations of 'the morrice-dancers on Plough-Monday – "just one ha'penny, sir, only one ha'penny, please"'.[60] A teacher recorded that two morris dancers appeared in the school at Stevington in Bedfordshire on Plough Monday in 1870 'frightening the children' (though several of the boys had absented themselves, quite possibly to participate in festivities).[61]

A rather confused account from Ashley on the eve of Plough Monday in 1873 described how a fight broke out over a singing contest when some morris dancers were present, but it is not clear if they were the instigators, the victims, or just became involved.[62] On Boxing Day in 1857 a travelling fight between rival gangs of gipsy fiddlers took place in several Cambridge pubs over who should play for a party of morris dancers, either for dancing that day, or in anticipation of a forthcoming plough-jagging. One of the families involved, the Shaws, had

[54] *Cambridge Chronicle*, 12 January 1861.
[55] Bradtke, 'Molly Dancing', p. 262.
[56] 'Wortley MSS, Field Notes on Plough Monday in Fulbourn'.
[57] *Cambridge Independent Press*, 13 January 1888.
[58] *Cambridge Independent Press*, 12 January 1894.

[59] *Calendar ... Huntingdonshire*. I am grateful to Liam Sims at Cambridge University Library for his help in accessing this item.
[60] *Huntingdon, Bedford & Peterborough Gazette*, 16 September 1837.
[61] 'Stevington School Logbook', p. 222.
[62] *Bury Free Press*, 15 February 1873.

been in a similar tussle eleven years before when they and another family had been playing for two groups of dancers who met in a pub, and proceeded to insult each other's playing.[63] Towards the end of the century the landlord of the Three Horseshoes pub in Great Chesterford in Essex used to bar his door against 'rowdy and drunken molly dancers'.[64]

We shall turn to molly dancing shortly, but first it's worth looking at some of the other aspects of rowdiness associated with dancing in East Anglia. A term sometimes used to describe the dancers is 'truculent rustics', a phrase taken from a Cambridge news report of 1845 which described how on Plough Monday:[65]

> *the town was infested by predatory bands of truculent rustics, dressed in an outlandish and savage guise, who paraded our streets in companies of six or eight, and after executing a wild and somewhat terrific kind of dance, they surrounded passengers, and made violent incursions into shops, demanding money, which their vehemence of manner and uncouth appearance were very successful in obtaining from timid women, nervous tradesfolks, and small boys. These parties continued to levy contributions until the evening commenced, when they were succeeded by a band of beggars, whose attributes were ghostly and witch-like: with blackened faces and spectral apparel, these appearances startled the town from its propriety from dusk to midnight. They suddenly came upon the affrighted wayfarer with long sticks, and demanded of him halfpence, to the sound of 'mump, mump'.*

There is little here to suggest a specific kind of dance with a set of distinct customary appurtenances, but after describing the morris dancers in Cambridge Hannah Gawthrop added 'At night the men, whom we call Mummers, would come with blackened faces knocking on our doors and singing: "Mump, mump ..."'.[66] She seems to imply that these were the same men as the dancers, but it is not certain. Enid Porter reported 'rough dancing' at Bottisham, where 'the men daubed their faces and danced to rough music of pots and pans'.[67]

Another instance of 'mumping' with no association with dance was recorded at Chesterton on Plough Monday in 1870, when 'several groups of fossil-diggers and boys of the labouring classes who were armed with thick sticks and some with masks on, went through the principal part of the parish for the purpose of what is vulgarly termed "mumping", and to collect pence from those who had not been ready to start the intruders off at once'. After a fight the police intervened. They described one participant, saying that 'his face was quite black. He had on an old straw hat, and an old coat stuffed with straw to make him appear high-backed, and some women's petticoats ... he was dressed in a similar way to a woman.'[68] The same issue of the newspaper carried a report that in Cambridge the same day, 'the town was unusually full of yokels dressed in all sorts of ludicrous costumes, who levied black mail wherever it was possible, and afterwards spent the proceeds, in many instances, in making themselves inebriated'.[69] At Brandon Creek rough music, sticks beating on pails and tin baths, accompanied the plough's journey round the village and 'if any housewife refused to donate a copper or two, the "females" in the Plough gang took off the long-legged drawers they wore and tied them around her neck', singing an insulting song.[70] The fictional events in *Ralf Skirlaugh* in Lincolnshire also included a suggestion of a rough-music satire on unpopular members of the community.

[63] *Cambridge Independent Press*, 2 January 1858; *Cambridge Independent Press*, 17 January 1846.
[64] 'Molly (and Morris) Dancing'.
[65] *Cambridge Independent Press, 18 January 1845.*
[66] Porter, p. 103.
[67] Porter, p. 129.
[68] *Cambridge Independent Press*, 15 January 1870 [a].
[69] *Cambridge Independent Press*, 15 January 1870 [b].
[70] Humphries, p. 7.

These descriptions sound very like what was later called 'hummy dancing', performed around Thetford in the late 19th and early 20th centuries. The fullest description is in local writer W.G. Clarke's 1925 book *In Breckland Wilds*, referring to the 1890s:[71]

> *'Hummy dancers' are associated with Thetford and Boxing Day. Until about thirty years ago, and on a few occasions since, bands of young men dressed in absurd costumes and black faces, paraded the streets and sometimes gave a performance. Some of each party wore female costumes and these were chased round and round by their partners who struck their padded backs with wooden ladles. These resounding thwacks were accompanied by the yells of both strikers and stricken. The band usually consisted of a man who played on fire-irons, another on a frying pan, some home-made stringed instruments from which a humming sound was evoked, possibly the origin of the term 'Hummy dancers'.*

Russell Wortley noted from one old participant that there were three male-'female' couples with blacked faces, the men's backs being stuffed with rags to give a hump-backed appearance, which the 'women' struck with wooden bats. There was no plough and the participants were not aware of Plough Monday customs.[72]

The Thetford commentator who in 1875 reproduced the election expenses list, possibly from the June 1790 election, also noted 'allusions to garland-makers, hummer dancers, and the like'; but the list itself has 'two garland makers, six stavesmen'.[73] It seems the writer misinterpreted a reference to 'stavesmen' (privately hired guards, widely used at elections) as a reference to hummer dancers carrying staves.

An anomalous 1823 report from Hitchin in Hertfordshire – which may be seen as a western outlier of the east-of-England orbit – described a May-day custom with two men, faces blacked, one with a broom and one cross-dressed as 'Mad Moll and her husband', two men as Lord and Lady, he beribboned and holding a sword, 'she' in white muslin and ribbons, and six or seven pairs of dancers, all men, half of them dressed as women. Three musicians accompanied them. The characters and costumes suggest affinities with Plough Monday, but the time of year and blacking (coming before the influence of minstrelsy) suggest links to sweeps' May-day customs.[74]

Mumping and hummy dancing are at the edges of the semantic spectrum spreading from morris dancing at the core. Another strand which emerged in the second half of the 19th century was molly dancing. The earliest descriptions using this name by participants relate to this period, although this is most likely a consequence of when the information was gathered. Our main sources for information about the dance are Joseph Needham, Arthur Peck and Russell Wortley, who conducted their researches from the 1930s on, speaking to old men who had danced in their youth 50-60 years before. Some participants who probably danced around the 1870s averred that 'the dancing was called "Molly" or "Morris" dancing' indiscriminately.[75] The dances described to Needham and Peck were straightforward country dances, done by the male molly dancers during the day and as mixed-couple social dances in the evening. This may underlie Josiah Chater's otherwise uncorroborated note in his diary for 1845:[76]

> *12 Jan. 1845. The first thing this morning was the morris dancers it being Plough Monday. They did kick up such a row as I never heard in all my life: all day long: men, women and boys.*

[71] Clarke, W.G., pp. 167-68.
[72] 'Wortley MSS, Thetford … Notes on Interview Re. Hummy Dancers'; 'Wortley MSS, Thetford … Jimmy Nichols'.
[73] H., A.L.
[74] Hone, 1:283-84.
[75] Needham and Peck, p. 80.
[76] Porter, p. 103.

Part of the problem with identifying strands in local traditions in the area is that the contemporary accounts often do not specify anything other than 'dances' and other apparently variable associated elements of custom – such as the plough, the solicitations and threats, which may also occur without a record of accompanying dancing. Adducing them now as specific evidence of morris, molly, hummy or other types of dancing, and teasing out the differences between them, if any, is primarily an exercise in speculation. The earliest evidence we have for the use of 'molly' in the area (apart from as the single character of Molly or Bessy associated with dances) is from 1866, but it implies an already existing practice:[77]

> We were reminded by parties of 'Mollies' perambulating the streets that Plough Monday had again come round. The genuine Mollies did not muster so numerously as in the previous year, but the occasion gave an opportunity to numbers of small boys to deck themselves with a piece of ribbon, and importune pedestrians for 'jes one ha'penny for a ploughboy'; to many of these urchins we should imagine that the question to define a plough would be as great a poser as a stiff problem.

This exemplifies the difficulty – nowhere does the account mention dancing, but it does imply that a plough should be associated with the custom. Two of the few contemporary references are from Histon in 1898 when 'the gaily dressed band of "Molly Dancers" were conspicuous by their absence' and in 1899 when 'The "Molly Dancers" were not represented, as the fellows that generally formed this band have gone away or found something to do. There is no one "out of work" in the parish at present.'[78]

When Russell Wortley investigated from the 1930s on, the information at Fulbourn in 1935 typified what he was told. His informant was the concertina player for the molly dancers. There were six dancers, three of whom were dressed as women; there was a cadger, and himself as musician. Whippers accompanied the dancers in the day and a plough at night. Similarly, at Balsham there were eight molly dancers, four dressed as women. They performed on Boxing Day, while the plough came out on Plough Monday. The membership of the two groups overlapped.[79] Wortley's informant at Withersfield, on the other hand, said that the molly dancers took the plough round, and at Girton the molly dancers are said to have taken a plough on wheels with them and danced around it.[80]

At Castle Camps when many were out of work the molly dancers dressed up with 'different bits and pieces', some wearing skirts, and blacked their faces. There was a similar story at West Wickham where three or four couples danced, some wearing skirts, some wearing tall hats, having blacked their faces. In this case the same people took the plough round (the implication being that this was a separate exercise). Unemployment was also a driver at Little Wilbraham, where the molly dancers also had blacked faces and some wore women's clothes. At West Wratting they performed around Christmastime, some wearing women's skirts.[81]

Outside of East Anglia there are scattered references to 'molly dancers'. As far back as Plough Monday in 1853 a report from Market Harborough used the term:[82]

[77] *Cambridge Chronicle*, 13 January 1866.
[78] *Cambridge Independent Press*, 14 January 1898; *Cambridge Independent Press*, 13 January 1899.
[79] 'Wortley MSS, Field Note on Balsham Molly Dancers'; 'Wortley MSS, Field Notes on Plough Monday in Fulbourn'; 'Wortley MSS, Field Note on Informant Mrs Pluck'.
[80] 'Wortley MSS, Field Notes ... on Weston Colville'; 'Wortley MSS, Field Note on Girton'.
[81] 'Wortley MSS, Field Note on West Wratting Molly Dancers'; 'Wortley MSS, Field Notes ... on Bartlow'; 'Wortley MSS, Field Notes ... on Weston Colville'; 'Wortley MSS, Field Note on Little Wilbraham'.
[82] *Northampton Mercury*, 15 January 1853.

An unusual number of 'ploughboys' visited Harborough on Monday last. One party attracted much notice, as it was composed of four couples of dancers, besides 'moggies, mollies, n****rs', etc. We believe that the greater part of these were not real 'ploughboys', but a party of stocking-makers from Kibworth, who went out for a 'spree'.

At Castleton in Derbyshire in the mid 19th century the morris dancers were sometimes called 'molly dancers',[83] and Philip Wentworth described the men accompanying the rushcart at Blackley near Manchester as 'what were called here "Molly Dancers", and by the poets "Morris", or "Morrice" dancers'.[84] One member of the Failsworth team taught by Mick Coleman from Oldham before World War I seemed to equate 'molly dancers' with the carnival morris then developing (see Chapter 26), who were 'not proper morris dancers'; but another of the team identified his team as the 'Failsworth Molly Dancers'.[85] Later in the 20th century, on May Day boys in Manchester would dress up in women's clothes and colour their faces, and perambulate singing 'Molly Dancers kicking up a row' – they too being called 'molly dancers'.[86] In the 1920s 'molly dancers' were advertised in the 'Daisy Day' procession to raise hospital funds in Ancoats, Manchester.[87] It's possible, however, that in this case the 'mollies' were the rigid slings (braided ropes) sometimes held in north-west morris dancing.[88]

The evidence indicates that, in East Anglia at least, the 'molly' element relates to the cross-dressing, rather than deriving or descending from the word 'morris'. The word is attested in the sense of an effeminate or homosexual male from the early 18th century.[89]

Through perusal of the records from across much of eastern England we have seen that morris dancers were more or less loosely associated with the plough jags and Plough Monday customs. Sometimes they were identified as one and the same; at other times there was a looser association, where they were distinct elements but may have had participants in common; and sometimes the two were seen as completely distinct, the association being little more than appearing around the same time. Within the relation to plough customs there were links to both plough jagging and the plough play, and beyond that to the more general mummers' play. Where the dancing is described it is indistinguishable from social country dancing. There were no distinct choreographic elements such as particular steps, or stick clashing, and bells and handkerchiefs were rarely mentioned. Dancers usually wore ribbons. There was a fool and a man-woman Molly, and in some cases half the dancers, though male, dressed as women (a feature which enhances the incorporation of social dances), while the 'real' men wore tall hats. Sometimes a lord and lady (who may incorporate the Moll), more ornately dressed than the rest, headed a double file of performers. Blacked faces were common, especially in the later period, but the evidence of the use of other colours suggests that other traditional disguising customs contribute to this as much as or more than the influence of minstrelsy. There are few records in the east midlands after the 1880s.

In East Anglia the situation is further complicated by the presence and influence of additional customs of mumping, hummy dancing and rough music. Here and in the practice of plough jagging in general it was easy for the solicitation element to develop into more overtly threatening behaviours. With the loss of most of the characteristic elements of morris dancing, and the superseding of the word itself by the word 'molly' to describe the dancers in Cambridgeshire in the second half of the 19th century, it is hard to maintain that 'morris dancing' survived in the area. The decline seen in the west is mirrored in these eastern areas.

[83] Addy and Kidson, pp. 412, 415.
[84] Wentworth, p. 58.
[85] Pilling, 'Failsworth'.
[86] 'Manchester May Day Tradition'.

[87] Heaney, Winifred.
[88] Howison and Bentley, 'North-west Morris', p. 47.
[89] 'Molly' (OED).

Chapter 17

North-west morris 1801-1850

In the first half of the 19th century morris dancing continued to flourish in the north-west of England. The chief loci were the industrial and industrializing towns to the east of Manchester in the context of rushbearing, as in the later 18th century, but there remained some outliers indicative of a different character, which we shall consider first (Figure 17.1).

At a masquerade on the occasion of the septennial Preston Guild procession in 1822 'morris dancers' participated, but these are likely to be of the kind who appeared at other high-society masquerades of the era, rather than a processional morris. There are no records of morris dancers in the detailed accounts of the Preston Guild procession itself at this time.[1]

On Whit Monday in 1817 Chester was 'disgraced by the fooleries of some dozen idle fellows, bedizened with rags and tinsel, calling themselves Morice Dancers, who, after performing a variety of antics, with less grace than so many baboons, conceived themselves entitled, judging from their very urgent solicitations, for payment, for their extravagances'. The curmudgeonly reporter would have liked to see their dancing 'quickened by the application of General Washington's whip' but acknowledged that they had been well rewarded.[2] While these dancers were not well received by this reporter from the *Chester Chronicle*, such views were in a minority in the region.

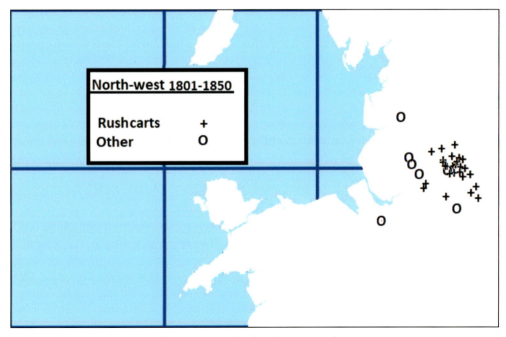

Figure 17.1: Morris dancing associated with rushcarts and other activities, 1801-1850.

---

[1] 'Preston Guild Masquerade', p. 37.

[2] *Chester Chronicle*, 30 May 1817.

The association with maypoles found in the 18th century lingered into the 19th. At Culcheth, near Leigh, there was a tradition of 'a plot of land given to the villagers in the reign of Queen Elizabeth ... for the use of the inhabitants of the olden time to practice ancient sports of the maurice or morris dance', upon which a maypole stood, still present in 1846. The pole was reported to have been erected by a member of the Withington family, who came to Culcheth Hall in 1824.[3] This piece of land with maypole, dedicated to morris dancing, echoes the similar tradition at Abram just four miles north of Culcheth, which we briefly encountered in the 18th century. The first detailed account of the tradition at Abram describes the event which took place on St Swithin's day, 15 July 1850, although the reason for the choice of this date is obscure. The *Wigan Times* reported that the dancers were young bachelors, with handkerchiefs which 'they strike against each other, as we might suppose the ancient morris dancers did with their staves or swords'. They wore beribboned white linen shirts, and trousers. There was a 'Belle' – a woman, not a cross-dressing man – who had a 'protector' holding a garland, and a fool. A dance was performed around the Belle. The reporter was pleased that 'the men, generally, were sober, and conducted themselves with strict propriety and quietness'. Somewhat enigmatically, the reporter added that 'For two or three days previously, we understand, a spurious company of morris dancers have been out, but with little success'.[4] The Abram tradition has echoes of older practices: the maypole, the association with the young men of the parish, and the obeisance towards a lady and her lord, all reminiscent of the Whitsun-ale morris in the south midlands.

Eccles wakes continued to be a major festivity, and in 1822 Joseph Parry painted pictures of the event. In one of them are three male and three female dancers waving handkerchiefs in the air, who appear to be dancing a hey (figure-of-eight) (Figure 17.2). Burton thought that 'the artist has drawn freely on his imagination, and the scene is quite unlike the village of Eccles',[5] but in fact the proportions and general features of the church depicted (though not the details) do match the parish church at Eccles, seen from the Market Place, and an undated but possibly contemporary pamphlet describing the picture identifies 'the morris dancing lads and lasses, in special costume for the occasion ... [f]lourishing their white scarfes'.[6] The women have dresses of different colours; the men share salmon pink colours in their shirts and waistcoats, but wear variously coloured trousers (and not breeches). They are dancing in front of a garlanded horse drawing a rushcart. Charlotte Burne recorded her aunt's memories of the rushcart at Radcliffe, near Bury, around 1830, also involving both male and female morris dancers.[7] The rushcarts were indeed the focus for most of the morris dancing in the first half of the century in the north-west.

Although the focus of rushcart activity was in the industrial and industrializing communities north and east of Manchester, rushcart ceremonies were also present on the Cheshire plain. The morris dancing recorded at Wilmslow in 1780 continued into the 19th century. In 1886 a correspondent wrote to Robert Holland that 'I know from my grandfather and grandmother that there was formerly a rush-bearing at Wilmslow, with the accompaniment of Morris Dancing, &c. A Mary Massey ... being the presiding genius at this Morris Dancing'.[8] Mary Massey died in 1830, aged 64, so this recollection must be from the early years of the century.[9] Rushbearing with morris dancers was certainly still practised at Lymm in 1817, when

3 *Manchester Times*, 10 July 1846.
4 Bearon, 'Abram Morris Dance', pp. 59-60.
5 Burton, Alfred, p. 164.
6 A., F.S.
7 Burne, 'Reminiscences', p. 204.
8 Holland, Robert, p. 295.
9 'Mary Massey'.

Figure 17.2: Joseph Parry, 'Eccles Wakes Fair, 1822' (detail) (Image © Salford Museum & Art Gallery, 1954-98).

(following a description of the construction of the rushcart by an unidentified witness) 'The cart thus loaded goes round to the neighbouring seats, preceded by male and female Morris Dancers, who perform a peculiar dance at each house, and are attended by a man in female attire (something between the fool and the Maid Maryan), who jingles a bell to the tune, and holds a large wooden ladle for money'.[10] The male and female dancers corroborate the scene depicted by Parry for Eccles five years later, and there is a man-woman – usually known in the north-west as 'Bessy' – collecting in a ladle. The Bessy, with ladle, is depicted in a painting of the Lymm rushbearing made around 1850 (Figure 17.3). Here, however, the dancers are all male. There are eight of them, in two lines four abreast, waving handkerchiefs. They wear straw hats, white shirts and trousers, long coloured sashes and some ribbons, including below the knee, but with no bells attached.

The four greys drawing the rushcart are confirmed by a newspaper account of the event in 1848, when there were rumours that the festival would be prohibited. The *Manchester Courier* celebrated the fact that the town was smartened up each year for the occasion, and that the event took place:[11]

> On Saturday there was a rushcart, drawn by four greys (hence the cognomen of Lymn greys), accompanied by morris Dancers and a band of musicians. On Monday the Foresters, Druids, and teetotallers, had each a procession, preceded by excellent bands of music. Then followed the old English sports of running in sacks, pitching the bars, &c., and whip for horses, belonging to Lymn and the surrounding townships. On Tuesday there was a repetition of Monday's sports. The rush bearing has passed off with the greatest spirit.

[10] Ormerod, 1:lxxix-lxxxii.

[11] *Manchester Courier*, 19 August 1848.

Figure 17.3: 'The Rush-bearers, Lymm, Cheshire' (Image © York Castle Museum, YORCM: DA7636).

Two years later, one 'Julius' describing the rushcart procession at Lymm, wrote:[12]

> *The cart is drawn round the parish by three or four spirited horses, decked out with ribbons, – the collars being surrounded with small bells. It is attended by morris-dancers, dressed in strange style, – men in women's clothes, &c. One big man in woman's clothes, with his face blacked, has a belt round his waist, to which is attached a large bell, and carries a ladle, in which he collects money from the spectators. The company stop and dance at the principal public-houses in their route, and then proceed to the parish church (!), where the rushes are deposited, and the garlands hung up very conspicuously, to remain till the next year.*

These three separate accounts, and the painting, provide a confusing and contradictory picture. The dancers are all men, or men and women, or men with some dressed as women. The Bessy has her face blacked according to one account, but not in the painting. The fact that three of these pieces of evidence come within two years of each other (though may represent perceptions from some time earlier) makes reconciliation of the accounts even more difficult. Julius also described a similar practice at Warburton, two miles from Lymm, but declared it not to be 'in such grand style'.

The Manchester artist Warwick Brookes sketched a scene of rushcart and dancers at Bowdon, five miles from Lymm, *c*. 1850, but confusingly described it as 'May Day at Bowden' (Figure 17.4). All of the figures in Brookes's sketch seem youthful. The ten or more dancers appear to be young males. Like the Lymm dancers they are wearing beribboned straw hats and shirts, with long sashes, and trousers with ribbons (but not, apparently, bells) around their lower legs, and are carrying handkerchiefs. There is no sign of a fool of Bessy.

---

[12] Julius.

Figure 17.4: Warwick Brookes, 'May Day at Bowden, Cheshire' (Image © Victoria and Albert Museum, London, 624-1886).

The numbers of dancers in many rushcart processions could reach double figures. Also in Cheshire, but at the edge of the Pennines, Macclesfield's celebrations on the coronation of George IV included 'ten couple of morris Dancers, fantastically dressed, whose performances excited universal admiration'.[13] This was a rare instance of official civic support in the area. In Chapel-en-le-Frith, Derbyshire, the rushbearing reported in 1758 was possibly still maintained 80 years later. A somewhat confusing report of the wakes there described how 'A vehicle, superbly adorned with garlands, evergreens, and banners, was drawn through the town by eight horses. Ten couple of morris dancers were thus conveyed; preceded by a splendid garland two yards diameter, and reaching four yards height.'[14] It may be that the report has merged the description of a rushcart and that of the accompanying dancers. In nearby Hayfield and New Mills newspaper reports of the wakes record morris dancers in 1836 and 1837; a much later report, supposedly relating to the time before 1818, claimed that 'Morris dancers, gaily dressed, danced in front of the public-houses to music supplied by the Old Reed Band, after which there was the usual "'lowance"'.[15] The writer may be conflating the cessation of collecting rushes for the church in that year with later accounts of dancing at public houses.

Still in Derbyshire, but at the edge of the industrial satellite towns of Manchester, Ebenezer Rhodes described the Glossop rushcart in 1824 being 'preceded by groups of dancers and a band of music', but is not explicit about the nature of the dancing.[16] As Figure 17.1 (p. 273) shows, rushcarts and morris dancers were thick on the ground in those satellite towns. Parishes were large, often with several townships within them, all growing apace with the influx of people

[15] *Stockport Advertiser*, 7 October 1836; *Stockport Advertiser*, 6 October 1837; *Ashton-under-Lyne Reporter*, 10 September 1898. I am grateful to Roger Bryant for bringing these to my attention.

[16] Rhodes, p. 203.

[13] *Chester Courant*, 24 July 1821.

[14] *Derbyshire Courier*, 21 July 1838.

to the industrial towns as well as the natural increase in population. Roger Elbourne has noted that this did not lead to a breakdown in or disruption of community events,[17] though there was rivalry. At Rochdale, described in 1844:[18]

> *...the neighbourhood being very populous, there are sometimes eight or nine rush carts, each having its band, etc., and they not unfrequently meet in one of the narrow streets, when generally a pretty stout battle takes place for precedence, as it is well known that those who arrive the first at the church always receive a donation of five shillings.*

Joseph Bradbury recalled seeing twelve rushcarts in Saddleworth after the 1830 parliamentary election, and often seeing five on other occasions from five townships, with four more townships co-operating to provide a sixth.[19] Alfred Burton described a painting of Saddleworth wakes from around that time, showing four rushcarts gathered, with 'All the humours of the fair ... the morris-dancers caper on the left hand; barrels of beer are being emptied by thirsty souls; and a donkey creates confusion in one corner by running away, upsetting everything in its way'.[20]

Elijah Ridings noted that the four townships of Newton Heath, Moston, Failsworth and Droylsden provided the Newton Heath rushcart on a rotating basis.[21] Rushcarts and dancers went from community to community. In 1830 the Stalybridge rushcart, preceded by twenty or more morris dancers, came to Mottram-in-Longdendale, but then moved on down the road to Hollingworth 'owing to some jealousy with the landlords', to the chagrin of the Mottram populace.[22] There could be even larger numbers of dancers, reflecting the trend noted above. The Hyde rushcart in 1819 was drawn by 24 horses supplied by the various mills, and 'forty couples' of morris dancers.[23]

As churches replaced their rush-strewn earthen floors (and as nineteenth-century sensibilities began once more, as in the 16th century, to view community festivals associated with churches as inappropriate), the rushcart became a more secular element of the general wakes-week holidays. A commentator on Rochdale in 1844 observed that 'in most places the rushes are sold after the festivity, which, from having no small portion of a religious character, has degenerated into mere holiday-making'.[24] The antiquary John Harland said in 1868 'now the church is generally the last place thought of in this festival, which has degenerated into mere rustic saturnalia', and noted the dwindling number of rushcarts appearing in Rochdale, from six or eight in the early part of the century to one or two in his day.[25]

Often publicans took the role of organizing a 'secular' rushcart. When in 1842 a rushcart, probably from Cheetham, came to the neighbouring settlement of Broughton on 20 August, an observer recorded that 'Two Men are appointed by the Landlord as Master of the Ceremonies they have a Band of Musicians, Men to Dance, provide Flags, Banners &c. for all of which they are responsible paying all and receiving all'. The dancers, 20 on this occasion, 'found it very difficult to Keep their equilibrium from the effects of fatigue a hot Sun and numberless draughts of double X'.[26]

Rushcarts and morris dancers would travel into the centre of Manchester to perform in the hope of collecting more money. Alfred Burton wrote:[27]

---

[17] Elbourne, p. 51.
[18] *Pictorial History*, p. 250.
[19] Bradbury, pp. 253-54.
[20] Burton, Alfred, pp. 80-81.
[21] Ridings, p. 168.
[22] Holden, p. 217.
[23] Stringfellow, p. 101.
[24] *Pictorial History*, p. 250.
[25] Baines, 1:503.
[26] Stringfellow, pp.53-54.
[27] Burton, Alfred, p. 63.

Manchester had no rush-cart of its own but every year a number of carts visited the town from the out-townships, some coming as far as from Oldham and Rochdale. They were always looked forward to, and liberally treated, and the inhabitants had thus the opportunity of inspecting the rival carts, and criticising the proficiency or otherwise of the morris-dancers who accompanied them.

As Burton notes, this was also an opportunity to display and trumpet a community's prosperity, craftsmanship and artistry measured against those of other communities. Of course, this led to fights between teams, as a Rochdale observer noted in *The Gentleman's Magazine* in 1843:[28]

A spirit of rivalry exists amongst the neighbouring villages, as to which shall produce the best cart and banner, and sometimes a serious fracas takes place between the parties....

The morris dancing sometimes proved a helpful distraction for criminal elements in the crowd. On 11 August 1849 the morris dancers and rushcart from Cheetham wakes were in Deansgate in the centre of the city when a boy was caught picking the pocket of a woman spectator.[29] Four weeks later another juvenile pickpocket was sentenced to three months in gaol and a whipping for picking the pockets of two women in Ancoats, on the northern edge of the city centre, as they 'were gazing at the antics of the morrice dancers who accompanied the rush-cart from Gorton wakes'.[30] Traffic was two-way, especially after the introduction of the railways: at the Stalybridge wakes in 1850 'On Monday [22 July], the rush cart, accompanied by the morris dancers, were a great source of attraction, and several of the light-fingered gentlemen from Manchester were very busy'.[31]

Fights were of course common, especially when dancers moved from their home territories. As the Gorton rushcart made its way to Manchester in 1829 the accompanying band struck up the anti-Irish tune 'Croppy Lie Down' as the procession entered the Irish quarter:[32]

instantly the war-whoop was sounded, and hundreds of the 'boys' immediately commenced an unequal war on the rash and unfortunate offenders. The assailants were armed with brooms, pokers, tongs, knobsticks, etc.; the musicians turned their implements into implements of war and defence, music for once having failed to charm the savage breast. The dancers tript their light fantastic toes, Lancashire fashion, upon the posteriors of their opponents. The rush-cart was mounted by two Irishmen; the drivers, alarmed for the safety of the plate which adorned it, lashed their horses; one scalader [climber] contrived to escape, but the other was detained, and driven to Gorton in gallant style, and upon him the Gortonians wreaked their fury. The old fool wisely enough turned his regalia, an old broom, into a weapon of offence and defence. Many of the dancers being nimble of foot, commenced a speedy retreat, recollecting that

'He who fights and runs away
Will live to fight another day.'

At intervals throughout the day, 'odd dancers' might be seen stealthily approaching the village, covered with wounds and glory, their dresses, plumes, and ribbons woefully dishevelled and torn.

Just after the middle of the century a similar battle took place when the rushcart and morris dancers again entered the Irish quarter: 'they got near to a Roman Catholic chapel ... and

---

[28] 'Great Musgrave Church'.
[29] *Manchester Courier,* 18 August 1849.
[30] *Manchester Courier,* 8 September 1849.
[31] *Manchester Times,* 27 July 1850.
[32] Burton, Alfred, pp. 59-60.

were dancing to one of their favourite tunes, "The Girl I Left Behind Me," when a large body of Irishmen mistaking it for "The Battle of the Boyne," and construing it into an insult, burst upon them with sticks, and beat and maltreated them in a most disgraceful manner'. Three dancers were severely injured.[33]

Fighting was not inevitable. The *Manchester Times and Gazette* reported that at Mottram-in-Longdendale in 1836 'Everything was conducted peaceably and with such regularity that in the two days' perambulation, amidst such an immense number of people, not one single accident occurred'.[34] Of course, reports depend to a large extent on the attitudes and prejudices of the correspondents and the journals and newspapers. 'Zemia' wrote of the Unsworth wakes, near Bury, in 1838 that 'The most attractive accompaniment of the modern wake is the Rush-cart', and continued in enthusiastic vein:[35]

> *Ever and anon, during its mighty progress through the village, the rush-cart stops before a gentleman's house; the windows are thrown open, the family appear to welcome it, the children run out to receive it, and the servants are not kept quite aloof: the horses shake their plumed heads, and jingle a merry peal on the bells with which they are plentifully garnished; the motley group 'exercise their dancing feet' with infinite alacrity and some skill; the rustic musicians pour forth their liveliest strains; the elevated heroes of the pageant, i.e. those on top of the rush-cart, wave ribands and handkerchiefs in token of joyful participation; and young and old, rich and poor, rejoice in the exuberant gaiety of the hour.*

At Radcliffe the same year the reporting of the wakes themselves was neutral, focusing mainly on the arrest of eight men for conducting a bull-baiting (the practice, though previously a significant feature of wakes, having been outlawed three years before). The account provides a good description of the variety of entertainments on offer:[36]

> *...the wakes were held as usual at Radcliffe, where there were morris dancers, bands of music, a rush cart, a horse race, wheelbarrow race, a foot race, fiddling match, smoking for a pound of tobacco, by ladies; tea drinking, by six of the oldest ladies of the parish; grinning through a collar, for a flitch of bacon; catching a pig, with a shaved and soaped tail; dancing, swarming the pole, &c., &c. The constables stated that they had no wish to abate any of those amusements which did not occasion cruelty to animals...*

The *Manchester Courier*'s reporter for Ashton-under-Lyne and Dukinfield wrote in both 1846 and 1849 that the wakes 'have been kept up with much spirit'.[37] In 1846 'The rush-cart was considered to be much finer than usual, and the Morris-dancers accompanying it showed themselves off to as much advantage as ribbons, garlands, &c., could assist them in doing'; while in 1849 'A large rush-cart was drawn through Dukinfield by eight horses, lent for the purpose by several gentlemen in the neighbourhood. The rush cart was occupied by a full complement of morris dancers and a band of music.' 'Occupied' suggests the dancers rode in the cart, as implied at Chapel-en-le-Frith 11 years earlier; however, a full rushcart has no room for dancers, except for the one or two privileged to ride atop the rushes.

The comment about 'the full complement of morris dancers' draws attention to the fact that they were not always present. There are dozens of accounts of rush-cart celebrations which do not mention dancers, but in most cases we cannot know if this was because they were absent,

[33] *News of the World*, 17 August 1851.
[34] *Manchester Times*, 17 September 1836.
[35] Zemia, p. 482.
[36] *Manchester Courier*, 22 September 1838.
[37] *Manchester Courier*, 22 August 1846; *Manchester Courier*, 25 August 1846.

or present but not mentioned. In 1825 Jessie Lee wrote to Hone's *Year Book* that rushcarts were accompanied by 'a band of music, and sometimes a set of morris dancers'.[38] In his account of Middleton wakes Samuel Bamford was more explicit: 'If the party can go to the expence of having a set of morrice-dancers, and feel inclined to undertake the trouble, some score or two of young men, with hats trimmed and decked out ... precede the drawers' of the rushcart.[39] Zemia, on the other hand, described Unsworth's rushcart's 'inseparable attendants, a band of morris dancers, in grotesque livery'.[40]

––––––––––

It is not surprising that literary evocations tended to view the rushcarts and morris through rose-tinted spectacles. They also tell us much about the characteristics of the dance in the north-west. In his poem on 'Newton Heath Wakes' Elijah Ridings fondly remembered 'rush-carts green on many a mound' and 'the nimble morris-dancers, / The blithe, fantastic, antic prancers / Bedeck'd in gaudiest profusion / With ribbons in a sweet confusion'.[41] The popular dialect author Ben Brierley thinly disguised his native Failsworth as 'Hazelworth ... famous for its rushbearings. It turned out the neatest cart, and the most thoroughly drilled troupe of Morris-dancers.' He described how 'grey haired villagers, helped over the hill by stalwart sons and buxom daughters, visiting, came to feast their eyes by a look at the rush-cart and the attendant Morris-dancers! How their hearts seemed to leap when the bells jingled, and the music of the dance struck up ... the lads moving through the graceful Morris-dance, and the lasses beside them half-wishing they might be allowed to join, and who will follow to adjust a detached ribbon or replace a stray flower.'[42]

Manchester-born William Harrison Ainsworth was a major Victorian literary figure. His best-known novel *The Lancashire Witches*, published in 1849, is based on the Pendle witch trials of 1612, and contains an account of a May-day festivity. Ainsworth had done his research and knew from Strutt, Douce and similar authorities what an early Stuart May Day should include. Maid Marion is Queen of the May, Robin Hood, Friar Tuck and all the other characters of that legend are present, and a hobby horse, fool and pipe-and-taborer, but Ainsworth grafted on what was clearly his own experience from his childhood. He had lived in the 1810s in King Street in the centre of Manchester, and in Cheetham, which had its own rushcart and morris dancers. The imagined May procession in his novel is anachronistically accompanied by a vividly described rushcart:[43]

> *In the rear of the performers in the pageant came the rush-cart, drawn by a team of eight stout horses, with their manes and tails tied with ribands, their collars fringed with red and yellow worsted, and hung with bells, which jingled blithely at every movement, and their heads decked with flowers. The cart itself consisted of an enormous pile of rushes, banded and twisted together, rising to a considerable height, and terminated in a sharp ridge, like the point of a Gothic window. The sides and top were decorated with flowers and ribands, and there were caves in the front and at the back, and on the space within them, which was covered with white paper, were strings of gaudy flowers, embedded in moss, amongst which were suspended all the ornaments and finery that could be collected for the occasion: to wit, flagons of silver, spoons, ladles, chains, watches, and bracelets, so as to make a brave and resplendent show. The wonder was, how articles of so much value would be trusted forth on*

---

[38] Lee, Jessie.
[39] Bamford, p. 152.
[40] Zemia, p. 482.

[41] Ridings, p. 137.
[42] Brierley, pp. 96, 97, 99.
[43] Ainsworth, William Harrison, pp. 26-27.

such an occasion; but nothing was ever lost. On the top of the rush-cart, and bestriding its sharp ridges, sat half a dozen men, habited somewhat like the morris-dancers, in garments bedecked with tinsel and ribands, holding garlands formed by hoops, decorated with flowers, and attached to poles ornamented with silver paper, cut into various figures and devices, and diminishing gradually in size as they rose to a point, where they were crowned with wreaths of daffodils.

The antiquaries' descriptions of maypoles were overridden by Ainsworth's first-hand experience of a hand-held one: 'a stout staff elevated some six feet above the head of the bearer, with a coronal of flowers atop, and four long garlands hanging down, each held by a morris-dancer'. The dancers' costumes have an admixture of Stuart and modern elements. The men are 'attired in a graceful costume, which set off their light active figures to advantage, consisting of a slashed jerkin of black and white velvet, with cut sleeves left open so as to reveal the snowy shirt beneath, white hose, and shoes of black Spanish leather with large roses. Ribands were everywhere in their dresses – ribands and tinsel adorned their caps, ribands crossed their hose, and ribands were tied around their arms. In either hand they held a long white handkerchief knotted with ribands.' There are also female morris dancers, 'habited in white, decorated like the dresses of the men; they had ribands and wreaths of flowers round their heads, bows in their hair, and in their hands long white knotted handkerchiefs'.

Ainsworth's account is so detailed that it must derive from close observation. It is one of the earliest pieces of evidence for the use of knotted handkerchiefs, a distinctive feature of north-west morris later in the century. Several of the earlier sources – including the pictures from Eccles and Lymm – have handkerchiefs held loose. In his poems describing Newton Heath wakes around 1830, Ridings refers to the dancers 'Waving white 'kerchiefs in the air'[44] and Frances Kemble wrote of the dancers at Heaton 'with their handkerchiefs flying',[45] each implying free movement. On the other hand, around 1840 the dancers at Hurst, near Ashton-under-Lyne, carried 'two large white cotton handkerchiefs, or cloths, tightly rolled up and tied at intervals with ribbons'.[46] In his account of 'Hazelworth' wakes, Ben Brierley writes of 'a flourishing of knotted white pocket handkerchiefs'.[47] One report from the 1830s says that the dancers:[48]

...came two by two, each provided with a small bell and a handkerchief, and, as the procession moved on, ... performed a symphony with the bell which they held in the one hand, while they kept time jointly by their own movements and the waving of their handkerchiefs. The dance chiefly consisted in each, as the procession moved on in a measured step, alternately turning quite round, and occupying the interval of these revolutions by waving the handkerchiefs, which was held by one corner, in a manner to harmonise with his own movements, all the time maintaining his part in the musical performance by the hand-bell which the Lancashire youths so well manage.

Although the combination of bell and handkerchief is otherwise unattested, this is a very circumstantial account by an eyewitness in the centre of Manchester, and it strongly suggests an unknotted handkerchief. The picture of rushcart and morris dancers in the centre of Manchester painted by Alexander Wilson in 1821 (Figure 17.5) also shows dancers holding handkerchiefs which appear to be unknotted. By 1850, however, the theatre critic of the *Manchester Times*, reviewing Macfarren's *King Charles the Second*, complained that the morris

[44] Ridings, p. 137.
[45] Kemble, 2:184.
[46] Howison and Bentley, 'North-west Morris', p. 47.
[47] Brierley, p. 99.
[48] Locke.

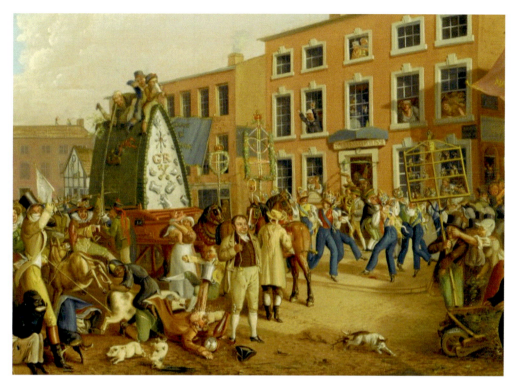

Figure 17.5: Alexander Wilson, 'Rush Bearing at Long Millgate, Manchester' (detail) (Image: Sphinx Fine Art).

dancers' costumes were '"too theatrical", and that the true English garb, with its knotted white handkerchief, effectively got up, as he could do it, would have harmonised better with the scene, and been equally striking'.[49]

Wilson's picture is very informative thanks to the clarity of detail. It shows six male dancers in trousers and lightweight shoes, wearing hats covered with flowers and with ribbons, surmounted by small garland hoops; they have white shirts with pleated sleeves, waistcoats of various colours, and blue sashes matching the trousers. They do not wear bells. Three more men in the same costume are standing behind the horses, and garlands are being carried on poles. The accompanying band of music includes a French horn player.

The lack of bells was a feature noticed by several commentators who expected them from their knowledge of antiquarian sources. Jessie Lee's account to William Hone spoke of 'a number of young men as Morris dancers, but without the appendage of bells, followed by young women bearing garlands'.[50] Annie Williamson's memories of Fallowfield included morris dancers; she espoused the theory of a 'Moorish' origin via Spain, but said 'it was not exactly a Morris Dance, because there were no castanets, in later days not even bells', implying a memory of their disappearance.[51]

Samuel Bamford spoke of 'the jingle of morrice-bells' on the evening before the rushcart procession, as 'the lads having borrowed each his collar of bells at neighbouring farm houses, would hang them on their necks and come jingling them home'.[52] However, it is more likely

[49] *Manchester Times*, 23 October 1850.
[50] Lee, Jessie.
[51] Williamson, p. 101.
[52] Bamford, p. 149.

that Bamford was referring to the bells worn by the drawers of the cart, as this too was a common practice. A newspaper correspondent of the *Manchester Times* said that in 1889 he had 'witnessed, many times, large parties of morris dancers with rush carts dance and prance and shake their bells along Yorkshire-street and Drake-street, Rochdale'.[53] Another writer the same year, describing Unsworth around 1840, mentions 'two or three couples of the boldest and bravest [yoked to the cart] in front with 'ringle bells' across their shoulders', in front of them, the band, and in front of the band, the morris dancers numbering about a dozen. He goes on to describe the dancers with their handkerchiefs, and the drawing team 'with jingling bells, the stretchers up, ribbons flying, they canter on, from side to side, with a lilting step'.[54]

Frances Kemble spoke in her memories from 1830 of the rushcart procession at Heaton with 'twelve country lads and lasses, dancing the real old morris dance'. They were accompanied by a band, a fool with bladder and stick, and two characters representing Adam and Eve.[55] An account probably relating to the Bolton area, published in 1849 but referring to events much earlier, also described both male and female dancers (with handkerchiefs, but with no mention of bells), and a fool, but a different supernumerary character:[56]

> The cart was drawn by four, and sometimes six fine horses, adorned with ribbons and bells, that jingled merrily as they walked. A dozen young men and women, streaming with ribbons and waving handkerchiefs, preceded the rush-cart, dancing the morris-dance. There was a shepherdess (with a lamb in a basket) carrying a crook, a bower borne over her head, and invariably two watches at her side; there was the fool, a hideous figure in a horrid mask, with onions for earrings, belabouring the crowd with an inflated bladder at the end of a pole.

In *Scarsdale*, his 1860 novel of Pennine community life, Sir James Kay-Shuttleworth, who was born in Rochdale, described the rushcart procession. Thirty young men in pairs, in white shirts, ribbons and flowered hats, were yoked in couples, holding a stave between them which was attached to a rope with which to draw the cart. They were practising some dances. Another 30 men were in couples behind the cart, to hold it on downhill stretches. Four men held poles from which hung a large banner depicting Scarsdale scenes and emblems. A fool was mounted on a donkey. 'Before the cart started for Rochdale ... a country dance was formed on each side of the road, it being the privilege of the young men yoked in the cart to choose their partners from the prettiest country girls – nothing loth for such a distinction'. The dance apparently lasted half an hour.[57]

A picture showing similar yoked pairs and a banner appeared in a descriptive account of festivities around Bury published in 1844 (Figure 17.6). It is clear that the men holding the banner are dancing as they proceed. The text accompanying the picture confirms the fool riding a donkey, and describes the young men (30 or 40, yoked in couples) 'gaily dressed, the favourite style being straw hats with light blue ribbons, white shirt sleeves tied with many-coloured ribbons, the brightest handkerchiefs possible for sashes, and ribbons again below the knee'. They are flanked by others dressed similarly, carrying whips.[58]

The ambiguities in and discrepancies between the different accounts suggest a widespread practice of morris dancing embedded in an overarching cultural milieu centred around rushcarts. The men pulling the carts (when horses were not used), or those in similar costume accompanying it, cracking whips, carrying banners, or engaged specifically as 'morris

[53] L., T.
[54] H., W.
[55] Kemble, 2:184.
[56] Grandmamma, p. 90.
[57] Shuttleworth, 1:201-03.
[58] *Pictorial History*, pp. 249-50.

Figure 17.6: 'Rushbearing' (in The Pictorial History of the County of Lancashire, *p. 249. London: Routledge, 1844).*

dancers', and the women in the procession, carrying garlands and/or dancing, all fell under a general penumbra which observers, or the participants themselves, might characterize as 'morris dancing'. Those drawing the cart were often described as carrying bells; the morris dancers, when separately identified, less so. Any of them – morris dancers proper, whippers, banner and garland carriers, cart-drawers, might dance in procession, and might take part in set-piece dances at the various halts along the way. The second edition of Edward Baines's history of Lancashire, edited by John Harland in 1868, was explicit in describing the rushcart procession in Rochdale, pausing to dance at inns along the route:[59]

> ... a kind of obtuse pyramid of rushes, erected on a cart, is highly ornamented in front, and surmounted by a splendid garland. To the vehicle so laden a number of young men, from thirty to forty, wearing white jackets and ornamented with silver articles, ribbons, and flowers, are harnessed in pairs. ... The procession then advances to the town, and, on arriving in front of each of the inns, a kind of morris-dance is performed by the men in harness, who jingle copper bells, and beat, or rather stamp, time with their wooden shoes – the clown, who is dressed in fancy attire, all the while collecting money to refresh the actors in the grotesque exhibition.

One element specifically identified with the morris dance at these events was the tune. Of course, dozens of popular tunes in common currency were used, as the accounts above show, but there are also several references to two distinct pieces of music used in association with the dance. Burton, quoting John Higson's account of the rushcart at Gorton in 1804, says that 'the dancers, in couples, tripped it on the "light fantastic toe" to the tune of the "Morris dance", etc.' In 1859 Samuel Bamford gave the words to the tune at Middleton:[60]

> *My new shoon they are so good,*
> *I cou'd doance morris if I wou'd;*
> *An' if hat an' sark be drest,*
> *I will doance morris wi' the best.*

These are words to the tune later identified by Anne Gilchrist as 'Long Morris' (Figure 17.7).

[59] Baines, 1:503.   [60] Bamford, p. 152.

i. LONG MORRIS

Moston Rush-cart Version of Tune

(*Sung*) Cheese and bread, the old cow's head,   Roast - ed in a lan - tern,
or Mor-ris Dance is a ve - ry pret-ty tune,   I can dance in my new shoon,

lan - tern;   A bit for me and a bit for thee, And a bit for mor-ris
my new shoon;   This is it, and that is it, And this is mor-ris

dan - cers,   A bit for me, &c.
dan-cing;   My old fa - ther broke his leg, And so it was a-chan-cing.

Figure 17.7: 'Long Morris' (in Anne G. Gilchrist, 'The Lancashire Rush-Cart and Morris-Dance', Journal of the English Folk Dance Society, 2nd series, 1 (1927): 17-27 (p. 17)).

Gilchrist points out that the tune, widely used in the north-west to accompany the processional dance, is a variant of that used in the Helston furry dance in Cornwall; it is also used by morris dancers in Derbyshire, for example the Derbyshire morris dance 'Winster Processional'.[61] In 1840 Chappell published a version of it in his *A Collection of English National Airs* as 'A morris dance, common in Lancashire and Derbyshire'.[62] Its use over a wide area suggests a long-standing association with the morris dance.

The second distinctive tune, also reproduced by Gilchrist, is 'Cross Morris' (Figure 17.8). This is a specific tune used to conclude the dance. No matter what the tune being played, at the call to 'cross morris' the music switches to this tune and a specific sequence of steps is performed, during which the dancers switch sides and return.

ii. CROSS MORRIS

Figure 17.8: 'Cross Morris' (in Anne G. Gilchrist, 'The Lancashire Rush-Cart and Morris-Dance', Journal of the English Folk Dance Society, 2nd series, 1 (1927): 17-27 (p. 17)).

[61] Gilchrist, 'Lancashire Rush-cart', p. 23; Sharp, 'Winster Morris Dance'.

[62] Chappell, 1:52, 2:109.

Writing of the dancers at Unsworth around 1840, 'W.H.' described the band 'playing Morris dance ... The dancers cross and cross, and step along with a rhythmic trip'.[63] More explicitly, Elijah Ridings's poem about the wakes mentions not just 'crossing here, re-crossing there' but also exhorts the dancers 'Come bustle, lads, for one dance more, / And then *cross morris* three times o'er'.[64] In his *Tales and Sketches of Lancashire Life* Ben Brierley recalled exactly the same command:[65]

> *I hear Old Senty call out, 'Cross Morris, three times o'er', and the band suddenly changes its tune, and there is a shuffling of feet and a rustling of ribbons, and a flourishing of knotted white pocket handkerchiefs, that is gladdening to look upon and listen to.*

It is only towards the end of the century that we find more detailed evidence for the kinds of steps and figures used. The complexity surviving then (for which see Chapter 24) suggests that in this period the community support around the performance of morris dancing in the north-west matched that of the Whitsun-ale morris in the maintenance of high standards of costume, artistry and choreography.

In January 1844 the Manchester Mechanics' Institution (a body established in 1824 to provide practical technical and scientific education, mainly to young workers) introduced to its annual Christmas party some 'novel associations ... the yule-log, the boar's head, the morris-dance, and the wassail-bowl.'[66] By 1849 these elements had become a major part of the evening's entertainment. There were 'the boar's head and carol, the wassail bowl, Old Father Christmas, Snap Dragon, and his mummers, ancient play of St George & the Dragon, the waits, children at haymaking, harvest home, Maid Marian and the morris dance, dancing round the maypole, sword dancing, hand-bell ringing'.[67] Non-members' tickets for the event at the Free Trade Hall were much in demand, selling at eight times their face value of 2s 6d.[68] It even made the pages of the *Illustrated London News*:[69]

> *A maypole, 'wreathed with garlands gay', was erected in the centre of the hall; and Maid Marian, as 'Queen of the May', awarded her presents and favours. The 'morris dance' was performed by about twenty rustics, decked with ribbons, bells, sashes, and other badges; and, as they danced, they sang a portion of an old song. So well was this dance liked, that it was loudly encored. 'The sword dance', which still lingers as a Christmas custom in the counties of Northumberland and Durham, was given by a number of youths in appropriate attire, decorated with ribbons of the gayest hues.*

The 'rustics' were in fact boys from the factory of the major cotton manufacturer J.A. Turner who were enrolled in the Mechanics' Institution, and 'the lads who danced the morris dance might be found at night in the classes, studying arithmetic'. There were 16 of them, 'dressed in white trousers, their hats decked with ribbons, and their coats studded all over with little tinkling bells', who danced around the maypole. This might be seen as a theatrical representation bearing little relation to the dances in the local community, but in 1852 a report referred to the 'agreeable chorus' of the morris tune, "The Morris dance is a very pretty tune, / Which I can dance in my new shoon' – which are the words to the 'Long Morris' referred to above. The authenticity was enhanced by the rushcart, which in 1849 was 'no mimic affair, but a real rush cart constructed for the festivity by Mr. Partington, of Whitley-lane, who keeps the

[63] H., W.
[64] Ridings, pp. 137, 139.
[65] Brierley, p. 99.
[66] *Manchester Times*, 20 January 1844.

[67] *Manchester Courier*, 30 December 1848.
[68] *Manchester Courier*, 6 January 1849.
[69] *Illustrated London News*, 13 January 1849.

inn there, known as The Rush Cart, whose father before him was a celebrated builder of those remnants of old custom, and who himself declared this to be a perfect model'. The same boys performed a sword dance, but we have no further information about the kind of dance they actually did, nor about the source of it.[70]

The performances at the Mechanics' Institution Christmas parties blended elements of pageant and theatre with the experience of many of the participants and audience who would have seen morris dancers and rushcarts in the streets of the city for themselves, although the newspaper's report suggests that rushcarts were already in decline. The performances at the Christmas parties foreshadow the further evolution of morris dancing in the north-west, but to put them in perspective we need first to look at developments in the staging of fêtes and festivals across the country during the century.

[70] *Manchester Courier*, 6 January 1849; *Manchester Courier*,
7 February 1849; *Manchester Courier*, 18 December 1852.

Chapter 18

Fêtes and festivals

We left the theatrical scene with morris dances and maypoles intertwined on the stage at the pleasure gardens and at major fêtes such as the Scottish fête at Holland Park in 1851, but falling from favour in the London theatres at least. Morris dancing remained popular at the somewhat more down-market pleasure grounds. These could still attract the chief dancing masters: Niccolo Deulin was responsible for the 'rural fete, called May-day, or Village Sports, including the Old English Morris Dance' in the Royal Grecian Saloon at the Eagle Tavern on 3 May 1843.[1] The proprietor of the tavern was T. Rouse, and three years later he was at the White Conduit Gardens, where he had 'a splendid maypole, around which the Old English morris-dancers, accompanied by Friar Tuck and Little John, marched in rustic procession'.[2] The Royal Pavilion Gardens at North Woolwich boasted 'the Maypole and Morris Dance, by Artistes of celebrity' in 1856, and the same in 1859, naming eight leading women and a *corps de ballet*.[3] The gardens continued to stage morris dances until at least 1880.[4] The South London Palace in 1870 put on a ballet inspired by Tennyson's 'The May Queen', in which 'Little Eva, a charming little dancer, is crowned the "Queen of May"'. She and four other women led a *corps de ballet* of nearly fifty artistes, and 'The Morris dance, in which they indulge, is exceedingly pretty, and the complicated devices into which the coloured ribbons are twisted would put the celebrated Gordian knot completely in the shade'.[5]

Provincial pleasure gardens presented similar events. On Whit Monday in 1848 the *Stamford Mercury* announced that the proprietor of the Vauxhall gardens at Boston 'intends bringing forward the old English morris dance, in illustration of the manners of the 16th and 17th centuries; introducing among other characters Jack in the Green, Margery Maypole, and Much the Miller'.[6] In 1852 a 'Gorgeous carnival' at Bingley Hall in Birmingham included a *grand bal masque* with 'the old English May pole dance ... introduced by a Company of Morris Dancers, engaged for the occasion'.[7]

In the provinces, however, short festivals and fêtes on holidays and for charitable purposes were now more characteristic arenas for morris dances than the permanent venues. Some of these were recorded relatively early in the century. In 1817 Major Mason, of Necton Hall in Norfolk, attempted to impose some decorum to the local Whitsuntide festivities by instituting the 'Necton Guild'. He introduced a maypole and morris dancing with other 'rustic sports' which in 1820 attracted a 'highly respectable assemblage of genteel company' according to the *Norfolk Chronicle*.[8] Heading the procession to Necton Hall were 'Master Beadle of the Guild, with a halberd; six boys and girls, Maypole dancers, two and two, hand in hand; Band of Music; Maskers, or morris-dancers fancifully attired, two and two', followed by several other dignitaries, office-holders and groups, including a second set of morris dancers. A first-hand sketch of the event (Figure 18.1) shows a slightly different scene. Dancers dance about the maypole (which is of the older kind, with garlands and no ribbons) but these are said to be

---

[1] *Morning Advertiser*, 3 May 1843.
[2] *Morning Advertiser*, 16 September 1846.
[3] *Morning Advertiser*, 8 September 1856; *Shoreditch Observer*, 18 June 1859.
[4] *Referee*, 6 September 1880.
[5] *Era*, 1 May 1870.
[6] *Stamford Mercury*, 9 June 1848.
[7] *Aris's Birmingham Gazette*, 22 March 1852.
[8] *Norfolk Chronicle*, 27 May 1820.

Figure 18.1: 'Necton Guild' (in William Hone, The Every Day Book, *ii, 336. London: William Tegg, [1868])*

the morris dancers 'in grotesque dresses; the men with fanciful figured print waistcoat and small clothes, decked with bows; and the women in coloured skirts, trimmed like stage dresses for Spanish girls, with French toques instead of caps'. [9] A figure wearing bells accompanies a maid in front of the dancers. The event was very much dependent upon the initiative of Major Mason. When he and his family were abroad at the time of the 1824 guild, 'the procession ... was omitted; "the Mayor" and his retinue of morris dancers, &c., not appearing *en costume*', though 16 children at the school founded by him did dance around the maypole. [10]

[9] K., 'Necton Guild'.

[10] *Norfolk Chronicle*, 12 June 1824.

By the mid century a variety of celebrations was engaging morris dancers. Military bands and an equestrian troop entertained the spectators who attended 'numerously and very respectably' the 'Grand rural fete' of the Printers' Pension Society at Bromley in 1846, and 'the morris dancers also met their share of praise'.[11] Undergraduates at Trinity College, Cambridge erected a maypole in 1844 and guided a large number of children around it, led by 'one pretty little girl, dressed grotesquely as "Maid Marian", with her three colleagues after the old morris dance fashion'.[12]

In 1860 the Windsor and Eton Literary and Scientific Institution held a fete at Ankerwyke which made only a modest profit (partly on account of poor weather) of just over £12 on an expenditure of nearly £71. The largest element of expenditure was on music (just over £24) but £8 10s was also spent in hiring morris dancers.[13] In Bury St Edmunds at the friendly societies' gala in 1870 a 'miniature ballet troupe (introduced this year for the first time) ... took the hearts of the ladies by storm by their graceful movements in the Garland dance and the May Pole Morris dance, once so popular a pastime in old England'.[14]

The Deputy Lieutenant of Kent, Thomas Maryon Wilson, opened his grounds at Old Charlton for a fête in 1857 in aid of the Funds of the Royal Kent Dispensary, which 'succeeded in engaging the services of a Grand Ballet company' including 'sets of morris dancers', as well as other attractions such as acrobats, minstrels and a balloon ascent. Three years later he hosted a similar event, this time in aid of the Charlton 28th Kent Rifle Volunteers, with maypole and morris dancing, and this time the dancers were identified as 'twelve of Mr. Chapino's pupils'. They appeared again the following year, when 'the grand maypole and morris dance by M. Chapino's ballet troupe, who some time since performed at the Crystal Palace, received great applause'.[15]

M. Chapino's pupils were back at the Crystal Palace in 1862 when they performed a 'petite ballet divertissement' and there was a morris dance. This was an event directed by Nelson Lee,[16] a theatre manager who also arranged many of the Crystal Palace entertainments and wrote over two hundred pantomimes.[17] He collaborated with Chapino in providing a package of entertainments at dozens of fêtes across England, frequently including morris and maypole dances. Although Lee was organizing fête entertainments before 1860, the first joint enterprise we know of was at Colnbrook near Slough in 1861:[18]

> Our old friend Mr. Nelson Lee had been applied to for his aid ... but was confined only to the obtaining of Mons. Chapino's Ballet Troupe, and this of itself was no mean attraction. During the afternoon they performed in admirable style 'the Maypole dance', 'the morris dance', 'the Scotch dance' and 'Sir Roger de Coverley', and were vociferously cheered during the execution of each. We were sorry to find the little interesting trippers had not a stage erected for them, as it would have been less arduous for them to go through their difficult evolutions ... We can only say the pupils did their task admirably, and reflected great credit on their instructor, Mons. Chapino.

By the time of the Foresters' Fete at Rickmansworth in 1865 the newspapers were able to speak of 'Mr Lee's attractive galaxy of performers' which included 'the old English morris

---

[11] *West Kent Guardian*, 18 July 1846.
[12] *Devizes and Wiltshire Gazette*, 23 May 1844.
[13] *Windsor and Eton Express*, 3 November 1860.
[14] *Bury Free Press*, 23 July 1870.

[15] *Morning Chronicle*, 27 June 1857; *Morning Chronicle*, 13 September 1860; *Naval & Military Gazette*, 24 August 1861.
[16] *London Evening Standard*, 10 June 1862.
[17] 'Mr. Nelson Lee'; 'Lee, Nelson'.
[18] *Uxbridge & West Drayton Gazette*, 10 August 1861.

dance' by the Chapino Ballet Troupe.[19] At Hounslow the following year 'An old English Morris dance by M. Chapino's fairy tribe brought Mr. Nelson Lee's division of the day's amusement to an end'.[20] The *Middlesex Chronicle* reported that at Kneller Hall Park in Whitton in 1867 Lee's entertainment included a comical concert, a maypole dance by Chapino's 'Troupe of Juveniles', a second concert, a minstrel show, Chapino's troupe returning for a morris dance, clowns, the 'amazing Lightning Zouave Drill' by 'Captain Austin, a distinguished American officer', more comedy, and concluding with Chapino's troupe once again performing the 'Old English dance of Sir Roger de Coverley'.[21] In 1871 the organizers of the Newbury Flower Show, seeking additional attractions, 'engaged Mr. Nelson Lee, who brought down a company, including a Japannese [*sic*] juggler, ballet and morris dancers, and punch and judy'.[22]

The press had difficulty with Chapino's name. At Woburn on 28 July 1862 'An old morris dance was provided by M. Champino's pupils' and the Denham fete the following day had 'the morris-dance by M. Chipino's pupils'. In 1867 'M. Chapiono's ballet troupe' were performing the dances.[23] Their appearances were not confined to the home counties; they may even have ventured as far north as Bradford in Yorkshire in 1866, where a gala included 'Champion's grand ballet troupe' performing morris and maypole dances.[24] In December 1862 they were certainly in Nottingham, headlining for five nights' entertainment at the Mechanics' Hall, performing their usual mix of maypole, morris and dances of all the nations of the British Isles.[25] They did not perform solely under Lee's management; in 1870 they were part of the London Star Gala company's programme at the Chertsey Literary and Scientific Institution annual fête.[26]

'Chapino' was in fact Charles Lupino, part of a family with extensive theatrical dancing connections.[27] His troupe (he was joint proprietor of a 'College for Dancing') were juveniles. At the Uxbridge Philanthropic Festival in 1866 the weather was unfavourable, and 'the Chapino band accomplished an Old English Morris dance under difficulties and with many falls, which the charming and diminutive dancers took all in good part, and appeared to regard as fun'.[28] Many of the dancers at such events were juveniles, like Chapino's troupe. At the People's Fête in Sheffield in 1858 the 'Enfant Corps Danseuse' performed 'a new Set of Figure and Costume Dances, introducing the Morris Dance, &c.'[29]

Theatrical impresarios like Nelson Lee were well placed to provide such entertainments. At the Grand Floral Fête in Sittingbourne in 1860 'Mr. J. Seaton, Professor of Callisthenics, from her Majesty's Theatre', was responsible for the morris dancing, old English sports, archery, bowls, football and Aunt Sally.[30] Further afield, 'Miss Lizzie Gilbert's Liliputian Ballet Troupe', 12 strong, offered 'their successful Summer spectacle, "A May-Day Festival, or Rustic Revels on the Village Green", introducing ... Roger de Coverley, Garland Dance, the May-pole Plaiting, the Morris Dance, and many other pretty and picturesque groupings' at Bristol Zoo in 1870. A month later they presented the spectacle at the Oddfellows' Fête in Cirencester.[31] In a theatrical engagement at the Alhambra Palace in Hull in 1873 they had become 'Miss

[19] *Herts Guardian*, 5 August 1865; *Uxbridge & West Drayton Gazette*, 29 July 1865.
[20] *Uxbridge & West Drayton Gazette*, 17 July 1866.
[21] *Middlesex Chronicle*, 20 July 1867.
[22] *Newbury Weekly News*, 31 August 1871.
[23] *Bedfordshire Mercury*, 2 August 1862; *Windsor and Eton Express*, 2 August 1862; *Berkshire Chronicle*, 22 June 1867.
[24] *Leeds Times*, 26 May 1866.

[25] *Nottingham Journal*, 2 December 1862.
[26] *Surrey Advertiser*, 9 July 1870.
[27] Judge, 'Tradition', p. 8.
[28] 'Balls'; *Uxbridge & West Drayton Gazette*, 4 August 1866.
[29] *Sheffield Daily Telegraph*, 8 July 1858.
[30] *Maidstone Journal*, 25 August 1860.
[31] *Western Daily Press*, 3 June 1870; *Wilts and Gloucestershire Standard*, 18 June 1870.

Lizzie Gilbert's world-famed juvenile ballet troupe (12 in number) from the Crystal Palace'.[32] At Allen's Varieties, Burnley, six years after that they had 'a new ballet, entitled, 'The Morris Dancers', with new songs, choruses and entirely new dresses', and two months later were performing in Morecambe Gardens.[33] 'Madame Ramsden's celebrated ballet troupe of thirty children, introducing "La Petite Ninny" (the youngest singer and dancer in the world)' performed 'The Gathering of the Clans', maypole and morris dances at the Queen's Recreation Grounds in Barnsley in July 1870 and at the Botanical Gardens in Sheffield the following month, advertising themselves as 'at liberty for fetes and galas'.[34] In the 1880s Madame Katti Lanner's pupils were providing the morris dances at the Crystal Palace, in 1883 as part of a 'May Queen' opera.[35]

Providing juvenile morris and maypole dancers was a flourishing business across the country. In 1864 the Midland Counties Gala Company organized an event at Witham in Lincolnshire which included 'morris dances by a band of children'.[36] Sutherland's sixteen-strong Juvenile Ballet Troupe were advertising their services including morris and maypole dances, jigs and gavottes for theatres, halls and fetes in May 1890. By December there were 20 in the company and they had added flings, hornpipes and Chinese dances to their repertoire for Christmas.[37] The following year Sutherland wrote an 'original, romantic, domestic drama', *Donnybrook*, with morris dances and Irish jigs arranged by his wife. This was staged at Chatham in August not with the ballet troupe, but with 20 local children. The same arrangement was in place at the staging in Hereford in February 1893 and with 30 local children at Hartlepool in February 1894.[38]

A wider variety of people evidently now felt able to teach morris dances to young people. For example, the annual temperance fête at Rippingale in Lincolnshire in the late 1890s had 21 boy morris dancers taught by the local schoolmaster.[39] The use of local children was also facilitated by the presence of local dancing academies offering morris dances among their repertoires. The Misses Thompson arrived in Burton-on-Trent from London in 1893 to open their Academy of Dancing, offering tuition not just in all the fashionable ballroom dances but also a morris dance, tambourine dance and skirt dances in Burton and surrounding towns. Two years later they had added highland fling, Irish jig, gipsy dance and castanet and fan dances to their offering.[40]

The Ladies College at Hackney may well have embraced such an opportunity. At its annual concert and soirée in 1872 over 200 pupils took part in their morris dance.[41] At the Farningham May Queen festival in Kent at the Home for Little Boys in 1879, the morris dancers who danced around the maypole were boys from the school naval training ship Shaftesbury, from the Electric Telegraph Department and from the Royal Military Asylum (for children of serving soldiers).[42] For Ye Olde Englishe Fayre organized with full civic support in Banbury in 1882, a troupe of 24 children in 'appropriate' costumes underwent several weeks' training, while eight morris dancers and their piper were 'drilled under the eye of an experienced manager',

[32] *Hull Packet*, 28 February 1873.
[33] *Burnley Express*, 22 March 1879; *Bradford Observer*, 29 May 1879.
[34] *Barnsley Independent*, 30 July 1870; *Era*, 31 July 1870.
[35] *Morning Post*, 20 October 1883; *Morning Post*, 4 August 1885.
[36] *Stamford Mercury*, 10 June 1864.
[37] *Era*, 31 May 1890; *Stage*, 19 September 1890.

[38] *Chatham News*, 22 August 1891; *Hereford Journal*, 18 February 1893; *Hartlepool Northern Daily Mail*, 6 February 1894.
[39] *Grantham Journal*, 6 July 1895.
[40] *Burton Chronicle*, 31 August 1893; *Burton Chronicle*, 29 August 1895.
[41] *Hackney and Kingsland Gazette*, 10 January 1872.
[42] *Morning Post*, 19 May 1879.

and were so popular that an encore was demanded.[43] At the distinctly middle-class Primrose League fête in Epping in 1892 'Mrs Water's amateur troupe' performed some morris dances. They appeared again 18 months later at a fancy-dress ball in aid of the Chipping Ongar Cricket Club, explicitly named as 'Mrs. Waters' Morris Dancers', and three weeks after that 'Mrs. Waters and her troupe of old English morris dances' [sic] performed at a Sawbridgeworth Primrose League meeting.[44] The use of children emphasised the evocation of an image of innocent and carefree bygone times.

There were many events where morris dancers appeared but we simply do not know if they were amateurs, professionals, semi-professionals, adults or children, nor what kind of performance was involved. One such was the Christmas treat at the Andover workhouse in 1881, when '"Ye anciente Morris Dancers" gave the delighted inmates a dramatic representation of "Kinge George of Merrie England"' – this may have been a mummers' play. Morris dancers appeared along with Turks, Zulus, Robin Hood and others in a Guy Fawkes procession in Maidstone in 1883.[45] The Grand Easter Festival at the Royal Agricultural Hall in Islington advertised for 'thirty-two ladies, for maypole and morris dancing' in 1888.[46]

One series of events which provides more information is the 'Grand Carnival and Torchlight Procession' at Ryde on the Isle of Wight at the end of the 1880s. In 1888 this included an 'Arab Chief ...; car [with] – Red Riding Hood – performances en route; twelve ghosts; Ryde Town Band; twelve morris dancers, one hundred children with Chinese lanterns, tambourines, &c. and other delights'.[47] The following year the participants were organized into troupes. One troupe consisted of 'eight dancing birds covered with bells, ridden by four gentlemen and four ladies dressed as frogs, foxes, dogs, cats and rabbits; these birds also danced Sir Roger de Coverley', against whom the troupe of 'twelve morris dancers in grotesque and fancy dresses, dancing and singing' must surely have struggled.[48] Three months later a case came to court in which the local tailor successfully sued one of the organizers for payment. He had spent 5s 6d on twelve suits for the morris dancers, who were all men; but said he had also had to train the dancers and that 'time at rehearsals, going to Shanklin to teach eight morris dancers [to] dance Sir Roger de Coverley' also merited payment. It's quite clear that in his mind at least, dancing birds covered with bells and ridden by assorted animals were as much morris dancers as the twelve in 'ordinary' grotesque dresses, and that 'Sir Roger de Coverley' was a morris-dance tune.[49]

Sherborne in Dorset instituted a major series of May-day pageants in the 1860s with a Jack-in-the-Green, maypole, May Queen with maids of honour, Lord of Misrule, Robin Hood and company, morris dancers and mummers, drawn from the children of the local National Schools.[50] The high point of this genre of popular entertainment was probably the series of carnivals organized during the 1890s at St Mary Cray in Kent by the local paper-mill owner E.H. Joynson. Like Sherborne, it had the panoply of May-day (and other) characters: Jack-in-the-Green, Robin Hood and entourage, John Barleycorn, jester, hobby horse, maids of honour – 'twelve dainty little maidens in white dresses, with crowns and garlands of summer flowers, and the twelve healthy country lads in smock frocks and hats, heavy boots and grey stockings,

[43] *Banbury Guardian*, 20 April 1882; *Banbury Guardian*, 27 April 1882.
[44] *Chelmsford Chronicle*, 24 June 1892; *Chelmsford Chronicle*, 26 January 1894; *East Anglian Daily Times*, 17 February 1894.
[45] *Montgomeryshire Express*, 20 November 1883.
[46] *Era*, 17 March 1888.
[47] *Isle of Wight Observer*, 18 August 1888.
[48] *Isle of Wight County Press*, 17 August 1889.
[49] *Isle of Wight County Press*, 9 November 1889; *Portsmouth Evening News*, 7 November 1889.
[50] *Sherborne Mercury*, 7 May 1861.

with whom they were to plait the Maypole'. There were 'six boys with animal heads ... and little bells at their wrists and ankles'. A group of 32 morris dancers appeared, and in an echo of earlier fêtes, they were taught by the *maître de ballet* at Drury Lane Theatre, Paul Valentine.[51] The female maypole dancers wore semi-classical costumes, and an accompanying illustration in the local newspaper showed that these had more of a Grecian than English country look. The news report stated that Joynson had himself designed all the costumes.[52] *The Era* said that Valentine's morris dance had been voted 'the biggest thing in the show', with three encores.[53] The following year's carnival attracted over 25,000 visitors and merited an entire special edition of the local newspaper. There were 16 morris-dance girls wearing bodices and skirts in various pastel shades and 30 adult males comprising Robin Hood's 'merrie men', who wore brown jerkins and green breeches, as did the 16 male morris dancers, also wearing feathered hats. Great play was made of the dances, again arranged by Paul Valentine, and conducted by Joynson himself. There were maypole dances, pastoral dances, rose dances, card dances, and morris dances. Rather enigmatically, 'A new feature was introduced into the Morris Dances this year, in the shape of a fantastic and pretty step'.[54] The *Kentish Mercury* gave a more detailed account:[55]

> Very quaint and pretty was the sight as the couples tripped in procession up the field, the bright colours of the maidens' figured gowns harmonising well with the pale green and stone coloured tunics of their partners. Particularly fascinating was the rhythm of the measure, danced to the strains of the old air by Godfrey known as 'The Curly-headed Plough Boy'. The men held a staff in each hand, and tapped those of their comrades as they passed one another in turn, the maidens meanwhile footing it in the centre of the circle. Then, with a change in the music, each girl robbed her partner of a staff, and again the couples passed in reversing circles, the tapping of the sticks being repeated with the same pleasing effect. At the conclusion of the Dance, whose various graceful figures and poses we would fain describe in detail, the couples returned in procession down the field, and made their bow to the occupants of the grandstand, who heartily applauded their performance.

Fred Godfrey was the bandmaster of the Coldstream Guards and a prolific composer and in this case, arranger. By 1895 – the last year of which we have a report – the carnival had become a 'children's carnival', the morris dance was being performed by 16 children of each sex. The boys wore blue or red striped tunics and red and white breeches, the girls dresses in pastel shades.[56]

The development of morris in fêtes and festivals saw the imagined morris of the London professionals reach out to embrace juveniles in May-day and other celebrations across the country. This helps to put into a broader context the evolution of morris dancing in Derbyshire and in the north-west in the latter half of the 19th century, where the morris fêtes came into contact with the dance in its community manifestations, and to which we shall now turn.

The north-west corner of Derbyshire looks across to the industrial towns circling Manchester, and the communities of the district participated in the rushbearing and associated traditions of that region. We have encountered morris dancing in that style at Chapel-en-le-Frith, Glossop, Hayfield and New Mills. In the south-east of the county there were traces of the Christmas

51   *Bromley & District Times*, 8 May 1891.
52   *Graphic*, 9 May 1891.
53   *Era*, 9 May 1891.
54   *Bromley & District Times*, 10 May 1892.
55   *Kentish Mercury*, 13 May 1892.
56   *Bromley & District Times*, 14 June 1895.

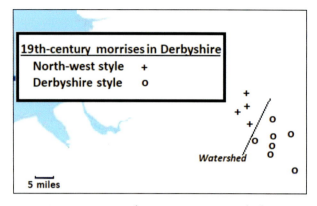

Figure 18.2: Nineteenth-century morrises in Derbyshire

morris-dancing traditions associated with the east of England. Between the two there is a small group of predominantly mining communities in the eastern Peak district whose morris dances exhibited distinctive features. They are geographically close to the rushbearing communities but lie on the other side of the line of the watershed separating west-flowing from east-flowing rivers, connected by the pass at Bar Moor Clough (Figure 18.2).

The earliest nineteenth-century reference is from Eyam. This is the village to which the ambiguous entry in the 1743 accounts of Richard Temple of Stowe may relate (p. 169). In 1802 several newspapers reported the death of Edward Dooley, a 'poor and infirm' miner who was playing the fiddle for a group of young men at a hilltop known as Eyam Edge, practising for an event the following Monday, when 'he suddenly laid down his fiddle, stretched himself, and expired'. An oratorio was due to be performed in a benefit concert for him at the parish church the following day, and this went ahead for the support of his aged mother.[57] Although described as 'infirm', he was only 37; the record of his burial on 30 August 1802 states that he was a 'Musician who died as he was going to play to some young People the Morris dance'.[58] The only other indication of dancing at Eyam is an 1873 antiquarian enquiry as to whether morris dancing was still practised there, and this enquiry probably derived ultimately from the 1802 reports.[59]

The only indication of rushbearing in these communities of the eastern Peak district comes much earlier, in the middle of the 18th century. The Castleton garland ceremony is well attested in the 19th century without any association with rushbearing, but in 1749 the Castleton churchwardens' accounts have:[60]

	£	s	d
Pd. At the Rush Cart for ale	0	1	8
Pd. For an iron Rod to hang ye singers [sc. ringers] garland in	0	0	8

Garlands are often associated with rushcart customs, but these usually take place in wakes weeks (the first week in September in Castleton), and none has the type of garland associated with Castleton since descriptive records began, which adorns the entire top half of the body of a man on horseback.

Most of what we know of the history of the Castleton garland custom comes from an article by Sidney Addy, who witnessed the event in 1900 and interviewed several of the participants and the older inhabitants of the village.[61] Addy described how a 'King' and 'Queen' ride around the village on 29 May, the King wearing the bell-shaped garland of flowers covering his head and upper body. They proceed around the village accompanied by morris dancers and a band,

[57] *Derby Mercury*, 9 September 1802.
[58] 'Edward Dooley'.
[59] Derwent.
[60] Robinson, Joseph Barlow, p. 21.
[61] Addy and Kidson.

after which the garland is hoisted to the top of the church tower, where it is left on display. The date of 29 May, and the custom of villagers' wearing sprigs of oak leaf, strongly indicate a link with the celebration of Oak Apple Day arising from the Restoration in 1660, but local historian Frank Parker has argued that the wearing of oak could equally be an expression of support for George III from 1760 on.[62] What is certain is that the custom continued to evolve throughout the 19th century and beyond.

Addy found evidence for the existence of the different elements of the custom at least from the early years of the 19th century, but he found no indication of a link with rushbearing during that time. The garland custom was overseen by the bell-ringers of the church, as indicated in the 1749 churchwardens' entry. The dancers were retinue to the 'King' and 'Queen', but Addy was told that until about 1850 the characters were called simply 'the man and woman', and that ringers called them 'the man that carries the garland' and 'the lady'. The woman/Queen was in fact male, and the development from one to the other is indicated by the fact that the crown worn by the character was a recent innovation in Addy's day, the character having worn a bonnet until 1896. A description of the costume in 1883 said:[63]

> The King wore a scarlet jacket covered with rosettes and streamers of ribbon ... Her Majesty the Queen ... wore a gaily trimmed bonnet, and veil, a cape, printed dress, and other elegant female attire, besides a scarlet parasol and a bouquet of flowers.

Ostensibly the King and Queen were elected each year but it was customary to elect the same people every time, if possible. The morris dancers were 'old men dressed in their Sunday clothes' according to one of Addy's informants; 'elderly men and young men' according to the 1883 report. There are no further indications of the costume, or of bells worn or handkerchiefs held. Men with besoms used to precede them to clear the way, but by Addy's time the Queen circling the dancers fulfilled that role. The tune used during the procession was a variant on the 'Long Morris' tune of the north-west. Addy was told that the dance was 'two steps out and two steps in, and then they twist around'.

The most elaborate expression of the distinctive Derbyshire morris is that of Winster. Winster too had a King (dressed in military costume) and Queen, but on foot, not mounted. A witch also took part, with blackened face and a besom, and a fool dressed as a pierrot clown. There were 16 dancers in two files of eight; the dancers in the left file wore flowered hats and were known as the 'ladies' side, but all the roles were taken by men.[64] A fool is not unexpected but the presence of a witch character is unusual. We saw earlier that dancers in Plough Monday customs sometimes had a witch as a 'Maid Marion' character, but that is all. The men in the Winster 'ladies' side did not cross-dress like the Plough Monday dancers, but simply added the token flowers to their hats.

Our earliest knowledge of the Winster dance is only from 1863, when the *Derby Mercury* reported that 'The morris dancers (the young men of the place) added greatly to the hilarity of the feast. Their characteristic parts were well sustained, their dresses smart in the extreme, their dancing and music very good, and they collected nearly [£]20'.[65] Performance was apparently intermittent in the 19th century (and certainly in the 20th). At the next reference ten years later, in 1873, the report suggests that this is a revival of a defunct practice:[66]

---

[62] Parker, Frank, 1: at 21:30.
[63] *Nottinghamshire Guardian*, 15 June 1883.
[64] Sharp and MacIlwaine, *Morris Book, Part III* (1924), pp. 73-74.
[65] *Derby Mercury*, 8 July 1863.
[66] *Derbyshire Times*, 9 July 1873.

The Morris Dance is one of the most time honoured customs of the place, but has not been observed for the last few years. It has now, happily been received [sic], and it is much to be hoped will not be again allowed to fall into disuse.

The chairman at the annual feast of the Foresters that year was the antiquary Llewellynn Jewitt, who had moved into Winster Hall in 1868, and Georgina Smith has suggested that he may have been instrumental in the revival of the dancing.[67] The news report in the *Derbyshire Mercury* is of 16 young men, with ribbons, rosettes, and flowers, their dances 'executed with precision'. They danced on several days during the week, and had a 'Queen and her military attendant, ... the clown and the witch' .

Despite this revival, there are no reports for several years thereafter, and in 1876 and 1877 the Buxton morris dancers (who were quite different, as we shall see) were engaged for Winster's annual flower show, which was instituted in 1875.[68] In 1882 the regular 'Gleanings in the Peak' column in the *Derbyshire Times* spoke in general terms of 'music and morris dancing' in Peak villages and went on to say that 'At Winster last week the inhabitants made the most of the custom', without being any more specific.[69] The flower show was revived in 1890, and in 1891 Winster morris dancers, 'a somewhat primitive company', performed, but the 'Gleanings in the Peak' columnist in the same newspaper was more charitable, speaking of his 'pleasure to witness a very old-fashioned sort of amusement':[70]

The custom of looking upon Morris-dancers was common years ago, now it is very rare. I need not attempt to give any description of the primitive enjoyment. Yet to see the slashing swordsman walking in soldier-like fashion at the head of the troupe, followed by the fiddler and accordian player, the frisky fellows with flowing ribbons in pretty costumes, was both strange and of some antiquity. I doubt whether there is a band of Morris-dancers in Derbyshire today, except the company at Winster.

When Cecil Sharp saw them in 1908 he wrote that 'Until twenty or thirty years ago the dances were performed annually in June, but since then they have been danced only on special occasions'. He reported a hobby horse had been present in the past, though there is no other record of one associated with the custom at Winster. A photograph of a group of performers at Winster Hall around 1870 exists and does show a horse as described, but the nature of the performing group is not known, although they might be mummers. Nonetheless, knowledge of the photograph may underlie what Sharp was told. As at Castleton, processional dancing alternated with stationary dances, but at Winster there were several distinct stationary dances. Most of them simply had country-dance figures and the dancers held handkerchiefs but did not wear bells.[71]

Before Sharp encountered them, Winster morris dancers are known with certainty only from brief reports in 1863, 1873 and 1891, with some evidence of their absence in other years. Despite the opinion of the author of 'Gleanings in the Peak' in 1891, other groups of Derbyshire morris dancers were performing, and for Tideswell there is strong evidence of dancing in 1797 and continuing throughout the second half of the 19th century.

---

[67] Smith, Georgina.
[68] *Derby Mercury*, 16 August 1876; *Derbyshire Times*, 18 August 1877.
[69] *Derbyshire Times*, 8 July 1882.
[70] *Derbyshire Times*, 21 August 1891; *Derbyshire Times*, 22 August 1891.
[71] Sharp and MacIlwaine, *Morris Book, Part III* (1924), pp. 73,75; Cawte, *Ritual Animal Disguise*, pp. 120-23.

The vicar of Tideswell noted in his diary in 1797 (probably in wakes week, in June) 'Great morris dancing today led by John Potts dressed in regimentals'.[72] This implies a ceremonial figure like that at Winster. He had apparently been lost by the time of the earliest newspaper report in 1845, when at the Oddfellows' club feast 'An interesting party of morris-dancers (about forty), engaged by the Odd Fellows, and attended by the Tideswell band, delighted the inhabitants and visitors by dancing in a line through the streets.'[73] There are brief reports of their doing the same in every decade thereafter. That of 1863 describes how:[74]

> ...about 70 of the younger members commenced the usual Morris-dance, headed by the banners and band of the club. This scene is one peculiar to the Peak, and is remarkable for its elegance of appearance, the white shirt sleeves, and sweethearts' white pocket handkerchiefs waving in irregular but determinate order through the streets, as the dance traverses the town.

In 1898 the nature of 'the merry tripping of a host of morris dancers' was described in more detail: 'The bells jingled, the countrymen gracefully wound in and out of their fellows, the handkerchiefs fluttered in the breeze'. The dance was closely tied to the Oddfellows benefit club. The members of the lodge did their dance 'with their scarves and regalia', implying that these appurtenances were relevant to both the lodge ceremonial and the dance. Although by this time the Oddfellows were primarily a friendly society providing benefits to members, their origins were in the quasi-masonic trade guilds and they retained some of the practices emphasising bonds of membership, and it may be that the dancing was an element in this. The report added that the lodge had been in existence for 68 years (i.e., from 1830) and 'the custom of morris dancing at the lodge festival has not once been omitted',[75] but all other aspects of any associated ceremony had been lost.

By the time Sharp saw it in 1910 the dance consisted of a simple processing and crossing movement, with the hands (carrying handkerchiefs) thrown up at intervals.[76] Towards the end of this period performing the dance became more of a social occasion. Sharp was told that the dancers took part in the formal feast procession on Monday in ordinary clothes, and in the evening removed their coats and used handkerchiefs in the dance, performed both in procession and stationary. On the Thursday, schoolchildren and adults of both sexes joined the dance, and on Saturday it was repeated by the younger members of the Oddfellows.[77]

A very similar association of morris dancing at the Oddfellows' feast was found at Taddington, three miles away, and was reported in the local press between 1875 and the end of the century. If anything this was even less formalized than at Tideswell. There was little in the way of costume, the men – 16 of them – in their ordinary clothes, simply wearing the Oddfellows' sash and holding handkerchiefs. Dancers crossed and re-crossed in procession, sometimes joining hands. A photograph taken around the end of the century shows eight dancers performing, in front of other club members, their banner, a band, and spectators (Figure 18.3).[78]

Taddington gives the impression of having lost many of the distinctive elements of a morris dance by the time it was described and photographed. Just two miles from Taddington is the village of Flagg, and there are brief reports of morris dancers in costume there in the 1850s. On the Wednesday of the club feast week, 28 June 1854:[79]

[72] Brown, Thomas. I am grateful to Ian Russell for bringing this to my attention.
[73] *Sheffield & Rotherham Independent*, 28 June 1845.
[74] *Derby Mercury*, 23 September 1863.
[75] *Derbyshire Times*, 2 July 1898.
[76] Sharp and MacIlwaine, *Morris Book, Part I* (1912), pp. 118-20.
[77] Sharp and MacIlwaine, *Morris Book, Part I* (1912), p. 118
[78] *High Peak News*, 22 May 1875; Bathe.
[79] *Derbyshire Courier*, 8 July 1854.

Figure 18.3: Taddington morris dance, club feast day, c. 1900 (Image courtesy of University of Sheffield Library, Dave Bathe collection, ACT/97-003/P/1792z).

The ancient Morris dancing was well executed by twenty young men who had spared no pains in making themselves perfect, and in having a characteristic and uniform dress with flowing ribbons, &c. The day proved fine, and after dancing through the village headed by the efficient band and large flags, they settled on a green platform kindly lent for the purpose, where there was a good store of refreshments provided.

The whole celebration was apparently arranged by the young men of the village, who then chaired one of their members around in honour of the successful week, perhaps suggesting this was a new event. Two years later the promised entertainments included 'the ribbon dance ... by twelve little girls, the morris dance by young men'.[80] We know no more of the Flagg morris dancers, but the added presence of the girls in 1856 followed close on developments in the morris dancing tradition at Buxton which were more far-reaching and had widespread effects.

The complex events at Buxton have been chronicled by Roy Judge and much of what follows derives from his careful analysis.[81] The custom of well-dressing – decorating a public well with arrangements of petals – was known in several Derbyshire villages but was instituted in Buxton only in 1840 when the Duke of Devonshire (resident at nearby Chatsworth) provided a new water supply to the town. Morris dancers were first reported at the festival in 1843. The reporter from the *Buxton Herald* was impressed with what may have been their inaugural appearance:[82]

[80] *Derbyshire Courier*, 28 June 1856.
[81] Judge, 'Tradition'.
[82] *Buxton Herald*, 6 July 1843.

Often as we have seen this very ancient amusement practised in various parts of the country we never saw it so well and elegantly performed before. The Buxton Morris dancers may fearlessly throw down the gauntlet to all the Morris dancers in the Peak, if not to the whole county. The inflexions of body exhibited by every one were of a kind exceedingly surprising. We never felt more pleasure in looking on any other kind of dancing; and we shall, with the Buxton public, be delighted to hear of a speedy announcement of another morris dance at Buxton, by the same incomparable dancers.

The following year the dancers, who were all young men, varied their programme by interspersing quadrilles with the morris dance. We learn that they also held not handkerchiefs but sprigs of evergreen in their hands. Their costume consisted of white trousers, black waistcoat over a shirt, straw hat and green ribbons (but bells were not mentioned).[83] They were accompanied by the Duke of Devonshire's and other bands.

In 1847 they did not perform, as the local press recorded, 'owing to some cause or other, which we have not heard explained'.[84] When they are next reported in 1849, it seems that they have incorporated supernumerary figures previously absent:[85]

The Morris-dancers started about two o'clock to perambulate the town, and we were sorry to observe that they were escorted by two very foolish men in women's clothes, whose absence would have been more creditable than their company. It was a disgusting accompaniment to what would otherwise have been a pleasing part of the day's amusements. To be accompanied by a fool was bad enough, but this was too bad. We would advise the young men who take part in the dance to discard such companionship next year.

This is the only indication of such supernumeraries, though it may imply a fool had been present in earlier years. Two years later they introduced another innovation, the local press announcing that they would 'renew the ancient custom of the maypole or ribbon dance'.[86] The 'ribbon' indicates that this was a plaited maypole dance, which can only have been inspired by the inclusion of such dances in the middle-class fêtes and festivals then spreading into the provinces from the London gardens. Buxton well-dressing itself certainly had middle-class origins and pretensions. Two years on again, 1853, and another innovation: 'a party of fourteen young girls, dressed in white with blue satin, &c., danced a morris dance to the strains of the Buxton Band'. The innocence of the scene was emphasised, one newspaper recording 'their little feet dancing the merry dance as they move along, and ever and anon waving gay garlands over their heads'. The precise form of these garlands is not clear. The young men (one report calls them 'boys') were still present too, but in their morris dance 'they got into a state of confusion, and had to stop'.[87]

In 1853 the girls were reported as being between ten and 15 years old. In 1855 they were about ten, and in 1856 'the youngest [was] little more than four years old'.[88] The press (and probably the organizers) promoted the 'young innocence' imagery, and in 1855 the girls were judged 'a great improvement on a lot of lubberly hobbedehoys, who seldom get through the maze without a blunder'.[89] The girls, on the other hand, were a marketable commodity. It was probably they who appeared, accompanied by the Tideswell Band, at the Chelmorton

[83] *Buxton Herald,* 29 June 1844.
[84] *Manchester Courier,* 30 June 1847.
[85] *Buxton Herald,* 30 June 1849.
[86] *Buxton Herald,* 21 June 1851.

[87] *Buxton Herald,* 25 June 1853; *Nottinghamshire Guardian,* 30 June 1853.
[88] *Manchester Times,* 18 June 1853; *Buxton Herald,* 23 June 1855; *Buxton Advertiser,* 27 June 1856.
[89] *Buxton Herald,* 23 June 1855.

well-flowering in early July 1855, and certainly they who graced the Grand Temperance Gala in Macclesfield at the end of that month, bringing garlands and their maypole, performing schottisches and waltzes in addition to the morris dance. They returned to the same venue for a fête in October, and were back in Buxton itself at a Grand Gala Day in September the following year when the 'little morris dancers' performed.[90]

In 1856, the *Buxton Advertiser* reported that 'by far the best feature on the occasion [of the well dressing] was the performance of the little Morris Dancers', and they appeared again the following year.[91] In 1858, however, the press regretted the absence of the girls. Instead there was 'a number of morris dancers, young men and boys, from Chapel-en-le-Frith, whose appearance, though very picturesque, was a poor substitute'.[92] Chapel-en-le-Frith was over the crest of the High Peak and its dancers were part of the rushcart tradition. No maypole is mentioned. In 1859 there was 'a band of village youths, decorated with many-coloured ribbons'. There was a maypole but they also performed 'a variety of pleasing and grotesque dances, the most successful being the Cocoa Nut dance'.[93] Coconut dances were a popular entertainment derived from the stage, but certainly considered suitable only for boys or men.[94]

In 1860 'our little townsfolk, the Morris Dancers ... in their Sailor-like costume' plaited the maypole. The reports of 1861-62 do not mention the sex of the dancers. Chambers's *Book of Days* reported in 1862 that 'Formerly they were little girls dressed in white muslin; but as this was considered objectionable, they have been replaced by young men gaily decorated with ribbons, who come dancing down the hill, and when they reach the pole in the centre of the crescent fasten the long ribbons to it, and in mystic evolutions plait them into a variety of forms, as they execute what is called the Ribbon Dance'.[95] Although the writer was correct as regards the return of male dancers from 1858, the report created confusion in later years when the passage was often repeated as if current, although in fact matters had taken a fresh turn.

There certainly were boys (local, not from Chapel-en-le-Frith) in 1860 and 1861, as in 1861 William Boam of Buxton was sued by a local shoemaker for payment for shoes made for his son in those two years: 'the boy wanted them for morris-dancing at the Buxton well-dressings'. Probably this was Boam's son Henry, twelve in 1861, or possibly William, seven.[96] In 1863 the railway came to Buxton, and the authorities were so busy preparing for the influx of visitors on excursion trains that some elements were dropped. 'But where were the morris dancers?' asked the *Derbyshire Times*.[97] In 1864 they were back, and from this point it is only the girls who appear. A picture of the event shows them being watched by large crowds as they plait the maypole, dressed in white, with blue Garibaldi jackets and white straw hats (Figure 18.4).[98] Crowds of literally thousands watched their performances, and great play was made of their epitome of innocence:[99]

> *Their very fair complexions, flowing curls, and cheerful faces, with their fairy like movements, won the admiration of all, forming as they did a most beautiful bouquet of youth and loveliness.*

[90] *Staffordshire Sentinel*, 28 July 1855; *Staffordshire Sentinel*, 11 August 1855; *Staffordshire Sentinel*, 6 October 1855; *Buxton Herald*, 11 September 1856.

[91] *Buxton Advertiser*, 27 June 1856; *Buxton Herald*, 25 June 1857.

[92] *Buxton Advertiser*, 26 June 1858.

[93] *Buxton Advertiser*, 11 June 1859; *Buxton Herald*, 23 June 1859.

[94] Bearon, 'Coconut Dances'.

[95] *Buxton Herald*, 28 June 1860; *Derbyshire Courier*, 29 June 1861; Chambers, 1:819.

[96] *Glossop Record*, 8 November 1862; 'William Boam' (1861 census).

[97] *Derbyshire Times*, 4 July 1863.

[98] *Nottinghamshire Guardian*, 1 July 1864.

[99] *Derbyshire Times*, 26 June 1872.

They appeared every year for decades thereafter. In 1880 'on the suggestion of a lady in the town' the Garibaldi jackets and sailor hats were replaced by a better fitting sash and a more fashionable hat.[100] In 1883 a May Queen was introduced, reflecting the growing interest in May festivals across the country.[101] New costumes were again introduced: 'Following the May Queen in her chair of state were the twelve morris dancers all dressed in elegant Dolly Varden costumes with Mother Hubbard bonnets to match'.[102] In 1891 they appeared in the national costumes of the four nations of the kingdom.[103]

We do not know how the first dancers learned the art of plaiting the maypole. The early accounts suggest that it was grafted on to the existing men's performance rather unsuccessfully before they were supplanted by the girls. The first named trainer in 1855 was William Worrall, a local stonemason employing six people in 1861.[104] By 1866 another local tradesman, shoemaker Robert Sumner, was training them and did so for the next decade.[105] From 1875 until the 1890s a William Evans

Figure 18.4: 'Annual ceremony of well dressing at Buxton, Derbyshire' (detail), Illustrated Times, *9 July 1864, p. 24.*

(not identified with certainty) took the role.[106] A trainer was certainly needed: when Matlock initiated a well dressing in 1865 their maypole 'had been reared and decked with streamers, but for want of a leader initiated into the mysteries of the maypole dance this was the least successful feature in the day's programme', according to the *Derby Mercury*.[107]

The morris dancers, as one of the chief attractions, were also relatively expensive. In 1855, in an overall expenditure of just under £33 (of which £13 was for the well dressing itself), Worrall was paid £1 8s to provide the dancers. In 1860 he was paid 16s for the training, and providing maypole and ribbons, plus £1 5s for hats and bells (the only indication that the dancers wore bells at all). The following year the dancers received £3 10s out of an overall expenditure of just under £50.[108] These payments were augmented by collections taken from the public as the girls danced, and in 1873 £15 was collected.[109] They performed over several days at Buxton, but when they were hired to perform at the Bakewell flower show in 1889 they received £4 10s just for the day.[110] At Buxton in 1889 each dancer received £1, amid rumours that the festival

[100] *Buxton Advertiser*, 26 June 1880.
[101] *Buxton Herald*, 20 June 1883.
[102] *Buxton Advertiser,* 28 June 1884.
[103] *Sheffield Independent*, 26 June 1891.
[104] *Buxton Herald,* 9 July 1857; 'William Worrall' (1861 census).
[105] *Sheffield Independent*, 19 June 1866; 'Robert Sumner' (1861 census).
[106] *Derbyshire Times*, 19 June 1875.
[107] *Derby Mercury*, 24 May 1865.
[108] *Buxton Herald*, 9 July 1857; Judge, 'Tradition', p. 10; *Buxton Advertiser*, 6 July 1861.
[109] *Buxton Herald,* 22 May 1873.
[110] *Sheffield Daily Telegraph*, 30 August 1889.

was not making money.[111] The intensity of their exertions at Buxton was the ostensible reason for restricting their appearances to the Gardens in 1879, for admission to which patrons had to pay, when in previous years their performances at several spots in town had been free to observe. However, this proved unpopular, such that the following year the decision became 'the great bone of contention' in the planning of the festival, and public dancing was restored, 'though it has lost the committee a great deal of monetary support'.[112]

The Buxton morris dancers were advertised as 'far-famed' and on more than one occasion, as 'far-farmed' – maybe a misprint, but they did travel to events at Macclesfield (a temperance gala) as early as 1855, Ashton-under-Lyne, Chesterfield, Sheffield, Southport (60 miles away), Bakewell and even Winster, perhaps suggesting that the indigenous team there was dormant.[113] Imitative well-dressing and maypole-cum-morris events sprang up in several communities round about. Ashton-under-Lyne trained up its own dancers in preference to the expense of hiring the Buxton girls, there were similar ceremonies at Endon and Milton in Staffordshire, and an entirely commercial spin-off at Rudyard Lake Hotel, near Leek.[114]

The other bastion of morris dancing in Derbyshire, Castleton, continued to evolve when from 1897 girls replaced the men in the morris dance, 'and the women who have dressed up their children in lieu of [the men] are talking of introducing a well-dressing'. Although they apparently continued to do the dance as performed by the men, they adopted a feature of north-west morris dancing in holding and waving a stick with ribbons in each hand.[115]

Derbyshire morris dances appear to have been rather simple choreographically, but at Castleton and Winster retained some features reminiscent of the old church ales in the presence of lord and lady and other supernumerary figures. What began at Buxton as a set of morris dancers in similar mould was supplanted quite quickly and consciously by a tradition based on the theatrical maypole morris of the fêtes and pleasure gardens, employing young girls to project the image of carefree innocence. Despite its obvious origin in the commercial exploitation of the festival this transition was then adopted as a genuine expression of the community, presaging similar developments in the industrial north-west.

[111] *Derbyshire Times*, 26 June 1886.
[112] *Buxton Herald*, 19 June 1879; *Buxton Advertiser*, 26 June 1880.
[113] Judge, 'Tradition', p. 12; *Staffordshire Sentinel*, 28 July 1855; *Derbyshire Times*, 16 July 1870; *Derbyshire Times*, 12 August 1871; *Sheffield Independent*, 13 August 1874; *Derbyshire Courier*, 5 August 1876; *Derbyshire Times*, 18 August 1877; *Sheffield Daily Telegraph*, 30 August 1889.
[114] Judge, 'Tradition', pp. 12-14.
[115] Addy and Kidson, pp. 419, 421, 427.

Chapter 19
The decline of the rushcarts

We left the north-west morris at the Manchester Mechanics' Institute Christmas party in 1852, blending elements of theatrical pageantry with local authenticity in the shape of a rushcart and the use of a tune strongly associated with the region's morris dancing (see Chapter 17). It was not an isolated example. The Oddfellows' Literary Institution in Rochdale explicitly followed the Manchester example in 1850 by holding a festival on Christmas Eve in which 'The Maypole was erected in the centre of the hall, and the morris dancers performed their evolutions round it'.[1] On 6 January 1865 the Rusholme Public Hall and Library's Christmas party illustrated the evocation of a blend of customs when 'the mummers and rustics ... raised the village Maypole, and a party of juvenile members in "gaye attyre" executed the sword dance, morris dance and peace egg'. (The 'peace-egg' is a mummers' play normally performed at Easter.) The Levenshulme Mechanics' Institution had a similar Christmas event in 1868.[2]

Professional entertainment venues also sought to incorporate morris dances in an 'authentic' setting. At the commercial 'Belle Vue wakes' in 1859 (Belle Vue Gardens being a major Manchester pleasure park) there were morris dancers and a rushcart, which also paraded the city streets. The dancers were described as 'lads' and the party of 20 was paid £8 10s.[3] In 1864 the morris dancers from Roundthorn, near Oldham, appeared on the local stage between the main entertainments.[4] The Christmas pantomime of 'Mother Goose' at the Prince's Theatre in Manchester in 1864 had '40 children, in proper costume, and with a real rush-cart, executing the Morris dance, under the superintendence of an old professor of this provincial pastime'. The 'old professor' was Joe Hilton, of Failsworth, who asked for 3s 6d a day plus beer money, but agreed to a single payment of one guinea (£1 1s) in lieu. The Failsworth dialect writer Ben Brierley, who mediated Hilton's engagement, led the all-girl ensemble at the first rehearsal. The band even used the 'Cross Morris' tune (discussed on pp. 286-87), expressed in the *Manchester Times* as 'dancers cross buttocks three times over', for the appropriate part of the dance.[5] Evidently Hilton was quite happy to have the dance performed by young girls instead of adult men.

Rushcarts were still appearing at several locations. At Middleton in 1852 there were four rushcarts with morris dancers. Despite the potential for rivalry, the local newspaper reporter commented on the peaceable manner and overall temperance of the wakes.[6] The towns and villages immediately to the east of Manchester were still fertile ground in this period. Within three miles of Ashton-under-Lyne were Gorton, Failsworth, Audenshaw, Denton, Dukinfield, Droylsden, Hurst, Stalybridge, Hyde and Millbrook, all with recorded rushcarts and morris dancers, often appearing in each others' communities in a custom mirroring that of the Whitsun-ale morris of the south midlands, with each community vying to turn out the best spectacle.

At the Stalybridge wakes in 1868 the local correspondent expected several rushcarts with their morris dancers and anticipated that the rivalry between them would raise the standards.[7]

---

[1] *Manchester Courier*, 28 December 1850.
[2] *Ashton Weekly Reporter*, 2 January 1869.
[3] *Era*, 11 September 1859; 'Belle Vue Gardens'.
[4] Judge, 'Old English Morris Dance', p. 338.
[5] *Manchester Times*, 31 December 1864; *Manchester Times*, 16 November 1889.
[6] *Manchester Courier*, 28 August 1852.
[7] *Ashton Weekly Reporter*, 18 July 1868.

The Millbrook cart turned out accompanied by a garland cart, which was a subsidiary cart decorated with the garlands which in other circumstances were carried on poles, or adorned the horses pulling the rushcart.[8] Dukinfield made an effort that year to establish a separate wakes celebration, but the draw of Ashton-under-Lyne just a mile away was too great. Two or three sets of morris dancers who appeared at Dukinfield soon moved on to Ashton.[9] Several sets of dancers, all based at local pubs, held suppers at the end of the wakes week. The Millbrook team met at a local beer seller's, and agreed in future to patronize Stalybridge wakes in preference to those at Mottram-in-Longdendale. The team had apparently already voted with their feet, for the *Glossop Record* complained about the absence of their rushcart and dancers from the Mottram wakes.[10] 'Everybody congratulated everybody else', including the dancers, whippers, collectors and 'Besom Bet', 'especial allusion being made to the ladies who had so freely contributed articles for the use of dancers' – presumably referring to elements of their costumes.[11] At Ashton relations were a little more strained. The 'west enders' based at the Craven Heifer inn won the prize for morris dancing at Dukinfield, but the rival 'east enders' from the Golden Lion came out top in the subsequent fight, 'several of them [the west-enders] being disabled from dancing next day, and the principal whip cracker getting his whip broken'.[12] The press also reported 'several sets of younger dancers', one of whom had a small rushcart in a coal waggon.[13]

Despite the fighting, some elements of decorum were observed. The lavish costumes of the dancers were displayed for the populace to admire at the home-base pub of each set, and the local reporter praised the 'very tasteful' costumes of the west-enders, 'the ornamentation employed being such as must have cost a great deal of scheming and labour'. The Millbrook dancers were careful to thank 'the Stalybridge police for the kind manner in which they assisted and protected those who took part in the dancing'.[14] The latter possibly refers to some scuffles that reportedly took place among the spectators while the dancers performed.[15]

The Saddleworth wakes had met with similar approval in 1854, when 'About five o'clock in the evening, the Greenfield rushcart and morris-dancers began to march through the district, and arrived at the church about eight in a very orderly well conducted manner. There was none of that brutal party faction fighting, which disgraced this happy time in former years; a strong proof, we think, that people are becoming wiser.'[16] Four years later 'The time-honoured wakes, with their rush-bearing, rush-carts, and Morris-dancing, seem to have lost none of their charms of attraction in this locality', the reporter being particularly in favour of the annual general sprucing up of the neighbourhood in readiness for them.[17] The reporter made a similar observation the following year, and noted the excitement engendered by the rushcarts and morris dancers:[18]

> *About six o'clock on Saturday evening, the residents of Uppermill were warned by the approaching bands of the 'fife and drum', that the wakes had opened, and that rush-carts and morris-dancers were perambulating the district. The sound of music, coupled with the shouting of the assembled multitude, who followed in the wake of the rush-carts, had a most attractive effect upon the good folks of Uppermill; for as soon as it was generally known that the Running-hill rush-cart was entering the village by New-street, and the Friezland cart*

---

8   *Ashton Weekly Reporter,* 25 July 1868 [a].
9   *Ashton Weekly Reporter,* 8 August 1868 [b].
10 *Glossop Record,* 22 August 1868.
11 *Ashton Weekly Reporter,* 15 August 1868.
12 *Ashton Weekly Reporter,* 22 August 1868 [b].
13 *Ashton Weekly Reporter,* 22 August 1868 [a].
14 *Ashton Weekly Reporter,* 15 August 1868.
15 *Ashton Weekly Reporter,* 25 July 1868 [b]; *Ashton Weekly Reporter,* 8 August 1868 [a].
16 *Huddersfield Chronicle,* 2 September 1854.
17 *Huddersfield Chronicle,* 28 August 1858.
18 *Huddersfield Chronicle,* 27 August 1859.

by Wadelock, every house was deserted by the old wives and maidens, who flocked into the streets to gaze at the grotesque gambols of the rustics who accompanied these carts.

The reporting was very much dependent on the attitudes of the individual reporters. Two years later a much more negative image of the Saddleworth wakes was painted:[19]

On Saturday last this much looked for holiday by the youthful part of the community was ushered in by the appearance of three rush-carts from different parts of the Greenfield valley. They had with them the usual accompaniments of drum and fife, and the shouting upro[a]rious rustic clowns, yoked into long rope and pole-traces. Thus they drag the carts along with antics and capers, obstructing the road and calling at every public-house and beerhouse along their various routes. The three rush-carts were in the village of Uppermill altogether about eight o'clock p.m., and the streets were thronged with people for more than an hour, so that it was dangerous to pass along the street. The capers of the half drunken Morris dancers with the different rush-carts seemed to excite the attention of the whole of the residents who thronged about them, and appeared to be quite delighted at the grotesque gambols of the silly rustics. ... Thus closed the annual wakes of Greenfield, Uppermill and Dobcross, and with the exception of the disorderly group of foolish young men who accompanied the rush-carts, all passed over in a quiet and orderly manner.

The Ashton-under-Lyne and Oldham-Saddleworth areas were two strongholds of rushcarts and morris dancers in the period from 1850, where they remained common enough for inter-community rivalry to foster their development. A few other communities also maintained their support of them. Morris dancers continued to appear with a rushcart at Lymm in Cheshire, where the publicans of the village were the prime movers in the cart's construction.[20] An advertisement for the wakes at Radcliffe in 1858 mentioned rushcart and morris dancers, but the following year the morris dancers were advertised without the rushcart.[21] Morris dancers were becoming detached from their rushcarts: at the Oldham wakes in 1862 and 1863 they performed separately from any rushcart.[22]

The mid century was a pivotal point at which the close association between morris dancers and rushcarts began to dissolve. In several instances deliberate efforts were made to revive or maintain the customs. Samuel Bamford, whose *Early Days* memoir of 1848 had reminisced about the morris dancers and rushcarts at Middleton, was involved in the Blackley Mechanics' Institute initiative in 1858 to restore the perceived former innocence of the wakes. It had been the Blackley rushcart lads and morris dancers who had in 1851 engaged in a furious fight with local Irishmen on the way into Manchester. Bamford's intentions included the desire 'to arrange processions with dancing, music and choral singing'. At two o'clock on Monday 2 August 'a procession, consisting of a band of music, morris dancers, several waggons or cars, decorated with gay flags and banners, and containing the female members of the institution, followed by the male members, proceeded through the village'.[23]

At Heywood in 1868 there was a mixed message:[24]

The Wakes have worn an aspect this year that has not been known for a number of years past. The barbarous custom of men drawing a rushcart through the streets has again been resorted

[19] *Huddersfield Chronicle*, 31 August 1861.
[20] *Warrington Guardian*, 19 August 1865.
[21] *Bury Times*, 18 September 1858; *Bury Times*, 10 September 1859.
[22] Helm, 'Rush-carts', p. 26.
[23] Poole, p. 20.
[24] *Rochdale Observer*, 8 August 1868.

to. There has been the gay appearance of Morris Dancers parading the streets. Booths, and stalls of various kinds have been very numerous, and, on the whole, it may be considered that they have been the busiest wakes this season, that has been known for a length of time.

At Middleton the morris dancers came together in 1865 after a break of about eight years, but without a rushcart. They were based at the Turn of Luck pub, and were accompanied by the Rhodes Brass Band and women bearing garlands, collecting £27 in two days' performances. By 1878 a rushcart had re-appeared.[25] The 1882 report in the *Middleton Albion*, however, which named dancers and described their appearance, omits mention of one, and added that the rain probably reduced their income to the extent that 'it is doubtful if they will ever turn out again'.[26] Nevertheless, the dancers were back the following year with a rushcart. They were still performing in 1886, evidenced by a photograph, but again with no evidence of a rushcart (Figure 19.1).[27] They are wearing trousers but no bells, and their hats are profusely decorated with flowers. They are holding slings, the braided ropes which supplanted the knotted handkerchiefs in most places during the century.

Three years later a correspondent of the *Manchester Times* painted a much gloomier picture:[28]

I was at Oldham and Middleton some weeks ago at their wakes, and at both places morris dancing was on the programme. A number of poor boys made an honest endeavour to fulfil

Figure 19.1: The Middleton morris dancers, 1886 (in John Graham, Lancashire and Cheshire Morris Dances, *p.xvi. London: J. Curwen & Sons, 1911).*

[25] Poole, pp. 18-19.
[26] *Middleton Albion*, 26 August 1882.
[27] Poole, pp. 18-19.
[28] *Manchester Times*, 30 November 1889.

the promise of the programme, and I fear a large majority of the people present thought they did fulfil it. But alas! how forcibly the performance reminded one that morris is dead – for ever dead! Not a note of morris. What music the boys were struggling with I do not know; I got out of hearing as soon as possible.

Even in the heart of rushcart territory, there was a sense that rushcarts were becoming peripheral to the proceedings. Sometimes substitutes for rushcarts were created. At the Ashton-under-Lyne wakes in 1874 the reporter praised an effort to recapture the rushcart heyday while disparaging an innovative substitute:[29]

The ancient custom of morris dancing has this year been revived with greater success than ever before during the last four or five-and-twenty years. The Hurst Brook lads have at great expense made a cart such as our grandfathers were accustomed to, and the decorations of the morris dancers are most lavish. Altogether this is a most creditable display, and will no doubt prove successful as a monetary speculation. Other bands of Morris dancers sprang up in various parts of the town, one of which marshalled a 'flower cart' in the shape of a church of flowers. This was a good effort, but there was none which had the same popularity as that from Hurst Brook.

The following month a rushcart was made 'in the old style' at Gorton; and in the same year a three-ton rushcart drawn by nine horses and preceded by 20 morris dancers went from Failsworth wakes to the centre of Manchester.[30] A few years earlier in Dukinfield, 'One of the rush carts was a remarkable one, and quite on a new model. A miniature church, constructed of ornamental paper and flowers of endless variety, had been erected by some adept artificers on a substantial cart drawn by ... grey and chestnut ponies.'[31]

Burton describes how children in Levenshulme morris-danced in front of a small cart. Such carts, constructed by children, were known as 'skedlock' carts (skedlock is charlock, used in place of rushes to decorate the carts).[32] Another common substitute for the rushcart was the coal cart. Paradoxically, the earliest reference I have found to coal carts at wakes alludes to their discontinuance. Though Middleton had four rushcarts in 1852, five years earlier the reporter of the wakes there wrote 'There have been no rush carts as on former occasions ... The working classes at Middleton and the neighbourhood, have for several years past discontinued the dragging of rushcarts and coal carts for the purpose of obtaining free drink, now regarding these as foolish sports.'[33] The *Manchester Times* reporter of the Denton wakes in 1849 felt the need to explain. After describing the rushcart drawn by decorated horses and preceded by morris dancers, he adds, 'The next feature of attraction was the procession of the "coal cart", being a cart-load of large lumps of coal, the estimated weight of which was four tons four cwt'.[34] Likewise, the reporter of the Heywood wakes in 1850 added an explanatory note, seeing it as evidence of decline:[35]

There was but one rush cart; but, as a competitor, a cart filled with large pieces of coal was dragged through the town by some 40 colliers. This is a sad falling off in the observance of village customs, for Heywood was formerly a noted place for rush carts, and about thirty years ago no less than twelve were drawn on the Saturday, and 18 on the Monday, exclusive of several carts with coal drawn by the colliers.

[29] *Hyde & Glossop Weekly News*, 22 August 1874.
[30] Burton, Alfred, pp. 61-62; *Manchester Evening News*, 26 August 1874.
[31] *Ashton Weekly Reporter*, 28 August 1869 [b].
[32] Burton, Alfred, pp. 51-55.
[33] *Manchester Times*, 24 August 1847.
[34] *Manchester Times*, 15 August 1849.
[35] *Manchester Courier*, 10 August 1850.

Coal mining was a major industry in the areas of east Manchester and Oldham, and the use of coal instead of rushes was evidently an adaptation better to reflect the lives of those industrial communities. Coal carts were also reported along with the rushcarts at the Ashton-under-Lyne wakes in 1854 and 1862.[36] The issue of the *Ashton Weekly Reporter* which described the innovative Dukinfield rushcart in 1869 also described the various carts and sets of dancers at Ashton, in some detail:[37]

> *This wakes we had only one rush cart, and that of an inferior character. The large waggon of rushes, ornamented with tinsel and even silver plate, with decorations really artistic, in vogue some years ago, has given place to a smaller cartload of rushes, very sparsely decorated. The six or eight horses of old have been superseded by half that number, and the garlands were not up to par. The morris dancers were certainly very skilful, and did their duty very well indeed, headed by a sooty-faced youth, in women's apparel and tattered garments, 'doing the fool', and well did he fulfil his office. Though the dancers were rather younger than the 'rush cart lads' of the days of yore, they were well patronised, particularly so as they had the field to themselves. They were sixteen in number, and were gaily decked in ribbons and rosettes, as usual. Then came the garland cart, which was certainly a very neat piece of workmanship, and the morris dancers were quite up to the mark. Then came a juvenile rush cart, drawn by a 'Jerusalem pony' [donkey], and two or three morris dancers, who did more falling out over the receipt than they did dancing. All combined, the rush carts and morris dancers were rather below mediocrity, and it is to be hoped, if the custom is continued, that next year will see a cart of the old stamp - a large waggon of rushes profusely ornamented, six or eight fine horses, with large beautiful garlands and gingling collar bells, and a set of morris dancers and a band with colours and crackers of the old stamp.*

Just three weeks earlier the same newspaper – and possibly the same reporter – had remarked upon a similar decline at the Mossley wakes:[38]

> *With some few exceptions, Roughtown has not failed to send a rush cart to the wakes; indeed, the 'owd teauners' resolved that there should be a rush cart this year, but their hearts failed them, and their efforts dwindled to a wreath or garland of flowers, which was erected in a cart, and drawn through the streets, preceded by Morris dancers.*

Though the wakes continued to flourish as a general holiday, the community investment necessary for rushcarts was certainly disappearing by the 1870s. Theresa Buckland has pointed to some of the countervailing factors: the curtailment of wakes holidays thanks to increasing industrialization, the availability of cheap railway excursions at holiday times, and reforming campaigns of Nonconformists and the temperance movement.[39] It may have been such a campaign in Rochdale in the 1860s which led to the circumstance Alfred Burton relates, of how around 1868 'James Dearden, Esq., of Rochdale, finding that no rush-carts came to Rochdale, offered a prize of ten guineas for the most handsome that came, five guineas for the next best, and one guinea for each that came. About twenty appeared, and a number also turned up the following year.' Dearden was a local J.P. and lord of the manor of Rochdale.[40] That such a monetary incentive produced results is indicative of the level of investment needed, and of the confidence required that such an investment would pay off. Burton implies that Dearden's initiative was not long-lasting, and that thereafter the decline continued.[41]

---

[36] *Manchester Courier*, 26 August 1854; *Ashton Weekly Reporter*, 23 August 1862.
[37] *Ashton Weekly Reporter*, 28 August 1869 [a].
[38] *Ashton Weekly Reporter*, 7 August 1869.

[39] Buckland, 'Hollo!', pp. 38-39.
[40] 'James Griffith Dearden'.
[41] Burton, Alfred, p. 73.

Another indication of the sums involved comes from Romiley, near Hyde, in 1873:[42]

> *The garland cart and morris dancers: we hear that £7 was subscribed towards these wakes novelties, and that the receipts therefrom amounted to about £14. After paying instrumentalists, dancers, &c., £1 10s was left over towards the next years' festival.*

The implied payments to performers, amounting to £5 10s, suggest a maximum of around 10s each (for eight dancers and three musicians) and proportionately less for every additional person. The following year there were certainly twelve dancers, who performed on the Monday and Tuesday of wakes week, accompanied by two whippers-in, four collectors and the Bredbury and Romiley Brass Band.[43] At Dukinfield in 1864 the pay was 2s 6d a day for the two days of the wakes. Twenty colliers were hired, and they collected between £10 and £12 on top of their pay.[44]

A significant event took place in Hyde which heralded a new direction for morris dancing in the region. A mayor of the town, Thomas Middleton, described it much later in these terms:[45]

> *Although there had been morris-dancing in Hyde as far back as folk could remember, there was no regular troupe of dancers with a continuous history until the formation of the Godley Hill Royal Morris Dancers... Godley, previously a township of Mottram parish, is now part of the borough; Godley Hill has always been regarded as the centre point of the township's activities, and on its crest stands an old inn, formerly known as Godley Hall, which became the headquarters of the Godley Hill dancers for at least sixty years. The troupe was started by John Godley, Samuel Harrison, and Charles Brooks, of Godley Hill, and Samuel Ratcliffe, of Hattersley, who made up the first single set. They were taught by the Mottram morris-dancers, and in a few months a full set of sixteen was made up. ... The rushcart, which headed the procession, was a work of art.*

Middleton misdates the formation to 1855. In fact, the first such rushcart appeared in 1862, and during the 1870s the dancers regularly advertised themselves as having been founded in 1861.[46] In 1861 John Godley was a thirty-year-old hatter (one of the town's major trades) living at home with his parents. Samuel Harrison was either a clogger or a lodge keeper at a cotton mill; both candidate Harrisons traceable in the census were about forty.[47] Such local tradesmen were slightly higher in social standing than the factory hands of earlier teams.

The dancers certainly retained the approval of the local élite, who 'assisted them handsomely', and by 1863 they had already grown to 24 in number.[48] Their advertisements in the local press (Figure 19.2) show a confidence in their abilities. 'A comparative stranger' wrote that year that 'Another feature I noticed ... was the Morris Dancers, whose mode of procedure in parading the streets of the town is better known to Hydeonians than to myself, therefore I will say nothing in respect to them beyond this, that their vigorous dancing and picturesque dress appeared to be very beneficial to the common purse'.[49] The Godley Hill dancers also seized opportunities to expand their sphere of performance, as when in 1878 they followed the holiday crowds to Southport and danced there for two days. They also danced at commercial venues such as Belle Vue.[50]

[42] *Hyde & Glossop Weekly News*, 26 July 1873.
[43] *Hyde & Glossop Weekly News*, 18 July 1874; *Hyde & Glossop Weekly News*, 25 July 1874.
[44] *Ashton Weekly Reporter*, 1 October 1864.
[45] Middleton, p. 52.
[46] Buckland, 'Hollo!', pp. 39-41.

[47] 'John Godley' (1871 census); 'Samuel Harrison, b.1821' (1861 census); 'Samuel Harrison, b.1822' (1861 census).
[48] Buckland, 'Hollo!', p. 43.
[49] Comparative Stranger.
[50] Buckland, 'Hollo!', p. 44.

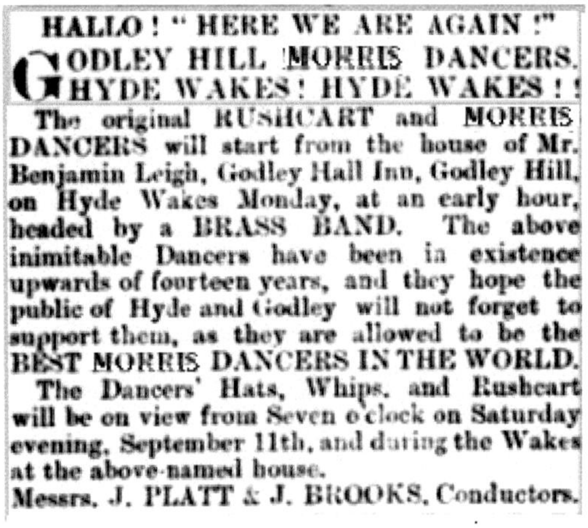

HALLO ! " HERE WE ARE AGAIN !"
GODLEY HILL MORRIS DANCERS.
HYDE WAKES ! HYDE WAKES ! !

The original RUSHCART and MORRIS DANCERS will start from the house of Mr. Benjamin Leigh, Godley Hall Inn, Godley Hill, on Hyde Wakes Monday, at an early hour, headed by a BRASS BAND. The above inimitable Dancers have been in existence upwards of fourteen years, and they hope the public of Hyde and Godley will not forget to support them, as they are allowed to be the BEST MORRIS DANCERS IN THE WORLD.

The Dancers' Hats, Whips, and Rushcart will be on view from Seven o'clock on Saturday evening, September 11th, and during the Wakes at the above-named house.

Messrs. J. PLATT & J. BROOKS, Conductors.

Figure 19.2: Godley Hill Morris Dancers advertisement, Hyde & Glossop Weekly News, and North Cheshire Herald, *11 September 1875, p. 1.*

While the vestiges of a custom associated with maypoles survived in central Lancashire, the century had been dominated by the burgeoning of rushcarts and their associated morris dancers in the industrial suburbs around Manchester, followed by the decline of the carts but the survival of the dance teams at the wakes holidays. The dances were performed mainly by large sets of adult men, but with some indication, particular in the western half of the area, that women might join in the dance. Bells were often dispensed with, but the handkerchiefs underwent a development of first being knotted, then becoming tightly braided slings.

At the same time juvenile troupes of dancers, often trained in ballet and dancing schools, took part in re-creations of May Day and 'Merrie England' throughout the 1860s and 1870s, and supplanted male dancers at Buxton. A rather carping reporter of the Hyde wakes in 1879 was perhaps reflecting this when he wrote 'It seems absurd that Morris dancing should be confined to the male sex, when the effect would be more picturesque and charming if there were a few pretty girls amongst them' – much the same sentiment as had been expressed at Buxton in the 1850s. The same reporter recorded morris dancers from Ashton, Oldham and Stockport at the wakes, and added 'We heard several enquirers as to how it happened that the Godley Hill lot, who have gained so much celebrity abroad, failed to put in an appearance at their own Wakes'.[51] It may well have been a consequence of their burgeoning fame. The Godley Hill Morris Dancers were to play a crucial role in developments at the end of the century.

[51] *Hyde & Glossop Weekly News,* 16 August 1879.

Chapter 20

Carnival processions

We do not know where the Godley Hill dancers were during the Hyde wakes in 1879, but from 1878 they began a long association with the May festivities at Knutsford, some 15 miles away on the Cheshire plain. Knutsford had instituted a festival in 1864, primarily as a children's procession and treat with the crowning of a May Queen and dancing round a maypole. Following a collapsed spectator stand in 1876 and bolting horses in the 1877 procession, the organization of the event was put under new management for 1878 and it immediately began to increase in scope and splendour.[1] This is when the Godley Hill Morris Dancers were first invited to join the procession, the start of a fifty-year association. It may have arisen from the chance circumstance that Joseph Brooks, one of the team's two 'conductors', had been born in Knutsford.[2] Where other festivals of this kind engaged dancing schools and similar establishments to provide constructed imaginings of morris dances, the report of Knutsford's that year pointed out that 'the procession included a body of genuine morris dancers'.[3] In 1880 'The Altrincham temperance band furnished music for the morris dancers (adults), whose attractive dress and well-executed movements made them one of the most effective features in the procession'.[4] The parenthetical comment again indicates an awareness of the difference between the Godley Hill dancers and the usual dancing fare at May festivals.

There are no reports of the Godley Hill dancers being associated with the fighting that often accompanied wakes and rushcarts. Another account styled them 'professional morris dancers'.[5] The reports also drew attention to the high 'production values' the dancers brought to their performances. In 1881 there were 'sixteen stalwart men, fantastically dressed in various coloured cloths, their heads enwreathed with flowers', and in 1883 a 'well-trained body of men, who were exceedingly smart'.[6] Knutsford was a paid engagement for which they received £15 in 1885 and £16 in 1887.[7] The Godley Hill men also replaced speculative excursions to seaside resorts by paid engagements at them. In 1883 they were part of 'Professor Le Mare's Old English Sports and Garden Party Company' performing at Southport Botanic Gardens along with the Hyde Borough Brass Band and advertising their availability for other engagements. They appeared there again the following year.[8] Given the anachronistic presence of the Hyde Borough Brass Band at the production of T.J. Dibdin's drama *Kenilworth* at the Hyde Theatre Royal in 1883, the morris dancers also performing may well have been Godley Hill, on the professional stage.[9]

The Knutsford May festivities were by the 1880s enormous in scale, and attracted press attention nationwide.[10] There had been earlier occasions of morris dances at organized Cheshire fêtes, but these had been on a smaller scale, such as the twelve boys and girls who performed at the annual May festival at Arley in 1857, and the 'customary morris dance' at Astbury in 1864.[11] At Over, near Winsford, a May festival was inaugurated in 1880. This was,

---

1 Leach, Joan.
2 Buckland, 'Hollo!', p. 44.
3 *Cheshire Observer*, 4 May 1878.
4 *Manchester Courier*, 3 May 1880.
5 *Hyde & Glossop Weekly News*, 8 May 1880.
6 *Liverpool Echo*, 14 May 1881; *Nantwich Guardian*, 5 May 1883.

7 *Manchester Courier*, 2 May 1885; *Alderley & Wilmslow Advertiser*, 22 July 1887.
8 *Era*, 8 September 1883; *Preston Herald*, 9 July 1884.
9 *Era*, 20 October 1883.
10 For example *Nottingham Evening Post*, 2 May 1889.
11 *Manchester Courier*, 9 May 1857; *Chester Courant*, 11 May 1864.

like Knutsford in its early days, primarily a children's procession and treat. By the third event, in 1882, 1500 children were involved, drawn in from the surrounding villages, and including some, trained by the ladies at Over Hall, who performed maypole and morris dances.[12] In 1884 there were over 2000 children, including 40 morris dancers and 40 maypole dancers.[13] In 1886 this rose to 80 boy morris dancers and 80 girl maypole dancers. In a comment perhaps directed at Knutsford, the *Manchester Courier*'s reporter added, 'if the professional morris and Maypole dancers who gad about the country for payment could have seen these children who stay at home and dance for the love of it they would have hid their heads in shame'.[14]

Large-scale community May festivals were also developing on the Lancashire plain. The *Bolton Evening News* reported in 1878 on the festivals at Worsley (begun in 1876) and Ince, each drawing thousands of spectators. The same article recorded the inaugural visit of the Godley Hill dancers to Knutsford, adding that they danced around the maypole at the conclusion of the ceremonies.[15] By 1881 Worsley had introduced morris dancers in addition to maypole dancers, flower girls, beefeaters, and various characters including Robin Hood. In 1883 the May festival had moved to August in the expectation of predictably better weather and consequently been renamed as a Rose Queen festival. The morris dancers danced around the maypole before the streamers were added for a plaited maypole dance.[16] At Ince, meanwhile, an advertisement for the 1881 May-day festivities (in aid of Wigan Infirmary) proclaimed the 'engagement of the famous "Abram Morris Dancers" and their Silver Garland, who appear once within every 21 years'.[17] Ince is less than three miles from Abram, where a morris dance around a maypole was said to be enacted by tradition every 21 years, as the advertisement states. In fact the precise term between documented appearances was more fluid. The dance was certainly performed in 1850, and the newspaper account then implies that events took place in 1794, 1814 and 1832 (see pp. 183 and 274). It was probably performed in the late 1860s.[18] The dance had been done in Abram on the weekend before St Swithin's day in 1880,[19] and it is possible that the team performed out of step with the supposed calendrical cycle because of the emerging interest in having morris dancers in festivals. At Ince they had the advantage of being able to provide a ready-made maypole-based tradition, unlike the other sides dancing in the north-west. There were also suggestions that the Abram dancers were active in 1888 and 1889, when the Wigan Infirmary sought their services.[20]

At Golborne, two miles from Abram, a May Queen festival was instituted in 1879. The 1884 festival had a procession of over forty elements, including morris dancers trained by one Thomas Berwick, whose team 'went through the ancient "May pole dance" in a manner that did credit to themselves and their tutor'.[21] Three years later the morris dance was described as 'a new feature at the festival', and it was performed by '18 young men, who were instructed by Mr. Perrin, of Abram'.[22] Another account speaks of 'the Abram May-pole dancers' who 'gave the ancient 'Morris dance', waving their white handkerchiefs in the air to the 'merrie music', and in a subsequent dance plaited the maypole.[23] The availability of local tradition which could inform the presentation of a May festival was a factor in the development of north-west morris in the ensuing decades.

[12] *Northwich Guardian*, 10 May 1882.
[13] 'Liverpool Mercury', 12 May 1884.
[14] *Manchester Courier*, 24 May 1886.
[15] *Bolton Evening News*, 2 May 1878.
[16] *Thanet Advertiser*, 7 May 1881; *Manchester Courier*, 4 August 1883.
[17] *Wigan Observer*, 2 April 1881.
[18] Bearon, 'Abram Morris Dance', pp. 60-61.
[19] Bearon, 'Abram Morris Dance', pp. 55-56.
[20] Bearon, 'Abram Morris Dance', p. 62.
[21] *Leigh Chronicle*, 9 May 1884.
[22] *Northwich Guardian*, 11 May 1887.
[23] *Leigh Chronicle*, 13 May 1887.

The explosion in the staging of May Queen and Rose Queen festivals that took place primarily in Lancashire from the 1890s, and the consequent florescence of morris dancing, has been documented in some significant publications upon which much of this chapter relies. Johnny Haslett has compiled an impressive and virtually comprehensive documentation of the newspaper sources for carnivals and galas in west Lancashire, the first volume of which covers the period to 1900.[24] Pruw Boswell has investigated in depth the histories of two particularly influential groups of teams emanating from Preston and from Horwich,[25] and Theresa Buckland has grounded the developments in their socio-cultural context.[26]

The key event in this process can be identified quite clearly. At the Knutsford festival on 1 May 1890 'a deputation from Leyland attended for the purpose of obtaining information as to the Morris Dancers which are about to be introduced into the Leyland Festival'.[27] The festival itself had been inaugurated the previous year. Some of the advertisements emphasised that there would be 'genuine morris dancers'.[28] This was the same phrase as had been used to describe the Godley Hill dancers in Knutsford in 1878. Knowing that morris dancing was practised outside of staged festivals, and having available relatively locally a form of the dance suited to procession through the streets, clearly led to a desire to promote 'authenticity' in the presentation of these spectacles. There may also have been an implicit expectation that 'genuine' morris dancers would be adult men. Hence the Leyland deputation's 35-mile journey to Knutsford to learn from the Godley Hill men. Their incorporation of morris dances into the Leyland festival was an innovation that was rapidly copied across Lancashire, leading to a proliferation of teams and to innovation in the dancing.

Performing just four weeks after the deputation to Knutsford, the Leyland morris dancers were well received. At Chorley, seven miles to the south-east, a festival inspired by Leyland's of the previous year had been arranged, and the *Preston Herald* commented that 'the committee received considerable assistance from Leyland friends, the engagement of the Morris dancers being one of the judicious investments'.[29] When they performed there just over a week later, the Leyland men 'claimed a large share of attention'.[30] The speed at which they had been assembled may underlie the comment in the first report that after the crowning of the Rose Queen, 'The Morris Dancers gave another exhibition of their one figure'. Reports identify the 'conductor' as a Mr Rose: this was John Rose, a fifty-three-year-old Leyland greengrocer.[31]

The following year there were morris dancers at the Leyland festival once more but no circumstantial account of them was given. However, the Leyland dancers did appear 'in costume' at Blackpool on 25 July 1891, accompanied by the Leyland Subscription Brass Band, and were now able to perform 'several of their latest dances'. They went speculatively, but were then engaged by the pier company to attract visitors to the pier.[32] Chorley, meanwhile, had evidently decided to follow Leyland's lead and have its own troupe of 'Morris dancers, 29 in number, under the leadership of Mr. H. Gent, who had very satisfactorily filled the post of trainer for them'. Harry Gent was, like John Rose, a local tradesman, being a fifty-five-year-old clogmaker,[33] and it is clear that local tradesmen rather than dancing masters filled the role of initiator and trainer for several teams. The Chorley team were apparently young men,

[24] Haslett.
[25] Boswell, *Morris Dancing ... Preston*; Boswell, *Morris Dancing ... Horwich*.
[26] Buckland, 'Institutions'.
[27] Boswell, *Morris Dancing ... Preston*, p. 4.
[28] *Lancashire Evening Post*, 24 May 1890.
[29] *Preston Herald*, 11 June 1890.
[30] *Lancashire Evening Post*, 7 June 1890.
[31] 'John Rose' (1891 census).
[32] *Preston Chronicle*, 25 July 1891; *Preston Chronicle*, 1 August 1891.
[33] Boswell, *Morris Dancing ... Preston*, p. 5; 'Henry Gent' (1891 census).

as the *Preston Herald* implied when it reported that after the Chorley Rifle Volunteers 'then followed what many young ladies considered the nicest picture of the procession – the 29 Morris dancers. They were really a fine and picturesque group.'[34] They were said to perform a 'Caledonian dance' and a 'Spanish dance'.[35]

At Horwich the committee for the newly planned Rose Queen festival duly made a pilgrimage to Knutsford in 1891. A ballot was held to determine contributions to the festival, and the Independent Methodist School was initially selected to provide the morris dancers, but in the event the Chorley morris dancers performed.[36] At both Chorley and Horwich the festivals inspired children of those communities to stage imitation festivals, including morris dancers. There were at least two such festivals in Chorley, while at Horwich the dancers were ten boys between nine and 14 years old.[37] At Ashton-in-Makerfield the same year some 'boy morris dancers' were in training for the May Queen festival and were 'one of the principal features of the procession'.[38] Some juvenile dancers performed at the Adlington rose festival.[39] The rapid introduction of the involvement of children into these civic festivals echoed events at Buxton and was to stimulate the developments of the following decades.

At the third harvest festival in Hindley Green, near Wigan, in August 1891, one Henry (Harry) Taylor taught juvenile maypole dancers and morris dancers, the latter being a 'new class'.[40] One report indicated that the Chorley morris dancers also performed.[41] The event inspired a group of young men to form a Hindley Green team in November that year. About 60 dancers and supporters partook of a tea at their formation, and three months later 100 attended a similar gathering.[42] Their first outing was apparently to Golborne, four miles away, which in previous years had used dancers trained in Abram. The local reporter noted that 'they varied previous programmes by going through their quaint dance as they moved along the streets. The novelty proved very acceptable.' The reporter was less enamoured of their arena performance: they 'gave a pleasing display, in which they introduced several dances, which, though good, were just a trifle too long'.[43] Naturally, they danced at the next Hindley Green harvest festival, under the captaincy of Harry Taylor, who had trained the *ad hoc* dancers the previous year. The report spoke of 'a real Morris dance'.[44] The following year, 1893, there was a 'May-pole dance by 24 girls, Royal circle dance by Morris dancers, revolving ballad dance [*sic*] by 36 girls, and old Morris dance', phrases indicating of an awareness of stage and community strands of dancing and of pre-existing morris dances, and possible evidence of a link with nearby Abram's circle dance.[45]

Meanwhile plans were being made for Preston's 1892 Rose festival, which coincided with a royal visit to open a town dock on 25 June. The festival committee sought the participation of the Leyland dancers, who at first refused, apparently seeing Preston's as a rival to their own festival. However, the Chorley dancers accepted, whereupon the Leyland men also agreed.[46] The event was a great success and within two weeks two separate advertisements appeared in the *Lancashire Evening Post*.[47] The first was on 2 July:

[34] *Preston Herald*, 10 June 1891.
[35] *Lancashire Evening Post*, 6 June 1891.
[36] Haslett, 1:25, 28, 39-43.
[37] Haslett, 1:38, 44.
[38] Haslett, 1:27.
[39] Haslett, 1:44.
[40] *Leigh Chronicle*, 14 August 1891; *Leigh Chronicle*, 4 September 1891.
[41] Haslett, 1:44.
[42] Haslett, 1:46, 49.
[43] *Leigh Chronicle*, 13 May 1892.
[44] *Leigh Chronicle*, 22 July 1892.
[45] Haslett, 1:101.
[46] *Lancashire Evening Post*, 11 June 1892; *Lancashire Evening Post*, 17 June 1892.
[47] *Lancashire Evening Post*, 3 July 1892, *Lancashire Evening Post*, 8 July 1892.

PRESTON MORRIS DANCERS. –Dancing Master, Mr. J. SPENCER. – A MEETING of the above Class will be held on WEDNESDAY NEXT, at the MOOR PARK DANCING ACADEMY, Aqueduct-street, at 7 30 p.m.

The second appeared on 8 July:

The Preston Royal Morris Dancers have Vacancies for a number of respectable YOUNG MEN. – Apply, York Hotel, Church-street, Monday evening, July 11th, at 8 15. P.S. – No boys need apply.

The Preston Morris Dancers were officially sanctioned, under mayoral patronage, after Spencer and a James Livingstone approached the Rose festival committee, and soon had 24 dancers, who demonstrated their skills in a dress rehearsal for their inaugural performance at a parade to raise funds for lifeboats on 24 September. Spencer provided the tuition free of charge at his dancing academy, and local tradesmen supplied the costumes.[48] Spencer, of course, had a commercial interest in promoting the team under the aegis of his dancing academy, but that was a recent development in his career. In 1891 he was still a worker in a cotton factory, as was his team secretary James Livingstone.[49] The opportunity afforded by morris dancing may even have been the stimulus for his change of profession.

Two weeks later the Preston Morris Dancers performed during half time at the Preston North End football match, to a mixed reception according to the *Preston Herald*, perhaps reflecting their inexperience:[50]

The interval was a little longer than usual, as the ground was given up for a little time to the Morris dancers, who did a little collecting on their own account, we believe. The innovation was variously looked at. Some liked it, and some did not. More it is hardly necessary to add, except that they had to 'double' before they had gone quite round the ground, for the place they danced on was wanted for sterner work.

Although the Preston Royal Morris Dancers had yet to make an appearance, there appears to have been some rivalry. The Preston Royal team took out an advertisement to state that 'The Preston Royal Morris Dancers wish to Inform the Public that they have NO CONNECTION with any Dancing Room class or with any other Morris Dancers that have appeared in Public' (including what may have been a dig at the artificiality of a dancing room), while the Preston Morris Dancers took out an advertisement on the day of the football match to state that they, 'who took part in the Lifeboat Saturday Procession, beg to inform the public that they are in NO WAY CONNECTED with the organisation which styles itself Preston "Royal" Morris Dancers'.[51]

Spencer's team ran a regular prize draw as a source of revenue, and by April 1893 they had become 'The Preston Morris Dancers Co., Ltd' and had a large room to hire out.[52] Earlier that year they had participated in a charity football gala at Everton Football Club, where 'the theatrical team numbered over half a hundred, many of them being Preston Morris dance[r]s, who displayed more than a superficial knowledge of the game'. They went on that evening to perform as an interlude to the pantomime 'Little Bo-peep' at the Rotunda theatre

[48] *Preston Herald*, 24 September 1892.
[49] 'James Spencer' (1891 census); 'James Livingstone' (1891 census).
[50] *Preston Herald*, 12 October 1892.

[51] *Lancashire Evening Post*, 5 September 1892; *Preston Chronicle*, 8 October 1892.
[52] *Preston Herald*, 24 December 1892; *Preston Chronicle*, 11 March 1893; *Preston Chronicle*, 22 April 1893.

in Liverpool, which announced that 'The celebrated Preston Morris Dancers will appear in full costume, with augmented orchestral accompaniment'.[53] This for a team that had first performed in public less than six months previously; like the Godley Hill team, they had a talent for self-promotion. They received travelling expenses (£8 11s 6d) for the football gala. Three weeks later they appeared on stage again at the last night of the pantomime 'Cinderella' at the Prince's Theatre in Preston itself.[54] Later in the year they danced in Blackburn in aid of hospital funds, collecting in the street. They collected £19, from which they deducted £14 in expenses.[55]

The Preston Royal Morris Dancers were established by Harry Gent, who had led the Chorley team. They made their first appearance on 17 October 1892 when they gave the opening display dance at the Preston Amalgamated Friendly Societies' ball.[56] Pruw Boswell has suggested that Gent could not simultaneously lead the Chorley and Preston Royal teams,[57] and there is no later record of his dancing with Chorley, but at the Chorley team's annual ball in November 1892 he was presented with a gold medal for his services, and said 'he was quite willing to do in the future what he had done in the past'.[58] Four months later Preston Royal opened the Oddfellows' ball, on which occasion also 'the Foresters' Male and Female Morris Dancers contributed greatly to the enjoyment of the proceedings'.[59] In March Preston Royal danced in aid of 'distressed card-room hands' (presumably on strike) at Bolton, 20 miles away, accompanied by the local Halliwell Brass Band, and the following month danced at the 'Old English sports and gala' at Halliwell.[60]

We know nothing more of the Foresters' Male and Female Morris Dancers. They were one of the literally dozens of teams which sprang up in the aftermath of the appearance of the Leyland and Chorley teams. Another example was the Bamber Bridge team, which may have been juveniles, and which turned out at the royal visit to Preston in 1892 and thereafter at the 'Penwortham Banquet' fête the following month and at the Preston Band of Hope Harvest Queen festival in September, but are otherwise unknown.[61] Just a few weeks after the Leyland team's debut in 1891, the village fête at nearby Farington had morris dancers, apparently juveniles, and again the following year. In 1893 the 'Farington Morris Dancers' organized a ball, and the village's 1893 Rose Queen festival featured the team. Later that year they organized a fête in conjunction with the Farington Brass Band. This suggests an adult team, but their conductor H. Blackhurst was the one who had trained the initial dancers. They held further fund-raising balls in December 1893 and 1894, but there is no evidence of further activity.[62]

The economic aspect was important in securing the services of a good morris team. When Thomas Powys, Baron Lilford of Bank Hall in Tarleton was seeking a team for his son's wedding festivities in 1894 his under-secretary, Henry Dandy, approached the Chorley dancers, who wanted an extra £2 for a Wednesday afternoon performance over a Saturday one on account of losing wages by accepting a weekday engagement. Dandy then approached Leyland morris dancers, but was told 'they do not perform out of their own parish'. He asked Lord Lilford's

[53] *Cricket and Football Field*, 4 February 1893; *Liverpool Mercury*, 1 February 1893.
[54] *Preston Herald*, 22 February 1893.
[55] *Liverpool Mercury*, 4 March 1893; *Blackburn Standard*, 9 September 1893.
[56] *Preston Herald*, 19 October 1892.
[57] Boswell, *Morris Dancing ... Preston*, p. 9.

[58] Haslett, 1:86.
[59] *Preston Chronicle*, 18 February 1893.
[60] *Preston Chronicle*, 13 March 1893; *Bolton Evening News*, 14 April 1893.
[61] *Preston Chronicle*, 25 June 1892; *Preston Herald*, 27 July 1892; *Preston Chronicle*, 3 September 1892.
[62] Haslett, 1:37, 53, 57, 89, 99-100, 121, 123, 163.

agent if he could proceed with Chorley so as to be able to tell the Hoole Band the music they would require.[63]

Many of the juvenile teams were associated with schools, most often Roman Catholic schools. Preston was a particular hub. Some events may have been in the wider tradition of fête entertainments, as the children's morris dance at St Paul's school in Preston in 1892, but the annual field days of both St Augustine's and St Ignatius's schools on successive Saturdays in 1896 featured juvenile morris dancers in procession.[64] Teams from St Ignatius's performed over several years. Besides their field days which continued to the end of the century, they were an advertised attraction at a fête in St Helen's in 1894 and performed in the Lifeboat Saturday processions in Preston in 1895 and 1896.[65] (Lifeboat processions, starting with Manchester's in 1891 – the first charity procession – became very popular during the 1890s and morris dancers frequently participated.) St Walburge's boys' team was similarly long-lasting, starting with a performance for a local Jesuit's anniversary in 1893, performing at field days from 1893 to 1900 and the Preston Rose festival in 1894, where they also performed physical and musical drills.[66] Elsewhere in Preston 'a few girls gave a new "morris Dance" much to the amusement of the rest' at St Thomas's, and there were 'Juvenile Morris Dancers' at St Wilfred's school, in 1893; and morris dancers performed at St Mary's school bazaar in 1897.[67] At Wigan, morris dancers from both St John's and St Patrick's schools took part in the Catholic Whitsuntide processions and Lifeboat Saturdays from 1896 on.[68] The movement spread as far as Keighley in Yorkshire, where at the Sunday schools' festival in 1897, 'A new feature was an exhibition of "morris dancing" through the streets by a troupe of little children belonging to the Catholic schools'.[69]

The 1893 Preston Rose festival on the bank holiday was a major event. Both Preston teams took part in the civic procession, Preston Royal coming in for particular praise, being given a 'deservedly cordial reception', and in addition the Preston Morris Dancers fielded a juvenile team of 24 boys and 24 girls.[70] All three also appeared at the Lifeboat Saturday parade in Preston in September.[71] By the following year the juveniles were billed as 'Mr. Spencer's Juvenile Morris Dancers' appearing with St Walburge's and Preston Royal (but not, apparently, the adult Preston Morris Dancers) at the Rose festival.[72] The Preston Morris Dancers were still active, collecting £5 11s 10d for the Victoria Hospital at Burnley, where they provided a 'novel and interesting spectacle' according to the *Burnley Gazette*.[73] In June they visited Lancaster to perform at the fire brigades' demonstration, where the reporter found their long display 'a bit wearisome', despite which they returned to the city for the sports gala in August. In July they attended Blackburn's first Lifeboat Saturday, and in September appeared at a cyclists' parade in Accrington.[74] The dancers went even further afield in later years, appearing at the Hospital Saturday procession in Birmingham in 1895 and the Lifeboat Saturday procession in Glasgow in 1896, where the 'clean braw laddies' attracted much praise.[75]

[63] Haslett, 1:153-54.
[64] Haslett, 1:230.
[65] Haslett, 1:134, 197, 202, 230, 235, 272, 307, 311.
[66] *Preston Herald*, 29 April 1893; Haslett, 1:114, 149, 154, 155, 193, 273, 289, 313.
[67] *Preston Herald*, 14 January 1893; *Preston Herald*, 11 March 1893; *Lancashire Evening Post*, 11 February 1897.
[68] Haslett, 1:220, 240, 266, 275-76, 281, 287-88, 290, 314-15.
[69] *Leeds Times*, 7 August 1897.

[70] *Preston Herald*, 9 August 1893.
[71] *Preston Herald*, 13 September 1893.
[72] *Lancashire Evening Post*, 7 August 1894.
[73] *Lancashire Evening Post*, 16 April 1894; *Burnley Gazette*, 12 May 1894.
[74] *Lancaster Guardian*, 9 June 1894; *Lancaster Guardian*, 28 July 1894; *Blackburn Standard*, 28 July 1894; *Lancashire Evening Post*, 10 September 1894.
[75] *Nottingham Evening Post*, 15 July 1895; *Preston Herald*, 20 June 1896.

The Preston Morris Dancers also engendered further teams. For many of their performances they engaged the juvenile Garland Band from Blackburn, and their cordial relations are chronicled in a series of letters to the children's section of the *Blackburn Standard* by the band's captain, William Hargreaves. In 1894 they danced in Darwen to raise funds for the band's uniforms.[76] In 1895 a band member wrote 'I think it would be very nice indeed to have a Band of Morris Dancers to go out along with our Band'.[77] Hargreaves went to Preston to see James Spencer, who agreed to help. He brought the adult team to perform in Blackburn and then at a social dance in aid of the new team, which trained over the winter.[78]

Colne was awarded borough status in 1895. The Preston Morris Dancers performed at the celebrations, 'and occasioned much amusement by their comical costume and merry brilliant dances as they capered about the streets'.[79] Five months later the local press reported that they had 'so excited the admiration of the spectators that a number of young men of our town resolved to learn the dance', and these gave an inaugural performance on 15 February 1896, dancing through the streets and organizing a general ball. They repeated the exercise on 14 March, collecting for the Colne Ambulance and Burnley Hospital funds.[80] Later that year they danced in Lifeboat Saturday processions at Nelson and Leeds. At the latter they were 'a welcome touch of old English pageantry', evincing pleasure that 'the good old custom survives' and giving 'to many, if not to most, their first glimpse of the wavering morrice' (referencing Milton's *Comus*) – somewhat ironic for a team in existence for less than a year.[81] In following years they performed at several charitable events, including raising funds for a poor children's seaside trip, an ambulance review at Barnoldswick and a charity parade in Colne.[82] At the last they appeared in the 'cyclists' section, as they had also formed themselves into the Colne Morris Dancers' Cycling Club, winning the prize for the best turn-out at a cycling parade in Accrington.[83] Traffic was two-way: in 1899 the Ormskirk cycling club fielded its own team of morris dancers.[84] The Colne dancers charged for their appearances at non-charity events. At the Nelson trades demonstration in 1899 their fee was £3 3s, out of a total of £31 3s for all the performers engaged for the procession.[85]

The Hindley Green morris dancers continued to flourish. At the end of a successful 1892 season they held a tea and social dance for themselves and friends, at which presentations were made to Harry Taylor their trainer and Robert Welch their accompanist during training.[86] They clearly had greater ambitions, for in 1895 they supplanted the Godley Hill dancers at Knutsford.[87] They did so again in 1898, though the Godley Hill dancers had appeared in 1896.[88] They also took part in the ubiquitous lifeboat processions, and at Blackburn's procession in 1898 both they and Spencer's (Preston) Juvenile Morris Dancers performed.[89]

After Horwich's initial engagement with the Chorley dancers in 1891 that town too initiated a home-grown team. A concert was held to raise money for costumes, and at their debut in the 1892 festival they were proudly announced to be 'all local men', whose 'dancing and evolutions, with their pretty costumes and wands, presented a very imposing sight'.[90] In 1894

[76] Hargreaves, 'Our Band Boys'.
[77] Astley.
[78] Hargreaves, Letter (1895); Hargreaves, Letter (1896).
[79] *Burnley Express*, 15 September 1895.
[80] Pilling, *Royal Morris*, pp. 3, 6.
[81] *Preston Herald*, 1 July 1896; *Leeds Mercury*, 6 July 1896.
[82] *Burnley Express*, 14 July 1897; *Craven Herald*, 20 August 1897; *Burnley Express*, 14 June 1899.
[83] *Burnley Express*, 8 September 1897.
[84] Haslett, 1:294.
[85] *Nelson Chronicle*, 27 October 1899.
[86] *Leigh Chronicle*, 11 November 1892.
[87] *Leigh Chronicle*, 3 May 1895.
[88] *Alderley & Wilmslow Advertiser*, 6 May 1898; *Northwich Guardian*, 6 May 1896.
[89] *Northern Daily Telegraph*, 4 July 1898.
[90] *Horwich Chronicle*, 26 March 1892; *Wigan Observer*, 20 July 1892.

they began calling themselves the 'Horwich Prize Medal Morris Dancers', possibly in response to another troupe calling themselves 'Horwich Morris Dancers'. A team of 'Horwich Junior Morris Dancers' appeared alongside the 'Horwich Senior and Prize Medal Morris Dancers' at the Horwich Rose queen festival in 1893.[91] The name capitalized on their success in a morris-dancing competition held at a Rochdale gala in July 1893, where they competed against a team from Oldham. The report in the *Rochdale Observer* made much of their ornate costumes and averred that the Oldham team 'did not seriously challenge the Horwich men'.[92] The criteria for judging the quality of a morris team had evidently moved on from the days of the rushcart tradition represented by Oldham. The Horwich men put the prize money towards the purchase of medals commemorating their achievement.[93] All the more embarrassing, then, that at a similar competition in Rochdale in 1895, the Horwich Junior Morris Dancers competed and carried off first prize, with the Horwich Prize Medal Morris Dancers being placed second.[94] Emulating Preston, they travelled further afield to the temperance gala at Lincoln in 1899. The *Lincolnshire Echo* reported that 'the very old custom of morris dancing is showing signs of revival, and [Horwich] carried off first prize at the last contest held at Bolton'.[95] Their appearance had been much anticipated, as the *Lincolnshire Chronicle*'s report suggests:[96]

> *Newland Mission brass band led the way, and immediately behind came the much-talked-of Horwich Morris Dancers, smartly attired in white jerseys and knickers of red plush. The party marched double-file, those in one row being distinguished by broad yellow sashes and those in the other by narrow blue ones, and at short intervals they broke into spirited dancing. At the rear of these came the Lancashire clown, 'Whimsical Dan', contentedly munching a muffin about 18 inches in diameter, and causing roars of laughter by his comical demeanour.*

'Whimsical Dan' was Dan Ouldcott, who often accompanied the team during the 1890s, and when he left the team appointed a new clown to fulfil the role.[97]

The employment of a clown or fool may have been an aspect of the Horwich team's links to older, rushcart-oriented, traditions of a fool or Besom Bet. The Rochdale report from 1893 mentioned that 'Each of the 25 members of the company carried plaited ribbon in his hands and swung and twisted it about when dancing'.[98] This use of slings also links the Horwich team to the older traditions of which Oldham were undoubtedly a part. It had been the subject of local discussion. At their first appearance in 1892 they used 'wands' – short beribboned sticks – but in 1893 they appeared with slings. The *Horwich Chronicle* reporter saw 'no reason why the wand was discarded by the dancers', but this drew a response from the team's trainer, Harry Barlow, that 'the dance gone through by the Horwich Morris Dancers would render the wand useless. The ropes carried by the Horwich Morris Dancers are the proper things to use, as in the real Morris dance exertions of the hands are equal to the feet. Thirty years ago in the country (Morris) dance the dancers used the blue and white plaid market handkerchief twisted and tied in a knot. To use the wand is not the Morris dance.' Harry Barlow and his son Thomas, who led and trained the team after his father died at the end of 1893, were born in Barton-upon-Irwell, scene of the eighteenth-century guising war, and evidently had knowledge of the older forms of dancing.[99]

[91] Haslett, 1:157, 165, 180; Boswell, *Morris dancing ... Horwich*, p. 9.
[92] *Rochdale Observer*, 26 July 1893.
[93] Boswell, *Morris Dancing ... Horwich*, p. 7.
[94] Haslett, 1:199.
[95] *Lincolnshire Echo*, 23 June 1899.
[96] *Lincolnshire Chronicle*, 27 June 1899.
[97] Boswell, *Morris Dancing ... Horwich*, pp. 8-9.
[98] *Rochdale Observer*, 26 July 1893.
[99] Boswell, *Morris Dancing ... Horwich*, pp. 6-7.

*Figure 20.1: Godley Hill Morris Dancers, 1882 (http://www.manchestermorrismen.org.uk/arc-photos/towns/
target42.html, CC 4.0 BY-SA).*

The earliest evidence of the use of wands or sticks instead of the handkerchiefs or slings of what the Barlows considered the old morris dance is the photograph of the Godley Hill dancers with their rushcart in 1882 (Figure 20.1).

Most of the information about north-west morris dances was collected in the mid twentieth century, when first-hand knowledge of nineteenth-century practice was hard to come by. It seems that knotted handkerchiefs or slings had supplanted loose handkerchiefs by the second half of the 19th century. Slings continued to be used in the Oldham area to the end of the century. A report from Oldham in 1884 described how the dancers 'twisted a little knot of decorated rope above their heads in a fashion indescribable'.[100] In the photograph of Middleton in 1886 (Figure 19.1 on p. 308) the dancers are holding slings. The Royton dance from the 1890s, later collected by Maud Karpeles, also used slings.[101] The development of rope slings from tightly knotted handkerchiefs is a natural evolution, but the introduction of wands is more problematic. They may simply be further stage in the evolution from slings. Dan Howison and Bernard Bentley saw them as contemporaneous alternatives, but the use of rope rather than wood in early examples of the wand type suggests that one developed from the other.[102] They may have evolved as 'handles' for the ribbons at the end; or they may be an importation from the dancing masters' conceptions of morris at May festivals, about which we have next to no choreographic information. The Godley Hill dancers' wands were beribboned only at one end, as were Leyland's, but the wands of later teams had ribbons at both ends, changing the nature of the movements that might be made with them.[103]

However wands developed, it seems that the Leyland deputation which went to Knutsford to learn from Godley Hill in 1890 adopted wands from them, and virtually all the teams that

[100] *London Evening Standard*, 15 September 1884.
[101] Karpeles, *Lancashire Morris Dance*, p. 13.
[102] Howison and Bentley, 'North-west Morris', p. 47.
[103] Boswell, *Morris Dancing ... Preston*, p. 15.

Figure 20.2: Leyland Morris Dancers with staves on the festival ground, 1890 (Photo courtesy of Roy Smith).

sprang up during the following decade followed Leyland, who at their first appearance had used 'gaily bedecked staves', visible in Figure 20.2.[104] Haslett identifies 47 named teams in west Lancashire in the period to 1900, and several more locations where a team performed but was not named.[105] Apart from Horwich, wherever there is sufficient detail in newspaper reports wands are indicated.

There is less information about footwear and stepping. Some teams wore clogs, others shoes, and some switched from one to the other. The 1884 description of Oldham has them wearing clogs. In 1896 the junior team at Horwich replaced boots by clogs, perhaps again under the influence of the Barlows' knowledge of older dance forms.[106] Analysis by Chas Marshall suggests that clogs were more prevalent in east Lancashire, in the old rushcart areas, and were almost absent from west Lancashire, also that they were preponderantly worn by the adult male teams.[107]

The dance from Royton collected by Maud Karpeles used a polka step, while many of the Lancashire plain teams employed a skipping step. Most of the evidence comes from a later period, and cannot be extended back to the 19th century with any confidence. However, most teams using the 'Cross Morris' tune had a specific step sequence associated with it, and had capers or spring-steps, suggesting a distinct choreography with analogies to the characteristic stepping of the south-midlands morris.

[104] *Preston Herald*, 31 May 1890.
[105] Haslett, 1:317-24.
[106] Haslett, 1:217.
[107] Marshall, Chas.

The professional approach first seen in the Godley Hill team was characteristic of many of the teams that sprang up in the north-west in the last decade of the 19th century. Godley Hill themselves must surely have been the kind of team the advertiser had in mind when placing a classified advertisement in the *Manchester Evening News* as early as 1886, seeking 'a brass band; also a respectable set of morris dancers, for an open-air juvenile party'.[108] No other team would have matched that description in the 1880s.

The picture of these new teams that is emerging puts them at the heart of life in the community. They had civic endorsement and engagement at processions. They organized fundraising balls, tea parties and prize draws. They performed for charity in aid of hospital funds and at lifeboat parades, but also in solidarity with strikers. Presentations of tokens of esteem were made to prominent members. They took paid engagements as far afield as Glasgow and Lincoln. The Preston Morris Dancers even formed themselves into a limited company. Most of the adult teams comprised working men, and participation in morris dancing gave them an opportunity to gain wider respect through their skill.

The teams took a pride in their appearance. The display of costumes was not new: both sets of Ashton-under-Lyne dancers puts their costumes on display before the 1868 wakes, and Godley Hill's hats were put on display more than once.[109] But for Preston Morris Dancers simply their appearance in full costume at their clubroom was something they felt they could advertise in the *Lancashire Evening Post* as an attraction in itself.[110] The Ashton-in-Makerfield

Figure 20.3: Preston Royal Morris Dancers, c. 1893 (Photo courtesy of Pruw Boswell).

[108] *Manchester Evening News*, 12 June 1886.
[109] *Ashton Weekly Reporter*, 22 August 1868 [a]; *Hyde & Glossop Weekly News*, 20 August 1870.
[110] *Lancashire Evening Post*, 5 August 1893.

May Queen festival in 1893 advertised 'maypole and morris dancers in entirely new costumes'.[111] When the Preston Juvenile Morris Dancers paraded at the RSPCA procession in 1894 they took a collection to pay for new costumes,[112] and when the Preston Royal Morris Dancers made their first appearance a highlight was their 'new Spanish costumes'.[113] The 'team photograph' of them taken around 1893 (Figure 20.3), shows this, and also the move away from the bead necklaces and flowered hats of the older, rushcart-based, teams. It reveals a more structured approach to the photographic image: they are seated in serried ranks like a sports team, unlike earlier photographs of dancers standing in quasi-set formation.

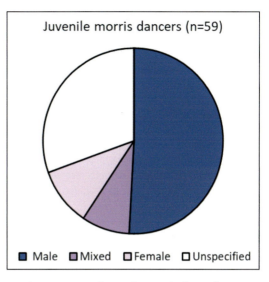

Figure 20.4: Juvenile morris teams in the north-west.

The first teams formed as a result of the Leyland initiative were adult men, like Godley Hill. Very soon a number of juvenile teams emerged. Some – like the Preston Juvenile Morris Dancers – were adjuncts of adult sides. Others were developments from the existing May festivals, adopting the processional element from the earlier north-west practice but possibly including other aspects of theatrically based festivals. Many of these juvenile sides were associated with local schools. Some have only a single recorded performance, others – such as St Ignatius's and St Walburge's from Preston – lasted several years, into the 20th century. The majority of the north-west juvenile teams were boys' teams, but there were also mixed and girls' teams (Figure 20.4), most of which were on the fringes of the area, in Cheshire and Cumbria. The report of the Adlington rose festival in 1895 commented on the 'new departure' of the introduction of girls: 'though perhaps some may argue in favour of the masculine gender alone, yet the most cautious would scarcely have dared to adversely criticise the display of Saturday'.[114]

Morris dancing spread to Cumbria in the 1890s. Keswick had been holding a May festival since 1885, instigated by the local clergyman. Cecil Sharp noted in 1911 that one J.T. Southworth taught the dancers at Keswick. He had learned the dance at Mawdesley, one of the teams near Preston that had been inspired by Leyland in 1893. However, Southworth was only 14 years old in 1893 when he learned in Mawdesley, and the Keswick carnival had already featured morris dancers in 1892, taught by W.F. Robinson. There were two groups of 12, one of boys and one of girls.[115] Similar patterns followed up to 1896.

The morris dancers in Cumbria from the 1890s were all children. The festival at Cockermouth was the idea of the local newspaper, the *West Cumberland Times*, to celebrate the third anniversary of its 'Cousin Charley's children's column' in 1894, and was billed as a 'Grand children's carnival and May festival'. The morris dancers (three sets of eight boys) had 'large hats, and ribbon twisted round their legs, and bells on their trousers and shoes'.[116]

[111] *Wigan Observer*, 6 May 1893.
[112] *Lancashire Evening Post*, 30 April 1894.
[113] *Preston Herald*, 19 October 1892.
[114] Haslett, 1:176.
[115] Allan, p. 188; *English Lakes Visitor*, 28 May 1892.
[116] *West Cumberland Times*, 21 April 1894; Scott.

In 1897 there were junior and senior morris dancers, 'a troupe of 50 Juvenile Jumpers, in addition to the usual sets of Dancers'. The 50 juniors were a mixed set, the 24 seniors a boys' team.[117] The jubilee celebrations at Workington saw an even larger number, 32 boys and 77 girls. The report gives details of their costumes:[118]

> The girl morris dancers were dressed mainly in national colours, and carried red, white, and blue sashes with bells at the ends. The boys wore knee breeches and white shirts, with red, white, and blue, ribbons from the breast with bells at the end of each ribbon. Their staffs were covered with red, white, and blue ribbon, bells again being fastened to each end, and both boys and girls had red, white and blue ribbons plaited on their stockings. The boys also wore straw hats specially purchased for the occasion, which were trimmed in a variety of styles but roses and the national colours always predominating.

The profuse use of bells and the plaited ribbons suggest the influence of the dancing masters' May festivals. One such was 'Professor' Oliver Cowper, who ran a dancing school in Workington.[119] His pupils entertained with morris dances at art exhibitions in Flimby in 1896 when 16 boys from Wyndham Row school performed, and 1899 when there were two large teams of girls: Netherton, with 29 dancers named, and Ellenborough, with 42. Where the children are named, a brief survey of census information indicates that the majority of performers of both sexes were in their early teens.[120] There were similar festivals at Moor Row from 1893 and Broughton Moor in 1896 (teams of 16 boys), and a girls' team at the jubilee celebrations in Aspatria in 1897.[121]

Apart from the single appearance of the Foresters' Male and Female Morris Dancers, female performers were usually young girls, performing under the aegis of some organizing body, be it a school or a festival committee. A slightly ambiguous report of the Lower Ince Rose Queen festival in 1896 refers to 'lady morris dancers attired in pink, white and blue cashmere' trained by male dancers from Hindley Green, but the context suggests they too may have been young girls.[122] One female team, however, did apparently operate as the independent men's teams did. These were the Royal Border Morris Dancers based in Foulridge, a small village just outside Colne, who performed in 1897:[123]

> Mr. Hartley Lee and his company, the 'Royal Border Morris Dancers', gave a performance last Saturday afternoon. The troupe consisted of sixteen girls, and starting from the station gates at 4-30 made a circuit of the village, finishing at Town Top. The movements were admirably executed, and called forth numerous expressions of high appreciation. The Waterside drum and fife band accompanied the procession, and altogether there was a very gay sight. It was the troupe's first turn out for the season. Collections were made en route, and realised £2 18s., and this goes towards furnishing the troupe with a set of bagpipes. The officers Mr. Hartley Lee (conductor), Mr. Fred Holgate (secretary) and Mr. Cookson (treasurer), are to be congratulated on the progress of the troupe, and on its great success in this its first appearance of the season.

---

[117] *West Cumberland Times*, 24 April 1897; *West Cumberland Times*, 28 April 1897; *West Cumberland Times*, 8 May 1897.
[118] *West Cumberland Times*, 23 June 1897, *Workington Star*, 25 June 1897.
[119] Mycock.
[120] *West Cumberland Times*, 5 September 1896; *West Cumberland Times*, 19 August 1899.
[121] *West Cumberland Times*, 27 May 1893; *West Cumberland Times*, 27 May 1896; *Carlisle Patriot*, 25 June 1897.
[122] Dann, p. 22.
[123] *Burnley Express*, 5 June 1897.

The following month they performed at the St John Ambulance Brigade fete in Nelson, and again in September, when they were described as 'a number of females dressed in Tartan plaids', collecting for themselves and the Nelson Ambulance Association.[124] Anthony Cookson, named as treasurer, had previously been a melodeon player for the Mossley morris dancers but had moved to Foulridge. The caption to a photograph of him in the archives of Manchester Morris Men suggests that the team also did Scottish dancing, accounting for the bagpipes and the tartan plaid. Ten years later he played for the men's team, the Colne Royal Morris Dancers.[125] His association with Mossley must have been brief, as in 1897 he was still only 21. (His daughter claimed he did not move to Foulridge until 1899.)[126] Hartley Lee was born in Bingley c. 1868, but living in Foulridge in 1891. Like Cookson, he was a cotton weaver, but by 1901 he had moved to Bootle and become a baker, so the Royal Border Morris Dancers may have been short-lived.[127] I have found no further records of their activity.

The morris dancers' occasional involvement with cycling which we noted earlier was not the only link between their dancing and other activities. The Preston Morris Dancers played charity football, but other teams fielded sides in their local football leagues even before the burgeoning of morris sides in the 1890s. In the 1880s the Victoria Morris Dancers were based at Heywood near Middleton. They provided entertainment at the Heywood Phoenix Bowling Club in 1884, and it may have been they who were the 'troupe of local morris dancers, who danced around the town for three days' at Heywood wakes in 1885, headed by a brass band. They were 'most tastefully dressed, and the graceful manner in which they went through their exercises was most creditable'.[128] Between the two events they played the Paved Brow Wanderers at football, and the following year the Wanderers played 'Heywood Morris Dancers'.[129] In 1892 and 1893 a team called the Deepdale Morris Dancers played football matches in the Preston area, losing heavily on each recorded occasion (Deepdale is, coincidentally, the home of Preston North End football club). However, there is no record of their performing any morris dances, and it may be that 'Morris Dancers' was simply an evocative epithet like other footballing names such as 'Wanderers' or 'Athletic'.[130]

The football matches give a sense of how well integrated the morris dancers were into their local communities, but the most cogent indication of community acceptance was the appearance at various fêtes and festivals of 'mock morris dancers' alongside 'real' morris dancers in affectionate parody of them. There was a general practice of having comic equivalents to parade elements in festivals. In place of 'Grenadier' and 'Coldstream' guards' bands there were 'Granny dear' and 'Cold cream' substitutes. The best description of mock morris dancers is from the Chorley Rose festival in 1892, almost immediately upon morris dancing reaching the area:[131]

> *Much diversion was caused by the mock Morris dancers, who in goggles, swallowtail coats, and coarse-canvas continuations [gaiters or trousers], trimmed with dainty lace, and carrying bladders instead of wands, executed a series of movements of a grotesque character, to music contributed by the band of the Cold Cream Guards, conducted by a*

[124] *Burnley Express*, 30 June 1897; *Burnley Gazette*, 22 September 1897.
[125] 'Mossley/Foulridge'.
[126] 'Anthony Cookson' (1901 census); Pilling, *Royal Morris*, p. 8; Pilling, 'Foulridge'.
[127] 'Hartley Lee' (1891 census); 'Hartly Lee' (1901 census).
[128] *Athletic News*, 6 August 1884; *Heywood Advertiser*, 7 August 1885.
[129] *Heywood Advertiser*, 17 April 1885; *Heywood Advertiser*, 26 February 1886.
[130] *Lancashire Evening Post*, 12 November 1892; *Lancashire Evening Post*, 21 October 1893; *Preston Herald*, 8 November 1893.
[131] Haslett, 1:66-67.

Teutonic looking Herr Von Bassoon, several members of which played concertinas, whilst the bulk had dummy clarionets.

The performance described later in the proceedings has the dancers belabouring each other with their bladders. A month later in the small festival at Whittle-le-Woods, 'Copying from similar affairs held in other villages ... There were morris dancers who were much admired, and mock morris dancers whose movements created great amusement'.[132] Over the next few years mock morris dancers appeared at fêtes in Adlington, Coppull, Horwich and Preston besides Chorley and Whittle-le-Woods.[133] A much earlier reference to 'sundry roving bands of music and mock morris dancers' at Hazel Grove wakes east of Manchester in 1871 is very likely the result of a reporter's failure to recognise 'real' morris dancers.[134]

In the explosion of fêtes and festivals in the north-west during the 1890s morris dancing was just one of many forms of dance put on display. At Hindley Green the morris-dance trainer Harry Taylor also coached the maypole, gipsy and Highland dancers.[135] At Fleetwood's diamond jubilee celebrations in 1897 a Mr Fox trained morris, maypole, skirt and tambourine dancers.[136] These were the kinds of dances in which the dancing academies up and down the country offered coaching, but in the north-west these were embedded with the community-based morris dances, or *vice versa*. With regard to the growth of juvenile teams, Theresa Buckland has noted that 'Morris dancing became one of several physical activities regarded as appropriate for children of both sexes to perform in a number of institutionalized contexts'.[137]

Garland dances were a particular element in the mix. The Chorley festival of 1891 advertised 'neat and charming dances; morris and garland dances'. The account of the festival did not mention a garland dance specifically, but apart from the morris dancers, whose 'Spanish' and 'Caledonian' dance we noted earlier (p. 316) there were country dances and a 'pretty dance by the bridesmaids'.[138] Garlands themselves were a frequent component of wakes and festivals, and it is difficult now to divine exactly how they fitted in to any given customary practice. The earliest references to garland dances are in the eighteenth-century theatre. We met earlier the staging of maypole and morris dances and a 'grand garland ballet' at the Leeds theatre in 1776 (see p. 157), and there was a similar performance using local talent at the Theatre Royal in Manchester in 1788, in a short play 'The Humours of Flixton Wakes', 'the whole to conclude with a sumptuous snig [eel] pye feast, and garland dance, by the lads from Flixton, Urmston, Stretford, &c.', reminiscent of the staging of 'Eccles wake' at the same theatre 11 years previously.[139] At the Duchess of St Albans's fête in 1829 the Covent Garden dancers 'traversed the grounds as Morrice dancers, and danced country dances, with garlands to the sound of pipe and tabor'.[140] The Viennese children's ballet visited London in 1845 performing dances with garlanded hoops, and were very influential; and in 1866 at a soirée in Grantham 'a bow of cane, surmounted by a coloured paper rosette' was held by each couple as they performed what the *Illustrated London News* described as a '"Morris dance" – a species of country dance'.[141] Many of the dancing academies had garland dances in their repertoire.

Garlands in north-west celebrations accompanied and adorned rushcarts before being hung in the church, and Jessie Lee described their being carried by young girls behind the morris

[132] Haslett, 1:78.
[133] For examples, see Haslett, 1:105, 121, 136-37, 190-92.
[134] *Hyde & Glossop Weekly News*, 19 August 1871.
[135] *Leigh Chronicle*, 22 July 1892.
[136] Haslett, 1:249.
[137] Buckland, 'Institutions', p. 53.

[138] Haslett, 1:26, 33-36.
[139] *Manchester Mercury*, 22 April 1788.
[140] *Morning Chronicle*, 22 June 1829.
[141] *Illustrated London News*, 19 April 1845. I am grateful to Theresa Buckland for drawing my attention to this; *Grantham Journal*, 8 December 1866.

dancers in the Rochdale rushbearing.[142] The paintings by Parry and Wilson (Figure 17.2 on p. 275 and Figure 17.5 on p. 283) show them carried aloft on poles and adorning the horse trappings. When the *Bury Times* described how at Radcliffe in 1859 'the morris dancers with their green grove and garlands continued their performances notwithstanding the rain', we do not know if the garlands were used in the dance or were simply an accompanying element.[143]

The Chorley garland dancers of 1891 were the first of several such during the 1890s. Most reports simply mention their presence, without further details. Besides the maypole, gipsy and Highland dances noted in the repertoire of Hindley Green's Harry Taylor, he also trained garland dancers, Scotch reel dancers, and skirt and 'ballad' dancers. His Hindley Green (Girl) Garland Dancers performed at the jubilee celebrations at Southport in 1897, where they 'carried hoops covered with paper flowers, which they waved with graceful effect during the dances which were heartily applauded'. The garland dancers from Hindley Green were operating in close conjunction with the morris dancers: the fee for both was met by a single payment of £15 4s.[144] In a development typical of the ways in which the custom was spread, the Hindley Green (Girl) Garland Dancers were the direct inspiration for a team at Ainsdale village fête three weeks later:[145]

> *A very pretty diversion was made in the afternoon's as well as the evening's proceedings by the performances of the Garland Dancers, a number of the schoolchildren who had been trained by Misses J. Crocker and Booth. The dances were arranged on the pattern of those of the Hindley dancers who visited Southport during the Jubilee fetes, and they were generally admired.*

Morris dancers in the north-west in the latter half of the 19th century were clearly players in a fluid, vibrant and popular suite of customs and festivals, imbibing influences from other dance forms, theatrical pageants and fêtes, and even appearing on the professional stage. The traffic may have been two-way. John Tiller, the theatre director who founded the Tiller Girls dance troupe, began his career in Manchester managing the Comedy Theatre, which included a children's dancing troupe. His first significant venture was to provide girls performing a coconut dance in the pantomime 'Robinson Crusoe' at the Prince of Wales Theatre in Liverpool in 1890. Soon after, his dancers were performing morris dances on the stage. At the Palace Theatre on the Isle of Man in 1893 'The Morris dances, the dance of the Troubadours, the rainbow dance, and the other scenes de ballet by the Tiller Troupes, are quite superb'. The following year Tiller's 'Harvest Home, or, Rustic Revels in ye Good Old Days' at the Empire Theatre in Cardiff featured the girls as morris dancers whose costume is reminiscent of those of the festival-based north-west morris (Figure 20.5).[146] Frederick Hamer claimed that the Tiller innovation of linking dancers in a chorus line was copied from the Royton morris, perhaps from the up-in-fours figure there.[147] This is unlikely, not least because the girls link arms round the waist, not at shoulder level as in up-in-fours, and because Tiller did not introduce the move until around 1910 when he was managing troupes worldwide, not just in the Manchester area.[148] Nonetheless, the environment in which both professional and amateur community-based dancing troupes were operating is certainly one conducive to mutual

[142] Lee, Jessie.
[143] *Bury Times*, 1 October 1859.
[144] Haslett, 1:137, 251, 256.
[145] Haslett, 1:257.

[146] 'John Tiller'; *Isle of Man Times*, 18 July 1893; *Western Mail*, 27 February 1894.
[147] Cawte, 'History', p. 93; Karpeles, *Lancashire Morris Dance*, pp. 24-25.
[148] Vernon, p. 41.

"HARVEST HOME" AT THE CARDIFF EMPIRE.

MORRIS DANCERS.

Figure 20.5: Tiller Girls as morris dancers, Western Mail,
27 February 1894, p. 6.

influence, and the two sticks shown in the illustration may show the influence of the festival morris. At the revival of the Jacobean *Maske of Flowers* at Gray's Inn in 1887, the morris dance therein called forth the comment 'the proper employment of two staves which each dancer holds in his hands is exceedingly complicated, and must require prolonged practice'.[149]

Unlike the dancers of the south-midlands morrises, the morris dancers of the north-west managed to adapt to the changing social conditions of the second half of the 19th century and to flourish. In the east of the area the dancers survived the decline of the rushcarts, appearing at general wakes festivities and in new contexts, including the professional theatre. Higher standards of behaviour enabled teams such as Godley Hill to prosper and to influence the increasingly popular May and Rose Queen festivals of the region. Their pivotal encounter with the deputation from Leyland to Knutsford in 1890 led to the establishment of dozens of teams in Lancashire and Cheshire in the closing decade of the century, and a melding of elements of the older local tradition with the concepts of Victorian May festivals. The participation of juveniles was one aspect of this, and when the developments reached Cumbria morris dancing there was exclusively done by juveniles. There are several indications that commentators, and presumably the general populace, were aware of the changing nature of performance. Costumes also developed, sometimes with a 'Spanish' look, and the use of wands based on Godley Hill's practice. The trainers, often semi-professionals, sought to cater for the variety of dances required by festival organizers, opening the possibility for different dance elements, such as garlands, to enter the repertoire. We shall see that when change swept the country at the beginning of the next century the strength of the north-west morris enabled it to respond in a distinctive way.

---

[149] *Times*, 8 July 1887.

Chapter 21

Other morrises

During the first half of the 19th century in the south midlands and for the whole century in the north-west, morris dancing remained an expression of community cohesion. In the west and east midlands it continued to be widespread, as often as not to relieve hardship, but many of its distinctive elements became diluted into a blend of customary activities. However, morris dancing crops up in a variety of unrelated contexts outside of these areas. In most cases we know nothing of the dance and little about the circumstances of performance.

In Salisbury the giant and Hob-nob the hobby horse belonging to the Tailors' Company continued to parade from time to time with morris dancers. The dancers appeared with the giant and Hob-nob at the jubilee of George III in 1809 and the christening of the Prince of Wales in 1842. At the passing of the Reform Bill in 1832 the Tailors' Company declined to appear in the procession as their funds were low. They lent the giant and Hob-nob to the city corporation, but no morris dancers appeared.[1] A book of doggerel verse published in 1844 by Frances Child has a picture which shows the giant and dancers next to the author's home in The Close in Salisbury. The depiction may be fanciful (the bells are not the usual crotals, and the picture shows a Maid Marion figure not otherwise known in Salisbury), but the giant at least (identified as St Christopher) is accurately drawn, and the poem itself refers to the presence of Maid Marion wearing morris bells (Figure 21.1).[2]

The Salisbury dancers appeared again at the 1856 peace celebrations after the Crimean War and for the marriage of the Prince of Wales in 1863.[3] By this time there were only four members of the Tailors' Company[4] and we do not know how dancers were recruited or from where, but it would not have been from within their ranks. Those who performed at the visit of the Prince of Wales in 1872 certainly met with disapprobation, despite having been much anticipated in the preparations for the event. The *London Daily News* reported:[5]

> *The authorities had evidently not put themselves to any trouble in rendering the procession worth looking at. The morris dancers, who might have been dressed with some attempt at disguise, were attired in white smockfrocks, adorned with a few paper flowers, in which costume they hopped about, very much after the fashion of a bear on hot iron.*

This might be seen as a metropolitan reporter's disdain for the provinces, but the *Aldershot Military Gazette* was also unimpressed:[6]

> *The pageant of St. Christpoher [sic] to-day was really very ridiculous. The figure of the giant was draped in tawdry calico; Hob-nob, his equerry, was not half frolicsome enough; the horrid dragon, who, of course, represents the power of evil, made all the fun, by running after all the presentable girls; and as for the morris-dancers, in their bits of cheap finery, they soon got tired, and were content to drink at nearly every public-house, and to collect money in a tin box from those who would give it.*

---

[1] Haskins, pp. 210, 401-02.
[2] Child, p. 93.
[3] *Salisbury and Winchester Journal*, 31 May 1856; *Devizes and Wiltshire Gazette*, 12 March 1863.
[4] Haskins, p. 216.
[5] *London Daily News*, 12 September 1872.
[6] *Aldershot Military Gazette*, 14 September 1872.

Figure 21.1: Giant and morris dancers at Salisbury (in Frances Child, The Spinster at Home in The Close at Salisbury, *facing p. 96. Salisbury: W.R. Brodie, 1844).*

The *Londonderry Standard* was even more condemnatory:[7]

> ...*the morris-dancers turn out to be a disgusting failure. Some half-dozen ill-looking fellows jump about the giant as though it were a Jack-in-the-Green; two of them are dressed up as*

---

[7] *Londonderry Standard*, 14 September 1872.

women, and the others have a few ribbons attached to nondescript attire which might easily be reduced to the simplest elements. ... St. Christopher, with his dancers and musicians – who, by-the-by, did not disdain to demand contributions, for no specified purpose - blocked up one thoroughfare after another from ten o'clock, when the procession set out from St. Anne's-street, till nearly six, when the giant was restored to his corner in the Museum, where, let us hope, he will long remain undisturbed.

The Tailors' Company itself, reduced to two men, was wound up in 1880.[8] It would not have been surprising if that were also the end of morris dancing in the city, but it was back for the royal jubilee in 1887. This was a much more organized event, with costumes supplied by a town tailor, in which after the procession through the town 'Giant, Hob-Nob, and Morris Dancers [are] to take up position near Market-house, at a point indicated by Sergt.-Major Ball'.[9]

The dancers appeared again alongside the giant and Hob-nob at the wedding of the Duke of York (the future George V) in 1893 and at the queen's diamond jubilee in 1897. In 1893 their appearance was put in the hands of a local carriagemaker and a grocer.[10] One does not get the sense in their appearances of a continuity of tradition, and their dance was disregarded to the extent that when scholars began to take a specific interest in morris dances after the turn of the century, no one appears to have visited the town to investigate it.

There are some indications in the golden jubilee celebrations of morris dancing surviving in nearby communities. Young men and boys morris-danced at Wishford, and there were dancers at Laverstock just outside Salisbury too. They were elements in torchlit processions, and the dancers at Wishford also carried and played stringed instruments, and may have owed more to nineteenth-century conceptions than to any community-based practice.[11]

While the dancers certainly appeared in Salisbury and nearby, sporadic reports across the south of England also suggest traces of morris dancing, though in several cases there is overlap or confusion with related customs. At Winchester on the occasion of the coronation of George IV in 1823, 'A party of young men, from the neighbouring village of Otterbourne, fancifully habited as Morris Dancers, accompanied by a band of music, and preceded by an elegant flag, visited different parts of this city in the course of the day, and exhibited some skill in this ancient amusement'.[12] In a scenario reminiscent of the Derbyshire morris, or which may simply be a description of a village social dance, at the Yetminster Friendly Society's annual feast in 1878 the members walked in procession around the village, then at the rear of the White Hart Inn 'the "morris dance" was heartily engaged in by a large party'.[13]

The author of a review of Douce's *Illustrations of Shakspeare* in 1808 declared he had seen morris dancers in Brighton thirty years previously,[14] but other reports from along the south coast suggest a blurring of perceptions. The coming-of-age of the 15th Duke of Norfolk took place at Arundel on 27 December 1868, and as part of the celebrations 'a band of five youthful morris dancers of very local extraction, and remarkably costumed ... performed a drama, in the wind and the rain, in front of the Norfolk Arms, and their melancholy earnestness, their funereal

[8] Haskins, p. 216.
[9] *Salisbury Times*, 4 June 1887; *Salisbury Times*, 18 June 1887.
[10] *Salisbury Times*, 28 July 1893; *Salisbury and Winchester Journal*, 26 June 1897.
[11] *Salisbury and Winchester Journal*, 2 July 1887 [b]; *Salisbury and Winchester Journal*, 2 July 1887 [a].
[12] *Hampshire Chronicle*, 21 July 1823.
[13] *Western Gazette*, 14 June 1878.
[14] 'Illustrations', p. 468.

mode of going through the comic passages were depressingly funny'. They were reported to have swords, and pills for a quack doctor.[15] This is clearly a mummers' play. The *Kentish Gazette* reported from Canterbury on May Day in 1858 that 'the chimney-sweepers danced their customary morris-dance, collected their usual half-pence or unfrequent shillings'.[16] In 1880 the local correspondent of the *Hastings and St Leonards Observer* lamented that only one Jack-in-the-Green 'with a company of morris-dancers' was to be seen in Hastings over the past few years, and wondered if the performers were truly still representative of a family-based sweeps' custom.[17] Sweeps also turned out at Gravesend on three days that year, reportedly performing with a Jack-in-the-Green and morris dancers on the Monday and Tuesday as well as Saturday 1 May. The *Gravesend Reporter* suggested that this was a result of their 'having evidently created a disinclination to settle down to work'.[18] At the same time we should note many reports of Jack-in-the-Green, including from Gravesend and Hastings, which do not make the automatic equation with morris dancers.[19] Nonetheless, sweeps' May-day celebrations were also equated with morris dancing in the capital. When two sweeps were brought before the magistrate for begging in Regent Street in 1833, the reporter applauded their acquittal, exclaiming 'What! Deprive us of the last remnant of "May-day Games" – of Jack-in-the-Green and his troop of morris dancers'.[20] The antiquary John Timbs's encounter with sweeps on May Day in the Old Change in 1837 'made us suspect the partial if not entire identity of the morrice dance and the sweeps' Saturnalia'.[21]

The London reporter of the *Aberdeen Weekly Journal* painted a very broad-brush picture for May Day in 1881, admiring the decorated dray horses but being rather dismissive of 'rude efforts ... made by ingenious youths to fabricate the Maypole, the attendant Queen, Morrice dancers, and mummers'. In 1886 one 'W.S.' was equally admiring of the dray horses but complained that 'the morris dancing has for many years been monopolised by the riff-raff of St. Giles, who for the sake of a few coppers keep up a shabby remembrance of this festival and Guy Fawkes-day'.[22] On a cold May Day in 1896 the London correspondent of the *Leicester Journal* 'saw one or two poor little attempts by shivering children to revive the lost art of morris-dancing'.[23] The overall impression from the capital is of a pitiable dying sweeps' custom, taken to be the last remnants of a more estimable morris-dancing tradition. Roy Judge's work has demonstrated the quite separate origins of the Jack-in-the-Green as an eighteenth-century sweeps' solicitation custom, and with typical understatement he noted that 'problems can begin to arise when too much reliance is placed on ... intuitive insight'.[24]

In the west country two different equations were made linking morris dancing with other customs. One was with mumming or more broadly with 'guise' or 'geese' dancing, itself a portmanteau term which could embrace an admixture of different elements of a winter house-visiting or processional custom, in many cases incorporating a mummers' play. There is evidence of the custom from the 18th century.[25] As early as 1803 Richard Polwhele wrote in his *History of Cornwall*: 'Geese-dance, i.e. guise, or disguise-dance – for so the Cornish pronounce guise. The geese-dancers of Cornwall answer to the mummers of Devon, and the morrice dancers of Oxfordshire, &c.'[26] Following Polwhele, another writer on Cornish customs in 1879 averred that 'The Cornish "guise-dancers" are not (as some

15 *Sheffield Daily Telegraph*, 30 December 1868.
16 *Kentish Gazette*, 4 May 1858.
17 *Hastings and St Leonards Observer*, 8 May 1880.
18 *Gravesend Reporter*, 8 May 1880.
19 Judge, *Jack-in-the-Green*, pp. 144-52.
20 *Leeds Times*, 9 May 1833.

21 Timbs, p. 281.
22 *Aberdeen Weekly Journal*, 3 May 1881; S., W.
23 *Leicester Journal*, 8 May 1896.
24 Judge, *Jack-in-the-Green*, p. 84.
25 Goskar and Goskar.
26 Polwhele, 3:58.

guide books say) 'something distinctively Celtic': they are just the old morris-dancers who have disappeared elsewhere'.[27]

An 1830 account of a Cornish mummers' play claimed that the performers were 'dressed out somewhat in the style of Morris dancers, in their shirt sleeves and white trowsers, much decorated with ribbons and handkerchiefs, each carrying a drawn sword in his hand, if they can be procured, otherwise a cudgel'.[28] In Devon, the landlord of the Church House inn in Stoke Gabriel was summoned for 'keeping a disorderly house on Christmas-day' in 1858, when 'there was a party of morris-dancers, or mummers, in the house carrying on a regular representation'.[29]

In the heart of the guise-dancing area at Gulval, Penzance, in 1859, a man described as one of a group of morris dancers made unwanted sexual advances to a passing young woman and was charged with assaulting her. The judge fined him, and noted that 'there was no harm or disgrace in morris-dancing itself, and it used to be an innocent pastime, but of late it had been accompanied by much mischief and had degenerated from a harmless amusement into an annoyance'.[30] In a general piece about 'geese-dancing' the *Cornish Telegraph* explained that it 'consists in a number of young men so disguising themselves in various costumes as not to be recognised', and 'Accompanied by martial music, the company of morris-dancers, in their gaudy liveries, scarfs, laces, and bells, and headed by their commander, went about from place to place, giving full vent to their merriment'.[31] (The author had read Stubbes's *Anatomy of Abuses* and may have incorporated some of his description from there.)

The other west-country thread was the link with Cornish May customs. The Helston furry dance – a mixed-couple longways dance processing through the streets and into and out of the houses in the village – has long been seen as analogous to, or a form of, a morris dance. The earliest printing of the Helston tune by Edward Jones in 1802 described how the May excursioners 'return to the Town in a Morrice-dance; both the Ladies and Gentlemen elegantly dressed in their summer attirement, and adorned with nosegays, and accompanied with minstrels, who play for the dancers this traditional May-Tune'.[32] 'An occasional correspondent' of the *Royal Cornwall Gazette* in 1804 wrote of May games, 'In some places, these games were nothing more than a Morris Dance (as in Helston, at present) in which Robin Hood and his associates were the principal personages'.[33] A century later Cecil Sharp had no hesitation in appropriating the Helston dance for inclusion in *The Morris Book*.[34] An additional tantalizing hint of connection is in the tune used for the dance, which Jones even described as the 'traditional' tune. It is essentially the same as that used in Derbyshire and the north-west morris dances, where it is the 'Long Morris'. The dance in Winster, which, though the performers were all male until recently, has 'men's' and 'women's' sides (see Chapter 18), was seen as another point of contact. Attempts have been made to find a common origin, but as Dave Bathe wrote in his description of Derbyshire morris dancing:[35]

> *The notion that the popularity of the tune in Derbyshire and Cornwall, together with their possession of similar processional dances, is linked to the migration of Cornish tin miners to work in the Peak District lead mining industry is now legendary. However, no conclusive link between the Derbyshire and Cornish traditions has been established.*

[27] *Cornishman*, 8 May 1879.
[28] Sandys.
[29] *Trewman's Exeter Flying Post*, 20 January 1859.
[30] *Cornish Telegraph*, 19 January 1859.
[31] *Cornish Telegraph*, 21 December 1859.
[32] Jones, Edward, p. 96.
[33] Occasional Correspondent.
[34] Sharp and Butterworth, pp. 96-102.
[35] Bathe, p. 35.

Similarly speculative attempts have likewise been made to explain the use of the same tune in north-west morris by adducing the migration of Derbyshire workers to the industrializing districts around Manchester.

The west-country hobby-horse traditions have also proved rich sources for morris-dance connections, based on the profusion of Tudor and Stuart references associating the hobby horse with the dance. When Sabine Baring-Gould noted the Padstow May-day song he immediately alluded to the presence of hobby horse and morris dance in Fletcher's *Women Pleas'd*.[36] Writing of the Minehead hobby horse in 1893, the *West Somerset Free Press* noted that 'Degenerate the custom may be, but, such as it is, there is no difficulty in recognising it to be a veritable fragment of the time when May-day was the carnival par excellence of rural merry-making and the hobby-horse, with its comical caperings, supplied the necessary low comedy to the pretty pageant of Robin Hood and Maid Marian, or the gaiety of the morris dance'.[37] For all that, there are no contemporary references associating hobby horses with the morris at Minehead or elsewhere in the west country. Christopher Cawte has noted hobby horses at Penzance, Combe Martin and Dunster (close to Minehead).[38] Following the International Folk-lore Congress in London in 1891, the folklorist Wladyslaw Lach-Szyrma (a Devonian living in Cornwall) enquired in the *Western Morning News*, 'Are there any Morris dances in Devon now?' but elicited no reply.[39]

The hobby-horse dance at Abbot's Bromley, which by the late 19th century was being called a horn dance,[40] was still seen as a morris dance. A writer in 1850 describing the 'Moresque Dance (vulgarly called a Morris Dance)' stated that although the dance in general was widespread, it was dying out, but could be seen, 'still continued with apparent zest' at Abbot's Bromley.[41] The dance had been reckoned to be, or to be like, a morris dance by observers since the 17th century, but apart from the fact that it is done by men as a seasonal custom it has little to link it with morris dancing.

There is rather more evidence for morris dancing in North Wales in the dance also known as the 'Cadi ha' (literally, summer pole, i.e., maypole). The earliest reference is from the rector of Llanarmon in 1815, describing Whitsun 'morrice-dancers' with ribbons, and bells at the knees, accompanied by a fool and a man-woman.[42] The surveyor William Holden recorded in his diary on 7 May 1829 that 'The Colliers who work at Sir T Mostyn mines visited Parkgate [Wirral] decorated with ribbons & fantastically dressed, bearing a flag with the insignia of their calling. Mr. O informed me they were celebrating (Old) May Day' [*recte* 12 May], and he recorded a paltry payment of 1½d to the 'Morris Dancers'.[43] The eponymous colliery village of Mostyn is on the Welsh coast, in Flintshire. The flag, and the dancers' profession, bring to mind the morris dancers of the Forest of Dean at the other end of the Welsh border.

In his work on Welsh folk dances Hugh Mellor thought that regular dancing in the area, possibly from Capel Curig, Abergele and Mostyn, stopped in the 1860s, but he describes a dance seen near Bagillt before World War I. There were eight male dancers in double file, carrying handkerchiefs, one side possibly wearing hats to betoken 'maids' (reminiscent of Derbyshire). The dance was akin to a simple longways country dance; the tune was a variant of the 'Long Morris' tune used in in Derbyshire, the north-west and at Helston.[44] Mellor was uncertain of

[36] 'Baring-Gould MSS'.
[37] *West Somerset Free Press*, 6 May 1893.
[38] Cawte, *Ritual Animal Disguise*, pp. 167-68, 174-77.
[39] Szyrma.
[40] Cawte, *Ritual Animal Disguise*, p. 69.
[41] *Derbyshire Advertiser*, 27 September 1850.
[42] Blake.
[43] Holden, pp. 58, 135.
[44] Mellor, pp. 11, 16-21.

the exact places but some confirmation can be found in newspaper reports. At Rhyl on Whit Tuesday in 1849 and Abergele the following day a commentator (who was promoting rational recreation for the working classes) saw 'a troop of men, bedizened in many coloured rags and ribbons, their faces painted, and performing all sorts of loutish, awkward antics; accompanied by the discordant tones of a broken-winded fife, and the discordant tootings of a brass horn', and was told they were morris dancers. In 1877 we find morris dancers again at Mostyn, where the villagers celebrated the coming of age of the future 3rd Baron Mostyn.[45]

Two parties of morris dancers were reported at Rhosllanerchrugog on May day in 1885 and 'several bands of morris dancers' at Pontblyddyn and Leeswood in 1894.[46] The reporter from Mold in 1893, however, was pleased to write that things had improved since the days when 'we used to be plagued with the Morris dancers, when dirty children put more soot than usual on their faces, and then set to dancing and begging'.[47] Lady Lewis said that she found traces of the dance 'among the very poor in Mold, who beg on that day'.[48]

Some instances may not even have involved dancing at all. In 1842, 'Nimrod', writing of Erddig, near Wrexham, recalled 'the morris-dancers at Easter', but they may well have been pace-eggers performing the Eastertide version of the mummers' play.[49] The Cadi ha does appear, however, to have been a dance tradition with the characteristics of morris dancing in north Wales, possibly linked to maypoles. On admittedly scant evidence, in the absence of cultural embedding in wider custom it seems to have remained relatively simple in form until its demise around the end of the century.

One final Welsh record serves mainly to highlight our ignorance. It is at the wrong time, in the wrong place, and by the wrong people to fit into this narrative. On Boxing Day 1840 at Newport in Monmouthshire there was an affray with knives and cudgels after 'a large party of Irishmen, who had been engaged in a Morris Dance throughout the day, came to the Bush [a pub] and commenced drinking', after which one attempted to leave without paying.[50] Events in Ireland (where evidence of morris dancing is in any case minimal) are beyond the scope of this survey, but I cannot resist alluding to the even more bizarre report in the *Dublin Evening Mail* regarding Holywell Boarding School in County Wicklow, where at the half-year examinations in 1848, in addition to honours awarded in Greek, Latin, Bible history and more recondite subjects such as personal deportment and map drawing, two boys were apparently awarded honours in morris dancing.[51]

At various times sword dancers have been called morris dancers. Choreographically, sword dancing is intrinsically different from morris dancing, and for that reason it is out of scope for this book and we shall only treat of it here in so far as we need to consider the interface between them. There are two strands in sword dancing. Each of them consists of hilt-and-point dances, in which the dancers are linked by holding the ends of their own and their neighbour's swords, only released for short periods for specific manoeuvres. The short-sword or rapper dances found predominantly in Northumberland and Durham use flexible strips of steel with handles at each end, and use that flexibility to weave intricate patterns or 'knots' with them. The longsword dances, nowadays based mainly in Yorkshire, use rigid swords

[45] *Kent & Sussex Courier*, 4 May 1877.
[46] *Wrexham Advertiser*, 9 May 1885; *Wrexham Advertiser*, 5 May 1894.
[47] *Wrexham Advertiser*, 6 May 1893.
[48] 'Cadi Ha'.
[49] Nimrod, p. 288.
[50] *Monmouthshire Merlin*, 2 January 1841.
[51] *Dublin Evening Mail*, 26 June 1848.

and simpler figures. Two major works provide a history and description of rapper dances: Christopher Cawte's 1981 article 'A History of the Rapper Dance' and Phil Heaton's book *Rapper* (2012).[52] Longsword still awaits a comprehensive history. The chapters on Great Britain and England in Stephen Corrsin's book *Sword Dancing in Europe* (1997) (which also discusses rapper dancing) are the best overview, and Paul Davenport's *Under the Rose* includes much relevant longsword source material from Yorkshire.[53] Ivor Allsop's substantial *Longsword Dances from Traditional and Manuscript Sources* describes the dances in detail but with little or no contextual or historical information.[54]

Sword dancing appears to be a relatively modern phenomenon in England, with a clear picture of performance only emerging in the second half of the 18th century. There are a few literary allusions linking swords with morris in the late Tudor period (see pp. 145-46). The Blundell family in Lancashire mentioned sword dances in 1638 and 1712 (for the latter, see p. 187; the dancers had to be specially taught).[55] The Revesby play (see Chapter 12) is an example of the ways in which different elements of cultural practice can come together. Sword and morris dances, plough customs and mummers' plays (broadly defined) were intermingled. Similar mixing of concepts can be found in the areas most associated with sword dancing.

The majority of references are from writers giving a name to what they see – or in some cases don't see – be it sword, morris or another designation. It may be first-hand observation, or itself derived indirectly and interpreted. The 1864 *Handbook for Travellers in Durham and Northumberland* tells us that in Hartlepool, 'Yule logs are scrupulously burnt and yule-cakes eaten at Christmas, when exhibitions of sword-dancers go about the streets'. When this book was reviewed in the *Saturday Review*, the reviewer paraphrased, but with what for our purposes is a crucial alteration: '... yule-cakes are eaten at Christmas. Morris-dancers still go their rounds.'[56] At this remove we cannot tell if the change arises from the reviewer's presumption from ignorance or has equal descriptive validity with the original text. The *Morning Chronicle* in 1850 alluded to 'the sword dance, as exhibited by guisers or mummers' in Northumberland and (while noting that it was much more common thirty years previously) said that it still flourished 'as morris-dancers in Yorkshire still circle the maypole'.[57] It is a pity we have no other indication of their doing so. 'A Sheffield Christmas of Bygone Days' of 1872 speaks of ten or 12 morris dancers, with a dancing master, with pairs taking hold of a loose string garland of artificial flowers, 'with which they perform many evolutions'; and contrasts this with sword dancers forming a lock with the swords.[58] The loose garland suggests that perhaps the writer has in mind the morris of the stage dancing masters. Despite the oddities in the characterization of morris dances, the point of both of these reports is that sword dancing is seen as different from morris dancing. *The Times* of 1 January 1878, on the other hand, was happy to make the equation:[59]

> *Years ago, before screw colliers came into use, sailing colliers, as a rule, used to lay up for a month or six weeks in the depth of winter, and most of the pits were unemployed over that period. Many of the pitmen at that time used to come to the towns in companies 'sword dancing', an ancient Northern form of Morris dancing.*

Local writers may have been more knowledgeable. The engraver Thomas Bewick wrote of his youth in the 1770s at Prudhoe, just outside Newcastle-upon-Tyne, and the 'buzz occasioned

---

[52] Cawte, 'History'; Heaton.
[53] Corrsin, pp.85-94, 183-236; Davenport, Paul D.
[54] Allsop.
[55] Corrsin, pp. 93-94.

[56] *Handbook*, p. 116; 'Murray's Handbook'.
[57] *Morning Chronicle*, 16 January 1850.
[58] *Sheffield & Rotherham Independent*, 21 December 1872.
[59] *Times*, 1 January 1878.

by 'foulpleughs' (morrice or sword dancers)'.[60] This suggests the inclusion of the dance as part of a plough custom. Similar associations are found in Yorkshire. On the north bank of the Humber estuary, in the Holderness area, some reports resemble those south of the estuary, as that from 1877 noting that ploughmen 'go round the towns and villages dragging a plough ... stopping occasionally to perform a rude morrice dance round their implement of labour'.[61] Over time the dance was seen more often as an autonomous custom, with residual elements of drama in the introductory song. When the *York Herald* reported that 'Bands of sword and Morris dancers visited the town during the day' on Boxing Day 1887 it clearly had two distinct groups in mind. The 'morris dancers' may have been mummers, but they were not the sword dancers.[62]

One of the more considered opinions, if a little confused, came as early as 1829 in an article on 'Christmas and the New Year' in *The Newcastle Magazine* by its editor, William Mitchell. He wrote:[63]

> We have likewise what are called sword dancers, who seem to be a species of morrice dancers; but how the name morris or morrice dancers, meaning Moorish dancers, ever came to be applied to the dancers so called in this country, is a matter of strong dispute among antiquaries. Most probably the name originates in the dance itself having been copied from the Moors, not in the dancers having been Moorish. Many of our common steps in dancing are from Spain, and probably the Spaniards themselves had them from the Moors. The Morrisco [sic] is defined as a dance in which bells are gingled, and staves or swords clashed. Now the clashing of staves or swords is precisely what is practised by our northern sword dancers. Staves appear to be the common implements now-a-days, but swords are remembered to have been used.

Mitchell has consulted his Johnson and other authorities. The oddest statement is that staves have supplanted swords in the sword dance. It may be that he is thinking of the thin wooden laths sometimes used in longsword dances, or is trying to reconcile Johnson's definition with his own observations. An account almost contemporary with this was related at second hand decades later, but is datable to c.1829, and describes rapper swords of the modern design, 'swords... of flexible iron, with a handle at each end'.[64] Cawte has noted that the use of swords with such flexibility was dependent on the manufacture of steel of sufficient quality, which was not available before the 18th century.[65] Until then sword dancing in the area must have borne more resemblance to the longsword dances of Yorkshire.

In a few cases we have evidence from the performers themselves. The sword dancers from Cumberland who performed in London in 1788 (see pp. 153-55) certainly called themselves morris dancers, but their knowing handout may well have taken its cue from the current antiquarian thinking. The Earsdon sword dancers in Northumberland and Grenoside in Yorkshire each called themselves 'morris dancers'.[66] In the case of Earsdon this was regularly picked up by the press. Over several decades the Earsdon dancers provided a Christmas entertainment at Alnwick Castle. The report from 1873 is typical:[67]

> Before the beautiful tree was despoiled of its gifts, a party of Morris dancers from Backworth and Earsdon, gave an entertainment for the amusement of those assembled. The dancers

[60] Bewick, pp. 80-81.
[61] Ross, Frederick, Stead and Holderness, p. 61 (sv fond-pleeaf).
[62] *York Herald*, 27 December 1887.
[63] 'Christmas', p. 6.
[64] Cawte, 'History', p. 81.
[65] Cawte, 'History', pp. 101-02.
[66] Sharp, *Sword Dances*, 1:54-82.
[67] *Alnwick Mercury*, 11 January 1873.

this year were by far the best that have ever attended Alnwick Castle, and they won for themselves repeated rounds of applause as they went through their most graceful evolutions.

On the other hand, in 1887 John Stokoe, writing in detail about the Earsdon dancers, including their performances at Alnwick, termed them 'sword dancers' only.[68]

There are two ways in which sword dancing may have come to be identified as a kind of morris dancing, including by its performers. The first is through the association with other elements of a custom, where the name 'drifts' across; for example, the term being broadened to refer to any kind of dance attached to a solicitation custom (such as the plough jags), then being re-applied in the more specific case of a sword dance being associated with such a custom. The other is through antiquarian influence. Charles Atkinson, a minor Northumbrian author, published a short story, *The Water-whelmed*, in 1831, which includes a detailed scene of preparations for a sword dance, and makes explicit reference to the antiquarian sources:[69]

And what, asks the southern reader, did all this mean? To him an explanation is due. The male part of the company, then, comprised a band of 'sword dancers', of whom most of the different collieries formerly mustered their respective corps during the festivities at Christmas. ... The practice seems clearly a vestige of the old English Morrice games: but as we have neither Strutt nor Brand at elbow, we will not plunge into the question.

Although the practitioners may not have read such sources, and were probably for the most part illiterate, that does not mean that the ideas were unknown, and they might readily be adopted by the dancers as a validation of the custom by reference to its supposed antiquity.

While in some parts of the country morris dancing was becoming a rare sight, and in others was becoming a major popular recreation, the popularity of morris dances on the stage continued and began to spill over into the concert hall. George Alexander Macfarren, who had arranged some of Chappell's collection of national English airs, wrote the opera *King Charles II* in 1848, which contained a morris dance. We noted above (pp. 282-83) the *Manchester Times*'s criticism of the inaccurate staging of the dance in Manchester. His music for the morris dance was also performed as an independent orchestral piece at Jullien concerts (promenade concerts of light orchestral music).[70] Macfarren also composed a cantata 'May Day' in 1856[71] and in the same year harmonized what was termed 'a collection of morris dances, from 1589 to 1622' for a lecture series by the eminent composer and music historian Charles Salaman. At the London lecture in 1857 'Salaman's spirited and highly characteristic performance of a morris dance (1622) was enthusiastically re-demanded'.[72]

Lectures on early music frequently utilized supposed morris-dance tunes to enliven the event. Sometimes these were simply local events. A Hull surgeon, John Henry Gibson, lectured more than once in the city on 'The Poetry and Music of the Ballad', in which a colleague 'Jonathan Hay gave a few examples of May-day and Morris dances on the flute'.[73] When the Reverend W.D.V. Duncombe lectured on 'English Music' at Kingstone, Herefordshire in 1863 he played 'Trip and Go' (mentioned adjacent to the morris dance in Nashe's *Summers Last Will and*

---

[68] Stokoe.
[69] Atkinson, Charles, p. 150.
[70] For example, *Northern Whig*, 5 January 1850; *Hull Packet*, 18 January 1850.

[71] *Daily News*, 27 January 1859.
[72] *Morning Post*, 26 February 1857.
[73] *Hull Advertiser*, 26 January 1861; *Hull and Eastern Counties Herald*, 1 April 1869; *Hull Packet*, 21 March 1873.

Testament) as a morris dance.[74] One of the more eminent lecturers was the Professor of Music at Oxford, Sir Frederick Ouseley, who included 'Staines Morris' in his lecture on 'English Dance Music in Olden Time'.[75] Madame Hoffman was more of a professional lecturer. She lectured on 'Ballad Lore' in London, Birmingham, Plymouth and elsewhere in the 1880s in an event described as being 'calculated as much for diversion as for instruction' and featuring 'the morris dance with bells'.[76]

For nearly 25 years William Birch's operetta *The Merrie Men of Sherwood Forest* was a popular work, receiving its first performance in 1867 and being staged over 50 times in the remainder of the century, often in concert performances. Not unnaturally, it had a morris dance. When it was staged at a choral concert in Tewkesbury in 1870, 'A morris dance chorus seemed to electrify the audience', and it was encored. At the Reading Choral Union concert a month later it 'seemed to carry the audience away' and was again encored.[77] When it went to Ashton-under-Lyne, however, 'the morris dance in the second act was a decided failure; and by no means equal to the occasional gambols of our rush-cart lads'.[78] Nonetheless, the work was well suited for amateur performance and continued to be popular. The Horbury Choral Society in Yorkshire presented it twice in three months in 1876.[79] It even became a staple at school concerts; at the Cheltenham and County School prize-giving in 1887, 'The Wedding March (instrumental) and the Morrice Dance were played with the vigour and dash that Mr. Birch evidently inten[d]ed should be thrown into them'.[80]

A compilation of 'English national airs' which included a morris dance was created by one of the Godfrey brothers (variously attributed to Frederick, bandmaster of the Coldstream Guards, or his brother Daniel, bandmaster of the Grenadier Guards), and was a popular band piece at concerts during the 1870s and occasionally afterwards. It was probably based on Chappell's publication, which identified five pieces as morris dances but only one – the 'Long Morris' tune of Derbyshire and the north-west – which simply bore the title 'A Morris Dance'.[81] Both Birch and Godfrey were eclipsed, however, by Edward German's incidental music for the play *Henry VIII*, first performed in 1892. His 'Three Dances' – 'Morris Dance', 'Shepherd's Dance' and 'Torch Dance' – proved enormously popular, and the 'Morris Dance' was performed either alone or (more often) with the other dances nearly 350 times over the next eight years. On the same day in August 1894 it was performed at the Lowestoft Marine Regatta and the Eckington Flower Show in Derbyshire, and two days later at an end-of-the-pier concert in Hastings.[82] Like Birch's piece, it frequently featured in school concerts and was it still being played a century later.[83] Over 20 other compositions called 'Morris Dance' were published in the second half of the 19th century, half of these in its last five years.

Sometimes the different worlds almost collided. The *Wellington Journal* of 9 February 1895 carried a piece on page 5 about a charity concert held to provide funds for charities supporting those laid out of work by the severe frost, at which German's 'Morris Dance' and 'Shepherd's Dance' were played as a violin solo by a Miss Edith Austin. On page 8 the newspaper reported on the frozen-out boatmen of Worcester 'going about as morris-dancers'.[84]

---

[74] *Hereford Journal*, 14 March 1863.
[75] *Pateley Bridge & Nidderdale Herald*, 26 January 1889.
[76] *Hackney and Kingsland Gazette*, 2 October 1885.
[77] *Gloucester Journal*, 29 January 1870; *Berkshire Chronicle*, 26 February 1870.
[78] *Ashton Weekly Reporter*, 18 March 1871.
[79] *Ossett Observer*, 4 March 1876; *Ossett Observer*, 10 June 1876.
[80] *Cheltenham Examiner*, 8 August 1883.
[81] Chappell, 1:52; 2:109.
[82] *Norfolk News*, 25 August 1894; *Derbyshire Courier*, 25 August 1894; *Hastings and St Leonards Observer*, 1 September 1894.
[83] Northern Sinfonia of England and Hickox.
[84] *Wellington Journal*, 9 February 1895 [a]; *Wellington Journal*, 9 February 1895 [b].

With the pervasive presence of morris dances on the stage, in 'Merrie England' events, May festivals, dancing academies and music concerts, it is not surprising that they should feature in society balls, where those attending could take part in a morris dance as opposed to merely watching a performance. The earliest example is from 1864 when at a ball at the High Sheriff of Essex's seat in Ingatestone, bad weather forced the morris dance inside – the intended staging out of doors suggests that this was perhaps a maypole dance.[85] In 1865 at a ball in aid of the Grantham Dispensary, the patron of the event, the Hon. Mrs Welby, introduced a 'new and effective dance, called the Morris dance'. This was probably the same dance as was on the programme at the Grantham Literary Institution soirée the following year, where it was described as 'a species of country dance the effect of which was extremely pretty, each couple being provided with a bow of cane, surmounted by a coloured paper rosette',[86] suggesting the import of a garland dance from the theatrically inspired May-day festivals.

It was another decade before a different morris dance appeared in society ballrooms. When the Earl and Countess De La War arranged their tenants' ball at Buckhurst in Sussex on New Year's Day in 1874, 'a country dance, called the "Morris Dance", was much in request, and very pretty to look upon'. At a grand ball there in 1875, 'the revival of an old country dance, called the "Morris Dance"', in which the dancers held and waved coloured ribbons aloft, was the encored highlight of the evening.[87] The juvenile party arranged by the Marchioness of Salisbury at Hatfield House on New Year's Eve in 1874 involved dressing up to represent Queen Elizabeth's court, and in this case pairs of dancers held a ribbon between them, 'the different couples circling in and out beneath the bright ribbons they held above their heads'.[88] At the 2nd Duke of Cornwall's Light Infantry ball in November 1887 'twenty-four couples engaged in an old English Morris dance; pink, black and French grey, plaited ribbons being used', suggesting that this was a dance around a maypole.[89] In the same month Princess Louise (daughter of Queen Victoria) led off the tenants' ball at Naworth Castle in a morris dance. Six years later a correspondent said the morris dance was done annually at the tenants' balls there, and described how 'Two sticks (somewhat like barbers' poles in miniature) tied at the top and having there a tassel, are used in the dance. The dance is not difficult to learn, neither does it require as much energy as waltzes, &c.'[90] This is a different dance again; its closest parallel is perhaps the loose garland string of flowers reported at Sheffield in 1872 (see p. 338).

Ardern Holt, a guru on the subject of fancy-dress balls, suggested in 1888 that 'The "Morris" dance is carried out after the fashion of the "Pavane", all the dancers wearing bells',[91] but in 1897 she advocated something different:[92]

> *...those who take part in it must be dressed in the costumes of Edward III's time, and go through a sort of country dance with a toe and heel step, waving handkerchiefs over their heads.*

From the mid 1890s the predominant form seems to have been the dancers individually holding long ribbons which they waved through the air. Several reports simply mention a 'morris dance' among the elements of an evening's programme, suggesting that it was being

---

[85] *Chelmsford Chronicle*, 1 April 1864.
[86] *Grantham Journal*, 30 December 1865; *Grantham Journal*, 8 December 1866.
[87] *Kent & Sussex Courier*, 9 January 1874; *Kent & Sussex Courier*, 17 December 1875.
[88] *Hertford Mercury*, 9 January 1875.
[89] *Western Morning News*, 5 November 1887.
[90] Cracoe.
[91] Holt, 'Dances'.
[92] Holt, 'Amusements'.

danced widely and did not need further comment. The account of the balls at Peckforton and Oulton in Cheshire in 1894 captured the atmosphere:[93]

> *Picturesqueness was very happily introduced into the up-to-date prosaic atmosphere of a country ball the other day, and I do not doubt that the Morris dance will ere long rival the pas de quartre [sic] in popularity even in London. The dance is less of a romp than Sir Roger de Coverley. The dancers stand in two long lines holding the ends of gaily coloured ribbons, which they twist and turn about in the maze of the measure. The waving of arms and the fluttering of rainbow ribbon ends through the air has a very charming effect. Merriment reigned both at Peckforton and at Oulton, when the Morris dance was in full swing. Everybody voted it capital fun, and hoped to 'meet' it again very shortly.*

We noted earlier the dancing academies' introduction of morris dances into their curricula. Theresa Buckland has drawn attention to the growth in popularity in the 1880s and 1890s of 'the fancy dance repertoire, which operated both as amusement, and as display'.[94] Madame and Mr Demery's Private Academy of Dancing and Deportment in Bedford offered 'morris dance of the present century' in 1894, followed later by 'new morris dance'. They also offered special terms for school enrolments.[95] The academies were not only teaching children. When 'the pupils and friends of Miss Henderson and Miss Colford, the well-known professors of dancing' put on the last dance of their season at Hampstead Conservatoire in 1897, the *Hampstead and Highgate Express* informs us that the children performed various fancy dances including a skirt dance and a hornpipe, but the adults performed others, including a morris dance.[96] The publisher J. Curwen & Sons brought out an action song 'Merry Morris Dancers' for performance by children in schools. It was usually acted out by six boys, though larger numbers and girls' performances are also known. So, for example, at the annual concert at Tewkesbury by children attending the British Schools in 1894, it was described as 'an action song by six boys, their lively motions and bright dresses making quite a pretty scene'.[97]

Outside its strongholds in the south midlands and north-west, and the variety of solicitation customs in the west midlands and east of England which brought morris dancing into association with mummers' plays, plough customs and black-face minstrelsy, there was a variety of other ways in which people could encounter what they perceived as morris dancing. Hobby-horse customs in the south-west and at Abbot's Bromley, sweeps' May-day celebrations in London and elsewhere, and sword dances in the north of England could all be interpreted as morris dances. They could be seen and heard on the stage, at festivals and in concerts. Anybody could take part in one at a society ball or in an action song in school. It is not surprising that a new generation of antiquaries began to take an interest.

---

[93] *Shields Daily News*, 1 May 1894.
[94] Buckland, 'Dance', p. 37.
[95] *Bedfordshire Times*, 4 August 1894, *Bedfordshire Times*, 8 December 1894.
[96] *Hampstead & Highgate Express*, 3 April 1897.
[97] *Tewkesbury Register*, 21 April 1894.

Chapter 22

Fin de siècle

At the start of the 19th century Douce had put the study of morris dancing on a firm, if limited footing, but suggested that as a live form it was already dying out. He and his fellow antiquaries did give people confidence that they knew what morris dancing was, and just as importantly how its spirit could be recaptured in entertaining recreations of the imagined days of Good Queen Bess and Merrie England – celebrating, as Douce put it, its ancientness and its Englishness. Although drawing upon Strutt for atmosphere – his fiction was perhaps more compelling than Douce's or Brand's reliance on early texts alone – the morris dance that emerged in the theatres and pleasure gardens was also influenced by the ideas of the theatrical dancing masters, and quite possibly by encounters with itinerant morris dancers on the streets of London. Much as the morris of the 16th century had filtered down from the court and the guilds to the parishes and provinces, the morris of 'Merrie England' spread from the metropolitan theatres and pleasure gardens to the provinces and the more downmarket pleasure gardens, or local fêtes and festivals. At the same time premium was placed on performance by juveniles, often by young girls, capturing the supposed innocence of May Day.

Meanwhile, we have seen how in communities across the country morris dancing was surviving in various forms and to various degrees. The handkerchief dances performed primarily in the spring months in the Forest of Dean and Derbyshire, and probably the Cadi ha in north Wales, were in all probability the lineal successors to the morris dances of the Tudor and Stuart periods, but lacking the degree of embedding in whole-community customs to sustain the complexity found in other areas. In the east midlands and East Anglia morris dancing became just one in a variety of winter solicitation customs, and the name spread from one form to another, embracing mumming and plough customs, and in the north-east the sword dance. In the west midlands a distinctive choreography, the bedlam morris, based on stick-clashing dances had emerged, but – as in the east of England – it became primarily a solicitation custom associated with winter. At Lichfield, virtually the only place where bedlam morris had enjoyed civic support, that fell away and would later be replaced by dancing on the May festival pattern (see Chapter 25).

The stick dances spilled over into the south-midlands area where the most direct lineal successor of the Tudor and Stuart morris, the morris of the Whitsun ale, was still popular at the start of the century. The community festival of the Whitsun ale and the rivalry between communities encouraged the maintenance and development of the complexity of the dance form. However, the rapid falling away of community engagement in the second half of the century meant that by the closing years of the century it was maintained only in a few places, none of them with the support afforded by a Whitsun ale.

By the close of the 19th century the only area where morris dancing continued to flourish, and even to spread, was the north-west of England. Here the rushbearing festivals, providing contextual community support broadly equivalent to that provided by the Whitsun ale in the south midlands, continued to be popular in the first half of the century, and the morris dance thrived with them. Factory work in the industrial north-west encouraged all workers in a district to have their holiday at the same time, and this facilitated a successful translation of rushbearing into a popular secular wakes holiday. None the less, the construction of a rushcart in those circumstances seemed less relevant, and that element began to disappear. Perhaps commencing with the influence of Buxton's transition of morris dancing to female dancers performing around a maypole, morris dances began to be associated with the May festivals of the area. However, because there was a vibrant local tradition, there was a distinct impetus to embrace some kind of 'authenticity' in the presentation of morris dances. This extended to the theatre as well as the fêtes and festivals. The introduction of the Godley Hill dancers to the Knutsford May procession in 1878 was a key moment in this progression. The processional nature of the north-west morris dances also made it easy to incorporate them in the May processions (as a distinct element of May festivals) of the area. The delegation despatched from Leyland to the Godley Hill dancers at Knutsford in 1890 to learn about morris dancing was the spur for the explosion of morris dancing across Lancashire, and into Cheshire and Cumbria, in the last decade of the century. It also increased the participation of juveniles of both sexes. The adult teams remained predominantly male, but sometimes in association with juvenile teams. There was an increase in the professionalization of the activity, and its perception as a straightforward entertainment for hire. Though the dancers still took collections while they danced, dancing was more often for an officially sanctioned civic function, or for a charitable purpose. Towns in the north-west took civic pride in the distinctiveness of the region and celebrated its cultural manifestations.

The premium put on 'authenticity' and 'real' morris dancing in the north-west found reflection in a different way elsewhere, through the activities of two antiquaries who engaged with the south-midlands morris. D'Arcy Ferris was a professional musician who in 1884 re-invented himself as a 'Designer and Director of Fetes, Festivities, Festivals, and Functions'.[1] Roy Judge has made a thorough examination of his role in relation to morris dancing. He shows that Ferris's early efforts were very much in 'Ye Olde Merrie Englande' vein (he was keen on mock-Tudor spelling). Ferris's account of the Christmas festivities at Southam in January 1885 includes the following:[2]

> Mummers appear on the scene, and dance the fifteenth century Morris dance. They should be nine in number [there were in fact four], and dressed with streamers and bells. They wear masks of lions, bears and goats, and make noises like these animals.

Shortly thereafter he began to do some historical research in a quest for accuracy. In August 1885 he arranged a summer festival at Lockinge, near Wantage, for which he announced 'Ye Morris daunce shal be daunced bye laddes of ye royal burgh of Wantage', and a month later he organized a similar fête at Grimston, where the dance was performed by nine boys from the York Industrial School. Ferris later said that these were handkerchief dances, but 'not very correct'.[3] In the autumn of 1885 he began to look for information about morris dancing, having decided that he wanted to revive authentic morris dancing as Shakespeare would have known it. This meant finding 'rustics' rather than theatrical artistes. He had a musical colleague in Bidford, a town with Shakespearean associations in popular legend, who put him in touch with one William Trotman, who had danced in the Bledington area, and who brought together a team of local youths plus David Millen, an older former morris dancer probably

---

[1] Judge, 'D'Arcy Ferris', p. 444.
[2] Judge, 'D'Arcy Ferris', p. 445.
[3] Judge, 'D'Arcy Ferris', p. 447.

from Ramsden in the Wychwoods. There were also contacts with older Bidford men who had previously danced.[4] From this group of people Ferris formed the Shakespearean Bidford Morris Dancers.

In addition to hunting for 'real' dancers, Ferris wanted authentic materials and authentic dances. These came from two kinds of source: the network of contacts Ferris was making, and his knowledge as a cultural historian who had done his research. Trotman evidently got some bell pads from a colleague in the Bledington area. Ferris acquired a tabor from Brackley, but had more difficulty in obtaining a pipe. He found the pipe-and-taborer Joe Powell of Bucknell but he would not part with his instrument. Ferris was some way into his programme of events before he eventually obtained one, and several performances had fiddle accompaniment instead. Although no south-midlands team had a hobby horse, Ferris knew that a Shakespearean morris team should have one, so a hobby horse was made along the lines of the one shown in the Betley window, whose image had been reproduced several times in antiquarian books and journals since its first publication in 1778.

Elaine Bradtke has analysed the sources of the revived Bidford repertoire. Ferris's musician was sent to Ilmington, a Warwickshire village nine miles from Bidford, with its own history of morris dancing, to learn the tunes from an old pipe-and-taborer. Later the Bidford men met the former Ilmington team to learn more dances, and some of the tunes and dances probably come from there. More of the repertoire probably came from the Bledington area, via Trotman and his contacts, while some tunes may be from Bidford itself.[5] This was primarily a south-midlands side performing dances from that repertoire. Two tunes and dances came from Ferris. One was the dance 'Bluff King Hal', for which Ferris adopted the tune 'Staines Morris'. The dance includes figures not found elsewhere in south-midlands morris, such as dancing in a ring with linked hands, and may reflect elements which Ferris had seen in theatrical environments.[6] The other dance was 'Merry-go-round', in which the dancers hold sticks radially like the spokes of a wheel as they dance in a circle. The tune which Ferris supplied for this was 'Morisque' from Arbeau's *Orchésographie*. The inspiration for the dance appears to be the newspaper report from the industrial west midlands in 1884, in which a correspondent of the *Birmingham Weekly Post*, 'H.W.', recalled seeing dancers some fifty years before:[7]

> *The figures of the dance were, as well as I can recollect, commenced by the dancers standing in two rows, then advancing and striking sticks which they held in their hands and retiring, and then changing sides and placing the points of their sticks in the centre, forming a circle, and going round to the right and left.*

The dance is illustrated in the photograph of the team taken outside the Falcon Inn in Bidford on 23 January 1886 (Figure 22.1). The picture also shows the hobby horse, and Ferris himself standing on the cart, costumed as Lord of Misrule.

Ferris contracted with the team for six months of public performances during the first half of 1886, in which he gave lectures on the morris dance and the team performed. The bells and pipe and tabor were displayed as exhibits. It was presented as primarily an antiquarian demonstration, to convey historical information rather than provide entertainment pure and simple. Although the early performances were enthusiastically received, later ones were less

---

[4] Judge, 'D'Arcy Ferris', p. 449.
[5] Bradtke, 'John Robbins', p. 46.
[6] Bacon, Lionel, pp. 71, 73.
[7] W., H.

Figure 22.1: Shakespearean Bidford Morris Dancers outside the Falcon Inn (in Roy Judge, 'D'Arcy Ferris and the Bidford Morris', Folk Music Journal, 4.5 (1984), 443-80 (p. 456)).

so, and Ferris found himself 'asking indulgence for "any uncouthness or rusticity that might be apparent"'.[8] The contract with the team was not renewed upon expiry.

The enterprise was not without consequences. It renewed interest in the dances in local communities. For example, the Ilmington team started dancing again after a twenty-year break. A combined Longborough and Lower Swell Morris (mentioned earlier, see p. 235) appeared. The dancer who supplied Ferris with his bells asked for them back so as to go out with his morris team. The Bidford team continued to appear, turning up at the Chipping Campden Floral Fete ten years later and in Stratford-upon-Avon a decade after that, and would re-emerge as a participant in the revival of morris dancing 20 years later.[9] The Chipping Campden team itself started dancing again in 1896 after a forty-year break.[10] Ferris continued to include morris dances in his displays and may have incorporated some of what he had learned from his Bidford experience, but at the Irish Exhibition which he organized at Olympia in 1888 the display seems to have been based on theatrical and antiquarian models.[11]

One extraordinary event which took place on 3 May 1892 and was reported in *The Queen* magazine was in all likelihood an indirect consequence of Ferris's initiative:[12]

> *Mrs W.C.H. Burne and the Morris Dancers gave an enjoyable Fancy Dress Ball at the Eyre Assembly Rooms, St. John's Wood on the 3rd inst. The hosts wore the Morris dress, and*

---

[8] Judge, 'D'Arcy Ferris', pp. 460-66.
[9] Judge, 'D'Arcy Ferris', pp. 471, 473, 474-75.
[10] Chandler, *Ribbons*, p. 74.

[11] Judge, 'Merrie England', p. 126.
[12] 'Mrs. W.C.H. Burne'.

danced quaint dances once or twice during the evening. One was an Oxfordshire Morris containing four figures. This dance was only recently gathered in Wychwood Forest; but unfortunately the traditional tunes have not yet been recovered. A second performance was a stage morris, and a third, 'La Boulangère', was danced by the morris dancers with eight shepherdesses.

Mrs W.C.H. Burne was the sister-in-law of the luminary of the Folklore Society and author of *Shropshire Folk-lore*, Charlotte Burne. Charlotte herself was at the ball, in the guise of Queen Anne; the society's president, Laurence Gomme, was also present as a roundhead, as was another prominent folklorist, T.F. Ordish, who attended as a Yorkshire yokel. A few months earlier Ordish had apparently approached Ferris to enquire about including a morris dance in a forthcoming Folklore Society *conversazione*. Ferris in turn contacted Thomas Curtis of the Brackley morris dancers, whom he had first encountered in his 1886 investigations. Charlotte Burne wrote to Mrs Gomme, 'I think it would be best if Mr Darcy de Ferrars would send a man up to London to give the Mortlake men a few lessons'.[13] In the event no morris transpired at the *conversazione*, but it may be that Ferris put them in touch with David Millen, his Bidford dancer from the Wychwoods, and that the dance at the ball was the result.

The ball combined in one evening a semi-authentic morris dance, a stage morris and a much more fanciful pastoral *divertissement*. Sadly, there seems to have been no follow-up to this event. But Ferris had shown that it was possible for middle- or upper-class researchers to go and find, and to present to middle-class audiences, morris dances as performed in communities. He paved the way for the next antiquary to venture into this field, Percy Manning, although it seems the paths of the two did not cross.

Percy Manning was an Oxford antiquary of independent means who devoted much of his life to collecting material and information about his adopted county of Oxfordshire, after arriving in Oxford in 1888 as an undergraduate. His primary interest was archaeology, but he went much further in that he was interested in objects and records from all periods of history, and extended that into collecting the intangible heritage of folklore and custom.[14] His first encounter with custom came when he encountered children with a May garland at his mother's home in Watford in 1893.[15] This led him on a quest to acquire the material relics of May customs, in the form of garlands and maces (posies of flowers arranged on short staves). In this he enlisted the help of the autodidact labourer Thomas Carter, with whom he worked closely over several years. Carter did much of the fieldwork on Manning's behalf.[16] On Carter's visit to Bampton in his searches he encountered Hannah Wells, who told him in July 1894 that in Bampton the May garlands were displayed on Whit Monday when the morris dancers performed. As soon as Manning learned of this he was anxious to acquire not just May relics but also the material culture associated with the dance – costume, bells, cake-tin with sword, pipe and tabor.[17] By the end of 1894 Manning was able to display at an exhibition on Oxfordshire history a dancer's costume, cake-tin and maces from Bampton, together with a pipe from Bampton and tabor from Deddington, a pair of bell pads from Headington, maces and a money box from Kirtlington, and a pipe-and-tabor from Leafield.[18]

[13] Judge, 'Merrie England', p. 128.
[14] Heaney, Michael, 'Percy Manning – a Life'.
[15] Manning, 'May-day'.
[16] Heaney, Michael, 'Thomas James Carter's Role'.
[17] Heaney, Michael, 'Percy Manning, Thomas Carter', pp. 91-93.
[18] *Catalogue*, p. 10.

Carter also collected verbal information for Manning about the dancers and dancing from many places in Oxfordshire and its immediate surrounds. His notes, though brief, are a mine of information, and Manning was the first to assemble this kind of material on morris dancing. They have enabled us to build a much more rounded picture of dancing in the area and have informed detailed work such as that of Keith Chandler in documenting the lives and experiences of the dancers.[19] Manning sent Carter out with a specific set of questions covering when dancing took place, who was involved, the costume, and memorable incidents. The responses from Wheatley are typical:[20]

> *Wheatley, Oxon.*   *Whitsuntide*
> *As existing in 1860*
> *Six dancers*   x   *Thos. Brookes, labourer*
>   *James Ring*   "
>   x   *Will. Putt*   "
>   x   *George Putt*   "
>   x   *Nathaniel Putt*   "
>   x   *Christopher Tombs*   "
> *Costume – pleated shirts, trousers, tall hat, red, orange & blue ribbons, sticks, & handkerchiefs*
> *Squire – with bladder & cow's tail*
>   x   *Thomas Gome, labourer*
> *Pipe & tabour – x*   *Old Tom Hall of Islip*
> *Foreman & treasurer – x*   *James Brooks, labourer.*
> *They practised all the winter in Munt's hovel, and were the best set on that side of the county.*
> *The dancing went on all Whitsun Week.*
> *(from Charles Shepherd, aged <blank>, of Wheatley, labourer. Sept. 1894. T.J.C.)*
> *[x now dead]*

In most cases Carter was collecting information about a previous generation of dancing. By the time Manning became interested, only two Oxfordshire teams were still active, at Bampton and Eynsham.

Manning's research led to a lecture for the Folklore Society and an article in *Folk-lore* in 1897.[21] This in turn engendered another round of collecting, in the course of which Manning encountered a photograph of the Headington Quarry team (Figure 22.2). The picture was taken around 1875 (though Manning thought 1864).[22] The team had stopped dancing around 1880, but Manning discovered that some of the dancers pictured were alive and conceived the idea of encouraging the team to re-form. The result was a concert at the Corn Exchange in Oxford on 13 March 1899, at which dances by the Headington Quarry men were interspersed with folk songs (as the term was understood at the time) by colleagues of Manning's friend, the Oxford organist and music seller Charles Taphouse. Manning later described the event in these terms:[23]

> *I had picked up a photograph taken in 1864, of the dancers, and I discovered that two of the men, James Hedges & Jack Horwood, who were represented in that photo, were still living in Headington. With Carter's aid, I persuaded them to get a side together in the Autumn of 1898, which practised under the tuition of Hedges & Horwood during the winter. By the*

---

19   Chandler, *Morris Dancing ... Aspects.*
20   'Manning MSS, Wheatley'.
21   Manning, 'Some Oxfordshire Seasonal Festivals'.
22   Heaney, Michael, Grant and Judge.
23   Manning, 'Notes on the Revival'.

Figure 22.2: Headington Quarry Morris Dancers, c. 1875 (Image © Historic England CC71:00070).

spring they were ready to dance and were provided with the necessary dress and equipment, on the exact lines of my old photo. The whole training was carried on by themselves, without any interference from me or from any outside source, so that there was <u>no possibility of contaminating the pure tradition</u>. (This is the great danger of today.)

Manning's aims were quite different from Ferris's. Ferris wanted to recreate a flavour of a lost romantic England; Manning wanted to have a living relic, with an archaeologist's eye to preserving the integrity of the object. This is not to say there was no eye to image: the local press billed them as 'Ye Olde Headyngton Morris Dancers'.[24]

Manning went on to say that 'Morris dancing at once jumped back into public favour at Headington, and the dancers used to go about and give performances on their own account'. Their musician at the concert and afterwards was Mark Cox, a fiddler, who, new to the morris, picked up the tunes by ear as they were whistled to him in preparation for the concert. They danced again at Whitsun 1899, when they were photographed by Henry Taunt.[25] They also took advantage of the wider opportunities for performance in the 1890s, adopting the 'olde' tag and performing at new kinds of venues. The local newspaper reported that on 13 December 1899 they came out to support fundraising for the Boer War:[26]

In the hope of further increasing the total of the local Transvaal War Fund, the members of the St. Clement's Gymnastic Class gave a concert and gymnastic display on Wednesday evening at the Constitutional Hall, Cowley-road. ... A further attraction was the appearance of 'Ye Olde Headyngton Morrys Dancers', whose quaint antics greatly amused the company.

[24] *Jackson's Oxford Journal*, 18 March 1899.
[25] Grant, 'When Punch Met Merry', p. 646.   [26] *Jackson's Oxford Journal*, 16 December 1899.

Thirteen days later, on Boxing Day, they decided to dance around Headington to earn money, as most of them, being labourers, were out of work because of the weather. Mark Cox, who was a servant at Magdalen College, was not affected by the weather, so would have been at work. In consequence, William Kimber was the musician, playing the concertina. On their summer circuit of Headington they had called at Sandfield Cottage, the home of Mrs Dora Birch, who had invited them to return at any time, so the dancers made their way there and performed five dances.[27] Mrs Birch's son-in-law was a guest in the house and was very struck by what he saw. He was Cecil Sharp, and this encounter proved to be a pivotal moment which determined much of the course of the development of morris dancing over the next century.

---

[27]   Grant, 'When Punch Met Merry', pp. 650-51.

Part V: Revival (1899 – present)

Chapter 23

Defining a revival

At the time of the encounter between Cecil Sharp and William Kimber morris dancing was both everywhere and nowhere. As Roy Judge has pointed out, the word conjured up several kinds of image, and we have seen its manifold manifestations in choral pieces, children's action songs, theatrical pageants and more. The erudite 9th edition of *Encyclopaedia Britannica*, on the other hand, declared morris dancing 'now wholly discontinued'.[1] Judge's review of the last decade of the century captures the myriad theatrical, musical and festive ways in which the public could encounter and engage with morris dancing, while at the same time believing it was something of the past.

Cecil Sharp himself was part of this environment. Born into a middle-class merchant's family in 1859, he was a keen amateur musician in his youth, and continued to pursue his musical interests even though pressured by his family into more staid regular employment. From 1882 to 1892 he was in Australia, working first in a bank then in legal offices, but from 1889 he finally committed himself to a career in music and became co-director of the Adelaide College of Music.[2] In 1890 he composed a comic opera, *Sylvia*, which included a morris dance.[3] From 1896, after his return to London, he was Principal of the Hampstead Conservatoire. This was a part-time post, and he was also music master at Ludgrove preparatory school. As Principal of the Conservatoire he may well have witnessed the morris dance performed there in 1897 by the pupils of the Misses Henderson and Colford.

On Boxing Day 1899 Sharp was struck by his encounter with the Headington Quarry morris dancers and invited their musician on the occasion, William Kimber, to return the following day, when Sharp transcribed several of Kimber's morris-dance tunes. For the moment, that was the end of it. Sharp did what any composer of his day might do and incorporated the tunes into a 'Suite for Small Orchestra' for performance at his Conservatoire, and moved on.[4]

Like many of his contemporaries, Sharp was influenced by the popular criticism of English music that it had produced no composers of note, and by the parallel thread that celebrated the grounding of composed music in the traditions of the composer's homeland. In Sharp's case this was expressed as an interest in the Englishness of the songs taught in schools, including his own, and in 1903 he decided to search for original material among the rural population of England.[5] On 22 August he collected his first folk song, 'Seeds of Love', from John England, the gardener of his old friend Charles Marson, vicar of Hambridge in Somerset.[6] This was the event which galvanized him, resulting in the publication of *English Folk-songs for Schools* in collaboration with Sabine Baring-Gould in 1906.[7] Within a couple of months of collecting his first folk songs he was lecturing on the subject, and in July 1905 Herbert MacIlwaine, musical director of the Espérance Club, read a news report about his work. The Espérance Club was a charity aiming to support and enrich the lives of working-class London girls, both materially and through the encouragement of song, dance and drama. The girls had already learned

---

[1] Judge, 'Merrie England', pp. 124-25.
[2] Heaney, Michael, 'Sharp'.
[3] Judge, 'Merrie England', p. 127.
[4] Judge, 'Merrie England', p. 135.

[5] Karpeles, *Cecil Sharp*, p. 31.
[6] Heaney, Michael, 'Sharp'.
[7] Gould and Sharp.

Figure 23.1: Espérance morris dancers (in Mary Neal, The Espérance Morris Book, *2nd ed., p. xiv. London: J. Curwen, 1910).*

Scottish and Irish dances, in these cases from Scottish and Irish nationals. The club's founder, Mary Neal, went to see Sharp in September 1905 to investigate the possibilities for her girls to learn English folk songs. A month later she was back to ask him about English folk dances. All he had were the tunes collected from Kimber six years previously. Sharp gave Neal the contact details he had noted and she went to find Kimber, bringing him and his cousin to the Espérance Club to teach the girls morris dances. They were first performed at the club's 1905 Christmas party before several prominent supporters, who encouraged Neal to present them to a wider audience in public performance.[8]

The resultant public performance on 3 April 1906 was a quasi-dramatic presentation, 'An English Pastoral' by Herbert MacIlwaine, which must have had much in common with the romantic stagings of 'Merrie England' over the past decades in theatres, pleasure gardens and at festivals. It was preceded by a lecture on folk song by Cecil Sharp, primarily making a plea for English folk song and dance to be incorporated into the school curriculum. In this concert MacIlwaine and Neal succeeded where Ferris and Manning had failed, in presenting 'authentic' morris dancing in a performance context which matched the cultural sentiments and expectations of the audience. The event was a resounding success, and within weeks the girls of the Espérance Club were in demand to travel across the country to teach the morris dances they had learned (Figure 23.1).[9] These were primarily stick and handkerchief dances from the Headington Quarry repertoire.

Sharp and Neal moved quickly to capitalize on their success by producing a handbook to assist in the teaching of the dances. Sharp met Kimber at the Espérance Club on 25 May 1906 and

---

[8] Kidson and Neal, pp. 161-63.   [9] Judge, 'Mary Neal', p. 551.

Figure 23.2: Notation for the cross-step (in Cecil J. Sharp and Herbert C. MacIlwaine, The Morris Book, *Part II, p.12. London: Novello, 1909).*

noted some tunes from him, while MacIlwaine took the lead in devising a notation expressive enough to capture the dance movements, which were noted from the dancing of the Espérance girls. It allowed steps and hand movements to be matched against the music (Figure 23.2).[10] The notation was further developed for subsequent publications. A week after that meeting Sharp, MacIlwaine and Neal met the Bidford dancers at Foxlydiate House near Redditch. Lady Margesson, the owner, had invited the Bidford men to train youngsters to perform in a pastoral play which she had written.[11] The personnel of the Bidford team was largely that of 1886; they had continued to perform over the next twenty years, and had participated in Shakespearean festivals in Stratford and, earlier in 1906, in the theatrical production of *Pan's Anniversary* there.[12] Sharp noted the tunes with a sketchy indication of the dance,[13] and three of the dances were included, along with the Headington dances, in *The Morris Book*, written in July 1906 and published by Novello and Co. at the end of April 1907 under Sharp's and MacIlwaine's names.[14] In the historical introduction Sharp adopted the standpoint that the dance was of Moorish origin, though much altered. In vindication of his views on the antiquity of folk music and the dance, he pointed out that the tune of the Bidford 'Morris Off' was identical to the 'Morisque' of Arbeau published 350 years before, an observation which would cause him embarrassment when he learned in 1910 of Ferris's role in introducing it to Bidford (see Chapter 22).[15]

Sharp at this stage was primarily interested in tunes. When he heard two labourers whistling morris tunes while repairing the sewers outside his house on 6 July 1906, he noted a couple of their tunes but more importantly obtained from them the address of John Mason, who was later to provide him not only with several morris-dance tunes, but also with crucial further contacts. These included the address of the elder sewerman's father, William Hathaway, which would eventually lead to Sharp's encountering the major Gloucestershire morris dances.[16] But when he met Mason and Hathaway in the spring of 1907 he noted only tunes, and did not pursue the dances.[17]

Relations between Sharp and Neal began to deteriorate around six months after the publication of *The Morris Book*, when a conference was arranged at the Goupil Gallery to establish an association to steer the future direction of the folk-dance revival. The subsequent rancorous

[10] Townsend, A.D., pp. 60-61.
[11] Sutcliffe, David, 'Margesson, Lady Isabel'.
[12] Judge, 'Merrie England', p. 136.
[13] 'Sharp MSS, Bidford Morris Tunes'.
[14] Sharp and MacIlwaine, *Morris Book, Part I* (1907), p. 7.

[15] Sharp and MacIlwaine, *Morris Book, Part I* (1907), pp. 13-15.
[16] Burgess.
[17] Judge, 'Cecil Sharp', pp. 200-01.

debate between and mutual excoriation of the opposing parties has been documented in detail in their respective biographies, and in a balanced assessment by Roy Judge.[18] Neal's approach was that one should learn directly from traditional dancers and that those who had learned directly should then pass on their knowledge to others. Variability in performance was an inevitable concomitant of this, originating with the traditional dancers themselves. Sharp adopted a more authoritarian approach relying on strict adherence to a canonical form of the dance, determined by expert collectors. The morris-dance scholar Matt Simons –and Judge before him – have downplayed the sense that here were two dichotomous and incompatible views on the dance, pointing out that despite the tensions Sharp and Neal continued to work together in many respects in the two years 1907-1909. Simons, however, does draw out the essence of the differences:[19]

> Whilst for Sharp the crux of authenticity resided in the dances, for Neal it was the dancers themselves who represented the genuine articles. The former assumed morris was an artefact of English culture, which required careful and exacting arbitration. By contrast, Neal's morris was an intuitive dance, transmitted through imitative learning. Sharp's view privileged a corpus of art, music, and literature as representative of the English national character.

The analysis by the folk-music scholar Chris Bearman highlights another of the fault lines developing between Sharp and Neal:[20]

> Neal conceived the Association and its committee as a body of friends gathered to help her, while Sharp conceived it as a public society and tried to impose the constitution and forms usual in other public societies such as the Folk Song Society.

Bearman adds that a consequence of Neal's conception was that she wanted a quasi-autocratic controlling role, an expansion of her Espérance Club aiming to aid her work in helping children, especially the disadvantaged. After the failure to reach agreement at the conference, Neal formed her own Association for the Revival and Practice of Folk Music as a separate entity from the Espérance Club. Sharp had no role in it.

According to the transcript of the conference Sharp complained – only half jokingly – that he had been promoting the virtues of folk music (primarily song) but that when it became popular it was through Neal's efforts and she would have the credit.[21] At first he was content to distinguish between collecting and popularization through performing, and to identify himself with the former, to which he gave primacy; but as Neal began to contact and use other traditional dancers he felt threatened. His view as it developed was that there was a 'correct' way of morris dancing and that deviations from it were 'degenerate'. However, during 1908 and 1909 his experience of collecting remained relatively limited. He saw the Winster dancers in June 1908 – the first occasion on which he transcribed dances himself – and the following month met and collected dances from the former Sherborne (Gloucestershire) dancer George Simpson.[22] In January 1909 he met Sam Bennett of Ilmington but was not impressed, seeing him as the instigator of a revival rather than as a traditional performer.[23]

Although Sharp was now definitely interested in folk dance, it was in 1908 still secondary to folk song. MacIlwaine seems to have been the main actor in the preparation of *The Morris Book, Part*

---

[18] Karpeles, *Cecil Sharp*; Neal; Judge, 'Mary Neal'.
[19] Simons, 'Morris Men', p. 32.
[20] Bearman, p. 94.

[21] 'Verbatim Report'.
[22] Townsend, A.D., pp. 62-63.
[23] 'Sharp MSS, Ilmington'.

II during the first part of the year. However, Sharp's visit to Winster and his independent collection of dances there, the realization that there was more to discover from the likes of Simpson and the Gloucestershire fiddlers, and his increasing unhappiness with the direction the movement was taking under Neal led to a delay in the production of this second part, and when it was published there was no reference to or acknowledgement of the Espérance contribution. The preface included an implicit criticism of their dancing:[24]

Figure 23.3: William Kimber, 1912 (Image courtesy of Vaughan Williams Memorial Library, Photograph Collection mo/Hea/1912+/358).

> *... we have noticed in the would-be Morris dancer a tendency to be over-strenuous, to adopt, upon occasion, even a hoydenish manner of execution. These are utterly alien to the spirit of the dance; for although it is characterized by forcefulness, strength, and even a certain abandonment, it is at the same time always an exhibition of high spirits under perfect control.*

When *The Morris Book, Part II* appeared in 1909 Sharp only had more Headington dances to offer, together with the Winster processional dance.[25] His conception of the dance as an art form was undoubtedly influenced by the fact that he had a young and fit exponent in William Kimber, who was aged just 27 when Sharp first met him in 1899. The Master of the Worshipful Company of Musicians described him in 1911 as 'nothing less than a Greek statue ... his grace and movements are absolutely classic' (Figure 23.3).[26] Kimber's dancing became the yardstick against which other dancers were judged.

However, dancers were variable. Dave Townsend has drawn attention to a letter from Espérance's (and at that time, Sharp's) main teacher, Florrie Warren, to Sharp in June 1909 before a morris-dance competition he was to judge. She had noticed that Kimber had changed the way he performed one of the steps and asked Sharp 'to decide which one we ought to teach ... according to the way he dances now the way we have been dancing is incorrect'.[27] In addition the steps performed by George Simpson, whom he had met at the beginning of the year, were altogether different from Kimber's (though Sharp did not note the steps until a later visit).

In the summer of 1909 Sharp rented a house in Stow-on-the Wold as a base from which to collect songs and dances. From here, following the leads in Percy Manning's 1897 article

---

[24] Judge, 'Cecil Sharp', pp. 207-08.
[25] Sharp and MacIlwaine, *Morris Book, Part II*, p. 6.
[26] *Musical Times*, 1 March 1911.
[27] Townsend, A.D., p. 64.

in *Folk-lore*, he went to Bampton, where he met William Wells. At this first meeting Sharp noted Wells's tunes but not his dances. He met the Ilmington team again, George Steptoe at Leafield and Michael Handy (a second, older source for Ilmington), and collected fragmentary information about several other morrises. Some of these fragments were gleaned from a visit to the Forest of Dean, while notes about Pershore and other west-midlands dances were gathered from a brief visit there.[28]

Sharp's other major informant during the sojourn at Stow-on-the-Wold was the musician Charles Benfield, who told Sharp about the dances from Bledington. There were several visits to and by Wells, and it seems MacIlwaine was summoned to Stow to help Sharp note down the Bampton dance steps.[29] However, Wells's style must have caused Sharp some inner anguish. He still had not seen a full Bampton team dance, but when he led Maud Karpeles, Ralph Vaughan Williams and some folk-dance students there for the Whit-Monday dancing in 1910, he forewarned them that 'we should not see the dances performed in the way that he had taught them, for already they had seriously deteriorated'.[30]

At the beginning of 1910 Sharp encountered the full extant Eynsham team, whose style of dancing was again markedly different from everything he had encountered before. He was impressed by their vigour ('as fine an exhibition of morris dancing as it has ever been my good fortune to see') but was unable to grasp the fluidity of the dances' structure, averring that the 'Brighton Camp' dance 'was their only one, although for variety's sake they performed it to different tunes'.[31] When the third part of *The Morris Book* came out in 1910, Sharp was moving towards a reconceptualized view of the morris dance. He wrote, 'Our experience proves that each village where Morris dancing survives has its own tradition, its own dances, and its own special methods of performance'; and he gave details of the villages from which the dances originated.[32] By the time of the fifth book in 1914, the entire organization was based upon village 'traditions', a reconception which was to shape the development of morris dancing over the next century.[33] *The Morris Book, Part III*, meanwhile, published in 1910, contained dances from Bampton, Eynsham, Bledington and Brackley. In the introduction Sharp felt ready to make some general assertions, including his view that 'in Worcestershire, Herefordshire and, so far as our investigation goes, in the northern counties, Morris dancing has undoubtedly fallen on evil days and become decadent.[34] The assertion about Worcestershire and Herefordshire was partly based on his own brief excursions to the area the previous year, but was also no doubt influenced by his reading of Charlotte Burne's work on Shropshire folklore.[35] However, there is no evidence that Sharp had investigated the north-west morris at this time, and as we have seen, it was flourishing at the end of the 19th century and continued to do so as Sharp was writing.

During this period Sharp had been taking steps to distance himself from Mary Neal's club. He was cultivating his relationship with the Chelsea College of Physical Education, part of the South Western Polytechnic. The relationship had begun with Espérance's Florrie Warren teaching the polytechnic's students, but in September 1909 a School of Morris Dancing was established there with Sharp as Director.[36] Both Sharp and Neal recognised the advantages

---

[28] Judge, 'Cecil Sharp', pp. 214-23.
[29] 'William Wells', p. 10.
[30] Karpeles, *Cecil Sharp*, p. 96. I am grateful to Derek Schofield for identifying this reference for me.
[31] Sharp and MacIlwaine, *Morris Book, Part III* (1924), pp. 83-84.

[32] Sharp and MacIlwaine, *Morris Book, Part III* (1910), p. 10.
[33] Sharp and Butterworth, *Morris Book, Part V*, pp. 5-8.
[34] Sharp and MacIlwaine, *Morris Book, Part III* (1910), p. 10.
[35] Burne, *Shropshire Folk-lore*.
[36] Judge, 'Mary Neal', pp. 557, 560.

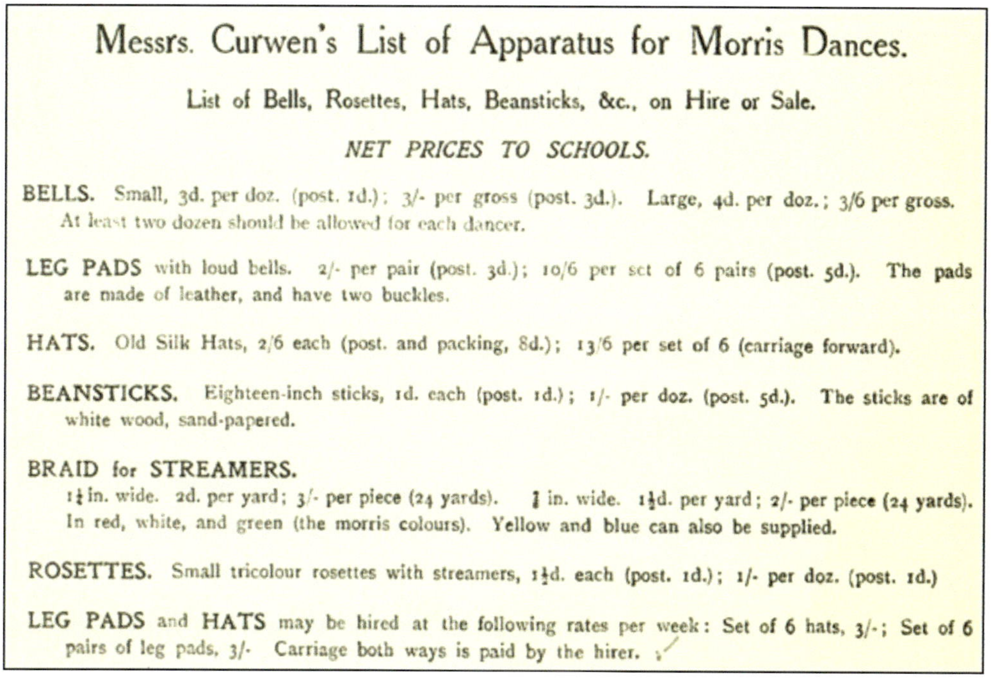

Messrs. Curwen's List of Apparatus for Morris Dances.

List of Bells, Rosettes, Hats, Beansticks, &c., on Hire or Sale.

NET PRICES TO SCHOOLS.

BELLS. Small, 3d. per doz. (post. 1d.); 3/- per gross (post. 3d.). Large, 4d. per doz.; 3/6 per gross. At least two dozen should be allowed for each dancer.

LEG PADS with loud bells. 2/- per pair (post. 3d.); 10/6 per set of 6 pairs (post. 5d.). The pads are made of leather, and have two buckles.

HATS. Old Silk Hats, 2/6 each (post. and packing, 8d.); 13/6 per set of 6 (carriage forward).

BEANSTICKS. Eighteen-inch sticks, 1d. each (post. 1d.); 1/- per doz. (post. 5d.). The sticks are of white wood, sand-papered.

BRAID for STREAMERS.
1¼ in. wide. 2d. per yard; 3/- per piece (24 yards). ⅞ in. wide. 1½d. per yard; 2/- per piece (24 yards). In red, white, and green (the morris colours). Yellow and blue can also be supplied.

ROSETTES. Small tricolour rosettes with streamers, 1½d. each (post. 1d.); 1/- per doz. (post. 1d.)

LEG PADS and **HATS** may be hired at the following rates per week: Set of 6 hats, 3/-; Set of 6 pairs of leg pads, 3/- Carriage both ways is paid by the hirer.

Figure 23.4: 'Messrs. Curwen's List of Apparatus for Morris Dances' (in Mary Neal, The Espérance Morris Book, Part II, p. 52. London: J. Curwen & Sons, 1912).

of getting morris dancing (and folk song) into school curricula, and this was a significant advance in the right direction for Sharp. Another key element was the Stratford Shakespeare Festival, which had become a showcase for the revival in folk music. By 1909 it had become the Stratford Festival of Folk Song and Dance with Sharp, Neal and MacIlwaine in an uneasy relationship as judges together with a prominent and influential Inspector of Schools, Edward Burrows, who initially enthusiastically embraced Neal's initiatives but later supported Sharp's conception of the movement.[37]

Novello began to distribute *The Morris Book* with flyers for Sharp's new School of Morris Dancing. Neal was dependent on the books for teaching but could not countenance promoting what was a rival to her own classes. This was the spur leading to her transforming the Association for the Revival and Practice of Folk Music into the Espérance Guild of Morris Dancers and the publication in 1910 by J. Curwen & Sons of her *The Espérance Morris Book*, with dances from Headington, Bidford, Ilmington and Abingdon (though they were not identified as such).[38] Curwen were already in the business of supplying equipment to schools in support of their music publications, and offered a complete set of 'apparatus for morris dances' to accompany the books (Figure 23.4).

The dispute between Sharp and Neal became public in an acrimonious outburst of letters to the press in May-June 1910, including accusations that Sharp was 'arrogat[ing] to himself the position of Pope', and challenges to Kimber's authority as the arbiter of the correct way to dance the Headington Quarry dances, after Neal contacted Joe Trafford, Mark Cox and other

---

[37] Judge, 'Mary Neal', p. 558.   [38] Judge, 'Mary Neal', p. 561.

older members of the Headington Quarry team.[39] From that point the two were irretrievably irreconcilable.

Sharp met D'Arcy Ferris in 1910 and, while it alerted him to the eclectic origins of the Bidford dances, the meeting also put Sharp on the trail of the Kirkby Malzeard sword dancers, whom Ferris had engaged for the Ripon millenary celebrations in 1886.[40] This rapidly led to the publication of the first of Sharp's sword-dance books in 1911, where he laid out in some detail his new view of the overall nature and relationships of morris dancing, sword dancing and the mummers' play as relict survivals of primitive rites, summarized as:[41]

> *In Morris, sword-dance, and play we seem to intercept three stages of development, arrested and turned to its own uses by the civilized and social idea of entertainment: in the Oxford Morris-customs the earliest sacramental rite; in the sword-dance the later human sacrifice; in the mumming play the still later half-magical presentment of nature's annual death and renewal.*

The book also included the Abbot's Bromley horn dance, where it was clear to Sharp that the horns 'recall the sacramental wearing of the skin of the sacred and sacrificed animal'. These views – similar ones were already being expressed by Neal[42] – embodied the 'cultural survivals' thesis originated by E.B. Tylor and popularized especially in J.G. Frazer's 1890 work *The Golden Bough*.[43] Frazer suggested that various contemporary customs in civilized societies, including May lords and the Jack-in-the-Green, were hangovers from rituals in primitive agrarian societies involving the death of a mock king to encourage the crops to grow. Tied to this was the idea that such ancient and deep-rooted practices were an expression of the racial as well as cultural identity of the English.

The ascription to primitive origins indirectly strengthened the feeling entertained by both Sharp and Neal that male dancers were to be encouraged, and preferred to women's or girls' dancing, though both recognised the pragmatic benefits in allowing the participation of women and girls. Neal was first off the mark with a team of boys in January 1910, while in February Sharp was still writing 'I am very anxious to have a men's side at my command'.[44] A flyer for folk-dance classes in Oxford in 1911, organized from Sharp's Chelsea school, declared that 'The "morris" is in origin a religious or ceremonial dance, confined to the initiated who pass it on with strict insistence upon correctness and, if possible uniformity'.[45] In the second edition of *The Morris Book, Part I* in 1912, a quite different work from the first edition rewritten to accommodate Sharp's revised view of the village-based tradition and the history of the dance, and expunging all mention of the Espérance Club, Sharp wrote:[46]

> *The Morris is, traditionally, a man's dance. Since, however, it was revived a few years ago it has been freely performed by women and children. Although this is not strictly in accordance with ancient usage, no great violence will be done to tradition so long as the dance is performed by members of one sex only. … Women, however, would be advised to avoid those dances in which essentially masculine movements as the 'Gallery', the 'Kick-jump', &c., occur. … The performers were picked men, chosen, after competition with other aspirants, because of their agility and the possession of certain specific qualities.*

---

[39] Judge, 'Mary Neal', pp. 563-66.
[40] Judge, 'Mary Neal', p. 557.
[41] Sharp, *Sword Dances*, 1:32-33.
[42] Bearman, p. 69.
[43] Frazer.

[44] Judge, 'Mary Neal', p. 562.
[45] Judge, 'Branch', pp. 91-92.
[46] Sharp and MacIlwaine, *Morris Book, Part I* (1912), pp. 42-43.

Figure 23.5: EFDS men's demonstration team, 1912 (Image courtesy of Vaughan Williams Memorial Library, Photograph Collection mo/EFDS/1912/13013).

By this time Sharp had the upper hand in the arguments. In the summer of 1911 he gained control of the influential Stratford festival, and on 6 December 1911 the English Folk Dance Society (EFDS) was established with Sharp at its head, based on an informal Folk Dance Club which had been organized by Maud Karpeles and her sister Helen, who had learned morris dancing at Sharp's Chelsea classes. At last Sharp was able to field a team of adult male dancers, representing the new Society (Figure 23.5).[47]

By this stage Sharp had encountered the most elaborate of the south-midlands morris dances, from Leafield (known as Fieldtown), Longborough, Bledington and Sherborne (Gloucestershire). These he published in *The Morris Book, Part IV* (1911) and *Part V* (1913). *Part V* was published under the names of Sharp and the composer George Butterworth, who was undertaking his own morris-dance collecting with notable success at Badby and Bucknell.[48] Butterworth recorded the trials and tribulations of hunting for dances at the latter place in his 'Diary of Morris Dance Hunting'.[49] He was one of the seven men who were the core of the EFDS men's demonstration team, and it is likely that Sharp saw him as his eventual successor at the helm of the EFDS; but he and three others of the team died during World War I.

The EFDS was a membership-based organization. It held examinations and issued certificates of competence in morris dancing (and other folk-dance forms), and rapidly grew in strength. At the end of 1913 the society had 280 full personal members, but in addition also had 20 branches across the country whose membership when recorded about three months later was probably over 2000 (there were 1585 in the 12 branches which reported numbers). The educational impetus was captured in the report of the Cheltenham branch: 'This Branch was formed in March, 1913, and has 165 members, over one hundred of whom are elementary

---

[47] Karpeles, *Cecil Sharp*, pp. 86, 116.
[48] Karpeles, *Cecil Sharp*, p. 108. [49] Wortley and Dawney.

school teachers'.[50] Although membership of the society proper was expensive at one guinea (£1 1s), branch membership could be had for as little as 1s. As Bearman points out, 'By this encouragement of a mass membership at low cost, the EFDS had far wider influence and a much broader base of support than the Esperance organisation could ever claim'.[51] Although the society's activity was inevitably curtailed during the war, it rapidly bounced back, with a strong demand for teachers. The Christmas vacation school in 1919 was attended by over 400 students and was visited by the President of the Board of Education at the head of a high-level Board of Education delegation.[52] The advent of the war did, however, spell the end for the Espérance movement. Mary Neal described its demise:[53]

> Our men dancers joined the army, the girls were scattered, the children could not come out in the evenings because of air raids. So the Club closed down and in 1918 it was impossible to begin again. The world had changed.

The Morris Book, Part V in 1913 was seen by Sharp as concluding the series. He wrote:[54]

> The area ... within which the Morris Dance has flourished within the last half-century ... is more or less clearly defined; and as this part of England has now been pretty closely investigated.

This was not quite true, for in 1919 he met William Walton of Adderbury, and the dances from there were included in the revision of *The Morris Book, Part II* later that year. In the revision of *Part III*, published in the year of his death, 1924, Sharp added a dance from Wheatley (collected in 1921) and one from Abingdon (collected in 1922, though first encountered in 1910). He published revised editions of parts I-III of *The Morris Book*, and these, together with parts IV and V, contained 81 morris dances from 17 locations. Fourteen of these places were in the south midlands and three in Derbyshire. Anomalously, as they were not called morris dances, the books also included the Helston furry dance and a comic three-person dance from Wyresdale in Lancashire. For decades thereafter these became the morris-dance canon, afforced by a few more collected primarily in the 1920s and 1930s.

The map of Sharp's collecting of dances is remarkably limited. It is more or less confined to the south midlands for morris dances and the north-east for sword dances. His sole record from the east of England appears to be the note he made of the occurrence of 'morris dancers' (without a dance notation) on Plough Monday around Littleport in Cambridgeshire when he visited on 8 September 1911.[55] We have noted his dismissal of the west-midlands dances in the introduction to *The Morris Book, Part III*, after a brief collecting spell, and his scorn for the north-west morris in the same sentence, though there is no evidence that he had seen any north-west dances at that stage.

In 1911, the year after his dismissal of the north-west morris, Sharp did note down in some detail the dance at Keswick, imported from Mawdesley near Preston (see Chapter 20), but he did not proceed to publish it. Instead he published the Wyresdale dance (collected in 1912), which has neither grace, nor choreographic similarity, nor the name of morris, its sole link being the use of the 'Greensleeves' tune used in south-midlands morris jigs. The reasons for these occasional excursions to Cumbria remain unclear. Neither was part of an extended sojourn. He met the person who became his preferred singer and protégée, Mattie Kay, at a concert in Walton-le-

[50] Croft, p. 16; 'News from the Branches'.
[51] Bearman, pp. 99-100.
[52] Croft, p. 10.
[53] Neal.
[54] Sharp and Butterworth, *Morris Book, Part V*, p. 7.
[55] 'Sharp MSS, Plough Monday'.

Dale near Preston when visiting his brother-in-law Walter Birch around 1900,[56] so it is possible he had seen one of the many sides in that area on such a visit. He must have been aware of the publication of John Graham's *Lancashire and Cheshire Morris Dances* by the rival firm Curwen in 1911.[57]

For Sharp, the idea of a 'folk' tradition relied on communal and almost unwitting evolution. In *The Morris Book, Part IV* he described the elaborate Sherborne and Leafield dances in some awe as 'the natural expression and unaided invention of the "untutored" country yokel'.[58] As he saw them as relics of ancient practices, it was easy from there to perceive that the dances could only exist in rural areas relatively untouched – untainted – by contemporary society and influences or by interventions from individuals bringing their own agency to the process. Hence his discomfiture on learning of D'Arcy Ferris's role in the Bidford repertoire, and his excising those dances from the second edition of *The Morris Book, Part I*. His dismissal of Sam Bennett's Ilmington team has similar elements, though is more complex. He wrote on 28 April 1910 to Alice Gomme, 'Miss N[eal] contemplates having the Ilmington Morris to London as examples of the traditional dance. These men only started operations 2 or 3 years ago and are very uncouth as well as untraditional dancers.'[59] Bennett had probably been inspired by reading of the 1906 revival, but could draw on local sources in Ilmington (themselves inspired by the Bidford revival of 1886). He was an enterprising fruit merchant capable of promoting his activities, and having been criticised by Sharp he worked with Mary Neal. He followed the Bidford – D'Arcy Ferris's – example in introducing a hobby horse to the Ilmington team.[60]

Sharp met Thomas Cadd of Yardley Gobion in 1910. Cadd had been asked 'a few years ago' to remember the Brackley dances he had seen, and imitated, as a boy around 1875, when he would have been a teenager. This was for a typical village May festival under the aegis of the local gentry. E.D. Mackerness suggested that the Yardley Gobion morris dancers appeared regularly between 1880 and 1920, but Cadd was only 17 in 1880 and census information shows him to be living in the parental home in Preston Bissett in 1881. He told Sharp that he had spent time moving around the country, chiefly in what were in fact the areas in Lancashire with a strong rushcart tradition, but by the 1891 census he had married a woman from Preston Bissett and they had their first child there in 1886, moving to Yardley Gobion by 1889 when their second child was born.[61] The morris dancing is attested from 1893. Apart from teaching the dancers, Cadd accompanied them as a Robin-Hood-cum-fool figure, and a hobby horse was introduced.[62] Clearly the Yardley Gobion morris did not fit Sharp's model for a traditional folk dance, because he knew who created it and knew of the 'non-peasant' involvement. Roy Judge has noted that Cadd's creativity 'encapsulates the problems which Cecil Sharp was going to meet when he tried to come to terms with the morris, crucially the difficulties connected with the continuity and creation of tradition'.[63]

There are similar examples where the interplay of influences may have led to anomalous results. In 1887 there had been an 'international morris dance' at Deddington, a village with its own morris history. There were nine dancers representing different nationalities, with an 'Italian' playing the barrel-organ.[64] They may well have appeared at intervals thereafter, but

[56] Karpeles, *Cecil Sharp*, p. 24; 'Walter De H Birch' (1901 census).
[57] Graham.
[58] Sharp, *Morris Book, Part IV*, p. 10.
[59] 'Sharp MSS, Correspondence with Alice Bertha Gomme'.
[60] Sutcliffe, David, 'Bennett, Sam'.
[61] Karpeles, 'Yardley Gobion Morris'; Mackerness; 'Thomas Cadd' (1881 census); 'Thomas Cadd' (1891 census).
[62] Warren.
[63] Judge, 'Merrie England', p. 134.
[64] *Banbury Advertiser*, 21 April 1887.

25 years later *Oxford Journal Illustrated* carried a picture of another such team from there.[65] Deddington may originally have been inspired by similar 'international morris dances' performed at Banbury in 1884 as part of an 'international fete'.[66] Such interfaces were not new. When the Littlemore Asylum just outside Oxford held its Christmas party in 1858 a 'morris dance, in character, by six of the attendants' was enthusiastically cheered, and was repeated in 1861, when the press noted that such dances 'are in a great measure peculiar to this neighbourhood'.[67] Around the same time in Sheffield there were 'queer doings' at the workhouse Christmas party in 1861 when 'women, with blackened faces, were kissing officers [of the workhouse], who kissed them in return; and the able-bodied paupers were kissing an officer's wife. The "mummers" and "Morris dancers" feats were enacted.'[68]

Among the reasons for Sharp's neglect of the north-west morris dances may be that they had widespread community support at all levels of society in industrial areas at the forefront of contemporary society, so did not fit the aetiological narrative he had constructed to explain the morris dances and sword dances he had found. This was certainly the view of Maud Karpeles, who was Sharp's close associate and in many ways guardian of his legacy (both metaphorically and literally: she was literary executrix of his estate). She did, however collect more from the west midlands after his death (see Chapter 15); and published details of the Royton north-west morris dance in 1930. What she said therein about the north-west tradition, however, is illuminating:[69]

> Unlike the traditional Morris of the Midlands, the Lancashire dance has attracted the attention of a wide public, and its very popularity has perhaps been its undoing.
>
> The Morris Dance is a great feature at the Lancashire Carnivals, which attract large crowds of spectators. On these occasions the dancers perform not only for display, but to compete against rival teams, and this has undoubtedly had an adverse effect on the dancing. The performers, instead of adhering to the traditional mode of dancing, have been tempted to introduce new features and develop the dance on lines that are calculated to win the approbation of the judge and the audience. Furthermore, many teams are trained especially to take part in the Carnivals and appear under the title of Morris Dancers, although they have, in fact, little or no knowledge of the traditional dance.
>
> In this way, false standards have been set up - or, as one dancer put it, 'the dance has been infringed' - and it seemed as though the genuine traditional Lancashire Morris was a thing of the past.

Karpeles was, therefore, pleased to find the Royton dance as it had been done at the beginning of the century, and it formed the basis of her published description. The north-west morris had indeed developed further since the end of the 19th century, and we shall consider those developments in the next chapter, but two things stand out in her assessment. One is that competition encourages innovation and is to be deprecated, although similar competitions had been a stimulus for many of the south-midlands teams which she admired. The other is that while she and Sharp decried the decline of the south-midlands morris in the 19th century, the popularity of the north-west morris was equally deleterious to its health. It seems that morris dancing was something that had to be rescued from its environment, whether it was neglected or embraced by its communities.

---

[65] *Oxford Journal Illustrated*, 26 April 1911.
[66] *Banbury Guardian*, 23 October 1884.
[67] *Oxford Chronicle*, 1 January 1859; *Jackson's Oxford Journal*, 5 January 1861.
[68] *Sheffield Independent*, 2 January 1862.
[69] Karpeles, *Lancashire Morris Dance*, p. 5.

Chapter 24

North-west morris 1900-1930

While the revival led by the Espérance Club and the English Folk Dance Society meant that in most parts of the country this rapidly became the form in which most people encountered morris dancing, in the north-west of England a more complex picture developed over the first part of the century. Four differing strands can be distinguished. First is the successor to the morris of the rushcarts. Second is its derivative, the festival-based morris that developed from Leyland in the 1890s and swept the area. Third is the competitive carnival morris that developed in turn from the festival morris. Fourth is the revival morris, which made inroads into the region much as it did across the rest of the country. The first three to some extent formed an overlapping continuum of influences which acted upon each other, but all were also influenced by the revival.

As a result of the enormous popularity of carnivals and festivals dozens of teams were formed. Some of these were transient, or only performed in a limited sphere – perhaps the annual village fête, or local temperance galas – while others endured over decades, gaining a strong reputation. The latter often had trainers who became well known for their skills. The performance contexts also varied. Street parades required different dances from displays at festival venues. The morris dances were performed along with a variety of other dances, from maypole to 'Grecian', presented at the same events, and often taught by, and even performed by, the same people. Festivals awarded prizes for morris and other entertainments, and these developed into competitions, influencing the style of dancing. Over time the changing performance contexts, in conjunction with the effects of World War I, led to a shift in the age and gender of the participants, from adult men to juvenile girls. Towards the end of the period, dancing by juvenile girls in carnival competitions was the predominant form, leaving the other forms ripe for 'revival' in their own right.

By the beginning of the 20th century rushcarts had all but disappeared. The few that were seen were constructed as memorials to olden days in civic celebrations such as those for the coronations of Edward VII in 1902 and George V in 1911, as for example at Didsbury, where a boys' team accompanied a rushcart on both occasions. A similar event took place in Droylsden in 1906.[1] In the former strongholds of the rushcarts the associated morris dancers sometimes survived independently. At Ashton-under-Lyne there were two sets in the period up to World War I, the 'Charlestown Lads' and the 'Cotton Street Lads'. ('Lads' was a common appellation for morris dancers, probably on the basis of the 'Rushcart Lads' tune – the 'Long Morris' – used for the dance.) They came out to collect for charity, including for the Whitehaven mine disaster of 1910, when according to one of the dancers they were given £20 to get new costumes.[2]

In Oldham the landlord at the Rope and Anchor pub paid for costumes for a team known as 'Mr Goray's Morris Dancers', apparently comprising both youths' and adult men's teams. They would have liked a rushcart but, as one of the dancers told the researcher Dan Howison, they 'never got that far'.[3] The identity of 'Mr Goray' has not been traced. The team reformed

---

[1] Stringfellow, pp. 64-65, 68; Howison, 'Didsbury'.
[2] Howison and Bentley, 'Ashton-under-Lyne'. [3] Howison, 'Oldham'.

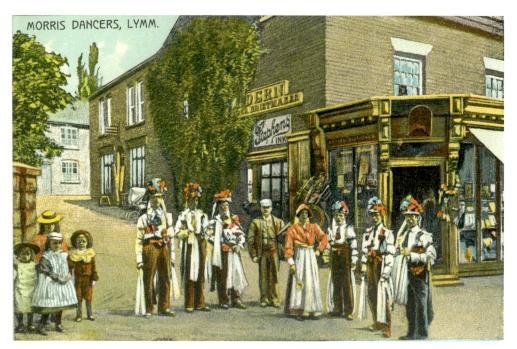

Figure 24.1: Oughtrington (Lymm) Morris Dancers, 1904 (Photo courtesy of Duncan Broomhead).

and continued for a couple of years after the war. Likewise, the team at Mossley was still going in 1923, when they were photographed outside their base at the Stamford Arms.[4] The fortunes of Oldham were closely linked to events at Royton, two miles north, where a dancer named Mick Coleman started a team in 1891. He may have learned the dance in his youth from his father in Oldham. The Royton team danced at all the local wakes, but also made excursions further afield, to seaside resorts. In 1895 one Jimmy Cheetham was the leader in Royton, and two families heavily involved were the McDermotts and the Irwins. Cheetham and members of the other families moved to Oldham around 1909.[5] By this time Mick Coleman was in Failsworth (four miles away along the road to Manchester), training a team there,[6] and his younger brother Jimmy Coleman re-formed a team in Royton, including Lees Kershaw, a concertina player and dancer. A short-lived rival team under Jim McDermott merged with them around 1912. Michael Higgins of a later Royton team suggested that 'it is conceivable that all the dancers in the by-now four teams could pass for the severed parts of one big one'.[7] Coleman's Royton team continued after World War I as Royton Central Morris Dancers, including Colemans, Kershaw and McDermotts.[8] These were the people whom Maud Karpeles was to meet in 1928 (see p. 379).

Lymm's rushcart limped into the beginning of the century with a team of dancers based at nearby Oughtrington. A 1904 postcard (Figure 24.1) shows what was by then a very old-fashioned image: six dancers in flowered hats, holding large loose handkerchiefs, and accompanied by a Bessy with ladle. They are wearing trousers, but no bells. Although the postcard shows an adult team, in the previous year the local newspaper had lamented that

---

[4] Cleary.
[5] Higgins.
[6] Pilling, 'Failsworth'.

[7] Higgins, p. 86.
[8] Schofield, 'Different Sort', p. 205.

'Even the morris dancers are reduced to one troup, and those boys, in place of two serious parties of gaily-bedecked men'.[9]

Other former rushcart areas followed the wider pattern of participating in carnivals and festivals. At Middleton a boys' team danced in the 1920s, and at nearby Middleton Junction a girls' team based at Jumbo Methodist Chapel was established before the war and continued throughout the inter-war years, but retaining the older practices of wearing clogs and holding slings.[10]

The Horwich Prize Medal men were still dancing up to World War I, performing as far afield as Sheffield. They also continued to use slings and wear clogs in the manner of the older teams associated with rushcarts, though the rest of the costume was akin to that of other local sides and they were firmly embedded in the milieu of May and Rose festivals. In 1906 they held a social evening to raise money for new costumes, and also ran a regular prize draw to raise funds.[11] There was also a troupe of mixed juvenile dancers in the town in the early years of the century. After the war a women's troupe based at St John's in Horwich performed for a few years.[12]

The Preston Morris Dancers under James Spencer continued to perform in the early years of the century, often accompanied by the juvenile team under his brother Tom Spencer. The juveniles were termed 'Comic Morris Dancers' at the poor children's treat in 1902.[13] Tom Spencer's niece was adamant that they continued until 1910 when the whole family emigrated; but James Spencer was still in Preston in 1911, as a hotel keeper.[14] The last recorded activity was an advertisement calling the juvenile team to practice in July 1905, but Tom Spencer and his daughter Ethel trained child dancers for the Preston Labour Association gala in 1910 and the Co-operative Society field day in 1911. At the latter the dancers performed Irish jigs and Scottish reels, as well as 'ye olde English Morris dance' and 'the modern Morris dance, not a little behind its predecessors'.[15] We do not know what the reporter perceived as 'olde' and what they designated 'modern', but it is clear that different types of morris dance were coming together, performed by the same groups in the same events.

The Rose Queen festival at Clayton-le-Moors hired the dancers from Whalley until they disbanded in 1903, but the organizers still wanted dancers so they engaged one of the Whalley men to teach a newly recruited local men's team, who danced up to World War I and re-formed for a few years afterwards. The *Accrington Observer* commented, 'In former years the morris dancing has been done by a number of young men from Whalley. The latter, now, are broken up and young men from ... schools have had to take on the duty. Trained and led by Mr Exton of Whalley, the twelve who took part in the dances ... performed admirably and all through the town their efforts were admired.' In the 1912 Rose Queen procession the adult male Clayton-le-Moors Prize Morris Dancers were followed by the Garland Dancers, described as 'a troupe of 16 girl Morris Dancers'.[16] Garland dances using semi-circular flowered hoops were by this stage seen as an appropriate part of a morris team's repertoire.

At Crewe several teams formed at the turn of the century to perform at festivals were based around the railway workshops, including the Crewe Original team, the Crewe Royal team

9   Bibby, 'History'.
10 Howison, 'Middleton'; Howison, 'Middleton Junction'.
11 Haslett, 2:215-16; Haslett, 3:137.
12 Boswell, *Morris Dancing ... Horwich*, pp. 12, 17-19.
13 Haslett, 2:65.74.
14 Boswell, *Morris Dancing ... Preston*, p. 7; 'James Spencer' (1911 census).
15 Haslett, 2:176; Haslett, 3:29, 70.
16 Haslett, 2:209; Haslett, 3:91.

(trained by David Billington, who had learned the dance in Preston), and 'Crewe Annamese Morris Dancers', an adult women's troupe who renamed themselves after just one year as the 'Crewe Alexandra Troupe of Lady Morris Dancers'.[17]

Richard Porter, a dancer with the Hindley Green men's side in the 1890s, trained a mixed juvenile troupe there from 1910, when they (and maypole dancers, also trained by Porter) were a new feature which 'considerably enlivened the procession' at the annual carters' festival. Porter re-formed them again after World War I; he also knew the Abram circle dance and was one of Maud Karpeles's informants for it in 1931.[18]

The Leyland Morris Dancers were one of the few men's teams which carried on into the 20th century and revived after World War I. They continued to perform primarily at the Leyland May festival, and to receive considerable civic support, embraced by the great and good of the community. One of their number, master butcher John Lord, led the team for some years and was on the festival's executive committee from 1895 until at least 1921. In the meantime he had risen to become chairman of the district council, and a magistrate. In 1922 he was chief marshal of the pageant. The men's team, at least, broadened their repertoire in acknowledgement of the folk-dance revival, performing the Flamborough sword dance at the Leyland May festival in 1914.[19]

Alfred Croasdale had led the Blackburn Prize Jazz Band (a comic band with associated men's morris dancers) before World War I, and his daughter formed a team of young girls to accompany the band after it, with half the girls dressed as boys.[20] They won prizes in the morris-dancing category at Haslingden in 1924, and (with the band) in the 'character' category of Burnley carnival. At Nelson in 1926 they won third prize in the morris-dancing category, but on this occasion they were billed as 'Blackburn Comic' morris dancers in the mock morris tradition.[21] The combination of morris dancers associated with comedy bands (often styled 'jazz' bands) recurs through the period, continuing the thread which began in the 1890s.

Many of the juvenile teams were associated with schools. The Roman Catholic St Walburge's school team at Preston was long-lasting, with a single trainer, Thomas Fitzgerald, for around 25 years from 1906. Likewise, the Wigan St John's team of boys performed for 60 years from 1895 to 1954. They were organized by their headmaster before the war but the revival afterwards in 1925 was credited to Father Fitzmaurice, the rector 'who was fully compensated for his successful effort to have them reintroduced by seeing the keen and enthusiastic interest manifested in the dances by the people'. At the Market Place 'so eager was the crowd to see to the best advantage that they encroached upon the space required by the dancers, who were forced to curtail their performance'.[22]

Other teams were associated with charitable organizations. The Boys' Refuge in Bootle was a residential school for homeless Catholic children which had a morris team at the start of the 20th century. They disappear from the records, however, after the Liverpool septicentennial pageant of 1907. At this event the band stopped playing before the boys had finished their programme. The boys carried on 'until an official kindly intimated that it was very good, but it was all that was wanted'. The following day the same happened, except that the boys had

[17] Buckland and Howison.
[18] Haslett, 3:8; Haslett, 4:134, 163; Bearon, 'Abram Morris Dance', pp. 52-53.
[19] Haslett, 4:177.
[20] *Dance Goes On*, p. 11.
[21] Haslett, 4:133, 139, 173.
[22] Boswell, *Morris Dancing ... Preston*, pp. 10, 13; Haslett, 4:148.

astutely brought their own school band who played simultaneously, and continued when the first band stopped.[23]

The Bensonians from Altrincham were described as a troupe of gymnasts but none the less they won the prize as the best morris dancers at a Chorley festival (a 'Rag Day') in 1928. This was an event typical of the emerging pattern of competitive dancing. Several women's teams were present besides the Bensonians: the Winton Prize Troupe of morris dancers, whose shakers ('tassels') were remarked upon; the Pink & White Morris Dancers; the Chorley Rose Buds, in clogs; the Black & Amber morris dancers from Hyde, and the Edge Fold Troupe from Walkden.[24] Shakers are dense bunches of ribbon at each end of a short handle, similar to cheerleaders' pompoms, which developed from the beribboned wands of the Godley Hill style.

The Lemocreme Girls were a troupe of workers from the lemon-curd manufacturer of that name in Urmston near Manchester in 1925-1927. They won second prize in the morris-dancing competition at Hindley carnival in 1925 (behind Horwich) and first prize in the competition at the Chorley East Ward carnival later that year, after the Chorley committee had reversed its resolve of the previous year that they would not have a competition as it would 'interfere with the playing of the bands for ordinary dancing'. The Lemocreme Girls were also known as 'ballet dancers', however, and at the 1926 Chorley Rose festival performed what was called a 'pageantry dance'.[25]

At the Blackpool railwaymen's flower show in 1928 prizes were awarded to five teams, in a 'descriptive dancing' competition exemplifying the diversification of dancing repertoire as the competition atmosphere took hold. These were the Desert Dream Dancers from Crewe, the Sea Maidens (Whitechurch), St Walburge's Morris Dancers (the Preston team with a history dating back to 1894), and two more Crewe teams, the Lido Ladies and Les Toupes. The judges were the principals of local dancing schools but we do not have any description of the dances done on this occasion.[26]

At Beetham near Lancaster morris dancing was the most popular feature of the village fête in 1910, taught by 'Miss Sealby, a very clever teacher from the London Esperance Club'. At the Patriotic Fete six years later, however, when almost all children at the local school took part, the sword and morris dances that were performed were evidently from Sharp's repertoire, as the reporter followed Sharp's philosophy in noting that 'The Morris is essentially, like the sword dance, a man's dance'. At Adlington in 1914 the school children gave 'old-time folk singing and dancing' from the EFDS repertoire. Blackpool held an annual dance competition in the 1920s and in 1922 a folk-dance competition was introduced, using the EFDS repertoire.[27]

When a mixed group of juvenile morris dancers from the Victoria Settlement club in Liverpool entertained at the Holy Trinity bazaar in Formby in 1911, they were 'carrying the cake and sword and asking the spectators to follow up the custom to "wish the dancers good luck, and cut a bit of the cake and put some money in the box"'.[28] This group had first been taught by Espérance teachers, but by this time was being taught in the EFDS style.[29] The village of Mellor had an active EFDS-based group in the 1920s, with performances of the Helston furry dance and the adult male morris dancers performing the Tideswell Processional at their fête in 1922 – one of

[23] Haslett, 2:245.
[24] Haslett, 4:220.
[25] Haslett, 4:138, 163, 166, 176.
[26] Haslett, 4:219.

[27] Haslett, 3:26, 177; Haslett, 4:69.
[28] Haslett, 3:63.
[29] Heathman, 'Revival', p. 143.

the few dances published by Sharp which could be incorporated into the context of the carnival procession. In 1924 they performed sword and handkerchief dances at the village fête.[30]

Blackburn had a strong EFDS branch and the EFDS repertoire made up the morris dances at Blackburn's May Queen and Pageant for War festivals in 1915 and its Shakespeare tercentenary celebrations in 1916. At the same time the Misses Hindley ran a dancing academy there whose pupils danced a morris dance at its fancy-dress ball in 1908, and in 1924 they were still teaching, providing morris dances and national dances at the Band of Hope festival.[31] At the Leyland May festival in 1913 not only were there the Leyland Morris Dancers, but the girls from Balshaw Grammar School danced 'How D'ye Do Sir' and other dances from the EFDS repertoire.[32]

At Accrington's hospital fete in 1927, Jesse Healey (who had trained the local morris teams before World War I) and his son judged the morris-dancing competition, which had categories for senior and junior morris dancers and for 'dancing of a similar type, but other than the real Lancashire morris dancing'. The latter was won by the Merrions of Bromley Cross near Bolton, while the Lyceum dancers did a sailor's hornpipe, but 'owing to lack of time the children were unable to perform in the correct costumes, having to do the dance in their Morris dancing dress, which rather spoiled the effect'. There had evidently been some tension at previous fêtes when the morris dancers stopped to perform *en route*, so the competition was held in the arena after the procession.[33]

St Philip's school in Southport had morris and maypole dancers trained by the school caretaker John Silversides in the early years of the century. They performed free of charge at the 1902 Southport gala but were allowed 1s for refreshments, and appeared at lifeboat parades in subsequent years.[34] When they re-emerged at school open days after World War I, however, it was to dance the EFDS repertoire, including the Tideswell Processional, 'Rigs of Marlow', and 'Bean Setting'.[35] The Linaker Street school in the town had EFDS dances at its May Queen pageant in 1914 and continued through the war and beyond, but the Olive Leaf Tent Rechabites (the local branch of a temperance society) performed in the north-west style throughout the 1920s.[36] When the EFDS-based men's team the Mellor Morris Dancers won the morris-dancing competition at Ribchester's May pageant in 1925, the runners up were the Blackburn Prize Morris Dancers and the Padiham Unity Club dancers came third – both of the latter dancing in the north-west festival style, with associated 'jazz' bands.[37]

The evolution in the morris-dance repertory was noted by the Bolton author Allen Clarke, reporting on Lytham's Rose festival in the *Blackpool Gazette* in 1919:[38]

> There were also girl morris dancers, tripping to the fine music of Elton Concertina Band. But why didn't the band play the good old Morris tunes to the dancing? There is no fitter music for the Morris dance than the old tunes to which it was originally danced, such as the jolly "Ninety Five, 'Long Morris', Nancy Dawson', 'A Hundred Pipers', 'Buttered Pease', etc.

Clarke complained again in 1920 'why don't the bands play the fine old Morris dance tunes instead of modern music?' He wrote this at the end of an encomium for Tom Bibby of Poulton-le-Fylde, at the Carleton gala:[39]

---

[30] Haslett, 4:86, 133.
[31] Haslett, 2:248; Haslett, 4:116.
[32] Haslett, 3:124-125.
[33] Haslett, 4:198.
[34] Haslett, 2:47.
[35] Haslett, 4:109.
[36] Haslett, 3:152; Haslett, 4:107, 160, 217, 232.
[37] Haslett, 4:142.
[38] Haslett, 3:257-58.
[39] Haslett, 4:28.

Here we were gladdened by the resplendent spectacle of Tom Bibby, old in head but young in the feet, the trainer (for I don't know how many years, but one man told me he recollected him at the job 30 years ago) of the girls and boy Morris dancers and Maypole dancers. Tom's cap was made of a little Union Jack with ribbons hanging behind, and he wore a white shirt with a salmon sash from shoulder to hip and claret coloured velvet knee breeches, and white stockings, and the sight of him took one back to the Merrie England of Shakespeare's time ... A jolly soul Tom, fond of the children and full of life. It was amusing to hear him have his joke with the aged woman visitor from Blackpool, who declared that he 'looked bonny', and to listen to the tale of the woman who had 'come in a sharrybanc frae Owdham' ... but it was best to see him in the field, leading his clever juveniles at their dancing, there he was in his element, graceful and delightful.

Clarke was highlighting the central role of trainers in the developing strands of morris dancing in the north-west. Bibby, a window cleaner by trade, had been training dancers at Poulton since at least 1906.[40] In subsequent years he was described as a 'veteran expert', but in the early days his local dominance was not assured. At the 1909 Poulton Club Day the organizing committee did not go straight to Bibby but put out invitations to tender to supply adult or juvenile morris dancers. In the end Bibby's mixed juvenile troupe did win out.[41] In 1912 the Espérance Club's musical director Clive Carey noted him as a possible contact for morris dancing but is not known to have followed this up.[42] Bibby also trained maypole dancers at Carleton in 1919 and a mixed juvenile troupe of morris dancers for the Bispham gala in 1924.[43]

The team at Nelson in the 1920s was a mixed team in which all dressed alike so as not to constrain the formation of the dancing set. They were trained by Emery Raw, who claimed he 'invented' the dance they did. From informants' accounts, Emery Raw's 'invention' was clearly directly derivative of the dances of the area. On the basis of the success of Raw's team the owners of a local ballroom also organized a team.[44] Raw was, in 1911, a house decorator by trade. Several noted trainers and organizers were not professionally involved in dance but followed other trades. This was a process of community creativity and transmission which belied Sharp's view of folk dance. Like Thomas Cadd at Yardley Gobion, and no doubt like many others, Raw brought his own agency to the process.

There were occasionally debates about the use of children. The planners of the gala at Ormskirk in 1906 looked at the Bickerstaffe dancers but, noting that they were children, thought that 'grown ups should be engaged' because children 'can't get on fast enough'; on the other hand, they 'looked far nicer than young men and women'. Two years later, however, the team was hired and was described as 'the chief attraction' of the fête.[45]

A T. Bretherton regularly trained juvenile morris dancers for the Lytham Rose Queen festival but in 1907 there were misgivings among the organizing committee. They were unhappy about the inclusion of a cake-walk the previous year, as a dance unsuitable for children. Moreover, Bretherton could only supply 16 children instead of the desired 20. They decided to hire the 16 provided the cake-walk was excluded. This was not the end of issues around Bretherton. In 1904 he had charged £5 for the services of his dancers; by 1908 it was £5.50 and when he raised

---

[40] Haslett, 2:206; Haslett, 4:80; 'Thomas Bibby' (1911 census).
[41] Haslett, 2:287, 302.
[42] Pilling, 'Leyland'.
[43] Haslett, 3:262; Haslett, 4:127.
[44] Howison, 'Nelson'; Pilling, 'Nelson'.
[45] Haslett, 2:207, 277.

the fee to £7 in 1909 the committee baulked at hiring them.[46] After the war, however, he was back, with his wife, in charge of a girls' troupe. His wife continued to organize it alone and then with her daughter in the second half of the 1920s.[47]

At the Ormskirk gala in 1905 £7 was also the fee, but for two companies, of 20 boys and 24 girls. The boys were trained by J.H. Carr, a local grocer, who performed this role between 1903 and 1912.[48] The Melia family and a Miss Matthews trained the girls, who also presented a maypole dance, and in the 1904 procession they won 'the admiration of the crowd, and were a credit to their trainer', despite which the reporter had doubts:[49]

> *The girl Morris Dancers are very good, and make a pretty spectacle, but their performances are not those of skilful and experienced young men, and there are one or two troupes in Lancashire who could be got down to provide the 'real thing', and who would prove a great attraction.*

At the same event the following year, for which we have a photograph showing the dancers (Figure 24.2), the reporter took an opposite view:[50]

> *...the girl Morris Dancers at various points in the march went through their interesting exercises with a skill and precision not excelled by the regular Morris Dancers whose performances were once so marked a feature at Lancashire fairs and wakes.*

At Longridge, however, when the organizing committee for the coronation festivities in 1902 advertised for 'young men over seventeen wishing to join the Morris Dancers, or boys and

Figure 24.2: Ormskirk St Anne's Morris Dancers, 1905 (Photo courtesy of Pruw Boswell).

---

[46] Haslett, 2:136, 142, 228, 233, 285.
[47] Haslett, 4:52, 82, 97, 104, 152, 176, 195, 195, 201, 226.
[48] Haslett, 2:114, 157-58; Haslett, 3:106.

[49] Haslett, 2:145.
[50] Haslett, 2:169.

girls under seventeen wishing to join the May Pole dancers', they had few volunteers for the morris. In the following years a group of schoolchildren morris-danced at Longridge's annual guild procession.[51]

The team at Adlington was mixed, but some of the girls dressed as boys as there were not enough boys to make up their file in the dance.[52] At Padiham there was an all-girls team but one file dressed as boys.[53] The Bury carnival procession in 1924 featured girls morris dancing, pierrots, another troupe of girls dancing under a banner proclaiming the 'Bolton United Veterans' Prize Jazz Band & Morris Dancers', a team of women morris dancers, half of them dressed as men, and a fourth team of women dressed androgynously in knickerbockers.[54]

There were morris dancers at Gisburn in Yorkshire before World War I,[55] but when their leader Fred Thurogood revived it after the war it was a mixed team with the men dancing on one side in the processional and the women on the other. The dance was one of the few north-west dances to published, in 1934. It consisted primarily of a walk, in procession, with the dancers crossing from time to time and occasionally using a skipping step. The ribbons normally found at the end of the short hand-held sticks had been replaced by bells.[56] At Clitheroe Chris Winckley, leader of the pre-war men's team, trained a women's team after the war was over.[57] When the Leyland parish of St James held a rose festival in 1923 a sixteen-strong women's side performed, trained by a local cotton weaver Walter Cowburn.[58] The aftermath of the war had also empowered women to take more active roles as trainers and instigators of morris dancing. At Eccleston in the 1920s a group of girl morris dancers performed in the church 'walking day' procession each year. Various names were given as trainers but census records show that they were all single women working as cotton weavers in the local mill.[59]

Charles Fidler of Stockport was described by his daughter as a 'dancing master' who compèred at local dances in his spare time, and trained female maypole and male morris dancers for the 1897 jubilee.[60] He did all these things, but his primary occupation was in fact as an engine driver.[61] His son Peter ran a chip shop, but also was secretary to the town's Silver Band, and took over the dancers after his father's death in 1911, continuing into the 1930s. He also taught morris dancing to local schools. The Fidlers' team was apparently mixed at first (though some stated it was boys only), but later girls only, and around 1924 the team replaced clogs with plimsolls, and tambourines with paper shakers. His daughter, however, said the team kept to the 'old style'.[62]

Although most of the trainers were amateurs, many were active for several years. In 1900 the Park Cycling Club at Lancaster introduced morris dancing by a mixed set of children into their annual cycle parade. They were trained by W. Clarke, the captain of the club.[63] There is no indication of how or from where he obtained the knowledge to do so, but he was able to provide piano accompaniment in indoor settings. The team was 50 strong, wore 'Swiss' costumes and the girls carried fans and tambourines, and in 1902, castanets. They gained a strong reputation and regularly visited Bradford, 50 miles away, in support of hospital fundraising, for which events the girls wore nurses' uniforms. They likewise performed to

[51] Haslett, 2:31, 33, 143, 182, 214.
[52] Boswell, *Morris Dancing ... Horwich*, p. 15.
[53] Pilling, 'Padiham'.
[54] *Bury Carnival.*
[55] Haslett, 3:16, 33, 48, 63, 88, 126.
[56] Douglas, Leta M., pp. [6-7].
[57] Howison and Bentley, 'North-west Morris', p. 45.
[58] Haslett, 4:109.
[59] Haslett, 4:24, 50, 215; 'Isabella Blackburn' (1911 census); 'Alice Mackrael' (1911 census).
[60] Howison, 'Stockport'.
[61] 'Fidler, Charles Burgess'.
[62] Froome; Howison, 'Stockport'.
[63] Haslett, 1:310-11.

fund-raise at Guiseley, near Leeds, where they were 'voted best in show in the huge procession'. It is clear that 'morris dancing' was being interpreted very freely, and that the dancers put on a varied programme.[64] At Lancaster's William Smith festival in 1910 they danced in procession to the festival arena, where their programme was:

1. *'Morris Dance', round the track;*
2. *'Physical Culture Drill', 1st Prize in Bradford 1908;*
3. *'Floral Maze Dance', 1st Prize in Leeds, 1909;*
4. *'Empire Flag Drill';*
5. *'Finale Dance' round the track.*

At the coronation festivities in 1911 they broadened their repertoire to include 'For King and Empire' with cord bearers representing the four constituent nations, floral courtiers, and a 'miniature king and queen', an addition so popular it was staged at least twice more during the year.[65] They resumed under Clarke after the war, and at the peace celebrations in Lancaster in addition to morris dancing they put on the flag drill and maze dances from a decade before, as well as a Highland fling. By 1921 they also had a 'statue dance'. They were still going strong in 1928: at the Morecambe carnival three teams were awarded prizes, but their pride must have been dented by the judges' pronouncement that they considered the Lancaster Morris Dancers to be the best, although they had declined to compete.[66] Clarke, it seems, built a successful thirty-year career as a morris-dance trainer on the basis of an apparently spontaneous decision to enliven his cycling club's parade.

The team from Mobberley in Cheshire first learned from Cecil Sharp's books after the war but the following year were taught by local women. Over the years the team moved from having two sides (men and women), to men only, then a mixed juvenile team. At the same time their repertoire developed, embracing dances in the north-west style, and they continued to modify their style of dancing for competition purposes as the judging criteria evolved.[67] They also adopted costumes typical of the north-west teams of the period, comprising in 1927 'white suits sashed and cross-gartered with blue ribbons and ... blue gipsy handkerchiefs tied on their heads. Their Morris sticks were gay affairs finished at the end with huge fluffy balls of blue and white paper.'[68]

The headmaster at Aughton near Ormskirk saw the dancers from Mobberley and invited them to dance at Aughton's carnival. They were then invited to teach local dancers in 1928, and the Belles of Aughton appeared with them at the carnival. The following year there were both Belles and 'Lads from the Village' ('sixteen hefty Aughton lads', echoing the earlier favoured epithet of 'rushcart lads'). They followed the Mobberley dancers in costume, with 'gypsy' headscarves and 'shillelaghs', the name sometimes given to the shakers that developed from the beribboned sticks. Shakers with dense bunches of streamers at both ends of a short stick had already been in use for some time. The earliest clear evidence is a picture of the Helmshore Morris Dancers (a mixed juvenile troupe) holding some at Musbury church pageant in 1911 (Figure 24.3). Later that year, the Lads, two troupes of the Belles and morris dancers from St Anne's, Ormskirk performed at the Ormskirk Police Gala, including a 'massed exhibition of country dances'.[69]

[64] Haslett, 2:53, 174, 211, 243, 271, 299.
[65] Haslett, 3:45, 63, 67.
[66] Haslett, 3:264; Haslett, 4:212.
[67] 'Mobberley Morris'; Howison, 'Godley Hill'.

[68] Haslett, 4:191.
[69] Haslett, 4:208, 219, 222-23; Howison, 'Middleton'; Howison, 'Aughton'.

Figure 24.3: Helmshore Morris Dancers, Musbury church pageant, 1911 (in Johnny Haslett, Morris Dancers and Rose Queens, *3:73. Leyland: Fairhaven Press, 2017, credited to Helmshore Local History Society).*

The practitioners were very much aware of the changes taking place in morris dancing, as witness the statements about styles of dancing in competitions. Fred Egerton, who had danced with the Goostrey team after World War I, said in 1962 (when the team still survived) that the dance was 'not the same – more of a display dance'.[70]

The association of morris dances with other dances as entertainment was widespread. A photograph of a procession at Whitworth near Rochdale in 1910 shows a group of 'nutters' (coconut dancers) followed by a group identified as morris dancers holding garlands.[71] A film of the Rose Queen procession at Clayton-le-Moors in 1908 shows the men's team and a girls' team of morris dancers, another team of female dancers, a group of boys in black-face, women doing Scottish dancing, a troupe doing 'Grecian' dances and set of couples in top hat and tails, or in evening dresses, all of whom are apparently male.[72]

The stationary dances for competitive purpose in a festival arena began to overtake the processional dances. Pruw Boswell has noted how the Horwich Prize girls' morris team altered their 'step-up' figure from eight simple forward steps to four forwards and four back, 'with the arm movements becoming more exaggerated, the arms being held stiffly and moved in time to the music in the manner of marching soldiers'.[73] An element of precision drilling came to be favoured by judges, and the introduction of novel and intricate figures to heighten interest. The Spick and Span dancers from Chorley, for example, devised figures named 'The Dragon' and 'The Snake'.[74] Spick and Span were formed specifically to dance in competitions, but their trainer was a former Hindley Green dancer, Bobby Goodman.[75] The local press reported that

[70] Howison, 'Goostrey'.
[71] 'Whitworth Nutters'.
[72] *Procession.*

[73] Boswell, 'Trends', p. 9.
[74] Boswell, 'Trends', pp. 11, 23.
[75] Boswell, 'Trends', p. 16.

they had an accompanying 'jazz' band and wore 'striking light-blue costumes with red sashes' which 'made a bright splash of colour'.[76] Although the dance was undergoing rapid change, this was evolutionary development from older styles rather than their being supplanted by an entirely new form.

The effects of the changing style are exemplified in the notes made by Dan Howison in 1960 when he interviewed Mrs Hamilton of Hyde, who at the time trained girls for morris competitions in carnivals, about the developments from the Godley Hill dance:[77]

> *Learnt the dance from four Godley men ... about 1920 ... Their team consisted of 16 girls, and they danced at various places ... where there were older judges who knew the old style of Morris and would judge it properly. But when the new style came in ('with arms bend and so on') they broke up because they no longer won prizes. This was about the beginning of the second World War. They did the same dance as the men, but wore different costume ... Does not think much of the present style of dancing (which her team does) but sees no alternative, since she says today's judges wouldn't appreciate the old style.*

> *...they went on doing the old style as long as they could, then adopted the new arm movements, while keeping the old steps and figures. The first teams dancing in the new style were ... a team from Altrincham, the Mobberley team and the 'Bensonians' ... led by Eric Benson.*

In Oldham a Mrs Schofield was a member of a girls' team which found it was losing points in carnival competitions while they still wore clogs (which were ineffective on the turf of a carnival arena), so they switched to pumps, and at the same time replaced their slings with shakers.[78] Jack Fosbrook trained a girls' team in Stockport between the two world wars. They retained the style of the older morris dancers while carnival judges still appreciated the old style, including wearing clogs, but Fosbrook ignored his girls' requests to move from slings to shakers.[79]

By 1930 most of the adult men's teams had disappeared, the end stage in a process which had begun in the 19th century with the abandonment of rushcarts and the evolution of the Godley Hill performances at Knutsford into the burgeoning of morris dances starting at Leyland and spreading across Lancashire and into the neighbouring counties. Boys' teams appeared soon after the start of this process, followed by mixed (mainly juvenile) and girls' teams. By the 1920s girls' teams predominated. Undoubtedly World War I had an effect, reducing the availability of male dancers and empowering women, but it only reinforced trends that were already in play. The changes in the gender and age of participants are shown in Figure 24.4. Although not many women's teams are indicated in the figure, they may be underrepresented, as newspaper reports may have described them as 'girls', and in the absence of any counter-indication I have taken that at face value. Throughout the period there are teams – predominantly juvenile – whose gender is not specified in the reports. In the last five-year period there were 17 of them. They are not represented in the figure.

Maud Karpeles's views on these developments were quoted at the end of Chapter 23. When she saw a carnival-style morris at Winsford in 1928 she wrote 'The dance gave the impression of musical drill and has evidently kept very few of its traditional characteristics', and 'I am

---

[76] Haslett, 4:148.
[77] Howison, 'Godley Hill'.
[78] 'Morris Dancing – Oldham'.
[79] Austin.

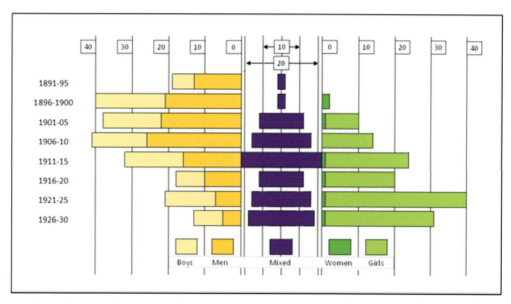

Figure 24.4: Gender balance of north-west morris teams, 1891-1930 (excluding teams of unknown gender).

told this is the kind of dance that usually passes for Morris, in Cheshire'.[80] Some years later she dismissed a morris from Lower Peover as 'similar to the usual pseudo-Cheshire morris'.[81] Film of the Over Peover Rose Queen carnival in 1938 shows separate men's and women's teams dancing what appears to be the same dance, holding shakers and dancing with a high-raised knee.[82]

Karpeles, however, did delight in finding and publishing in 1928 the dance as it used to be performed at Royton, where it had retained its 'purity and completeness'.[83] It had a complexity in stepping and figures matching that of the south-midlands morris. There were walking steps, polka steps and capers. Besides the widespread north-west figures of dancing in file and a variety of cross-over movements, in some sequences the dancers formed ranks four abreast. In all, Karpeles described nine different steps and 24 different figures in the dance. This was the first published description of the north-west morris dance in sufficient detail to allow people to teach and learn it from a book (the earlier publication by John Graham[84] lacked clarity and rigour). It marked the point at which the north-west morris – in this form at least – was incorporated into the revival of morris dancing under the aegis of the English Folk Dance Society. The sides dancing in the styles dismissed by Karpeles continued on their own trajectory for another forty years outside the ambit of the 'folk-dance revival'.

---

[80] 'Karpeles MSS, Oldfield Morris'.
[81] 'Karpeles MSS, Peover Morris'.
[82] *Peover (Cheshire) Carnival.*

[83] Karpeles, *Lancashire Morris Dance*, p. 5.
[84] Graham.

Chapter 25

The revival after Sharp

When Cecil Sharp and George Butterworth published *The Morris Book, Part V* in 1913 its reviewer called it 'a last gleaning'.[1] Sharp had done little collecting after that publication, and with his death the impression was very much that there was a closed canon of morris dances. He had certainly promoted himself as the sole authority. While Sharp was in his last illness in 1924, he was visited by a group of Cambridge University men, soon to constitute themselves more formally into a morris club, who had decided to visit the villages from which Sharp had collected morris dances, and to perform those dances there. They called themselves the 'Travelling Morrice'. For his part, Sharp perceived this as a threat to his role as unique authority on and sole arbiter of the morris. He told Douglas Kennedy that when they visited, 'he felt rather like a suspected person visited by the flying squad who had decided not to press a charge before collecting supporting evidence from certain elderly persons who would be able to help them with their enquiries'.[2] By this stage Sharp's conception of the morris had won out over Mary Neal's, but the Travelling Morrice tour heralded a movement away from the perpetuation of the dance in the classroom and other formal settings, towards returning it as a living form to communities. The tours – for they became annual – did lead to the collecting of more dances. Although the Travelling Morrice was autonomous, the EFDS remained the sole vehicle for dissemination, and the newly collected dances from the south-midlands morris villages of Leafield, Longborough and Bledington were published in the society's journal.[3]

Despite their new approach to performance the Cambridge men thoroughly espoused Sharp's view of the dance's ritual antecedents and quasi-spiritual qualities. One Cambridge man, Rolf Gardiner, spoke of folk dance as 'an expression of the new wordless religion which is throbbing in the earth to-day'.[4] Gardiner was one of the prime instigators of the Travelling Morrice, and he saw membership of a morris team as a *Blutsbrüderschaft* ('blood-brotherhood'),[5] an élite group of men forged into a unity, partly by athletic dancing ability but also involving ideas of racial bonds and innate class superiority. The dance itself was for him a 'masculine ritual of soil fertility and local tradition'.[6] He was a complex figure with what Matt Simons has called 'fascistic' leanings, and his prickly personality endeared him to few.[7] The Cambridge men perhaps indulgently dismissed many of his idiosyncrasies as 'Rolfery',[8] and although Gardiner was a prime mover behind the team, other members did not embrace his philosophies wholesale. They viewed the tours as holidays as much as any kind of pilgrimage, and cultivating links with the locals was often pursued in the village pub embracing the romanticized image of 'quaffing' beer referred to as 'nectar';[9] but the distance between the more privileged dancers and the old working men of the villages remained.

---

[1] Barker.
[2] Kennedy, 'Folk Dance Revival', p. 88.
[3] Schofield, R. Kenworthy, 'Morris dances from Field Town'; Schofield, R. Kenworthy, 'Morris dances from Longborough'; Schofield, R. Kenworthy, 'Morris dances from Bledington'.

[4] Cited in Heathman, 'Revival', p. 158.
[5] Cited in Heathman, 'Revival', p. 167.
[6] Gardiner, Rolf, p. 53.
[7] Simons, 'Morris Men', p. 83.
[8] Simons, 'Morris Men' pp. 120-23.
[9] Simons, 'Pilgrimages', p. 142.

Cambridge Morris Men came into being as a club in October 1924, soon after the first Travelling Morrice tour.[10] They were part of a movement which Matt Simons has characterized as an element in a general desire to 'reassert manliness' after World War I.[11] By the early 1930s there was a handful of clubs of male dancers who had learned their dancing with the EFDS but had an independent existence beyond its formal classes and demonstrations. Like Cambridge, Oxford University also had an associated team. The other locus of development was Thaxted in Essex, whose Anglo-Catholic Christian socialist 'Red Vicar' Conrad Noel had embraced morris dancing in 1910 when his wife approached the Espérance Guild to teach the residents of the town. Katie Palmer Heathman has noted that 'the beginnings of morris in Thaxted were firmly rooted in the social ethos of Neal's Espérance Club'. By 1911 there were 60 dancers, performing to large audiences.[12] The club resumed after World War I but, given the demise of the Espérance Club, looked to the EFDS for guidance. By 1925 Miriam Noel had persuaded the women in the team to confine themselves to country dances, leaving the morris for the men.[13]

One regular attender at Conrad Noel's church services was Alec Hunter of Letchworth. Hunter was a textile craftsman (he had left Oxford University after just two terms to pursue his craft) whose vision of England embraced Christian socialism, the Arts and Crafts movement and the quasi-utopian ideal embodied in Letchworth Garden City.[14] He was a key mover in establishing and organizing the local EFDS branch there, and his own prowess as a dancer was such that he was asked to join the EFDS's demonstration morris team. He trained the Letchworth team to a similarly high standard. As Simons puts it, 'Morris dance in Letchworth resembled one manifestation of an enlightened way of living, borrowing from representations of the past in contemporary practice'.[15]

Hunter's affinity with Conrad Noel's Thaxted led to occasions for joint dances by the teams from the two communities, starting in the early 1920s. Hunter also maintained links with the Cambridge Morris Men, attending their first feast as an honoured guest in 1925 (along with Douglas Kennedy, the new Director of the EFDS following Sharp's death), and joining the Travelling Morrice for their second and third tours. Hunter's experience on the tours led to the inauguration of regular public morris dancing in Thaxted in 1926, which led in turn to other informally organized meetings of morris men's teams and to the institution in 1927 of regular meetings in Thaxted closely tied to church services there.[16]

On 2 November 1933 the Cambridge Morris Men met and discussed the formation of an 'informal federation' of men's morris clubs, deciding to sound out the clubs at Oxford, Letchworth and Thaxted about the proposal. The initiative came from the eminent biochemist and sinologist Joseph Needham, the Squire (leader) of the club, and the Bagman (secretary) Arthur Peck. The East Surrey Morris Men (a team established in 1926) were later consulted, and by the time the Cambridge men formally instituted the federation, to be known as the Morris Ring, on 14 April 1934 the London-based Greensleeves Morris Men (also founded in 1926) had been added to the list. The objects of the Ring were stated to be 'to encourage the dancing of the morris, and to preserve its traditions, to bring into contact all existing Morris Men's Clubs or sides and to encourage the formation of others'. Needham's letter to Greensleeves sums up the attitude of the Ring's founders:[17]

---

[10] Abson, 'Travelling Morrice'.
[11] Simons, 'From Country Gardens', p. 238.
[12] Heathman, 'I Ring', pp. 125-27.
[13] Simons, 'Morris Men' p. 56.

[14] Simons, 'Morris Men' p. 127.
[15] Simons, 'Morris Men' pp. 138-39, 146.
[16] Simons, 'Morris Men' pp. 147, 149, 151, 153.
[17] Ross, Bob, p. 305.

The whole position arises owing to a certain failure of the E.F.D.S. to understand the optimum conditions for the flourishing of the Morris. These conditions are the close association together of men, and men only, in a club, with activities which include spontaneously organised meetings and tours.

The Morris Ring grew rapidly. By the time of its official inaugural meeting on 20 August 1934 at Cecil Sharp House, headquarters of the EFDS, a further seven clubs had joined. Another half dozen joined each year till the outbreak of war in 1939, at which time the membership was 39 clubs from all over the country (including one Dutch club), and 110 men from 17 clubs attended the last pre-war meeting at Thaxted.[18] Hunter was elected its first 'Squire'.

Despite Needham's characterization of the EFDS's 'failure', ties between the EFDS and the Morris Ring remained close. The society had by then merged with the Folk-song Society to become the English Folk Dance and Song Society, EFDSS. Most dancers learned to dance in EFDSS classes, and the magazine *E.F.D.S. news* (which retained the pre-merger initials) carried regular reports on the Ring. Douglas Kennedy wrote about the upcoming Thaxted meeting in the April 1936 issue:[19]

Although 'The Ring' consists of Morris Clubs, there is nothing to stop individual dancers from coming to Thaxted. They will be taken care of and made into teams. It is one of the ways in which Morris dancers can be encouraged. The Ring is anxious to help in the formation of men's clubs. They can only arise around some individual already interested. What is not generally known is that the Ring and the E.F.D.S. can help to build up a club round an interested individual by supplying instruction and information of every kind.

Although the EFDSS clearly embraced the Morris Ring, the latter's exclusive maleness did engender some wry comment among the society's members. One wrote anonymously a lampoon 'broadside ballad' to be sung to the morris tune 'Beaux of London City':[20]

When times were bad some novices had
To learn their first steps from a girl.
'Twas all effervescence, neglecting the essence,
The oyster – omitting the pearl.
What men want is Morris,
For Morris is our ploy,
What it means to us
We can never discuss,
But it's felt by each true-hearted boy.

– and had Kenworthy Schofield (the second Squire of the Ring) say:

What we want is Morris
And what we want is a Ring,
Where neither our Sweethearts
Nor mothers can come
Nor our Wives even get a look in.

EFDSS Director Douglas Kennedy presented the Ring's first Squire Alec Hunter with a staff of office (which Hunter had in fact designed). Kennedy had declined to become the Ring's first

---

[18] Abson, 'Morris Ring', p. 297.
[19] Kennedy, 'Men's Morris'.
[20] 'Morris Ring'.

Squire himself in a gesture to help the new organization to develop a separate identity, but accepted the role just a few years later in 1938.[21] In 1955 the EFDSS added a badge of office (also designed by Hunter) to the regalia.[22] Each club admitted to the Ring was also presented with a staff as token of their status. Following the practice of the Cambridge Morris Men there was an annual formal dinner (a 'feast'). The link to the Established Church at Thaxted led to a Church of England service being a regular element of Ring meetings. These ritual symbols and practices shared their characteristics with other primarily male groups such as friendly societies and the Freemasons. A ritual of admission was introduced for new Squires, who must dance a solo jig, and dancing a jig in public has also become an initiation rite for dancers in many older club sides before they are allowed to wear all elements of the team's costume.

Morris dancing was now thoroughly embedded within the 'establishment', no matter how left-wing or socialist some of its upper-middle-class practitioners might be. Each of the two ancient universities was a stronghold. At Oxford this had been the case as far back as 1913, when the 'Dancing Dons', including Sharp's demonstration-team dancer Reginald Tiddy of Trinity College, caused a sensation when they performed on stage in the Oxford University Dramatic Society production of *The Shoemakers' Holiday*.[23]

In 1923 the Oxford University branch of the EFDS had initiated a practice which has become widespread. The May Morning ceremony at Oxford, when choristers sing a Latin hymn from Magdalen College tower at 6 a.m., exudes timeless piety, although it is a tradition which has constantly developed and changed over its five-hundred-year history. By the late 19th century it had even acquired an aura of being a Christianized ancient ritual.[24] Half a mile down the road the Oxford sweeps paraded a Jack-in-the-Green on the same day into the early years of the 20th century.[25] The University morris dancers introduced morris dancing immediately after the hymn singing, 'as a free gift to the city, in gratitude for the long and lovely survival here of the May-day celebrations', saying, 'we are dancing for the pleasure of those who have deserved well by rising early, for our own pleasure, and in obedience to the Shakespearean dictum "A morris for May day"', and they later added a Jack-in-the-Green to the festivities.[26] The connection of morris and May Day had been tenuous at best, and none of the morris teams encountered by Sharp and enshrined in *The Morris Book* had danced then. Nor was 6 a.m. strictly dawn; but the practice of many modern teams of dancing at dawn on May Day derives from this initiative.

———————————

Those at the Cambridge meeting of 2 November 1933 which founded the Morris Ring agreed 'not to invite traditional teams such as the Chipping Campden Men'.[27] There was a strong awareness of the distinction between 'tradition' and 'revival', arising primarily from Sharp's emphasis on the primacy of 'traditional authority'. 'Traditional' teams were held in reverence by dancers in revival teams, even though in the case of Chipping Campden the team had come together (been 'revived') only the previous year as a direct result of the Travelling Morrice's visit to the town.[28] Despite the initial decision, individual morris dancers from these teams who had been instrumental in the revival, such as William Kimber of Headington Quarry and William Wells of Bampton, were frequent guests at the Ring's meetings, and in 1937 the teams from Abingdon and Bampton joined the Ring.[29]

---

[21] Abson, 'Morris Ring', pp. 298-99.
[22] Russell.
[23] Judge, 'Branch', p. 94.
[24] Judge, 'May Morning'.
[25] Judge, *Jack-in-the-Green*, pp. 164-75.
[26] Judge, 'May Morning', pp. 33-34.
[27] Ross, Bob, p. 302.
[28] Simons, 'Pilgrimages', p. 147.
[29] Abson, 'Morris Ring', pp. 297-98.

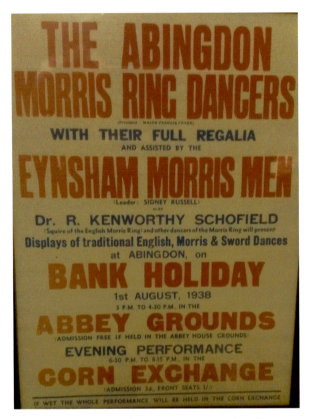

In the first half of the 20th century outside the north-west very few groups with an ancestry antedating the EFD(S)S revival were still active. The revival was based around the south-midlands traditions, so it was not surprising that those communities were the focus of efforts to sustain or revive them. Despite Sharp's reliance on William Kimber, there was no active team from Headington Quarry in the initial stages of the revival. Kimber recruited a team in 1910 which was active till the outbreak of World War I and he re-formed it in 1920. There are occasional reports of activity in the following decade but when the Oxford Morris Men (a city-based, not university, side) were formed in 1938, several of its members were Headington Quarry men, there being no extant team by then. In the inter-war period Kimber was also active elsewhere, teaching teams for the Oxford City Police, the Morris Motors Social Club in Oxford and the British

Figure 25.1: Poster advertising a meeting at Abingdon, 1 August 1938 (Photo © Michael Heaney).

Workman (a Headington labour club), as well as performing at EFDSS functions.[30] He was also a frequent attender and honoured guest at meetings of the Morris Ring throughout the 1930s.[31]

The Eynsham men continued to dance in their village five miles west of Oxford, relatively unnoticed outside their own community, during the 1920s. A team performed in the village for George V's silver jubilee in 1935 and again on the occasion of the coronation of George VI in 1937, and shortly afterwards the Travelling Morrice met and filmed them.[32] Likewise, the Abingdon men, who had paraded through the town (but did not dance) at the silver jubilee, got a team together for the 1937 coronation. They were encouraged by a local enthusiast, Francis Fryer of Wargrave Hall, who became their 'president' (separate from their traditional leader, the mock mayor of Ock Street).[33] They immediately joined the Morris Ring at its Thaxted meeting in June 1937.[34] The Abingdon and Eynsham teams performed together at an event in Abingdon the following year, for which a poster described the Abingdon men as the 'Abingdon Morris Ring Dancers' and the Ring's Squire, Kenworthy Schofield, was present. Other Morris Ring dancers were present to supply further elements of the programme, although this was not an official meeting of Ring clubs (Figure 25.1).

[30] Grant, 'Headington Quarry'.
[31] 'Log of the 1st Meeting'; 'Log of the 6th Meeting'; 'Log of the 9th Meeting'; 'Log of the 12th Meeting'; 'Log of the 16th Meeting'.
[32] *Eynsham Morris.*
[33] Leach, *Mr. Hemmings' Morris Dancers.*
[34] Abson, 'Morris Ring', p. 297.

At the same meeting in Thaxted at which Abingdon joined the Morris Ring, a Bampton team joined. The Bampton men were the only south-midlands team to continue with scarcely any interruption throughout the first half of the century. Sharp's original contact for the Bampton team, William Wells, drew attention to the Bampton morris's credentials as 'the oldest set of morris-dancers in or out of Oxfordshire' in an interview with the national newspaper *Daily News* in 1910.[35] He was the team's conduit for contact with the wider world, as in 1914 when they were invited to perform at the Reading Regatta; and he was the driving force behind the team's continuation during World War I and its prompt revival afterwards.[36] In 1920 'men from London motored down to take snapshots of the dancing', and in 1921 the team advertised their impending Whit Monday appearance in the local press.[37]

Although Wells was the most prominent of the performers at the time, other members in the extended family network that constituted the core of the team (see Figure 14.6 on p. 236) also felt they could speak for it, especially as the team could now command fees for their appearances instead of soliciting contributions from the audience. Wells later claimed that during the Whit Monday dancing in 1925 the dancer Billy Flux, son-in-law of Thomas 'Buscot' Tanner, was approached by its organizer to dance at an 'Olde Englishe Fayre' at Stanford-in-the-Vale, at which Queen Victoria's granddaughter Princess Helena Victoria was the principal guest. Flux and the Tanner family apparently agreed the terms without consulting Wells, who took umbrage thereby. Wells agreed to honour the booking but vowed not to play the music for them again. At the next Whit Monday he did indeed refuse to play, and the team had trouble finding a replacement musician, resulting in the unusual sight of their eventual substitute fiddler, one Bertie Clarke of Carterton, playing the tunes reading from Cecil Sharp's books propped on a music stand. The *Witney Gazette* report stressed the credentials of the team (implicitly downplaying Wells's importance):[38]

> ...the Bampton morris-men hold an unbroken record of Four hundred years, and during the whole of that period there has always been one at least bearing the name of Tanner. The present head, who is an old dancer and whose grandfather and father also followed the craft, has three sons and a son-in-law among the performers, and his name is Tanner.

The following year Wells had trained a new team of his own (Figure 25.2), and both teams danced on Whit Monday. The *Witney Gazette's* reporter this time evidently had the benefit of Wells's side of the affair:[39]

> ...the late troup deserted their veteran fiddler, Mr. Wm. Wells, who has been connected with Bampton Morris dancing for forty years and its guiding light for the greater part of that period, and imported a musician, a circumstance which decidedly spoils the parochial character of the pastime that has existed for more than four hundred years. Not to be daunted, Mr. Wells collected another band of young men, and in an incredibly short space of time turned them into an efficient troup of dancers, whose performance was a source of wonder and delight during the whole of Whit-Monday.

In 1928 the EFDS stalwart and member of the society's morris demonstration team Kenneth Constable observed both Bampton teams as they danced. The Ilmington morris fiddler Sam Bennett had joined Clarke to play for the Tanner set, but also played for EFDS country dancers

[35] Chandler, *Morris Dancing at Bampton*, p. 5.
[36] Chandler, *Morris Dancing at Bampton*, pp. 29-30.
[37] Chandler, *Bampton Morris Dancers*, pp. 11-12.
[38] Chandler, *Bampton Morris Dancers*, p. 14.
[39] Chandler, *Bampton Morris Dancers*, p. 16

Figure 25.2: William Wells's team Bampton, 6 June 1927 (Image courtesy of Vaughan Williams Memorial Library, mo/Bam/1927/9242).

while the morris dancers watched – the villagers' not unreasonable proprietary response to which was, according to Constable, 'Bampton dancing should be for Bampton folks'. Constable made several observations about differences from the dances as published in *The Morris Book*, noting 'The diversity of footing, especially in the half-gip, is truly mathematical, but the arms will shock the uninitiated most'; and as for Wells himself, 'Words cannot describe and photographs only faintly portray its gambolling unorthodoxy'.[40] `This pattern continued until 1933. Thereafter Wells's team survived, and the Tanner team appeared only three times more, in 1938, 1939 and 1941.[41]

Outside the south midlands the situation was very different. Christopher Cawte had described the dancing at Orleton in Herefordshire in the 1920s as the 'nadir' of the morris dance in the west midlands and I characterized it as exemplifying the erosion in distinctiveness and the incorporation of other elements including black-face minstrelsy (see Chapter 15). Other west-midlands events seen as morris dancing during the first part of the 20th century are equally diffuse, and the ascription of 'morris' may be imposed on them by the observer. So the Aston-on-Clun group called 'mummers' but describing their activities as 'n****ring' find their way into Cawte's description of west-midlands morris dancing. The activities of children in Broseley singing minstrel songs up to 1950 are also included.[42] Most such performances were not noted at the time but were recalled when researchers looking for traces of morris dancing made enquiries decades later.[43] An exception was the Much Wenlock morris dances. After the dancers were interviewed by the BBC in 1935 Maud Karpeles noted two tunes from one of the performers in 1937.[44] Just after World War II Geoffrey Mendham met a possibly related team

[40] Constable.
[41] Chandler, 'Archival Morris Photographs'.
[42] Cawte, 'Morris Dance', pp. 201, 203.

[43] Jones, Dave, pp. 13-17.
[44] Jones, Dave, p. 40; 'Karpeles MSS, Much Wenlock Morris'.

Figure 25.3: Westwood Morris Men, Much Wenlock, 1949 (Photo © Arthur Blake).

there, calling themselves the Westwood Morris Men (presumably from Stretton Westwood nearby). They had blacked faces and performed a dance with sticks to bones and tambourine accompaniment around a melodeon player.[45] (Figure 25.3)

Karpeles had also collected the Upton-on-Severn dances, for which purpose a former dancer gathered a team together which continued to dance for a short time afterwards, appearing at a village fête the following year.[46] Karpeles published the dances a few years later.[47]

The Travelling Morrice's excursions to the Cotswolds alerted them to the passing of old dancers there, and as a result two members, Joseph Needham and Arthur Peck, determined to seek out also without delay the remnants of molly dancing in Cambridgeshire.[48] They found the practice still extant at Little Downham (Figure 25.4) and published an account of the dances in 1933. There were six men: a money collector, musician playing the accordion, and four dancers (one of whom was a 'Betty') dancing in couples. Needham and Peck published details of the dances but concluded that 'the dancing has unfortunately degenerated so much that all clues to its original form are lost'.[49] The Little Downham molly dancers continued until 1937, but attracted only the occasional slight attention of the local press.[50]

Despite these occasional interactions with surviving elements of the custom, apart from the Upton-on-Severn dances neither west-midlands morris nor molly dancing were incorporated into the revivalist repertoire at this stage. The dances were noted for the record, rather than with an eye to their revival.

---

[45] Mendham.
[46] 'Karpeles MSS, Upton-on-Severn Morris'; Jones, Dave, p. 58.
[47] Karpeles, 'Upton-on-Severn Morris Dances'.
[48] Simons, 'Morris Men', p. 193.
[49] Needham and Peck, p. 85.
[50] Frampton, *Necessary*, pp. 10-11.

Figure 25.4: Molly dancers at Little Downham, Plough Monday, 1932 (Photo by William Palmer courtesy of John Jenner © Elizabeth Heydeman).

The north-west morris continued to tread a different path. The publication in 1930 of Maud Karpeles's book describing the Royton morris dance led to the team re-forming and performing at the EFDS's Royal Albert Hall festival that year.[51] The team continued to dance throughout the 1930s (and a boys' side was revived after World War II). Meanwhile Dorothea Haworth of Manley, in Cheshire, who had become interested in folk dancing while at Oxford University, invited Bob MacDermott of the Royton team to teach the dance there in 1934. The Manley team did not use Karpeles's book but learned directly from MacDermott, who continued to be associated with the team until his death in 1962.[52] The Royton dance, with all its trappings including most of the costume, was in effect transplanted to Manley; the team did no other dances but continued to develop the dance in its new home (Figure 25.5).

In the early 1930s the Manchester branch of the EFD(S)S had a men's morris team, which at some point developed enough of a separate identity to be enrolled as a club in the Morris Ring in 1936. The branch minutes for 3 February 1936 record that 'It was decided that the Men's Morris Side should affiliate with the Morris Ring, the Branch paying the Annual Subscriptions'.[53] Bob MacDermott had taught them the Royton dance in 1933-34. In 1937 they learned the dance of the recently defunct Godley Hill team and performed it at the Alderley Edge Festival in 1938, retaining the usual EFDSS costume for south-midlands morris, except for donning flowered hats.[54] The north-western dances did not sit easily with the south-midlands repertoire of the Ring sides; the radically different costume and footwear involved

[51] Schofield, Derek, 'Different Sort', p. 203.
[52] Schofield, Derek, 'Different Sort', pp. 206-07.
[53] Ashman, Keith, p. 5.
[54] Tallis.

Figure 25.5: Manley Morris Dancers, Chester, 2007 (Photo © Derek Schofield).

militated against 'quick-change' transformations. This may have been one reason why, despite Karpeles's publication, few clubs in the Morris Ring adopted the Royton or other published north-west dances into their repertoire.

In March 1936 the Manchester EFDSS branch also had demonstrated to them the dance from Mill Brow (Millbrook in Stalybridge) which had been revived by the local scout troop and taught by a Millbrook dancer from the turn of the century, a Mr Pollitt. They noted that 'The dance, steps, figures and tunes, are very much on the same lines as the "Royton Dance", but lacks [sic] the elaboration, the intricate stepping and slinging that the "Royton Dance" has achieved'.[55] Surprisingly, the Manchester Morris Men/EFDSS team apparently made no effort to incorporate the dance into their repertoire or even to note it down. At the Morris Ring meeting in Longridge near Preston in May 1939 the assembled dancers saw the dance from nearby Goosnargh, performed by a mixed juvenile set. The dance was noted by Fred Hamer, who had grown up in Longridge but on becoming a teacher had moved to Bedford in 1931, where he became interested in morris dancing and founded the Bedford Morris Men, which joined the Ring in 1936. One of the minor researchers into the dances, he published his researches on the south-midlands-style Brackley and Hinton dances, but not the north-west material.[56]

In 1911 John Graham had published a rather confused account taken from the dances at Godley Hill, Failsworth and Middleton. For some reason neither the EFD(S)S nor the Morris Ring picked up the baton to any great extent. Only Maud Karpeles published the material she had

---

[55] 'Manchester and District Branch'.

[56] 'Hamer MSS'; Loveless; Hamer, 'Hinton and Brackley Morris'.

collected. Each of her published descriptions represented a rather atypical dance: Royton for its complexity, Abram for its circular formation, and Lymm for its general conservatism in the face of the mainstream developments in the north-west morris, which Karpeles deprecated.[57] The north-west dances on the whole continued to evolve along their own path, and did little to inform the revival elsewhere.

We noted earlier (p. 362) Cecil Sharp's view that the morris dance was linked to sword dancing and the mummers' play as relict survivals of primitive rites, and that as such they were the evolutionary expression of English racial and cultural identity, and thereby of national identity. Embracing this explanation enabled twentieth-century men and women to tap into rose-tinted views of Englishness and to reconnect with its distant past. The survivals theory became the orthodoxy for much of the century. For example, Iolo Williams felt able to say, in his *English Folk Song and Dance* of 1935, that 'In the Morris and Processional dances, therefore, one may see the survival of a primitive festival of the spring, which may, at various times in its career, have included both human and animal sacrifice', while admitting that 'thoughts such as these will hardly be the first to rise in the spectator's mind to-day, unless they have been put there by reading'.[58] Douglas Kennedy wrote in 1949, 'the word "Moorish" was used in the sense of "pagan", and the Morris was a pagan dance ... probably indigenous to these Islands as far back as Roman times'.[59]

The presumption of an extremely ancient past allowed folklorists to look even further afield to European parallels. Rodney Gallop wrote in 1934:[60]

> There is no question that the English Morris dance is closely related to the similar dances (whether called Morisco or not) of the rest of Europe, and it is impossible to propound an answer to the question of its origin without taking into account the evidence furnished by other countries.

Douglas Kennedy wrote that 'Our picture of the English Morris as a man's ritual, linked with the pre-Christian Lenten festival, would be blurred and fragmentary if it reflected only the English survival'. He even went so far as to postulate connections between individual elements of choreography, noting that the Basque dancers used a 'strikingly similar step' to the galley step of the south-midlands morris.[61] The most frequent analogy made was with dances or mock battles featuring Moors and Christians. But even the loosest of correlations could be used, without even a similarity in name. At the International Folk Dance Festival organized by the EFDSS in 1935, the Romanian scholar Romulus Vuia stated 'I do not think it necessary to stress the fact that the English Sword and Morris dancers are the distant British variation of the Roumanian Călușari'.[62]

Within England Sharp had already included the Abbot's Bromley horn dance and Helston furry dance in his publications, and we have seen that these were on occasion referred to as 'morris dances'. The Britannia Coconut Dancers of Bacup were also brought into the ambit, by their own initiative. The dancers participated in several of the dancing competitions which we have seen were prevalent in the north-west, and which often offered prizes in different

---

[57] Graham; Karpeles, *Lancashire Morris Dance*; Karpeles, 'Abram Morris Dance'; Karpeles and Helm.
[58] Williams, Iolo, pp. 154-56.
[59] Kennedy, *England's Dances*, p. 44.

[60] Gallop, p. 123.
[61] Kennedy, *England's Dances*, pp. 36, 127.
[62] Vuia, p. 105.

Figure 25.6: Britannia Coconut Dancers, Bacup, Easter Saturday, 2014 (Photo © Derek Schofield).

categories of dance. The Britannia Coconut Dancers sought and received authentication from the EFDSS that theirs was a genuine morris dance, so as to validate their participation in such contests.[63] It is, in fact, most probably an adaptation of nineteenth-century caricature stage representations of African or Pacific islanders to street performance, and the association with morris dancing is a result of their overlapping performance contexts (Figure 25.6).[64] The current team's account, in 2020, of the black-face element is that it derives from their 'unique [coal-]mining tradition'.[65] The Bacup dancers were also protective of their dance as intellectual property and thereby an exploitable commodity. They sought an agreement with the EFDS that their dances would not be copied or published, and in return undertook to 'make no alteration without first consulting and discussing same with the Society'. As Theresa Buckland points out, this is reflective of the EFDS's view that change is degenerative of 'pure' tradition.[66] In embracing Sharp's conceptions, EFDSS branches and morris clubs also used to perform sword dances in parallel with morris dances. EFDSS branches also included country dances.

The only serious attempt to provide a research-based analysis of the nature and history of morris dancing came from Joseph Needham in his 'The Geographical Distribution of English Ceremonial Dance Traditions', published in 1936.[67] This was by far the most significant contribution to the study since Douce's in 1807. Needham created a comprehensive listing of all the known dance customs, classified according to type. He categorized the dances geographically, primarily morris and sword, but including unique instances such as the Abbot's Bromley horn dance. He was the first to use the term 'north-western morris' as opposed to 'the

63 Buckland, 'In a Word', p. 54.
64 Buckland, 'Black Faces'.
65 'Official Britannia Coconut Dancers Press Statement'.
66 Buckland, 'In a Word', p. 53.
67 Needham.

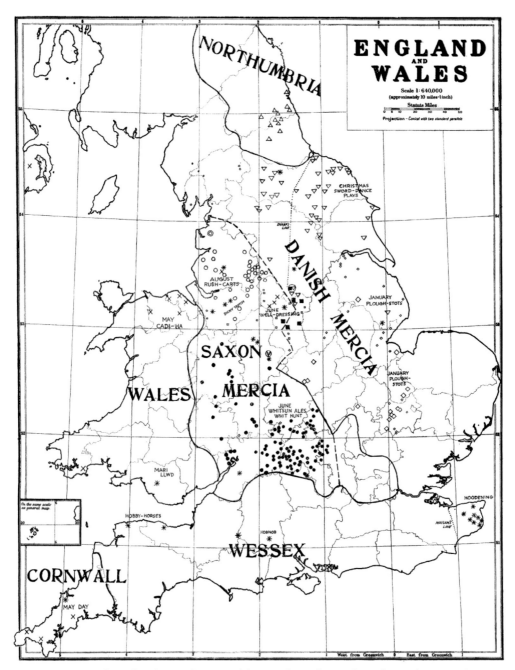

Figure 25.7: Joseph Needham's map of ceremonial dance traditions (in Joseph Needham, 'The Geographical Distribution of English Ceremonial Dance Traditions', Journal of the English Folk Dance and Song Society, 3, no. 1 (1936): 1-45 (following p. 38) by permission of the Needham Research Library).

Lancashire' and/or 'Cheshire morris'. He introduced 'Cotswold morris' for the dances of the south midlands, including within the term the Forest of Dean and west-midlands morrises. In addition to the geographical categorization, he provided classifications for ancillary customs such as well dressing and rushcarts. He made a decision to omit all evidence before 1800, on the grounds that for more remote periods it is difficult to assign a classification to a dance with any certainty. He also plotted the tabular listing of occurrences on a map (Figure 25.7).

The fundamental weakness in Needham's analysis lies in the superimposition onto the map of the regions of Anglo-Saxon England, and his presumption that correlation implies causation. As he had excluded all the pre-1800 evidence (some of which would in any case disrupt his geography), this required a one-thousand-year leap of the imagination to posit a causal connection.

There is much additional historical detail in the article. Following Sharp, Needham linked the use of the word 'morris' to the practice of face-blackening, although the evidence for it is weak. He separated out the name from the dance, and noted the rather indiscriminate use of the word 'morris':[68]

> ...if the term ' Morris' was given indiscriminately to all groups of celebrants whose faces were blackened or who were otherwise disguised, no judgments as to the relationships of the various rites which they performed can be made simply on the ground that they were called Morrisers. It is thus valueless to assert that there is a close genetic connection between Morris and Sword dancers on the ground that Sword dancers were often called Morris dancers. Nor can we assume a connection between the Morris dancers and the Mummers, on the ground that the latter were often called Morrisers. I would suggest that in probing the origin of the various dance-types and their geographical distribution we should pay more attention to their internal structure and less to their names.

He considered two of the origin theories, that morris dances developed from the sword dances, and that they derived from processions. This led him on to cite Roman processions, adducing as relevant in this context the paper streamers at the ends of the short sticks held by dancers in the Cheshire festivals, which we have seen was in fact a development within the 50 years before Needham's article.

For all its weaknesses, Needham's article provided an essential reference tool for future researchers. It was generally accepted that the name was late medieval but the dance was older. Douglas Kennedy, paraphrasing Needham's observations, noted that 'Its geographical distribution in England relates it to the oldest settlements in England'.[69]

After the hiatus in activities for the duration of World War II the Morris Ring became the predominant force in the development of morris dancing. The EFDSS under Douglas Kennedy moved away from presenting itself primarily as a pedagogical organization focused on standards of achievement, and emphasised instead popular participation in country dancing. The society abolished its examination structure for dancing in 1956.[70] Although the EFDSS did continue to provide tuition, the main impetus now came through learning within clubs, fostered by the Morris Ring. The pattern for its meetings was set at the first public post-war meeting in 1949: an ale (a private informal social gathering, taking over the name from Whitsun ales) on a Friday evening, division into smaller groups for tours of the local area followed by massed dancing and a formal feast on the Saturday, and a church service (almost invariably Church of England, very occasionally Methodist) and more massed dancing on

---

[68] Needham, pp. 26-27.
[69] Kennedy, *England's Dances*, p. 44.
[70] Heaney, Michael, 'Kennedy'.

the Sunday.[71] Pre-war meetings had often included an instructional element prior to public performance of the dances practised. Instruction was for a while left much more in the hands of the clubs, but in 1957 the Ring decided to provide more formal teaching sessions, and the first such, with the avowed purpose being 'to provide instruction in Cotswold Morris in view of the importance of all the clubs working for and maintaining a high dancing standard' was held as its 62nd meeting at the EFDSS headquarters Cecil Sharp House in March 1958.[72]

Meanwhile the Ring was experiencing a re-expansion following the inevitable falling-off during World War II. The Ring recognised 'a great necessity for a drive to form new clubs'. Of the 39 member clubs of 1939, by 1946 and the end of World War II only eight were still dancing, with a further seven hoping to restart.[73] Although only a minority of clubs usually attended any given meeting, by the time of the 70th meeting in Headington Quarry in 1959, 395 men representing 39 clubs attended.[74] The Ring was probably at its peak (in terms of influence if not of numbers) some years later, in the 1970s. Its Squire in 1976, Morris Sunderland, was reported as saying at the record of its 162nd meeting that:[75]

> the number of clubs now in the Ring was 122; he had let in 33 clubs hitherto in his term of office – and two more that night made it 35. Eighty-nine clubs were still outside the Ring; many of them did not want to join the Ring; they did not appreciate the fellowship of the Ring.

The mid 1970s were a turning point for several reasons, but the Ring could celebrate its growth and diversification. 'Traditional' teams (those with a history predating the revival) had already begun joining before World War II and now more joined. The Headington Quarry team not only joined shortly after their revival in 1948, but their leader Jim Phillips became Squire of the Ring from 1958 to 1960.[76] His team now began to perform not only the Headington Quarry dances but also others from the EFDSS repertoire, and added a rapper dance to the mummers' play performed on Boxing Day each year. In offering a variety of folk entertainments it mirrored the practice of many modern revival morris clubs.

The Morris Ring itself formally declared in 1949 that it was acceptable for member clubs to perform sword dances at its meetings,[77] and the 41st meeting in 1953 was organized by the King's Men of Newcastle who demonstrated the High Spen rapper dance with the former leader of the High Spen team. The Squire of the Ring said in response that 'in his view the Sword dance and the Morris dance were two expressions of the English men's dance and that both should come into the Ring on an equal footing'.[78] The revived High Spen team was the first solely sword-dancing team to come to a Ring meeting, in 1955, and it was joined there by the Holy Name Scouts Sword Team from Manchester. At the following meeting the Whitby Boys Sword Team and the Winlaton Sword Dancers took part.[79] The third arm of Sharp's ritual triad, the mummers' play, remained mainly as a secondary activity for morris clubs, but in 1970 the Ring admitted its first pure mummers' team, the Coventry Mummers, founded four years earlier.[80]

---

[71] 'Log of the 234th Meeting'.
[72] 'Log of the 62nd Meeting'.
[73] 'Log of the 21st Meeting'.
[74] 'Log of the 70th Meeting'.
[75] 'Log of the 162nd Meeting'.

[76] 'Past Squires'.
[77] 'Log of the 29th Meeting'.
[78] 'Log of the 41st Meeting'.
[79] 'Log of the 52nd Meeting'; 'Log of the 53rd Meeting'.
[80] 'Log of the 53rd Meeting'; 'Log of the 123rd Meeting'.

Although the Manley Morris Dancers joined the Morris Ring in 1953, they took little active part in its meetings,[81] and the Ring remained predominantly an organization of teams performing the dances of the south midlands. As a fresh generation took up morris dancing, however, a new spirit of research began to develop in the north-west during the 1950s and 60s. In 1960 Daniel Howison and Bernard Bentley of the Manchester Morris Men published a survey of the north-west morris, collating earlier research (notably by Maud Karpeles) and giving references to several unpublished dances. They noted:[82]

> *Not only is there much important information hidden in local newspaper files and libraries, but there are still men alive who actually performed the dance in their youth, and it is essential that these men should be sought out before it is too late. The fact that nine of the twenty-one full versions and two of the three fragmentary ones have been recovered since 1952 suggests that there is still a great deal of material available, and if this is not to perish irrevocably, the task of collecting it must be undertaken with the utmost urgency.*

Much of the later work had been done by Howison and Bentley themselves, but their fellow member Julian Pilling was a third assiduous collector. In 1963 he taught dances from Longridge, Nelson and Colne at Ring instructional meetings.[83] Pilling taught the local Failsworth dance to boys at the school of another member, Jim Mainland, and members of that team went on to found or join a number of other teams.[84] In 1967 Pilling re-formed the Colne Royal Morris Men, consciously changing from the former name of 'Dancers' 'in accordance with modern practice and understanding'. He wrote that:[85]

> *The dance represents that which was taught ... in the 1930s ... supplemented by knowledge gained from members of the 1908-1914 team. It aims at authenticity, for the modern attitude to the traditional dance is a purist one...*

The issue of the EFDSS journal which carried Howison and Bentley's article also carried 'A Geographical Index of the Ceremonial Dance in Great Britain' by Christopher Cawte, Alex Helm, Roger Marriott and Norman Peacock.[86] This significantly expanded and updated Joseph Needham's work, including all the known references back to the 16th century, and introducing a more fine-grained classification, including a distinction between the south-midland 'Cotswold' and west-midland '(Welsh) Border'. It was arranged by county, so allowing easy comparison of neighbouring instances. Apart from the element of theorizing inherent in assigning classifications, it eschewed the advancement of any theoretical or historical interpretation of the data. It remains an essential basis for research over 60 years later.

The introduction of the 'Border' concept was expanded in Cawte's 1963 article on 'The Morris Dance in Herefordshire, Shropshire and Worcestershire',[87] which fully introduced the term 'Border morris'. This was a more restrictive scope than that of the west-midlands morris described in these pages, as it did not include the dances of the industrial west midlands of Birmingham and south Staffordshire, nor of Lichfield.

A few years before Cawte published on border morris, the Lichfield dances had undergone further development in unusual circumstances. The original bedlam-style dancers had disappeared during the 1870s, and from the 1890s troupes of boys danced before a May cart. At

---

81 Schofield, *All Step Up*, p. 60.
82 Howison and Bentley, 'North-west Morris', p. 53.
83 'Log of the 86th Meeting'; 'Log of the 91st Meeting'.
84 Schofield, Derek, 'Which Past?', p. 97.

85 Pilling, *Royal Morris*, p. 14.
86 Cawte, Helm, Marriott and Peacock.
87 Cawte, 'Morris Dance'.

various times these comprised a troupe trained by Charles George, a clerk in a local brewery; boys from the local Midland Truant School; and in 1908 and 1909 the Juvenile Morris Dancers from Stafford, hired for £4 10s. After World War I another local man trained dancers, and in 1927 there was also a girls' team. From 1929 into the 1930s the English Electric Morris Dancers from Stafford were engaged (English Electric was an engineering firm). All of these seem to have been dancers in the north-west festival style.[88]

In 1954 three dancers from local clubs in the Morris Ring appealed in the local paper for information about the dancing at the Lichfield Greenhill Bower. This resulted in a series of anonymous communications providing what were purported to be manuscript notes of the dances, made in the 1890s. Additionally, tunes were whistled to the recipients in anonymous telephone calls. A few elements in the choreography seemed to relate to fragmentary information gleaned from older inhabitants of Lichfield, but it was very largely similar to, or derivative of, the complex morris of the south midlands, with both stick and handkerchief dances and jigs, while the steps included capers and galleys.[89] Even at the time the editor of the journal publishing the dances commented that 'The furtiveness and elaborate anonymity with which the Manuscripts of the dance notations and even two of the tunes have passed to the hands and ears of the investigators prompted the suspicion that it has all been a hoax'.[90] Nevertheless, the dances were enthusiastically adopted and rapidly passed into the general morris-dance repertoire, and have been popular in performance ever since. However, two pieces of evidence demonstrate that the story of their recovery cannot be taken at face value. The first is circumstantial. When the dances were ostensibly recovered the only available model for choreography was the morris of the south midlands as promulgated by the EFDSS and the Morris Ring, but with our more detailed knowledge of the history of the dance and its antecedents in Lichfield there is no way in which that history could produce dances of the kind described in the notes and telephone calls. The second is more damning. The manuscript notes were said to have been made in the 1890s, but in 1984 analysis showed that the paper on which they were written was made after 1930. The strong implication is that they were devised in 1954 by one of the participants in their 'recovery'.[91]

The Lichfield dances were promoted primarily through a series of instructional meetings organized by the Morris Ring. At many of these meetings in the 1960s the instructors included Roy Dommett. Dommett was, in his day job, Britain's chief missile scientist, a role he necessarily kept to himself.[92] He was also a keen morris dancer and a researcher, and assiduously collected and transcribed almost all of the manuscript sources for morris dances. Moreover, he began to film contemporary performance all over the country. He was responsible for popularizing, often through typescript booklets accompanying the instructionals, some of the neglected south-midlands dances not published by Sharp, for example the dances from Oddington (Gloucestershire), Ascot-under-Wychwood, Ducklington and Stanton Harcourt. At the 97th Ring meeting in London in 1965, 'discussion began with views on Roy Dommett's booklets on Abingdon, Bampton, Oddington, Wheatley, and Ilmington; the meeting acknowledged the value of his work in collecting a mass of material'.[93] The eventual outcome was *A Handbook of Morris Dances*, published in 1974 in ring-bound form by the Morris Ring.[94] It came out under the name of Lionel Bacon, past Squire of the Ring, but owed much to Dommett's work. He later

[88] Judge, 'Morris in Lichfield', pp. 145-47.
[89] Everett, Phillips and Helm.
[90] Jackson, Sara E.
[91] Judge, 'Morris in Lichfield', pp. 132, 148-52.
[92] *Times*, 19 January 2016.
[93] 'Log of the 97th Meeting'.
[94] Bacon, Lionel.

said 'It would probably sell well if it had got Lionel Bacon's name on it and it wouldn't sell it [*sic*] if had got my name on it, and I went along with that', adding that given his professional work and the generally left-wing leanings of the folk movement at the time, he was happy to keep his head down.[95]

'Bacon', as it became known, rapidly became the morris dancer's bible. Not only did it have the neglected dances from south-midlands communities, it included several west-midlands dances, and those from Lichfield. Winster was included, but not Sharp's other published Derbyshire dance from Tideswell. Bacon explained the omission as 'the fact that women and children participate in the dancing now led me to classify it with Helston rather than Winster'.[96] This was a handbook for morris men only. The glaring omission was the dances of the north-west, for which even the dances already published were omitted. The main repository of knowledge about the north-west dances was by now the Manchester Morris Men, thanks to the work of Dan Howison, Bernard Bentley, Julian Pilling and others. Howison said later that he had 'deliberately not published any of [his] notations because [he] didn't want the north-west morris to go the way of Cotswold, and become a dance that any revival team might do, whether they operated in Ormskirk or Orpington'. [97] The work by Dommett and others culminating in the publication of Bacon's handbook represented the high point for the path of the revival as initiated by Sharp and continued by the Morris Ring. Reservations of the kind expressed by Howison were among the factors driving significant changes in the following decades.

---

[95] Dommett and Heaney.
[96] Bacon, Lionel, p. v.

[97] Schofield, Derek, 'Which Past?', p. 103.

Chapter 26

The second revival

The period around 1970 saw an explosion of interest in folk music and the emergence of folk rock, with groups such as Fairport Convention, Steeleye Span and the Albion Band at the forefront. Ashley Hutchings was a founder member of all three groups, and independently produced the *Morris On* album in 1972, featuring a variety of morris-dance tunes and related songs.[1] He followed this in 1976 with *Rattlebone and Ploughjack*, containing readings and music relating to what were now being called border morris and molly dancing.[2] Several folk clubs had associated morris teams. For example, the Herga Folk club in Pinner not only had song and music sessions but organized ceilidhs, and around 1970 its members formed Herga Morris. That team in turn spawned several others in the surrounding area.[3] In Lancaster the local folk club started the John o'Gaunt Morris Men in 1966 as a south-midlands and sword-dancing side but soon switched to north-west morris. Their example inspired the creation of other teams dancing north-west morris, such as Garstang Morris Dancers in 1970.[4]

Bacon's *Handbook* excluded all 'newly composed dances or variants', with the sole exception of 'Balance the Straw' in the style of Leafield, which had become an established part of the repertoire.[5] By this time the contents of *The Morris Book* were no longer being treated as a

Figure 26.1: Gloucestershire Old Spot Morris Dancers, Cheltenham 1973
(Photo courtesy of Bernie Cherry © Paddy O'Biernes).

[1] Hutchings et.al., *Morris On.*
[2] Hutchings et.al., *Rattlebone.*
[3] Herga Folk Club.
[4] Schofield, Derek, 'Which Past?', p. 97.
[5] Bacon, Lionel, pp. ii, 149, 321.

canonical bible, and other new dances were being created. An early example was 'Old Harry' in the Longborough style, taught by Westminster Morris Men in 1964, and Roy Dommett has indicated that the Westminster team introduced other new dances around the same time.[6] In the 1970s innovation grew apace. The Sheffield City Morris Men, formed in 1975, dance mainly in what they call the 'Medup' ('made up') tradition, based upon the published Upton-on-Severn style.[7]

Other teams were moving away from the Morris Ring's model in different ways. The Gloucestershire Old Spot Morris Dancers were formed in 1972, and danced only the dances from Longborough, aiming for a high standard of performance. They slowed the music so as to jump high in the slow capers and to emphasise the accuracy in stepping and formation (Figure 26.1).

One member described it thus:[8]

> We tried to fly! To jump in the air and stay there for a few seconds and not come down till the music said. I've heard it said that Old Spot had such high leaps, but that's not true, we never leaped. All the steps were tight and controlled, and up in the air. We would practise jumping on to a table from a stand-still, both feet leaving the ground together. It was practise, practise, practise, not just once a week in the practice hall, but every day and all day, whenever you had the chance. Dancing as a set – there was no room for individuality – you had your single and double jigs for that. It was tight controlled steps together, as one man, keeping in line across and down the set. We had some swank, and we did it - we learnt to fly!

They wore white trainers for greater agility, instead of adhering to the EFDSS and Morris Ring norm of black leather shoes. Several sides copied them, giving rise to the term 'white-shoe' morris. Among them were Ducklington Morris, not only based in Ducklington but also performing the dances from that village.[9] This was another aspect of the broadening base of the morris in the 1970s and 80s – the re-establishment of teams in places from which dances had been collected. One of the first were the Adderbury Morris Men, founded by Tim Radford and Brian Sheppard in 1974 and first dancing in public in 1975. Very soon afterwards the team split over differences in approach to interpretation and membership, giving rise to a second team, the Adderbury Village Morris Men, and both teams have (in 2022) proved long-lasting.[10]

Some teams had more tenuous links with their history than others. Both Ducklington and Adderbury had to rely on the written sources left by previous collectors. At Winster, where the morris team was revived in 1977, they had the benefit of previous revivals in the 1920s and 1950s and contacts with older dancers.[11] At Eynsham, where the team re-formed after a forty-year break in 1979, three of the 1930s side were still alive, but for costume the team eschewed that of the 1930s and went back to the smocks of the team dancing at the beginning of the century, re-creating as much as reviving the past (Figure 26.2).

The urge to step beyond the repertoire of *The Morris Book* and its additions in the EFDSS's journals led also to a renewed interest in the dances of the west midlands, christened 'border' morris in 1963 by Christopher Cawte.[12] Roy Dommett organized a workshop on the topic in

---

[6] 'Log of the 92nd Meeting'; Dommett, 'Extension', p. 40.
[7] Eyre, Newman and Delamere.
[8] Langsbury.
[9] Marshall, Chris.
[10] *They Throw Away Discord*, p. 21.
[11] Ford, Geoff.
[12] Cawte, 'Morris Dance', p. 206.

Figure 26.2: Eynsham morris, c. 1900 and 2022 (Images courtesy of Vaughan Williams Memorial Library, Photograph Collection mo/ Eyn/1900+/10998, and © Julia Parker).

Ledbury in 1972 and this led to the formation of The Original Welsh Border Morris Men in 1973. This was an *ad hoc* grouping of dancers from other teams, initially from Faithful City Morris Men of Worcester and Silurian Morris of Ledbury, who met (and meet) annually shortly before Christmas.[13]

Some teams had included the occasional border morris dance in their repertoire, but none was making these dances the main focus of their performances. The first team dedicated solely to performing border morris were the Shropshire Bedlams, founded in 1975 by the celebrated folk musician John Kirkpatrick when he moved to Shropshire. He had previously learned south-midlands morris as a member of Hammersmith Morris Men but then followed up the border morris references from Cawte and Dommett. These remnants lacked the recent shared experience of a celebratory and sometimes competitive performance context which had furthered the development of distinctive styles in the south midlands and the north-west, so Kirkpatrick's drawing together of the dances from different localities in the west midlands inevitably led, quite consciously on his part, to the elaboration of a distinctive style melding elements of the different remnants. Like the Gloucestershire Old Spot Morris Dancers, he wanted a single style performed well, rather than a miscellany of different styles that had been the hallmark of most Morris Ring teams. He wrote 'It was a golden opportunity to introduce something new into morris dancing'. He 'just made up' their characteristic step (step hop, step hop, step, step, step hop), admitting 'there's no traditional basis for this pattern of stepping in Border morris or anything else, really'.[14] The team wore tattered jackets to provide imposing bulk, and blacked up, according to Kirkpatrick, because 'I *like* to look frightening'. They peppered the dances with random arm movements, whoops and yells, doing everything 'at full tilt', including energetic stick clashing (Figure 26.3).[15] The name – taken from the seventeenth-century Shrewsbury

---

[13] Welshbordermorris.
[14] Kirkpatrick, pp. 18-19,23.

[15] Kirkpatrick, pp. 24-25.

Figure 26.3: Shropshire Bedlams at Whitby Folk Week, 2007 (Photo © Derek Schofield).

references – captured the atmosphere of frenzy which Kirkpatrick wanted to cultivate (within the disciplined choreography).

Like Kirkpatrick, Dave Jones, one of the Silurian Morris founders of The Original Welsh Border Morris Men, had researched the border morris dances and spoken to the few performers surviving who had performed in the early years of the century. He persuaded his team to switch to a wholly border-morris repertoire and to a change of costume in 1979. Until then the team had danced mainly south-midlands dances with appropriate costume, just adding face blacking for border dances on their annual Boxing Day tour. The team now adopted black faces, shirts with tatters and tail-coats, based on the costume worn at Upton-on Severn at the start of the century.[16]

Around the same time Gordon Ashman, who with little experience had just been made squire of what he described as 'the second-worst side in the world', the Ironmen from Ironbridge, successfully proposed that the team change to performing border morris. He consulted the same reference sources as Kirkpatrick, and adopted tatters, with clogs (uniquely, for border morris) and black faces. They gave their first performance in October 1980, at an old people's hospital:[17]

> We burst in through the door, noisy, rough, frightening. We didn't kill any with fright, though we might have done. We were full of vigour and performing. And this, of course, was a huge difference. This was something we had never done before as a Cotswold Morris side. We were performing.

Border morris appeared to be liberating in contrast to the more restrained performance of most revival teams based on the south-midlands style, with their emphasis on precise steps and regular formations. Roy Dommett wrote:[18]

---

[16] Silurian Morris.
[17] Ashman, 'With One Bound', pp. 109-10.
[18] Dommett, 'Introduction'.

The impact of the Shropshire Bedlams on their first visit to the Sidmouth Folk Festival cannot be exaggerated. The tremendous showmanship and sense of fun, elements largely missing from Festival Morris, grabbed the attention and suddenly the dances made sense.

The style grew rapidly in popularity. Within the decade there were around 20 teams dancing only border morris, and more were including it within a broader repertoire.

Cecil Sharp had described the morris of Herefordshire and Worcestershire as being 'in a state of decadence',[19] that is, that it had decayed from the elaborate morris of the south midlands into something simpler. The opposite view now began to be expressed, that it represented 'the oldest, most basic, least civilised antics of our dancing ancestors'.[20] This view formed a bridge back to an association with paganism, albeit it in its modern form, not as the survival envisaged in Frazer's *The Golden Bough* but as a practised lifestyle.[21] One early such team were The Witchmen, who since the early 1980s, according to their website, have danced 'Morris from the Daarkside [*sic*] where pagan ritual dance meets street entertainment'.[22]

Another unlikely linking strand was the fictional 'dark morris' of Terry Pratchett's *Discworld* series, explicitly contrasting with the white costume of most sides performing south-midlands dances. It was first mentioned in *Reaper Man* (1991) and elaborated upon in *Wintersmith* (2001), in which 'Tiffany is taken one icy midnight to a leafy clearing in a leafless wood, where six men, their faces blacked and wearing black clothes, dance to the powerful beat of a silent drum'.[23] Researcher Chloe Middleton-Metcalfe has suggested that by 2016 over one third of a corpus of 155 teams dancing border morris had costumes which could be described as 'black', with a further eleven described as 'Gothic'.[24]

Border morris had provided a new approach and a new repertoire in this revival, and in the same vein others turned to molly dancing, which likewise afforded a less structured discipline outside the south-midlands dances, and a set of dances to which they could bring their own interpretations. In 1974 William Palmer published his recollections of collecting molly dances at Little Downham in 1933.[25] Ashley Hutchings's release of *Rattlebone and Ploughjack* in 1976[26] also stimulated a revived interest in molly dancing as a form of morris dancing. Cambridge Morris Men began to perform the dances in 1977 as a winter variant, local to the area, of their standard morris-dance repertoire.[27] In the same year the Mepal Molly Men were formed at the instigation of local resident Brian Cookham, initially following up on Palmer's article and meeting two survivors from Palmer's 1933 encounter.[28] They continue to perform as faithfully as possible a re-creation of those dances, avoiding for the most part formal practice, and elaborate or uniform costume. They appear rarely outside Mepal itself on Plough Monday and the Whittlesea straw-bear festival the following weekend.[29]

The Seven Champions emerged in 1977 from the Kent group the Headcorn Morris Dancers, as a result of dissatisfaction with the limitations of the standard south-midlands-based repertoire of that team. They initially intended to perform molly dances but in their first year performed a mummers' play, taking their name from the version collected from nearby Shoreham. One member intimated that they looked to molly dancing because 'it was dissimilar to what other groups were doing, and it had

[19] Sharp and MacIlwaine, *Morris Book, Part I* (1912), p. 21.
[20] Hutchings.
[21] Letcher, pp. 105-06.
[22] Witchmen.
[23] Pratchett and Simpson, p. 320.
[24] Metcalfe, p. 5.

[25] Palmer, William.
[26] Hutchings et.al., *Rattlebone*.
[27] Bradtke, 'Molly Dancing',p. 94.
[28] Frampton, George, 'Mepal Molly Men'.
[29] Bradtke, 'Molly Dancing', p. 92.

potential for creative expansion'. This was an explicit avowal of innovation over the re-enactment of the sources as received, and mindful of the fact that they were not resident in the area where molly dancing had been practised.[30] They took their initial repertoire from the few published sources, enlarged by the publication by Russell Wortley and Cyril Papworth of four more dances in 1978.[31] All of these were very close choreographically to social country dances, but the team then consciously expanded and amended the dances.[32] The costume evoked that of the early twentieth-century labourer, with collarless shirt, corduroy trousers with lollygags (twine tied below the knee) and hobnailed boots, but incongruously with top hats and sashes. There were no bells or handkerchiefs. Unlike the earlier molly dancers, only the man-woman Molly himself cross-dressed (though later a second Molly was added). They blacked their faces. The Seven Champions' dancing style was a slow heavy-footed stomp, emphasised by the hobnailed boots, with strong arm movements, and was to some degree a self-parodying form entirely lacking in grace, but strongly rhythmical (Figure 26.4). The parody is strengthened by a fakelore history involving treacle mines.[33]

Several of the teams which have sprung up in the revival of interest have taken the Seven Champions' interpretation as their model for the dance. Even those who adopt a different style acknowledge the influence, as evidenced by Tony Forster of Pig Dyke Molly of Peterborough, founded in 1984:[34]

In style of dancing, we are a tribute to Seven Champs - our tribute is that we react strongly against it. Champs style works brilliantly, but it just isn't all there is, though widely copied,

Figure 26.4: Seven Champions Molly Dancers at Kirtlington Lamb Ale, 2013
(Photo: Mike Finn: https://www.flickr.com/photos/mwf2005/8935155284/ CC-BY 2.0).

[30] Bradtke, 'Molly Dancing', p. 118.
[31] Wortley and Papworth.
[32] Frampton, George, 'Repertoire?', pp. 67-71.

[33] Bradtke, 'Molly Dancing', pp. 123-24.
[34] Forster, 'About Molly Dancing'.

and is no more 'correct' than any other style. So we base all our dance patterns on 'social'
structure rather than Morris structure (sequence of figures repeated rather than figure/
chorus), and we dance fast, trying to give a feeling of exuberance and movement and flux
rather than fist-punching military discipline.

Pig Dyke Molly only dance between late November and January, as do the Norwich Shitwitches, who also did not wish to be a 'Seven Champions clone' and decided on only the briefest specification of costume 'to avoid uniformity and create a shambolic appearance, which seemed to the team to constitute the Molly'.[35]

In the north-west, as in the south midlands, it was feasible to move to new styles and repertoire by establishing teams in communities which had a previous history of morris dancing. Leyland were among the earliest. They had re-formed in 1966 on the initiative of the daughter of a former dancer, again with the help of other former dancers, and performed not just the local dances but also other north-west and some south-midlands dances.[36] In 1974 a new team was formed at Saddleworth to revive its rushcart. The dance notation had been lost, so Derek Froome of the Manchester Morris Men used his team's unpublished collections to create a new dance based on other local sources. A similar process took place the same year at Gorton.[37] The revived Horwich Prize Medal Morris Men arose from the local folk-song club in 1975, performing a variety of north-west dances.[38] By the end of the 1970s 15 teams had been formed in the region to perform the north-west dances.[39]

Geoff Hughes of Manchester Morris Men had started the Rumworth Morris in Bolton to concentrate on the north-west repertoire, as opposed to the Manchester men's more general approach. He was also aware of the Abram dance when, living locally, he saw an application to make the space in Abram known as Morris Dancer's Ground into common land. This led in time to the revival of the dance in 1984, and over the next few years efforts were made to recreate more faithfully the practices of the Abram dancers in 1880 and 1901.[40]

Teams outside the north-west also began to take an interest. Earlsdon Morris Men from Coventry were formed after a Coventry Mummers player saw Colne Royal Morris Men at a Morris Ring meeting and determined to form a team to dance that style. Derek Froome taught them the Colne dance and they began performance in 1973. The revived Colne team under Julian Pilling adopted a proprietary attitude and placed an advertisement in *English Dance and Song* asserting that performance of the Colne dance by other teams amounted to theft of their intellectual property.[41] This approach reflected the close association between dance and regional identity expressed by Dan Howison (see p. 397), and voiced again by Roger Edwards, founder of Garstang Morris Men:[42]

Personally, I don't like people in places like Devon or somewhere dancing North West Morris,
it just doesn't seem right. How can a Southerner for instance be something he isn't? You are
a product of where you live, and your own area is ingrained in you, as part of your character.

Despite this commonly held view, Derek Froome was also instrumental in the adoption of a north-west repertoire by the Chanctonbury Ring Morris Men based in Sussex, when members

[35] Forster, *Molly*, pp. 30-31.
[36] Smith, Roy.
[37] Schofield, Derek, 'Which Past?', p. 98.
[38] Higson.

[39] Schofield, Derek, *All Step Up*, p. 99.
[40] Hughes, 'Abram Morris Dance'.
[41] Earlsdon Morris; 'Colne Royal Morris Men'.
[42] 'Garstang Morris', p. 12.

of the team attended a workshop on dances from Milnrow, Colne and Ashton-under-Lyne which he led in 1975. The team continued to perform south-midlands dances but there were almost two clubs within the team, with separate practice nights for the two styles. The debate within the club about the preponderance of or preference for one or the other style continued for decades, but four other clubs in the area began dancing the north-west style as a result of seeing the Chanctonbury Ring team.[43]

Much of the increase in the numbers of teams dancing north-west was driven by the founding of women's teams, but this was part of a much broader movement challenging the male-only practices of morris clubs and the Morris Ring. The 1971 Sidmouth Folk Festival proved a trigger point. A festival workshop on 'ritual dance' was organized, but several female ticket-holders were refused entry on the grounds of their sex. Roy Dommett, present at the festival, arranged an unofficial workshop for them. One attender was Betty Reynolds, who with her husband Tony ('Tubby') ran the Bath University Folk Dance Society. The frustration of women folk-dance enthusiasts at the exclusive maleness of morris teams can be seen in her later comments on the birth of the movement:[44]

> I have followed Tubby morris dancing for sixteen years, either sitting or standing quietly, always watching and listening, at practices, Ring meetings and days of dancing.

No longer content to watch from the sidelines, she taught dances learned at the workshop – those from White Ladies Aston as border morris and Runcorn as north-west – to women at the club, and they first danced in public as Bath City Women's Morris in 1972 (Figure 26.5).[45] When wives and girlfriends of the male morris teams visiting events organized at Bath saw the women's side they were enthused, and this led to Betty Reynolds organizing a workshop for women dancers in 1973, led by Roy Dommett. About forty women from Bath, Cardiff, Cheltenham and Oxford University were taught south-midlands dances from Wheatley and Ilmington and garland dances from the north-west. Shortly afterwards the Cheltenham participants formed the core of England's Glory Ladies Morris.[46]

The following year the Cheltenham team organized another instructional meeting at which the idea was raised of an organization to support women's teams, the male-only Morris Ring being closed to them. The five teams at the meeting asked Betty Reynolds and Bath City Women's Morris to take the proposal forward and an advertisement announcing the 'Women's Morris Federation of Teams' appeared in *English Dance and Song*. The advertisement brought an enthusiastic response from both active and potential teams. Thirteen teams attended the federation's inaugural meeting in October 1975.[47] Less than three years later there were over 70 member teams.[48] One of the founders of the Poynton Jemmers team wrote that at least six teams arose as a consequence of a single event, the 'women's ritual dance' workshop held at Sidmouth in 1975.[49]

The early nineteen-seventies saw the growth of the Women's Liberation Movement, which held its first conference in Oxford in 1970, and the burgeoning of women's morris was part of the wider challenge to male dominance in society. There were specific practical issues for women's teams, however. Two pressing topics were repertoire and costume.

[43] Goddard and Bassford.
[44] 'Betty Reynolds'.
[45] Buckland, 'Liberating Tradition', pp. 314-15.
[46] Parker, Val, 'Women's Morris Federation', pp. 282-83.
[47] Parker, Val, 'Women's Morris Federation', pp. 285-86.
[48] Joyce, p. 12.
[49] Mettam.

Figure 26.5 Bath City Women's Morris at Bath Abbey courtyard in their second year of dancing, 1973
(Photo © Val Parker).

The repertoire was determined partly by what was available, as Lionel Bacon's *Handbook* was seen as the jealously guarded property of the Morris Ring, who were the sole outlet for sales, though some women's teams had access. Several of the early teams were taught south-midlands dances by supportive members of local men's sides. Roy Dommett continued to teach at workshops and the Sidmouth Folk Festival morris workshops opened to women.[50]

Other significant factors were historical precedent and 'suitability'. By pointing to past practice, women's teams could counter the argument that morris dancing had always been purely a men's dance. The Ilmington fiddler Sam Bennett had taught a girls' team in 1912, and the women's team Windsor Morris were just one among many who decided that the Ilmington dances were 'politically correct at the time for a women's side' and less antagonistic towards the men's teams.[51] The north-west dances such as that from Runcorn were a particularly fruitful ground for two reasons: the historical precedent for women dancing was very strong, and they were comparatively neglected by the men's teams, so again minimizing direct conflict with men's practice. The federation also advised women's teams against performing those dances from communities where male teams still appeared, such as Bampton and Headington. Considerations of what was thought appropriate for women, as adjudged by women themselves, but also in views expressed by male dancers, led to the avoidance at first of dances containing galley steps, or energetic slow capers such as those from Longborough.[52]

The presence of galleys and slow capers in some south-midlands dances led a number of women's women's teams to resolve the issue the other way, by adopting trousers instead of skirts. Windsor Morris actively decided that they wanted to dance with strength and vigour, so

[50] Wearing, 'What to Dance?', pp. 268-69.
[51] Neill, p. 2.   [52] Wearing, 'What to Dance?', pp. 269-70.

changed to trousers in 1978.[53] Many teams went through rapid changes in costume, with long skirts (reminiscent of the costumes of the Espérance girls), but also shorter skirts, trousers or breeches. Sally Wearing cites the case of Holden's Goldens, a team from Wolverhampton, who wore long skirts in 1976 and short skirts in 1977 before settling on trousers in 1978.[54] The revival of teams in former dancing communities took the form of a women's team at Bucknell. Naturally they based their costume on that of the nineteenth-century men's team (Figure 26.6). Choice of costume was less of an issue for those teams performing north-west dances, and skirts were very much the norm. Their problems were in establishing repertoire from largely unpublished sources.

Male reaction to the development of women's morris dancing was often negative, sometimes even hostile. The Squire of the Morris Ring at the inception of the Women's Morris Federation, Morris Sunderland, went to see the Cardiff team in 1975 and was reported to have said at a subsequent Ring meeting that 'men must respect the girls; they could not be stopped', suggesting that the most that could be done would be to encourage them to do something else.[55] Sunderland's successor as Squire, David Welti, wrote to the second issue of *Morris Matters* (a magazine established by Windsor Morris and generally reflective of the Women's Morris Federation's perspective) in 1978 and adduced the several reasons why he deprecated women's morris dancing. These were that morris dancing is more than just recreation, but has

Figure 26.6: Bucknell Morris, c. 1987 (Photo © Lindsay Seagrim-Trinder).

[53] Dixon, p. 23.
[54] Wearing, 'What to Dance?', p. 274.

[55] 'Log of the 151st Meeting'.

its roots as 'an integral part of a pre-Christian religion'; that purported evidence of women's morris dances is not substantiated; that having too many clubs would 'dilute' it; that women dancing would drive men away; and that he would prefer to see women 'dancing something suitable in a feminine way' and not to 'ape men', although he acknowledged that women dancing could encourage men to raise their standards.[56] In the following issue John Wilson of Towersey Morris Men described events at the Morris Ring's annual general meeting, which were more overtly hostile:[57]

> No-one spoke in favour of admitting women to the Ring and as a general summary, the feeling was that women should not be admitted to the Ring or to individual sides and should be discouraged from dancing morris in public.

There was even concern about female musicians playing for men's sides. Wilson wrote that David Welti reported on refusing admission to the Ring to one side on those grounds, and that he received whole-hearted endorsement of his stance. Wilson went on to add his own views – that morris dancing was traditionally male, and one should not break with tradition; it evoked victory and fighting, and men were better at those activities. He attributed women's interest primarily to advancing the cause of women's liberation. Unsurprisingly, these views gave rise to rebuttals. Rose Jones of Holden's Goldens found Welti's views 'patronising' and pointed out that many male dancers lacked strength, or pride in performance.[58] Sally Wearing objected to Wilson's attribution of motives, putting joy of dancing and performance first.[59] Val Parker took up the appeal to 'tradition':[60]

> How is it that certain morris men can happily disregard the appropriate seasons, dance in isolation from the rites which used to accompany the morris, perform Oxfordshire village customs in alien counties, wear kit bearing little resemblance to pre-Revival costume, play instruments unknown to the morris even a hundred years ago, display hobby-horses which were re-introduced in the late nineteenth century with little or no idea of their original function, and yet debar women in the name of so-called 'purism'?

Although Julian Pilling had derived substantial information about north-west morris from women who had danced in teams, when he was approached for help by Sue Allan, wanting to revive the dance in Ulverston, he replied 'I have no knowledge that I am prepared to pass on to instigators of women's morris'.[61] The irony of this attitude was not lost on female dancers who were aware of the history. One noted:[62]

> ...there were ... teams like the little girls in Horwich – when there weren't enough men to carry on the Horwich men's team after the First World War, the leader of the men's team taught the girls and they kept it going. So when the Horwich men reformed, there were still some women living who could teach the men again, and so the Horwich men now dance what was originally the Horwich men's dance - though it's been through the girls' team in the meantime.

Pruw Boswell noted of John o'Gaunt Morris Men's decision to revive the old Lancaster processional and garland dances that 'both the dances from Lancaster were originally danced by a team of children, boys and girls, and both had to be re-choreographed and re-named before they became suitable for performance by the men'.[63]

---

[56] Welti.
[57] Wilson, p. 13.
[58] Jones, Rose.
[59] Wearing, 'Infuriated'.

[60] Parker, Val, 'Letter'.
[61] Allan, p. 189.
[62] 'Morris Matters Talks to Jenny Potts', p. 17.
[63] Boswell, 'Lancashire Legacy', p. 111.

Despite the views of the Morris Ring many men gave their support. People such as Tubby Reynolds and Roy Dommett were indefatigable in teaching at workshops and providing information on dances, while at the same time being regular participants in Ring activities. Several men's teams had more or less formal associations with women's teams. For example, Martha Rhoden's Tuppenny Dish were closely linked to the Shropshire Bedlams. Kesteven Morris were founded in 1976 and fielded a men's team dancing mainly south-midlands dances and rapper and a women's team dancing south-midlands, north-west and molly dances.[64] Several teams were formed by 'morris widows' (wives and girlfriends) of men's teams. Bourne Bumpers ('widows' of Bourne River Morris Men), Knots of May (Chanctonbury Ring Morris Men) and Meridian (Blackheath Morris Men) all arose in this way.[65]

Although north-west morris was a popular choice for women's teams, the largely unpublished repertoire was an obstacle to finding dances, and this situation encouraged the further seeking out and collecting of dances. Jenny Potts, founder of Rivington Morris, a women's team based in the north-west, obtained details of the Marston dance from the Women's Morris Federation, but from local contacts revived dances from Blackburn and Ormskirk.[66] Tim and Jan Beasant and the Poynton Jemmers team (Figure 26.7) revisited Marston and collected the dance anew. The Beasants also collected dances from Lostock Gralam and Stockport.[67] At Stockport the dances of the teams taught by the Fidler family were re-incarnated in the Fidler's Fancy team.[68] In 1988 the federation published a selection of north-west dances to meet the need for an easily available repertoire.[69]

Figure 26.7: Poynton Jemmers in 1991 (Photo © Derek Schofield).

[64] 'Kesteven Morris'.
[65] Neill, pp. [4, 9, 11].
[66] 'Morris Matters Talks to Jenny Potts', pp. 16-17.
[67] Beasant, Beasant, Cohen and Poynton Jemmers; Beasant and Beasant; 'Stockport Premier Morris Dance'.
[68] Fidler's Fancy Morris.
[69] Owen, Trefor.

The Women's Morris Federation was created initially 'for practising women's sides only', but the question of opening the membership to mixed or male teams very soon arose. A motion to remove the word 'women's' from the name and the constitution was defeated at the third annual general meeting in 1977. In 1980 a proposal to remove the word just from the name of the federation was defeated. However, the same meeting opted to admit mixed and joint sides ('mixed' being sides in which both sexes danced together, 'joint' where there were separate teams of men and women within the club), while continuing to bar men-only sides. This last barrier was lifted in 1982, and the following year the name was changed to 'The Morris Federation'.[70]

The impetus to broaden membership criteria was clearly there from the inception of the new federation, and the establishment in 1979 of a third morris organization, Open Morris, which embraced all gender mixes from the start was undoubtedly a factor. Open Morris was founded by a mixed side ineligible to join either of the existing associations under their constitutions at that time. The three bodies existed in an uneasy relationship for several years, though attendance at each other's annual meetings was instituted, and informal annual joint meetings. They began to collaborate more formally when the provisions of a proposed new Licensing Act threatened to introduce regulations prohibiting a number of kinds of entertainments, including morris dancing, without a local authority licence. The three organizations gathered the support of the EFDSS and the Musicians' Union to lobby Parliament to exempt informal entertainments of this kind.[71] Their efforts met with success, and the following provision was added to the Act:[72]

> The provision of any entertainment or entertainment facilities is not to be regarded as the provision of regulated entertainment for the purposes of this Act to the extent that it consists of the provision of—
>
> (a) a performance of morris dancing or any dancing of a similar nature or a performance of unamplified, live music as an integral part of such a performance, or
>
> (b) facilities for enabling persons to take part in entertainment of a description falling within paragraph (a).

The experience led to more formal co-operation via the Joint Morris Organisations, dealing with practical matters such as the arrangement of insurance for morris clubs, publicity in the form of joint displays of dancing, and continuing advocacy on behalf of morris dancing.

Meanwhile carnival morris had continued to evolve away from its origins in north-west morris. By the late 20th century they were entirely different communities. Geoff Hughes of the Rumworth Morris (a north-west morris team) described how in 1995:[73]

> Earlier this summer Rumworth took part in Boothstown Carnival and were placed immediately behind a Carnival Morris Troupe. As is usual for these events there were several holdups to the procession including one particularly lengthy halt... As is our custom we continued to dance during this rather lengthy static period, and the girls, after watching for a minute or two began to imitate the steps and figures of our dance. After a few minutes of this one girl was heard to remark to her friend 'It's just like real morris dancing!'

---

[70] Parker, Val, 'Women's Morris Federation', p. 292.
[71] Adamson.
[72] Licensing Act, Schedule 1, §11.
[73] Hughes, 'Carnival Morris'.

Duncan Broomhead has charted the evolution of the Goostrey Morris Dancers in the period after World War II.[74] The team was founded as a men's team in 1907, re-formed as a mixed team after World War I and competed in several carnivals, including Goostrey's own Rose Day festival. At the request of the festival committee the team re-formed again after World War II, and in 1950 competitions were held at the festival. By this time rules had been introduced to formalize adjudication of the teams. The morris teams of the time continued to dance in carnival processions as well as in arena performances, and in the latter Goostrey stayed with the two-line formation of the road procession when other teams had abandoned it for their arena dances. By the mid 1950s they were the among the last few remaining mixed teams, but after the untimely death of three male dancers at the end of the decade Goostrey too became an all-female group. They adapted more to the overall style of carnival morris dancers, changing their stepping to match the polka step with high leg lift of the other teams. The team folded on the retirement of their trainer Elsie Maddocks in 1969, but she later taught the dance to the Poynton Jemmers as they revived north-west dances.

The mainstream revival morris community very much ignored carnival morris. The designation 'fluffy' appears to have arisen soon after World War II. The earliest known use is contained in some notes sent by Fred Hamer (Squire of the Ring then, or shortly thereafter) to the EFDSS Director Douglas Kennedy in 1950, listing his view of the 'traditional' and 'untraditional' elements in '"fluffy" dancing'. The 'traditional' elements included the step ('a feminine attempt to produce the precision of the Lancashire traditional step'), the shakers, the multiples of four dancers in the formation, the use of leaders, and some of the figures. 'Untraditional' were the music, most of the figures, the costume, theatricality ('better done in the theatre … It has no earthy quality and completely lacks spontaneity'), the trainers' liberty to invent ('They have no sense of the continuity of tradition'), and of course the sex of the dancers.[75] Once one subtracts the inherent biases of the writer, this is an informative summary of the relationship between the two forms as they drew apart. Though Hamer recognised the occasional tune played by the bands as coming from the older repertoire, teams danced to 'any old march'. In the period since he wrote, the music has changed from live accompaniment to recordings, primarily from contemporary pop music.

The term 'fluffy' may derive from the shakers as they developed from the beribboned sticks of the earlier teams. The report of the Mobberley team in 1927 (see p. 376) whose 'Morris sticks were gay affairs finished at the end with huge fluffy balls of blue and white paper' hints at the perceptions which may have given rise to it. In later usage it sometimes had derogatory connotations. Only a minority within the carnival-morris community use the term 'fluffy morris' among themselves to designate the dance.

According to Broomhead, the Goostrey Rose Day festival morris competitions continued until 1988, when they were discontinued by the committee. Ian McKinnon, principal of the carnival morris Silverdale Sapphires Morris troupe from Newcastle-under-Lyme and a competition adjudicator, attributed this to the general societal conditions of the early years of the Thatcher government, and teenage girls' opting for Saturday jobs, so making themselves unavailable for the carnival competitions generally held on the same day. Some teams initiated Sunday competitions divorced from carnivals, and the process was self-reinforcing. The more teams participated in Sunday competitions, the fewer were available for Saturday carnivals, and the

---

[74] Broomhead.   [75] Hamer, 'Traditional Elements'.

fewer the dancers available for carnivals, the more the carnival organizers discontinued the competitions. McKinnon writes:[76]

> *Morris dancing and Entertaining competitions were now taken 'off the streets' and away from the valuable outside exposure and funding that they had enjoyed previously, into the ghetto-like existence of weekly indoor competitions against the same range of opponents, week in, week out.*

('Entertaining' in this context is a specific competition category allied to carnival morris but including some of the more gymnastic or acrobatic elements introduced by such teams as the Bensonians of Altrincham after World War I.)

Geoff Bibby put forward an alternative view that saw the developments as directed by the wishes of the participants themselves, but with the same end result:[77]

> *The troupes became increasingly less interested in the processions, which tired everyone out, because they attended the fetes solely to win the competitions. When there were many troupes, these competitions would take all or most of the day, which didn't always suit the organisers. Nowadays the troupes arrange their own competition venues and invite the other troupes to attend and compete. This means that the carnival morris troupes have become a rarer sight at village fetes and are not seen so much in open public performance in any great numbers.*

Lucy Wright reports that by the mid 2000s troupe attendance at carnivals had declined dramatically as the teams abandoned the carnival circuit in favour of private competitions in indoor venues.[78]

McKinnon compiled a list of carnival teams *circa* 2014, identifying 656 teams active since World War II. Despite his characterization of the competitive carnival-morris environment as 'ghetto-like', it continued to flourish, and over 200 teams were active at the time he compiled the list.[79] There are several organizations overseeing the competitions, among them the Manchester and North East Cheshire Carnival Organisation (MANECCO), the English Town and Country Carnival Organisation (ETACCO) and the Mid-Cheshire Independent Adjudicating Panel (MCIAP).

The formal adjudication rules are complex. The troupe's entry to and exit from the dancing arena, their costume, timing, their deportment, the technicalities of the dance steps and arm movements are all scrutinized in detail, and points awarded or deducted under each heading. The leader of the troupe is marked separately. McKinnon describes three kinds of step – the down step, or Lancashire morris step; the pas-de-bas, and the kick-step – and the elements to look for in adjudicating them. For the Lancashire morris step, which he describes as 'the basic Fluffy Morris step for decades' (Figure 26.8), he writes:[80]

> *The free foot is lifted, toe pointed vertically downwards, with the lower part of the leg angled slightly inwards across the shin of the supporting leg ... At the top of the free foot's travel, it may, or may not physically touch the knee of the supporting leg and then it slides down, across the supporting leg but clear of it and at an angle to it. The toes of the free foot touch the ground at a point on the opposite side of the supporting foot. The free foot now becomes the supporting foot. One beat after it has landed, the other foot begins its ascent to the level of the knee of the supporting leg. ... At all times the heels are kept clear of the floor.*

---

[76] McKinnon, 'Fiddling'.
[77] Bibby, 'Morris Dancing in Lymm', p. 51.
[78] Wright, 'Sequins', p. 339.
[79] McKinnon, 'List'.
[80] McKinnon, *Fluffy Morris*, p. 9.

Figure 26.8: Orcadia Morris Dancers from Skelmersdale, at Pier Head Village, Liverpool, 2017 (Photo © Lucy Wright).

Lucy Wright has described this as 'a precise and driving triple step strongly reminiscent of the "ranting" [polka step] found in clog morris'.[81]

Great importance is attached to costumes, which are refreshed regularly. The standard costume consists of short, fluted dresses with padded shoulders and wide bell sleeves, identical for the whole team (exception for minor variations to signify the leader and mascot). Points are deducted if team members appear wearing damaged or worn costumes. Troupes compete to have the most striking and innovative dresses. Despite their elaborate nature and the requirement for strict uniformity, they are mainly hand-made by volunteers, and less affluent teams may sometimes buy complete sets second-hand when a wealthier team updates its costume.[82]

The effects of disparities between the ages of dancers (sometimes noted as a problem in the early festival processions) have been dealt with by the strict delineation of defined age categories. Each organization words the definitions slightly differently, but ETACCO are typical. 'Babies' (aged 6 and under) must dance for at least 2 minutes in competitions; 'Dinkies' (9 and under) at least 3 minutes; 'Tinies' (12 and under) at least 4 minutes; 'Juniors' (16 and under) and 'Seniors' (any age) at least 6 minutes.[83]

Stratification by age helps to ensure that teams are matched in ability in the intense weekly competitions each summer, leading to a final 'end of season' competition at which the teams judged best over the summer compete. Dance routines are guarded zealously. There is a strong family-based network of trainers and supporters, and girls stay in the community as they progress up the 'lines' to senior level. Lucy Wright cites the experience of the chief costume-maker for the Orcadia Morris Dancers, whose mother and aunt had trained teams and made costumes. She danced for over 40 years before retiring to focus on training and dressmaking herself.[84]

---

81 Wright, 'Sequins', p. 337.
82 Wright, 'Girls' Carnival Morris Dancing', p. 30.
83 E.T.A.C.C.O.
84 Wright, 'Girls' Carnival Morris Dancing', p. 33.

The closing decades of the 20th century saw morris dancing moving away from Sharp's vision of a rescued ancient rite towards a greater sense of the morris as a tradition rooted in community. In evaluating the contribution made by the Seven Champions Molly Dancers, George Frampton wrote:[85]

> *What has been achieved is to put a distinct style into a perceived vision of 'Molly dancing', much in the same way as the Gloucestershire Old Spot Morris dancers have done with the Longborough tradition, or the Shropshire Bedlams with Welsh Border Morris.*

Ironically, the Seven Champions were not based in their traditional community, but they did inspire other teams in East Anglia. 'Single tradition' teams, some based in villages and towns that had fielded teams in the past, flourished. The north-west in particular took pride in the ownership of its dances. The historical antecedents of north-west dances also gave some external legitimation – if they needed it – to women's dancing as they began to participate. Although carnival morris, the daughter of the north-west style, continued along its independent path, the folk-revival community began to take more than derogatory notice of it. An early instance of rapprochement was the Dancing England concert of 1984. This was one of an annual series of concerts showcasing English traditional dance and related customs. The 1984 event featured the Platt Bridge Morris team of carnival dancers, and after a brief description of the characteristics of the style, the programme concluded:[86]

> *We trust that you will enjoy this display of the Platt Bridge 'Antoinettes', and will agree that the Fluffy morris, which at present is danced by over sixty troupes in the North-west, Cheshire and North Wales is thriving and is a worthy descendant of the older North-West Morris.*

---

[85] Frampton, George, 'Repertoire?', p. 79.   [86] *Dancing England*, p. [5].

Chapter 27

The modern English morris dance

By the end of the twentieth century the strands of morris dancing had emerged in the multifarious forms in which you are likely to encounter it today. We have traced, in so far as we can, how these strands arose and evolved over nearly 600 years. There comes a point at which the narrative stops being history and becomes social observation. The dance and dancers continue to evolve. In 2018 the Morris Ring finally agreed to accept female dancers in clubs. Votes in favour were 87% of those cast.[1] This was bowing to the inevitable, and ended a forty-year debate within the Ring; but in the meantime the Morris Federation has become dominant among the three morris organizations. At the end of 2021 the Morris Federation had 498 member teams, the Morris Ring 177 (down from 192 in 2000) and Open Morris 137. Each organization has a minority of non-morris members: sword dance, mumming, clog and step dancing are all represented, and a very small number of clubs are members of more than one organization. Those whose interest in morris dancing had been awoken by the folk-music boom of the 1970s are reaching the end of their dancing lives, and with them that generation of morris teams is disappearing. The demise of Green Man's Morris of Birmingham is typical. It was founded a little earlier than the boom, in 1955, but 60 years later members were talking to other local teams, also in decline, about joint performances, and in 2017 decided to close. Paul Oldhams wrote in *The Morris Ring Circular:*[2]

> Some of our men have joined other clubs, but for most, the end of Green Man has meant the end of our dancing days. The Lichfield Bower procession which we led for 60 years has been left in the capable feet of the ladies of Three Spires Morris.

The same issue of *The Morris Ring Circular* recorded the demise of the One Day Wonders Travelling Morris after thirty years, as the team aged and failed to recruit new members.[3]

Jack Worth of Headington Quarry Morris Dancers and a statistician by profession has conducted several surveys of morris dancing clubs over the past decade. His morris census of 2020, like its predecessors in 2014 and 2017, was offered to teams in the three organizations, but not to carnival morris teams. The respondents were self-selected, so may not give an entirely accurate picture. It shows an ageing population of dancers, from an estimated average age of 52 in 2014 to 53 in 2017 and 55 in 2020, though absolute numbers of dancers increased from 12,800 in 2014 to 13,600 in 2020. Recruitment to Morris Ring sides at just over one recruit per year was markedly less than that to Morris Federation and Open Morris teams, who each attracted half as many again. Most new recruits (63%) are female.[4]

The practice of blacking up, adopted primarily by border morris and some molly teams and arising in the first instance from the example of the Shropshire Bedlams, had been problematical for some time. When Derek Schofield wrote about the issue in *EDS* magazine in 2005, pointing out that the evidence for blacking up before the advent of black-face minstrelsy was minimal, and that the alternative origin stories such as disguise, poaching, or mining were lacking in supporting evidence, there were still plenty of responses supporting the

[1] 'Squire Eddie Worrall'.
[2] Oldhams, p. 8.
[3] Oldaker,
[4] Worth, p. 18.

practice. Ian Anderson, editor of *fRoots* magazine, thought 'there's a big difference between intentionally giving offence and deliberately choosing to take it when none is intended', while Bob Cross, the Squire of the Morris Ring, affirmed that 'the issue on blacking up needs no further discussion. The Morris Ring support the clubs that use disguise and will continue to support them.'[5] Seven of the eight responses defended the practice, as did letters in the following issue of *EDS*.

Despite the resistance in some quarters, teams were beginning to instigate change. The Shropshire Bedlams moved from black-face to mask-wearing in 2016. In the same year the Seven Champions Molly Dancers moved from full black-face to a black diagonal across one side of the face. The English Folk Dance and Song Society followed the lead of some folk festivals and 'made a decision to no longer engage black-face morris sides for EFDSS events, education activities or any other activities'. Chief Executive Katy Spicer wrote:[6]

> *Most dance sides do not present morris dancing as a consciously authentic historical reconstruction, but as contemporary entertainment, and so are moving away from black faces to ensure their performance is relevant, entertaining and inclusive in the 21st century.*

Opinion among dancers had certainly shifted. Even ignoring the supposed origin of black-face in morris dancing or the intent of the dancers today, the fact that black-face minstrelsy existed, based clearly on racial prejudice in the context of enslavement, had a significant bearing on public perception.

The rapid growth of the Black Lives Matter campaign after the death of George Floyd in the USA on 25 May 2020 led the Joint Morris Organisations to issue a statement just six weeks later:[7]

> *Our traditions do not operate in a vacuum. While no morris dancer wants to cause offence, we must recognise that full face black or other skin tone makeup is a practice that has the potential to cause deep hurt. Morris is a living tradition and it is right that it has always adapted and evolved to reflect society. Over the past few years, many morris teams have already proactively taken the decision to stop using full face black makeup to avoid causing offence or hurt. We now believe we must take further steps to ensure the continued relevance and inclusivity of the tradition. The Joint Morris Organisations (The Morris Federation, The Morris Ring, and Open Morris) have therefore agreed that each of them will take action to eliminate this practice from their membership. Teams that continue to use full face black or other skin tone make up will find they are no longer part of the mainstream morris community, be covered by JMO public liability insurance, or invited to take part in events organised or sponsored by the JMO.*

The respective organizations duly amended their constitutions to achieve this aim.

The acknowledgement that morris dancing is more than just the re-creation of an old custom manifested itself in other ways too. There is more attention given to the dance as a performance art. Alex Merry has founded two young female groups. The first is the Belles of London City, who say of themselves, 'Vibrant, energetic, challenging and delightfully eccentric, the Belles of London City will break all of your stereotypes about Morris dancing',

---

[5] Schofield, Derek, 'Black and White Issue'.
[6] Spicer, Katy.   [7] 'Calling Time'.

Figure 27.1: Boss Morris at Stroud Folk Festival, 2019 (Photo © Stephen Rowley).

and that they 'offer an eclectic range of performances, workshops and experiences based on traditional folk for modern audiences'.[8] On moving to Stroud in Gloucestershire, Merry established the Boss Morris team, who describe themselves as 'an eclectic group of professional performers, dancers, musicians, artists and a horde of magical beasts who create tailored performances for vibrant and exciting events' (Figure 27.1).[9] One member of the team said of morris as generally practised, 'I think for a really long time it's been stuck in a time warp'.[10]

The musician and dancer Laurel Swift devised Morris Offspring in 2003, 'a ten-year project bringing morris dance and music to the stage exploring the form's creative and choreographic possibilities, and capturing images of morris through artwork, photography and film.'[11] The emphasis was on crafted stage performance using young dancers, most of whom were children of dancers who were involved in the folk revival of the 1970s, and Swift saw it as the next step in the evolution of the tradition. The majority of these initiatives still take south-midlands morris as their starting point. The Demon Barbers roadshow was another theatrical initiative, but reached further, including sword dance and hip-hop in the repertoire and looking for cross-overs between the styles.[12]

---

8 'Belles of London City'.
9 Boss Morris.
10 Leonard.

11 Swift.
12 Barber and Walker.

There have been several kinds of reasons why people have indulged in morris dancing. The first is as an artistic performance, a display of skill, grace and creativity to impress the spectators. The second is as an affirmation of community cohesiveness. Third is as a solicitation custom to alleviate poverty, earn extra income, or collect for charity. Fourth is as a re-creation of the imagined past. Fifth is simply the opportunity for shared personal enjoyment and development. Often more than one element is present at the same time.

Artistic performance is the route by which morris dancing apparently came into England in the 15th century, but after its initial popularity it declined as a primary motivation for presenting dances. It returned in the theatrical presentations of the 18th and 19th centuries, and the musical compositions of the 19th, although coming from a different conception of the morris. It eventually paved the way for the late-nineteenth-century revivals culminating in Sharp's and Neal's initiatives at the beginning of the 20th century, which also took inspiration from the re-creation of an imagined past. Skill in performance is also at the root of competitive dancing, and competitions between teams at Whitsun ales no doubt contributed to the development of complexity in the south-midlands dances. More recently competitions in north-west festivals have led to the rapid evolution in the style of performance, resulting in the emergence of carnival morris. In both the early EFD(S)S examination structure and the strict rules of interpretation which have evolved in carnival morris, however, over-detailed judgemental scrutiny of the minutiae of performance can be thought to have had a stultifying effect. It may even have unintended consequences. Lucy Wright avers that the characteristic bell sleeves of carnival-morris costume were introduced by the dancers to lessen the possibility of being marked down for incorrect arm movements.[13]

The way in which the artistic morris of the court transmuted into the community-affirming morris of the church ale remains speculative. It may be that it was triggered at Kingston-upon-Thames in one of those chance encounters of the kind that also led to the presence of the Godley Hill dancers in Knutsford and so to the efflorescence of the festival and carnival morris, or occasioned by Sharp's mother-in-law taking up residence for a few years in Headington. It was not mirrored across the continent of Europe. Whatever the case, morris dancing became one of the major symbols of community spirit in the church ale and civic processions. In the late 16th and the 17th centuries that community loyalty spilled over from purely local expression into the religious and the wider civic community, and morris dancing became a badge signifying one's adherence to a particular cause in those culture wars.

After the Restoration morris dancing remained as an expression of community cohesion primarily in the Whitsun ales of the south midlands and the rushcart processions of the north-west, with some remnants in Derbyshire and the Forest of Dean. In these places it kept a clear identity as a dance form, and skill in performance remained a factor both for pride in community and in attracting the opposite sex. It also affirmed the continuity of belonging to the community, that this was an activity hallowed by repetition over the years, by ancientness.

Elsewhere – in the west and east midlands, and in East Anglia – the distinctiveness of the morris dance was diminished as it blurred into other customs, and it became primarily a solicitation for money. Solicitation had always been a part of the communal festival, to defray the costs of the ale or to meet the outlay for the dancers' costumes, but solicitation for its own sake was taken as an indicator of poverty, of life on the edge of the community rather than at its heart.

---

[13] Wright, 'Sequins', p. 341.

South-midlands dancers were aware of that shift and adduced it as one of the reasons for the decline in dancing in the region. Solicitation for charitable purposes was a significant feature of the north-west festivals and processions in particular and has transmuted into the practice of the majority of contemporary teams.

In the north-west the transition was made from the church-centred festival of rushbearing to civic-centred processions and May-queen festivals. This also involved a migration from the industrial towns mainly east of Manchester to the Lancashire and Cheshire plain, but with enough continuity and commonality of experience for it to be seen as relatively seamless and for the roots to be recognised. The transition also involved an injection of historical re-creation of the romanticised innocent May Day of Merrie England. The sense of history – the ancient Englishness of the dance – had been identifiable since the late 16th century in the Kenilworth extravaganza for Queen Elizabeth and the protestation of the morris fiddler from Herne when hauled before the mayor in Canterbury in 1589. It was also present in the seventeenth-century struggles as they too touched upon the nature of Englishness. Thereafter antiquaries and lexicographers attempted to put flesh on the historical bones, providing the theatrical dancing-masters with a quasi-authentic basis for nineteenth-century perceptions of the dance.

At the end of the 19th century antiquarian research moved into what we would now call fieldwork, as D'Arcy Ferris, Percy Manning, Cecil Sharp and Mary Neal went to find 'real' morris dancers as exponents of living history. The influence of Sharp and his EFDS in particular shaped the course of morris dancing throughout the 20th century, replacing transmission of the dance within communities by teaching at first in classes and then in clubs, available to all – or at least to all men, as the century progressed – and without local roots. This opened the way to a new kind of participation, morris dancing as a hobby – to keep fit, meet people, and make friends in a convivial atmosphere.

Nearly all the morris dancing we see today is now the result of collecting done by those with an interest in recreating morris dancing as it was done at some time in the past. For almost all of the commentators of the 19th century, morris dancing was either extinct or nearly so, and Sharp's sense that he was rescuing it persists. Trish Winter and Simon Keegan-Phipps write:[14]

> *The idea that the English have been blind to, or need to search for their own folk traditions presents the performance of English folk within a narrative of discovery ... [the subject's] discovery of their personal identity is tied up with the discovery, or rediscovery, of English folk traditions. We saw this narrative, for example, in the film Way of the Morris...*

This path to discovery was one element in the resurgence of teams performing dances specific to a locality, often their own. It was one of the drivers of those whom Theresa Buckland called the 'neo-traditionalists', seeking to re-affirm the local identity and local ownership of dances in the communities whence they came.[15] Several commentators have expressed the view that the English seem to be ashamed of their national culture, or that to celebrate it embraces far-right nationalism. The British National Party certainly sought to exploit Englishness in folk, to the dismay of the vast majority of folk musicians and dancers.[16] Another approach was to look back to an imaginary pre-Christian ritual and conjoin it with another modern re-creation in neo-paganism. This was yet another appeal to the ancientness of the dance.

---

[14] Winter and Keegan-Phipps, p. 139.
[15] Buckland, 'Being Traditional' p. 203.   [16] Winter and Keegan-Phipps, pp. 153-56.

Morris dancing as recreation for its own sake is on a par with innumerable other sports and pastimes available to people today. It can be physically demanding, a point recognised by Sharp and educationalists before him in promoting it among schoolchildren, and also by those teams embracing 'white-shoe' morris. On the other hand, if dancers are dancing primarily for their own enjoyment or to socialize with fellow team members rather than to entertain spectators, it can be less entertaining as a spectacle.

All of the other reasons for dancing which have driven the history of morris dancing over nearly 600 years are alive today. There is a revived performance ethic. There can be a strong sense of community cohesion, particularly in areas where morris dancing was common in the past, but in some cases 'revival' teams have been performing in their communities for longer than the lifespan of many 'traditional' teams. Although soliciting money as a remedy for destitution or poverty has gone, teams still collect money to defray expenses or support a charity. The appeal to the past – keeping alive a tradition, connecting to a community's roots, evocation of a timeless Merrie England, imagining a link to ancient paganism – is still a significant driving force. Julian Pilling wrote about its constant re-invention:[17]

> There is no ritual in morris and it is in no way a 'ritual' dance. Dances of the morris type have always been subject to conscious revival. Sometimes it is the dance as before and sometimes it is the new dance but always it is our old customs being revived. The tradition of morris is the tradition of revival.

Carnival morris certainly shares the performance ethic and values artistry, even if most of its activity now takes place in an inward-looking community of families, fellow performers and past performers. What it most obviously lacks in contrast to the rest of the morris dancing world is an appeal to the past, except for adherence to rules of performance laid down a few decades ago. Over the past few years Lucy Wright has done invaluable work in drawing attention to carnival morris as a valid 'folk' tradition. However, she writes of it (terming it 'girls' morris'):[18]

> I am ... acutely aware that describing girls' morris as a folk dance may in itself be problematic, not least because to date nobody I have encountered in the girls' morris dancing community has expressed any specific wish to be acknowledged in this way. As such, it could be argued that my persistent pushing for the reevaluation of girls' morris dancing in the context of the English folk movement imposes upon girls' morris dancing an interpretation and even sense of enfranchisement that it <u>does not actively want</u>.

She goes on to say that one justification for her approach is that it gives us a window into a contemporary folk process, given that we cannot go back to interrogate dancers from previous times about their life experience and the role morris dancing played in it.

I have reached a similar conclusion by a rather different route, by way of a thought experiment. Morris dancing as practised had remained relatively neglected until Cecil Sharp encountered it in 1899. What if that event had happened not in 1899, but in 1999? What would he have found? It is highly likely that there would be no vestige of the dance as performed in most of the areas where traces could be found in 1899 and the immediately following decades. South-midlands morris was reduced to a handful of active teams in 1899, and their subsequent survival has been to no small degree the result of the enthusiasm and interest of Sharp and

---

[17] Pilling, 'Wild Morisco', p. 18. [18] Wright, 'This Girl', p. 311.

those who followed him. Likewise, the subsequent collecting of dances in the west midlands and East Anglia took place within the framework of the structures he established. The dance in the Forest of Dean and north Wales would have been forgotten, and a similar fate is likely to have overtaken the Derbyshire morris. The north-west morris alone would have survived, but without the activities of dancers in clubs in the 1950s and after, resulting ultimately from Sharp's revival, the older forms which continued to around the middle of the twentieth century would probably have been lost.

Sharp did not, of course, go looking for morris dancing in 1899, it was something he encountered by chance. Realistically, the only morris dancing he could have encountered by chance in 1999 is girls' carnival morris. It is the one form of morris dancing which has not been affected by the feedback loop to the past that is the revival initiated by Sharp, celebrating its ancientness and its Englishness. It is a contemporary dance form, not a re-creation of a past dance form. It is the modern English morris dance.

Bibliography

Following the practice adopted in *Annals of Early Morris*, ecclesiastical visitation articles have been treated in a particular way in the bibliography. Visitation articles generally have extremely long, formulaic titles, and are listed and cited in bibliographies and catalogues under a variety of headings. The most certain way of identifying them, and the few locations where they may be found, is to give their numbers in the two major listings of British early printed books, the STC (*A Short-title Catalogue of Books Printed in England, Scotland & Ireland and of English Books Printed abroad, 1475-1640*, first compiled by A.W. Pollard & G.R. Redgrave. 2nd ed., revised & enlarged, begun by W.A. Jackson & F.S. Ferguson, completed by Katherine F. Pantzer. London: The Bibliographical Society, 1976-1986) and Wing (*Short-title Catalogue of Books Printed in England, Scotland, Ireland, Wales, and British America and of English Books Printed in Other Countries, 1641-1700*, compiled by Donald Wing. 2nd ed., revised and enlarged. New York: Index Committee of the Modern Language Association of America, 1972-1988). Such articles are given in references as 'V.A.' followed by the ecclesiastical jurisdiction and the date, and the appropriate reference number in the relevant early-book catalogue, e.g., 'V.A. *Diocese of Lincoln* (1580) (STC 10230.5)'. They are listed in place-name order. In the few cases not listed in these sources I have given full bibliographic details.

Although the core manuscripts of Cecil Sharp (his Folk Dance Notes, Folk Words and Folk Tunes) are kept at Clare College, Cambridge, I have cited from the copies at the Vaughan Williams Memorial Library, as these are directly linked to the digitized versions available from the library's digital resources.

Entries under newspapers are listed chronologically under each title. Other entries are listed alphabetically.

A. 'The Passionate Morrice'. In *Tell-Troths New-Yeares Gift …, and, The Passionate Morrice*, edited by Frederick J. Furnivall, 47–105. New Shakspere Society Publications. Series 6, Shakspere's England 2. London: Trübner, 1876.

A., F.S. 'Eccles Wakes'. *Manchester Times*, 31 May 1895.

Aberdeen Weekly Journal. 'Latest London News', 3 May 1881.

Abson, Walter. 'The Morris Ring'. *The Morris Dancer* 3, no. 10 (2003): 293–99.

Abson, Walter. 'The Travelling Morrice'. *The Morris Dancer* 2, no. 2 (1986): 23–24.

Adamson, Stephen. 'The Three Morris Organisations Trafalgar Square, November 2003'. *The Morris Ring Circular* 46 (2004): 5.

Addy, S.O., and Frank Kidson. 'Garland Day at Castleton'. *Folklore* 12, no. 4 (1901): 394–430.

'Adelphi'. *The Literary Gazette*, no. 882 (14 December 1833): 796.

The Adelphi Theatre Project. 'Dance, Entertainment, and Spectacles'. Accessed 30 October 2022. https://www.umass.edu/AdelphiTheatreCalendar/entr.htm.

The Age. [Letter], 11 May 1828.

The Age. 'Surrey Zoological Gardens', 22 June 1834.

An Agreeable Companion. London: Printed for and sold by Robert Goodman, Norwich, 1742.

Ainsworth, Robert. *Thesaurus Linguae Latinae Compendiarius, or, A Compendious Dictionary of the Latin Tongue, Designed for the Use of the British Nations*. London: Printed for J.J. and P. Knapton, 1736.

Ainsworth, William Harrison. *The Lancashire Witches*. London: Printed for private circulation only, 1849.

An Alarm to Judgement. [London?], 1678.

Aldershot Military Gazette. 'Salisbury on the off Day', 14 September 1872.

Alderley & Wilmslow Advertiser. 'The "Royal May Day" Festivities', 22 July 1887.

Alderley & Wilmslow Advertiser. 'Festival at Knutsford: Crowning the May Queen', 6 May 1898.

Alemán, Mateo. *The Rogue, or, The Life of Guzman de Alfarache*. London: Printed [by Eliot's Court Press and George Eld] for Edward Blount, 1623.

Alford, Violet. 'The Maypole: An Engraving of 1751'. *Journal of the English Folk Dance and Song Society* 4, no. 4 (1943): 146–48.

Alford, Violet. *Sword Dance and Drama*. London: Merlin Press, 1962.

'Alice Mackrael in Household of James Mackrael, "England and Wales Census, 1911"'. Chorley, RG14/121, p.1. 1911 census. Accessed 30 October 2022. https://www.familysearch.org/ark:/61903/1:1:X49Q-XTH.

Allan, Sue. 'Merrie England, May Day and More: Morris Dances in Cumbria in the Early Twentieth Century'. In *The Histories of the Morris in Britain*, edited by Michael Heaney, 179–201. London: English Folk Dance and Song Society & Historical Dance Society, 2018.

Allsop, Ivor. *Longsword Dances from Traditional and Manuscript Sources*, edited by Anthony G. Barrand. Brattleboro: Northern Harmony Publishing Company, 1996.

Alnwick Mercury. 'Christmas and New Year's Festivities at Alnwick Castle', 11 January 1873.

Anglo, Sydney. 'The Court Festivals of Henry VII: A Study Based upon the Account Books of John Heron, Treasurer of the Chamber'. *Bulletin of the John Rylands Library* 43, no. 1 (1960): 12–45.

Anglo, Sydney. *Spectacle, Pageantry, and Early Tudor Policy*. 2nd ed. Oxford-Warburg Studies. Oxford: Clarendon Press, 1997.

Another Collection of Philosophical Conferences of the French Virtuosi upon Questions of All Sorts for the Improving of Natural Knowledg [sic] Made in the Assembly of the Beaux Esprits at Paris.... London: Printed for Thomas Dring and John Starkey, 1665.

'Anthony Cookson in Household of Sarah Cookson, "England and Wales Census, 1901"'. Burnley, RG13/83/234, p. 34. 1901 census. Accessed 30 October 2022. https://www.familysearch.org/ark:/61903/1:1:X9KM-3CB.

Apollo's Banquet: Short Rules and Directions for Practitioners on the Violin with a Collection of Old Country Dances. London: John Playford, 1670.

Arbeau, Thoinot. *Orchésographie: Et Traicte en Forme de Dialogue, par Lequel Toutes Personnes Peuvent Facilement Apprendre & Practiquer l'Honneste Exercice des Dances*. Lengres: Imprimé par Jehan des Preyz, 1589.

Arbor. 'Tree Pruning [Letter]'. *Eddowes's Journal*, 25 December 1878.

Archaeologos. 'Jottings by the Way, in South Staffordshire. – V. Wednesbury, Willenhall and Darlaston'. *Birmingham Daily Post*, 20 April 1868.

'Archdeaconry of Berkshire Act Book, BRO: D/A2/C16, f. 89'. REED Online. Accessed 30 October 2022. https://ereed.library.utoronto.ca/records/berks-ridm187707360/.

'Archdeaconry of Stafford Visitation Act Book [a], LRO: B/V/1/31, f. [140v]'. REED Online. Accessed 15 February 2022. https://ereed.library.utoronto.ca/records/staff-ridm55187152/.

'Archdeaconry of Stafford Visitation Act Book [b], LRO: B/V/1/38, f. [24v]'. REED Online. Accessed 30 October 2022. https://ereed.library.utoronto.ca/records/staff-ridm55090384.

'Archdeacon's Court Book'. MS X.2.4. Canterbury Cathedral Archives.

Aris's Birmingham Gazette. 'The Gorgeous Carnival at Bingley Hall [Advertisement]', 22 March 1852.

Armstrong, Edward A. 'The Crane Dance in East and West'. *Antiquity* 17, no. 66 (1987): 71-76.

'Arthur of Bradly'. In *The Second Part of Merry Drollery, or, A Collection of Jovial Poems, Merry Songs, Witty Drolleries, ...* collected by W.N., C.B., R.S., J.G., Lovers of Wit, 125-28. London: Printed by J.W. for P.H., 1661.

'Articles Objected against Mr Tho. Wilson, Minister of Otham in Kent, April 29. 1635, with His Answers Thereunto, Presented May 28. 1635'. In *The Life and Death of Mr Tho. Wilson, Minister of Maidstone, in the County of Kent*, 67–91. [London?], 1672.

Articles of Visitation and Enquiry Concerning Matters Ecclesiastical: Exhibited to the Ministers, Churchwardens and Sidemen of Every Parish within the Diocese of Norwich in the Episcopal and Primary Visitation of the Right Reverend Father in God William... Lord Bishop of Norwich. London: Printed for R. Clavel, 1686.

Ashman, Gordon. 'Customs in Conflict: The Morris Dance in the Shrewsbury and Ironbridge Area of Shropshire'. *Traditional Dance* 5/6 (1988): 135–58.

Ashman, Gordon. Personal Communication to the Author, *c.* 1986.

Ashman, Gordon. 'With One Bound They Were Free: From the Cotswolds to the Welsh Border in One Stride'. *Lore & Language* 6, no. 2 (1987): 105–16.

Ashman, Keith. *Manchester Morris Men: The Early Years*. [Manchester]: Manchester Morris Men, 2010.

Ashton, John. *Social Life in the Reign of Queen Anne*. London: Chatto & Windus, 1904.

The Ashton Weekly Reporter, and Stalybridge and Dukinfield Chronicle. 'The Wakes', 23 August 1862.

The Ashton Weekly Reporter, and Stalybridge and Dukinfield Chronicle. 'The Wakes', 1 October 1864.

The Ashton Weekly Reporter, and Stalybridge and Dukinfield Chronicle. 'The Forthcoming Wakes', 18 July 1868.

The Ashton Weekly Reporter, and Stalybridge and Dukinfield Chronicle. 'Stalybridge Wakes: The Rush Cart and Garland Cart', 25 July 1868 [a].

The Ashton Weekly Reporter, and Stalybridge and Dukinfield Chronicle. 'Interfering with the Morris Dancers and Assaulting the Police', 25 July 1868 [b].

The Ashton Weekly Reporter, and Stalybridge and Dukinfield Chronicle. 'The Melee about the Morris Dancers', 8 August 1868 [a].

The Ashton Weekly Reporter, and Stalybridge and Dukinfield Chronicle. 'The Wakes', 8 August 1868 [b].

The Ashton Weekly Reporter, and Stalybridge and Dukinfield Chronicle. 'The Rushcart at the Wakes', 15 August 1868.

The Ashton Weekly Reporter, and Stalybridge and Dukinfield Chronicle. 'Ashton Wakes', 22 August 1868 [a].

The Ashton Weekly Reporter, and Stalybridge and Dukinfield Chronicle. 'Fight between the Morris Dancers', 22 August 1868 [b].

The Ashton Weekly Reporter, and Stalybridge and Dukinfield Chronicle. 'Christmas Entertainment at Levenshulme', 2 January 1869.

The Ashton Weekly Reporter, and Stalybridge and Dukinfield Chronicle. 'Mossley: The Wakes', 7 August 1869.

The Ashton Weekly Reporter, and Stalybridge and Dukinfield Chronicle. 'The Rush Carts', 28 August 1869 [a].

The Ashton Weekly Reporter, and Stalybridge and Dukinfield Chronicle. 'The Wakes', 28 August 1869 [b].

The Ashton Weekly Reporter, and Stalybridge and Dukinfield Chronicle. 'The Operetta of Robin Hood', 18 March 1871.

Ashton-under-Lyne Reporter. [News Item], 10 September 1898.

Astley, Alice. 'Morris Dancers Would Be Nice'. *Blackburn Standard*, 28 September 1895.

'Aston Abbotts Churchwardens' Accounts'. PR 7/5/1. Buckinghamshire Record Office.

Athletic News. 'Heywood Phoenix Bowling Club', 6 August 1884.

Atkins, Maurice. *Cataplus, or, Æneas, His Descent to Hell, a Mock Poem in Imitation of the Sixth Book of Virgil's Æneis, in English Burlesque*. London: Printed for Maurice Atkins, 1672.

Atkinson, Charles. 'The Water-whelmed [by] the Author of Derwentwater'. *The Englishman's Magazine* 2, no. 2 (1831): 149–65.

Atkinson, Tom. *Elizabethan Winchester*. London: Faber and Faber, 1963.

Aubrey, John. 'The Country Revell'. MS Aubrey 21, ff. 4-22. Bodleian Libraries.

Aughterson, Kate. *The English Renaissance: An Anthology of Sources and Documents*. London: Routledge, 1998.

Austin, Liza. 'Fosbrook's Stockport Premier Morris Dancers'. *Folk Buzz* 16 (1986): 26.

Author of *Westminster Drollery*. 'The Little Children's Figure Dance'. In *Mock Songs and Joking Poems, by the Author of Westminster Drollery*, 95–96. London: Printed for William Birtch, 1675.

Author of *Westminster Drollery*. 'A Song on the Dance Called the Morris'. In *Mock Songs and Joking Poems, by the Author of Westminster Drollery*, 93–95. London: Printed for William Birtch, 1675.

Avery, E.L. *The London Stage 1660-1800*. 5 vols. Carbondale: Southern Illinois University Press, 1960–1968.

Bacon, Francis. *History Naturall and Experimentall, of Life and Death, or, Of the Prolongation of Life*, edited by William Rawley. Lond: I. Haviland for W. Lee and H. Mosley, 1638.

Bacon, Lionel. *A Handbook of Morris Dances*. The Morris Ring, 1974.

Bailey, Nathan. *The Antiquities of London and Westminster*. London: Printed for J. Osborn, 1734.

Bailey, Nathan. *Dictionarium Britannicum, or, A More Compleat Universal Etymological English Dictionary than Any Extant*. London: Printed for T. Cox, 1730.

Bailey, Nathan. *An Universal Etymological Dictionary*. London: Printed for E. Bell, 1721.

Baines, Edward. *The History of the County Palatine and Duchy of Lancaster*, edited by John Harland. New, revised and improved ed. 2 vols. Liverpool: Routledge, 1868.

Baker, Anne Elizabeth. *Glossary of Northamptonshire Words and Phrases*. 2 vols. London: John Russell Smith, 1854.

Baker, George. *The History and Antiquities of the County of Northampton*. 2 vols. London: John Bowyer Nichols and Son, 1822–1830.

Baldwin, Elizabeth, David George, and David Mills, eds. *Lancashire Including Isle of Man Addenda*. Records of Early English Drama, 2009. Accessed 30 October 2022. https://reed.utoronto.ca/wp-content/uploads/2013/12/LancashireAddenda.pdf.

'Balls and Dancing Every Evening'. In *Diprose's London Guide*, 30. London: T. Wilks, 1862.

Bamford, Samuel. *Early Days*. 2nd ed., revised. Manchester: Heywood, 1859.

Banbury Advertiser. 'Deddington: Easter Market', 21 April 1887.

Banbury Guardian. 'Woodstock', 5 June 1851.

Banbury Guardian. 'Woodstock', 12 June 1851.

Banbury Guardian. 'Ye Olde Englishe Fayre', 20 April 1882.

Banbury Guardian. 'The Old English Fair at the Exchange Hall', 27 April 1882.

Banbury Guardian. [Advertisement], 23 October 1884.

Barber, Damien, and Bobak Walker. 'Time Gentlemen Please'. People Dancing. Accessed 30 October 2022. https://www.communitydance.org.uk/DB/animated-library/time-gentlemen-please.

Barfield, Samuel. *Thatcham, Berks, and Its Manors*, edited by James Parker. 2 vols. Oxford: James Parker, 1901.

'Baring-Gould MSS, Songs of the West, 216, Personal Copy Padstow May-Day Song'. 5203M, 2:195. Devon Heritage Centre. Accessed 30 October 2022. https://www.vwml.org/record/SBG/1/2/411.

Barker, E. Phillips. 'A Last Gleaning'. *English Folk-Dance Society's Journal* 1, no. 1 (1914): 9–11.

Barley, Michael W. 'Plough Plays in the East Midlands'. *Journal of the English Folk Dance and Song Society* 7, no. 2 (1953): 68–95.

Barnard, E.A.B. *A Seventeenth Century Country Gentleman: Sir Francis Throckmorton, 1640-80*. Cambridge: Heffer, 1944.

Barnsley Independent. 'Opening of the Queen's Recreation Grounds, Barnsley', 30 July 1870.

Barrow, Henry. *A Brief Discoverie of the False Church*. 1590. Dort?: s.n., 1591.

Barrow, Henry. *Mr Henry Barrowes Platform*. [London?]: s.n., 1611.

Barton, B.T. *Historical Gleanings of Bolton and District*. 3 vols. Bolton, 1881–1883.

Bath Chronicle. [News Item], 8 November 1866.

Bathe, Dave. 'Oddfellows and Morris Dancing in a Peak District Village'. *Folk Music Journal* 5, no. 1 (1985): 4–47.

Baxter, Richard. 'The Divine Appointment of the Lord's Day'. In *The Practical Works of the Late Reverend and Pious Mr. Richard Baxter*, edited by William Orme, 13:363–516. London: James Duncan, 1830.

Beard, Thomas, and W. Taylor. *The Theatre of Gods Judgements*. 4th ed. London: Printed by S.I. and M.H., 1648.

Bearman, Christopher James. 'The English Folk Movement 1898-1914'. Doctoral dissertation, University of Hull, 2001. Accessed 8 September 2022. https://hydra.hull.ac.uk/assets/hull:5448a/content.

Bearon, Peter. 'The Abram Morris Dance and the Abram Morris Dancer's Ground'. *Folk Music Journal* 12, no. 1 (2021): 52–75.

Bearon, Peter. 'Coconut Dances in Lancashire, Mallorca, Provence and on the Nineteenth-Century Stage'. In *The Histories of the Morris in Britain*, edited by Michael Heaney, 87–111. London: English Folk Dance and Song Society & Historical Dance Society, 2018.

Beasant, Tim, and Jan Beasant. 'Morris in Lostock Gralam'. *Buzz* 6 (1983–1984): 13–17.

Beasant, Tim, Jan Beasant, Anne Cohen and Poynton Jemmers. 'The Marston Processional Morris Dance'. *English Dance and Song* 43, no. 2 (1981): 4–5.

Beaufort, Lady Margaret. [Lady Margaret Beaufort, Household Accounts]. MS D 91.20. St John's College, Cambridge.

Beaumont, Charles. 'Masque of the Inner Temple and Gray's Inn'. In *The Dramatic Works in the Beaumont and Fletcher Canon*, edited by Fredson Bowers, 1:111–44. Cambridge: Cambridge University Press, 1966-1996.

Beaumont, Charles, and John Fletcher. 'The Knight of the Burning Pestle'. In *The Dramatic*

Works in the Beaumont and Fletcher Canon, edited by Fredson Bowers, 1:1–110. Cambridge: Cambridge University Press, 1966-1996.

Bedfordshire Mercury. 'Woburn: The Annual Holiday', 2 August 1862.

Bedfordshire Times and Independent. [Advertisement], 4 August 1894.

Bedfordshire Times and Independent. [Advertisement], 8 December 1894.

'Bedlam, n.' In *OED Online*. Oxford University Press. Accessed 20 February 2022. https://www.oed.com/view/Entry/16879.

Behn, Aphra. *The Rover, or, The Banish't Cavaliers: As It Is Acted at His Royal Highness the Duke's Theatre*. London: Printed for John Amery, 1677.

'Belle Vue Gardens, Receipt Sheets', 7 September 1859. F.4.2.5(i). Chetham's Library.

'The Belles of London City'. Accessed 3 March 2022. https://www.bellesoflondoncity.co.uk/.

Bennet, John. *Mirror of the Soul: The Diary of an Early Methodist Preacher, John Bennet, 1714-1754*, edited by S.R. Valentine. Peterborough: Methodist Publishing House, 2002.

Berington, Thomas. *News from the Dead, or, The Monthly Packet of True Intelligence from the Other World*. London, 1756.

Berkshire Chronicle. 'Ancient Borough Custom', 23 June 1849.

Berkshire Chronicle. [Advertisement], 22 June 1867.

Berkshire Chronicle. 'Performance of Mr. Birch's Operettas', 26 February 1870.

Berrow's Worcester Journal. 'The Weather', 18 January 1838.

Berrow's Worcester Journal. 'A Matrimonial Exposure at Upton', 3 March 1855.

Berrow's Worcester Journal. 'Distress in the City', 29 January 1881.

'Betty Reynolds - President'. *Morris Matters* 1, no. 1 (1978): 2.

Bewick, Thomas. *A Memoir of Thomas Bewick, Written by Himself*. Gateshead: Jane Bewick, 1862.

Bibby, Geoff. 'A History of Morris Dancing in and around Lymm and Statham'. The Lymm Morris Archive. Accessed 30 October 2022. http://www.lymm-morris.org.uk/Lymm_Book/.

Bibby, Geoff. 'Morris Dancing in Lymm: Revival of the Old Dance and Development of the New'. *The Morris Dancer* 4, no. 2 (2010): 40–54.

Bicester Herald. 'Royal Marriage Festivities at Buckingham', 27 March 1863.

Bilstonian. 'Local Notes and Queries, [1447]: Morris Dancers'. *Birmingham Weekly Post*, 3 May 1884.

Birmingham Daily Post. 'The Iron Trade', 30 January 1868.

Birmingham Journal. 'The Carpet-weavers' Strike', 27 August 1853.

Blackburn Standard. 'Donations to Blackburn and East Lancashire Infirmary', 9 September 1893.

Blackburn Standard. 'A Tribute to Heroism', 28 July 1894.

Blake, Lois. 'The Morris in Wales'. *Journal of the English Folk Dance and Song Society* 9, no. 1 (1960): 56–57.

Blenheim Papers. 'Accounts, Woodstock Election, 1727, in Correspondence and Papers Relating to Woodstock Estate and Borough, and to Other Estates in the Area, 1710-1741, Blenheim Papers Vol. 368'. Add. MS 61468. British Library.

Blount, Thomas. *Glossographia, or, A Dictionary, Interpreting All Such Hard Words ... as Are Now Used*. London: Printed by Tho. Newcomb, 1656.

Blount, Thomas. *Glossographia Anglicana Nova*. London: Printed for Dan. Brown, 1707.

Blount, Thomas. *Tenures of Land & Customs of Manors*, edited by William Carew Hazlitt. England: England: Reeves and Turner, 1874.

Blundell, Nicholas. *The great diurnal of Nicholas Blundell of Little Crosby, Lancashire*, edited by Frank Tyrer and J.J. Bagley. 3 vols. Chester: Record Society of Lancashire and Cheshire, 1968–1972.

Boas, F.S. 'James I at Oxford in 1605'. *Malone Society Collections* 1, no. 3 (1909): 247–59.

Boase, G.C. 'Flexmore, Richard (1824–1860), Clown'. Oxford Dictionary of National Biography. Accessed 30 October 2022. https://doi.org/10.1093/ref:odnb/9745.

'Bobbing Joe'. In *The English Dancing Master*, 7. London: Printed by Thomas Harper, and are to be sold by John Playford, 1651.

Bolton Evening News. 'Crowning of May Queens', 2 May 1878.

Bolton Evening News. [Advertisement], 14 April 1893.

'The Book of the Fraternity or Gild of the Holy Trinity of Luton'. Z486/1. Bedfordshire Archives.

'A Booke Conteyning the Manner and Order of a Watch to Be Used in the Cittie of London'. In

The Harleian Miscellany, IX, 389–408. London: White and Cochrane, 1812.

Borfet, Abiel. *Postliminia Caroli II: The Palingenesy, or, Second-Birth, of Charles the Second to His Kingly Life*. London: Printed for M. Wright, 1660.

Boss Morris. 'About Boss …' Accessed 3 March 2022. https://www.bossmorris.com/about.

Boswell, Pruw. 'The Lancashire Legacy'. In *Morris: The Legacy of the Past: Proceedings of a One Day Conference on Morris Dancing, Birmingham, 20th April, 1996*, 111–15. London: The Morris Ring, the Morris Federation, and Open Morris, 1996.

Boswell, Pruw. *Morris Dancing on the Lancashire Plain: The Horwich Inquiry*. Bamber Bridge: Claughton Press for the Morris Ring, 1984.

Boswell, Pruw. *Morris Dancing on the Lancashire Plain: The Preston Tradition*. Bamber Bridge: Claughton Press for the Morris Ring, 1981.

Boswell, Pruw. 'Trends in Morris Dancing on the Lancashire Plain'. *Traditional Dance* 5/6 (1988): 1–25.

Bradbury, Joseph. *Saddleworth Sketches*. Oldham: Hirst & Rennie, 1871.

Bradford Observer. [Advertisement], 29 May 1879.

Bradtke, Elaine. 'John Robbins and the Shakespearean Bidford Morris Tune Repertoire'. In *Routes and Roots*, edited by Ian Russell and Chris Goertzen, 34–50. Aberdeen: The Elphinstone Institute, 2012.

Bradtke, Elaine. 'Molly Dancing and the Seven Champions: Postmodernism and the Re-Invention of Tradition'. Doctoral dissertation, University of Maryland, 1997.

Brand, John. *Observations on Popular Antiquities: Including the Whole of Mr. Bourne's Antiquitates Vulgares*. Newcastle upon Tyne: Printed by T. Saint, 1777.

Brand, John. *Observations upon Popular Antiquities*, edited by Henry Ellis. Revised. 2 vols. London: F.C. and J. Rivington, 1813.

Brathwait, Richard. *A Cater-Character, Throwne out of a Boxe by an Experience'd Gamester*. London: Imprinted by F.K, 1631.

Brathwait, Richard. 'Upon Kempe and His Morice'. In *The Good Wife, or, A Care One amongst Women [by] Mesophilus*, sig. f(v). London: Printed for Richard Redmer, 1618.

'Bray Churchwardens' Accounts 1602-1707'. D/P23/5/1. Berkshire Record Office.

Breton, Nicholas. 'The Mother's Blessing'. In *The Works in Prose and Verse of Nicholas Breton*, edited by Alexander B. Grosart, 1:m, 1879.

Breton, Nicholas. 'Pasquils Passe, and Passeth Not'. In *The Works in Prose and Verse of Nicholas Breton*, edited by Alexander B. Grosart, 1:g, 1879.

Breton, Nicholas. 'A Poste with a Packet of Mad Letters'. In *The Works in Prose and Verse of Nicholas Breton*, edited by Alexander B. Grosart, 2:h, 1879.

Brewer, J.S., and R.H. Brodie, eds. *Letters and Papers, Foreign and Domestic, of the Reign of Henry VIII: Preserved in the Public Record Office, the British Museum, and Elsewhere*. 2nd ed. revised and greatly enlarged. Vol. 1. London: H.M.S.O., 1920.

Brewer, J.S., James Gairdner, and R.H. Brodie, eds. *Letters and Papers, Foreign and Domestic, of the Reign of Henry VIII: Preserved in the Public Record Office, the British Museum, and Elsewhere in England*. 23 vols in 35 vols. London: H.M.S.O., 1862–1932.

Brewer, Thomas. *The Country Girle: A Comedie, as It Hath Beene Often Acted with Much Applause: Never Printed Before*. London: Printed for A.R., 1647.

A Bricklayer. 'Bricklayers and Morris-Dancers'. *Shrewsbury Chronicle*, 24 February 1865.

Brierley, Ben. 'Rushbearing!' In *Tales and Sketches of Lancashire Life*, by Ben Brierley, 95–107. Manchester: John Heywood, 1862–1863.

Brinkworth, Edwin Robert Courtney. *Shakespeare and the Bawdy Court of Stratford*. London: Phillimore, 1972.

Briscoe, Marianne G. 'Deserts of Desire: Reading across the Midlands'. *Fifteenth-century Studies* 13, no. 213 (1988): 263–73.

Bromley & District Times. 'May Day Carnival at St. Mary Cray', 8 May 1891.

Bromley & District Times. [News Item], 10 May 1892, Special Cray edition.

Bromley & District Times. 'Children's Carnival at St. Mary Cray', 14 June 1895.

'Brook Green Fair'. *The New Monthly Magazine and Literary Journal* 4, no. 13 (January 1822): 554–61.

'Brooks Wright (Bef.1709-1762)'. Wikitree. Accessed 3 October 2022. https://www.wikitree.com/wiki/Wright-33037.

Broomhead, Duncan. 'Goostrey Morris Dancers – a Journey to the Carnival'. *Morris Matters* 39, no. 1 (2020): 1–9.

Brown, Cedric C. 'The Chirk Castle Entertainment of 1634'. *Milton Quarterly* 11, no. 3 (1977): 76–86.

Brown, John. *A Compendious History of the British Churches in England, Scotland, Ireland, and America.* [Glasgow: Printed by John Bryce], 1784.

Brown, Rawdon, Horatio F. Brown, and A. B. Hinds, eds. *Calendar of State Papers and Manuscripts, Relating to English Affairs, Existing in the Archives and Collections of Venice, and in Other Libraries of Northern Italy.* 38 vols in 40 vols. London: Longman, Green, Longman, Roberts and Green, 1864–1947.

Brown, Thomas. 'Diaries of the Rev. Thomas Brown, Schoolmaster and Vicar of Tideswell'. D7676/Bag C/321. Derbyshire Record Office.

Bruce, John, ed. *Calendar of State Papers, Domestic Series, of the Reign of Charles I.* 23 vols. London: Longman, Green, 1858–1897.

Brunel, Antoine de. *A Journey into Spain.* London: Printed for Henry Herringman, 1670.

Brydges, Sir Egerton, and Joseph Haslewood. *The British Bibliographer.* 4 vols. London: T. Bensley, 1810–1814.

Buckingham Express. 'Stowe: School Treat', 13 June 1868.

Buckinghamshire Herald. [News Item], 21 September 1844.

Buckland, Theresa. 'Being Traditional: Authentic Selves and Others in Researching Late-Twentieth-Century Northwest Morris Dancing'. In *Dancing from Past to Present: Nation, Culture, Identities*, edited by Theresa Buckland, 199–227. Madison: University of Wisconsin Press, 2006.

Buckland, Theresa. 'Black Faces, Garlands, and Coconuts: Exotic Dances on Street and Stage'. *Dance Research Journal* 22, no. 2 (1990): 1–12.

Buckland, Theresa. 'Dance and Cultural Memory: Interpreting "Fin de Siècle" Performances of "Olde England"'. *Dance Research* 31, no. 1 (2013): 29–66.

Buckland, Theresa. '"Hollo! Here We Are Again!": Godley Hill Morris Dancers: A Study in Longevity'. *Traditional Dance* 2 (1983): 37–57.

Buckland, Theresa. '"In a Word We Are Unique": Ownership and Control in an English Dance Custom'. In *Step Change*, edited by Georgina Boyes, 49–59. London: Francis Boutle, 2001.

Buckland, Theresa. 'Institutions and Ideology in the Dissemination of Morris Dances in the Northwest of England'. *Yearbook for Traditional Music* 23 (1991): 53–67.

Buckland, Theresa. 'Liberating Tradition: Gender Politics in Late Twentieth Century English Revivalist Morris Dancing'. In *Folklore Revival Movements in Europe Post 1950: Shifting Contexts and Perspectives*, edited by D. Stavělová and Theresa Buckland, 311-30. Prague: Institute of Ethnology, Academy of Sciences, 2019.

Buckland, Theresa, and Dan Howison. 'Morris Dancers in Crewe before the First World War'. *English Dance and Song* 42, no. 2 (1980): 10–13.

Bucks Herald. 'Yardley Hastings', 2 June 1855.

Bullokar, John. *An English Expositor, or, Compleat Dictionary ...,* edited by A Lover of the Arts. 3rd time revised. London: Printed by J. Field, 1663.

Bunting, W.B. *The Parish Church of St Thomas à Becket, Chapel-en-le-Frith.* Manchester: Sherratt & Hughes, 1925.

Burgess, Paul. 'The Mystery of the Whistling Sewermen'. *Folk Music Journal* 8, no. 2 (2002): 178–94.

Burn, Richard. *The Justice of the Peace, and Parish Officer.* 2nd ed. 2 vols. London: Printed by Henry Lintot, 1756.

Burnaby, William. *The Satyr of Titus Petronius Arbiter, a Roman Knight: With Its Fragments, Recover'd at Belgrade, Made English.* London: Printed for Samuel Briscoe, 1694.

Burne, Charlotte Sophia. 'Reminiscences of Lancashire and Cheshire When George IV. Was King'. *Folklore* 20, no. 2 (1909): 203–7.

Burne, Charlotte Sophia. *Shropshire Folk-lore.* London: Trübner, 1883.

Burnley Express. [Advertisement], 22 March 1879.

Burnley Express. 'Charter Day at Colne', 15 September 1895.

Burnley Express. 'Foulridge', 5 June 1897.

Burnley Express. [Advertisement], 30 June 1897.

Burnley Express. 'The Poor Children's Trip', 14 July 1897.

Burnley Express. 'Cyclist Success', 8 September 1897.

Burnley Express. 'Costume Parade at Colne', 14 June 1899.

Burnley Gazette. 'Victoria Hospital', 12 May 1894.

Burnley Gazette. 'Morris Dancers', 22 September 1897.

Burton, Alfred. *Rushbearing.* Manchester: Brook and Chrystal, 1891.

Burton, Henry. *A Brief Answer to a Late Treatise of the Sabbath Day.* Amsterdam: J.F. Stam, 1635.

Burton, Henry. *A Divine Tragedie Lately Acted, or, A Collection of Sundrie Memorable Examples of Gods*

Judgements upon Sabbath-Breakers. [2nd ed. London?], 1641.

Burton, Henry. *A Replie to a Relation, of the Conference between William Laude and Mr. Fisher the Jesuite*. [Amsterdam: Cloppenburg Press], 1640.

Burton, Henry. *A Tryall of Private Devotions*. 1628. Facs. English Experience 856. Amsterdam: Theatrum Orbis Terrarum, 1977.

Burton, Samuel. *A Sermon Preached at the Generall Assises in Warwicke, the Third of March, Being the First Friday in Lent, 1619*. London: Printed by W. Stansby for Nathaniel Butter, 1620.

Burton, William. *Ten Sermons upon the First, Second, Third and Fourth Verses of the Sixt of Matthew*. London: By Richard Field for Thomas Man, 1602.

Burton Chronicle. 'Dancing, Deportment and Calisthenics [Advertisement]', 31 August 1893.

Burton Chronicle. 'Dancing, Deportment and Calisthenics [Advertisement]', 29 August 1895.

The Bury and Norwich Post, or, Suffolk, Norfolk, Essex, and Cambridge Advertiser. [News Item], 12 May 1802.

The Bury and Norwich Post, or, Suffolk, Norfolk, Essex, and Cambridge Advertiser. [News Item], 13 May 1807.

The Bury and Norwich Post, or, Suffolk, Norfolk, Essex, and Cambridge Advertiser. [News Item], 26 December 1821.

Bury Carnival, Saturday September 6th 1924 [Video], 1924. Accessed 3 October 2022. https://vimeo.com/451886098.

Bury Free Press. 'The Bury St. Edmund's Gala', 23 July 1870.

Bury Free Press. 'Assault and Broken Leg', 15 February 1873.

Bury Times. [Advertisement], 18 September 1858.

Bury Times. [Advertisement], 10 September 1859.

Bury Times. 'The Wakes', 1 October 1859.

Butler, Samuel. 'Fragments of an Intended Second Part of ... Satyr'. In *The Genuine Remains in Verse and Prose of Mr Samuel Butler*, edited by R. Thyer, 1:213-27. London: Printed for J. and R. Tonson, 1759.

Buxton Advertiser. 'The Well-Dressing of 1856', 27 June 1856.

Buxton Advertiser. [News Item], 26 June 1858.

Buxton Advertiser. 'The Well-Flowering', 11 June 1859.

Buxton Advertiser. 'Buxton Well-Flowering', 6 July 1861.

Buxton Advertiser. [News Item], 26 June 1880.

Buxton Advertiser. 'Crowning the May Queen', 28 June 1884.

Buxton Herald. 'Buxton Well-Dressing', 6 July 1843.

Buxton Herald. 'Visit of the King of Saxony', 29 June 1844.

Buxton Herald. 'The Buxton Well Flowering of 1849', 30 June 1849.

Buxton Herald. [Advertisement], 21 June 1851.

Buxton Herald. 'The Well-Dressing', 25 June 1853.

Buxton Herald. 'Buxton Well Flowering', 23 June 1855.

Buxton Herald. [Advertisement], 11 September 1856.

Buxton Herald. 'Buxton Well-Dressing Festivities', 25 June 1857.

Buxton Herald. 'Buxton Well Flowering', 9 July 1857.

Buxton Herald. 'Buxton Well Flowering: Midsummer 1859', 23 June 1859.

Buxton Herald. 'Buxton Well-Flowering', 28 June 1860.

Buxton Herald. 'Well-Dressing', 22 May 1873.

Buxton Herald. 'Buxton Well Dressing', 19 June 1879.

Buxton Herald. 'Buxton Well-Dressing 1883', 20 June 1883.

Byng, John. *The Torrington Diaries: Containing the Tours through England and Wales of the Hon. John Byng (Later Fifth Viscount Torrington) between the Years 1781 and 1794*. 4 vols. London: Eyre & Spottiswoode, 1934–1938.

Byrd, William. 'The Morris'. In *My Ladye Nevells Booke*, edited by Hilda Andrews, 39. London: Curwen, 1926.

'Cadi Ha'. *Journal of the Welsh Folk Song Society* 3, no. 1 (1930): 69–74.

Calendar of the Manuscripts of the Most Hon. the Marquis of Salisbury, K.G., &c. ...Preserved at Hatfield House, Hertfordshire. 24 vols. London: HMSO, 1883.

Calendar: (The Calendar of Every-Day Reference, Huntingdonshire), 1845.

'Calling Time on Full-Face Black Makeup'. The Morris Federation. Accessed 3 October 2022. https://www.morrisfed.org.uk/2020/07/03/calling-time-on-full-face-black-makeup/.

Cambridge Chronicle and Journal. 'Plough Monday', 14 January 1854.

Cambridge Chronicle and Journal. 'Godmanchester: Plough Monday', 12 January 1861.

Cambridge Chronicle and Journal. 'Plough Monday', 13 January 1866.

Cambridge Independent Press. 'Plough Monday', 18 January 1845.

Cambridge Independent Press. 'Plough Monday', 17 January 1846.

Cambridge Independent Press. 'Four "Merry Gipsies Are We"', 2 January 1858.

Cambridge Independent Press. 'Plough Monday', 15 January 1859.

Cambridge Independent Press. 'Chesterton: Brutal Assault', 15 January 1870 [a].

Cambridge Independent Press. 'Plough Monday', 15 January 1870 [b].

Cambridge Independent Press. 'Plough Monday', 13 January 1888.

Cambridge Independent Press. 'Stretham', 12 January 1894.

Cambridge Independent Press. 'Histon: Plough Monday', 14 January 1898.

Cambridge Independent Press. 'Histon: Plough Monday', 13 January 1899.

Capell, Edward. *Notes and Various Readings to Shakespeare, Part the First*. London: Printed for Edw. and Cha. Dilly, 1774.

Carew, Richard. *The Survey of Cornwall*. London: Printed by S.S. for John Jaggard, 1602.

Carlisle Patriot. 'Cumberland 200 Years Ago', 8 January 1897.

Carlisle Patriot. 'Aspatria', 25 June 1897.

Carter, J. 'Lincoln's Inn'. *The Gentleman's Magazine: And Historical Chronicle* 87 (June 1817): 518.

'[Cartwright Papers], Account Book 1691-1722'. ML/1306. Northamptonshire Archives.

'[Cartwright Papers], Account Book 1722-1735'. ML/1307. Northamptonshire Archives.

Casanova, Giacomo. *History of My Life*, translated by Willard R. Trask. 12 vols. London: Longmans, 1966.

The Case between the Managers of the Two Theatres, and Their Principal Actors, Fairly Stated, and Submitted to the Town. London: Printed for J. Roberts, 1743.

Caswell, T. 'Morris Dancing'. *Bye-Gones Relating to Wales and the Border Counties* n.s. 12 (24 May 1911): 61–62.

A Catalogue of Objects Illustrating the History and Antiquities of Oxford, and of the Neighbourhood. [Oxford]: Oxford Architectural and Historical Society, 1894.

Catherine of Braganza. 'Accounts of the Queen's Privy Purse: Signature of Catherine of Braganza, 1663-1668'. 1-WORSLEY/6. Lincolnshire Archives.

Catlin, Edward. 'Poems Addressed to Pestell'. In *The Poems of Thomas Pestell*, edited by Hannah Buchan, 122-23. Oxford: Blackwell, 1940.

Cavendish, Margaret, Duchess of Newcastle. 'The Second Part of the Lady Contemplation'. In *Playes Written by the Thrice Noble, Illustrious and Excellent Princess, the Lady Marchioness of Newcastle*, 212–46. London: Printed by A. Warren, 1662.

Cavendish, Margaret, Duchess of Newcastle. 'Youths Glory, and Deaths Banquet'. In *Playes Written by the Thrice Noble, Illustrious and Excellent Princess, the Lady Marchioness of Newcastle*, 122–80. London: Printed by A. Warren, 1662.

Cavendish, William. '[A Treatise on Government]'. In *A Catalogue of Letters and Other Historical Documents Exhibited in the Library at Welbeck*, compiled by S. Arthur Strong, 173–226. London: John Murray, 1903.

Cawte, E.C. 'Early Records of a Rushcart at Didsbury'. *Folklore* 72, no. 1 (1961): 330–37.

Cawte, E.C. 'A History of the Rapper Dance'. *Folk Music Journal* 4, no. 2 (1981): 79–116.

Cawte, E.C. 'The Morris Dance in Herefordshire, Shropshire and Worcestershire'. *Journal of the English Folk Dance and Song Society* 9, no. 4 (1963): 197–212.

Cawte, E.C. Personal Communication to the Author, 19 August 1986.

Cawte, E.C. *Ritual Animal Disguise: A Historical and Geographical Study of Animal Disguise in the British Isles*. Mistletoe Series. Cambridge: D.S. Brewer for the Folklore Society, 1978.

Cawte, E.C., Alex Helm, Roger Marriott, and Norman Peacock. 'A Geographical Index of the Ceremonial Dance in Great Britain'. *Journal of the English Folk Dance and Song Society* 9, no. 1 (1960): ii, 1–41.

Chamberlain, Robert. *The Swaggering Damsel: A Comedy*. London: Printed by Tho. Cotes, for Andrew Crooke, 1640.

Chambers, Robert, ed. *The Book of Days, a Miscellany of Popular Antiquities*. 2 vols. London: W. & R. Chambers, 1863–1864.

'A Chancery Case Arising out of Sir Humphrey Gilbert's 1578 Voyage'. In *New American*

World, Vol. III: English Plans for North America: The Roanoke Voyages, New England Voyages, edited by David B. Quinn, 204–09. London: Macmillan, 1985.

Chandler, Keith. 'The Archival Morris Photographs, 4: "The Old 'Uns and the Young 'uns", Bampton, Oxfordshire, 1927'. *English Dance & Song* 47, no. 3 (1985): 26–28.

Chandler, Keith. *Bampton Morris Dancers 1915-1945: The Newspaper Accounts.* Eynsham: Chandler Publications, 1986.

Chandler, Keith. *Morris Dancing at Bampton until 1914.* Minster Lovell: Chandler Publications, 1983.

Chandler, Keith. *Morris Dancing in the English South Midlands, 1660-1900: Aspects of Social and Cultural History.* CD-ROM MTCD250. Musical Traditions, 2002.

Chandler, Keith. *Morris Dancing in the English South Midlands, 1660-1900: A Chronological Gazetteer.* Enfield Lock: Hisarlik Press, for the Folklore Society, 1993.

Chandler, Keith. 'Morris Dancing in the Forest of Dean'. In *Morris Dancing in the English South Midlands, Musical Traditions Supplement No 3,* CD-ROM MTCD250. Musical Traditions, 2002.

Chandler, Keith. 'Popular Culture in Microcosm: The Manuscript Diaries of Richard Heritage of Marsh Gibbon, Buckinghamshire'. *Folk Music Journal* 9, no. 1 (2006): 5–55.

Chandler, Keith. *'Ribbons, Bells and Squeaking Fiddles': The Social History of Morris Dancing in the English South Midlands, 1660-1900.* Enfield Lock: Hisarlik Press, for the Folklore Society, 1993.

Chandler, Keith. *'Taking an Annual Circuit': Peripatetic Rural Morris Dancers in London and the Home Counties.* Eynsham: Chandler Publications, 1984.

Chappell, William. *A Collection of English National Airs.* 2 vols. London: Chappell, 1840.

Chatham News. [Advertisement], 22 August 1891.

Chaworth, Sir Thomas. [Will]. In *Testamenta Eboracensia, Part II,* no. 179, 220–29. Surtees Society 30. Durham: Surtees Society, 1885.

Chelmsford Chronicle. 'Grand Ball at the Hyde', 1 April 1864.

Chelmsford Chronicle. 'Primrose League Fete', 24 June 1892.

Chelmsford Chronicle. 'A Grand Fancy Dress Concert', 26 January 1894.

Cheltenham Chronicle. 'The Weather and Its Effects', 20 February 1855.

Cheltenham Examiner. 'The Cheltenham and County School (Mr. West's)', 8 August 1883.

Cheltenham Mercury. 'Signs of Hard Times', 29 January 1881.

Chepstow Weekly Advertiser. 'Grand Bazaar and Historical Fete at Chepstow Castle', 2 August 1890.

Cheshire Observer. 'Knutsford: Mayday Festivities', 4 May 1878.

Chester Chronicle. 'Singular Instance of Longevity', 10 July 1789.

Chester Chronicle. [News Item], 30 May 1817.

Chester Courant. 'Macclesfield', 24 July 1821.

Chester Courant. 'May Day at Astbury', 11 May 1864.

Child, Frances. *The Spinster at Home in The Close at Salisbury.* Salisbury: W.R. Brodie, 1844.

'Christmas and the New Year'. *The Newcastle Magazine* 8, no. 1 (1829): 1–7.

The Christmas Prince, edited by Frederick S. Boas. Malone Society Reprints. Oxford: Malone Society, 1922.

Die Chroniken der Deutschen Städte vom 14. bis 16. Jahrhundert. 32 vols. Leipzig: S. Hirzel, 1862–1917.

The Cities Loyalty Display'd, or, The Four Famous and Renowned Fabricks in the City of London Exactly Described. London, 1661.

The Citizen. 'Forest of Dean Miners' Association', 3 July 1884.

The Citizen. 'Town of Ye Man of Ross', 1 September 1884.

Clarke, Samuel. *The Lives of Two and Twenty English Divines.* London: Printed by A[braham] M[iller] for Thomas Underhill and John Rothwell in Pauls Church-yard, 1660.

Clarke, W.G. *In Breckland Wilds.* London: Robert Scott, 1925.

Clarkson, Christopher. *The History of Richmond, in the County of York.* Richmond: Printed by and for T. Bowman, 1814.

Claydon House. '[Account Books]'. MSS 4/5/41, 42, 47, 49, 51. Claydon House.

Cleary, Dennis. 'Stamford Arms 1923'. NW07330. Manchester Morris Men's archives.

Cleveland, Joseph. *The Character of a London Diurnall,* 1644.

Clifford, Jesse. *My Reminiscences of Charlbury.* Gloucester: John Bellows, 1892.

Clifford, John. 'Personal Account Book of John Clifford, 1673/4-1679'. D149/A26. Gloucestershire Archives.

Clopper, Lawrence M., ed. *Records of Early English Drama: Chester*. Manchester: Manchester University Press, 1979.

Codrington, Robert. *Heptameron, or, The History of the Fortunate Lovers... by ... Margaret de Valoys, Queen of Navarre ...now Made English*. London: Printed by F.L. for Nath: Ekins, 1654.

Cokain, Aston. *Trappolin Creduto Principe, or, Trappolin Suppos'd a Prince*. London: Printed by W.G. and are to be sold by Isaac Pridmore, 1658.

Coldewey, John C. 'Plays and "Play" in Early English Drama'. *Research Opportunities in Renaissance Drama* 28 (1985): 181–88.

Cole, William. *The Bletchley Diary of the Rev. William Cole 1765-67*, edited by Frances Griffin Stokes. London: Constable, 1931.

Collier, John Payne. *The History of English Dramatic Poetry to the Time of Shakespeare: And Annals of the Stage to the Restoration*. 3 vols. London: John Murray, 1831.

Collinson, John. *The Beauties of British Antiquity*. London: Printed for the author, 1779.

'The Colne Royal Morris Men [Advertisement]'. *English Dance and Song* 38, no. 3 (1976): 87.

A Comparative Stranger. 'At the Wakes'. *Hyde & Glossop Weekly News, and North Cheshire Herald*, 18 September 1857.

The Complete Vocabulary in English and French, and in French and English. London: Printed for G. G. J. and J. Robinson, 1785.

C[onstable], K.B. 'Bampton, May 28th, 1928'. *E.F.D.S. News* 18 (1928): 113–14.

Constitutions and Canons Ecclesiasticall. London: By Robert Barker, 1604.

Cooke, Alexander. *More Worke for a Masse-priest*. London: Printed by William Jones, 1621.

Copinger, Walter Arthur, 1847-1910, ed. *County of Suffolk: Its History as Disclosed by Existing Records and Other Documents*. 5 vols. London: Sotheran, 1904.

The Cornish Telegraph. 'West Penwith Justices' Petty Sessions', 19 January 1859.

The Cornish Telegraph. [News Item], 21 December 1859.

Cornishman. 'Cornish Customs in May', 8 May 1879.

Corrsin, Stephen D. *Sword Dancing in Europe: A History*. Enfield Lock: Hisarlik Press, for the Folklore Society, 1997.

Cotgrave, Randle. *A Dictionarie of the French and English Tongues*. London, 1611.

Cotton, Charles. *Burlesque upon Burlesque, or, The Scoffer Scoft: Being Some of Lucians Dialogues*. London: Printed for Henry Brome ..., 1675.

'Country Dance, n.' In *OED Online*. Oxford University Press. Accessed 3 October 2022. https://www.oed.com/view/Entry/43087.

The Country Journal, or, The Craftsman. [News Item], 11 November 1727.

A Country Layman. *A Letter to Mr. Archdeacon Eachard: Wherein Are Some Remarks on the Stuarts Family and Archbishop Laud*. London: Printed for R. F, 1728.

A Countryman. 'Plough Monday'. *Leicester Journal*, 15 January 1864.

Courtly Masquing Ayres: Containing Almaines, Ayres, Corants, Sarabands, Moriscos, Jiggs, &c. London: Printed by W. Godbid for John Playford, 1662.

'Covent Garden'. *Theatrical Journal* 1, no. 10 (February 1840): 85–86.

Coventry Herald. 'Reminiscences of a Pedestrian', 5 May 1854.

Coventry Herald. 'Rugby Petty Sessions', 20 January 1865.

Coventry Standard. 'The Brinklow Morris Dancers', 27 January 1865.

Coverdale, Miles. 'The Old Faith'. In *Writings and Translations of Myles Coverdale*, 1–83. Parker Society 13. Cambridge: University Press, 1844.

Cracoe. 'Morris Dance in the North of England'. *Newcastle Chronicle*, 4 March 1893.

Craftsman, or, Say's Weekly Journal. [News Item], 20 April 1771.

Crashaw, William. *The Sermon Preached at the Crosse, Feb. xiiij. 1607*. London: By H. L[ownes]. for Edmond Weaver, 1608.

Craven Herald. 'Ambulance Review and Demonstration', 20 August 1897.

Cricket and Football Field. 'Theatrical Football Match', 4 February 1893.

Croft, W.D. 'Sixteen Years' Progress'. *Journal of the English Folk Dance Society* 2nd series, 1 (1927): 3–16.

Croker, Thomas Crofton. *Researches in the South of Ireland*. London: John Murray, 1824.

Cunnington, Benjamin Howard. *Records of the County of Wilts: Being Extracts from the Quarter Sessions Great Rolls of the Seventeenth Century*. Devizes: George Simpson, 1932.

Curzon, Henry. *The Universal Library, or, Compleat Summary of Science*. 2 vols. London: Printed for George Sawbridge, 1712.

Daily Advertiser. [Letter], 27 July 1743.

Daily Advertiser. [Advertisement], 22 August 1743.

Daily Advertiser. [Advertisement], 27 August 1743.

Daily Advertiser. [Advertisement], 10 September 1743.

Daily Advertiser. [Advertisement], 15 September 1743.

Daily Advertiser. [Advertisement], 19 September 1743.

Daily Advertiser. [Advertisement], 7 October 1743.

Daily Advertiser. [Advertisement], 17 October 1743.

Daily Advertiser. [Advertisement], 3 November 1743.

Daily Advertiser. [Advertisement], 25 August 1744.

Daily Advertiser. 'London: Bartholomew Fair', 23 August 1745.

Daily Courant. [Advertisement], 10 January 1716.

Daily Journal. 'Jack Sheppard's Epistle', 16 November 1724.

Daily Journal. [Advertisement], 17 January 1730.

Daily Journal. [Advertisement], 21 March 1730.

Daily News. 'The Musical Society of London', 27 January 1859.

Daily News. 'Royal Cremorne Gardens', 14 June 1859.

Daily Post. [News Item], 13 October 1722.

Daily Post. [Advertisement], 19 November 1725.

Daily Post and General Advertiser. [Advertisement], 27 August 1743.

The Dance Goes On: North West Processional Morris around Pendle. [Roughlee]: Malkin Morris, 2019.

Dancing England (Number 6) [Programme]. Stapleford: Dancing England, 1984.

The Dancing Master, III. London: Printed by William Pearson, 1727.

Daniel, Samuel. 'The Queen's Arcadia'. In *The Poetical Works of Mr. Samuel Daniel*, 155–224. London: Printed for Robert Gosling [et al.], 1718.

Dann, Tony. 'The Famous Old Hindley Green Morris Dancers'. *English Dance & Song* 45, no. 1 (1983): 22–24.

Dasent, John Roche, ed. *Acts of the Privy Council of England: New Series Vol. 22, A.D. 1591-2*. London: H.M.S.O, 1901.

Davenant, Sir William. 'The Rivals'. In *The Dramatic Works of Sir William D'Avenant*, 5:213–94. Dramatists of the Restoration. Edinburgh: William Paterson, 1872-1874.

Davenport, Barbara. 'Barbara Davenport's Accounts'. 2664/3/2D/2/51. Wiltshire and Swindon History Centre.

Davenport family. 'Household Bills for the Davenports'. 2664/2/4B/47. Wiltshire and Swindon History Centre.

Davenport, Henry. 'Bills for Henry Davenport and Mrs Davenport'. 2664/3/2D/2/59. Wiltshire and Swindon History Centre.

Davenport, Mrs. 'Bills for Mrs Davenport and Others'. 2664/3/2D/2/58. Wiltshire and Swindon History Centre.

Davenport, Paul D. *Forgotten Morris.* 2nd ed. Mosborough: South Riding Folk Network, 1997.

Davis, Cecil T. 'Wandsworth Churchwardens' Accounts from 1558 to 1573'. *Surrey Archaeological Collections* 17 (1902): 135–75.

Dawson, Giles E., ed. *Records of Plays and Players in Kent 1450-1652.* Malone Society Collections 7. Oxford: Malone Society, 1965.

Day, Cyrus L. 'Thomas Randolph's Part in the Authorship of Hey for Honesty'. *PMLA: Publications of the Modern Language Association of America* 41, no. 2 (1926): 325–34.

Daye, Anne. 'Morris and Masque at the Jacobean Court'. In *The Histories of the Morris in Britain*, edited by Michael Heaney, 19–31. London: English Folk Dance and Song Society & Historical Dance Society, 2018.

Daye, Anne. 'The Revellers Are Entering: Shakespeare and Masquing Practice in Tudor and Stuart England'. In *The Oxford Handbook for Shakespeare and Dance*, edited by Brandon Shaw and Lindsey McCulloch, 107–31. Oxford: Oxford University Press, 2019.

Dean Forest (Mines) Act 1838.

Defoe, Daniel. *The Great Law of Subordination Consider'd, or, The Insolence and Unsufferable Behaviour of Servants in England Duly Enquir'd into.* London: Sold by S. Harding, W. Lewis, [etc.], 1724.

Defoe, Daniel. *The Storm, or, A Collection of the Most Remarkable Casualties and Disasters Which Happen'd in the Late Dreadful Tempest, Both by Sea and Land.* London: Printed for G. Sawbridge, 1704.

Dekker, Thomas. 'The Shoemakers' Holiday'. In *The Dramatic Works of Thomas Dekker*, edited by Fredson Bowers, 1:7–104. Cambridge: Cambridge University Press, 1953.

Dekker, Thomas, and Thomas Middleton. 'The Roaring Girl'. In *The Dramatic Works of Thomas Dekker*, edited by Fredson Bowers, 3:1–112. Cambridge: Cambridge University Press, 1953.

Dekker, Thomas, and William Rowley. 'The Witch of Edmonton'. In *The Dramatic Works of Thomas Dekker*, edited by Fredson Bowers, 3:481–568. Cambridge: Cambridge University Press, 1953.

Dekker, Thomas, and John Webster. 'Westward Ho'. In *The Dramatic Works of Thomas Dekker*, edited by Fredson Bowers, 2:311–405. Cambridge: Cambridge University Press, 1953.

Democritus Ridens, or, Comus and Momus. Vol. 10, 1681.

Derby Mercury. [News Item], 9 September 1802.

Derby Mercury. 'Winster: The Wakes', 8 July 1863.

Derby Mercury. 'Tideswell', 23 September 1863.

Derby Mercury. 'Matlock Bath Well Dressing', 24 May 1865.

Derby Mercury. 'Winster Flower Show', 16 August 1876.

Derbyshire Advertiser and Journal. 'Moresque Dances', 27 September 1850.

Derbyshire Courier. 'Chapel-en-le-Frith', 21 July 1838.

Derbyshire Courier. 'Flagg Wakes and Well-dressing', 8 July 1854.

Derbyshire Courier. 'Flagg Well-dressing', 28 June 1856.

Derbyshire Courier. 'Buxton Well-flowering', 29 June 1861.

Derbyshire Courier. 'Winster', 5 August 1876.

Derbyshire Courier. 'Eckington Flower Show', 25 August 1894.

Derbyshire Times and Chesterfield Herald. 'The Buxton Well Dressing', 4 July 1863.

Derbyshire Times and Chesterfield Herald. [Advertisement], 16 July 1870.

Derbyshire Times and Chesterfield Herald. [Advertisement], 12 August 1871.

Derbyshire Times and Chesterfield Herald. 'Buxton: The Well-dressing', 26 June 1872.

Derbyshire Times and Chesterfield Herald. 'Winster: The Wakes', 9 July 1873.

Derbyshire Times and Chesterfield Herald. 'The Buxton Well Dressing', 19 June 1875.

Derbyshire Times and Chesterfield Herald. 'Winster', 18 August 1877.

Derbyshire Times and Chesterfield Herald. 'Gleanings in the Peak', 8 July 1882.

Derbyshire Times and Chesterfield Herald. 'Gleanings in the Peak', 26 June 1886.

Derbyshire Times and Chesterfield Herald. 'Winster Flower Show', 21 August 1891.

Derbyshire Times and Chesterfield Herald. 'Gleanings in the Peak', 22 August 1891.

Derbyshire Times and Chesterfield Herald. 'Festival at Tideswell', 2 July 1898.

Derwent. 'The Morris Dance at Eyam'. *Derbyshire Times and Chesterfield Herald*, 24 May 1873.

'Description of Bush Fair'. *The Loyal Observator, or, Collins's Weekly Journal*, no. 44 (5 October 1723): 2.

Devizes and Wiltshire Gazette. 'May-day at Cambridge', 23 May 1844.

Devizes and Wiltshire Gazette. 'Salisbury', 12 March 1863.

D'Ewes, Sir Simonds. *The Journal of Sir Simonds D'Ewes from the Beginning of the Long Parliament to the Opening of the Trial of the Earl of Stafford*. New Haven: Yale University Press, 1923.

Dibdin, Charles. *Liberty-hall, or, A Test of Good Fellowship: A Comic Opera*. London: Printed for the author, 1784.

Dickson, Thomas, James Balfour Paul, C. T. McInnes, and Athol L. Murray, eds. *Accounts of the Lord High Treasurer of Scotland = Compota Thesaurariorum Regum Scotorum*. 13 vols. Edinburgh: H. M. General Register House: Her Majesty's Stationery Office, 1877.

Dietz, Brian. *The Port and Trade of Early Elizabethan London: Documents*. London Record Society 8. London: London Record Society, 1972.

'Diocese and Archdeaconry of Chichester, Detection Book, September 1615-July 1617 [Churchwardens' Presentments, Cocking/West Lavington]'. Ep/I/17/17. West Sussex Record Office.

Dixon, Shirley. 'Women in Trousers – a Perspective'. *Morris Matters* 27, no. 2 (2008): 22–24.

'The Dixton Manor Paintings'. The Wilson. Accessed 3 October 2022. https://www.cheltenhammuseum.org.uk/collection/the-dixton-manor-paintings/.

Dommett, Roy. 'Extension of the Repertoire and Newly Conceived Traditions'. *Lore & Language* 6, no. 2 (1987): 33–64.

Dommett, Roy. 'Introduction'. Border Morris. Accessed 3 October 2022. http://www.opread.force9.co.uk/RoyDommet/BorderNotes/Introduction.htm.

Dommett, Roy. *Roy Dommett's Morris Notes*, edited by Anthony G. Barrand. 2nd ed. 10 vols. Easthampton, Mass: CDSS of America, 1986.

Dommett, Roy, and Michael Heaney. 'Conversation between Roy Dommett and Mike Heaney, with Transcript', 24 March 2015. SOUND/EFD/1. Vaughan Williams Memorial Library.

Done, John. *A Miscellania of Morall, Theologicall and Philosophicall Sentences* [sic]: *Worthy Observation*. London: Printed for John Sweeting, 1650.

Douce, Francis. *Illustrations of Shakspeare*. 2 vols. London: Longman Hurst, Rees & Orme, 1807.

Douce, Francis. 'On the Ancient English Morris Dance'. In *Illustrations of Shakspeare*, 2:429–82. London: Longman Hurst, Rees & Orme, 1807.

Douch, H.L. 'Household Accounts at Lanherne'. *Journal of the Royal Institution of Cornwall* n.s. 2, no. 1 (1953): 25–32.

Douglas, Audrey W., and Peter Greenfield, eds. *Records of Early English Drama: Cumberland, Westmorland, Gloucestershire*. Toronto: University of Toronto Press, 1986.

Douglas, Gawin. *The Aeneid of Virgil, Translated into Scottish Verse*. 2 vols. Edinburgh: Bannatyne Club, 1839.

Douglas, George, ed. 'Christes Kirk of the Green'. In *The Book of Scottish Poetry*, 176–83. London: Fisher Unwin, 1911.

Douglas, Leta M. *Three More Dances of the Yorkshire Dales*. 2nd ed. Giggleswick: The author, 1934.

Drake, Nathan. *Shakspeare and His Times*. 2 vols. London: T. Cadell and W. Davies, 1817.

Drinkwater, C.H. 'Shrewsbury Trade Guilds: The Glovers' Company [2nd Paper]'. *Shropshire Archaeological and Natural History Society* 1st series, 10 (1887): 33–95.

Dublin Evening Mail. 'Holywell Boarding School', 26 June 1848.

Duffett, Thomas. *The Empress of Morocco: A Farce*. London: Printed for Simon Neal, 1674.

Duffett, Thomas. *Psyche Debauch'd: A Comedy*. London: Printed for John Smith, 1678.

Dumfries and Galloway Standard. 'The Scottish Society's Fete', 16 July 1851.

Dunbar, William. 'Aganis the Solistaris in Court'. In *The Poems of William Dunbar*, edited by James Kinsley, 71. Oxford: Clarendon Press, 1979.

Dunkin, John. *The History and Antiquities of Bicester*. London: Richard and Arthur Captor, 1816.

Dunlop, Robert. 'Morris Dancing at Kirtlington Lamb Ale'. In *The Histories of the Morris in Britain*, edited by Michael Heaney, 251–61. London: English Folk Dance and Song Society & Historical Dance Society, 2018.

Dunmow Flitch Trials. 'The History of the Dunmow Flitch Trials'. Accessed 3 October 2022. https://www.dunmowflitchtrials.co.uk/history/.

D'Urfey, Thomas. *Madam Fickle, or, The Witty False One: A Comedy*. London: Printed by T.N. for James Magnes and Rich. Bentley …, 1677.

Duros, Edward. 'The Water-whelmed'. *The Englishman's Magazine* 2, no. 2 (1831): 149–65.

Durston, Chris. 'Lords of Misrule: The Puritan War on Christmas'. *History Today* 35, no. 12 (1985): 7–14.

Dutton, Sir John, 'Cash Account Book, 1709-1744'. D678/1/F12/2/1. Gloucestershire Archives.

Dymond, D. 'Three Entertainers from Tudor Suffolk'. *REED Newsletter* 16, no. 1 (1991): 2–5.

E.T.A.C.C.O. 'Rules'. Accessed 3 October 2022. https://etacco1.webs.com/rules.htm.

Earlsdon Morris. 'A Brief History'. Accessed 3 October 2022. http://www.earlsdonmorrismen.org.uk/history.html.

Earwaker, J.P. *East Cheshire: Past and Present, or, A History of the Hundred of Macclesfield*. 2 vols. London: John Parsons, 1877–1880.

East Anglian Daily Times. [News Item], 17 February 1894.

'Edward Dooley, "England, Derbyshire, Church of England Parish Registers, 1537-1918"'. FamilySearch. Accessed 3 October 2022. https://www.familysearch.org/ark:/61903/1:1:QPZV-2Q41.

Eglin, John. *The Imaginary Autocrat: Beau Nash and the Invention of Bath*. London: Profile, 2005.

Elbourne, Roger. *Music and Tradition in Early Industrial Lancashire, 1780-1840*. Woodbridge: D.S. Brewer for the Folklore Society, 1980.

Eliot, John. *Ortho-epia Gallica*. London: Printed by [Richard Field for] John Wolfe, 1593.

'Elizabeth Cromwell Her Gittare Book: The Morice Dance'. MS Mus. 139, f. 5. Harvard Houghton Library.

Ellis, W. Patterson. 'The Churchwardens' Accounts of the Parish of St. Mary, Thame [Pt.19]'. *Berks, Bucks and Oxon Archaeological Journal* 19 (1913): 20–24.

Elrington, C.R., ed. 'Parishes: Alderton with Dixton'. In *A History of the County of Gloucester: Volume 6*, 189–97. London: Institute for Historical Research, 1965.

'Ely Diocesan Act Book, Visitation Book, 1593-1594'. Cambridge. GBR/0012/EDR B/2/14. Cambridge University Library.

'Ely Diocesan Act Book, 1600-1606'. Cambridge. GBR/0012/EDR B/2/21. Cambridge University Library.

'Ely Diocesan Act Book, Visitation Book, 1601-1603'. Cambridge. GBR/0012/EDR B/2/18. Cambridge University Library.

'Ely Diocesan Act Book, 1609-1610'. Cambridge. GBR/0012/EDR B/2/30. Cambridge University Library.

'Ely Diocesan Act Book, 1614-1618'. Cambridge. GBR/0012/EDR B/2/35. Cambridge University Library.

Elyot, Thomas, and Thomas Cooper. *Bibliotheca Eliotæ = Eliotis librarie.* London: In the house of Thomas Berthelet, 1548.

Emmison, Frederick George. *Elizabethan Life: Morals & the Church Courts.* Essex Record Office Publications. Chelmsford: Essex County Council, 1970.

Emmison, Frederick George. 'Tithes, Perambulations and Sabbath-Breach in Elizabethan Essex'. In *Tribute to an Antiquary: Essays Presented to Marc Fitch by Some of His Friends,* edited by Frederick George Emmison and Roy Stephens, 177–215. Leopard's Head Press, 1976.

'England's Joy, or, A Relation of the Most Remarkable Passages, from His Majesty's Arrival at Dover, to His Entrance at Whitehall'. In *An English Garner: Stuart Tracts 1603-1693,* 425–30. Westminster: Constable, 1903.

The English Dancing Master. London: Printed by Thomas Harper, and are to be sold by John Playford, 1651.

English Lakes Visitor. 'May Show at Keswick', 28 May 1892.

The Era. [News Item], 12 August 1855.

The Era. 'Provincial Theatricals', 11 September 1859.

The Era. 'Alhambra Palace, Leicester Square', 23 October 1859.

The Era. [Advertisement], 8 April 1860.

The Era. 'The South London Palace', 1 May 1870.

The Era. [Advertisement], 31 July 1870.

The Era. 'Hengler's Cirque: The Dunmow Revels', 17 March 1872.

The Era. [Advertisement], 8 September 1883.

The Era. 'Hyde: Theatre Royal', 20 October 1883.

The Era. [Advertisement], 17 March 1888.

The Era. [Advertisement], 31 May 1890.

The Era. [News Item], 9 May 1891.

Evans, Arthur Benoni. *Leicestershire Words, Phrases, and Proverbs.* London: W. Pickering, 1848.

Evans, Arthur Benoni. *Leicestershire Words, Phrases, and Proverbs,* edited by Sebastian Evans. [Revised ed.]. London: Trübner, 1881.

The Evening Post. [Advertisement], 12 March 1724.

Everett, W., F.C. Phillips, and Alex Helm. 'Lichfield Morris: The Story of the Recovery of a "Lost" Tradition'. *Journal of the English Folk Dance and Song Society* 8, no. 2 (1957): 83–104.

The Examiner. 'Three Grand Galas', 26 July 1851.

The Excursion down the Wye from Ross to Monmouth. [Monmouth]: Printed and sold by [Charles Heath], 1799.

'Expenses for the Election of Knights of the Shire for the County of Wiltshire'. AC 109/785. Wiltshire and Swindon History Centre.

Eynsham Morris. 2nd ed. Eynsham: Eynsham Morris, 1990.

Eyre, Dave, John Newman, and Peter Delamere. 'The Origins of Sheffield City Morris Men: Medup, We Did It Our Way'. *Lore & Language* 6, no. 2 (1987): 83–97.

'The Famouus Hystory off George a Greene Pinder off the Towne off Wakefeild'. In *Plays and Poems of Robert Greene,* edited by J. Churton Collins, 2:167–77. Oxford: University Press, 1905.

Fane, Mildmay. 'Raguaillo d'Oceano'. In *Mildmay Fane's Raguaillo d'Oceano, 1640, and Candy Restored, 1641,* edited by Clifford Leech. Materialien Zur Kunde Des Älteren Englischen Dramas 15. Louvain: Librairie universitaire, 1938.

Farley, Henry. *St. Paules-Church Her Bill for the Parliament.* London: G. Eld for R. Milbourne, 1621.

Farmiloe, James Ernest, and Rosita Nixseaman. *Elizabethan Churchwardens' Accounts.* Bedfordshire Historical Record Society 33. Streatley: Bedfordshire Historical Records Society, 1953.

Farnaby, Giles. 'Kempe's Morris'. In *Keyboard Music,* by Giles Farnaby and Richard Farnaby, edited by Richard Marlow. London: Royal Musical Association, 1965.

Father Frank. 'Local Notes and Queries, [1450]: Morris Dancers'. *Birmingham Weekly Post,* 3 May 1884.

Featly, Daniel, Martin Day, Richard Sibbs, and Thomas Taylor. Θρηνοικοσ, *The House of Mourning: Furnished with Directions for Preparations to Meditations of Consolations at the Hour of Death.* London: Printed by John Dawson, for R[alph] M[abbe and Nicholas Bourne], 1640.

Fennor, William. *Cornu-Copiæ, Pasquils Night-Cap, or, Antidot for the Head-Ache.* London: Printed for Thomas Thorp, 1612.

Fennor, William. *Pasquil's Palinodia and His Progresse to the Taverne.* London: Printed for Thomas Snodham, 1619.

Fetherston, Christopher. *A Dialogue agaynst Light, Lewde, and Lascivious Dauncing.* London: By Thomas Dawson, 1582.

Feuillerat, Albert Gabriel, ed. *Documents Relating to the Revels at Court in the Time of King Edward VI and Queen Mary, the Loseley Manuscripts.* Materialien zur Kunde d. Älteren Engl. Dramas 44. Louvain: Uystpruyst, 1914.

'Fidler, Charles Burgess'. In *Wills and Administrations, 1911.* Probate service, n.d.

Fidlers Fancy Morris. 'What Do We Dance'. Accessed 3 October 2022. https://fidlersfancy.weebly.com/dances.html.

'The Fidler's Morris'. In *The Dancing Master,* 17th ed., 299. London: Printed by W. Pearson, 1721.

Fiennes, Celia. *The Journeys of Celia Fiennes.* London: Cresset Press, 1972.

Firth, C.H., and R.S. Rait, eds. 'An Ordinance for Ejecting Scandalous, Ignorant and Insufficient Ministers and Schoolmasters'. In *Acts and Ordinances of the Interregnum, 1642-1660,* 2:968–90. London: H.M.S.O, 1911.

Fishwick, Henry. *History of the Parish of Rochdale.* Rochdale, 1875.

Flecknoe, Richard. *Animadversions on a Petition Delivered to the Honourable House of Parliament by Several of the Godly Party in the County of Salop....* [London], 1653.

Fletcher, John. 'Women Pleas'd'. In *The Dramatic Works in the Beaumont and Fletcher Canon,* edited by Fredson Bowers, 5:441–538. Cambridge: Cambridge University Press, 1966.

Fletcher, John, and William Shakespeare. *Two Noble Kinsmen.* Lincoln, Nebr.: University of Nebraska Press, 1970.

Florio, John. *A Worlde of Wordes, or, Most Copious, and Exact Dictionarie in Italian and English.* London: By Arnold Hatfield for Edw. Blount, 1598.

Ford, Geoff. 'Winster Morris Celebrate 40 Years of Dancing'. Great British life: Derbyshire life, 25 June 2018. Accessed 3 October 2022. https://www.greatbritishlife.co.uk/people/winster-morris-6514702.

Ford, John. 'Love's Sacrifice'. In *The Works of John Ford,* edited by Alexander Dyce and William Gifford. New ed., 2:1–108. London: Lawrence and Bullen, 1895.

Forrest, John. *The History of Morris Dancing, 1458-1750.* Cambridge: James Clarke, 1999.

Forrest, John, and Michael Heaney. 'Charting Early Morris'. *Folk Music Journal* 6, no. 2 (1991): 169–86.

Forster, Tony. 'About Molly Dancing and Pig Dyke Molly'. Pig Dyke Molly. Accessed 3 October 2022. https://www.pigdyke.co.uk/what-is-molly.php.

Forster, Tony. *Molly: Dancing into the Twenty-first Century.* Morris Federation, 2002.

Foster, C.W. *Lincoln Episcopal Records in the Time of Thomas Cooper, S.T.P., Bishop of Lincoln, A.D. 1571 to A.D. 1584.* Publications of the Lincoln Record Society. Lincoln: Lincoln Record Society, 1912.

Frampton, George. 'The Mepal Molly Men'. *Morris Matters* 16, no. 2 (1997): 9–15.

Frampton, George. *Necessary to Keep up the Day.* Marden: The author, 1994.

Frampton, George. 'A Penny for the Ploughboys ...'. *The Morris Dancer* 2, no. 8 (1989): 121–24.

Frampton, George. 'Repertoire? – Or Repartee?: The Seven Champions Molly Dancers 1977-1987'. *Lore & Language* 6, no. 2 (1987): 65–81.

Frampton, T. Shipdem. 'St. Mary's Church Minster, Isle of Thanet: List of Vicars'. *Archaeologia Cantiana* 25 (1902): 97–112.

Frazer, J.G. *The Golden Bough: A Study in Comparative Religion.* 2 vols. London: Macmillan, 1890.

Frere, W.H., ed. 'V.A. Province of York (1571)'. In *Visitation Articles and Injunctions of the Period of the Reformation,* 1:253–73. Alcuin Club Collections 14–16. London: Longmans, Green, 1910.

Froome, Derek. 'Stockport Morris'. NW09570. Manchester Morris Men's archives.

A Full Answer to a Scandalous Pamphlet, Intituled, A Character of a London Diurnall. London: Printed by F.P. for Francis Coles and Lawrence Blaikeloke, 1645.

Fuller, John. 'Cash Book of Estate and Personal Income and Expenditure of John Fuller (1680-1745), May 1731 - Sept 1745'. SAS/RF 15/28. East Sussex Record Office.

Fuller, Thomas. *The History of the Worthies of England.* London: Printed by J. G[rismond]. W. L[eybourne]. and W. G[odbid]., 1662.

G., W.H. 'Local Notes and Queries, [1483]: Morris Dancers'. *Birmingham Weekly Post,* 7 June 1884.

Gage, John. *The History and Antiquities of Hengrave, in Suffolk.* London: James Carpenter, Joseph Booker and John Deck, 1822.

Gairdner, James. 'The Spousells of the Princess Mary, Daughter of Henry VII, to Charles Prince of Castile, A.D. 1508'. In *Camden Miscellany, IX,* 2nd item. London: Camden Society, 1893.

Gallini, Giovanni-Andrea. *A Treatise on the Art of Dancing.* London: Printed for the author, 1762.

Gallop, Rodney. 'The Origins of the Morris Dance'. *Journal of the English Folk Dance and Song Society* 1, no. 3 (1934): 122–29.

Galloway, David, ed. *Records of Early English Drama: Norwich, 1540-1642.* Toronto: University of Toronto Press, 1984.

Galloway, David, and John M. Wasson, eds. *Records of Plays and Players in Norfolk and Suffolk.* Malone Society Collections 11. Oxford: Malone Society, 1981.

Gardiner, Dorothy. *Historic Haven: The Story of Sandwich.* Derby: Pilgrim Press, 1954.

Gardiner, Edward I. 'Stowe School Treat'. *Buckingham Express*, 13 June 1868.

Gardiner, Rolf. 'Music, Noise and the Land'. *Wessex: Letters from Springhead* 3, no. 3 (1951): 51–54.

Garry, Francis N.A., and A.G. Garry. *The Churchwardens' Accounts of the Parish of St. Mary's, Reading, Berks, 1550-1662.* Reading: Printed by Edward J. Blackwell, 1893.

'Garstang Morris: "Straight Lads from Lancashire"'. *Morris Matters* 7, no. 2 (1984): 8–12.

Gataker, Thomas. *A Discours Apologetical; Wherein Lilies Lewd and Lowd Lies in His Merlin or Pasquil for the Yeere 1654, Are Clerly Laid Open.* London: Printed by R. Ibbotson for Thomas Newberry, 1654.

Gaule, John. *An Admonition Moving to Moderation.* London: Printed by Henry Lloyd and Roger Vaughan, for Henry Brome, 1660.

Gazophylacium Anglicanum: Containing the Derivation of English Words, Proper and Common. London: Printed by E.H. and W.H., 1689.

Geckle, George L. *John Marston's Drama: Themes, Images, Sources.* Rutherford, N.J.: Fairleigh Dickinson University Press, 1980.

Geisberg, Max. *Verzeichnis der Kupferstiche Israhels van Meckenem †1503.* Studien zur deutschen Kunstgeschichte 58. Strassburg: J.H.E. Heitz, 1905.

General Evening Post. [News Item], 15–17 February 1774.

General Evening Post. [Advertisement], 3–6 December 1785.

Gent, I.M. *The Most Famous and Renowned Historie, of That Woorthie and Illustrous Knight Mervine.* London: By R. Blower and Val. Sims, 1612.

'George Augustus Rowell (1804-1892): St Sepulchre's Cemetery, Oxford'. People Buried in St Sepulchre's Cemetery, Oxford. Accessed 3 October 2022. http://www.stsepulchres.org.uk/burials/rowell_george_augustus.html.

Gerard, Thomas. 'Expenses Account Book of Sir Thomas Gerard of Garswood, Ashton-in-Makerfield, 5 Feb 1752-15 Jul 1759'. DP/481. Lancashire Archives.

The Ghost, or, The Woman Wears the Breeches: A Comedy Written in the Year MDCXL. London: Printed by William Bentley for Thomas Heath, 1653.

Gibson, Richard. 'Accounts of Richard Gibson for Revels etc: Stuffs Purchased, Workmanship, Wages, 1-12 Hen VIII'. E 36/217. The National Archives.

Gilbert, Samuel. *The Florists Vade-mecum.* London: Printed for Thomas Simmons, 1682.

Gilchrist, Anne G. 'A Carved Morris Panel from Lancaster Castle'. *Journal of the English Folk Dance and Song Society* 1, no. 2 (1933): 86–88.

Gilchrist, Anne G. 'The Lancashire Rush-cart and Morris-dance'. *Journal of the English Folk Dance Society* 2nd series, 1 (1927): 17–27.

Gilpin, George. *The Beehive of the Romishe Churche* [by Philip van Marnix van Sant Aldegonde] ... Translated out of Dutch into English by George Gilpin the Elder. London, 1580.

Gisborne, Thomas. *An Enquiry into the Duties of the Female Sex.* London: T. Cadell jun. and W. Davies, 1797.

Glapthorne, Henry. *Argalus and Parthenia.* London: Printed by R. Bishop for Daniel Pakeman, 1639.

Glasgow Herald. 'The Scottish Fete at Holland Park', 14 July 1851.

Glasscock, J.L., ed. *The Records of St. Michael's Parish Church, Bishop's Stortford.* London: Elliot Stock, 1882.

Glossop Record. 'Chapel-en-le-Frith County Court', 8 November 1862.

Glossop Record. 'Mottram: The Wakes', 22 August 1868.

Gloucester Chronicle. 'The Frost', 7 January 1854.

Gloucester Journal. 'Aenigma', 23 May 1727.

Gloucester Journal. [Letter], 30 May 1727.

Gloucester Journal. [News Item], 22 May 1733.

Gloucester Journal. [Advertisement], 1 May 1744.

Gloucester Journal. 'The Festivities at Ross', 21 June 1851.

Gloucester Journal. [News Item], 17 February 1855.

Gloucester Journal. 'Westbury-on-Severn', 30 May 1863.

Gloucester Journal. 'Newnham', 16 May 1868.

Gloucester Journal. 'Choral Concert', 29 January 1870.

Gloucester Journal. 'May Hill', 12 June 1875.

Goddard, Sean, and Ed Bassford. 'Consequences of Bringing North-West Morris to South-East England: The Chanctonbury Ring Effect'. In *The Histories of the Morris in Britain*, edited by Michael Heaney, 215–49. London: English Folk Dance and Song Society & Historical Dance Society, 2018.

Goldsmid, Edmund. '9: III of Hearts: Cromwell Pypeth unto Fairfax [Playing Card]'. In *Explanatory Notes of a Pack of Playing Cards, Temp Charles II, Forming a Complete Political Satire of the Commonwealth*. Edinburgh: E. & G. Goldsmid, 1886.

Goldsmiths' Company, 'A. 1444. 22 Hen. VI—1516. 7 Hen. VIII. [Wardens' Accounts and Court Minutes]'. Goldsmith's Company, MS 1520. Goldsmith's Library.

Good Fellows Must Go Learn to Dance [Broadside]. London: William Gryffith, 1569; and in *The Ballad Literature and Popular Music of the Olden Time*, 1:246. London: Chappell, 1859.

Goodwin, John. Ὑβριστοδικαι, *The Obstructours of Justice, or, A Defence of the Honourable Sentence Passed upon the Late King*. London: Printed for Henry Cripps, and Lodowick Lloyd, 1649.

Goskar, Tom, and Tehmina Goskar. 'Historical Guise Dancing and Its Music'. Cornish Trad [Blog], 22 September 2019. Accessed 3 October 2022. https://www.cornishtrad.com/guisedancing/historical-guise-dancing-and-its-music/.

Gosson, Stephen. *Playes Confuted in Five Actions*. London: Imprinted for Thomas Gosson, 1582.

Gottfried, Robert Steven. *Bury St. Edmunds and the Urban Crisis, 1290-1539*. Princeton: Princeton University Press, 1982.

Gould, Sabine Baring-, and Cecil J. Sharp, eds. *English Folk-songs for Schools*. London: J. Curwen & Sons, 1906.

Gouldman, Francis. *A Copious Dictionary in Three Parts*. London: Printed by John Field, 1664.

Graham, John. *Lancashire and Cheshire Morris Dances*. London: J. Curwen & Sons, 1911.

'Grandmamma'. *Chambers's Edinburgh Journal*, no. 293 (1849): 90–91.

Grant, Bob. 'Headington Quarry and Its Morris Dancers: A Brief Chronology up to 1961'. *The Morris Dancer* 2, no. 10 (2010): 153–62.

Grant, Bob. 'When Punch Met Merry'. *Folk Music Journal* 7, no. 5 (1999): 644–55.

Grantham Journal. 'Grantham Dispensary Ball', 30 December 1865.

Grantham Journal. 'Literary Institution Soiree', 8 December 1866.

Grantham Journal. 'Little Bytham', 28 January 1882.

Grantham Journal. 'Castle Bytham', 20 January 1883.

Grantham Journal. 'Rippingale: Temperance', 6 July 1895.

The Graphic. 'May-Day Sports at St. Mary Cray', 9 May 1891.

Gras, Norman Scott Brien. *The Early English Customs System: A Documentary Study of the Institutional and Economic History of the Customs from the Thirteenth to the Sixteenth Century*. Cambridge: Harvard University Press, 1918.

Gravesend Reporter, North Kent and South Essex Advertiser. 'Sweeps' Day', 8 May 1880.

'Great Marlow Churchwardens' Account Book, 1593-1674'. PR 140/5/1. Buckinghamshire Record Office.

'Great Musgrave Church, Westmoreland'. *The Gentleman's Magazine: And Historical Chronicle* 20 (1843): 572–73.

Green, David. *Blenheim Palace*. London: Country Life, 1951.

Green, Mary Anne Everett. *Calendar of State Papers, Domestic Series, of the Reign of James I: Preserved in the State Paper Department of Her Majesty's Public Record Office*. 5 vols. London: Longman, Brown, Green, Longmans, & Roberts, 1857.

Greene, Robert. 'Frier Bacon and Frier Bongay'. In *Plays and Poems of Robert Greene*, edited by J. Churton Collins, 2:15–78. Oxford: University Press, 1905.

Greene, Robert. 'Greene's Farewell to Folly'. In *The Life and Complete Works in Prose and Verse of Robert Greene*, edited by Alexander B. Grosart, 9:225–348. London: Privately printed, 1881.

Greene, Robert. 'Groats-worth of Witte, Boughte with a Million of Repentance'. In *The Life and Complete Works in Prose and Verse of Robert Greene*, edited by Alexander B. Grosart, 12:95–150. London: Privately printed, 1881.

Greene, Robert. 'A Quip for an Upstart Courtier'. In *The Life and Complete Works in Prose and Verse of Robert Greene*, edited by Alexander B. Grosart, 11:209–94. London: Privately printed, 1881.

Greenfield, Peter H. 'Entertainments of Henry, Lord Berkeley, 1593-4 and 1600-5'. *Records of Early English Drama Newsletter* 8, no. 1 (1983): 12–24.

Greg. '192: Morrice Dancing'. *Shropshire Notes and Queries*, 19 June 1885: 61.

Gregory, George. *Essays Historical and Moral.* 2nd ed. London: Printed for J. Johnson, 1788.

Grey, Anthony. 'Account Book of Anthony Grey, 11th Earl of Kent, 1670-77'. L31/121. Bedfordshire Archives and Records Service.

Grose, Francis. *The Antiquities of England and Wales.* 8 vols. London: Printed for S. Hooper, 1782–1787.

Gutch, Eliza, and Mabel Peacock. *Examples of Printed Folk-lore Concerning Lincolnshire.* London: Nutt, 1908.

Gutch, John. *A Lytell Geste of Robyn Hode.* 2 vols. London: Longman, Brown, Green, Longmans, 1847.

H., A.L. 'A Curious Election Document'. *Norwich Mercury*, 13 January 1875.

H., W. 'Rushbearing'. *Manchester Times*, 14 December 1889.

Hackney and Kingsland Gazette. 'Ladies College, Albion Hall', 10 January 1872.

Hackney and Kingsland Gazette. 'St Mark's Institute, West Hackney, Syllabus of Entertainments', 2 October 1885.

Hall, Edward, and Richard Grafton. *Hall's Chronicle: Containing the History of England* [1550], edited by Henry Ellis. London: Printed for J. Johnson, 1809.

Hall, Thomas. *Funebria Floræ, the Downfall of May-Games.* 2nd ed., corrected. London: Printed by Henry Mortlock, 1661.

Hamer, Fred. 'The Hinton and Brackley Morris'. *Journal of the English Folk Dance and Song Society* 7, no. 4 (1955): 205–17.

Hamer, Fred. 'Traditional Elements in "Fluffy" Dancing', 1950. I am grateful to Duncan Broomhead for supplying me with a copy of this typescript.

'Hamer MSS, Longridge'. Folder 9: North West Morris (FBH/1/9), p. 16. Vaughan Williams Memorial Library.

Hampshire Chronicle. [News Item], 21 July 1823.

Hampstead & Highgate Express. 'Miss Henderson's Dances', 3 April 1897.

Handbook for Travellers in Durham and Northumberland. London: John Murray, 1864.

Harbage, Alfred. *Annals of English Drama, 975-1700: An Analytical Record of All Plays, Extant or Lost, Chronologically Arranged and Indexed by Authors, Titles, Dramatic Companies, Etc.*, edited by Sylvia S. Wagonheim. 3rd ed. London: Routledge, 1989.

Harbage, Alfred. 'The Authorship of *The Christmas Prince*'. *Modern Language Notes* 50, no. 8 (1935): 501–05.

Hargreaves, William. [Letter]. *Blackburn Standard*, 19 October 1895.

Hargreaves, William. [Letter]. *Blackburn Standard*, 14 March 1896.

Hargreaves, William. 'Our Band Boys'. *Blackburn Standard*, 25 August 1894.

Harland, John. 'Lancashire and Cheshire Transcripts'. GB.127 MS f 942.72 H72 (book 6, f.1). Manchester Libraries, Information and Archives.

Harland, John, and Thomas Turner Wilkinson. *Lancashire Legends, Traditions, Pageants, Sports, &c.* London: Routledge, 1873.

Harrington, F. *The History of Eccles and Barton's Contentious Guising War*, by F. H**r**g**n. [Manchester], 1777.

Harris, Barbara J. *Edward Stafford, Third Duke of Buckingham, 1478-1521.* Stanford, California: Stanford University Press, 1986.

Harris, William. *An Historical and Critical Account of the Life and Writings of Charles I King of Great Britain.* London: Printed for R. Griffiths and C. Henderson, 1758.

Harrop, Peter. *Mummers' Plays Revisited.* Abingdon: Routledge, 2019.

Harsnett, Samuel. *A Declaration of Egregious Popish Impostures.* London: Printed by James Roberts, 1603.

Hartland, Ethel M. 'Karpeles MSS, [Letter to Cecil Sharp, 30 August 1913]'. MK/7/6. Vaughan Williams Memorial Library. Accessed 3 October 2022. https://www.vwml.org/record/MK/7/6.

Hartlepool Northern Daily Mail. 'The Alhambra', 6 February 1894.

'Hartley Lee, "England and Wales Census, 1891"'. Burnley, RG12/3382/161, p. 11. 1891 census. Accessed 3 October 2022. https://www.familysearch.org/ark:/61903/1:1:QTR6-52M.

'Hartly Lee, "England and Wales Census, 1901"'. West Derby, RG13/44/97, p. 20. 1901 census. Accessed 3 October 2022. https://www.familysearch.org/ark:/61903/1:1:X9KL-T32.

Harvey, Richard. *Plaine Percevall the Peace-maker of England.* [London: R. Haney?], 1589.

Haskins, Charles Homer. *The Ancient Trade Guilds and Companies of Salisbury.* Salisbury: Journal Office, 1912.

Haslett, Johnny, ed. *Morris Dancers and Rose Queens.* 4 vols. Leyland: Fairhaven Press, 2005–2021.

Hastings and St Leonards Observer. 'Notes from Hastings', 8 May 1880.

Hastings and St Leonards Observer. 'Hastings Pier Concerts', 1 September 1894.

Hawkins, Sir John. *A General History of the Science and Practice of Music*. 5 vols. London: Printed for T. Payne and Son, 1776.

Haydocke, Richard. *A Tracte Containing the Artes of Curious Paintinge, Carvinge & Buildinge, Written First in Italian by J.P. Lomatius*. Oxford: Printed by J. Barnes, 1598.

Hayes, Edward. [Narrative of Sir Humphrey Gilbert's Last Expedition]. In *The Voyages and Colonising Enterprises of Sir Humphrey Gilbert*, edited by David Beers Quinn, 2:385–423. Hakluyt Society, Series 2, 83-84. London: Hakluyt Society, 1940.

Hays, Rosalind Conklin, C. Edward McGee, Sally L. Joyce, and Evelyn S. Newlyn, eds. *Records of Early English Drama: Dorset*, edited by Rosalind Conklin Hays and C.E. McGee; *Cornwall*, edited by Sally L. Joyce and Evelyn S. Newlyn. [Turnhout]: Brepols, 1999.

Head, James Roper. *A Sketch of an Act of Parliament to Permit, under Certain Regulations, in Wet and Casual Harvests, the Appropriation of Two Sundays in a Year, for the Purpose of Carrying and Securing Corn*. London: Printed for J. Debrett, 1797.

Heaney, Michael. 'Bloxham: A Lost Morris Tradition'. *English Dance and Song* 45, no. 2 (1983): 12–13.

Heaney, Michael. 'Disentangling the Wychwood Morrises'. *Traditional Dance* 3 (1985): 44–81.

Heaney, Michael. 'The Earliest Reference to the Morris Dance?' *Folk Music Journal* 8, no. 4 (2004): 513–15.

Heaney, Michael. 'Kennedy, Douglas Neil (1893–1988), Folk Musician and Dancer'. Oxford Dictionary of National Biography. Accessed 3 October 2022. https://doi.org/10.1093/ref:odnb/54871.

Heaney, Michael. 'A Morris Murder'. *The Morris Dancer* [1], no. 17 (1983): 4–7.

Heaney, Michael. 'Must Every Fiddler Play a Fiddle?' *Records of Early English Drama Newsletter* 11, no. 1 (1986): 10–11.

Heaney, Michael. 'Percy Manning – a Life'. In *Percy Manning: The Man Who Collected Oxfordshire*, edited by Michael Heaney, 1–47. Oxford: Archaeopress, 2017.

Heaney, Michael. 'Percy Manning, Thomas Carter and the Revival of Morris Dancing'. In *Percy Manning: The Man Who Collected Oxfordshire*, edited by Michael Heaney, 91–117. Oxford: Archaeopress, 2017.

Heaney, Michael. 'Sharp, Cecil James (1859–1924), Collector of English Folk-Songs and Dances'. *Oxford Dictionary of National Biography*. Accessed 3 October 2022. https://doi.org/10.1093/ref:odnb/36040.

Heaney, Michael. 'Thomas James Carter's Role in the Collection of Oxfordshire Antiquities, Fossils and Folklore'. *Oxoniensia* 83 (2018): 101–37.

Heaney, Michael. 'Trunkles'. *The Morris Dancer* 2, no. 9 (1990): 136–39.

Heaney, Michael. '"With Scarfes and Garters as You Please": An Exploratory Essay in the Economics of the Morris'. *Folk Music Journal* 6, no. 4 (1993): 491–505.

Heaney, Michael, and John Forrest. *Annals of Early Morris*. CECTAL Bibliographical and Special Series 6. Sheffield: Centre for English Cultural Tradition and Language in association with the Morris Ring, 1991.

Heaney, Michael, and John Forrest. 'An Antedating for the "Morris Dance"'. *Notes and Queries* 49, no. 2 (2002): 190–93.

Heaney, Michael, Bob Grant and Roy Judge, '"Copy gp Morice dancers Mr Manning"', *English Dance and Song*, 43, no. 2 (1981): 14-16.

Heaney, Winifred. Author's interview, 13 March 1983.

Heanley, R.M. 'The Vikings: Traces of Their Folklore in Marshland'. *Saga-book* 3 (1901–1903): 35–62.

Heath, James. *The Glories and Magnificent Triumphs of the Blessed Restitution of His Sacred Majesty K. Charles II*. London: Printed and are to be sold by N.G., R.H. and O.T. ..., 1662.

Heathman, Katie Palmer. '"I Ring for the General Dance": Morris and Englishness in the Work of Conrad Noel'. In *The Histories of the Morris in Britain*, edited by Michael Heaney, 115–31. London: English Folk Dance and Song Society & Historical Dance Society, 2018.

Heathman, Katie Palmer. 'Revival: The Transformative Potential of English Folksong and Dance, 1890-1940'. Doctoral dissertation, University of Leicester, 2016. Accessed 3 October 2022. https://leicester.figshare.com/ articles/thesis/Revival_The_Transformative_ Potential_of_English_Folksong_and_ Dance_1890-1940/10122410/1.

Heaton, Phil. *Rapper: The Miners' Sword Dance of North-east England*. London: EFDSS, 2012.

Heffer, Arthur. 'The Tour of the Travelling Morrice'. *E.F.D.S. News*, no. 9 (May 1925): 247–60.

Helm, Alex. 'Rush-carts of the North-west of England'. *Folk Life* 8 (1970): 20–31.

Helm MSS, 'Manuscript notebook relating to A Geographical Index of the Ceremonial Dance in Great Britain, vol. 23'. HELM/A/1/23. University College London Library.

'Henry Gent, "England and Wales Census, 1891"'. Chorley, RG12/3424/89, p. 2. 1891 census. Accessed 3 October 2022. https://www.familysearch.org/ark:/61903/1:1:79ZP-H3Z.

Heraclitus Ridens: At a Dialogue between Jest and Earnest Concerning the Times. Vol. 15, 1681.

Herbert, Sir Thomas. *A Relation of Some Yeares Travaile Begunne Anno 1626. into Afrique and the Greater Asia*. London: Printed by William Stansby, 1634.

Herbert, Sir Thomas. *Some Yeares Travels into Divers Parts of Asia and Afrique*. Revised and enlarged. London: Printed by R[ichard] Bi[sho]p for Jacob Blome and Richard Bishop, 1638.

Hereford Journal. 'Lecture on English Music', 14 March 1863.

Hereford Journal. [Advertisement], 18 February 1893.

Hereford Times. 'Cleobury Mortimer: Rejoicings at the Coming of Age of G.E. Wicksted, Esq., of Shakenhurst Hall', 7 February 1857.

Hereford Times. 'Morris Dancers', 6 February 1858.

Hereford Times. 'Ross', 14 March 1863.

Herga Folk Club. 'Club History'. Accessed 3 October 2022. http://folk4all.net/HergaHistory.htm.

Herrick, Robert. 'The Country Life'. In *The Poetical Works of Robert Herrick*, edited by L.C. Martin, 229–31. Oxford: Clarendon Press, 1956.

Herrick, Robert. 'Hesperides'. In *The Poetical Works of Robert Herrick*, edited by L.C. Martin, 255. Oxford: Clarendon Press, 1956.

Herrick, Sir William. 'Financial Papers of Sir William Herrick, 1602-1623'. MS Eng. hist. c. 479. Bodleian Libraries.

Hertford Mercury and Reformer. 'Juvenile Fancy Ball at Hatfield House', 9 January 1875.

Herts Guardian, Agricultural Journal, and General Advertiser. 'Rickmansworth, Foresters' Fete', 5 August 1865.

Heywood, Thomas. 'The Fair Maid of the West, II, or, A Girle Worthe Gold'. In *The Dramatic Works of Thomas Heywood, Now First Collected with Illustrative Notes and a Memoir of the Author*, 2:339–424. London: J. Pearson, 1874.

Heywood Advertiser. 'Victoria Morris Dancers v. Paved Brow Wanderers', 17 April 1885.

Heywood Advertiser. 'Heywood Wakes', 7 August 1885.

Heywood Advertiser. 'Heywood Morris Dancers v. Paved Brow Wanderers', 26 February 1886.

Higgins, Michael. '"A Properly Conducted Morris Dance": The Role of Jimmy Cheetham before the Great War in Oldham and Royton, Lancashire'. *Traditional Dance* 4 (1986): 73–103.

High Peak News. 'Annual Feast of the "Adventure of the Peak" Lodge, Taddington', 22 May 1875.

Highfill, Philip H., Kalman A. Burnim, and Edward A. Langhans. 'Bullock, Mrs Hildebrand, Ann, Née Russell'. In *A Biographical Dictionary of Actors, Actresses, Musicians, Dancers, Managers & Other Stage Personnel in London, 1660-1800*, 2:405–08. Eighteenth Century Drama. Carbondale: Southern Illinois University Press, 1973–1993.

Highfill, Philip H., Kalman A. Burnim, and Edward A. Langhans. 'Delagarde, [Charles?]'. In *A Biographical Dictionary of Actors, Actresses, Musicians, Dancers, Managers & Other Stage Personnel in London, 1660-1800*, 4:279–80. Eighteenth Century Drama. Carbondale: Southern Illinois University Press, 1973–1993.

Highfill, Philip H., Kalman A. Burnim, and Edward A. Langhans. 'Dubois, Jean-Baptiste'. In *A Biographical Dictionary of Actors, Actresses, Musicians, Dancers, Managers & Other Stage Personnel in London, 1660-1800*, 4:483–85. Eighteenth Century Drama. Carbondale: Southern Illinois University Press, 1973–1993.

Highfill, Philip H., Kalman A. Burnim, and Edward A. Langhans. 'Ferrère, Auguste Frédéric Joseph?' In *A Biographical Dictionary of Actors, Actresses, Musicians, Dancers, Managers & Other Stage Personnel in London, 1660-1800*, 5:232–33. Eighteenth Century Drama. Carbondale: Southern Illinois University Press, 1973–1993.

Highfill, Philip H., Kalman A. Burnim, and Edward A. Langhans. 'Fuozi, Mlle'. In *A Biographical Dictionary of Actors, Actresses, Musicians, Dancers, Managers & Other Stage Personnel in London, 1660-1800*, 5:424–25. Eighteenth Century Drama. Carbondale: Southern Illinois University Press, 1973–1993.

Highfill, Philip H., Kalman A. Burnim, and Edward A. Langhans. 'Holland, John'. In *A Biographical*

Dictionary of Actors, Actresses, Musicians, Dancers, Managers & Other Stage Personnel in London, 1660-1800, 7:375–76. Eighteenth Century Drama. Carbondale: Southern Illinois University Press, 1973–1993.

Highfill, Philip H., Kalman A. Burnim, and Edward A. Langhans. 'Lassells, D'. In *A Biographical Dictionary of Actors, Actresses, Musicians, Dancers, Managers & Other Stage Personnel in London, 1660-1800*, 9:161. Eighteenth Century Drama. Carbondale: Southern Illinois University Press, 1973–1993.

Highfill, Philip H., Kalman A. Burnim, and Edward A. Langhans. 'Lawrence, Joseph'. In *A Biographical Dictionary of Actors, Actresses, Musicians, Dancers, Managers & Other Stage Personnel in London, 1660-1800*, 9:171–72. Eighteenth Century Drama. Carbondale: Southern Illinois University Press, 1973–1993.

Highfill, Philip H., Kalman A. Burnim, and Edward A. Langhans. 'Prince, Joseph'. In *A Biographical Dictionary of Actors, Actresses, Musicians, Dancers, Managers & Other Stage Personnel in London, 1660-1800*, 12:165–66. Eighteenth Century Drama. Carbondale: Southern Illinois University Press, 1973–1993.

Highfill, Philip H., Kalman A. Burnim, and Edward A. Langhans. 'Sala, Signora'. In *A Biographical Dictionary of Actors, Actresses, Musicians, Dancers, Managers & Other Stage Personnel in London, 1660-1800*, 13:176–77. Eighteenth Century Drama. Carbondale: Southern Illinois University Press, 1973–1993.

Highfill, Philip H., Kalman A. Burnim, and Edward A. Langhans. 'West, D'. In *A Biographical Dictionary of Actors, Actresses, Musicians, Dancers, Managers & Other Stage Personnel in London, 1660-1800*, 15:371–72. Eighteenth Century Drama. Carbondale: Southern Illinois University Press, 1973–1993.

Highfill, Philip H., Kalman A. Burnim, and Edward A. Langhans. 'West, Louisa Margaretta, Later Mrs Richard Suett, 1754-1832, Dancer'. In *A Biographical Dictionary of Actors, Actresses, Musicians, Dancers, Managers & Other Stage Personnel in London, 1660-1800*, 15:372–73. Eighteenth Century Drama. Carbondale: Southern Illinois University Press, 1973–1993.

Highfill, Philip H., Kalman A. Burnim, and Edward A. Langhans. 'West, William, b. c. 1757, Dancer, Choreographer, Ballet Master'. In *A Biographical Dictionary of Actors, Actresses, Musicians, Dancers, Managers & Other Stage Personnel in London, 1660-1800*, 16:1–2. Eighteenth Century Drama. Carbondale: Southern Illinois University Press, 1973–1993.

Higins, John. *Huloets Dictionarie Newelye Corrected, Amended, Set in Order and Enlarged*. Londini: In aedibus Thomae Marshij, 1572.

Higins, John. *The Nomenclator, or Remembrancer of Adrianus Junius ... and Now in English*. London: For Ralph Newberie, 1585.

Higson, Richard. 'Horwich Prize Medal Morris Men'. *The Morris Ring Circular* 12 (1987): [8-9].

Hill, Christopher. *Society and Puritanism in Pre-Revolutionary England*. London: Secker & Warburg, 1964.

Hill, T. 'Local Notes and Queries, [1479]: Morris Dancers'. *Birmingham Weekly Post*, 31 May 1884.

Hill, T. 'Local Notes and Queries, [1575]: Morris Dancers'. *Birmingham Weekly Post*, 20 September 1884.

The History of Cheltenham and Its Environs. Cheltenham: H. Ruff, 1803.

History of Parliament Online. 'Chaworth, Sir Thomas (d.1459), of Wiverton, Notts. and Alfreton, Derbys'. Accessed 3 October 2022. http://www.historyofparliamentonline.org/volume/1386-1421/member/chaworth-sir-thomas-1459.

History of Parliament Online. 'Spelman, Sir Henry (c.1564-1641), of the Barbican, London and Congham, Norf.' Accessed 3 October 2022. https://www.historyofparliamentonline.org/volume/1604-1629/member/spelman-sir-henry-1564-1641.

The History of Reynard the Fox, and Reynardine His Son: Written by an Eminent Statesman of the German Empire, and since Done into English. [London]: Printed for the booksellers of London and Westminster, 1700.

Hobbs, May Elliott. 'Memories of Cecil Sharp'. *E.F.D.S. News*, no. 8 (1924): 228–30.

Hobhouse, Edmund. *Church-wardens' Accounts of Croscombe, Pilton, Patton, Tintinhull, Morebath, and St. Michael's, Bath: Ranging from A.D. 1349 to 1560*. Somerset Record Society. London: Printed for subscribers, by the Somerset Record Society, 1890.

Hodgkinson, R. 'Extracts from the Act Books of the Archdeacons of Nottingham [Pt 1]'. *Transactions of the Thoroton Society* 29 (1925): 19–67.

H[odgkinson], R.F.B. 'Morris Dancing in Nottinghamshire in the Seventeenth Century'. *E.F.D.S. News* 10 (1925): 319–21.

Holden, William. *The Diaries of William Holden, 1829 and 1830*, edited by Jonathan Pepler. [Alsager]: Record Society of Lancashire and Cheshire, 2018.

Hole, Robert, ed. 'The Kings Morisck'. In *Parthenia In-violata, or, Mayden-musicke for the Virginalls and Bass-viol*. 1614. [Facs.] New York: New York Public Library, 1961, 54-55.

Holland, Philemon. *The Historie of the World, Commonly Called, The Natural Historie of C. Plinius Secundus,* translated into English. 2 vols. London: Printed by Adam Islip, 1601.

Holland, Robert. *A Glossary of Words Used in the County of Chester*. London: Trübner, 1886.

Holme, Randle. *The Academy of Armory*. Chester: For the author, 1688.

Holt, Ardern. 'Amusements for Children's Parties'. *The Queen*, 1 January 1898: 32.

Holt, Ardern. 'Dances Suitable for Fancy Balls'. *The Queen*, 29 December 1888: 34.

Holyday, Barton. Τεχνογαμια, or, *The Marriages of the Arts*. London: Printed by William Stansby, 1617.

Holyoke, Thomas. *A Large Dictionarie in Three Parts*. London: Printed by W. Rawlins for G. Sawbridge, 1677.

Hone, William. *The Every Day Book*. 2 vols. London: William Tegg, 1868.

Horman, William. *Vulgaria*. London, 1519. Facs. English experience. Amsterdam: Theatrum Orbis Terrarum, 1975.

Horwich Chronicle. [Advertisement], 26 March 1892.

'Household Accounts of Lord Monson 1767-1772'. MON/10/1/A/3. Lincolnshire archives.

'Household Accounts of Lord Monson 1781-1790'. MON/10/1/A/6. Lincolnshire archives.

Howell, James. *Dendrologia: Dodona's Grove, or, The Vocall Forrest*. [London]: By: T[homas]: B[adger]: for H: Mosley, 1640.

Howell, James. *Lexicon-tetraglotton, an English-French-Italian-Spanish Dictionary*. London: Printed by J.G. for Samuel Thomson, 1660.

Howell, James. *The True Informer, Who in the Following Discours, or Colloquy, Discovereth unto the World the Chiefe Causes of the Sad Distempers in Great Brittany, and Ireland*. Oxford [i.e., London]: Printed by Leonard Lichfield, 1643.

Howison, Daniel. 'Aughton (Nr Ormskirk)'. NW08060. Manchester Morris Men's archives.

Howison, Daniel. 'Didsbury'. NW02650-NW02660. Manchester Morris Men's archives.

Howison, Daniel. 'Godley Hill'. NW04270-NW04280. Manchester Morris Men's archives.

Howison, Daniel. 'Goostrey'. NW04560. Manchester Morris Men's archives.

Howison, Daniel. 'Middleton'. NW06370. Manchester Morris Men's archives.

Howison, Daniel. 'Middleton Junction'. NW06580. Manchester Morris Men's archives.

Howison, Daniel. 'Nelson (3)'. NW07590. Manchester Morris Men's archives.

Howison, Daniel. 'Oldham'. NW07880. Manchester Morris Men's archives.

Howison, Daniel. 'Stockport'. NW09650, NW09670, NW 09700, NW 09710. Manchester Morris Men's archives.

Howison, Daniel, and Bernard Bentley. 'Ashton-under-Lyne'. NW00680. Manchester Morris Men's archives.

Howison, Daniel, and Bernard Bentley. 'The North-west Morris: A General Survey'. *Journal of the English Folk Dance and Song Society* 9, no. 1 (1960): 42–55.

Howkins, Alun. 'The Taming of Whitsun'. In *Popular Culture and Class Conflict, 1590-1914*, edited by Eileen Yeo and Stephen Yeo, 187–208. Brighton: Harvester, 1981.

Howse, Violet Mary. *Stanford-in-the-Vale Churchwardens' Accounts 1552-1725*. Stanford-in-the-Vale: [The author], 1987.

The Huddersfield Chronicle and West Yorkshire Advertiser. 'Saddleworth: The Wakes', 2 September 1854.

The Huddersfield Chronicle and West Yorkshire Advertiser. 'Saddleworth: The Wakes', 28 August 1858.

The Huddersfield Chronicle and West Yorkshire Advertiser. 'Saddleworth: The Wakes', 27 August 1859.

The Huddersfield Chronicle and West Yorkshire Advertiser. 'Saddleworth: The Wakes', 31 August 1861.

Hughes, Geoff. 'The Abram Morris Dance: A Personal Account of Its Revival'. *English Dance and Song* 53, no. 2 (1991): 2–5.

Hughes, Geoff. 'Carnival Morris — the Real Stuff?' Listserv. Morris Dancing Discussion List, 10 October 1995. Accessed 3 October 2022. https://list.iupui.edu/sympa/arc/morris-l/1995-10/msg00102.html.

Hull Advertiser and Exchange Gazette. 'Mechanics' Institute', 26 January 1861.

Hull and Eastern Counties Herald. 'Hull Mechanics' Institute', 1 April 1869.

The Hull Packet and East Riding Times. [Advertisement], 18 January 1850.

The Hull Packet and East Riding Times. [Advertisement], 28 February 1873.

The Hull Packet and East Riding Times. 'Lecture on Old English Ballads', 21 March 1873.

'The Humble Petition of the Humerous and Diverting Company of Jack-Puddings...'. *The Political State of Great Britain* 56, no. 5 (November 1738): 453–54.

Humphries, Richard. *'...for a Bit of Sport...'.* Linton: R. & K. Humphries, 1986.

Huntingdon, Bedford & Peterborough Gazette. [News Item], 16 September 1837.

Huntriss, Yvonne S. 'Mummering and Niggering in Bloxham'. *Cake & Cockhorse* 7, no. 7 (1978): 219–25.

Hutchings, Ashley. '[Sleeve Notes]'. In *Rattlebone and Ploughjack.* HELP24. Island Records, 1976.

Hutchings, Ashley, et al. *Morris On.* HELP5. Island Records, 1972.

Hutchings, Ashley, et al. *Rattlebone and Ploughjack.* HELP24. Island Records, 1976.

Hutton, Ronald. *The Rise and Fall of Merry England: The Ritual Year 1400-1700.* Oxford: Oxford University Press, 1994.

Hutton, Ronald. *The Stations of the Sun: A History of the Ritual Year in Britain.* Oxford: Oxford University Press, 1996.

Hyde & Glossop Weekly News, and North Cheshire Herald. 'Mottram Wakes Rush Cart', 20 August 1870.

Hyde & Glossop Weekly News, and North Cheshire Herald. 'Hazel Grove Wakes', 19 August 1871.

Hyde & Glossop Weekly News, and North Cheshire Herald. 'Romiley', 26 July 1873.

Hyde & Glossop Weekly News, and North Cheshire Herald. '[Advertisements]', 18 July 1874.

Hyde & Glossop Weekly News, and North Cheshire Herald. [News Item], 25 July 1874.

Hyde & Glossop Weekly News, and North Cheshire Herald. 'Ashton Wakes', 22 August 1874.

Hyde & Glossop Weekly News, and North Cheshire Herald. 'The Morris Dancers', 16 August 1879.

Hyde & Glossop Weekly News, and North Cheshire Herald. 'Knutsford', 8 May 1880.

Illustrated London News. 'Madame Weiss and the Viennese Children', 19 April 1845.

Illustrated London News. 'Revival of Old Christmas Gambols at Manchester', 13 January 1849.

Illustrated London News. '"Worcestershire Mummers" – Painted by C. Cattermole', 15 January 1859.

'Illustrations of Shakspeare, and of Antient Manners [Review]'. *The Edinburgh Review* 12, no. 24 (1808): 449–68.

'The Informers Lecture to His Sons'. In *Rome Rhym'd to Death, Being a Collection of Choice Poems.* London: Printed for John How ..., 1683.

Ingram, Hastings. 'Account Book of Hastings Ingram'. CR2855. Warwickshire Record Office.

Ingram, Martin. *Church Courts, Sex and Marriage in England, 1570-1640.* Past and Present Publications. Cambridge: Cambridge University Press, 1987.

Ingram, Reginald W., ed. *Records of Early English Drama: Coventry.* Manchester: Manchester University Press, 1981.

'Instances of the Longevity or Length of Life in Some Persons'. *The New Wonderful Magazine and Marvellous Chronicle* 2, no. 13 (1 January 1794): 71–76.

'[Interrogation of Nicholas Saynt and Other Morris Dancers]', 1589. Quarter Sessions Examinations, CCA: CC/J/Q/388. Canterbury Cathedral Library.

Ironside, Gilbert. *Seven Questions of the Sabbath Briefly Disputed, after the Manner of the Schooles.* Oxford: Printed by Leonard Lichfield, 1637.

Irving, Washington. *Bracebridge Hall, or, The Humorists: A Medley by Geoffrey Crayon, Gent.*, edited by Herbert F. Smith. The Complete Works of Washington Irving 9. Boston, Mass: Twayne, 1977.

Isaac, Mr. *The Morris, a New Dance for the Year 1716*, 1716.

'Isabella Blackburn in Household of William Blackburn, "England and Wales Census, 1911"'. Chorley, RG14/173, p.1. 1911 census. Accessed 3 October 2022. https://www.familysearch.org/ark:/61903/1:1:X49Q-XLJ.

Isle of Man Times. 'An Evening of Delight', 18 July 1893.

Isle of Wight County Press and South of England Reporter. 'Grand Carnival at Ryde', 17 August 1889.

Isle of Wight County Press and South of England Reporter. 'Isle of Wight County Court: The Ryde Carnival', 9 November 1889.

Isle of Wight Observer. 'The Ryde Carnival', 18 August 1888.

Israhel van Meckenem, Goldschmied und Kupferstecher, †1503 in Bocholt: zur 450. Wiederkehr seines Todestages. Bocholt: s.n., 1953.

J., G. *Geography Epitomiz'd, or, The London Gazetteer.* London: Printed for Charles Rivington [et al.], 1718.

Jackson, John. *History of the City and County of Lichfield.* Lichfield: Printed and sold by John Jackson, 1795.

Jackson, Richard. [Will], *c.* 1510. Prerogative Court of Canterbury, 31 Bennett. The National Archives.

Jackson, Sara E. 'Editorial'. *Journal of the English Folk Dance and Song Society* 8, no. 2 (1957): iv.

'Jackson v. Swann, Bonde and Others'. PRO STAC 5/J22/16. The National Archives.

Jackson's Oxford Journal. [Announcement], 26 May 1753.

Jackson's Oxford Journal. [News Item], 23 June 1753.

Jackson's Oxford Journal. [News Item], 31 May 1766.

Jackson's Oxford Journal. [News Item], 22 October 1774.

Jackson's Oxford Journal. [Advertisement], 23 April 1785.

Jackson's Oxford Journal. [Advertisement], 23 May 1789.

Jackson's Oxford Journal. [News Item], 21 June 1794.

Jackson's Oxford Journal. 'Milton Whitsun Ale', 21 May 1808.

Jackson's Oxford Journal. 'Milton Whitsun Ale', 20 May 1809.

Jackson's Oxford Journal. 'Whitsuntide', 21 May 1825.

Jackson's Oxford Journal. 'Whitsun Ale at Milton-under-Wychwood', 17 May 1828.

Jackson's Oxford Journal. 'Forest of Wychwood Fair', 3 September 1831.

Jackson's Oxford Journal. '[Letter from] A Spectator', 16 June 1832.

Jackson's Oxford Journal. 'Origins of May-Poles and Whitsun-Ales', 13 May 1837.

Jackson's Oxford Journal. [News Item], 6 June 1837.

Jackson's Oxford Journal. 'Wychwood Forest', 7 September 1844.

Jackson's Oxford Journal. 'Wychwood Forest', 30 August 1845.

Jackson's Oxford Journal. 'Forest Fair', 19 September 1846.

Jackson's Oxford Journal. 'Revels at Kenilworth Castle', 18 August 1855.

Jackson's Oxford Journal. 'Littlemore Lunatic Asylum', 5 January 1861.

Jackson's Oxford Journal. 'Longborough', 28 March 1863.

Jackson's Oxford Journal. 'Exhibition of Morris Dancing – an Interesting Revival', 18 March 1899.

Jackson's Oxford Journal. 'At the Constitutional Hall', 16 December 1899.

James VI and I. 'The King's Majesties Declaration to His Subjects Concerning Lawfull Sports to Be Used'. In *Minor Prose Works of King James VI and I,* edited by James Craigie, 101–09. Scottish Text Society iv, 14. Edinburgh: Scottish Text Society, 1982.

'James Griffith Dearden 1839-1912'. DLO Yeomanry Personalities. Accessed 3 October 2022. https://sites.google.com/site/dloyeomanrypersonalities/officers/james-griffith-dearden-1839-1912.

'James Livingstone "England and Wales Census 1891"'. Preston, RG12/3429/10, p. 13. 1891 census. Accessed 3 October 2022. https://www.familysearch.org/ark:/61903/1:1/QR8T-PMM.

'James Spencer "England and Wales Census 1891"'. Preston, RG12/3429/48, p. 33. 1891 census. Accessed 3 October 2022. https://www.familysearch.org/ark:/61903/1:1/QRDP-5MM.

'James Spencer, "England and Wales Census, 1911"'. Preston, RG14/353/1. 1911 census. Accessed 3 October 2022. https://www.familysearch.org/ark:/61903/1:1/X497-JW5.

Jewitt, Llewellynn. 'On Ancient Customs and Sports of the County of Derby'. *Journal of the British Archaeological Association* 7 (1852): 199–210.

Jewitt, Llewellynn. 'On Ancient Customs and Sports of the County of Nottingham'. *Journal of the British Archaeological Association* 8 (1853): 229–40.

'John Godley, "England and Wales Census, 1871"'. Cheshire, RG09/2557/25/43. 1871 census. Accessed 3 October 2022. https://www.familysearch.org/ark:/61903/1:1/VBX2-B74.

'John Rose, "England and Wales Census, 1891"'. Chorley, RG12/3420/54, p. 3. 1891 census. Accessed 3 October 2022. https://www.familysearch.org/ark:/61903/1:1/7948-5PZ.

'John Tiller'. In *Wikipedia,* 3 October 2022. https://en.wikipedia.org/w/index.php?title=John_Tiller&oldid=1068324402.

Johnson, A. H. *The History of the Worshipful Company of the Drapers of London.* 5 vols. Oxford: Clarendon Press, 1914–1922.

Johnson, D. A., and David Vaisey, eds. *Staffordshire and the Great Rebellion*. Stafford: Staffordshire County Council, County Records Committee, 1964.

Johnson, Samuel. *A Dictionary of the English Language*. 2 vols. London: Printed for J. Knapton &c, 1756.

Johnson, Samuel. *The Letters of Samuel Johnson*. Hyde ed. 3 vols. Princeton: Princeton University Press, 1992.

Johnston, Alexandra F., and Margaret Rogerson, eds. *Records of Early English Drama: York*. Manchester: Manchester University Press, 1979.

Jones, Dave. *The Roots of Welsh Border Morris*. Revised ed. Putley: Anne Jones, 1995.

Jones, Edward. *The Bardic Museum of Primitive British Literature and Other Admirable Rarities: Forming the Second Volume of the Musical, Poetical, and Historical Relicks of the Welsh Bards and Druids*. London: A. Strahan, 1802.

Jones, Rose. 'Reply to David Welti'. *Morris Matters* 1, no. 3 (1978): 27–28.

Jonson, Ben. 'Bartholomew Fair'. In *The Cambridge Edition of the Works of Ben Jonson*, edited by David M. Bevington, Martin Butler, and Ian Donaldson, 4:253–428. Cambridge: Cambridge University Press, 2012.

Jonson, Ben. 'Every Man out of His Humour'. In *The Cambridge Edition of the Works of Ben Jonson*, edited by David M. Bevington, Martin Butler, and Ian Donaldson, 1:233–423. Cambridge: Cambridge University Press, 2012.

Jonson, Ben. 'A Particular Entertainment of the Queene and Prince Their Highnesse to Althrope'. In *The Cambridge Edition of the Works of Ben Jonson*, edited by David M. Bevington, Martin Butler, and Ian Donaldson, 2:393–417. Cambridge: Cambridge University Press, 2012.

Jonson, Ben, and F.G. Waldron. *The Sad Shepherd, or, A Tale of Robin Hood: A Fragment*. London: J. Nichols, 1783.

The Jovial May-pole Dancers, or, The Merry Morris. [London]: Printed for J. Deacon, [*c.* 1690].

Joyce, Jenny. 'Women's Morris Federation?' *Morris Matters* 1, no. 3 (1978): 12–13, 19.

Judge, Roy. 'A Branch of May'. *Folk Music Journal* 2, no. 2 (1971): 91–95.

Judge, Roy. 'Cecil Sharp and Morris, 1906-1909'. *Folk Music Journal* 8, no. 2 (2002): 195–228.

Judge, Roy. 'D'Arcy Ferris and the Bidford Morris'. *Folk Music Journal* 4, no. 5 (1984): 443–80.

Judge, Roy. *The Jack-in-the-Green*. 2nd ed. London: FLS Books, 2000.

Judge, Roy. 'Mary Neal and the Espérance Morris'. *Folk Music Journal* 5, no. 5 (1989): 545–91.

Judge, Roy. 'May Morning and Magdalen College, Oxford'. *Folklore* 97, no. 1 (1986): 15–40.

Judge, Roy. 'Merrie England and the Morris 1881-1910'. *Folklore* 104, no. 1/2 (1993): 124–43.

Judge, Roy. 'The Morris in Lichfield'. *Folklore* 103, no. 2 (1992): 131–59.

Judge, Roy. '"The Old English Morris Dance": Theatrical Morris, 1801–1880'. *Folk Music Journal* 7, no. 3 (1997): 311–50.

Judge, Roy. 'Tradition and the Plaited Maypole Dance'. *Traditional Dance* 2 (1983): 1–23.

Julius. 'The Horse's Head – Rush-Bearings'. *Notes and Queries* 1st series, 1, no. 17 (1850): 257–58.

Junius, Franciscus. *Etymologicum Anglicanum*, edited by E. Lye. Oxford: Printed at the Sheldonian Theatre, 1743.

K. 'Necton Guild'. In *The Every Day Book*, by William Hone, 335–38. London: William Tegg, 1868.

Karpeles, Maud. 'The Abram Morris Dance'. *Journal of the English Folk Dance and Song Society* 1, no. 1 (1932): 55–59.

Karpeles, Maud. *Cecil Sharp: His Life and Work*. London: Routledge & Kegan Paul, 1967.

Karpeles, Maud. *The Lancashire Morris Dance*. London: Novello, 1930.

Karpeles, Maud. 'Upton-on-Severn Morris Dances'. *Journal of the English Folk Dance and Song Society* 1, no. 2 (1933): 101–3.

Karpeles, Maud. 'Yardley Gobion Morris'. *Journal of the English Folk Dance and Song Society* 8, no. 1 (1956): 44–45.

Karpeles, Maud, and Alex Helm. 'The Lymm (Cheshire) Morris Dance'. *Journal of the English Folk Dance and Song Society* 6, no. 3 (1951): 100–01.

'Karpeles MSS, Forest of Dean'. MK/7/7. Vaughan Williams Memorial Library. Accessed 3 October 2022. https://www.vwml.org/record/MK/7/7.

'Karpeles MSS, Much Wenlock Morris Not for Joe / 3 Jolly Sheepskins'. MK/1/4/5346. Vaughan Williams Memorial Library. Accessed 3 October 2022. https://www.vwml.org/record/MK/1/4/5346.

'Karpeles MSS, Oldfield Morris: Information and Dance Figures'. MK/1/1/4545. Vaughan Williams Memorial Library. Accessed 3 October 2022. https://www.vwml.org/record/MK/1/1/4545.

'Karpeles MSS, Peover Morris'. MK/1/1/4962. Vaughan Williams Memorial Library.

'Karpeles MSS, Upton-on-Severn Morris: Information, Stick Dance and Handkerchief Dance'. MK/1/1/3375-3382. Vaughan Williams Memorial Library. Accessed 3 October 2022. https://www.vwml.org/record/MK/1/1/3375.

'Karpeles MSS, Worcestershire Morris: White Ladies Aston'. MK/1/1/4500-4502. Vaughan Williams Memorial Library. Accessed 3 October 2022. https://www.vwml.org/record/MK/1/1/4500.

Kelly, William. *Notices Illustrative of the Drama, and Other Popular Amusements, Chiefly in the Sixteenth and Seventeenth Centuries, Incidentally Illustrating Shakespeare and His Contemporaries.* London: John Russell Smith, 1865.

Kemble, Frances Ann. *Record of a Girlhood.* 3 vols. London: R. Bentley, 1878.

Kemp, William. *Kemps Nine Daies Wonder: Performed in a Daunce from London to Norwich,* edited by Alexander Dyce. Camden Society 11. London: J.B. Nichols and Son, 1840.

Kennedy, Douglas. *England's Dances: Folk Dancing To-day and Yesterday.* London: G. Bell, 1949.

Kennedy, Douglas. 'Folk Dance Revival'. *Folk Music Journal* 2, no. 2 (1971): 80–90.

Kennedy, Douglas. 'Men's Morris'. *E.F.D.S. News* 4, no. 12 (1936): 373–74.

Kent & Sussex Courier. 'Festivities at Buckhurst', 9 January 1874.

Kent & Sussex Courier. 'Grand Ball at Buckhurst', 17 December 1875.

Kent & Sussex Courier. 'Coming of Age Rejoicings at Mostyn, Flintshire', 4 May 1877.

Kentish Gazette. [News Item], 4 May 1858.

Kentish Mercury. 'May-day Games at St. Mary Cray', 13 May 1892.

Kerry, Charles. 'Antiquarian Papers [Microfilm]'. Z/354. Surrey History Centre.

Kerry, Charles. *The History and Antiquities of the Hundred of Bray, in the County of Berks.* London: Printed for the author by Savill and Edwards, 1861.

Kerry, Charles. *A History of the Municipal Church of St. Lawrence, Reading.* Reading: Published by the author, 1883.

Kersey, John. *Dictionarium Anglo-Britannicum, or, A General English Dictionary.* London: Printed by J. Wilde, 1708.

Kersey, John. *A New English Dictionary.* London: Printed for Henry Bonwicke, 1702.

'Kesteven Morris'. Accessed 3 October 2022. http://www.kestevenmorris.co.uk/index.htm.

Kettlewell, Mrs W.R. 'William Wells and the Bampton Morris'. *Country Dance and Song* 4 (1971): 9–12.

Kidderminster Times and Advertiser for Bewdley & Stourport. 'The Drink Again', 3 January 1874.

Kidson, Frank, and Mary Neal. *English Folk-song and Dance.* Cambridge: University Press, 1915.

'Kingston Parish Records: Churchwardens' Accounts Recording Receipts from Rents and Other Sources, 1503-1681'. Z/367/12 (KG2/2/1). Surrey History Centre.

Kipling, Gordon. *The Triumph of Honour: Burgundian Origins of the Elizabethan Renaissance.* Publications of the Sir Thomas Browne Institute. General Series. The Hague, Netherlands: Published for the Sir Thomas Browne Institute [by] Leiden University Press, 1977.

Kirby, Mary. *Leaflets from My Life.* London: Simpkin, Marshall & co, 1887.

Kirkpatrick, John. 'The Shropshire Bedlams'. *American Morris Newsletter* 23, no. 1 (2000): 17–33.

Klausner, David, ed. *Records of Early English Drama: Herefordshire, Worcestershire.* Toronto: University of Toronto Press, 1990.

Klausner, David, ed. *Records of Early English Drama: Wales.* London: British Library, 2005.

Knight, Francis A. *The Heart of Mendip.* London: Dent, 1915.

Knight, Stephen, and Thomas H. Ohlgren, eds. *Robin Hood and Other Outlaw Tales.* 2nd ed. Middle English Texts. Kalamazoo, Mich.: Medieval Institute Publications, 2000.

Knighton, C.S. 'Mennes, Sir John (1599-1671), Naval Officer'. Oxford Dictionary of National Biography. Accessed 3 October 2022. https://doi.org/10.1093/ref:odnb/18561.

Knowlton, Jean Elizabeth. 'Some Dances of the Stuart Masque Identified and Analyzed'. Doctoral dissertation, Indiana University, 1966.

L., T. 'Rushbearing'. *Manchester Times,* 7 December 1889.

Laborde, Léon Emmanuel. *Les Ducs de Bourgogne, Études sur les Lettres, les Arts et l'Industrie pendant le xve Siècle, Seconde Partie.* 3 vols. Paris: Plon Frères, 1849-52.

The Lady's Newspaper. 'Banquet to the Crimean Guards', 30 August 1856.

La Marche, Olivier de. *Mémoires d'Olivier de La Marche, Maître d'Hôtel et Capitaine des Gardes de Charles le Téméraire*. 4 vols. Paris: Librairie Renouard, 1883–1888.

Lancashire, Anne. *London Civic Theatre: City Drama and Pageantry from Roman Times to 1558*. Cambridge: Cambridge University Press, 2002.

Lancashire, Anne, and David John Parkinson, eds. *Records of Early English Drama: Civic London to 1558*. Cambridge: D.S. Brewer, 2015.

Lancashire, Ian. 'Orders for Twelfth Day and Night circa 1515 in the Second Northumberland Household Book'. *English Literary Renaissance* 10, no. 1 (1980): 7–45.

Lancashire Evening Post. [Advertisement], 24 May 1890.

Lancashire Evening Post. 'Rose Festival in Chorley', 7 June 1890.

Lancashire Evening Post. 'The Rose Festival at Chorley', 6 June 1891.

Lancashire Evening Post. 'The Rose Festival', 11 June 1892.

Lancashire Evening Post. 'The Rose Festival', 17 June 1892.

Lancashire Evening Post. [Advertisement], 3 July 1892.

Lancashire Evening Post. [Advertisement], 8 July 1892.

Lancashire Evening Post. [Advertisement], 5 September 1892.

Lancashire Evening Post. [Football Results], 12 November 1892.

Lancashire Evening Post. [Advertisement], 5 August 1893.

Lancashire Evening Post. [Football Results], 21 October 1893.

Lancashire Evening Post. 'Preston Morris Dancers at Burnley', 16 April 1894.

Lancashire Evening Post. [Advertisement], 30 April 1894.

Lancashire Evening Post. 'The Preston Rose Festival', 7 August 1894.

Lancashire Evening Post. 'Cyclists' Parade at Accrington', 10 September 1894.

Lancashire Evening Post. [Advertisement], 11 February 1897.

Lancaster Guardian. [Advertisement], 28 July 1894.

Lancaster Guardian. 'The Fire Brigades' Demonstration', 9 June 1894.

Langham, Robert. *Laneham's Letter Describing the Magnificent Pageants Presented before Queen Elizabeth, at Kenilworth Castle in 1575*. [Warwick]: John Merridew, 1774.

Langham, Robert. *A Letter*, edited by R. J. P. Kuin. Medieval and Renaissance Texts (Leiden, Netherlands). Leiden: E.J. Brill, 1983.

Langsbury, Ken. 'And Then It Happened!' Mustrad. Accessed 3 October 2022. https://www.mustrad.org.uk/articles/langsbry.htm.

Larwood, Jacob, and John Camden Hotten. *The History of Signboards, from Earliest Times to the Present Day*. 5th ed. London: J.C. Hotten, 1868.

Latimer, Hugh. 'The Sermon of Master Doctor Latimer, Preached on the Third Sunday in Advent, 1552'. In *Sermons by Hugh Latimer*, edited by George Elwes, 65–83. Parker Society 20. Cambridge: University Press, 1845.

Latimer, Hugh. 'The Sixth Sermon Preached before King Edward, April Twelfth, [1549]'. In *Sermons by Hugh Latimer*, edited by George Elwes, 194–215. Parker Society 20. Cambridge: University Press, 1845.

Leach, Joan. *The History of Knutsford Royal May Day*. Knutsford: J. Leach, 1987.

Leach, Jonathan. *Morris Dancing at Abingdon to 1914*. Eynsham: Chandler Publications, 1987.

Leach, Jonathan. *Mr. Hemmings' Morris Dancers: A Team with a Long History*. Abingdon: Mr. Hemmings' Morris Dancers, n.d.

Leanerd, John. *The Country Innocence, or, The Chamber-Maid Turn'd Quaker: A Comedy*. London: Printed for Charles Harper, 1677.

Leather, Ella M. *The Folk-lore of Herefordshire*. Hereford: Jakeman & Carver, 1912.

Lee, Frederick George. *The History, Description and Antiquities of the Prebendal Church of the Blessed Virgin Mary of Thame, in the County and Diocese of Oxford*. London: Mitchell and Hughes, 1883.

Lee, Frederick George. 'Oxfordshire Christmas Miracle Play'. *Notes and Queries* 5th series, 2, no. 52 (1874): 503–05.

L[ee], J[essie]. 'Rush Bearing in Lancashire'. In *The Year Book*, by William Hone, 552–53. London: Ward, Lock, Bowden & co, 1892.

'Lee, Nelson'. In *The Era Almanack*, 2nd ed., 23, 1868.

The Leeds Intelligencer. [Advertisement], 9 July 1776.

Leeds Mercury. 'Lifeboat Saturday in Leeds', 6 July 1896.

Leeds Times. 'May-Day Frolic', 9 May 1833.

Leeds Times. [News Item], 26 May 1866.

Leeds Times. 'Keighley', 7 August 1897.

The Leicester Chronicle, or, Commercial and Agricultural Advertiser. 'Leicester Cricket Ground', 7 September 1839.

Leicester Journal. 'Hinckley Petty Sessions', 12 January 1849.

Leicester Journal. 'Melton Mowbray', 15 January 1858.

Leicester Journal. 'Our London Letter', 8 May 1896.

Leicestershire Mercury. 'The Colliers', 21 May 1859.

Leigh, James. 'Personal Accounts of James Leigh, 1757-1758'. DR/18/31/869. Shakespeare Birthplace Trust Record Office.

Leigh Chronicle and Weekly District Advertiser. 'Crowning the May Queen at Golborne', 9 May 1884.

Leigh Chronicle and Weekly District Advertiser. 'Crowning the May Queen at Golborne', 13 May 1887.

Leigh Chronicle and Weekly District Advertiser. 'Hindley Green Harvest Queen Festival', 14 August 1891.

Leigh Chronicle and Weekly District Advertiser. 'Hindley Green: Picnic', 4 September 1891.

Leigh Chronicle and Weekly District Advertiser. 'Crowning the May Queen at Golborne', 13 May 1892.

Leigh Chronicle and Weekly District Advertiser. 'Hindley Green Harvest-Queen Festival', 22 July 1892.

Leigh Chronicle and Weekly District Advertiser. 'Hindley Green: Morris Dancers', 11 November 1892.

Leigh Chronicle and Weekly District Advertiser. 'The Hindley Green "Morris" Dancers', 3 May 1895.

Leland, John. *Joannis Lelandi Antiquarii De Rebus Britannicis Collectanea,* edited by Thomas Hearne. Editio altera. 6 vols. Londini: Apud Benj. White, 1774.

Lemon, Robert. *Calendar of State Papers, Domestic Series, of the Reigns of Edward VI, Mary, Elizabeth ...: Preserved in the State Paper Department of Her Majesty's Public Record Office.* 7 vols. London: Longman, Brown, Green, Longmans, & Roberts, 1856.

Leonard, Boudicca Fox-. 'Meet Boss Morris, the Stylish Young Women Making English Folk Dance Cool'. *The Telegraph,* 19 May 2019.

Letcher, Andy. 'Paganism and the British Folk Revival'. In *Pop Pagans: Paganism and Popular Music,* edited by Donna Weston and Andy Bennet, 91–109. Oxford: Routledge, 2014.

Licensing Act 2003 (2003).

Lichfield Mercury. 'Greenhill Bower', 4 June 1830.

Lillywhite, Bryant. *London Signs.* London: Allen & Unwin, 1972.

Lincoln, Rutland and Stamford Mercury. [Advertisement], 29 June 1792.

Lincoln, Rutland and Stamford Mercury. [News Item], 22 January 1821.

Lincoln, Rutland and Stamford Mercury. 'Sunday's and Tuesday's Posts', 24 May 1833.

Lincoln, Rutland and Stamford Mercury. 'Louth Borough Police', 7 January 1853.

Lincoln, Rutland and Stamford Mercury. [News Item], 15 January 1864.

Lincolnshire Chronicle. 'Melton Mowbray', 17 January 1851 [a].

Lincolnshire Chronicle. [News Item], 17 January 1851 [b].

Lincolnshire Chronicle. 'Plough Monday', 17 January 1851 [c].

Lincolnshire Chronicle. 'Plough Monday', 16 January 1852.

Lincolnshire Chronicle. [News Item], 30 December 1853.

Lincolnshire Chronicle. [News Item], 2 January 1857.

Lincolnshire Chronicle. 'Ingham – the Morris Dancers Again', 2 January 1864 [a].

Lincolnshire Chronicle. 'Metheringham – Morris Dancers', 2 January 1864 [b].

Lincolnshire Chronicle. [News Item], 14 January 1870.

Lincolnshire Chronicle. 'Christmas Eccentricities', 9 December 1870.

Lincolnshire Chronicle. 'Scunthorpe', 14 January 1876.

Lincolnshire Chronicle. 'Temperance Gala at Lincoln', 27 June 1899.

Lincolnshire Echo. 'Lincoln's Temperance Fete and Gala', 23 June 1899.

'List of Christmas Gifts to the Poor, to Servants and Prisoners by the Wyndham Then Arundell Family at Salisbury, Including Payments to Morris Dancers, 1744-1769, 1795-1797, Arundell of Wardour Castle'. 2667/23/5. Wiltshire and Swindon History Centre.

'List of Christmas Gifts to the Poor and to Servants, 1756-1785, Arundell of Wardour Castle'. 2667/23/6. Wiltshire and Swindon History Centre.

Lithgow, William. *The Totall Discourse, of the Rare Adventures, and Painefull Peregrinations of Long Nineteene Yeares Travailes from Scotland, to the Most Famous Kingdomes in Europe, Asia, and Affrica.* London: By J. Okes, 1640.

Little, Alice. 'The Whit-Horn'. England: the other within. Accessed 3 October 2022. https://

england.prm.ox.ac.uk/englishness-whit-horn. html.

Little, Thomas. *Confessions of an Oxonian*. 3 vols. London: J.J. Stockdale, 1826.

Liverpool Echo. 'Crowning the May Queen at Knutsford', 14 May 1881.

Liverpool Mercury. 'Fancy Dress Ball', 23 October 1840.

Liverpool Mercury. 'Hengler's', 11 March 1868.

Liverpool Mercury. 'May Day Festival at Over', 12 May 1884.

Liverpool Mercury. [Advertisement], 1 February 1893.

Liverpool Mercury. 'The Theatrical Football Match at Goodison Park', 4 March 1893.

Lloyd's Weekly Newspaper. 'Royal Surrey Zoological Gardens', 3 August 1845.

Lloyd's Weekly Newspaper. 'Royal Surrey Gardens', 30 August 1857.

Locke, E. 'The Rush Carts of Lancashire'. *Hereford Times*, 17 January 1846.

'Log of the 1st Meeting of the Morris Ring'. Morris Ring Logbook, 1.

'Log of the 6 Meeting of the Morris Ring'. Morris Ring Logbook, 1.

'Log of the 9th Meeting of the Morris Ring'. Morris Ring Logbook, 1.

'Log of the 12th Meeting of the Morris Ring'. Morris Ring Logbook, 1.

'Log of the 16th Meeting of the Morris Ring'. Morris Ring Logbook, 1.

'Log of the 21st Meeting of the Morris Ring'. Morris Ring Logbook, 1.

'Log of the 29th Meeting of the Morris Ring'. Morris Ring Logbook, 1.

'Log of the 41st Meeting of the Morris Ring'. Morris Ring Logbook, 2.

'Log of the 52nd Meeting of the Morris Ring'. Morris Ring Logbook, 3.

'Log of the 53rd Meeting of the Morris Ring'. Morris Ring Logbook, 3.

'Log of the 62nd Meeting of the Morris Ring'. Morris Ring Logbook, 3.

'Log of the 70th Meeting of the Morris Ring'. Morris Ring Logbook, 3.

'Log of the 86th Meeting of the Morris Ring'. Morris Ring Logbook, 4.

'Log of the 91st Meeting of the Morris Ring'. Morris Ring Logbook, 4.

'Log of the 92nd Meeting of the Morris Ring'. Morris Ring Logbook, 4.

'Log of the 97th Meeting of the Morris Ring'. Morris Ring Logbook, 4.

'Log of the 123rd Meeting of the Morris Ring'. Morris Ring Logbook, 6.

'Log of the 151st Meeting of the Morris Ring'. Morris Ring Logbook, 7.

'Log of the 162nd Meeting of the Morris Ring'. Morris Ring Logbook, 7.

'Log of the 234th Meeting of the Morris Ring'. Morris Ring Logbook, 8.

Lohrli, Anne. 'William S. Wickenden'. Dickens Journals Online. Accessed 3 October 2022. https://www.djo.org.uk/indexes/authors/ william-s-wickenden.html.

Lomazzo, Gio. Paolo. *Trattato dell'Arte della Pittura Scultura ed Architettura*. 3 vols. Roma: Presso Saverio Del-Monte Editore Proprietario, 1844.

London and Its Environs Described. London: Printed for R. and J. Dodsley, 1761.

London Chronicle. [Letter], 13–15 September 1763.

London Chronicle. 'Theatrical Intelligence', 1–3 December 1772.

London Courier and Evening Gazette. 'Covent Garden Theatre', 10 November 1824.

London Daily News. 'The Autumn Manoeuvres', 12 September 1872.

London Daily Post and General Advertiser. 'Marlborough, Oct. 19'. 26 October 1738.

London Daily Post and General Advertiser. 'Bartholomew Fair', 20 August 1739.

London Daily Post and General Advertiser. [Advertisement], 8 December 1743.

London Daily Post and General Advertiser. [Advertisement], 13–15 December 1743.

London Daily Post and General Advertiser. [Advertisement], 19–22 December 1743.

London Daily Post and General Advertiser. [Advertisement], 26–31 December 1743.

The London Evening Post. 'Bath, April 20', 23 April 1728.

The London Evening Post. [News Item], 2 March 1756.

London Evening Standard. 'Crystal Palace', 10 June 1862.

London Evening Standard. 'Hengler's Grand Cirque', 7 April 1874.

London Evening Standard. 'Going-off Clubs', 15 September 1884.

London Journal, [Letter], 17 April 1725.

Londonderry Standard. 'The Autumn Manoeuvres', 14 September 1872.

'The Loseley Manuscripts, Records of the More And More Molyneux Family of Loseley Park'. LM/1087/3/9/. Surrey History Centre.

Lowe, Barbara. 'Early Records of the Morris in England'. *Journal of the English Folk Dance and Song Society* 8, no. 2 (1957): 61–82.

Loveless, Kenneth. 'Frederick Hamer 1909-1969'. *Folk Music Journal* 2, no. 1 (1970): 71–72.

Loyd, Mathew. *The King Found at Southwell, and the Oxford Gigg Playd, and Sung at Witney Wakes.* London: Printed for F.L, 1646.

'Lucas Archive Account Book for 1671-1677, Lucas Archive Family Papers for Wrest Park'. L31/194. Bedfordshire Archives and Records Service.

'Lucas Archive, Correspondence, Correspondence to Jemima Yorke, Née Campbell from Her Father John Campbell, Lord Glenorchy, 3rd Earl of Breadalbane'. L30/9/17/45. Bedfordshire Archives and Records Service.

Lucius. 'Original Letters, Moral and Entertaining: Letter V: On Sunday Schools'. *Westminster Magazine*, September 1785, 477–79.

Lupton, Donald. *A Warre-like Treatise of the Pike, or, Some Experimentall Resolves, for Lessening the Number, and Disabling the Use of the Pike in Warre.* London: Printed by Richard Hodgkinsonne, 1642.

Lydgate, John. 'A Mumming at Hertford'. In *The Minor Poems of John Lydgate*, edited by H.N. McCracken, 675–82. Early English Text Society 192. London: Oxford University Press, 1911.

Lyly, John. 'A Whip for an Ape'. In *The Complete Works of John Lyly*, edited by R. Warwick Bond, 3:415–19. Oxford: University Press, 1902.

Lysons, Daniel. *The Environs of London: Being an Historical Account of the Towns, Villages, and Hamlets, within Twelve Miles of That Capital.* 4 vols. London: Printed by A. Strahan for T. Cadell in the Strand, 1792–1796.

M., M. '189: Morrice Dancing'. *Shropshire Notes and Queries*, 12 June 1885: 60.

Maas, Martha, ed. 'The Morris'. In *English Pastime Music 1630-1660: An Anthology of Keyboard Pieces*, 54. Madison: A-R Editions, 1974.

Macaulay, Aulay. *The History and Antiquities of Claybrook, in the County of Leicester.* London: Printed for the author, 1791.

Machyn, Henry. *The Diary of Henry Machyn, Citizen and Merchant-Taylor of London, from A.D. 1550 to A.D. 1563*, edited by John Gough Nichols. London: Printed for the Camden Society, by J. B. Nichols and Son, 1848.

Mackerness, E.D. 'The Yardley Gobion Morris'. *Journal of the English Folk Dance and Song Society* 7, no. 4 (1955): 216–17.

MacLaren, Archibald. *London out of Town, or, The Family Genius's: A Farce, with Songs.* London: Printed and sold for the author, 1809.

MacNally, Leonard. *Robin Hood, or, Sherwood Forest: A Comic Opera.* London: Printed by J. Almon, 1784.

Macready, William. *The Irishman in London, or, The Happy African: A Farce.* London: Printed by W. Woodfall, 1793.

'Maids Morris'. In *The Dancing Master*, 7th ed., 3rd supplement, 1. London: Printed by E. Jones for H. Playford, 1689.

Maidstone Journal and Kentish Advertiser. [Advertisement], 25 August 1860.

Maitland, J.A. Fuller, W. Barclay Squire, and Blanche Winogron, eds. 'The King's Morisco'. In *The Fitzwilliam Virginal Book*, Revised Dover ed., 2:373. New York: Dover, 1980.

Maitland, J.A. Fuller, W. Barclay Squire, and Blanche Winogron, eds. 'Put up Thy Dagger'. In *The Fitzwilliam Virginal Book*, Revised Dover ed., 2:72–73. New York: Dover, 1980.

'Manchester and District Branch'. *E.F.D.S. News* 4, no. 12 (1936): 398.

Manchester Courier and Lancashire General Advertiser. 'Bull-Baiting', 22 September 1838.

Manchester Courier and Lancashire General Advertiser. 'The Ashton and Dukinfield Wakes', 22 August 1846.

Manchester Courier and Lancashire General Advertiser. 'Ashton and Dukinfield Wakes', 25 August 1846.

Manchester Courier and Lancashire General Advertiser. 'Buxton Well Dressing', 30 June 1847.

Manchester Courier and Lancashire General Advertiser. 'Lymn [sic] Rushbearing', 19 August 1848.

Manchester Courier and Lancashire General Advertiser. 'Mechanics' Institution Annual Christmas Party [Advertisement]', 30 December 1848.

Manchester Courier and Lancashire General Advertiser. 'The Christmas Party of the Mechanics' Institution', 6 January 1849.

Manchester Courier and Lancashire General Advertiser. 'Manchester Mechanics' Institution Christmas Party', 7 February 1849.

Manchester Courier and Lancashire General Advertiser. 'Beware of Pickpockets', 18 August 1849.

Manchester Courier and Lancashire General Advertiser. 'A Juvenile Pickpocket', 8 September 1849.

Manchester Courier and Lancashire General Advertiser. 'Heywood Wakes', 10 August 1850.

Manchester Courier and Lancashire General Advertiser. 'The Oddfellows' Literary Institution', 28 December 1850.

Manchester Courier and Lancashire General Advertiser. 'Wakes', 28 August 1852.

Manchester Courier and Lancashire General Advertiser. 'Mechanics' Institution Christmas Party', 18 December 1852.

Manchester Courier and Lancashire General Advertiser. 'The Christmas Pantomime', 24 December 1853.

Manchester Courier and Lancashire General Advertiser. 'Ashton Wakes', 26 August 1854.

Manchester Courier and Lancashire General Advertiser. 'May-Day Festivities at Arley', 9 May 1857.

Manchester Courier and Lancashire General Advertiser. 'May Day Festivities: Knutsford', 3 May 1880.

Manchester Courier and Lancashire General Advertiser. 'Coronation of the Rose Queen at Worsley', 4 August 1883.

Manchester Courier and Lancashire General Advertiser. 'Coronation Day at Knutsford', 2 May 1885.

Manchester Courier and Lancashire General Advertiser. 'A Model May Festival', 24 May 1886.

Manchester Evening News. 'Local and District News', 26 August 1874.

Manchester Evening News. [Advertisement], 12 June 1886.

'The Manchester May Day Tradition of Molly Dancing'. BBC Radio 4 Making History. Accessed 3 October 2022. https://www.bbc.co.uk/radio4/history/making_history/makhist10_prog5d.shtml.

Manchester Mercury. [Advertisement], 25 February 1777.

Manchester Mercury. [Advertisement], 22 April 1788.

The Manchester Times and Gazette. 'Mottram in Longdendale', 17 September 1836.

The Manchester Times. 'The Christmas Party at the Mechanics' Institution', 20 January 1844.

The Manchester Times. 'Leigh: Public Rejoicings', 10 July 1846.

The Manchester Times. 'The Middleton Wakes', 24 August 1847.

The Manchester Times. 'Denton Wakes'. 15 August 1849.

The Manchester Times. 'Stalybridge Wakes', 27 July 1850.

The Manchester Times. 'Theatre Royal', 23 October 1850.

The Manchester Times. 'Buxton: The Well Dressing', 18 June 1853.

The Manchester Times. 'Christmas Pantomimes: Prince's Theatre: Mother Goose', 31 December 1864.

The Manchester Times. 'Rushbearing and Morris Dancers', 16 November 1889.

The Manchester Times. 'Rushbearing', 30 November 1889.

'Mander & Mitchenson Theatre Collection, [Newscutting]'. MM/REF/TH/GR/PAN/4, p. 125. University of Bristol Theatre Collection.

Manners, Charles. *The Manuscripts of His Grace, the Duke of Rutland, G.C.B., Preserved at Belvoir Castle.* 4 vols. London: H.M.S.O., 1888–1905.

Manning, Percy. 'May-day at Watford, Herts.' *Folk-lore* 4, no. 3 (1893): 403–04.

Manning, Percy. 'Notes on the Revival of Morris Dancing'. MS Top. Oxon d.200, ff. 62-65. Bodleian Libraries.

Manning, Percy. 'Some Oxfordshire Seasonal Festivals: With Notes on Morris-dancing in Oxfordshire'. *Folk-lore* 8, no. 4 (1897): 307–24.

'Manning MSS, Ascot-under-Wychwood'. MS Top. Oxon d.200, f. 133. Bodleian Libraries.

'Manning MSS, Deddington'. MS Top. Oxon d.200, f. 173. Bodleian Libraries.

'Manning MSS, [Efforts to Obtain a Pipe and Tabor]'. MS Top. Oxon d.200, f. 73. Bodleian Libraries.

'Manning MSS, March Gobbin Morris'. MS Top. Oxon d.200, f. 231. Bodleian Libraries.

'Manning MSS, Wheatley'. MS Top. Oxon d.200, f. 244. Bodleian Libraries.

Mares, F.H. 'Norris, Henry (1661x5–1731), Actor'. Oxford Dictionary of National Biography. Accessed 3 October 2022. https://doi.org/10.1093/ref:odnb/20273.

Marriott, Roger. 'Staffordshire Morris'. *English Dance and Song* 21, no. 3 (1957): 106–7.

Marsh, Bower, and John Ainsworth. *Records of the Worshipful Company of Carpenters.* Oxford: Printed for the Company at the University Press, 1913–1968.

Marshall, Chas. 'Clog Morris – There's No Such Thing!' *Morris Matters* 11, no. 1 (1992): 19–25.

Marshall, Chris. 'A Brief History Of Ducklington Morris'. Ducklington Morris [Blog]. Accessed 3 October 2022. http://www.ducklingtonmorris.org.uk/ducklington-morris/a-brief-history-of-ducklington-morris/.

Marshall, Rosalind K. *Mary I.* London: H.M.S.O, 1993.

Marston, John. 'Histrio-mastix, or, The Player Whipt'. In *The Plays of John Marston,* edited by H. Harvey Wood, 3:243–302. Edinburgh: Oliver & Boyd, 1934–1939.

Marston, John. 'Jacke Drums Entertainment, or, The Comedie of Pasquill and Katherine'. In *The Plays of John Marston*, edited by H. Harvey Wood, 3:175–241. Edinburgh: Oliver & Boyd, 1934.

Marston, John. 'The Malcontent'. In *The Plays of John Marston*, edited by H. Harvey Wood, 1:135–217. Edinburgh: Oliver & Boyd, 1934–1939.

Martin Senior. 'The Just Censure and Reproof of Martin Junior'. In *The Marprelate Tracts 1588, 1589*, edited by W. Pierce, 335–81. London: James Clarke, 1911.

Martin the Metropolitan. 'Hay Any Worke for Cooper'. In *The Marprelate Tracts 1588, 1589*, edited by W. Pierce, 197–284. London: James Clarke, 1911.

'Mary Massey, England, Cheshire Bishop's Transcripts, 1598-1900'. FamilySearch. Accessed 3 October 2022. https://www.familysearch.org/ark:/61903/1:1:NCWL-GQV.

'Massingberd Mundy papers, Bailiff's or Steward's Day Book of Disbursements, House, Garden and Farm, 1655-1677'. 1-MM/6/1/4. Lincolnshire Archives.

Massinger, Philip. 'A Very Woman'. In *The Plays and Poems of Philip Massinger*, edited by Philip Edwards and Colin Gibson, 4:201–90. Oxford: Clarendon Press, 1976.

'The Maurice Daunce'. Add. MS 41996 F. British Library.

May, Thomas. *The Reigne of King Henry the Second Written in Seaven Bookes*. London: Printed by A[ugustine] M[atthewes and John Beale] for Benjamin Fisher, 1633.

'May Day'. *The Literary Chronicle and Weekly Review* 2, no. 51 (6 May 1820): 299–300.

Mayhew, Graham. *Tudor Rye*. Occasional Papers (University of Sussex. Centre for Continuing Education). Brighton: Falmer Centre for Continuing Education, University of Sussex, 1987.

McKinnon, Ian. 'Fiddling While the Carnival World Burns!' Troupes and Bands. Accessed 3 October 2022. http://outsiderobs.blogspot.com/2011/10/fiddling-while-carnival-world-burns.html.

McKinnon, Ian. *Fluffy Morris, or, The Art of Judging Carnival Display Morris Troupes*. 3rd (revised) – internet – ed. Accessed 3 October 2022. http://ccgi.ianmckinnon.plus.com/fluffypdf.pdf.

McKinnon, Ian. 'List of Past and Present Morris Troupes'. Troupes and Bands. Accessed 3 October 2022. http://ccgi.ianmckinnon.plus.com/trad_mor7.php.

McManus, Clare. 'Women and English Renaissance Drama: Making and Unmaking "The All-male Stage"'. *Literature Compass* 4, no. 3 (2007): 784–96.

Mellor, Hugh. *Welsh Folk Dances*. London: Novello, 1935.

Memoirs and Adventures of a Flea. 2 vols. London: Printed for T. Axtell, 1785.

Mendham, Geoffrey. 'Encounters with the Morris Dance in Shropshire'. *English Dance and Song* 18, no. 3 (1953/54): 100–02.

Mennes, John. *Recreation for Ingenious Head-peeces*. London: Printed by M. Simmons, 1654.

Mepham, W.A. 'The History of the Drama in Essex from the Fifteenth Century to the Present Time'. Doctoral dissertation, Queen Mary College, London, 1937.

Mercurio-Mastix Hibernicus. *A Muzzle for Cerberus, and His Three Whelps Mercurius Elencticus, Bellicus, and Melancholicus*. London: Printed for R. Smithurst, 1648.

Mercurius Elenticus. *The First Part of the Last Wil & Testament of Philip Earle of Pembrooke and Montgomery, Lord of Saint Quintin, &c. Now Knight of Berk-shire*. [London], 1649.

'The Mery Life of the Countriman'. MS Rawl. poet. 185, f. 19v. Bodleian Libraries.

Metcalfe, Chloe Middleton-. *The History and Development of Dark Border Morris*. Revised ed. Morris Federation, 2021. Accessed 3 October 2022. https://www.morrisfed.org.uk/wp-content/uploads/2021/10/The-History-and-Development-of-Dark-Border-Morris.pdf.

'Metropolitan Theatres'. *Theatrical Journal* 10, no. 519 (November 1849): 365–67.

Mettam, Ann. 'Poynton Jemmers 10th Anniversary'. *Folk Buzz* 15 (1985): 13–14.

Middlesex Chronicle. 'Grand Fete at Kneller Hall Park', 20 July 1867.

Middleton, Thomas. 'Rushbearing and Morris Dancing in North Cheshire'. *Transactions of the Lancashire and Cheshire Antiquarian Society* 60 (1949): 47–55.

Middleton Albion, [News Item], 26 August 1882.

Mill, Anna Jean. *Mediaeval Plays in Scotland*. St. Andrews University Publications. Edinburgh: W. Blackwood & Sons, 1927.

Millington, Peter. 'Folk Play Scripts Explorer'. Master Mummers, 14 May 2007. Accessed 3

October 2022. http://www.mastermummers. org/scripts/explorer.php.

Millington, Peter. 'Manning's Mummers' Plays'. In *Percy Manning: The Man Who Collected Oxfordshire*, edited by Michael Heaney, 173–219. Oxford: Archaeopress, 2017.

Milton, John. 'A Mask [Comus] … Presented at Ludlow Castle'. In *The Works of John Milton*, 1.1:85–123. New York: Columbia University Press, 1931.

Minsheu, John. *Ηγεμων Εις Τας Γλωσσας, Id Est, Ductor in Linguas, The Guide into Tongues*. London: apud Ioannem Browne, 1617.

'The Mobberley Morris'. *Buzz* 3 (1983): 20–23.

Moll, Henry. 'On Fucus'. In *Records of Early English Drama: Cambridge*, edited by Alan H. Nelson, 878–79. Toronto: University of Toronto Press, 1988.

'Moll Peatly'. In *The Dancing Master*, 3rd ed. [2nd supplement], 48. London: Printed by W.Godbid and are sold by J. Playford and Z. Watkins, 1665.

'"Molly, n.1".' Oxford English Dictionary. Accessed 3 October 2022. https://www.oed.com/view/ Entry/120943.

'Molly (and Morris) Dancing in Essex'. *Essex Folk News*, no. 40 (1983): 6–7.

Monmouthshire Beacon. 'The Coming of Age of Mr. J. Maclean Rolls: Garden Party at The Hendre', 9 May 1891.

Monmouthshire Merlin. '"Bush"-fighting; or the Irish at War', 2 January 1841.

Montgomeryshire Express. 'Guy Fawkes Celebration in Mid-Kent', 20 November 1883.

'Moorish, Adj. 2.' Oxford English Dictionary. Accessed 3 October 2022. https://www.oed. com/view/Entry/121982.

Moreau, Simeon. *A Tour to Cheltenham Spa, or, Gloucestershire Display'd*. Bath: Printed for the author, by R. Cruttwell, 1783.

'Morisco Gallyard'. Osborn Music MS 13, ff. 40v-41r [new foliation]. Yale Beinecke Library.

Morley, Thomas. 'Madrigalls to Foure Voices: The Firste Booke, XVIII'. In *English Madrigal Verse 1588-1632*, edited by E.H. Fellowes, 3rd ed., 143. Oxford: Oxford University Press, 2016.

Morning Advertiser. 'Royal Grecian Saloon [Advertisement]', 3 May 1843.

Morning Advertiser. 'White Conduit Gardens', 16 September 1846.

Morning Advertiser. 'Royal Pavilion Gardens [Advertisement]', 8 September 1856.

Morning Chronicle and London Advertiser. 'Theatrical Intelligence', 3 December 1772.

Morning Chronicle and London Advertiser. [News Item], 28 December 1772.

Morning Chronicle and London Advertiser. [Advertisement], 12 March 1774.

Morning Chronicle and London Advertiser. 'Pantheon Masquerade', 2 February 1788.

The Morning Chronicle. 'The Mirror of Fashion', 25 June 1819.

The Morning Chronicle. 'Royal Amphitheatre (Astley's), Westminster Bridge', 9 October 1820.

The Morning Chronicle. 'The Mirror of Fashion', 21 July 1821.

The Morning Chronicle. 'The Duchess of St. Alban's Fete', 22 June 1829.

The Morning Chronicle. [Advertisement], 22 March 1834.

The Morning Chronicle. 'The Rural Districts: Northern Counties – Northumberland: Letter XXVI', 16 January 1850.

The Morning Chronicle. 'The Scottish Fete at Holland Park', 11 July 1851.

The Morning Chronicle. [Announcement], 27 June 1857.

The Morning Chronicle. 'Kent Volunteer Rifle Corps: Grand Fete Champetre in Charlton Park', 13 September 1860.

The Morning Post. [News Item], 19 August 1800.

The Morning Post. 'Mrs. Thellusson's Masquerade', 2 June 1804.

The Morning Post. 'Fashionable World', 17 May 1805.

The Morning Post. 'Fashionable World', 14 June 1809.

The Morning Post. 'Albinia, Countess of Buckinghamshire's Masked Fete: Additional Particulars', 26 June 1815.

The Morning Post. 'Fashionable World', 25 June 1819.

The Morning Post. 'Almack's Masqued and Fancy Dress Ball', 7 July 1819.

The Morning Post. 'Sadler's Wells', 13 June 1821.

The Morning Post. 'The Grand Caledonian Fete', 1 June 1825.

The Morning Post. 'The Fancy Ball at Almack's', 8 June 1825.

The Morning Post. 'The Grand Fancy Ball at Almack's', 8 May 1826.

The Morning Post. 'The Fête Champêtre at Holly Grove, Highgate', 2 June 1834.

The Morning Post. 'The Farewell Fete at Holly Lodge', 18 June 1834.

The Morning Post. 'Royal Beulah Spa', 16 August 1836.

The Morning Post. 'Royal Beulah Spa', 20 August 1836.

The Morning Post. 'The Scottish Féte [*sic*]', 6 August 1852.

The Morning Post. 'Mr. Charles Salaman's Concert Lectures', 26 February 1857.

The Morning Post. 'Royal Dramatic College', 2 June 1860.

The Morning Post. 'Easter Amusements – Crystal Palace', 6 April 1868.

The Morning Post. 'The Home for Little Boys', 19 May 1879.

The Morning Post. 'Crystal Palace', 20 October 1883.

The Morning Post. [Advertisement], 4 August 1885.

Morrice Dancers at Revesby, Reproduced from the Manuscript at the British Library. Sheffield: CECTAL, 1976.

Morris, Claver. *The Diary of a West Country Physician*, edited by Edmund Hobhouse. London: Simpkin Marshall, 1934.

'Morris Dancing – Oldham'. NW07900. Manchester Morris Men's archives.

'Morris Matters Talks to Jenny Potts of Rivington'. *Morris Matters* 2, no. 4 (1979): 16–20.

'The Morris Ring'. *E.F.D.S. News* 4, no. 11 (1936): 359–60.

Moser, Joseph. 'Vestiges, Collected and Recollected'. *The European Magazine, and London Review* 50 (1806): 345–53.

'Mossley/Foulridge'. NW07420. Manchester Morris Men's archives. Accessed 3 October 2022. http://www.manchestermorrismen.org.uk/arc-photos/towns/target75.html.

Motley, Thomas. 'The Oxfordshire Fool, or, The Banbury Journal'. *Jackson's Oxford Journal*, 15 May 1753.

'Mr. Nelson Lee'. *The Players* 1, no. 18 (1860): 137–38.

'Mrs. W.C.H. Burne and the Morris Dancers', *The Queen*, 14 May 1892: 46.

Müller-Meiningen, Johanna. *Die Moriskentänzer und andere Arbeiten des Erasmus Grasser für das Alte Rathaus in München*. München: Schnell & Steiner, 1984.

Munday, Anthony. *The Downfall of Robert, Earl of Huntingdon*, edited by John C. Meagher. Oxford: Malone Society, 1965.

Munday, Anthony. *John a Kent & John a Cumber*, edited by M. St. Clare Byrne. Malone Society Reprints 49. London: Malone Society, 1923.

Munn, Thomas. *The Life of Thomas Munn, Alias, the Gentleman Brick-Maker, Alias, Tom the Smuggler, Who Was Executed ... for Robbing the Yarmouth Mail on the 20th of July Last*. London: Printed for Thomas Harris, 1750.

'Murray's Handbook for Durham and Northumberland [Review]'. *Saturday Review of Politics, Literature, Science and Art* 18 (1864): 403–04.

The Musical Times. 'The Musicians' Company', 1 March 1911.

A Musicall Banquet, Set Forth in Three Choice Varieties of Music. London: Printed by T.H. for John Benson, and John Playford, 1651.

Mycock, Sue. 'Whitehaven/Workington Dances'. NW09970. Manchester Morris Men's archives.

Myers, A.R. 'The Book of the Disguisings for the Coming of the Ambassadors of Flanders, December 1508'. *Historical Research: The Bulletin of the Institute of Historical Research* 54 (1981): 120–29.

Nabbes, Thomas. 'Covent Garden'. In *The Works of Thomas Nabbes*, edited by A.H. Bullen, 1:1–91. Old English Plays: New Series. London: Privately printed by Wyman & Sons, 1887.

Nabbes, Thomas. 'A Presentation Intended for the Prince His Highnesse on His Birth-Day'. In *The Works of Thomas Nabbes*, edited by A.H. Bullen, 2:256–68. London: Privately printed by Wyman & Sons, 1887.

Nabbes, Thomas. *The Springs Glorie Vindicating Love by Temperance against the Tenent, Sine Cerere & Baccho Friget Venus*. London: Printed by J[ohn] D[awson] for Charles Greene, 1638.

Nantwich Guardian. 'Knutsford', 5 May 1883.

Nashe, Thomas. 'Preface [to Sir Philip] Sidney's "Astrophel and Stella"'. In *The Works of Thomas Nashe*, edited by Ronald B. McKerrow, 3:327–33. Oxford: Blackwell, 1958.

Nashe, Thomas. 'The Returne of Pasquill'. In *The Works of Thomas Nashe*, edited by Ronald B. McKerrow, 1:65–103. Oxford: Blackwell, 1958.

Nashe, Thomas. 'Summers Last Will and Testament'. In *The Works of Thomas Nashe*, edited by Ronald B. McKerrow, 3:227–95. Oxford: Blackwell, 1958.

Naval & Military Gazette and Weekly Chronicle of the United Service. 'Kent', 24 August 1861.

Neal, Mary. 'As a Tale That Is Told: The Autobiography of a Victorian Woman'. Mary Neal MSS, MN/1/1. Vaughan Williams Memorial Library. Accessed 3 October 2022. https://www.vwml.org/record/MN/1/1.

Needham, Joseph. 'The Geographical Distribution of English Ceremonial Dance Traditions'. *Journal of the English Folk Dance and Song Society* 3, no. 1 (1936): 1–45.

Needham, Joseph, and Arthur Peck. 'Molly Dancing in East Anglia'. *Journal of the English Folk Dance and Song Society* 1, no. 2 (1933): 79–85.

Neill, Beth. *The Morris Federation: Twenty-one Years, 1975-1996.* [Windsor]: Morris Federation, 1996.

Nelson, Alan H, and John R. Elliott, eds. *Records of Early English Drama: Inns of Court.* 3 vols. Cambridge: D.S. Brewer, 2010.

Nelson Chronicle, Colne Observer and Clitheroe Division News, 'Nelson Trades Demonstration: Balance Sheet for 1899', 27 October 1899.

'[Nether] Alderley Churchwardens' Accounts 1721-1802'. P 143/3/2/1/1 and 2. Chester Records Office.

'A New Ballad of Bold Robin Hood, Shewing His Birth, Breeding, Valour, and Marriage at Tutbury Bull-Running'. In *The Roxburghe Ballads,* 3:440–48. Hertford: Ballad Society, 1869-1899.

A New Bull-bayting, or, A Match Play'd at the Town-Bull of Ely by Twelve Mungrills. Nod-lon [i.e., London]: Printed at the Sign of the [Bull], 1649.

A New Canting Dictionary. London, 1725.

'A New Touch of the Times, or, The Nations Consent for a Free Parliament'. In *The Pepys Ballads,* edited by Hyder Edward Rollins, 4:112–14. Cambridge, Mass: Harvard University Press, 1929-1932.

Newbury Weekly News and General Advertiser. 'Newbury Flower Show', 31 August 1871.

Newcome, Henry. *The Autobiography of Henry Newcome, M.A.,* edited by Richard Parkinson. 2 vols. Remains, Historical and Literary, Connected with the Palatine Counties of Lancaster and Chester 26–27. Manchester: Chetham Society, 1852.

Newes out of the West, or, The Character of a Mountebank. London, 1647.

'News from the Branches'. *English Folk-Dance Society's Journal* 1, no. 1 (1914): 28–32.

News of the World. [News Item], 17 August 1851.

Nimrod. 'My Life and Times'. *Fraser's Magazine for Town and Country* 25, no. 147 (1842): 288–303.

Norfolk Chronicle. 'Necton Guild', 27 May 1820.

Norfolk Chronicle. 'Necton Guild', 12 June 1824.

Norfolk News. 'Lowestoft Marine Regatta', 25 August 1894.

North, Thomas, ed. *The Accounts of the Churchwardens of S. Martin's, Leicester, 1489-1844.* Leicester: Samuel Clarke, 1884.

Northampton Mercury. [Advertisement], 6 October 1766.

Northampton Mercury. 'Market Harborough: Plough Monday', 15 January 1853.

Northampton Mercury. [News Item], 21 January 1865.

Northampton Mercury. 'The Brinklow Morris Dancers', 28 January 1865.

Northampton Mercury. 'Market Harborough: The Cattle Plague', 13 January 1866.

Northampton Mercury. 'Morris Dancers', 6 December 1884.

Northamptonshire Mercury. [Advertisement], 7 September 1747.

Northern Daily Telegraph. 'Blackburn: An Interesting Spectacle', 4 July 1898.

Northern Sinfonia of England, and Richard Hickox. *Three Dances from 'Henry VIII'.* CD. English Miniatures, CDC 7 49933 2. EMI, 1991.

Northern Whig. [Advertisement], 5 January 1850.

Northwich Guardian. 'May Festival at Over', 10 May 1882.

Northwich Guardian. 'Crowning of the May Queen at Golborne', 11 May 1887.

Northwich Guardian. 'Knutsford Royal May-Day Festivities', 6 May 1896.

Norwich Mercury. 'Norwich Election', 10 January 1835 [a].

Norwich Mercury. 'Thetford Election', 10 January 1835 [b].

Nottingham Evening Post. 'Crowning the May Queen in Cheshire', 2 May 1889.

Nottingham Evening Post. 'Birmingham Hospital Saturday', 15 July 1895.

Nottingham Journal. [Advertisement], 2 December 1862.

Nottinghamshire Guardian. 'A Gala Day at Buxton', 30 June 1853.

Nottinghamshire Guardian. 'A Party of Morris Dancers in Trouble', 8 January 1864.

Nottinghamshire Guardian. 'Buxton Well Flowering', 1 July 1864.

Nottinghamshire Guardian. 'Royal Oak Day', 15 June 1883.

Oakes, James. *The Oakes Diaries: Business, Politics and the Family in Bury St Edmunds, 1778-1827,* edited by Jane Fiske. 2 vols. Woodbridge: Boydell & Brewer, 1990–1991.

Ó Beaglaioch, C., C. Mac Cuirtin, and A. Mac Cuirtin. *The English-Irish Dictionary*. Paris: Seamus Guerin, 1732.

An Occasional Correspondent. 'Cornwalliana, No. XVI'. *Royal Cornwall Gazette*, 5 May 1804.

'The Official Britannia Coconut Dancers Press Statement - 30th July 2020'. Accessed 3 October 2022. https://www.coconutters.co.uk/the-official-britannia-coconut-dancers-press-statement.

Ogilby, John. *Asia: The First Part Being an Accurate Description of Persia, and the Several Provinces Thereof....* London: Printed by the author, 1673.

An Old Fogy. 'Christmas Visitors [Letter]'. *Derbyshire Times and Chesterfield Herald*, 6 January 1875.

'Old Meg of Herefordshire for a Mayd Marian and Hereford Towne for a Morris Daunce'. In *Records of Early English Drama: Herefordshire, Worcestershire*, edited by David N. Klausner, 125-36 [text], 280-82 [commentary]. Toronto: University of Toronto Press, 1990.

Oldaker, Joe. 'Just Wondering ... for Thirty Years'. *The Morris Ring Circular* 74 (2018): 11–13.

Oldhams, Paul. 'Green Man's Morris and Sword Club: The Final Chapter'. *The Morris Ring Circular* 74 (2018): 7–8.

'On Monday Next, Dec. 31, 1787, Horsemanship...'. In *Collectanea, or, A Collection of Advertisements and Paragraphs from the Newspapers, Relating to Various Subjects. Publick Exhibitions and Places of Amusement*, n.d. Accessed 31 October 2022. https://www.bl.uk/georgian-britain/articles/georgian-entertainment-from-pleasure-gardens-to-blood-sports.

'On the Burlesque Festivals of Former Ages'. *The Gentleman's Magazine: And Historical Chronicle*, October 1821, 320–23.

The Oracle and Daily Advertiser. 'Mrs. Walker's Masked Ball', 29 May 1800.

Ormerod, George. *The History of the County Palatine and City of Chester*, edited by T. Helsby. 2nd ed., revised and enlarged. 3 vols. London: George Routledge and Sons, 1882.

Ossett Observer. 'Choral Society's Concert', 4 March 1876.

Ossett Observer. 'Horbury Feast', 10 June 1876.

Owen, Dorothy M. 'Short Guides to Records: 8. Episcopal Visitation Books'. *History* 49, no. 166 (1964): 185–88.

Owen, Hugh, and John Brickdale Blakeway. *A History of Shrewsbury*. 2 vols. London: Harding, Lepard, 1825.

Owen, John. *A True Copy of the Welch Sermon Preached before the Two Princes, Prince Rupert and Prince Maurice, at Dover*. London: Printed for Thomas Bates ..., 1646.

Owen, Trefor. *North West Morris Dancing: A Selection from Trefor Owen's Collection*. Morris Federation, 1988.

Oxford Chronicle. 'Woodstock', 25 May 1844.

Oxford Chronicle and Reading Gazette. 'Littlemore Asylum Concert', 1 January 1859.

Oxford Chronicle and Reading Gazette. 'Milton-under-Wychwood', 21 March 1863.

Oxford Chronicle and Reading Gazette. 'Morris Dancers', 26 May 1866.

Oxford Journal Illustrated. 'International Morris Dancers', 26 April 1911.

Oxford Times. 'Bampton: Whit Monday', 10 June 1865.

Oxford Times. 'Kirtlington "Lamb Ale" – Lecture by Mr. T. Tindall-Wildridge', 17 February 1902.

Oxfordshire Weekly News. 'Shipton-under-Wychwood: Treat to Aged People', 22 May 1889.

Page, Christopher. *The Guitar in Tudor England*. Cambridge: Cambridge University Press, 2015.

Palmer, Philip. *Some Records of the Churches and Ancient Parish of the Holy and Undivided Trinity, Guildford*. Guildford: Lasham, 1888.

Palmer, William. 'Plough Monday 1933 at Little Downham'. *English Dance and Song* 36, no. 1 (1974): 24–25.

Palsgrave, John. *Lesclarcissement de La Langue Francoyse*. 1530. Scolar press facs. Menston: Scolar Press, 1969.

Parker, Frank. *The Origins and Survival of the Castleton Garland Ceremony [Video]*. 3 vols. Longstone Local History Group, 2019. Accessed 3 October 2022. https://youtu.be/6whBSfWvoYc.

Parker, Val. 'Letter, Reprinted from Rocking Horse'. *Morris Matters* 1, no. 4 (1978): 27.

Parker, Val. 'The Women's Morris Federation – from Start to Finish'. In *The Histories of the Morris in Britain*, edited by Michael Heaney, 279–93. London: English Folk Dance and Song Society & Historical Dance Society, 2018.

Parkinson, John. *Theatrum Botanicum = The Theater of Plants*. London: Printed by Tho. Cotes, 1640.

'Past Squires of the Morris Ring from 1934'. The Morris Ring. Accessed 3 October 2022. https://themorrisring.org/about-mr/history/past-squires.

Pateley Bridge & Nidderdale Herald. 'Harrogate Church Institute', 26 January 1889.

Peacock, Edward. *Ralf Skirlaugh, the Lincolnshire Squire: A Novel*. 3 vols. London: Chapman & Hall, 1870.

Peck, Francis. *New Memoirs of the Life and Poetical Works of Mr John Milton*. London, 1740.

Peck, William. *A Topographical Account of the Isle of Axholme*. 2 vols. Doncaster: Printed for the author, 1815.

The People. 'Twelfth Night in Town and Country', 17 January 1897.

Peover (Cheshire) Carnival 1938 & 1939 [Video], 2020. Accessed 3 October 2022. https://www.youtube.com/watch?v=zyXDgpzCqJw.

Pepys, Samuel. *The Diary of Samuel Pepys: A New and Complete Transcription*, edited by Robert Latham and William Matthews. 11 vols. London: G. Bell, 1970–1983.

'Peterborough Diocesan Records'. Correction book 70 (X 621). Northamptonshire Archives.

Pettitt, Thomas. 'English Folk Drama in the Eighteenth Century: A Defense of the "Revesby Sword Play"'. *Comparative Drama* 15, no. 1 (1981): 3–29.

Peyton, S.A. *The Churchwardens' Presentments in the Oxfordshire Peculiars of Dorchester, Thame, and Banbury*. Oxford: Oxfordshire Record Society, 1928.

Phillips, Edward. *The New World of English Words*. London: Printed for Nath. Brooke, 1658.

Phillips, Edward. *The New World of Words, or, Universal English Dictionary*, edited by John Kersey. 6th ed., Revised. London: Printed for J. Phillips, 1706.

The Pictorial History of the County of Lancashire. London: Routledge, 1844.

'The Pilgrimage to Parnassus'. In *The Three Parnassus Plays*, edited by J.B. Leishman, 93–132. London: Nicholson & Watson, 1949.

Pilling, Julian. 'Failsworth'. NW02910-NW2950. Manchester Morris Men's archives.

Pilling, Julian. 'Foulridge, Interview with Lilian Thornton, 29 April 1964'. NW03200. Manchester Morris Men's archives.

Pilling, Julian. 'Leyland'. NW05320. Manchester Morris Men's archives.

Pilling, Julian. 'Nelson (2)'. NW07570. Manchester Morris Men's archives.

Pilling, Julian. 'Padiham'. NW08180. Manchester Morris Men's archives.

Pilling, Julian. *The Royal Morris of Colne*. Colne: Colne Royal Morris Men, 1971.

Pilling, Julian. 'The Wild Morisco, or The Historical Morris'. *Dolmetsch Historical Dance Society Journal* 1, no. 8 (1978): 15–21.

P[lanché], J.R. 'Summer Merriment'. In *The Every Day Book*, by William Hone, 396–97. London: William Tegg, 1868.

Plot, Robert. *The Natural History of Stafford-shire*. Oxford: Printed at the Theatre, 1686.

The Poll of the Freeholders of Oxfordshire, Taken at the County Court Held in Oxford on the 17th of April, 1754. Oxford: Printed by W. Jackson, 1754.

Polwhele, Richard. *The History of Cornwall*. 3 vols. Falmouth: Cadell and Davies, 1803.

Poole, Robert. 'Samuel Bamford and Middleton Rushbearing'. *Manchester Region History Review* 8 (1994): 14–22.

'Popular Customs and Superstitions in Herefordshire, from Mr Fosbroke's *Aricomensia*'. *The Gentleman's Magazine: And Historical Chronicle* 92 (1822): 220–23.

Porter, Enid. *Cambridgeshire Customs and Folklore*. London: Routledge & Kegan Paul, 1969.

Portsmouth Evening News. 'A Carnival Dispute', 7 November 1889.

Potter, Humphrey Tristram. *A New Dictionary of All the Cant and Flash Languages, Both Ancient and Modern*. [London]: Printed by W. Mackintosh, 1795.

Pratchett, Terry, and Jacqueline Simpson. *The Folklore of Discworld*. London: Corgi, 2009.

Pressey, W.J. 'The Churchwardens' Accounts of West Tarring [Pt 11]'. *Sussex Notes and Queries* 4, no. 3 (1932): 80–85.

Preston, Michael J. 'The Oldest British Folk Play'. *Folklore Forum* 6, no. 3 (1973): 168–74.

Preston, Michael J., and Paul Smith, eds. '*A Petygree of the Plouboys or Modes Dancers Songs*': The Morris Dance at Revesby: A Facsimile of the 1779 Manuscript in the Lincolnshire Archives. Sheffield: NATCECT, 1999.

Preston Chronicle. 'Leyland, Farington & Lostock Hall: The Morris Dancers', 25 July 1891.

Preston Chronicle. 'Leyland, Farington & Lostock Hall: The Morris Dancers', 1 August 1891.

Preston Chronicle. 'Opening of the Dock', 25 June 1892.

Preston Chronicle. 'Band of Hope Festival', 3 September 1892.

Preston Chronicle. [Advertisement], 8 October 1892.

Preston Chronicle. 'Oddfellows' Ball', 18 February 1893.

Preston Chronicle. [Advertisement], 11 March 1893.

Preston Chronicle. 'The Preston Royal Morris Dancers', 11 March 1893.

Preston Chronicle. [Advertisement], 22 April 1893.

'Preston Guild Masquerade'. *The Calcutta Journal of Politics and General Literature* 2, no. 54 (1823): 37–38.

Preston Herald. [Advertisement], 9 July 1884.

Preston Herald. 'Royal Oak Day: May Festival at Leyland', 31 May 1890.

Preston Herald. 'Rose Festival in Chorley', 11 June 1890.

Preston Herald. 'The Chorley Rose Festival', 10 June 1891.

Preston Herald. 'Penwortham Banquet', 27 July 1892.

Preston Herald. 'The Preston Morris Dancers', 24 September 1892.

Preston Herald. 'Football Notes and Notions', 12 October 1892.

Preston Herald. 'Friendly Societies' Ball', 19 October 1892.

Preston Herald. [Advertisement], 24 December 1892.

Preston Herald. 'St. Thomas's Girls' School', 14 January 1893.

Preston Herald. 'The Prince's Theatre', 22 February 1893.

Preston Herald. 'Entertainment at St. Wilfrid's School', 11 March 1893.

Preston Herald. 'Silver Jubilee of the Rev. N.C. Papall, S.J., of Preston', 29 April 1893.

Preston Herald. 'Preston Rose Festival', 9 August 1893.

Preston Herald. 'Lifeboat Saturday in Preston', 13 September 1893.

Preston Herald. 'Fulwood Rangers v. Deepdale Morris Dancers', 8 November 1893.

Preston Herald. 'The Preston Morris Dancers', 20 June 1896.

Preston Herald. 'Nelson: Lifeboat Saturday', 1 July 1896.

Price, F.D. 'Stow, Campden and Winchcombe Deaneries in 1576, Part VIII'. *Evesham Journal*, 19 February 1938.

Prior, Mary. 'The Accounts of Thomas West of Wallingford, a Sixteenth-century Trader on the Thames'. *Oxoniensia* 46 (1981): 73–93.

Procession & Rose Queen Ceremony c1908 [Video]. NW Film Archive, NWFA 5953. Accessed 3 October 2022. https://vimeo.com/568866958.

Prynne, William. *The Antipathie of the English Lordly Prelacie, Both to Regall Monarchy, and Civill Unity*. London: Printed ... for Michael Sparke senior, 1641.

Prynne, William. *Histrio-mastix*. London: Printed by E.A., 1633.

Prynne, William. *A Looking-glasse for All Lordly Prelates*. [London?], 1636.

Prynne, William. *A Quench-coale, or, A Briefe Disquisition and Inquirie, in What Place of the Church or Chancell the Lords-table Ought to Be Situated, Especially When the Sacrament Is Administered?* [Amsterdam: Richt Right Press], 1637.

Prynne, William. *The Unbishoping of Timothy and Titus, or, A Briefe Elaborate Discourse, Proving Timothy to Be No Bishop...by a Well Wisher to God's Truth and People* [signing himself A.B.C. London?: Printed by J.F. Stam], 1636.

Prynne, William, and Henry Burton. *The Lord's Day, the Sabbath Day*. 2. ed, much enlarged. Amsterdam: J.F. Stam, 1636.

Public advertiser. 'Masquerade Intelligence', 4 February 1788.

Public advertiser. 'Vauxhall Masquerade', 6 June 1791.

Pugh, R.B., and Elizabeth Crittall, eds. 'Parliamentary History 1689-1832'. In *A History of the County of Wiltshire: Volume 5*, 195–230. London: Victoria County History. Accessed 3 October 2022. http://www.british-history.ac.uk/vch/wilts/vol5/pp195-230.

Purefoy, Elizabeth, and Henry Purefoy. *Purefoy Letters 1735-1753*, edited by G. Eland. London: Sidgwick & Jackson, 1931.

Purvis, J.S., ed. *Tudor Parish Documents of the Diocese of York: A Selection*. Cambridge: University Press, 1948.

R., W. 'Morris Dancers'. *Notes and Queries* 6th series, 5, no. 114 (1882): 176.

Rablet, Richard. *Cobbes Prophecies*. London: For private circulation, 1890.

Ralph, James. *The Touch-stone, or, Historical, Critical, Political, Philosophical, and Theological Essays on the Reigning Diversions of the Town*. London: Printed and sold by the booksellers of London and Westminster, 1728.

Ramsay, Laurence. *The Practise of the Divell*. London: for Timothie Rider, 1577.

Randolph, Thomas. 'Amyntas, or, The Impossible Dowry'. In *The Poems and Amyntas of Thomas Randolph*, edited by John Jay Parry. New Haven: Yale University Press, 1917.

Randolph, Thomas. 'The Muses' Looking-glass'. In *Poetical and Dramatic Works of Thomas Randolph, of Trinity College, Cambridge*, edited by William Carew Hazlitt, 1:173–266. London: Reeves and Turner, 1875.

Randolph, Thomas. *A Pleasant Comedie, Entituled Hey for Honesty, down with Knavery*, translated out of Aristophanes His Plutus. London, 1651.

Ratcliff, S.C., and H.C. Johnson, eds. *Quarter Sessions Order Book, Easter 1650-Epiphany 1657*. Warwick County Records 3. Warwick: L. Edgar Stephens, 1937.

Ratcliffe, Thomas. 'Old Time Country Dances'. *Nottinghamshire Guardian*, 21 February 1914.

Rawnsley, Eleanor F. *The Rushbearing in Grasmere and Ambleside*. [Kendal: Titus Wilson], 1953.

Reading Standard. [News item], 15 July 1914.

Read's Weekly Journal, or, British Gazetteer. 'Northampton June 7', 12 June 1731.

A Real Lover of Old English Pastimes. 'Dover's Meeting – Whitsun Sports'. *The Mirror of Literature, Amusement, and Instruction* 7, no. 199 (10 June 1826): 354–55.

Recreation for Ingenious Head-peeces. London: Printed by M. Simmons, 1650.

The Referee. 'North Woolwich Gardens [Advertisement]', 6 September 1880.

Rehin, George F. 'Blackface Street Minstrels in Victorian London and Its Resorts: Popular Culture and Its Racial Connotations as Revealed in Polite Opinion'. *The Journal of Popular Culture* 15, no. 1 (1981): 19–38.

[Report]. *The Gentleman's Magazine: And Historical Chronicle* 83 (June 1813): 525.

Report on Manuscripts in Various Collections. 8 vols. London: H.M.S.O, 1901–1914.

Revesby. 'General Accounts and Inventory for Revesby (1723-1725)'. U1590/A49/1. Kent Archives and Local History.

Reynolds's Weekly News. 'Cremorne Gardens', 8 September 1850.

Rhodes, Ebenezer. *Peak Scenery*. London: Longman Hurst, Rees, Orme, Brown, and Green, 1824.

Rich, Barnabe. *The Honestie of This Age, Proving by Good Circumstance That the World Was Never Honest till Now*, edited by Peter Cunningham. Early English Poetry, Ballads, and Popular Literature of the Middle Ages. London: Percy Society, 1844.

Rich, Barnabe. *The Irish Hubbub or, The English Hue and Crie*. London: Printed for John Marriot, 1618.

Rich, Barnabe. *Opinion Diefied* [sic]. London: Printed [by Thomas Dawson] for Thomas Adams, 1613.

'Richard Walker'. Centre for the Study of the Legacies of British Slavery. Accessed 3 October 2022. http://wwwdepts-live.ucl.ac.uk/lbs/person/view/2146635635.

Rickard, R.L., ed. *The Progress Notes of Warden Woodward Round the Oxfordshire Estates of New College, Oxford, 1659-1675*. Oxford: Oxfordshire Record Society, 1945.

Riden, Philip. *Household Accounts of William Cavendish, Lord Cavendish of Hardwick, 1597-1607*. 3 vols. Derbyshire Record Society 40–42. Chesterfield: Derbyshire Record Society, 2016.

Rider, John. *Bibliotheca Scholastica: A Double Dictionarie*. [Oxford]: Printed by Joseph Barnes, 1589.

Ridings, Elijah. 'Newton Heath Wakes'. In *Pictures of Life*, by Elijah Ridings, 135–44, 167–68. Manchester: Cathrall & Beresford, 1850.

Ritson, Joseph. *Robin Hood: A Collection of All the Ancient Poems, Songs and Ballads, Now Extant, Relative to That Celebrated English Outlaw*. 2nd ed. 2 vols. London: W. Pickering, 1832.

Rivers, Flo. 'Morris Dancing'. *Notes and Queries* 6th series, 9, no. 214 (1884): 90.

'Robert Sumner, "England and Wales Census, 1861"'. Derbyshire RG09/2545/28, p. 15. 1861 census. Accessed 3 October 2022. https://www.familysearch.org/ark:/61903/1:1:M7NF-N62.

Robertson, Jean, and D.J. Gordon, eds. *Calendar of Dramatic Records in the Books of the Livery Companies of London, 1485-1640*. Malone Society Collections 3. Oxford: Malone Society, 1954.

Robertson, William. *Phraseologia Generalis = A Full, Large, and General Phrase Book*. Cambridge: Printed by John Hayes and are to be sold by George Sawbridge, 1681.

Robinson, Charles J. *A History of the Mansions and Manors of Herefordshire*. London: Longmans, 1873.

Robinson, Joseph Barlow. *Derbyshire Gatherings*. London: J.R. Smith, 1866.

Rochdale Observer. 'Heywood Wakes', 8 August 1868.

Rochdale Observer. 'Rochdale Infirmary Gala', 26 July 1893.

Rochefort, César de. *The History of the Caribby-Islands*. London: Printed by J.M., 1666.

Rocke, Joan. 'The Mirror on the Plain'. *Cheshire Life*, November 1985, 36–37.

Roderick, John. *Y Geirlyfr Saesneg a Chymraeg*. Yn y Mwythig [Shrewsbury]: Argraphwyd gan Thomas Dusston, 1737.

Rogers, Pat. 'Johnson, Samuel (1709–1784), Author and Lexicographer'. Oxford Dictionary of National Biography. Accessed 3 October 2022. https://doi.org/10.1093/ref:odnb/14918.

Rogers, Richard. *Seven Treatises, Containing Such Direction as Is Gathered out of the Holie Scriptures.* London: F. Kyngston for T. Man, and R. Dexter, 1603.

Romburgh, Sophie van. 'Junius [Du Jon], Franciscus [Francis] (1591–1677), Philologist and Writer on Art'. Oxford Dictionary of National Biography. Accessed 3 October 2022. https://doi.org/10.1093/ref:odnb/15167.

Roper, W.O. 'The Missing History of Warton, by John Lucas'. *Transactions of the Historic Society of Lancashire & Cheshire* 38 (1886): 159–69.

Ross, Bob. 'Joseph Needham and the Foundation of the Morris Ring'. *The Morris Dancer* 3, no. 10 (2003): 299–305.

Ross, Frederick, Richard Stead, and Thomas Holderness. *A Glossary of Words Used in Holderness in the East-riding of Yorkshire.* London: Trübner, 1877. Accessed 3 October 2022. https://hdl.handle.net/2027/nnc1.cu11686308.

Roud, Steve. *The English Year.* London: Penguin, 2006.

Rowell, George Augustus. 'Notes on Some Old-Fashioned English Customs: The Mummers; the Morris-Dancers; Whitsun-Ales; Lamb-Ales'. *Folklore Journal* 4, no. 2 (1886): 97–109.

Roy, Donald. 'Planché, James Robinson (1796–1880), Playwright and Herald'. *Oxford Dictionary of National Biography.* Accessed 3 October 2022. https://doi.org/10.1093/ref:odnb/22351.

Rudder, Samuel. *A New History of Gloucestershire.* Cirencester: Printed by Samuel Rudder, 1779.

Rugby Advertiser. '"Plough Boys" in Trouble', 21 January 1865.

Rugby Advertiser. 'The Brinklow Morris Dancers', 28 January 1865.

Rugg, Thomas. *The Diurnal of Thomas Rugg, 1659-1661*, edited by William L. Sachse. Camden Third Series 91. London: Royal Historical Society, 1961.

The Run-Awyaes [sic] *Answer to a Booke Called, A Rodde for Runne-Awayes.* [London: A. Mathewes], 1625.

Russell, Ewart. [Notes]. *The Morris Dancer* [1], no. 3 (1979): 19–20.

Rycaut, Paul. *The Present State of the Ottoman Empire Containing the Maxims of the Turkish Politie.* London: Printed for John Starkey and Henry Brome, 1668.

S., F. '176: Morrice Dancing'. *Shropshire Notes and Queries*, 29 May 1885, 53–54.

S., H.R. 'Presentments, 1578'. *Northamptonshire Notes and Queries* 1 (1884): 57.

S., W. 'London Correspondence'. *Diss Express*, 7 May 1886.

Sabol, Andrew J., ed. 'The French Morris'. In *Four Hundred Songs and Dances of the Stuart Masque*, 237. Providence, R.I.: Brown University Press, 1978.

Sale, Jane. 'The Dixton Paintings'. *Gloucestershire History* 6 (1992): 12–16.

Salisbury, Jesse. *A Glossary of Words and Phrases Used in S.E. Worcestershire.* London: J. Salisbury, 1893.

Salisbury and Winchester Journal. [News Item], 13 October 1746.

Salisbury and Winchester Journal. 'Celebration of Peace', 31 May 1856.

Salisbury and Winchester Journal. 'Laverstock', 2 July 1887 [a].

Salisbury and Winchester Journal. 'Wishford', 2 July 1887 [b].

Salisbury and Winchester Journal. 'Jubilee Celebrations', 26 June 1897.

The Salisbury Times. 'Jubilee Gifts', 4 June 1887.

The Salisbury Times. 'Order of Procession', 18 June 1887.

The Salisbury Times. 'Royal Celebrations', 28 July 1893.

Salopian and West Midlands Monthly Illustrated Journal, December 1879. [Cutting supplied to the author by Gordon Ashman].

Sampson, William. *Vow Breaker, or, The Fayre Maide of Clifton*, edited by Hans Wallrath. Louvain: Uystpruyst, 1914.

'Samuel Harrison [b. 1821], "England and Wales Census, 1861"'. Cheshire RG09/2557/25/43. 1861 census. Accessed 3 October 2022. https://www.familysearch.org/ark:/61903/1:1:M7JQ-DMM.

'Samuel Harrison [b. 1822], "England and Wales Census, 1861"'. Cheshire RG09/2557/137/28. 1861 census. Accessed 3 October 2022. https://www.familysearch.org/ark:/61903/1:1:M7JQ-9JQ.

Sanderson, Robert, ed. 'De Warranto Speciale pro Georgio Duci Buckingham et Aliis'. In *Foedera, Conventiones, Literae et Cujuscunque Generis Acta Publica, Inter Reges Angliae, et Alios Quosvis Imperatores ... Ab Anno 1101*, 18:236–40. Londini: Per J. Tonson, 1704.

S[andys], W[illiam]. 'Christmas Drama of St. George'. *The Gentleman's Magazine: And Historical Chronicle* 100 (1830): 505–06.

Sanson, Nicholas. *Cosmography and Geography in Two Parts*. London: Printed by S. Roycroft, 1682.

Sanuto, Marino. *I Diarii di Marino Sanuto: (MCCCCXCVI-MDXXXIII) dall'Autografo Marciano Ital. cl. VII codd. CDXIX-CDLXXVII*. 58 vols. Venezia: F. Visentini, 1879-1903.

Schofield, Derek. *All Step Up: The History of the Manley Morris Dancers*. [Wistaston: The author], 2022.

Schofield, Derek. 'A Black and White Issue' [and responses]. *EDS* 67, no. 2 (2005): 12–14.

Schofield, Derek. 'A Different Sort of Revival: The Life and Times of the Manley Morris Dancers'. In *The Histories of the Morris in Britain*, edited by Michael Heaney, 203–14. London: English Folk Dance and Song Society & Historical Dance Society, 2018.

Schofield, Derek. 'Which Past? The Influences of Tradition and Revival on the North-West Morris'. In *Morris: The Legacy of the Past: Proceedings of a One Day Conference on Morris Dancing, Birmingham, 20th April, 1996*, 95–109. [London]: The Morris Ring, the Morris Federation, and Open Morris, 1996.

Schofield, R. Kenworthy. 'Morris Dances from Bledington'. *Journal of the English Folk Dance and Song Society* 1, no. 3 (1934): 147–51.

Schofield, R. Kenworthy. 'Morris Dances from Field Town'. *Journal of the English Folk Dance Society* 2nd series, 2 (1928): 22–28.

Schofield, R. Kenworthy. 'Morris Dances from Longborough'. *Journal of the English Folk Dance Society* 2nd series, 3 (1930): 51–57.

Scott, Agnes. [Letter]. *West Cumberland Times*, 28 April 1894.

'Scraps from a Notebook'. *Gentleman's Magazine* 100, no. 2 (July 1830): 23–25.

'The Second Part of the Return from Parnassus, or, The Scourge of Simony'. In *The Three Parnassus Plays*, edited by J.B. Leishman, 215–367. London: Nicholson & Watson, 1949.

'A Sentimental Journey [by] a Lady' [continuation]. *The Lady's Magazine, or, Entertaining Companion for the Fair Sex, Appropriated Solely to Their Use and Amusement* 3, no. 3 (March 1772): 97–104.

Settle, Elkanah. *The Empress of Morocco: A Tragedy with Sculptures, as It Is Acted at the Duke's Theatre*. London: Printed for William Cadema, 1673.

Seward, Anna. *Letters of Anna Seward, Written between the Years 1784 And 1807*. 6 vols. Edinburgh: Archibald Constable, 1811.

Shakespeare, William. *King Henry V*, edited by J. H. Walter. Arden Edition of the Works of William Shakespeare. London: Methuen, 1954.

Shakespeare, William. *The Second Part of King Henry VI*, edited by A.S. Cairncross. 3rd ed. Arden Edition of the Works of William Shakespeare. London: Methuen, 1957.

Shakespeare, William. *The Plays of William Shakespeare*, edited by Samuel Johnson. 8 vols. London: Printed for J. and R. Tonson &c., 1765.

Sharp, Cecil J. *The Morris Book, Part IV*. London: Novello, 1911.

Sharp, Cecil J. *The Sword Dances of Northern England, Together with the Horn Dance of Abbots Bromley*. 3 vols. London: Novello, 1912–1913.

Sharp, Cecil J. 'Winster Morris Dance and Processional'. In *Morris Dance Tunes: Set VI*, Revised ed., 2–3. London: Novello, 1912.

Sharp, Cecil J., and George Butterworth. *The Morris Book, Part V*. London: Novello, 1913.

Sharp, Cecil J., and Herbert C. MacIlwaine. *The Morris Book, Part I*. London: Novello, 1907.

Sharp, Cecil J., and Herbert C. MacIlwaine. *The Morris Book, Part I*. 2nd ed. London: Novello, 1912.

Sharp, Cecil J., and Herbert C. MacIlwaine. *The Morris Book, Part II*. London: Novello, 1909.

Sharp, Cecil J., and Herbert C. MacIlwaine. *The Morris Book, Part III*. London: Novello, 1910.

Sharp, Cecil J., and Herbert C. MacIlwaine. *The Morris Book, Part III*. 2nd ed. London: Novello, 1924.

'Sharp MSS, Ascott under Wychwood Morris'. Folk Dance Notes, vol. 2, pp. 41-45. Vaughan Williams Memorial Library. Accessed 3 October 2022. https://www.vwml.org/record/CJS2/11/2/41.

'Sharp MSS, Bidford Morris Tunes'. Folk Tunes, 947-954. Vaughan Williams Memorial Library. Accessed 3 October 2022. https://www.vwml.org/record/CJS2/10/947.

'Sharp MSS, Brimfield, Herefordshire'. Folk Dance Notes, vol. 1, p. 95. Vaughan Williams Memorial Library. Accessed 3 October 2022. https://www.vwml.org/record/CJS2/11/1/95.

'Sharp MSS, Cliffords Mesne Morris'. Folk Dance Notes, vol. 1, p. 188. Vaughan Williams Memorial Library. Accessed 3 October 2022. https://www.vwml.org/record/CJS2/11/1/188.

'Sharp MSS, Correspondence with Alice Bertha Gomme, 28 April 1910'. Sharp correspondence, CJS1/12/7/6/20. Vaughan Williams Memorial

Library. Accessed 3 October 2022. https://www.vwml.org/record/CJS1/12/7/6/20.

'Sharp MSS, Ducklington Morris'. Folk Dance Notes, vol. 1, pp. 144-147. Vaughan Williams Memorial Library. Accessed 3 October 2022. https://www.vwml.org/record/CJS2/11/1/144.

'Sharp MSS, Extracts from William Kimber's Letters'. Folk Dance Notes, vol. 1, p. 35. Vaughan Williams Memorial Library. Accessed 25 3 October 2022. https://www.vwml.org/record/CJS2/11/1/34.

'Sharp MSS, Finstock Morris'. Folk Dance Notes, vol. 2, pp. 129-130. Vaughan Williams Memorial Library. Accessed 3 October 2022. https://www.vwml.org/record/CJS2/11/2/129.

'Sharp MSS, Ilmington'. Folk Dance Notes, vol. 1, p. 187. Vaughan Williams Memorial Library. Accessed 3 October 2022. https://www.vwml.org/record/CJS2/11/1/187.

'Sharp MSS, Longhope'. Folk Dance Notes, vol. 1, p. 85. Vaughan Williams Memorial Library. Accessed 3 October 2022. https://www.vwml.org/record/CJS2/11/1/85a.

'Sharp MSS, [Mayhill]'. Folk Dance Notes, vol. 1, pp. 86-87. Vaughan Williams Memorial Library. Accessed 3 October 2022. https://www.vwml.org/record/CJS2/11/1/86.

'Sharp MSS, Minster Lovell Morris'. Folk Dance Notes, vol. 2, pp. 49-50. Vaughan Williams Memorial Library. Accessed 3 October 2022. https://www.vwml.org/record/CJS2/11/2/49.

'Sharp MSS, Mr Horne, "Morris Dancing", Transcript'. Folk Dance Notes, vol. 1, pp. 43-52. Vaughan Williams Memorial Library. Accessed 3 October 2022. https://www.vwml.org/record/CJS2/11/1/43.

'Sharp MSS, North Leigh Morris'. Folk Dance Notes, vol. 2, p. 126. Vaughan Williams Memorial Library. Accessed 3 October 2022. https://www.vwml.org/record/CJS2/11/2/126.

'Sharp MSS, Peopleton, Worcestershire'. Folk Dance Notes, vol. 1, pp. 90-91. Vaughan Williams Memorial Library. Accessed 3 October 2022. https://www.vwml.org/record/CJS2/11/1/90.

'Sharp MSS, Plough Monday'. Folk Dance Notes, vol. 2, pp. 39-40. Vaughan Williams Memorial Library. Accessed 3 October 2022. https://www.vwml.org/record/CJS2/11/2/39.

'Sharp MSS, Ruardean'. Folk Dance Notes, vol. 1, pp. 88-89. Vaughan Williams Memorial Library. Accessed 3 October 2022. https://www.vwml.org/record/CJS2/11/1/88.

'Sharp MSS, Spelsbury Morris and Chadlington Morris'. Folk Dance Notes, vol. 2, pp. 47. Vaughan Williams Memorial Library. Accessed 3 October 2022. https://www.vwml.org/record/CJS2/11/2/47.

'Sharp MSS, Weobley Morris Dance'. Folk words, p. 2193. Vaughan Williams Memorial Library. Accessed 3 October 2022. https://www.vwml.org/record/CJS2/9/2193.

Sharpe, J.A. 'Crime and Delinquency in an Essex Parish 1600-1640'. In Crime in England 1550-1800, edited by J.S. Cockburn, 90–109. London: Methuen, 1977.

Sharpe, Lewis. The Noble Stranger, as It Was Acted at the Private House in Salisbury Court, by Her Majesties Servants. London: Printed by I.O. for James Becket, 1640.

Shaw, Stebbing. History and Antiquities of Staffordshire. 2 vols. London: J. Nichols, 1798–1801.

The Sheffield & Rotherham Independent. 'Tideswell', 28 June 1845.

The Sheffield & Rotherham Independent. 'The Sheffield Christmas of Bygone Days', 21 December 1872.

Sheffield Daily Telegraph. [Advertisement], 8 July 1858.

Sheffield Daily Telegraph. 'Majority of the Duke of Norfolk', 30 December 1868.

Sheffield Daily Telegraph. 'Bakewell Flower Show', 30 August 1889.

Sheffield Independent. 'Sheffield Guardians' Meeting', 2 January 1862.

Sheffield Independent. 'Buxton Well Dressing', 19 June 1866.

Sheffield Independent. 'Bakewell Floral and Horticultural Society', 13 August 1874.

Sheffield Independent. 'Well Dressing Festival at Buxton', 26 June 1891.

Sherborne Mercury. 'Observance of May Day at Sherborne', 7 May 1861.

Sheridan, Thomas. A General Dictionary of the English Language. London: Printed [by William Strahan], 1780.

Shields Daily News. [News Item], 1 May 1894.

Shirley, James. 'The Bird in a Cage'. In The Dramatic Works and Poems of James Shirley, edited by William Gifford, 365–455. London: John Murray, 1833.

Shirley, James. *The Lady of Pleasure*, edited by Ronald Huebert. Manchester: Manchester University Press, 1986.

Shoreditch Observer. 'Royal Pavilion Gardens [Advertisement]', 18 June 1859.

Shrewsbury Chronicle. 'Christmas Minstrelsy', 31 December 1886.

Shuttleworth, Sir James Phillip Kay-. *Scarsdale, or, Life on the Lancashire and Yorkshire Border Thirty Years Ago.* 3 vols. London: Smith, Elder, 1860.

Sigma. 'Topical Notes'. *Buckinghamshire Herald*, 9 May 1891.

Silhill. 'Local Notes and Queries, [1448]: Morris Dancers'. *Birmingham Weekly Post*, 3 May 1884.

Silurian Morris. 'History'. Accessed 3 October 2022. http://www.silurianmorris.org.uk/history.

Simons, Matthew. 'From Country Gardens to British Festivals: The Morris Dance Revival, 1886-1951'. In *The Routledge Companion to English Folk Performance*, edited by Peter Harrop and Steve Roud, 225-47. London: Routledge, 2021.

Simons, Matthew. 'Morris Men: Dancing Englishness, c. 1905-1951'. Doctoral dissertation, De Montfort University, 2019. Accessed 3 October 2022. https://dora.dmu.ac.uk/bitstream/handle/2086/18685/SIMONS_DOCTORALTHESIS.pdf.

Simons, Matthew. '"Pilgrimages to Holy Places": The Travelling Morrice, 1924-1939'. In *The Histories of the Morris in Britain*, edited by Michael Heaney, 133–49. London: English Folk Dance and Song Society & Historical Dance Society, 2018.

Sisson, Charles Jasper. *Lost Plays of Shakespeare's Age.* Cambridge: University Press, 1936.

Slack, Paul. *The English Poor Law, 1531-1782.* Studies in Economic and Social History. Basingstoke: Macmillan Education, 1990.

Smith, Francis. *Clod-Pate's Ghost, or, A Dialogue between Justice Clod-Pate and His (Quondam) Clerk Honest Tom Ticklefoot.* [London], 1679.

Smith, Georgina. 'Winster Morris Dance: The Sources of an Oikotype'. *Traditional Dance* 1 (1982): 93–108.

Smith, J.R. 'The Suppression of "Pestiferous Dancing" in Essex'. *English Dance and Song* 36, no. 1 (1974): 9–11.

Smith, Roy. 'Morris History'. Lancashire Folk. Accessed 3 October 2022. https://www.lancashirefolk.co.uk/morris-history.

Snooke, William. 'The Diary of William Snooke, The Manor House, Bourton-on-the-Water, 1774, 1775, transcribed by J. Homfray'. GAL/52319GS, GAL/G2/52322GS. Gloucestershire Archives.

Somerset, Alan, ed. *Records of Early English Drama: Shropshire.* Toronto: University of Toronto Press, 1994.

Soriano Fuertes, Mariano. *Historia de la Música Española: Desde la Venida de los Fenicios hasta el Año de 1850.* 4 vols. Madrid: Martin y Salazar, 1855.

'Southampton Book of Fines'. SC5/3/1. Southampton Archives. (In personal communication to the author from T. James, 27 January 1986).

Speaight, George. 'Powell, Martin (d. in or before 1725), Puppet-showman'. Oxford Dictionary of National Biography. Accessed 3 October 2022. https://doi.org/10.1093/ref:odnb/22656.

The Spectator. [Advertisement], 7 August 1712.

Spelman, Sir Henry. *Vox Graculi, or, Jacke Dawes Prognostication.* London: By J. H[aviland and E. Allde?] for Nathaniell Butler, 1622.

Spencer, Robert, ed. 'The Moris'. In *The Mynshall Lute Book*, Facs., f. 8. Leeds: Boethius Press, 1975.

Spencer, Robert, ed. 'Stanes Morris'. In *The Trumbull Lute Book*, Facs., f. 9v. Clarabricken: Boethius Press, 1980.

Spicer, John. *The Sale of Salt, or, The Seasoning of Soules.* London: Printed by Nicholas Okes, 1611.

Spicer, Katy. 'Facing up to a Dancing Debate'. *EDS* 78, no. 4 (2016): 14–14.

'Squire Eddie Worrall Reflects on the ARM'. The Morris Ring. Accessed 3 October 2022. https://themorrisring.org/article/squire-eddie-worrall-reflects-arm.

The St. James's Chronicle. [Letter], 9 January 1768.

Stabel, Peter. 'Guilds in Late Medieval Flanders: Myths and Realities of Guild Life in an Export-Oriented Environment'. *Journal of Medieval History* 30, no. 2 (2004): 187–212.

Staffordshire Advertiser. 'Lichfield "Greenhill Bower"', 20 May 1837.

Staffordshire Advertiser. 'Lichfield Greenhill Bower [Advertisement]', 12 May 1849.

Staffordshire Advertiser. 'Trade of the District', 7 August 1858.

Staffordshire Advertiser. 'Lichfield Greenhill Bower', 2 June 1860.

Staffordshire Advertiser. 'Lichfield: The Greenhill Bower', 14 June 1862.

Staffordshire Sentinel and Commercial & General Advertiser. [Advertisement], 28 July 1855.

Staffordshire Sentinel and Commercial & General Advertiser. 'Grand Temperance Gala at Macclesfield', 11 August 1855.

Staffordshire Sentinel and Commercial & General Advertiser. 'The Anniversary of the Public Park at Macclesfield', 6 October 1855.

The Stage. [Advertisement], 19 September 1890.

Stamford Mercury. [News Item], 10 November 1820.

Stamford Mercury. [News Item], 30 December 1831.

Stamford Mercury. 'Boston Vauxhall', 9 June 1848.

Stamford Mercury. 'Morris Dancers at Church', 26 December 1862.

Stamford Mercury. 'Kesteven Police', 8 January 1864.

Stamford Mercury. 'Grand Gala', 10 June 1864.

Stamford Mercury. 'The Cattle Plague v Morris Dancers', 5 January 1866.

Stamford Mercury. 'Caistor', 4 January 1878.

Stamford Mercury. [News Item], 23 January 1880.

Stamford Mercury. 'Brigg Petty Sessions', 14 January 1881.

Stamford Mercury. 'Spilsby', 5 January 1883.

Stamford Mercury. 'Not Entitled to Wear Uniform', 11 December 1896.

The Standard. 'Royal Surrey Zoological Gardens', 17 May 1853.

The Standard. 'Easter Amusements – the Crystal Palace', 6 April 1858.

The Standard. 'Crystal Palace – Whitsuntide Holiday Amusements', 25 May 1858.

The Standard. [Review], 27 December 1860.

'Stanes Morris'. In *The English Dancing Master*, 87. London: Printed by Thomas Harper, and are to be sold by John Playford, 1651.

Stapleton, Mrs Bryan. *Three Oxfordshire Parishes.* Oxford: Clarendon Press, 1893.

The Star. [News Item], 9 August 1792.

Stevenson, Geo. Jno. 'Nottinghamshire Centenarians'. *Derbyshire Courier*, 12 January 1878.

'Stevington School Logbook, 1864-1881'. SDStevington3/1. Bedfordshire Archives.

Stockport Advertiser. [News Item], 7 October 1836.

Stockport Advertiser. [News Item], 6 October 1837.

'Stockport Premier Morris Dance'. NW09620-NW09640. Manchester Morris Men's archives.

Stockwood, John. 'A Sermon Preached at Paules Crosse on Barthelmew Day, Being the 24 of August 1578'. In *Harrison's Description of England in Shakspere's Youth*, edited by Frederick J. Furnivall, 4:327–39. London: Trübner; Chatto & Windus, 1877.

Stokes, James, ed. *Records of Early English Drama: Lincolnshire.* London: British Library, 2009.

Stokes, James, ed. *Records of Early English Drama: Somerset.* Toronto: University of Toronto Press, 1996.

Stokes, James. 'The Wells Cordwainers' Show: New Evidence Concerning Guild Entertainment in Somerset'. *Comparative Drama* 19, no. 4 (1985/86): 332–46.

Stokes, James. 'The Wells Shows of 1607'. In *Festive Drama: Papers from the Sixth Triennial Colloquium of the International Society for the Study of Medieval Theatre, Lancaster, 13-19 July, 1989*, edited by Meg Twycross, 132–56. Cambridge: D.S. Brewer, 1996.

Stokes, James. 'Women and Mimesis in Medieval and Renaissance Somerset (and Beyond)'. *Comparative Drama* 27, no. 2 (1993): 176–96.

Stokoe, John. 'Notes on the Sword Dancers' Song and Interlude'. *Monthly Chronicle of North-country Lore and Legend* 1 (1887): 462–65.

Stone, Percy G. 'The Ledger Book of Newport, I.W.,1567-1799 [Part 1]'. *The Antiquary* 48 (1912): 178–85.

Stone, Percy G. 'The Ledger Book of Newport, I.W.,1567-1799 [Part 2]'. *The Antiquary* 48 (1912): 211–18.

Stooks, Charles Drummond. *A History of Crondall and Yateley.* Winchester: Warren and Son, 1905.

Stow, John. *A Survey of London*, edited by Charles Lethbridge Kingsford. British History Online. Oxford: Clarendon Press, 1908. Accessed 3 October 2022. https://www.british-history.ac.uk/no-series/survey-of-london-stow/1603/pp99-104.

'Stowe MSS, Abstract of Monthly Accounts, 1842, 1843, 1844'. MS STG Accounts, box 196. Huntington Library.

'Stowe MSS, Bills for the Dresses for the Stowe Mores Dancer [*sic*], 1844 September 10'. MS STG Accounts, box 150. Huntington Library.

'Stowe MSS, [Buckingham Election Accounts 1741]'. MS STG Elections, Box 1, Folder 4. Huntington Library.

'Stowe MSS, Letter from Joseph Parrott to Henry Beauchamp, 13 May 1782'. MS STG Correspondence Box 225, Folder 17. Huntington Library.

'Stowe MSS, Letter from Richard Grenville, 2nd Duke of Buckingham and Chandos, to Mary Grenville, Duchess of Buckingham and Chandos, 18 July 1844'. MS STG Correspondence box 56, folder 10. Huntington Library.

'Stowe MSS, Payments by J. Poole, 1817-1821'. MS ST Volume 419. Huntington Library.

'Stowe MSS, Petition to 3rd Bart. to Support the R[ev]ival of the Ancient Custom of a Whisson Ale'. MS STTM Box 5, Folder 8. Huntington Library.

'Stowe MSS, Richard Temple, 2nd Earl Temple, Accounts 1732-1779'. MS ST Volume 164. Huntington Library.

'Stowe MSS, Richard Temple, 3rd Bart., Day Book 1680-1684'. MS ST Volume 175. Huntington Library.

'Stowe MSS, Richard Temple, 3rd Bart., Ledger Book 1677-1688'. MS ST Volume 152. Huntington Library.

'Stowe MSS, Richard Temple, 3rd Bart., Money Received and Payments Made 1720-1723'. MS ST Volume 162. Huntington Library.

'Stowe MSS, Stowe Household Accounts 1779-1818'. MS STG accounts box 146, bundle for 1790-1799. Huntington Library.

Stratford-upon-Avon. 'Chamberlains' Accounts, 1701-1730'. BRU/4/6. Shakespeare Birthplace Trust Record Archives.

Stratford-upon-Avon. 'Chamberlains' Accounts, 1730-1750'. BRU/4/7. Shakespeare Birthplace Trust Record Archives.

Streitberger, W.R. *Court Revels, 1485-1559*. Studies in Early English Drama 3. Toronto: University of Toronto Press, 1994.

Stringfellow, Garry. *Rushbearing & Rush Strewing in Churches across the Northern Counties*. Hebden Bridge: Northern Earth, 2018.

Stroud Journal. 'Dean Forest', 3 June 1871.

Strutt, Joseph. *Glig-gamena Angel-ðeod, or, The Sports and Pastimes of the People of England*. London: J. White, 1801.

Strutt, Joseph. *Queenhoo-hall: A Romance, and Ancient Times: A Drama*. 4 vols. Edinburgh: John Murray, 1808.

Stubbes, Philip. *Philip Stubbes's Anatomy of the Abuses in England in Shakspere's Youth, A.D. 1583*, edited by Frederick James Furnivall. 2 vols. London: N. Trübner, 1877.

The Suffolk Chronicle, or, Weekly General advertiser & County Express. [News Item], 6 July 1820.

Sun. 'Fete at Frogmore', 21 May 1795.

Sunday Observance Act 1625, Pub. L. No. 1 Car I c 1. Accessed 3 October 2022. https://en.wikisource.org/wiki/Sunday_Observance_Act_1625.

Surrey Advertiser. 'Chertsey Literary and Scientific Institution: The Fourth Grand Annual Rural Fete', 9 July 1870.

Sutcliffe, David. 'Bennett, Sam'. Cecil Sharp's People. Accessed 3 October 2022. https://cecilsharpspeople.org.uk/bennett-sam.html.

Sutcliffe, David. 'Margesson, Lady Isabel'. Cecil Sharp's People. Accessed 3 October 2022. https://cecilsharpspeople.org.uk/margesson-lady-isabel.html.

Sutcliffe, Matthew. *An Abridgement or Survey of Poperie*. London: M.Bradwood for C.Burbie, 1606.

Swift, Laurel. 'Morris Offspring'. Laurel Swift. Accessed 3 October 2022. https://web.archive.org/web/20210919161100/http://www.laurelswift.co.uk/morris-offspring/4590809935.

Swinnock, George. *The Life and Death of Mr. Tho. Wilson, Minister of Maidstone, in the County of Kent, M.A.* [London?], 1672.

Szyrma, W.S. Lach-. 'Folk Lore'. *Western Morning News*, 12 December 1891.

'Tailors' Guild Assembly Minute Book (1517-1575)'. G23/1/251. Wiltshire and Swindon History Centre.

'Tailors' Guild Assembly Minute Book (1575-1598)'. G23/1/252. Wiltshire and Swindon History Centre.

'Tailors' Guild Assembly Minute Book (1597-1631)'. G23/1/253. Wiltshire and Swindon History Centre.

'Tailors' Guild Assembly Minute Book (1631-1735)'. G23/1/254. Wiltshire and Swindon History Centre.

Tallis, John. 'The Lancashire Morris before the War'. *The Morris Dancer* 4, no. 1 (2010): 5-6.

Taplin, J.A. 'Local Notes and Queries, [1475]: Whitsun Ales'. *Birmingham Weekly Post*, 31 May 1884.

Taverner, William. *'Tis Well If It Takes: A Comedy*. London: Printed for John Pemberton, 1719.

Taylor, John. 'Incipit Johannes Strangways [Begins: This Gentleman ...]'. In *Coryat's Crudities*, by Thomas Coryate, sig. Bb2v-3. London: W. Cater, 1776.

Taylor, John. 'Incipit Johannes Strangways [Begins: Thou Cravest My Verse...]'. In *Coryat's Crudities*, by Thomas Coryate, sig. e4. London: W. Cater, 1776.

Taylor, John. *Mad Verse, Sad Verse, Glad Verse and Bad Verse*. [Oxford: Printed by Leonard Lichfield], 1644.

Taylor, John George. *Our Lady of Batersey: The Story of Battersea Church and Parish Told from Original Sources*. London: George White, 1925.

Taylor, Thomas. *Truth's Innocency and Simplicity Shining through the Conversion...* London: Printed and sold by T. Sowle ..., 1697.

Tebbutt, C.F. *Huntingdonshire Folklore*. St Ives: Friends of the Norris Museum, 1984.

Temple, Sir William. 'Of Health and Long Life'. In *The Works of William Temple*, 1:272–89. London: Churchill, 1720.

The Tewkesbury Register, and Agricultural Gazette. 'Annual Concert by Children Attending the British Schools', 21 April 1894.

Thanet Advertiser. 'Coronation of the May Queen at Worsley', 7 May 1881.

They Throw Away Discord .... Adderbury: Adderbury Morris Men, 1984.

Thomas, A.H., ed. *Calendar of Plea and Memoranda Rolls Preserved among the Archives of the Corporation of the City of London at the Guildhall*. 6 vols. Cambridge: Cambridge University Press, 1926–1961.

'Thomas Bibby, "England and Wales Census, 1911"'. Fylde, RG14/507/1. 1911 census. Accessed 3 October 2022. https://www.familysearch.org/ark:/61903/1:1:X49X-BCP.

'Thomas Cadd in Household of William Cadd, "England and Wales Census, 1881"'. Buckingham, RG11/1486/38, p. 1. 1881 census. Accessed 3 October 2022. https://www.familysearch.org/ark:/61903/1:1:Q27Z-1P5F.

'Thomas Cadd, "England and Wales Census, 1891"'. Pottersbury, RG12/1189/138, p. 12. 1891 census. Accessed 3 October 2022. https://www.familysearch.org/ark:/61903/1:1:42CJ-NW2.

'Thomas Furlonger (1744–1840)'. FamilySearch. Accessed 3 October 2022. https://www.familysearch.org/tree/person/sources/LWBM-VLV.

Thompson, Pishey. *The History and Antiquities of Boston*. Boston: John Noble, 1856.

Thornton, Edwin. 'Local Notes and Queries, [1456]: Morris Dancers'. *Birmingham Weekly Post*, 3 May 1884.

Thorp, Jennifer. 'Rank Outsider or Outsider of Rank: Mr Isaac's Dance "The Morris"'. In *The Histories of the Morris in Britain*, edited by Michael Heaney, 33–43. London: English Folk Dance and Song Society & Historical Dance Society, 2018.

Throckmorton Family. 'Detailed Disbursements by a Steward or Bailiff of the Throckmorton Family, [Apparently at Weston Underwood, Buckinghamshire], 1699-1733'. D/EWE/A1. Berkshire Record Office.

Timbs, John. 'The Morrice Dance'. *The Mirror of Literature, Amusement, and Instruction* 29, no. 832 (1837): 280–82.

The Times. 'Queen Square', 8 August 1817.

The Times. 'The Northumberland Pitmen', 1 January 1878.

The Times. 'The "Maske of Flowers" at Gray's Inn', 8 July 1887.

The Times. 'Roy Dommett', 19 January 2016.

Tollet, George. 'Mr. Tollet's Opinion Concerning the Morris Dancers upon His Window'. In *The Plays of William Shakspeare*, edited by Samuel Johnson and George Steevens, 2nd ed., 5:425-434 + plate following p. 434. London: Printed for C. Bathurst [&c.], 1778.

Townsend, A.D. 'Cecil James Sharp as Collector and Editor of Traditional Dance'. *Traditional Dance* 5/6 (1988): 53–76.

Townsend, James. *The Oxfordshire Dashwoods*. Oxford: Printed for private circulation, 1922.

Townshend, Aurelian. 'Albion's Triumph, Personated in a Maske at Court by the Kings Majestie and His Lords, the Sunday after Twelfe Night, 1631'. In *Aurelian Townshend's Poems and Masks*, edited by E.K. Chambers, 55–78. Tudor & Stuart Library. Oxford: Clarendon Press, 1912.

Toy, Spencer. *The History of Helston*. London: Oxford University Press, 1936.

A Transcript of the Registers of the Worshipful Company of Stationers, from 1640-1708 A.D. 3 vols. London, 1913–1914.

Trewman's Exeter Flying Post, or, Plymouth and Cornish Advertiser. 'Brixham – Petty Sessions', 20 January 1859.

'Triumph of Peace'. In *Records of Early English Drama: Inns of Court,* edited by Alan H. Nelson and John R. Elliott, 2:591–612. Cambridge: D.S. Brewer, 2010.

Tryon, Thomas. *A Way to Health, Long Life and Happiness*. London: Printed and sold by Andrew Sowle, 1683.

Turner, William. *A Compleat History of the Most Remarkable Providences Both of Judgment and*

Mercy, Which Have Hapned in This Present Age. London: Printed for John Dunton ..., 1697.

Twemlow, J.A., ed. *Liverpool Town Books*. 2 vols. Liverpool: Liverpool University Press, 1918.

Twisse, William. *Of the Morality of the Fourth Commandement as Still in Force to Binde Christians*. London: Printed by E.G. for John Rothwell, 1641.

Underdown, David. *Revel, Riot, and Rebellion: Popular Politics and Culture in England 1603-1660*. Oxford: Clarendon Press, 1985.

UNESCO. 'Processional Giants and Dragons in Belgium and France'. Intangible Cultural Heritage. Accessed 3 October 2022. https://ich.unesco.org/en/RL/processional-giants-and-dragons-in-belgium-and-france-00153.

Universal Spectator and Weekly Journal. [Comment], 9 December 1732.

Upton, John. *Critical Observations on Shakespeare*. London: Printed for G. Hawkins, 1748.

Urbeltz, Juan Antonio. *Morris Dances, Origin and Metaphor*, 2007.

Uxbridge & West Drayton Gazette. 'Colnbrook: Literary Institute Fete', 10 August 1861.

Uxbridge & West Drayton Gazette. 'Rickmansworth, Foresters' Rural Fete', 29 July 1865.

Uxbridge & West Drayton Gazette. 'Isleworth, Hounslow, Brentford, and Twickenham Philanthropic Societies' Fete', 17 July 1866.

Uxbridge & West Drayton Gazette. 'Grand Revival of the Uxbridge Philanthropic Festival', 4 August 1866.

V.A. Archdeaconry of Bedford. STC 10138. 1629.

V.A. Archdeaconry of Bedford. STC 10139. 1636.

V.A. Archdeaconry of Berkshire. STC 10141. 1631.

V.A. Archdeaconry of Berkshire. STC 10142. 1635.

V.A. Archdeaconry of Berkshire. STC 10142.5. 1638.

V.A. Diocese of Bristol. STC 10143. 1603.

V.A. Province of Canterbury. STC 10155. 1576.

V.A. Province of Canterbury. STC 10155.3. 1577.

V.A. Province of Canterbury. STC 10155.7. 1580.

V.A. Province of Canterbury. STC 10157. 1582.

V.A. Diocese of Carlisle. STC 10173. 1629.

V.A. Diocese of Carlisle. STC 10174. 1632.

V.A. Diocese of Chester. STC 10174.5. 1581.

V.A. Diocese of Chester. STC 10176.5. 1617.

V.A. Diocese of Chichester. STC 10179. 1586.

V.A. Diocese of Chichester. STC 10180. 1600.

V.A. Diocese of Chichester. STC 10185. 1638.

V.A. Diocese of Chichester. Wing C4026. 1662.

V.A. Diocese of Coventry and Lichfield. STC 10224. 1584.

V.A. Diocese of Coventry and Lichfield. STC 10226. 1610.

V.A. Diocese of Durham. Wing C4033. 1662.

V.A. Diocese of Exeter. STC 10203. 1579.

V.A. Diocese of Exeter. STC 10204. 1599.

V.A. Diocese of Gloucester and Bristol. STC 10209. 1594.

V.A. Archdeaconry of Leicester. STC 10222. 1613.

V.A. Diocese of Lincoln. STC 10230.5. 1580.

V.A. Diocese of Lincoln. STC 10231. 1585.

V.A. Diocese of Lincoln. STC 10232. 1588.

V.A. Diocese of Lincoln. STC 10233. 1591.

V.A. Diocese of Lincoln. STC 10234. 1594.

V.A. Diocese of Lincoln. STC 10235. 1598.

V.A. Diocese of Lincoln. STC 10235.5. 1601.

V.A. Diocese of Lincoln. STC 10236.5. 1607.

V.A. Diocese of Lincoln. STC 10239. 1618.

V.A. Diocese of Lincoln. STC 10240. 1622.

V.A. Diocese of Lincoln. Wing C4063. 1686.

V.A. Diocese of Llandaff. Wing C4051. 1662.

V.A. Diocese of London. STC 10251. 1577.

V.A. Diocese of London. STC 10251.5. 1583.

V.A. Diocese of London. STC 10252. 1586.

V.A. Diocese of London. STC 10252.5. 1589.

V.A. Diocese of London. STC 10253. 1598.

V.A. Diocese of London. STC 10254. 1601.

V.A. Diocese of London. STC 10255. 1604.

V.A. Archdeaconry of Norfolk. STC 10177. 1634.

V.A. Diocese of Norwich. STC 10300. 1638.

V.A. Archdeaconry of Nottingham. STC 10306. 1639.

V.A. Diocese of Oxford. STC 10308. 1619.

V.A. Diocese of Oxford. STC 10308.5. 1622.

V.A. Diocese of Oxford. STC 10310. 1629.

V.A. Diocese of Rochester. STC 10321.5. 1638.

V.A. Diocese of Salisbury. STC 10327. 1581.

V.A. Diocese of St David's. Wing C4082. 1662.

V.A. Diocese of Winchester. STC 10353. 1584.

V.A. Diocese of Winchester. STC 10356. 1597.

V.A. Diocese of Winchester. STC 10356.6. 1603.

V.A. Diocese of Winchester. STC 10361. 1628.

V.A. Province of York. STC 10375: part. 1571.

V.A. Province of York, 1577 & 1578. STC 10376. 1577.

V.A. Archdiocese of York. STC 10377.5. 1607.

V.A. Diocese of York. STC 10378. 1610.

V.A. Diocese of York. STC 10379. 1618.

V.A. Diocese of York. STC 10379.5. 1623.

V.A. Province of York. STC 10379.7. 1629.

V.A. Province of York. STC 10380. 1633.

V.A. Archdeaconry of York. STC 10381.7. 1635.

V.A. Archdeaconry of York. STC 10382. 1638.

'Varieties'. *Harlequin* 1, no. 2 (1829): 47–48.

Vavasour, Lady Margaret. [Will]. In *Testamenta Eboracensia, Part I*, no. 264, 362–64. Surtees Society 4. London: J.B. Nichols, 1863.

'Verbatim Report of the Goupil Gallery Meeting Nov. 1907'. Accessed 3 October 2022. https://www.maryneal.org/file-uploads/files/file/1907s1b.pdf.

Verney, Frances Parthenope, and Margaret Maria Williams-Hay Verney. *Memoirs of the Verney Family*. 4 vols. London: Longmans, Green, 1892–1899.

Verney, Margaret Maria Williams-Hay. *Verney Letters of the Eighteenth Century from the MSS. at Claydon House*. 2 vols. London: Benn, 1930.

Vernon, Doremy. *Tiller's Girls*. London: Robson, 1988.

Vicars, John. *Gods Arke Overtopping the Worlds Waves, or, The Third Part of the Parliamentary Chronicle*. London: Printed by M. Simons, and J. Macock, 1646.

Victoria and Albert Museum. 'Window'. Victoria and Albert Museum: Explore the Collections. Accessed 3 October 2022. http://collections.vam.ac.uk/item/O8054/.

'A View of the Rotundo, House & Gardens at Ranelagh with an Exact Representation of the Jubilee Ball as It Appeared May 24th 1759 Being the Birth Day of His Royal Highness George Prince of Wales'. Museum of London. Accessed 3 October 2022. https://collections.museumoflondon.org.uk/online/object/92742.html.

Vuia, R. 'The Roumanian Hobby-Horse, the Căluşari'. *Journal of the English Folk Dance and Song Society* 2 (1935): 97–108.

W.,H., 'Local Notes and Queries, [1452]: Morris Dancers'. *Birmingham Weekly Post*, 3 May 1884.

Wallis, John. 'A Letter ... to Mr Andrew Fletcher, Concerning the Strange Effects Reported of Musick in Former Times, beyond What Is to Be Found in Later Ages'. *Philosophical Transactions of the Royal Society* 20 (1698): 297–303.

Walpole, Horace. *A Catalogue of Engravers, Who Have Been Born or Resided in England*. [Twickenham], 1765.

Walsall Advertiser. [News Item], 2 August 1884.

'Walter De H Birch, "England and Wales Census, 1901"'. RG13/13/122, p.18. 1901 census. Accessed 3 October 2022. https://www.familysearch.org/ark:/61903/1:1:X9GX-SYV.

Wantage.'Churchwardens' Accounts for Wantage, 1564-1656'. MS Top. Berks c. 44 (SC53738). Bodleian Libraries.

Ward, J. 'IV. Extracts from the Church-Wardens Accompts of the Parish of St. Helen's, in Abington, Berkshire'. *Archaeologia* 1, no. 2 (1779): 11–23.

Ward, Robert. *Fucus, sive, Histriomastix*, edited by G.C. Moore-Smith. Cambridge: University Press, 1909.

Warner, Ferdinando. *The History of Ireland. Volume the First*. London: Printed for J. and R. Tonson, 1763.

Warner, William. *The First and Second Parts of Albions England*. London: By Thomas Orwin, for Thomas Cadman, 1589.

Warren, D. 'Yardley Morris', 4 July 2008. Accessed 3 October 2022. https://web.archive.org/web/20080704132432/http:/www.mkheritage.co.uk/yghg/school/morrisdance.html.

Warrington Guardian. 'Lymm Rushbearing', 19 August 1865.

Wase, Christopher. *Grati Falisci Cynegeticon, or, A Poem of Hunting, by Gratius the Faliscan, Englished*. London: Charles Adams, 1654.

Wasson, John M., ed. *Records of Early English Drama: Devon*. Toronto: University of Toronto Press, 1986.

Waterhouse, Edward. *Fortescutus Illustratus, or, A Commentary on That Nervous Treatise, De Laudibus Legum Angliæ, Written by Sir John Fortescue*. London: Printed by Tho. Roycroft, 1663.

Waterhouse, Edward. *The Gentlemans Monitor, or, A Sober Inspection into the Vertues, Vices, and Ordinary Means of the Rise and Decay of Men and Families*. London: Printed by T.R. for R. Royston ..., 1665.

'Wavertree'. NW09860. Manchester Morris Men's archives.

Wearing, Sally. 'Infuriated'. *Morris Matters* 1, no. 4 (1978): 24–26.

Wearing, Sally. 'What to Dance? What to Wear? The Repertoire and Costume of Morris Women in the 1970s'. In *The Histories of the Morris in Britain*, edited by Michael Heaney, 266–77. London: English Folk Dance and Song Society & Historical Dance Society, 2018.

Weaver, F.W., and G.N. Clark, eds. *Churchwardens' Accounts of Marston, Spelsbury, Pyrton*. Oxford: Oxfordshire Record Society, 1925.

Weaver, John. *Orchesography, or, The Art of Dancing, by Characters and Demonstrative Figures.... an Exact and Just Translation from the French [of Raoul-Auger Feuillet]*. London: Printed by H. Meere, 1706.

Weelkes, Thomas. 'Ayres or Phantasticke Spirites for Three Voices, XVIII'. In *English Madrigal Verse 1588-1632*, edited by E.H. Fellowes, 3rd ed., 294–304. Oxford: Oxford University Press, 2016.

Weelkes, Thomas. 'Madrigals of 5. and 6. Parts, Apt for the Viols and Voices, Pt.1, VII-VIII'. In *English Madrigal Verse 1588-1632*, edited by E.H. Fellowes, 3rd ed., 290–94. Oxford: Oxford University Press, 2016.

Weelkes, Thomas. 'Madrigals to 3, 4, 5 and 6 Voyces, XI'. In *English Madrigal Verse 1588-1632*, edited by E.H. Fellowes, 3rd ed., 282. Oxford: Oxford University Press, 2016.

Welker, Lorenz. 'Moresca und Moriskentanz: Rezeption des Fremden in Musik und Tanz in Spätmittelalter und Renaissance'. In *Die Münchner Moriskentänzer: Repräsentation und Performanz Städtischen Selbstverständniss*, edited by Iris Lauterbach and Thomas Weidner, 69-81. München: Zentralinstitut für Kunstgeschichte, 2013.

Wellington Journal. 'Charity Concert in Wellington', 9 February 1895 [a].

Wellington Journal. 'The Severe Weather', 9 February 1895 [b].

'Welsh Morris Dance'. In *The Third Book of the Compleat Country Dancing Master*, col. 103. London: Printed and sold by J. Walsh, 1735.

Welshbordermorris. 'History of OWBM'. Accessed 3 October 2022. https://welshbordermorris.blogspot.com/p/ears-2013-and-still-counting.html.

Welti, David. 'David Welti Writes to WMF'. *Morris Matters* 1, no. 2 (1978): 10–11.

Wentworth, Philip. *The History and Annals of Blackley and Neighbourhood*. Middleton: John Bagot, 1892.

West Cumberland Times. 'May Festival at Moor Row', 27 May 1893.

West Cumberland Times. [Advertisement], 21 April 1894.

West Cumberland Times. 'May Festival at Broughton Moor', 27 May 1896.

West Cumberland Times. 'Exhibition of Work and Art at Flimby', 5 September 1896.

West Cumberland Times. 'The Coming Festival', 24 April 1897.

West Cumberland Times. [Advertisement], 28 April 1897.

West Cumberland Times. 'The Children's Column', 8 May 1897.

West Cumberland Times. 'Jubilee Celebrations: Workington', 23 June 1897.

West Cumberland Times. 'Industrial and Art Exhibition at Flimby: Children's Carnival', 19 August 1899.

West Kent Guardian. 'Printers' Pension Society', 18 July 1846.

West Somerset Free Press. 'The "Hobby Horse" at Minehead', 6 May 1893.

Western Daily Mercury. 'The Bath and West of England Agricultural Society', 9 June 1863.

Western Daily Press. [Advertisement], 3 June 1870.

Western Gazette. 'Club Festival', 14 June 1878.

Western Mail. '"Harvest Home" at the Cardiff Empire', 27 February 1894.

Western Morning News. 'Ball at Plymouth Guildhall', 5 November 1887.

Wetenhale, Alice. [Will], 1458. Prerogative Court of Canterbury,Stokton 24-25. The National Archives.

White, Francis. *An Examination and Confutation of a Lawlesse Pamphlet, Intituled, A Briefe Answer to a Late Treatise of the Sabbath-Day*. London: Printed by R[ichard] B[adger] for Andrew Crooke, 1637.

The Whitehall Evening Post. [News Item], 26 October 1754.

Whitfield, Christopher, ed. *Robert Dover and the Cotswold Games*. London: Henry Sotheran, 1962.

'Whitworth Nutters and Whitworth Morris Dancers, July 30, 1910, Whitworth Parish Church Carnival'. NW10010. Manchester Morris Men's archives.

Wickenden, William S. [Letter]. *The Gentleman's Magazine: And Historical Chronicle* n.s. 92 (1822): 601–02.

Wickenden, William S. 'A Sketch of the Early Life of the Author'. In *Poems and Tales*, by William S Wickenden, xv–lxxv. London: Arthur Hall, Virtue & co., 1851.

Wickenden, William S. 'A Tale of the Forest of Dean'. *Household Words* 3, no. 72 (1851): 461–64.

Wigan Observer and District Advertiser. [Advertisement], 2 April 1881.

Wigan Observer and District Advertiser. 'Horwich Rose Festival', 20 July 1892.

Wigan Observer and District Advertiser. [Advertisement], 6 May 1893.

Wiles, David. *The Early Plays of Robin Hood*. Cambridge: D.S. Brewer, 1981.

Wilkes, Richard. 'Original Collections for the History of Staffordshire'. SMS 647. William Salt Library.

Willan, Thomas Stuart. *A Tudor Book of Rates [The Rates of the Customes House, 1582]*. Manchester: Manchester University Press, 1962.

'William Boam, "England and Wales Census, 1861"'. Derbyshire, RG09/2545/41, p. 42. 1861 census. Accessed 3 October 2022. https://www. familysearch.org/ark:/61903/1:1:M7NF-VZT.

'William Smith MSS, Biographical, Verse'. Archive WS/A/2/1. Oxford University Museum of Natural History.

'William Smith MSS, Diary, 1789'. Archive WS/B/001. Oxford University Museum of Natural History.

'William Smith MSS, The Whitsun Ale (Churchill) Accounts for 1721'. Archive WS/A/2/2. Oxford University Museum of Natural History.

'William Wells 1868-1953: Morris Dancer, Fiddler and Fool'. *Journal of the English Folk Dance and Song Society* 8, no. 1 (1956): 1–15.

'William Worrall, "England and Wales Census, 1861"'. Derbyshire RG09/2545/27, p. 13. 1861 census. Accessed 3 October 2022. https://www. familysearch.org/ark:/61903/1:1:M7NF-JGW.

Williams, A.R. 'An Early Memory, Typescript', 1931. LIB/COLL/GRQ 35/110-119. Vaughan Williams Memorial Library.

Williams, Iolo. *English Folk Song and Dance*. London: Longman, Green, 1935.

Williams, J.F. *The Early Churchwardens' Accounts of Hampshire*. Winchester: Warren and Son, 1913.

Williamson, Mrs W.C. *Sketches of Fallowfield and the Surrounding Manors, Past and Present*. Manchester: J. Heywood, 1888.

Willoughby, Gilbert Henry Heathcote-Drummond-. *Report on the Manuscripts of the Earl of Ancaster, Preserved at Grimsthorpe*. Hist. MSS. Comm. Dublin: H.M.S.O, 1907.

Willoughby, Maurice. Author's interview, 28 October 1982.

Wilson, John. 'Keeping Morris Masculine'. *Morris Matters* 1, no. 3 (1978): 13–15.

Wilts and Gloucestershire Standard. [Advertisement], 18 June 1870.

Windsor and Eton Express. 'Literary Institution – the Fete', 3 November 1860.

Windsor and Eton Express. 'The Denham Fete', 2 August 1862.

Winerock, Emily F. 'Churchyard Capers: The Controversial Use of Church Space for Dancing in Early Modern England'. In *The Sacralization of Space and Behavior in the Early Modern World*, edited by Jennifer Mara DeSilva, 233–56. Abingdon: Ashgate, 2015.

Winerock, Emily F. 'Competitive Capers: Gender, Gentility and Dancing in Early Modern England'. In *The Oxford Handbook of Dance and Competition*, edited by Sherril Dodds, 65–85. Oxford: Oxford University Press, 2019.

Winerock, Emily F. 'Reformation and Revelry: The Practices and Politics of Dancing in Early Modern England, c. 1550 – c. 1640'. Doctoral dissertation, University of Toronto, 2012. Accessed 3 October 2022. https://tspace. library.utoronto.ca/bitstream/1807/34965/3/ Winerock_Emily_F_201211_PhD_thesis.pdf.

Winkless, Dorothy. 'Five Tracy Diaries of the Eighteenth and Nineteenth Centuries'. In *The Sudeleys - Lords of Toddington*, 200–21. London: Manorial Society of Great Britain, 1987.

Winter, Trish, and Simon Keegan-Phipps. *Performing Englishness: Identity and Politics in a Contemporary Folk Resurgence*. Manchester: Manchester University Press, 2013.

'Winterslow Churchwardens' Accounts'. Winterslow. All Saints' Church.

Wise, Francis. *Some Enquiries Concerning the First Inhabitants Language Religion Learning and Letters of Europe*. Oxford: At the Theatre, 1758.

The Witchmen. 'Witchmen Pagan Morris Dancers'. Accessed 3 October 2022. http:// witchmen.com/.

Wither, George. *The Modern States-man*. London: Printed by Henry Hills, 1653.

Wither, George. *Salt upon Salt: Made out of Certain Ingenious Verses upon the Late Storm and the Death of His Highness Ensuing*. London: Printed for L. Chapman, 1659.

Witney Express and Oxfordshire and Midland Counties Herald. 'Bampton: Club Feasts', 9 June 1870.

Wolverhampton Chronicle and Staffordshire Advertiser. 'Death from Cold', 4 January 1837.

Wolverhampton Chronicle and Staffordshire Advertiser. 'The Colliers at Ironbridge', 19 October 1864.

Wood, Anthony à. *The History and Antiquities of the University of Oxford*, edited by John Gutch. 2 vols. Oxford: Printed for the editor, 1792–1796.

Wood, Anthony à. *The Life and Times of Anthony Wood, Antiquary, of Oxford, 1632-1695*, edited by Andrew Clark. 5 vols. Oxford: Clarendon Press, 1891.

Wood, Thomas. 'Thomas Wood, Accounts with Jos. Armstrong of Manchester, &c'. GB127. M62/1/2. Manchester Libraries, Information and Archives.

Wood, William. *New Englands Prospect: A True, Lively, and Experimentall Description of That Part of America, Commonly Called New England.* London: By Tho. Cotes, for Iohn Bellamie, 1634.

Wooders, Jameson. '"With Snail Shells Instead of Bells": Music, Morris Dancing, and the "Middling Sort" of People in Eighteenth-century Berkshire'. *Folk Music Journal* 10, no. 5 (2015): 550–74.

Worcester Herald. 'Celebration of the Majority of George Edmund Wicksted, Esq.', 7 February 1857.

Worcestershire Chronicle. 'Local Intelligence', 11 January 1854.

Worcestershire Chronicle. 'Upton-on-Severn', 28 February 1855.

Worcestershire Chronicle. 'Charge of Theft', 13 December 1879.

Worcestershire Chronicle. 'Stealing an Overcoat at Leigh', 10 January 1880.

Worcestershire Chronicle. 'Work Not Wanted', 29 January 1881.

Worcestershire Chronicle. 'Canal Boatmen out of Work at Worcester', 22 January 1887.

Worcestershire Chronicle. 'Gipsy Items, Names, and Customs', 31 May 1890.

Workington Star. 'Jubilee Day at Workington', 25 June 1897.

World and Fashionable Advertiser. [News Item], 1 June 1787.

World and Fashionable Advertiser. [News Item], 27 April 1789.

World and Fashionable Advertiser. [Advertisement], 1 May 1789.

World and Fashionable Advertiser. [News Item], 7 May 1789.

World and Fashionable Advertiser. [Advertisement], 11 May 1789.

Worth, Jack. 'Findings from the 2020 Morris Census'. Accessed 3 October 2022. https://www.morrisfed.org.uk/wp-content/uploads/2021/02/Findings-from-the-2020-Morris-Census-as-at-202012.pdf.

Wortley, Russell. 'The Bromsberrow Heath Morris Dances'. *English Dance and Song* 23, no. 4 (1959): 94–95.

Wortley, Russell. ''The Bucknell Morris'. *English Dance and Song* 37, no. 3 (1975): 105.

Wortley, Russell. 'Cotswold Olympicks [Letter]'. *The Times*, 2 July 1961.

Wortley, Russell. 'The Morris of the Dean Forest'. *English Dance and Song* 42, no. 1 (1980): 16–17.

Wortley, Russell, and Michael Dawney. 'George Butterworth's Diary of Morris Dance Hunting'. *Folk Music Journal* 3, no. 3 (1977): 193–202.

Wortley, Russell, and Cyril Papworth. 'Molly Dancing in South-west Cambridgeshire'. *English Dance and Song* 40, no. 2 (1978): 38–39.

'Wortley MSS, Field Note on Balsham Molly Dancers, Cambs., Taken from an Informant, Will Plumb, 29 Aug 1955'. 97-022/7/1/1. University of Sheffield Library.

'Wortley MSS, Field Note on Boxworth (Cambs.)'. 97-022/7/1/34. University of Sheffield Library.

'Wortley MSS, Field Note on Girton (Cambs.), Gathered from Informant Charles Huntlea'. 97-022/7/1/28. University of Sheffield Library.

'Wortley MSS, Field Note on Great Wilbraham (Cambs., 26 March 1938'. 97-022/7/1/31. University of Sheffield Library.

'Wortley MSS, Field Note on Informant Mrs Pluck of Oakington (Cambs.), 3 Jan 1957'. 97-022/7/1/42. University of Sheffield Library.

'Wortley MSS, Field Note on Little Wilbraham (Cambs.), 5 and 26 March 1938'. 97-022/7/1/30. University of Sheffield Library.

'Wortley MSS, Field Note ... on West Wickham (Cambs.), 3 September 1955'. 97-022/7/1/17. University of Sheffield Library.

'Wortley MSS, Field Note on West Wratting Molly Dancers, Cambs., Taken from an Informant, Mr Plumb, 29 Aug 1955'. 97-022/7/1/4. University of Sheffield Library.

'Wortley MSS, Field Notes ... on Bartlow, Castle Camps (Cambs.) and Ashdon (Essex), 17 Feb 1958'. 97-022/7/1/10. University of Sheffield Library.

'Wortley MSS, Field Notes on Comberton Molly Dancers, 1934-1937'. 97-022/7/1/23. University of Sheffield Library.

'Wortley MSS, Field Notes on Plough Monday in Fulbourn (Cambs.) 5 Jan 1935'. 97-022/7/1/27. University of Sheffield Library.

'Wortley MSS, Field Notes ... on Weston Colville, West Wratting, West Wickham (Cambs.), Withersfield (Suffolk), Balsham (Cambs.),

Great Thurlow, Great Bradley (Suffolk), Burrough Green, Dullingham and Horseheath (Cambs.), 11 Aug 1956'. 97-022/7/1/13. University of Sheffield Library.

'Wortley MSS, Mrs Bolton – Notes on Plough Monday in Great Sampford and Radwinter [Essex]'. 97-022/1/9/13/62. University of Sheffield Library.

'Wortley MSS, Notes on Cotswold Morris, Collected by Russell Wortley and Arthur Peck 1936-1938'. 97-022/1/7/5/41. University of Sheffield Library.

'Wortley MSS, Thetford [Norfolk] – Jimmy Nichols – Notes on Interview Re. Hummy Dancers Who Performed on Boxing Days [up to Second World War]'. 97-022/1/9/5/36-37. University of Sheffield Library.

'Wortley MSS, Thetford [Norfolk] – Notes on Interview Re. Hummy Dancers'. 97-022/1/9/5/32-33. University of Sheffield Library.

'Wortley MSS, Typed Details of the Costume Worn for Molly Dancing, from Information given by Joseph Kester between January 1948 and January 1950'. 97-022/7/1/49. University of Sheffield Library.

Wotton, Sir Henry. *A Parallell Betweene Roberte Late Earle of Essex, and George Late Duke of Buckingham*. London, 1641.

Wrexham Advertiser. 'Rhosllanerchrugog', 9 May 1885.

Wrexham Advertiser. 'Mold', 6 May 1893.

Wrexham Advertiser. 'Pontblyddyn and Leeswood', 5 May 1894.

Wright, Lucy. 'Girls' Carnival Morris Dancing and Material Practice'. *Yearbook for Traditional Music* 49 (2017): 26–47.

Wright, Lucy. '"Sequins, Bows and Pointed Toes": Girls' Carnival Morris – the "Other" Morris Dancing Community'. In *The Routledge Companion to English Folk Performance*, edited by Peter Harrop and Steve Roud, 336-54. London: Routledge, 2021.

Wright, Lucy. 'This Girl Can Morris Dance: Girls' Carnival Morris Dancing and the Politics of Participation'. In *The Histories of the Morris in Britain*, edited by Michael Heaney, 295-312. London: English Folk Dance and Song Society & Historical Dance Society, 2018.

'The Wye and Monmouthshire: No. IV'. *The Saturday Magazine* 13, no. 398 (1838): 97–98.

Wyndham, John. 'Account Book of John Wyndham of Norrington, 1720-1749'. DDWY/6/1/34. Somerset Heritage Centre.

York Herald. 'Ripon', 27 December 1887.

Zemia. 'Rural Festivals'. *New Monthly Magazine and Humorist* 54, no. 216 (1838): 474–82.

Zhdanov, Prokhor. *A New Dictionary English and Russian = Новой Словарь Англиской и Россійской*. В Санктпетербурге: при Тип. Шляхетнаго кадетскаго корпуса, 1784.

Index